Premium Auditing Applications

MW01264522

Premium Auditing Applications

Everett D. Randall, CPCU, CLU, APA
Vice President–Examinations
The Institutes

Coordinating Author

Lowell S. Young, CPCU, CLU, APA
Director of Curriculum
The Institutes

5th Edition • 7th Printing

The Institutes
720 Providence Road, Suite 100
Malvern, Pennsylvania 19355-3433

5th Edition · 7th Printing · August 2010

Library of Congress Control Number: 2006933270

ISBN 978-0-89463-312-6

Foreword

The Institutes are the trusted leader in delivering proven knowledge solutions that drive powerful business results for the risk management and property-casualty insurance industry. For more than 100 years, The Institutes have been meeting the industry's changing professional development needs with customer-driven products and services.

In conjunction with industry experts and members of the academic community, our Knowledge Resources Department develops our course and program content, including Institutes study materials. Practical and technical knowledge gained from Institutes courses enhances qualifications, improves performance, and contributes to professional growth—all of which drive results.

The Institutes' proven knowledge helps individuals and organizations achieve powerful results with a variety of flexible, customer-focused options:

Recognized Credentials—The Institutes offer an unmatched range of widely recognized and industry-respected specialty credentials. The Institutes' Chartered Property Casualty Underwriter (CPCU) professional designation is designed to provide a broad understanding of the property-casualty insurance industry. Depending on professional needs, CPCU students may select either a commercial insurance focus or a personal risk management and insurance focus and may choose from a variety of electives.

In addition, The Institutes offer certificate or designation programs in a variety of disciplines, including these:

Claims

Commercial underwriting

Fidelity and surety bonding

General insurance

Insurance accounting and finance

Insurance information technology

Insurance production and agency management

Insurance regulation and compliance

Management

Marine insurance

Personal insurance

Premium auditing

Quality insurance services

Reinsurance

Risk management

Surplus lines

Flexible Online Learning—The Institutes have an unmatched variety of technical insurance content covering topics from accounting to underwriting, which we now deliver through hundreds of online courses. These cost-effective self-study courses are a convenient way to fill gaps in technical knowledge in a matter of hours without ever leaving the office.

Continuing Education—A majority of The Institutes' courses are filed for CE credit in most states. We also deliver quality, affordable, online CE courses quickly and conveniently through our newest business unit, CEU.com. Visit www.CEU.com to learn more.

College Credits—Most Institutes courses carry college credit recommendations from the American Council on Education. A variety of courses also qualify for credits toward certain associate, bachelor's, and master's degrees at several prestigious colleges and universities. More information is available in the Student Services section of our Web site, www.TheInstitutes.org.

Custom Applications—The Institutes collaborate with corporate customers to utilize our trusted course content and flexible delivery options in developing customized solutions that help them achieve their unique organizational goals.

Insightful Analysis—Our Insurance Research Council (IRC) division conducts public policy research on important contemporary issues in property-casualty insurance and risk management. Visit www.ircweb.org to learn more or purchase its most recent studies.

The Institutes look forward to serving the risk management and property-casualty insurance industry for another 100 years. We welcome comments from our students and course leaders; your feedback helps us continue to improve the quality of our study materials.

Peter L. Miller, CPCU
President and CEO
The Institutes

Preface

Premium Auditing Applications is the textbook used for the APA 92 course. It is one of the textbooks used as part of the APA designation program. The APA program is designed to provide professional education in the specialized field of premium auditing.

This textbook describes a systematic process that can serve as a framework for premium determination in premium audits. The following summarizes the thirteen chapters of *Premium Auditing Applications*.

Chapter 1 provides an overview of insurance rates, including rating plans, ratemaking goals, and rate filings, as well as rate regulation—all of which influence the work of premium auditors.

Chapter 2 covers workers' compensation laws, rating bureaus for workers' compensation insurance, the Workers' Compensation and Employers' Liability Insurance Policy, and the *Basic Manual for Workers Compensation and Employers Liability Insurance*.

Chapters 3 and 4 cover the premium basis for workers' compensation and the resulting premium determination. *The Basic Manual*'s classification references, rules, and techniques are examined.

Chapter 5 describes workers' compensation relating to construction operations, including construction classifications, industry practices, and the construction process.

Chapter 6 provides an understanding of maritime workers' compensation and the federal laws associated with it to give a background for proper premium determination.

Chapters 7 and 8 describe commercial general liability insurance, its premium bases and classifications, and the resulting premium determination.

Chapter 9 covers business auto insurance, including the business auto coverage and the classification of trucks, tractors, and trailers necessary for premium determination.

Chapter 10 describes motor carrier insurance and premium determination, including the truckers' coverage form, motor carrier coverage, and premium bases necessary for premium determination.

Chapter 11 sets a framework for garage insurance, including the garage coverage form, declarations, and endorsements necessary for premium determination.

Chapter 12 examines various types of commercial property/inland marine insurance, the reasons for audits, and valuation concepts important for premium determination.

Chapter 13 covers other premium auditor roles, many associated with supporting the underwriting and claim departments of the insurer.

The Institutes appreciate the contributions of the following individuals, who served in an advisory capacity or reviewed one or more chapters in the book:

Marilyn J. Atkins, APA, CPIW

David G. Baker, APA

James C. Boone, APA

Sharon L. Carney, APA, CIPA

Raymond F. Cass, CPCU, APA, AU

Anthony J. Iacono

Gregory E. Jensen

Donna L. Marquette, APA, CIPA

Diana L. McCarthy, APA, ARM

James F. Mendyk, CPCU, APA, CIPA

Laura A. Pieters, APA

Donald S. Sutton, CPCU, APA, CIPA

Their thoughtful review of the material has contributed to making this text more relevant to current industry conditions. The Institutes remain equally thankful to individuals who contributed to the earlier development of texts for this course, although they are too numerous to name here. The current updated and revised text continues to reflect the valuable insight of these insurance professionals.

For more information about The Institutes' programs, please call our Customer Service Department at (800) 644-2101, e-mail us at customerservice@TheInstitutes.org, or visit our Web site at www.TheInstitutes.org.

Lowell S. Young

Contributing Authors

The Institutes and the author acknowledge with deep appreciation the work of the following contributing authors:

Martin J. Frappolli, CPCU, AIS
The Institutes

Robert J. Gibbons, PhD, CPCU, CLU
International Insurance Foundation

Connor M. Harrison, CPCU, AU, ARe
The Institutes

Jerome Trupin, CPCU, CLU, ChFC
Trupin Insurance Services

Contents

Direct Your Learning

Insurance Rates and Rate Regulation

Educational Objectives

After learning the content of this chapter and completing the corresponding course guide assignment, you should be able to:

▶ Describe the insurance concepts of causes of loss; physical, moral, and morale hazards; and the law of large numbers.

▶ Given the elements of ratemaking—including exposure unit, exposure base, and rate—calculate an insurance premium.

▶ Describe the following concepts:

- Exposure base characteristics
- Insurance rates
- Modifications to manual rates
- Rating classifications

▶ Describe ratemaking goals.

▶ Describe the process used to regulate insurance rates.

- Identify the goals of insurance rate regulation.
- Describe the major types of state rating laws, and discuss the advantages and disadvantages of these laws.

▶ Describe the rate filings processes and the role of insurance advisory organizations.

▶ Describe the changing landscape of state versus federal regulation of insurance.

▶ Define or describe each of the Key Words and Phrases for this chapter.

CHAPTER 1

Develop Your Perspective

What are the main topics covered in the chapter?

Insurance rates should generate premiums that adequately reflect the loss exposures for which insureds are charged based on rating plans that reflect appropriate exposure bases, rating classifications, and criteria for those classifications. The goals of ratemaking are to reflect correct rates per loss exposure and to produce rates that respond to changes in loss exposures, encourage loss control, provide for a reasonable profit, and are simple to understand and apply. State insurance regulation imposes ratemaking requirements.

Identify aspects of exposure bases used to develop premiums.

▶ How can exposure bases be sensitive to inflation?

▶ What makes an exposure base easy to determine?

▶ Why are some exposure bases difficult to manipulate?

Why is it important to learn these topics?

Insurance rates are the foundation for insurance premiums. Therefore, it is fundamental that premium auditors understand the mechanisms for developing those rates, the business conditions and regulatory requirements restricting rates that insurers charge, and the importance of accurately reporting required information to insurance advisory organizations and state rating bureaus.

Consider why insurers may be forced to charge a rate that is inadequate for the loss exposure that it represents.

▶ How are the premiums charged for insurance coverage determined to be fair and accurate?

▶ How can the inaccurate reporting of loss exposures cause the rates charged by insurers to be inaccurate?

How can you use what you will learn?

Examine the rating classes applied to the accounts that you audit.

▶ How may the rating classes be refined to more accurately represent the loss exposures of the business?

▶ What regulations limit or enhance the insurer's ability to establish fair and accurate insurance rates and premiums for insureds?

Insurance Rates and Rate Regulation

Premium auditing is the process necessary to determine the fair price of an insurance policy when the ultimate exposure is not known until the policy has expired. Premium auditors should have a sound understanding of fundamental insurance concepts as well as ratemaking concepts and goals, rating plans, rate regulation, and rate filings to effectively and efficiently perform their premium auditing tasks. This chapter provides an overview of these topics.

Insurance is a financial transaction. The two parties to an insurance contract agree to exchange financial claims with certain conditions attached. The parties use insurance to treat only financial losses. Insurance cannot restore nonfinancial losses, such as a loss in morale when a well-liked employee retires. Nor is insurance cost effective in treating all financial losses. Insurance is not effective in treating losses that are certain or accurately predictable for a single insured, such as maintenance costs associated with normal wear and tear on machinery. Insurance is most effective in treating accidental losses due to causes of loss that are to a large extent beyond the insured's control.

INSURANCE CONCEPTS

This section provides a brief overview of fundamental insurance concepts, including causes of loss, hazards, indemnification, and the law of large numbers. These concepts are fundamental to understanding insurance ratemaking.

A cause of loss (also called a peril) is the means by which property is damaged or destroyed. Many causes of loss are forces of nature, such as wind, flood, and earthquake. Other causes of loss can arise from the acts of people, such as robbery, burglary, and vandalism. Causes of loss are affected by hazards. A hazard is a condition that increases the frequency and/or severity of loss. Hazards can be divided into three categories: physical, moral, and morale.

A physical hazard is a tangible condition of property, persons, or operations that increases the frequency or severity of loss. For example, defective electric wiring increases the likelihood of fire. Likewise, an unlighted stairway increases the possibility that customers will trip and fall.

Moral and morale hazards both involve people's attitudes rather than the insured objects' physical attributes or physical environment. Moral hazard is a tendency for the insured (or persons associated with the insured) to intentionally cause a loss. For example, an insured may commit arson to collect the insurance proceeds if the proceeds would be worth more than the amount for which the insured could sell its intact goods. Likewise, an insured may file false claims or inflated claims to profit from the insurance payment.

Morale hazard arises from the insured's carelessness or indifference. The mere existence of an insurance contract can create a morale hazard. At times, insureds may exercise less care than they would otherwise because they know that insurance is likely to cover potential losses. An insured who does not exercise reasonable care in keeping the workplace safe, for example, may increase the chance of loss from fire, premises liability, and workers' compensation claims.

Insurers use several defenses to protect themselves against hazards, whether physical, moral, or morale. The underwriting process should detect excessive hazards. It should (1) require that the insured adopt the measures necessary to avoid or reduce hazards, (2) impose a premium sufficient to cover the losses resulting from those hazards, or (3) decline to provide coverage. When moral hazards exist, declination of coverage is the only alternative.

Insurers often provide financial incentives to insureds to correct physical hazards. For example, insurers use rating plans that require insureds to pay more in premiums when their losses have been excessive. Other rating plans provide rate credits when loss control practices, such as safety meetings, are used, whether they actually offset losses or not.

Insurance is a contractual arrangement whereby one party (the insurer) agrees to indemnify a second party (the insured) for financial losses that result from certain causes of loss. The contract may specifically list the causes of loss, or the contract may cover losses from all causes it does not specifically exclude. An insurance contract transfers the adverse financial effect of an insured loss from the insured to the insurer. Consequently, it reduces the effect of the various causes of loss on the insured and reduces the uncertainties to which the insured is subject.

Because an insurer enters into insurance contracts with many insureds, an insurer also reduces the uncertainties of the entire economic system. The law of large numbers is a mathematical principle stating that as the number of similar, independent exposure units increases, the relative accuracy of predictions about the future outcomes (losses) also increases. For example, a firm that owns only one car cannot project with acceptable accuracy the dollar amount of liability claims that will arise from using the car in any one year. However, an insurer that insures one million cars can project its annual losses with much greater accuracy. Therefore, by pooling many insureds' loss exposures, an insurer increases the accuracy of projecting losses and reduces uncertainty. The insurer can then allocate economic resources more efficiently.

Of course, an insurer can allocate economic resources efficiently only if it can properly allocate the loss cost among its various insureds. Equitably allocating the loss cost is the function of insurance rating plans. To promote an understanding of rating plans, the next section discusses important rate-making concepts.

RATEMAKING CONCEPTS

In an insurance policy, the insurer promises under certain conditions to indemnify the insured for certain kinds of losses occurring during the specified policy period. In return, the insured pays a premium, which is the applicable insurance rate multiplied by the number of applicable exposure units. An exposure unit is a unit of measurement of the exposure base used in premium calculations.

An exposure base is a variable that approximates the loss potential for a line of insurance. For example, payroll is a variable of the approximate loss potential for workers' compensation insurance because disability payments under workers' compensation insurance depend on the injured worker's payroll. Therefore, payroll is the exposure base for workers' compensation. In property insurance, the exposure base is the amount of insurance for covered property, such as buildings and/or contents. Examples of other exposure bases include gross sales, area, admissions, and total cost of a contract.

An exposure unit is a unit of measurement of the exposure base used in premium calculations. For example, the exposure unit in workers' compensation insurance is each $100 of payroll (or sales). The exposure unit is based primarily on common sense, convenience, or information technology requirements, rather than on statistical reasons. No statistical reasons exist for an insurer to choose the exposure unit to be each $100 of payroll rather than each $1,000 of payroll. In fact, exposure units can vary by line of insurance, even when the exposure base is the same. For example, an exposure base for commercial general liability (CGL) insurance can be the same as for workers' compensation insurance—that is, payroll. However, when the exposure base for CGL insurance is payroll, the exposure unit is $1,000, not $100 of payroll.

Many insurance policies have exposure bases that vary over time (for example, general liability policies have various exposure bases—payroll, gross sales, area/units, or cost—depending on the type of insured business). The premium auditor must determine what the actual exposure was when conducting the final premium audit. The final premium charged to the insured should accurately reflect the insured's exposure to loss covered by the policy.

The **rate** is the price of insurance per exposure unit that, when multiplied by the number of exposure units, determines the premium. Each classification has a different rate, depending on the expected probability of loss for that classification. Exhibit 1-1 illustrates how an insurer calculates an insurance premium.

Rate
The price of insurance per exposure unit that, when multiplied by the number of exposure units, determines the premium.

EXHIBIT 1-1

Calculation of an Insurance Premium

Premium = Rate × Number of exposure units.

Assume that the exposure base is gross sales and that the exposure unit is each $1,000 of gross sales. The rate for the insurance coverage is $1.35. ABC Company has $3,500,000 in gross sales.

ABC has 3,500 exposure units ($3,500,000 ÷ 1,000), so its premium would be:

$4,725 = $1.35 × 3,500.

Insurers base the insurance premium that insureds will pay on gross sales or payroll, for example, for the policy period. However, insureds do not know in advance what their gross sales or payroll will be for that period. If an insurer charged a flat premium, insureds may eventually pay more or less than their loss exposures would dictate. To avoid this, insurers set rates per exposure unit, and at the end of the policy period, insurers determine the exact number of exposure units (for example, each $100 of payroll) for the policy period. Insurers base the insured's final premium on the actual number of exposure units during the time period for which the insurers provided coverage. In many cases, the premium auditor determines the actual number of exposure units. In some cases, insurers may allow the insured to submit a report indicating the number of exposure units.

RATING PLANS

Rating plan
A set of directions that specify criteria of the exposure base, the exposure unit, and rate per exposure unit to determine premiums for a particular line of insurance.

An insurance rating plan provides an objective means for determining insurance premiums. A **rating plan** is a set of directions that specify criteria of the exposure base, the exposure unit, and rate per exposure unit to determine premiums for a particular line of insurance. The rating plan often defines the distinct classifications of insureds and their operations and an insurance rate for each rating classification, reflecting the different loss exposures involved. When one insured performs several distinct operations, the premium auditor may need to break down the total exposure units by classification, applying a different rate to each.

Exposure Base Characteristics

Exposure bases are chosen because they reflect the loss exposure assumed by the insurer. An exposure base should be an accurate measure, sensitive to inflation, easy to determine, difficult for the insured to manipulate, and acceptable to regulators and society. Most exposure bases do not exhibit all these characteristics to the same degree, nor do all insureds have loss exposures that are accurately measured by the most fitting exposure base. Consequently, insurers select exposure bases that most closely approach the ideal.

Accurate Measure

An exposure base should be an accurate measure of the magnitude of the insured loss exposure. The insured's expected losses should increase or decrease in the same proportion as the number of exposure units. An exposure base that is not an accurate measure would result in an inequitable insurance cost allocation, with some insureds paying less than their share of the insurance cost and others paying more than their share. As with any inequitable insurance cost allocation, such an exposure base would lead to adverse selection against the insurer and dissatisfaction among insureds.

As indicated, few exposure bases are ideal. For example, because of the variation in wage rates, payroll may not be an accurate measure of workers' compensation exposures. However, businesses retain payroll data for income tax and Social Security reporting purposes. The premium auditor can also obtain payroll data easily. The risk of criminal prosecution deters the insured from manipulating payroll data; consequently, these data are accurate for premium auditing purposes.

Sensitive to Inflation

An exposure base should also be sensitive to inflation. Otherwise, it would not reflect the true cost of insurance. For example, gross sales is used as the exposure base for liability insurance because inflation has an effect on the magnitude of liability losses. Gross sales as an exposure base is sensitive to inflation. Because gross sales tend to rise with inflation, the premium also rises without any change in the rate. If the exposure were not sensitive to inflation, insurers would have to increase the rate itself to obtain additional premium to cover rising loss costs because of inflation. The use of inflation-sensitive exposure bases enables insurers to ask for rate increases less often. Insurers prefer inflation-sensitive exposure bases because they correct themselves automatically for changes in inflation.

Easy to Determine

An exposure base should be easy to determine. Preferably, it should be directly determinable from the insured's records or from a relatively simple inspection of the insured's premises or operations. An exposure base that an insurer can measure only through lengthy research would result in excessive insurer expenses (or perhaps insureds' expenses), making premiums more expensive. However, using the same exposure base for different lines of insurance significantly reduces the effort required to determine the actual loss exposure for each.

Mileage would probably be a better exposure base than car-years (one vehicle insured for twelve months is one car-year) for auto insurance, and insurers use it in some cases. However, most insureds do not gather mileage statistics for other purposes, so the premium auditor would have to check the insured vehicles' odometers, a prohibitively expensive effort.

The number of customers entering the premises would probably be a better exposure base than floor area for determining premises liability. However, most businesses do not count customers entering the business premises, so an insurer cannot collect such data with reasonable ease and expense. Insurers do use the number of customers entering the premises for theaters and similar businesses that keep a count through ticket sales. Retail sales can partially determine customer count through gross sales.

Difficult for the Insured to Manipulate

An exposure base should be difficult for the insured to manipulate without detection. If manipulation is easy and safe, some insureds may manipulate exposure base information to reduce their premiums, thereby depriving the insurer of adequate revenue for the loss exposures assumed.

Acceptable to Regulators and Society

An exposure base should be acceptable to both regulators and society. Regulators in most states must approve an insurer's rating manual and rating plans. If an insurer proposes an exposure base that is not acceptable to the regulatory authority (or to other special interest groups who make their beliefs known to the regulator), the regulator is unlikely to approve the proposal.

Social acceptability of the exposure base is also a consideration. If an insurer were to propose an exposure base that is unacceptable to a large and/or vocal group, that group may be able to draw enough attention to its viewpoint to pressure the insurer not to use the exposure base. An extreme example is the rating base for hospital professional liability insurance. An insurer may determine that the loss exposure is closely related to the number of deaths that occur in the hospital over a time period. Although this measure may be statistically correlated to the loss exposure, society would probably disapprove of this method of measuring the exposure base.

Although unfair discrimination is more closely related to rate approval than to selecting an ideal exposure base, if an insurer were to propose an exposure base that unfairly discriminated against a group, both society and regulators would likely prevent the insurer from using the exposure base. An example is a proposal to use member contribution rates for pricing liability insurance on churches. If a certain denomination were known for having a higher contribution rate among members, charges of unfair discrimination would likely arise. Such an exposure base would also likely be socially unacceptable.

Insurance Rates

An insurance rate consists of the following three components: an expected loss component, an underwriting expense component, and an allowance for underwriting profit and contingencies. In practice, insurers usually combine the underwriting expense component and the allowance for profit and contingencies into a single element: the expense loading. The **expense loading** is the element in the gross rate that covers the insurer's underwriting expenses, profits, and contingencies. Determining the expected loss component (called the pure premium) is the most difficult part of the ratemaking process and involves the greatest uncertainty. The **pure premium** is the amount included in the rate per exposure unit required to pay losses. Insurers estimate the amount needed for expected losses based on past loss experience adjusted to reflect the following: probable future trends in inflation and accident frequency, and other factors that may cause future losses to differ from those incurred in the past. Insurers usually calculate the pure premium by dividing the dollar amount of losses incurred for some period of years (called the experience period) by the number of earned exposure units. The formula to calculate the pure premium is as follows:

Expense loading
The element in the gross rate that covers the insurer's underwriting expenses, profits, and contingencies.

Pure premium
The amount included in the rate per exposure unit required to pay losses.

$$\text{Pure premium} = \frac{\text{Dollar amount of losses incurred in the experience period}}{\text{Number of earned exposure units}}.$$

Therefore, if the losses and loss adjustment expenses incurred during the experience period (after adjustment for inflation and other factors) amounted to $1,270,000, and earned exposure units were 1,000,000 (for example, $100,000,000 of payroll), the pure premium would be calculated as follows:

$$\text{Pure premium} = \frac{\$1,270,000}{\$1,000,000} = \$1.27.$$

Because insurance rates depend so heavily on loss cost statistics and exposure unit statistics, insurers must gather and report those statistics with the utmost accuracy. Additionally, loss cost statistics of a single insurer are usually insufficient for the insurer to make reasonable forecasts of future losses. Consequently, insurers act collectively to gather loss cost data. An error in either the loss data or the exposure data will cause the resulting rates to be incorrect for the assumed loss exposures.

Insurers usually include their loss adjustment expenses in the pure premium for ratemaking purposes, but include all other expenses in the expense loading. The size of the total expense loading and the exact nature of expense categories vary by line of insurance. For example, for equipment breakdown (also called boiler and machinery) insurance, an insurer may allocate 35 percent of the premium to general administrative and loss control expenses, while allocating only 10 percent of the premium to those expenses for commercial fire insurance. The difference is largely due to the greater expenses incurred for loss control inspections under equipment breakdown insurance.

Exhibit 1-2 shows a hypothetical expense loading for one line of liability insurance. The expense categories are typical of those that insurers use for most lines of insurance, although the percentage allocated to each expense category varies by line of insurance.

EXHIBIT 1-2

Expense Loading for One Line of Liability Insurance

Expense Category	Percentage of Gross Rate
Total acquisition costs	29.5%
General expenses	10.7
Taxes, licenses, and fees	2.7
Total underwriting expenses	42.9%
Expected losses and loss adjustment expenses	57.1
Total expenses	100.0%

Gross rate

The pure premium divided by the sum of the expected percentage of losses and loss adjustment expenses.

Insurers usually calculate the gross rate for premiums, which includes all three rate components—expected loss, underwriting expense, and allowance for underwriting profit and contingencies. **Gross rate** is the pure premium divided by the sum of the expected percentage of losses and loss adjustment expenses. For example, if the pure premium for a given classification for liability coverage is $1.27 per $1,000 of payroll, and the expected loss percentage is 57.1 percent (as shown in Exhibit 1-2), then the gross rate would be calculated as follows:

$$\text{Gross rate} = \frac{\text{Pure premium}}{\text{Expected percentage of losses and loss adjustment expenses}}$$

$$= \$1.27 \div 0.571$$

$$= \$2.22.$$

The expected loss percentage equals 100 percent minus the percentage loading for expenses, profit, and contingencies.

As mentioned, insurers include a loading for underwriting profit and contingencies. (The contingency component of the expense loading reflects the possibility that the actual amount needed for losses incurred will exceed the amount included in the rate to pay them.) For many lines of insurance, this loading has been 5 percent of premiums. However, including a 5 percent loading for underwriting profit and contingencies does not mean that insurers always earn exactly 5 percent. In fact, they seldom do. Historical data indicate that industry underwriting profit has exceeded 5 percent only twice in nearly four decades.[1] Insurers also rely on investment income from the funds they hold for the time between collecting premiums and paying losses. In some states, insurers are required to reflect expected investment income experience in the calculation of the rate. Therefore, in those states, investment income is no longer available to make up any shortfall in underwriting profit because it is now part of that profit determination.

Modifications to Manual Rates

The **manual rate** is the rate found in a rating manual or a computerized rate table. The **manual premium** is the premium developed from applying the manual rate to the number of exposure units. Manual premiums can be subsequently modified to reflect the insured's loss experience or other factors for which the insurer has regulatory approval to consider in pricing. Later chapters describe the exposure bases, the classifications, and the modifications involved in determining the final premium for various lines of insurance.

Manual rate
The rate found in a rating manual or a computerized rate table.

Manual premium
The premium developed from applying the manual rate to the number of exposure units.

Rating Classifications

Generally, insurers attempt to spread the loss costs equitably over all insureds purchasing the insurance. Insurers can use the following three methods of spreading loss costs: charge all insureds the same rate for each line of insurance, set a different rate for each insured based on that insured's loss characteristics, or divide all insureds into relatively homogeneous classes and charge the same rate to each insured in a given class based on the average loss exposure of the class.

Insurers have used the first method—the same rate for all insureds—for some lines of insurance for which the loss exposure does not vary greatly among insureds, when sufficient information is not available to determine the extent of variation among insureds, or when the premium for each insured is too small to justify the expense of using either of the other two methods. However, when substantial variation exists in the loss costs of various insured groups, using the same rate can lead to considerable problems. In such cases, the same rate is too high for some insureds and too low for others. At the other end of the spectrum, the insurer may attempt to craft an individual rate for each insured.

An individually determined rate for each insured would seem to solve the problems caused by charging the same rate for all insureds. However, it creates its own problems. First, individual rating is expensive, so it would not be economically feasible except for loss exposures with a substantial premium. Second, individual rates would likely be subjective for many lines of insurance because precisely evaluating individual loss exposures is not possible. Third, individual rates based on subjective factors could lead to unfair discrimination, either intentional or unintentional. The compromise approach to either charging everyone the same rate or tailoring a rate for each loss exposure is to use class rates.

Class rating involves the creation of categories that reflect certain risk characteristics. Insureds are categorized and charged the average rate for the class. Class rating is more cost effective to apply than individual rating and only slightly more expensive than a same-rate method. A properly designed class rating scheme will include a class for each loss exposure.

Class rating increases the effectiveness of using the law of large numbers. The law of large numbers requires a large number of homogenous loss exposures. Classifying risks—categorizing by risk characteristics—makes the loss exposures being classified homogenous for insurance pricing purposes.

Insureds can also understand class rating. Paying a premium based on categories of risk characteristics makes more sense than everyone's paying the same rate or having a customized rate.

Class rating involves using an average rate for the class, with the rate being too high for some and too low for others. Class rating requires a well-planned classification system of loss exposures so that all insureds believe that they are paying a fair price.

In devising a classification system, insurers must strike a balance between complexity and simplicity. A complex classification system may have multiple factors and thereby result in hundreds of classifications. While a complex classification system may yield greater class homogeneity, it would likely sacrifice the possibility of having large numbers in each category. A simple classification system with relatively few classifications would have many loss exposures in each category, thereby making the average rate charged for each classification adequate for each classification as a whole. However, competitive forces in the insurance marketplace have often thwarted simple classification plans as competing insurers have expanded simple classifications to attract more desirable insureds.

RATEMAKING GOALS

Sound ratemaking is essential to an insurer's financial well-being. Inadequate rates produce losses for the insurer and could eventually lead to insolvency. Excessive rates could lead to loss of business to competitors. In support of sound ratemaking, an insurer should strive to achieve the following six goals:

1. Produce the correct rate per exposure unit
2. Produce stable rates
3. Respond promptly to changes in loss experience
4. Encourage loss control
5. Provide for profit and contingencies
6. Make ratemaking simple to understand and apply

Because these goals can have conflicting intents, insurer ratemaking efforts must strike a balance among the individual goals.

Produce the Correct Rate per Exposure Unit

Ratemaking should produce the correct rate per exposure unit. The correct rate is the amount adequate to cover losses and the insurer's expenses as well as to provide sufficient profit to attract capital. If the rate is not correct, in addition to risking loss of business and perhaps insolvency, the insurer faces other consequences. If the rate is too low to provide an adequate profit, it will result in inadequate capital to meet the public's insurance needs. If the rate is too high, it will result in dissatisfied customers and investigation by governmental agencies, and it will attract excessive capital (with resulting excessive competition) to the industry.

Produce Stable Rates

Insurance rates should be reasonably stable. Rapid changes in rates, especially price increases, are likely to lead to consumer dissatisfaction and regulatory problems. Insurers use three ratemaking methods to avoid undue rate fluctuations. These methods include:

- Use of a long experience period
- Statistical isolation of catastrophic losses
- Use of credibility factors

For some lines of insurance, such as earthquake insurance, in which losses naturally fluctuate widely by year, insurers customarily use a long experience period for ratemaking purposes. Insurers have used statistics for a fifteen-year period as the basis of rates for some lines of insurance so that a few unusually bad or unusually good years will not cause undue rate fluctuations. For a line of insurance with little loss fluctuation, a shorter period may be sufficient. A line of insurance with a small premium volume requires a longer experience period than one with a large premium volume.

Another ratemaking method that insurers use for catastrophe-prone lines of insurance is to exclude part or all of the catastrophe losses from the ratemaking statistics. The insurer then replaces the excluded losses with a catastrophe charge. This charge is calculated based on an even longer experience period. The insurer can also calculate the catastrophe charge based on national statistics, whereas the insurer may use state statistics in most other lines of insurance.

Credibility factors also provide rate stability. A **credibility factor** is the factor applied in ratemaking to adjust for the predictive value of loss data and used to minimize the variations in the rates that result from purely chance variations in losses. The credibility factor, which ranges from zero to one, is a measure of the predictive value of the past loss data as an indication of future expected losses. A certain amount of chance fluctuation exists in losses by year. The relative magnitude of fluctuation decreases as the number of exposure units increases. A large volume of past loss statistics permits an insurer to estimate future losses more accurately, provided all else remains the same,

Credibility factor
The factor applied in ratemaking to adjust for the predictive value of loss data and used to minimize the variations in the rates that result from purely chance variations in losses.

than does a small volume of loss statistics. Consequently, the credibility factor increases as the volume of statistics increases, although not necessarily in direct proportion to that increase.

Insurers usually base a rate increase on two sets of loss statistics. For example, insurers may base part of the rate change for a certain rating classification on the statewide loss statistics and part on the national loss statistics. If the credibility factor were 1.00 for a certain state for a certain classification, then the insurer would base the rate change totally on the statewide loss statistics. If the credibility factor were 0.70, then the insurer would base 70 percent of the rate change on the statewide loss statistics and 30 percent on the national loss statistics. Credibility factors serve to temper the effect of favorable or unfavorable loss experience.

Respond Promptly to Changes in Loss Experience

If an insurer is to remain solvent and competitive, its rates must respond promptly to changes in loss experience. Rates must increase when the loss frequency or severity increases, and decrease when they decrease. When loss experience changes rapidly, responsiveness and stability naturally conflict. A balance must be struck between these two goals.

Just as a long experience period tends to promote stability, a short experience period tends to promote responsiveness. Insurers have used an experience period as short as one year in some lines of insurance when responsiveness was particularly important.

Trend factor
An adjustment to loss data for a change in general economic conditions, such as inflation.

Using trend factors is another way to increase rate responsiveness. Insurers use a **trend factor** to adjust loss data for a change in general economic conditions, such as inflation.

If loss data analysis indicates a trend in loss frequency, loss severity, or both, the insurer projects the trend into the future to the midpoint of the period for which the insurer will use the rates. In the absence of trend factors, rates would always lag behind losses because insurers calculate rates for the future based on past loss experience. The lag would be particularly serious for insurers during periods of high inflation. However, inflation is not the only trend factor insurers use. Loss frequency or severity can change because of changes in laws, technology, business conditions, or other factors, such as benefit levels provided to injured workers under workers' compensation.

Merely projecting past trends into the future is not sufficient because the trend can increase, decrease, or even change directions before the insurer uses the rates. Actuaries can use econometric models to find a better way to adjust past loss data to reflect future conditions.

Merit rating plan
An insurance rating plan that either increases or decreases manual rates for a particular insured based on that insured's actual or expected loss experience.

Insurers have also used merit rating plans to promote rate responsiveness, especially for medium to large commercial and industrial accounts. A **merit rating plan** is an insurance rating plan that either increases or decreases manual rates for a particular insured based on that insured's actual or expected loss experience. Merit rating plans are also an important way to encourage loss control.

Encourage Loss Control

Several ratemaking techniques are used to encourage loss control. The simplest way to encourage loss control through ratemaking is to give direct rate credits (or to charge a lower premium) for specified loss control measures. For example, for burglary insurance, insurers give rate credits for superior safes and for acceptable alarm systems. Similarly, commercial property pricing reflects construction features as well as fire detection and fire suppression measures. Conversely, insurers apply rate surcharges for undesirable features. For example, an insured operating a company-owned aircraft pays a seat surcharge, which leads to a total workers' compensation premium that reflects the increase in loss exposure as the size of the aircraft increases.

Ratemaking can also reward the insured for successful loss control results instead of encouraging specific measures that the insurer expects to reduce losses. For example, merit rating plans include experience rating plans, retrospective rating plans, and schedule rating plans. Those rating plans are described next.

An **experience rating plan** is a rating plan that increases or reduces the premium for a future policy period based on the insured's own loss experience for a period in the recent past. For example, an insurer may determine an insured's rates for 20X9 on the basis of that insured's loss experience for the years 20X5, 20X6, and 20X7. The insurer would reduce the manual rates if the insured's losses were less than the average for the classification and increase them if the insured's losses were higher.

Experience rating plan
A rating plan that increases or reduces the premium for a future policy period based on the insured's own loss experience for a period in the recent past.

A **retrospective rating plan** is a rating plan that increases or reduces the premium for a given policy period based on the insured's own loss experience during the same policy period. Under such a plan, the insured pays the standard premium at the policy period's beginning and receives either a refund or a bill for an additional premium after the policy period's end, depending on the loss experience during the period. The policy contains a formula for calculating the retrospective premium adjustment. Retrospectively rated plans are especially effective for encouraging loss control because of the potential premium savings if losses are low. Alternatively, insurers sometimes require retrospectively rated plans as a condition of providing insurance for marginal accounts that may generate high losses.

Retrospective rating plan
A rating plan that increases or reduces the premium for a given policy period based on the insured's own loss experience during the same policy period.

Many regulatory authorities also permit insurers to use a schedule rating plan. A **schedule rating plan** is a rating plan that awards debits or credits based on specific categories, such as the care and condition of the premises or the selection and training of employees. The schedule debit or credit amount generally does not exceed 25 percent of the premium, and the insurer applies it to a previously calculated premium. The insurer first determines the premium using approved rates and then modifies that premium by

Schedule rating plan
A rating plan that awards debits or credits based on specific categories, such as the care and condition of the premises or the selection and training of employees.

the experience rating factor. The insurer further modifies the result by the schedule debit or credit percentage.

Provide for Profit and Contingencies

Rates include a provision for profit and contingencies. Insurers are entitled to a return on capital, and, consequently, profit is explicitly provided for in the rate. Despite the presumed accuracy of ratemaking in forecasting losses, insurers recognize that losses that were not contemplated in ratemaking may occur. For example, wind losses caused by hurricanes could exceed what was forecast because of an abnormal number of hurricanes. The provision in rates for contingencies reflects this possibility. Although insurers have expended much effort and expense on improving ratemaking, insurance rates are still only estimates of the amount that the insurer will need to cover losses and expenses and to provide for a profit and contingencies. Even the soundest ratemaking cannot consistently produce rates that are exactly correct for the loss exposure insured.

For most lines of insurance, the combined loading for profits and contingencies is usually 5 percent of the gross rate. This loading amount has been challenged by state regulators and others as being either too high or too low. Some contend that the loading should be lowered because of investment income on the line of insurance. Others contend that the 5 percent loading does not provide insurers with a sufficient return on capital.

Make Ratemaking Simple to Understand and Apply

A variety of people must understand ratemaking: underwriters, rate clerks, producers, and sometimes insureds, among others. Insurance personnel must understand ratemaking to apply rates and to explain them to others. Insureds must understand rates to be assured that they are not being overcharged and to understand what steps they can take to reduce insurance costs. If the insured does not understand ratemaking, ratemaking cannot achieve its goal of encouraging loss control. Consequently, ratemaking must be as simple as possible to understand.

RATE REGULATION

Regulatory authorities monitor insurer rating practices to ensure that rates are adequate, not excessive, and not unfairly discriminatory. States, not the federal government, are primarily responsible for rate regulation. Rate regulation might well be the regulatory activity that receives the most public attention. This section covers rate regulation goals, types of rating laws, and arguments for prior approval and open competition rating laws.

Property-casualty insurance pricing has historically been cyclical. The typical pattern is a few years of low rates, relaxed underwriting, and underwriting losses (soft market) followed by a few years of high rates, restrictive underwriting, and strong underwriting gains (hard market). This pattern is known as the underwriting cycle.

The underwriting cycle has strong, generally undesirable effects on the market and challenges all aspects of rate regulation. A full discussion of the underwriting cycle is beyond the scope of this text.

Insurance Rate Regulation Goals

The three major goals of rate regulation are to ensure that rates are:

1. Adequate
2. Not excessive
3. Not unfairly discriminatory

Adequate

The first goal of insurance rate regulation is that rates be adequate. Rates for a specific type of insurance should be high enough to pay all claims and expenses related to those rates. This requirement helps maintain insurer solvency. If rates are inadequate, an insurer might fail, and policyholders and third-party claimants would be financially harmed if their claims were not paid.

Several factors complicate the regulatory goal of having adequate rates:

- An insurer usually does not know what its actual expenses will be when the policy is sold. Premiums are paid in advance, but they might be insufficient to pay all related claims and expenses that occur later. An unexpected increase in claim frequency or severity can make the rate inadequate.

- Insurers might charge inadequate rates in response to keen price competition in order not to lose business.

- State rate approval systems might not approve insurers' requests for adequate rates for political reasons or because of disagreement over the level of requested rates.

- Unanticipated events might lead to higher losses than those projected when rates were set.

Although insurance rate adequacy is a goal of insurance regulation, no method of rate regulation guarantees that rates will be adequate.

Not Excessive

A second goal of insurance rate regulation is that rates not be excessive. Insurers should not earn excessive or unreasonable profits. Regulators have considerable latitude and discretion in determining whether rates are excessive for a given type of insurance, and they consider numerous factors. These factors include (1) the number of insurers selling a specific coverage in the rating territory, (2) the relative market share of competing insurers, (3) the degree of rate variation among the competing insurers, (4) past and prospective loss experience for a given type of insurance, (5) possibility of catastrophe losses,

(6) margin for underwriting profit and contingencies, (7) marketing expenses for a given type of insurance, and (8) special judgment factors that might apply to a given type of insurance.

Regulators sometimes use the fair rate of return approach in determining whether an insurer's rates are adequate or excessive. An insurer should expect at least some minimum rate of return on the equity invested in its insurance operations. An insurer's fair rate of return presumably should resemble the rate of return applicable to other types of businesses, especially if insurers are to attract investment capital. Many believe that the insurance business, by its nature, involves a higher degree of risk than many other businesses and that higher risks generally should be accompanied by higher returns. To date, little agreement exists as to what constitutes a fair rate of return for insurers.

Not Unfairly Discriminatory

The third goal of insurance rate regulation is that rates not be unfairly discriminatory. The word "discrimination," as usually used, carries negative connotations, but the word itself is neutral, implying only the ability to differentiate among things. Discrimination, in the neutral sense, is essential to insurance rating. However, insurers' discrimination must be fair and consistent. This means that loss exposures that are roughly similar regarding expected losses and expenses should be charged substantially similar rates. For example, two drivers age twenty-five operating similar vehicles in the same rating territory who buy the same type and amount of auto insurance from the same insurer should be charged similar rates.

Only unfair discrimination is prohibited, not *fair* discrimination. If loss exposures are substantially different in terms of expected losses and expenses, then different rates can be charged. For example, if a woman age twenty-five and another age sixty-five are in good health and purchase the same type and amount of life insurance from the same insurer, it is not unfair rate discrimination to charge the older woman a higher rate. The higher probability of death for a woman at age sixty-five clearly and fairly justifies a higher rate.

Types of Rating Laws

The rates that property-casualty insurers can charge in any state are affected by that state's rating laws. Generally, the major types of state rating laws are as follows:

- *Mandatory rate law.* Under a **mandatory rate law**, a state agency or rating bureau sets rates, and all licensed insurers are required to use them.

- *Prior approval law.* Under a **prior approval law**, rates must be approved by the state insurance department before they can be used. Insurers have criticized prior approval laws because there is often considerable delay in obtaining a rate increase. Consequently, a rate increase might be inadequate by the time it is approved. Furthermore, the statistical data required by the state insurance department might not be readily available.

Mandatory rate law
State law under which insurance rates are set by a state agency or rating bureau and all licensed insurers are required to use those rates.

Prior approval law
State law under which insurance rates must be approved by the state insurance department before they can be used.

- *File-and-use law.* Under a **file-and-use law**, rates have to be filed with the state insurance department, but they can then be used immediately. The department has the authority to disapprove the rates if they cannot be justified or if they violate state law. A file-and-use law overcomes the problems of delay associated with prior approval laws.

- *Use-and-file law.* Under a **use-and-file law**, which is a variation of the file-and-use law, insurers can change rates and later submit filing information that is subject to regulatory review.

- *Flex rating law.* Under a **flex rating law**, prior approval is required only if the new rates exceed a certain percentage above (and sometimes below) the rates filed previously. Insurers are permitted to increase or decrease their rates within the established range without prior approval. Typically, a range of 5 to 10 percent is permitted. Flex rating permits insurers to make rate adjustments quickly in response to changing market conditions and loss experience, but it prohibits wide swings within a short period of time. Flex rating also can restrict insurers from drastically reducing rates to increase market share. The result should be smoother insurance pricing cycles.

- *Open competition.* Under an **open competition system**, rates do not have to be filed with the state insurance department. Market prices driven by the economic laws of supply and demand, rather than the discretionary acts of regulators, determine the rates and availability. However, insurers might be required to furnish rate schedules and supporting statistical data to regulatory officials, and the state insurance department has the authority to monitor competition and to disapprove rates if necessary. The goals of adequate, nonexcessive, and equitable rates still apply.

These laws apply not only to rates for a new type of insurance, but also to rate changes.

Desirability of Strict Rate Regulation

Generally, consumer groups and politicians tend to support prior approval or other forms of strict regulation, while insurers and economists tend to support use-and-file and open competition.

Proponents of prior approval laws offer the following reasons for their position:

- Prior approval laws require insurers to justify their requests for rate increases with supporting actuarial data.

- Prior approval laws tend to promote insurer solvency. Because regulators review rate data, rates can be set at adequate levels to maintain insurer solvency.

- Prior approval laws keep rates reasonable and prevent insurers from charging excessive rates. Many people assume that insurers are earning excessive profits and that rates can be reduced only by direct government action.

File-and-use law
State law under which insurance rates must be filed with the state insurance department but can then be used immediately.

Use-and-file law
State law under which insurance rates can be put into effect with filing information subsequently submitted and subject to regulatory review.

Flex rating law
State law under which prior approval is required only if the new rates exceed a certain percentage above (and sometimes below) the rates previously filed.

Open competition system
A system under which rates do not have to be filed with the state insurance department.

Proponents of open competition offer the following reasons for their position:

- Prior approval laws might cause rate increases to be inadequate for writing profitable business. Inadequate rates might force insurers to reduce the amount of new business written or might even force them to withdraw from the market, which could lead to an insurance availability problem.

- Prior approval laws might distort incentives for controlling claim costs. This argument applies largely to auto insurance. To make auto insurance more affordable, regulators might reduce rates for drivers with the highest premiums by increasing rates for other drivers. Regulators might limit the rates insurers can charge drivers who are in a residual market plan or might restrict the use of age, gender, or territory as ratemaking variables. The result is that high-risk drivers are more likely to drive, they are more likely to purchase expensive cars, and they are less likely to exercise caution in preventing accidents and theft losses than if their rates were not subsidized.[2]

- Prior approval laws might lead insurers to abandon the state, increasing the number of drivers in residual market plans. Considerable evidence exists that in states with strict rate suppression, the proportion of drivers in residual market plans is much higher than in states with competitive rating laws. Under open competition, the equilibrium market price is determined by market forces, not by government regulators. Consequently, most drivers can be insured in the voluntary standard market by paying market prices.

- Open competition is less expensive to administer. Regulators are not required to review thousands of rate filings or to hold costly hearings. Consequently, the state insurance department's limited resources can be devoted to higher-priority areas, such as solvency regulation and consumer affairs.

- Open competition tends to overcome the limitations of prior approval laws. Open competition laws allow rates to be adjusted more quickly in response to changing economic and market conditions. Fewer political pressures are encountered, and the need for supporting actuarial data is reduced.

- Open competition among insurers keeps rates reasonable and equitable. Free market forces, rather than government intervention, curtail excessive rates.

RATE FILINGS

Virtually all states require insurers to file their rates with the state insurance regulators for at least some lines of insurance. The filings must include the rate schedules; explain the method by which the insurer determined the rates; and provide sufficient statistical data to show that loss experience, changes in law, or other factors necessitate the requested rate change.

An insurer can choose to prepare its own rate filings, and many insurers do so for at least some lines of insurance. Many small insurers, however, do not have a sufficiently large volume of business to calculate credible rates. Therefore, they share loss cost data with other insurers through membership in insurance advisory organizations or rating bureaus.

Insurance Advisory Organizations

Insurance advisory organizations are independent corporations that work with and on behalf of insurers that purchase or subscribe to their services. Advisory organizations primarily develop prospective loss costs and standard insurance policy forms. Sometimes, they also file loss costs and policy forms with the state on behalf of their member and subscribing insurers. They often provide other valuable services to participants in the insurance market and its regulators, such as the following:

- Developing rating systems
- Collecting and tabulating statistics
- Researching important insurance topics
- Providing a forum for discussing issues
- Educating insurers, insurance regulators, and the public about relevant issues
- Monitoring regulatory issues of concern to members

Insurers must pay a fee for the services of insurance advisory organizations. Well-known insurance advisory organizations include Insurance Services Office (ISO), the American Association of Insurance Services (AAIS), and the National Council on Compensation Insurance (NCCI).

Even though insurers that use advisory organizations' services are not required to use specific insurance rates or forms, advisory organizations impose a certain degree of uniformity. Relatively few insurers have the resources to independently develop the statistical data on which to base their own insurance rates or to develop policy forms, endorsements, and rating systems for many different coverages that also comply with many state regulations. Insurance consumers benefit from competition among insurers who base their rates on sound statistical data. Uniformity in insurance policies also makes it easier for consumers to comparison-shop.

Examples of Insurance Advisory Organizations

Many bureaus operate in the United States. Some operate throughout all or most of the country, and others operate in only one or a few states. This text describes only NCCI, ISO, and AAIS.

The **National Council on Compensation Insurance (NCCI)** is an insurance advisory organization that manages a database of workers' compensation insurance information, analyzes industry trends, prepares workers' compensation rate recommendations, assists in pricing legislation, and provides data products.

Insurance advisory organization
An independent corporation that works with and on behalf of insurers that purchase or subscribe to its services.

National Council on Compensation Insurance (NCCI)
An insurance advisory organization that manages a database of workers' compensation insurance information, analyzes industry trends, prepares workers' compensation rate recommendations, assists in pricing legislation, and provides data products.

NCCI works actively with regulators; insurers; trade associations; and business, industry, and labor coalitions to maintain a healthy workers' compensation system and to reduce the frequency of employee injuries. In many jurisdictions, NCCI acts as a statistical agent or adviser to state rating bureaus in several other states. NCCI gathers ratemaking data, calculates and files prospective loss costs (or rates) for its members, designs and administers experience and retrospective rating plans, and drafts standardized policy contracts for workers' compensation insurance. Virtually all insurers that write workers' compensation insurance in the U.S. are members or subscribers of NCCI or a state's rating bureau that relies on services provided by NCCI.

Insurance Services Office, Inc. (ISO)
An insurance advisory organization that provides analytical and decision-support products and services to the property-liability insurance industry.

Insurance Services Office, Inc. (ISO), is an insurance advisory organization that provides analytical and decision-support products and services to the property-casualty insurance industry. ISO is a multiple-line advisory service organization that provides prospective loss costs to the insurance industry. ISO functions as an insurance advisory organization for virtually all property and liability lines of insurance except workers' compensation, ocean marine, aviation, and surety bonds. Other insurance advisory organizations have jurisdiction over workers' compensation and surety bonds, but no insurance advisory organizations in the U.S. have jurisdiction over ocean marine and aviation insurance.

ISO performs all of the loss-cost advisory service functions, including fire insurance rating inspections of commercial buildings. It also inspects cities and towns to evaluate their fire defenses for fire insurance rating purposes. ISO operates nationally, and many property-casualty insurers are members or subscribers for at least some of its services.

American Association of Insurance Services (AAIS)
A national insurance advisory organization that develops policy forms, manual rules, and rating information used by U.S. property-casualty insurers.

The **American Association of Insurance Services (AAIS)** is a national insurance advisory organization that develops policy forms, manual rules, and rating information used by U.S. property-casualty insurers. AAIS is a product development resource for insurance providers. AAIS currently offers programs of forms, rules, and rating information for more than twenty lines of personal and commercial insurance; statistical reporting plans for all of those lines, plus auto; and support services for custom product development, state filings, actuarial analysis, automation, and training.

State rating bureau
An advisory organization that provides analytical and decision-support products and services to the property-casualty insurance industry.

A **state rating bureau** is an advisory organization that provides analytical and decision-support products and services to the property-casualty insurance industry. Two kinds of state rating bureaus exist: a state government's agencies and insurer-owned bureaus that serve a single state. However, member companies own and operate most state rating bureaus under the state regulatory authorities' supervision. Insurer-owned state rating bureaus exist in some states for workers' compensation and auto insurance. The states of California, Delaware, Hawaii, Indiana, Massachusetts, Michigan, Minnesota, New Jersey, New York, North Carolina, Pennsylvania, Texas, and Wyoming operate their own non-NCCI rating bureaus. Many of these largely follow NCCI rules for computing premiums and classifications, but California, Delaware, Texas, and Pennsylvania are notably different from NCCI in some aspects of classification and premium computation.

Some state rating bureaus are not large enough to support the technical staffs and data necessary to perform their duties. Also, insurers can more efficiently report all their statistics to a single bureau rather than reporting some to a national bureau and some to a state bureau. Consequently, state rating bureaus rely on insurance advisory organizations, principally ISO and NCCI, for technical advice and statistical and data processing services.

Rate Deviations

Many insurers that are members or subscribers of insurance advisory organizations do not adhere to all loss costs. A **deviation filing** is a request that an insurer files with state insurance regulators to deviate from insurance advisory organization-developed loss costs. Insurer deviations are usually presented as a percentage of loss costs. For example, an insurer may file a 15 percent downward deviation, which authorizes it to use rates 15 percent less than those filed.

Deviation filing
A request that an insurer files with state insurance regulators to deviate from insurance advisory organization-developed loss costs.

The insurer justifies deviation from the insurance advisory organization's prospective loss costs on the basis that the individual insurer's loss costs, for whatever reason, will be either higher or lower. Some states even require that all insurers (not just those filing deviations) justify that the loss costs proposed are representative of the insurer's expected loss costs.

Independent Filings

If an insurer elects not to join or subscribe to an insurance advisory organization, it must then calculate its own loss costs and expense costs and file its own final rates. In doing so, it must furnish state insurance regulators with sufficient data to demonstrate that its rates comply with the statutory requirements.

Some large insurers have sufficient data from their own experience to satisfy regulatory requirements. New or small insurers must use experience data from other insurers either combined with or instead of their own data. Insurers can obtain data directly from other insurers or from an insurance advisory organization. If the line of insurance is new, insurance data may not be available. Insurers may use data gathered by other industries or by governmental agencies in such cases.

An independent filing is more complex than a deviation filing because an independent filing must incorporate all the supporting data. An insurer bases a deviation filing on an insurance advisory organization's supporting data and includes only data sufficient to justify the deviation from their statistics. However, an independent filing has greater flexibility. A deviation is usually the same percentage deviation for all of an insured's classifications within a given line of insurance. An independent filing does not have that restriction. In fact, the classification system for an independent filing can differ substantially from that used by the insurance advisory organization. Of course, the flexibility has a price. The insurer submitting the independent filing must bear the entire cost of the necessary technical personnel to calculate its rates, prepare filings, and maintain the necessary contacts with state insurance regulators. Insurance advisory organization members and subscribers share such costs among themselves, reducing the expense borne by any one insurer.

Despite the disadvantages, independent filings have become increasingly important in recent years in some major lines of insurance. However, they are not nearly as common in property insurance, partially because of the need for engineers to inspect commercial buildings for rating purposes. Also, the lower loss frequency in property insurance requires a much larger body of data for sufficient credibility for ratemaking purposes. Few insurers could accumulate sufficient property insurance data solely from their own experience.

SUMMARY

Premium auditors should understand fundamental insurance concepts as well as ratemaking concepts to perform their premium auditing tasks effectively and efficiently. Fundamental insurance concepts include causes of loss, hazards, indemnification, and the law of large numbers. Ratemaking concepts include how to determine a premium by multiplying the rate times the applicable exposure units. The rate is the price of insurance per exposure unit.

A rating plan is a set of directions that specify criteria of the exposure base, the exposure unit, and the rate per exposure unit to determine premiums for a particular line of insurance. Exposure bases should be an accurate measure, sensitive to inflation, easy to determine, difficult for the insured to manipulate, and acceptable to regulators and society.

Insurance rates consist of an expected loss component, an expense component, and an allowance for underwriting profit and contingencies. The pure premium is the expected loss component in an insurance rate. The gross rate is determined by dividing the pure premium by the expected percentage of losses and loss adjustment expenses.

The manual rate is found in the rating manual before applying modifiers, as is done with experience or retrospectively rated plans. Multiplying the number of exposure units by the manual rate for the applicable classification produces the manual premium for a particular policy. Insurers can use the following three methods of spreading loss costs: charge all insureds the same rate for each line of insurance, set a different rate for each insured based on that insured's characteristics, or divide all insureds into relatively homogeneous classes and charge the same rate to each insured in a given class based on the average loss exposure of the class.

To promote sound ratemaking, an insurer should strive to achieve the following six goals:

1. Produce the correct rate per exposure unit
2. Produce stable rates
3. Respond promptly to changes in loss experience

4. Encourage loss control

5. Provide for profit and contingencies

6. Make ratemaking simple to understand and apply

Regulatory authorities monitor insurer rating practices to ensure that rates are adequate, not excessive, and not unfairly discriminatory. Although the federal government has sometimes exercised control over insurance rates to control rate inflation, the states are primarily responsible for rate regulation.

State regulatory laws can be classified according to the extent of state control of rates and the method by which the state implements that control. The six major regulatory rate law classes are (1) mandatory rate laws, (2) prior approval laws, (3) file-and-use laws, (4) use-and-file laws, (5) flex rating laws, and (6) open competition system.

Virtually all states require insurers to file their rates with state insurance regulators for at least some lines of insurance. The filings must include the rate schedules; explain the method by which the insurer determined the rates; and provide sufficient statistical data to show that loss experience, changes in law, or other factors necessitate the requested rate change. A rate filing may consist of a few or many pages, depending largely on the financial and political importance of the line of insurance.

Many insurers that are members or subscribers of insurance advisory organizations do not adhere to all loss costs. Some insurers file a request to deviate from the loss costs with the appropriate state insurance regulators. Those requests are called deviation filings.

If an insurer elects not to join or subscribe to an insurance advisory organization, it must calculate its own loss costs and expense costs and file its own rates. In doing so, it must furnish state insurance regulators with sufficient data to demonstrate that its rates comply with the statutory requirements.

CHAPTER NOTES

1. Industry underwriting profits, from 1967 through 2004, have not exceeded 5 percent since 1972. There has been an underwriting loss (combined ratio > 100) in twenty-six of the last thirty-eight years. A.M. Best Company, *Best's Aggregates & Averages*, Property/Casualty, 2005 edition (Oldwick, N.J.: A.M. Best Co., 2005), p. 398.

2. Scott E. Harrington, "Competition and Regulation in the Automobile Insurance Market" (paper prepared for distribution at the ABA National Institute on Insurance Competition and Pricing in the 1990s, Baltimore, Md., June 2–3, 1990), p. 6.

Direct Your Learning

Workers' Compensation Insurance

Educational Objectives

After learning the content of this chapter and completing the corresponding course guide assignment, you should be able to:

▶ Describe each of the following regarding workers' compensation insurance:

- Methods for meeting the employers' obligation
- Persons and employments covered
- Eligibility for benefits
- Benefits provided
- Benefit administration

▶ Summarize the coverage provided by the standard Workers' Compensation and Employers' Liability Insurance Policy, including the following:

- Contents of the information page of the policy and its use in a premium audit
- Standard provisions of the policy
- Common endorsements to the policy and their effect on premium determination and the premium audit

▶ Describe the purpose and the format of the *Basic Manual for Workers Compensation and Employers Liability Insurance*.

▶ Define or describe each of the Key Words and Phrases for this chapter.

CHAPTER 2

Develop Your Perspective

What are the main topics covered in the chapter?

This is the first of four chapters addressing workers' compensation insurance. This chapter begins with basic information about this coverage line, including workers' compensation laws; workers' compensation rating bureaus; and the standard policy, endorsements, and manual.

Identify the relationship between state workers' compensation laws and the coverage provided by the workers' compensation policy.

▶ How are coverage benefits provided tailored by each state?

▶ How can the workers' compensation laws accommodate the various coverage benefits required by each state?

Why is it important to learn about these topics?

Premium auditors perform more audits on workers' compensation policies than on any other kind of policy. Understanding the laws surrounding workers' compensation, the various rating bureaus, and the insurance policy associated with workers' compensation is fundamental for a premium auditor to be able to perform his or her job effectively. The NCCI *Basic Manual,* which provides for workers' compensation rules and classifications, and for rates and state exceptions, is a basic tool required to perform an audit.

Examine the parts of the standard workers' compensation policy and the *Basic Manual.*

▶ What questions about an audit would premium auditors be able to answer from these sources?

▶ How can the auditor use the *Basic Manual* to answer questions regarding the appropriate application of rates?

How can you use what you will learn?

Consider a premium auditor approaching an audit without this fundamental knowledge about workers' compensation.

▶ What types of errors or incorrect assumptions might an auditor make without understanding the relationship between workers' compensation laws and the policy coverage?

▶ How might misuse of the *Basic Manual* lead to an inaccurate audit report?

Workers' Compensation Insurance

This chapter describes workers' compensation laws, including methods for meeting employers' obligations. The chapter discusses persons and employments covered, as well as eligibility and benefits provided in workers' compensation. The Workers' Compensation and Employers' Liability Insurance Policy is discussed, as well as standard provisions and selected endorsements of the policy. Finally, the contents of the *Basic Manual for Workers Compensation and Employers Liability Insurance (Basic Manual)* are introduced.

Workers' compensation is the line of insurance requiring the largest number of premium audits. In 2004, workers' compensation premiums totaled about $37 billion, approximately 9 percent of all direct property-casualty insurance premium revenue.[1] The opportunity to earn significant investment income on amounts held in reserve for future claim payments further increases the importance of this line of business for insurers. Because this form of insurance provides compensation benefits to workers suffering injuries or diseases arising out of and in the course of their employment, it is also a major factor in protecting the welfare of the American labor force. The system distributes the costs of industrial accidents and occupational diseases among employers within the class of business so that the employer can add those costs to the product's price. Therefore, businesses do not pass those costs on to charitable organizations or government agencies. For the system to work properly, however, insurers must precisely and consistently apply extremely detailed rules and procedures regarding coverage, the premium basis, and the employers' classifications. As this and the next four chapters explain, those rules and procedures for workers' compensation present premium auditors with a challenging task.

WORKERS' COMPENSATION LAWS

Before states passed workers' compensation laws, injured workers could sue their employers under common law for damages resulting from the injury. The burden of proof was on the employee bringing the suit to establish that the employer was at fault for the injury. Defenses that employers usually offered were contributory negligence, assumption of risk, and the fellow servant rule.

Contributory negligence is a common-law defense that prevents a person who has been harmed from recovering damages if that person contributed in any way to his or her own harm. **Assumption of risk** is a defense to negligence that bars a plaintiff's recovery for harm caused by the defendant's

Contributory negligence
A common-law defense that prevents a person who has been harmed from recovering damages if that person contributed in any way to his or her own harm.

Assumption of risk
A defense to negligence that bars a plaintiff's recovery for harm caused by the defendant's negligence if the plaintiff voluntarily incurred the risk of harm.

Fellow servant rule
A common-law defense to negligence used by employers in tort suits brought by injured employees who sustained injuries during the course of business from the act or omission of a fellow employee.

negligence if the plaintiff voluntarily incurred the risk of harm. The **fellow servant rule** is a common-law defense to negligence used by employers in tort suits brought by injured employees who sustained injuries during the course of business from the act or omission of a fellow employee.

These common-law defenses made it difficult for employees to collect damages for their injuries. Also, employees often feared that suing their employers or testifying on behalf of fellow employees would cost them their jobs. Although some employees occasionally collected large settlements as a result of successful suits, most injured workers received no compensation at all. This situation gave rise to the following criticisms:

- Compensation to injured employees was insufficient in most cases.
- Wasteful prosecution of lawsuits consumed most of the cost of the employers' liability system.
- Court delays severely strained family finances even when compensation was adequate.
- The employers' liability system generated antagonism between employers and employees.

Because of these criticisms, governments enacted workers' compensation laws. The workers' compensation laws provide a type of no-fault protection. Covered employees suffering work-related injuries are automatically entitled to compensation benefits without having to prove their employer negligent. In return for such protection, the employee gives up the right to sue the employer and the law limits the employer's liability to the benefits defined by state statute.

Ideally, workers' compensation laws should function as follows:

- Provide sure, prompt, and reasonable income and medical benefits to work-accident victims, or income benefits to their dependents, regardless of fault
- Provide a single remedy for work-related injuries and thereby reduce delays, costs, and court workloads arising from litigation
- Relieve public and private charities of financial drains related to uncompensated industrial accidents
- Eliminate fees payment to lawyers and witnesses as well as time-consuming trials and appeals
- Encourage maximum employer interest in safety and rehabilitation through appropriate experience-rating mechanisms
- Promote frank study of accident causes (rather than concealment of fault), thereby reducing preventable accidents and human suffering

The details of specific workers' compensation laws vary considerably by state, and legislatures frequently amend them. Premium auditors must therefore have an up-to-date reference for the workers' compensation laws of any state in which they work. In general, they should know the methods permitted for employers to meet their obligation under the law, the persons and employ-ments covered by the law, the injuries and diseases covered by the law, and the benefits provided by the law. All of this is in addition to the obvious need for a premium auditor to be intimately familiar with the workers' compensa-tion manual rules and classifications that apply in each state. The following discussion is a summary of workers' compensation laws.

Methods for Meeting Employer's Obligation

Most workers' compensation statutes require employers to demonstrate the financial ability to pay any claims that may arise. The most common methods of meeting this obligation of insurance are the following:

- Voluntary private insurance
- Workers' compensation insurance plans
- State funds
- Employers mutual insurance companies
- Self-insurance
- Self-insured groups

Voluntary Private Insurance

The simplest way for an employer to meet the workers' compensation obligation is to obtain insurance from a private insurer licensed to write workers' compen-sation coverage in the state. In return for the premium, the insurer promises to pay the benefits required by law for any work-related injuries. In this way, the employer reduces the uncertainty involved in the cost of employee injuries and saves the administrative cost and burden of settling claims.

Workers' Compensation Insurance Plans

A business occasionally cannot obtain voluntary private insurance because it does not meet insurers' established underwriting criteria or insurers are reluctant to provide coverage in the state due to inadequate rates. Because workers' compensation insurance is compulsory, organizations that are unable to purchase this insurance would be unable to continue to operate. For this reason, all states have some type of involuntary mechanism to provide cover-age for firms that cannot obtain insurance in the voluntary market. The two primary residual market mechanisms for this purpose are workers' compensa-tion insurance plans and state funds. Workers' compensation insurance plans are a type of **assigned risk plan**, which is a state insurance program that makes insurance available to applicants rejected by private insurers; generally, insurers doing business in the state are assigned their proportionate share of applicants based on the total volume of insurance sold in the state. Assigned risk plans are often referred to as a **residual market (shared market)**, meaning the collective markets or facilities that make insurance available to those who cannot obtain coverage in the standard (voluntary) market.

Assigned risk plan
State insurance program that makes insurance available to applicants rejected by private insurers; generally, insurers doing business in the state are assigned their proportionate share of applicants based on the total volume of insurance sold in the state.

Residual market (shared market)
The collective markets or facilities that make insurance available to those who cannot obtain coverage in the standard (voluntary) market.

Workers' compensation insurance plans, also known as assigned risk plans or pools, are mandated by statute in many states to make workers' compensation insurance more widely available. An employer that private insurers have rejected can apply to the plan and obtain coverage.

All insurers selling workers' compensation insurance in a state are required to participate in the plan and receive their share of assignments. The way in which insurers participate and receive their assignments varies by state. Two general methods by which insurers receive their assignments are (1) the insurer is assigned the proportion of risks applying to the plan that corresponds to the proportion of the workers' compensation premium market share in that state, or (2) insurers form a reinsurance pooling arrangement to share the operating results of all assignments to the plan.

Servicing carrier
An insurer appointed to handle all of the functions of an insurer for those policies insured under a residual market plan.

Under the pooling arrangement, **servicing carriers** are insurers appointed to handle all of the functions of an insurer for those policies insured under a residual market plan. Servicing carriers are frequently used to handle the processing of the loss exposures submitted to the plan, including claim adjustment. Servicing carriers are paid a fee to cover their processing expenses and submit the remainder of the premiums to the pool along with any losses. Pool members share the premiums and losses.

National Pool (National Workers Compensation Reinsurance Pool)
An organization in which hazardous workers' compensation loss exposures assigned to insurers under various plans are reinsured by a pool in which all insurers proportionately participate.

The largest workers' compensation pool is the National Workers Compensation Reinsurance Pool (called the National Pool). The **National Pool** is an organization in which hazardous workers' compensation loss exposures assigned to insurers under various plans are reinsured by a pool in which all insurers proportionately participate. Although the National Pool is national in name, it operates in only thirty states. Insurers share in losses based on their voluntary workers' compensation premium in each state. Certain member insurers act as servicing insurers and receive a fee for providing policyholder services such as loss control, claim handling, and premium auditing. NCCI administers the National Pool.

State Funds

State fund
A state government entity that acts like an insurer, accepting any application for insurance in the state.

A **state fund** is a state government entity that acts like an insurer, accepting any application for insurance in the state. In approximately twenty states, state funds provide workers' compensation insurance. Most states established state funds to make workers' compensation insurance available soon after the states enacted workers' compensation laws. Therefore, no assigned risk plans exist in states with state funds. State funds include competitive state funds and monopolistic state funds.

Competitive state fund
A state government entity that operates alongside private insurers in providing workers' compensation insurance.

A **competitive state fund** is a state government entity that operates alongside private insurers in providing workers' compensation insurance. An employer with employees in such a state can choose to purchase insurance from either a commercial insurer or the state fund. In many states, the competitive state fund is the largest provider of workers' compensation insurance in the state, often providing one-third or more of the total workers' compensation premiums in the state. For example, the state funds in New York and California each rank in the top five providers of workers' compensation nationally, even though they provide workers' compensation in only one state.[2]

Five states (North Dakota, Ohio, Washington, West Virginia, and Wyoming) require all employers to purchase workers' compensation insurance through a monopolistic state fund. A **monopolistic state fund** is an exclusive fund that is the sole provider of workers' compensation insurance within the state. Because no private insurers are licensed to sell workers' compensation coverage in those states, they are generally called monopolistic funds by the workers' compensation insurance industry. Therefore, the standard workers' compensation policy that applies in other states cannot be used to provide workers' compensation coverage in those five states. The West Virginia legislature voted to change its monopolistic fund to a mutual company as of January 1, 2006, and to permit private insurers to compete for workers' compensation business in the state starting in 2008. Puerto Rico, the Virgin Islands, and all the Canadian provinces have monopolistic workers' compensation plans.

> **Monopolistic state fund**
> An exclusive fund that is the sole provider of workers' compensation insurance within the state.

Employers Mutual Insurance Companies

In recent years, instead of creating competitive state funds, a number of states have organized mutual insurance companies. For example, reacting to an availability crisis in workers' compensation insurance, the State of Maine created the Maine Employers Mutual Insurance Company. An **employers mutual insurance company** is an insurer that resembles competitive state funds and generally acts as the insurer of last resort in a state. However, it is not a semi-autonomous state agency. Rather, the legislature authorizes the employers mutual insurance companies to operate as domestic mutual insurers, but with continued oversight by the state. Often, the legislature guarantees the insurer's ability to maintain an adequate surplus to pay claims.

> **Employers mutual insurance company**
> An insurer that resembles competitive state funds and generally acts as the insurer of last resort in a state.

Self-Insurance

Almost all states allow employers to self-insure their workers' compensation loss exposure. **Self-insurance** is a loss retention plan in which an organization has formally decided to retain losses rather than purchase insurance; consequently, the organization keeps records of its losses and maintains a formal system to pay them. To qualify as a self-insurer, an employer usually must post a surety bond with the workers' compensation agency to guarantee the security of the benefit payments. Most states also require evidence of administrative capacity. Many self-insured firms purchase excess liability insurance (stop-loss insurance) to protect against catastrophic claims or the aggregation of losses. Self-insurance of workers' compensation exposures is usually practical only for large payroll employers.

> **Self-insurance**
> A loss retention plan in which an organization has formally decided to retain losses rather than purchase insurance; consequently, the organization keeps records of its losses and maintains a formal system to pay them.

Self-insurance operates best when an employer has a large number of employees to benefit from the law of large numbers. The self-insurer should establish safety engineering and claim adjustment services similar to those of insurers.

The self-insurer may also have to retain staff to handle claims, although employers usually outsource this work to third-party administrators (TPAs) that provide such services.

Self-Insured Groups

Self-insured group (pool or trust)
A group of employers in the same industry that jointly (as a whole) and severally (individually) guarantee payment of workers' compensation benefits to the employees of the group's members.

In a search for more economical ways for employers to meet their obligations under workers' compensation laws, many states have authorized the formation of self-insured groups. A **self-insured group (pool or trust)** consists of a group of employers in the same industry that jointly (as a whole) and severally (individually) guarantee payment of workers' compensation benefits to the employees of the group's members.

Because there is no insurer involved, the group retains an administrator to run the day-to-day operations and a TPA to manage claim administration. Sometimes the same organization provides both services. Self-insured groups usually purchase excess liability insurance to protect their members.

It is important that self-insured group participants understand the financial risk associated with self-insured groups. If the assets of the group are insufficient to cover the group's liabilities, each member would be subject to an assessment in order to fund the shortage—even members that had had no claims at all. This approach is in sharp contrast to commercial insurance. While there is always a possibility that an insurer may become insolvent, an insured would be responsible only for its own claims. In the case of a self-insured group, a member can be assessed for a shortage due to claims of other insureds, investment losses, mismanagement, or for any other cause. Because group members are jointly and severally liable, a member can be held responsible for the entire deficit, not just its proportionate share. It would then have the right to seek reimbursement from the other group members. Unlike most private insurers, self-insured groups are generally not covered by state guaranty funds.

Persons and Employments Covered

Workers' compensation applies to most employments, with some significant exceptions. One objective of workers' compensation laws is that coverage under the acts should encompass as many types of employment as possible. Workers' compensation laws do not cover all employments, but the trend has been to extend the coverage provided by those laws. It is estimated that 90 percent of all non-federal government employees come under the protection of workers' compensation laws.[3]

Workers' compensation statutes apply to virtually all industrial workers and most other kinds of private employment. Some states' laws, however, exempt employers with less than a stipulated number of employees. In addition, many statutes specifically exclude or exempt certain employments. Farm laborers, domestic servants, and casual employees are the most common exemptions. Employees subject to federal laws, such as the Federal Employees' Compensation Act, the Federal Employers' Liability Act, the Longshore and Harbor Workers' Compensation Act (LHWCA), and the Jones Act are also excluded.

The distinction between excluded and exempt employment is important. An excluded employment, such as a seaman subject to the Jones Act, is one that the law does not and will not cover. An exempt employment, such as domestic servants in many states, is one that the law does not have to cover, but that the law (and insurers) can cover. Some state laws use the terms interchangeably.

Many states provide workers' compensation protection for all or for certain classes of public employees, such as employees of municipalities and public schools. States do not cover classes of employees covered in federal compensation laws, such as federal government employees, maritime workers, and railroad workers in interstate commerce.

Definition of an Employee

Whether a person is entitled to protection under workers' compensation law depends on whether that person qualifies as an employee according to the law. A court ultimately decides disputed employment status based on the facts of the individual case. Some states' workers' compensation statutes, however, modify the common law definition of employee by specifically including or excluding certain occupations. For example, California considers real estate salespersons to be employees, whereas other states consider real estate salespersons to be independent contractors. Premium auditors must know how each state defines employees. In most cases, remuneration of employees, not independent contractors, is used to determine the final workers' compensation premium.

Jurisdiction of Employment

When a worker's occupation requires travel into another jurisdiction, questions frequently arise as to which workers' compensation law applies. Determining the applicable jurisdiction depends on the particular provisions of the law in question. Typical considerations include the place and nature of employment, the place where the employee was hired, the state in which the employee was intended to work, how long the employee has been away from the state in question, the employee's state of residence, and the jurisdiction of the employer's domicile. Different coverage and benefit provisions in the various jurisdictions further compound this problem. For example, a truck driver may live in State A, go to work for a trucking firm in State B, and drive through every state except Alaska and Hawaii as part of employment. According to the laws of many jurisdictions, if the driver is injured, he could file a workers' compensation claim in the state in which the injury occurred, in which employment was principally located, or in which the employer hired the employee. This situation allows the employee to select the jurisdiction with the most liberal benefits; there are often substantial differences in the benefits provided by different state laws.

Extraterritorial provision
Workers' compensation statute that extends the benefits of the state in which an employee was hired to an employee temporarily working and injured in another state.

Most state workers' compensation laws have **extraterritoriality provisions**, which are workers' compensation statutes that extend the benefits of the state in which an employee was hired to an employee temporarily working and injured in another state. These provisions apply even when the state where the injury occurred is not named in the policy. For example, an Iowa roofing firm takes on work in Indiana and sends its regular employees to work there temporarily. An employee who lived and regularly worked in Iowa, if injured while temporarily working in Indiana, is entitled to benefits under the Iowa workers' compensation law. Coverage is provided by the insurer covering the Iowa location, even though the accident occurred in Indiana and Indiana is not listed in the insured's policy. Most states limit this extraterritorial protection to employees temporarily outside the state. A potential problem for the employer is that the injured employee may also qualify for benefits under Indiana law. If the benefits under the Indiana law were greater than those provided by the Iowa law, the insurer would be responsible for no more than the benefits provided by Iowa law. If the employer hired some additional employees in Indiana in addition to its regular Iowa employees, those employees would not be covered by a policy that named only Iowa as a covered state. The method to treat this exposure is discussed later in this chapter. NCCI issued guidelines for premium auditors to use in assigning remuneration to the proper state in such cases; many insurers have their own guidelines, which they provide to auditors.

Eligibility for Benefits

Workers' compensation laws provide broad coverage for work-related injuries and occupational diseases. However, state laws have certain requirements that must be met in order for benefits to be payable. These requirements are established by state law and are not provisions of the workers' compensation policy. The policy automatically conforms to state law. This conformity means that if the state law considers an injury to be compensable, the policy must pay. These requirements generally include the following:

- There must be an impairment.
- The injury must be work related.
- The injury or disease must be covered.
- The employee must notify the employer of the injury.

Impairment

Impairment
A damage, weakening, or deterioration, especially caused by injury or disease.

Disability
A physical or mental impairment that substantially limits one or more of the major life activities of an individual.

There must be an impairment (which can be either temporary or permanent and either partial or total) or death in order for the policy to respond. **Impairment**, in medical terminology, is a damage, weakening, or deterioration, especially caused by injury or disease. A **disability** is a physical or mental impairment that substantially limits one or more of the major life activities of an individual. An employee is disabled when the impairment reduces the employee's ability to work in gainful activity. The extent of the disability may depend on the impairment and also on nonmedical factors such as the worker's age and education.

Work-Related

A covered workers' compensation injury or disease must arise out of and in the course of employment. That means that the injury must be causally related to the employment and occur while the employee is engaged in work-related activities. Some states have adopted the **positional risk doctrine**, which is a body of law used to determine whether an accident causing injury arose out of employment by considering whether the injury may not have occurred except that the employment put the employee in a position of danger. Just being on the job when an injury occurs makes the injury compensable. For example, in a state that has adopted the positional risk doctrine, an employee injured when an out-of-control car crashes through the storefront where he or she is working would be covered by workers' compensation law. The rationale for this doctrine is known as the "but for" principle of causation. That is, but for being at work, the employee would not have been injured. Other states hold that such an accident does not arise out of employment and would therefore not be covered by workers' compensation.[4]

Positional risk doctrine
A body of law used to determine whether an accident causing injury arose out of employment by considering whether the injury may not have occurred except that the employment put the employee in a position of danger.

Covered Injury or Disease

A covered injury or disease must cause the impairment in order for coverage to respond. The disability must be caused by an accidental injury. For an injury to be accidental, it must be unexpected; intentionally self-inflicted injuries are not covered. In addition, its occurrence must be definite in time—usually interpreted to mean a sudden event. A sudden onset of pain usually fits with this interpretation. For example, back strain from heavy lifting may occur gradually over a long period; however, if the straining suddenly culminates in back pain, it is usually compensable. Courts and workers' compensation administrative bureaus liberally interpret the "suddenness" requirement.

In contrast to traumatic injury, all state workers' compensation laws now also recognize occupational disease (as opposed to occupational injury), even though workers' compensation laws had no specific provisions for such. **Occupational disease** includes any chronic ailment that occurs with increased frequency in workers performing similar tasks or grouped in a particular industry. Coverage and interpretation, however, vary considerably. Some states cover only the occupational diseases that are listed under the law, but most states provide coverage for all occupational diseases. Because some diseases can be latent for a considerable time, such as asbestosis, many states allow an extended discovery period.

Occupational disease
Includes any chronic ailment that occurs with increased frequency in workers performing similar tasks or grouped in a particular industry.

Not every illness contracted by an employee while at work is classified as an occupational disease. For example, an employee who catches a cold from a fellow employee is not entitled to workers' compensation benefits. In general, a cause-and-effect relationship must exist between the occupation and the disease.

Notice of Injury

For an injury or disease to be covered, the injured employee must notify the employer of the occurrence. The law usually excuses the employee's failure to give notice if the employer knew about the accident or if the failure to give notice did not prejudice the employer's rights.

First report of injury
A notification submitted by an employer to the state workers' compensation agency when an injury to an employee is identified.

Once the employer knows about the injury, the employer must make a filing known as the **first report of injury**, which is a notification submitted by an employer to the state workers' compensation agency when an injury to an employee is identified. Insured employers generally send a report to the insurer, and it files the first report with the state administrative agency. Failure of the employer to give notice does not prejudice the employee's claim. See Exhibit 2-1 for an example of a first report of injury form.

Benefits Provided

The benefits provided by the various state workers' compensation laws include the following:

- Medical benefits
- Disability benefits
- Death benefits
- Rehabilitation benefits

Premium auditors must occasionally explain the benefits provided under workers' compensation laws to insureds, particularly when a legislated increase in benefits leads to an increase in insurance rates.

Medical Benefits

Compensable medical expenses amount to more than 50 percent of all workers' compensation benefits paid.[5] In all states, the workers' compensation law provides unlimited medical expense benefits. Those benefits include medical, hospital, surgical, and prescription drug expenses as well as other related medical care costs, including physical therapy and prosthetic devices.

Disability Benefits

Workers' compensation laws provide disability income benefits to compensate an injured employee for wage loss during periods of disability. Disability benefits can be classified as any of the following: temporary total disability, temporary partial disability, permanent total disability, and permanent partial disability.

EXHIBIT 2-1

First Report of Injury Form

ILLINOIS FORM 45: EMPLOYER'S FIRST REPORT OF INJURY

Please type or print.

Employer's FEIN	Date of report	Case or File #	Is this a lost workday case? Yes / No

Employer's name		Doing business as	

Employer's mailing address

Nature of business or service	SIC code

Name of workers' compensation carrier/admin.	Policy/Contract #	Self-insured? Yes / No

Employee's full name	Social Security #	Birthdate

Employee's mailing address	Employee's e-mail address

Male / Female	Married / Single	# Dependents	Employee's average weekly wage

Job title or occupation	Date hired

Time employee began work AM PM	Date and time of accident	Last day employee worked

If the employee died as a result of the accident, give the date of death.	Did the accident occur on the employer's premises? Yes / No

Address of accident

What was the employee doing when the accident occurred?

How did the accident occur?

What was the injury or illness? List the part of body affected and explain how it was affected.

What object or substance, if any, directly harmed the employee?

Name and address of physician/health care professional

If treatment was given away from the worksite, list the name and address of the place it was given.

Was the employee treated in an emergency room? Yes / No	Was the employee hospitalized overnight as an inpatient? Yes / No

Report prepared by	Signature	Title and telephone #

Please send this form to the ILLINOIS INDUSTRIAL COMMISSION 701 S. SECOND STREET   SPRINGFIELD, IL 62704. IC45 9/03

By law, employers must keep accurate records of all work-related injuries and illness (except for certain minor injuries). Employers shall report to the Commission all injuries resulting in the loss of more than three scheduled workdays. Filing this form does not affect liability under the Workers' Compensation Act and is not incriminatory in any sense. This information is confidential.

Temporary total disability (TTD)
A disability that prevents an injured worker from performing any job duties for a specific period but that ultimately allows the worker to resume all job duties.

Temporary partial disability (TPD)
A disability that prevents an injured worker from performing some job duties for a definite period.

Permanent total disability (PTD)
A disability that prevents an injured worker from ever being able to perform any job duties.

Permanent partial disability (PPD)
A disability due to an irreversible injury that allows an injured worker to resume some, but not all, job duties.

Most disabilities are temporary. Benefits for these disabilities can be either temporary total disability benefits or temporary partial disability benefits. **Temporary total disability (TTD)** is a disability that prevents an injured worker from performing any job duties for a specific period but that ultimately allows the worker to resume all job duties. **Temporary partial disability (TPD)** is a disability that prevents an injured worker from performing some job duties for a definite period. Insurers and employers have found that encouraging employees to return to work on a light-duty basis is an important loss-control technique that benefits both the employer and the employee.

Disability benefits are subject to a deductible in the form of a waiting period. Disability benefits—usually a per day amount—are not paid to a disabled worker until the waiting period expires. Such a waiting period eliminates minor, temporary disability claims. However, disability that continues beyond the waiting period is compensated. Additionally, most states provide compensation retroactively to the first day of disability for those claims that exceed the waiting period. This waiting period varies from two to seven days, depending on the state.

The law usually expresses the weekly benefit as a percentage of the employee's average weekly wage at the time of the disability onset. In addition, the laws place maximum and minimum amounts, which vary widely by state, on this weekly benefit. The states determine the weekly maximum and minimum amounts in various ways, but a common method is to fix the limits at a percentage of the state's average weekly wage.

Although cases of permanent disability are only a small minority of all disability claims, they account for a disproportionately large part of the total cost of workers' compensation benefits. Permanent disability can be categorized as permanent total disability or permanent partial disability. **Permanent total disability (PTD)** is a disability that prevents an injured worker from ever being able to perform any job duties. **Permanent partial disability (PPD)** is a disability due to an irreversible injury that allows an injured worker to resume some, but not all, job duties. With both of these types of disability, it is expected that the disability will be permanent.

The benefits provided for PTD are similar to those provided for temporary total disability: a percentage of the employee's average weekly wage subject to maximums and minimums. Some states limit PTD to a specified number of weeks or to a dollar amount.

PPD covers a partial disability that is expected to be permanent and compensates the injured worker for the possible decrease in future earnings. The degree of PPD is not measurable until the maximum medical improvement has been reached; therefore, an injured worker may receive TPD benefits starting at the time of the injury (after satisfying any waiting period) and then receive a PPD benefit when it is determined that a certain degree of disability is permanent.

The majority of states calculate PPD according to a schedule that allots a certain number of weeks of benefits to loss of use of particular bodily member, such as a hand, foot, eye, etc. The number of weeks is multiplied by the weekly benefit calculated for TTD. Partial loss of use of a bodily member generally results in an allowance equal to a percentage of total loss of use. For example, if total loss of use of the hand called for a 150-week benefit, a 20 percent loss of use of the hand would result in a 30-week benefit.

PPD awards are cited as one of the weaknesses of many current workers' compensation laws. Critics allege that much of the money for permanent partial disability goes to claimants who may be somewhat limited in their function due to an injury, but suffer little or no reduction in their earning ability.[6] PPD accounts for the second largest share of workers' compensation benefits.

Death Benefits

Death benefits payable to the worker's family include partial replacement of the worker's former weekly wage and a specified amount for burial expense. The wage loss replacement percentage depends primarily on the number and types of dependents and varies by state; for a surviving spouse with children, 66 $^2/_3$ percent is the most common death benefit, subject to a minimum and maximum benefit. Some states provide a maximum total benefit expressed as either a maximum amount or maximum time period for benefits. The burial expense allowance also varies by state, with $5,000 being the most common.

There has been a steady reduction in work-related fatalities, due partly to an increased emphasis on safety and partly to the shift in the U.S. economy from manufacturing to service industries. Death benefits now account for only a small percentage of the total cost of workers' compensation benefits.

Rehabilitation Benefits

Rehabilitation of injured workers is one of the goals of workers' compensation; every state law includes rehabilitation benefits. The primary rehabilitation benefit provided is the payment of expenses for complete medical treatment and medical rehabilitation. However, the employee may also benefit from vocational rehabilitation. Most workers' compensation laws provide a maintenance allowance to injured workers during rehabilitation. This allowance is in addition to other compensation benefits, and the state usually limits the amount of the allowance. Additional rehabilitation benefits are available from state agencies. In a number of states, employers (and therefore their insurers) are required to provide rehabilitation services, and injured employees are required to use them. Many insurers provide rehabilitation services extending beyond the laws' requirements. Rehabilitation is in everyone's interest; it saves the insurer and the insured money, it improves the injured employee's quality of life, and it reduces the burden on society of caring for individuals who cannot work.

Benefit Administration

Because of the compulsory and social nature of workers' compensation insurance, the state supervises the payment of benefits to ensure compliance with the law. Most states have a workers' compensation board or industrial commission with responsibility to administer the law. (Three states still use the courts instead of a specific administrative agency to administer claims.) The injured worker notifies the employer of the injury. The employer submits the injury report to the insurer, which then transmits the report to the administrative agency. Most states use a direct-payment system; under this system, the responsible party or its insurer pays the benefits immediately, and the administrative agency reviews the amounts paid to determine compliance with the law. In other states, if the employer does not contest the claim, the injured employee and the employer's insurer agree on a settlement. This agreement must comply with the workers' compensation law and is subject to review by the workers' compensation agency.

If the employer contests the claim, most states require a hearing by an administrative agency officer. The employer can appeal the hearing officer's decision to the workers' compensation board or commission and then to the appropriate court.

THE WORKERS' COMPENSATION AND EMPLOYERS' LIABILITY INSURANCE POLICY

The Workers' Compensation and Employers' Liability Insurance Policy combines blanket coverage for obligations imposed by the applicable state workers' compensation law and broad coverage for other employers' liability. This blanket coverage enables insureds to operate nationwide without having to make changes in their workers' compensation coverage for each state. For example, endorsements spare policyholders from having to revise the insurance program every time they establish a new location or make some other change in the business, which saves insurers the expense of modifying policies when the workers' compensation law changes.

A key workers' compensation policy feature is that it contains uniform provisions, even though workers' compensation benefits vary by state or jurisdiction. Insurers can use the same policy for basic coverages without endorsements because the states' compensation laws, not the policy provisions, govern the coverage conditions. The policy contract specifically incorporates the workers' compensation laws by reference. A premium auditor analyzing the coverage and benefits provided must therefore refer to the applicable statutes and the policy. Having all insurers using the standard policy, together with uniform underwriting rules, also enables insurance advisory organizations to provide uniform loss data.

The burden of determining the earned premium still falls on the premium auditor. The premium auditor has frequent contact with insureds.

Consequently, the premium auditor as a representative of the insurer should have a working knowledge of the Workers' Compensation and Employers' Liability Insurance Policy.

Information Page (Form Number WC 00 00 01 A)

A complete workers' compensation policy consists of an information page (WC 00 00 01 A), referred to as the declarations page in most other lines of insurance; a standard provisions Workers' Compensation and Employers' Liability Insurance Policy Form (WC 00 00 00 A); and any appropriate endorsements.

Terminology: Standard Policy and Form

The *Basic Manual* defines the term "standard policy" as including both the information page and the standard provisions form in this text. Generally, the insurance industry refers to the standard provisions without the information page.

Exhibit 2-2 shows the information page and the specific information about the insured that is needed to form a contract and to determine the earned premium. This information includes the following:

- The names of the insured(s) and the insurer
- The policy number
- What period the policy covers
- Coverage provided
- States in which coverage is provided
- A listing of the endorsements and schedules attached to the policy at inception
- Maximum amounts that the insurer will pay under the employers' liability coverage
- Classifications, estimated premium basis, and rates to be used
- Estimated annual premium to be charged, the annual minimum premium, and the expense constant

Some insurers include other items on the information page, such as the producer's name and code number; prior policy number, or "new" if the insurer did not previously provide coverage; policy issuance place and date; countersignature information; and so forth. In some states, some or all of this information is required by state laws or regulations.

Premium auditors should carefully examine the information page because much of the identifying information contained in it is essential for the premium audit. This information is not always complete. Premium auditors should review the information page with the insured to ensure that all the information is correct. The information page contains insured-specific

EXHIBIT 2-2

Workers' Compensation and Employers' Liability Information Page

WORKERS COMPENSATION AND EMPLOYERS LIABILITY INSURANCE POLICY

INFORMATION PAGE

Insurer:

```
┌──────────────────────────────────────────────┐
│              P O L I C Y   N O .               │
│ | | | | | | | | | | | | | | | | | | | | | | | │
└──────────────────────────────────────────────┘
```

1. **The Insured:** AMR Corporation   ___ Individual   ___ Partnership
    Mailing address: 2000 Industrial Highway   X Corporation or _____
    Workingtown, PA 19000

    Other workplaces not shown above:

2. **The policy period is from**   10/1/X3   **to**   10/1/X4   **at the insured's mailing address.**

3. A. **Workers Compensation Insurance: Part One of the policy applies to the Workers Compensation Law of the states listed here:**   PA

    B. **Employers Liability Insurance: Part Two of the policy applies to work in each state listed in Item 3.A. The limits of our liability under Part Two are:**

Bodily Injury by Accident	$ 100,000	each accident
Bodily Injury by Disease	$ 500,000	policy limit
Bodily Injury by Disease	$ 100,000	each employee

    C. **Other States Insurance: Part Three of the policy applies to the states, if any, listed here:**

    All except those listed in Item 3A and ME, ND, OH, WA, WV, WY and OR

    D. **This policy includes these endorsements and schedules:**

    See Schedule

4. **The premium for this policy will be determined by our Manuals of Rules, Classifications, Rates and Rating Plans. All information required below is subject to verification and change by audit.**

Classifications	Code No.	Premium Basis Total Estimated Annual Remuneration	Rate Per $100 of Remuneration	Estimated Annual Premium
Sheet Metal Shop	0454	300,000	11.53	34,590
Clerical Office	0953	275,000	.49	1,348
		Experience Modification of 1.382 Applied		13,728
		Estimated Premium Discount		(4,869)
		Total Estimated Annual Premium $		44,797

Minimum Premium $ 1,273   **Expense Constant $**   140

Countersigned by _____ A. M. Abel _____
                                    (authorized representative)

WC 00 00 01 A
© 1987 National Council on Compensation Insurance.

information that is essential to the premium audit because it serves as the basis for classification and pricing.

Each policy has a policy number that is unique to a particular insured. (All insurers use their own systems for numbering policies.) Policy numbers can include coding to provide added information about the policy, such as the issuing office/state, the expiration year, and the policyholder's account number.

Item 1—Information About the Insured

The first item gives essential information about the insured, including the following:

- The insured's name and mailing address
- The legal entity type, whether an individual, a partnership, a corporation, or another type
- Workplace locations other than those at the insured's mailing address

Additionally, the federal employer identification number for each entity insured under the policy and identifying numbers that a certain state may require are sometimes shown in Item 1.

Item 2—Coverage Period

Item 2 shows the policy's coverage period and the effective date and hour as well as the expiration date and hour. (The standard form does not include the inception and expiration time, but insurers uniformly use 12:01 AM for both.) Policy coverage begins and ends at 12:01 AM at the insured's address given in Item 1. Because this time is standard within the industry for workers' compensation policies, there is seldom an argument about when a policy covers an injury. If an accident occurs on a day when a policy from one insurer expires and another insurer's policy takes over, the expiring policy would cover injuries from accidents occurring before 12:01 AM of the expiration date, and the new policy would cover injuries occurring after that time.

Item 3—States Covered and Employers' Liability Limits

Item 3 shows the states in which coverage is provided by the policy and the limits of liability for employers' liability (EL).

The workers' compensation insurance section of the information page indicates the states in which workers' compensation coverage applies. The insurer will pay benefits required by the workers' compensation law of the state or states shown in Item 3.A. All states in which the insured conducts operations and in which the insurer is licensed to provide coverage should be listed. If a state in which the insured has operations at the policy inception is not listed, the policy states that it will not provide coverage unless the insurer is notified by the insured within thirty days of the policy's inception.

Item 3.B. shows the limits of liability under employers' liability coverage for bodily injury by accident and bodily injury by disease. The standard limits of liability are $100,000 for each accident for bodily injury by accident; $100,000 for each employee for bodily injury by disease; and $500,000 as a policy limit for bodily injury by disease. These liability limits are often abbreviated as $100/100/500. Higher limits are available. Exhibit 2-3 shows an excerpt from the *Basic Manual* that contains the factors to increase limits of liability. For example, the charge for a $500/500/500 limit is 1.7 percent of the premium for $100/100/500; if the premium is $50,000, the additional premium to increase the employers' liability limit to $500/500/500 would be $850.

Additional premiums to increase liability limits are subject to a minimum premium. For example, if an insured wanted $500/500/500 limits but had only a $5,000 premium at basic limits, the $85 premium ($5,000 × 0.017) would be subject to the $100 minimum premium.

An insured may commence operations in a state not listed in Item 3.A. or, as noted above, an employee may, under some circumstances, elect to make a claim under the workers' compensation law of another state. To provide coverage in such cases, the insured can request that another state's insurance be used by entering the names of the states in Item 3.C. When a state is listed in Item 3.C., the policy will provide coverage just as if that state had been listed in Item 3.A. However, insurers cannot list the monopolistic states nor any other states in which they are not licensed to provide workers' compensation insurance; some insurers will not list certain states in which, even though they are licensed, they are unwilling to provide workers' compensation insurance. Insureds should list states with known operations in Item 3.A. Item 3.C. is for contingency purposes.

The insurer lists all endorsements and schedules attached to the policy at inception under the Endorsements and Schedules item.

Item 4—Premium Determination Information

The information needed to calculate the estimated policy premium appears in Item 4.

The Classifications section describes the classifications assigned to the insured's business and shows the four-digit code number that corresponds to the manual classification assigned to the insured's operations. (Pennsylvania and Delaware use three-digit classification codes.) The insurer takes this description exactly from the appropriate workers' compensation manual.

The Premium Basis column contains the insured's estimate of what the total remuneration will be for the period covered by the policy. The insurer shows the estimated remunerations beside their respective classifications. On new policies, the insurer uses the estimates provided by the insured, which are sometimes verified by the insurer's loss control personnel when inspecting the insured's premises. On renewal policies, the payroll estimates are revised to reflect the values developed by the premium auditor.

EXHIBIT 2-3

Workers' Compensation and Employers' Liability Increased Limit Percentages

Bodily Injury by Accident / Each Accident Limit and Bodily Injury by Disease / Each Employee Limit ($000 Omitted)	Bodily Injury by Disease: Policy Limit ($000 Omitted)																		
	500	1,000	2,000	3,000	4,000	5,000	6,000	7,000	8,000	9,000	10,000	15,000	20,000	25,000	30,000	35,000	40,000	45,000	50,000
100	1.0	0.6	1.3	1.8	2.20	2.5	2.7	2.8	2.9	3.0	3.1	3.4	3.6	3.7	3.8	3.9	4.0	4.1	4.2
200	0.5	1.10	1.8	2.3	2.70	3.0	3.2	3.3	3.4	3.5	3.6	3.9	4.1	4.2	4.3	4.4	4.5	4.6	4.7
300	0.9	1.50	2.2	2.7	3.10	3.4	3.6	3.7	3.8	3.9	4.0	4.3	4.5	4.6	4.7	4.8	4.9	5.0	5.1
400	1.3	1.90	2.6	3.1	3.50	3.8	4.0	4.1	4.2	4.3	4.4	4.7	4.9	5.0	5.1	5.2	5.3	5.4	5.5
500	1.7	2.30	3.0	3.5	3.90	4.2	4.4	4.5	4.6	4.7	4.8	5.1	5.3	5.4	5.5	5.6	5.7	5.8	5.9
1,000		2.80	3.5	4.0	4.40	4.7	4.9	5.0	5.1	5.2	5.3	5.6	5.8	5.9	6.0	6.1	6.2	6.3	6.4
2,000			4.3	4.8	5.20	5.5	5.7	5.8	5.9	6.0	6.1	6.4	6.6	6.7	6.8	6.9	7.0	7.1	7.2
3,000				5.3	5.70	6.0	6.2	6.3	6.4	6.5	6.6	6.9	7.1	7.2	7.3	7.4	7.5	7.6	7.7
4,000					6.10	6.4	6.6	6.7	6.8	6.9	7.0	7.3	7.5	7.6	7.7	7.8	7.9	8.0	8.1
5,000						6.8	7.0	7.1	7.2	7.3	7.4	7.7	7.9	8.0	8.1	8.2	8.3	8.4	8.5
6,000							7.4	7.5	7.6	7.7	7.8	8.1	8.3	8.4	8.5	8.6	8.7	8.8	8.9
7,000								7.9	8.0	8.1	8.2	8.5	8.7	8.8	8.9	9.0	9.1	9.2	9.3
8,000									8.3	8.4	8.5	8.8	9.0	9.1	9.2	9.3	9.4	9.5	9.6
9,000										8.7	8.8	9.1	9.3	9.4	9.5	9.6	9.7	9.8	9.9
10,000											9.0	9.3	9.5	9.6	9.7	9.8	9.9	10.0	10.10
15,000												10.3	10.5	10.60	10.70	10.80	10.90	11.0	11.10
20,000													11.3	11.40	11.50	11.60	11.70	11.80	11.90
25,000														12.10	12.20	12.30	12.40	12.50	12.60
30,000															12.80	12.90	13.0	13.10	13.20
35,000																13.40	13.50	13.60	13.70
40,000																	13.90	14.00	14.10
45,000																		14.30	14.40
50,000																			14.70

Refer to Table 1A for Minimum Premiums.

Continued on next page

Table 1A—Minimum Premium For Increased Limits

Minimum Premium to be used when increasing the limits of employers liability under Part Two of a workers compensation and employers liability policy.

| LIMITS OF LIABILITY: | | | | | | |
| ARE GREATER THAN: | | | BUT NOT MORE THAN: | | | |
Bodily Injury By Accident (Each Accident Limit)	Bodily Injury By Disease (Each Employee Limit)	**Bodily Injury By Disease (Policy Limit)**	Bodily Injury By Accident (Each Accident Limit)	Bodily Injury By Disease (Each Employee Limit)	**Bodily Injury By Disease (Policy Limit)**	Minimum Premium For Increased Limits
100,000	100,000	**500,000**	500,000	500,000	**500,000**	$100
500,000	500,000	**500,000**	1,000,000	1,000,000	**1,000,000**	$150
1,000,000	1,000,000	**1,000,000**	5,000,000	5,000,000	5,000,000	$150 plus $25 for each 1,000,000 or part thereof in excess of a **Bodily Injury By Disease (Policy Limit)** of 1,000,000.
5,000,000	5,000,000	5,000,000	—	—	—	$250 plus $10 for each 1,000,000 or part thereof in excess of a **Bodily Injury By Disease (Policy Limit)** of 5,000,000.

The Rates column contains the rates applicable to the various classifications in the classifications column. (A separate rate applies for each classification.) The rate shown is the current rate for the state or states covered by the policy unless an approved independent filing or rate deviation applies. Usually the rate is per $100 of remuneration.

For the Estimated Annual Premium column, the insurer determines the estimated premium by multiplying the estimated remuneration by the rates for each classification.

The minimum premium is the lowest amount for which the insurer will issue the policy. Each classification carries its own minimum premium, which the manual lists with applicable rates in the state manual rate pages. For policies with multiple classifications, insurers use the highest minimum premium. Not all states impose minimum premium requirements.

Total estimated annual premium is the total of the individual estimated premiums shown in the column above it or on appropriate attached schedules. If the policy is subject to experience rating, the insurer must show the experience rating modification factor. If the state has approved schedule rating, the insurer must show the schedule rating information, when applicable. If a premium discount applies, the insurer may show that discount in Item 4, as well.

The **expense constant** is a flat charge to cover administration expenses, such as policy issuing, servicing, maintaining, recording, and auditing expenses. This flat charge applies to every workers' compensation policy regardless of the premium size. (The state rate pages indicate the expense constant.) The expense constant is included in the minimum premium for each classification. In some states, an insurer may include this expense in its loss cost multiplier and not charge a separate expense constant.

Expense constant
A flat charge to cover administration expenses, such as policy issuing, servicing, maintaining, recording, and auditing expenses.

The amount a policyholder pays at the beginning of a policy period, pending the determination of the actual premium owed, is the **deposit premium**, and the insurer can show it in Item 4. The deposit premium may be less than the total estimated annual premium if the insurer offers different payment options. Competitive pressures have forced insurers to reduce the deposit premium requirement to as little as one-twelfth of the total premium or less to retain desirable business. Some insurers offer large insureds cash flow plans that spread the premium payment over a much longer period. Under some of those plans, the insurer will bill the policyholder in the first year for the expense and profit/contingency portion of the premium plus the cost of losses paid in the first year. In following years, the insurer bills the policyholder for the losses and expenses as the insurer pays them.

Deposit premium
The amount a policyholder pays at the beginning of a policy period, pending the determination of the actual premium owed.

Insurers sometimes write policies on an interim adjustment basis. In such cases, the insurer may perform a premium audit or require the insured to report actual remuneration at monthly, quarterly, or semiannual intervals. The insurer then bills the insured based on the actual premium developed. The deposit premium is deducted from the final billing. When used, the premium adjustment intervals are shown in Item 4.

Standard Provisions Workers' Compensation and Employers' Liability Insurance Policy Form (WC 00 00 00)

The information page shows specific information about the insured. The standard provisions policy form contains the policy contract's general terms. Exhibit 2-4 is the 1992 standard provisions policy form.

The standard provisions policy form includes the General Section and six parts. Part One, Part Two, and Part Three describe three coverage types: workers' compensation, employers' liability, and other states insurance, respectively. The insured's duties in the event of a loss appear in Part Four. Part Five contains all the provisions relating to premium determination. Part Six lists the policy conditions.

General Section

The General Section explains the nature of the policy and defines important workers' compensation and employers' liability insurance terms.

The first paragraph explains that the policy is a contract and that the parties are "you" (the insured) and "us" (the insurer). The complete contract consists of the standard provisions policy form, the information page, and all endorsements and schedules listed on the information page. Any changes in the policy's provisions must be by endorsements issued by the insurer.

Paragraph B clarifies the named insureds under the policy. The insured is the employer named in Item 1 of the information page. The policy explicitly states that if that employer is a partnership, coverage applies to the partners only in their capacity as employer of that partnership's employees. Consequently, if a partner is also involved in an enterprise other than the entity named in the policy, and if that enterprise also has employees, there is no coverage under the policy for that enterprise. For example, a policy may insure the partnership of John Jones and Mary Smith, who operate a clothing store. If Mary also runs a business that provides dry cleaning services, there would be no coverage for workers' compensation claims by the dry cleaning service's employees under the policy covering the clothing store.

Paragraph C of the General Section defines workers' compensation law to mean "the workers or workmen's compensation law and occupational disease law of each state or territory named in Item 3.A. of the Information Page." Any amendments to the law in effect during the policy period are included, but this definition does not include any provisions of a statute that relate to nonoccupational disability benefits. Workers' compensation laws apply only to occupational injuries and disease. Five states (California, Hawaii, New Jersey, New York, and Rhode Island) and Puerto Rico mandate nonoccupational temporary disability benefits for employees disabled due to injury or sickness while off the job. Separate coverage is needed to comply with those laws.

EXHIBIT 2-4

1992 Edition Standard Workers' Compensation Policy Form

WORKERS COMPENSATION AND EMPLOYERS LIABILITY INSURANCE POLICY   **WC 00 00 00 A**

1st Reprint   Effective April 1, 1992   **Standard**

WORKERS COMPENSATION AND EMPLOYERS LIABILITY INSURANCE POLICY

In return for the payment of the premium and subject to all terms of this policy, we agree with you as follows:

GENERAL SECTION

A. The Policy

This policy includes at its effective date the Information Page and all endorsements and schedules listed there. It is a contract of insurance between you (the employer named in Item 1 of the Information Page) and us (the insurer named on the Information Page). The only agreements relating to this insurance are stated in this policy. The terms of this policy may not be changed or waived except by endorsement issued by us to be part of this policy.

B. Who Is Insured

You are insured if you are an employer named in Item 1 of the Information Page. If that employer is a partnership, and if you are one of its partners, you are insured, but only in your capacity as an employer of the partnership's employees.

C. Workers Compensation Law

Workers Compensation Law means the workers or workmen's compensation law and occupational disease law of each state or territory named in Item 3.A. of the Information Page. It includes any amendments to that law which are in effect during the policy period. It does not include any federal workers or workmen's compensation law, any federal occupational disease law or the provisions of any law that provide nonoccupational disability benefits.

D. State

State means any state of the United States of America, and the District of Columbia.

E. Locations

This policy covers all of your workplaces listed in Items 1 or 4 of the Information Page; and it covers all other workplaces in Item 3.A. states unless you have other insurance or are self-insured for such workplaces.

PART ONE
WORKERS COMPENSATION INSURANCE

A. How This Insurance Applies

This workers compensation insurance applies to bodily injury by accident or bodily injury by disease. Bodily injury includes resulting death.

1. Bodily injury by accident must occur during the policy period.

2. Bodily injury by disease must be caused or aggravated by the conditions of your employment. The employee's last day of last exposure to the conditions causing or aggravating such bodily injury by disease must occur during the policy period.

B. We Will Pay

We will pay promptly when due the benefits required of you by the workers compensation law.

C. We Will Defend

We have the right and duty to defend at our expense any claim, proceeding or suit against you for benefits payable by this insurance. We have the right to investigate and settle these claims, proceedings or suits.

We have no duty to defend a claim, proceeding or suit that is not covered by this insurance.

D. We Will Also Pay

We will also pay these costs, in addition to other amounts payable under this insurance, as part of any claim, proceeding or suit we defend:

1. reasonable expenses incurred at our request, but not loss of earnings;

2. premiums for bonds to release attachments and for appeal bonds in bond amounts up to the amount payable under this insurance;

3. litigation costs taxed against you;

4. interest on a judgment as required by law until we offer the amount due under this insurance; and

5. expenses we incur.

E. Other Insurance

We will not pay more than our share of benefits and costs covered by this insurance and other

1 of 6

Continued on next page

insurance or self-insurance. Subject to any limits of liability that may apply, all shares will be equal until the loss is paid. If any insurance or self-insurance is exhausted, the shares of all remaining insurance will be equal until the loss is paid.

F. **Payments You Must Make**

You are responsible for any payments in excess of the benefits regularly provided by the workers compensation law including those required because:

1. of your serious and willful misconduct;

2. you knowingly employ an employee in violation of law;

3. you fail to comply with a health or safety law or regulation; or

4. you discharge, coerce or otherwise discriminate against any employee in violation of the workers compensation law.

If we make any payments in excess of the benefits regularly provided by the workers compensation law on your behalf, you will reimburse us promptly.

G. **Recovery From Others**

We have your rights, and the rights of persons entitled to the benefits of this insurance, to recover our payments from anyone liable for the injury. You will do everything necessary to protect those rights for us and to help us enforce them.

H. **Statutory Provisions**

These statements apply where they are required by law.

1. As between an injured worker and us, we have notice of the injury when you have notice.

2. Your default or the bankruptcy or insolvency of you or your estate will not relieve us of our duties under this insurance after an injury occurs.

3. We are directly and primarily liable to any person entitled to the benefits payable by this insurance. Those persons may enforce our duties; so may an agency authorized by law. Enforcement may be against us or against you and us.

4. Jurisdiction over you is jurisdiction over us for purposes of the workers compensation law. We are bound by decisions against you under that law, subject to the provisions of this policy that are not in conflict with that law.

5. This insurance conforms to the parts of the

workers compensation law that apply to:

a. benefits payable by this insurance;

b. special taxes, payments into security or other special funds, and assessments payable by us under that law.

6. Terms of this insurance that conflict with the workers compensation law are changed by this statement to conform to that law.

Nothing in these paragraphs relieves you of your duties under this policy.

**PART TWO
EMPLOYERS LIABILITY INSURANCE**

A. **How This Insurance Applies**

This employers liability insurance applies to bodily injury by accident or bodily injury by disease. Bodily injury includes resulting death.

1. The bodily injury must arise out of and in the course of the injured employee's employment by you.

2. The employment must be necessary or incidental to your work in a state or territory listed in Item 3.A. of the Information Page.

3. Bodily injury by accident must occur during the policy period.

4. Bodily injury by disease must be caused or aggravated by the conditions of your employment. The employee's last day of last exposure to the conditions causing or aggravating such bodily injury by disease must occur during the policy period.

5. If you are sued, the original suit and any related legal actions for damages for bodily injury by accident or by disease must be brought in the United States of America, its territories or possessions, or Canada.

B. **We Will Pay**

We will pay all sums you legally must pay as damages because of bodily injury to your employees, provided the bodily injury is covered by this Employers Liability Insurance.

The damages we will pay, where recovery is permitted by law, include damages:

1. for which you are liable to a third party by reason of a claim or suit against you by that third party to recover the damages claimed

WORKERS COMPENSATION AND EMPLOYERS LIABILITY INSURANCE POLICY   WC 00 00 00 A

1st Reprint   Effective April 1, 1992   **Standard**

against such third party as a result of injury to your employee;

2. for care and loss of services; and

3. for consequential bodily injury to a spouse, child, parent, brother or sister of the injured employee;

provided that these damages are the direct consequence of bodily injury that arises out of and in the course of the injured employee's employment by you; and

4. because of bodily injury to your employee that arises out of and in the course of employment, claimed against you in a capacity other than as employer.

C. Exclusions

This insurance does not cover:

1. liability assumed under a contract. This exclusion does not apply to a warranty that your work will be done in a workmanlike manner;

2. punitive or exemplary damages because of bodily injury to an employee employed in violation of law;

3. bodily injury to an employee while employed in violation of law with your actual knowledge or the actual knowledge of any of your executive officers;

4. any obligation imposed by a workers compensation, occupational disease, unemployment compensation, or disability benefits law, or any similar law;

5. bodily injury intentionally caused or aggravated by you;

6. bodily injury occurring outside the United States of America, its territories or possessions, and Canada. This exclusion does not apply to bodily injury to a citizen or resident of the United States of America or Canada who is temporarily outside these countries;

7. damages arising out of coercion, criticism, demotion, evaluation, reassignment, discipline, defamation, harassment, humiliation, discrimination against or termination of any employee, or any personnel practices, policies, acts or omissions;

8. bodily injury to any person in work subject to the Longshore and Harbor Workers' Compensation Act (33 USC Sections 901–950), the Nonappropriated Fund Instrumentalities Act (5 USC Sections 8171–8173), the Outer Conti-

nental Shelf Lands Act (43 USC Sections 1331–1356), the Defense Base Act (42 USC Sections 1651–1654), the Federal Coal Mine Health and Safety Act of 1969 (30 USC Sections 901–942), any other federal workers or workmen's compensation law or other federal occupational disease law, or any amendments to these laws;

9. bodily injury to any person in work subject to the Federal Employers' Liability Act (45 USC Sections 51–60), any other federal laws obligating an employer to pay damages to an employee due to bodily injury arising out of or in the course of employment, or any amendments to those laws;

10. bodily injury to a master or member of the crew of any vessel;

11. fines or penalties imposed for violation of federal or state law; and

12. damages payable under the Migrant and Seasonal Agricultural Worker Protection Act (29 USC Sections 1801–1872) and under any other federal law awarding damages for violation of those laws or regulations issued thereunder, and any amendments to those laws.

D. We Will Defend

We have the right and duty to defend, at our expense, any claim, proceeding or suit against you for damages payable by this insurance. We have the right to investigate and settle these claims, proceedings and suits.

We have no duty to defend a claim, proceeding or suit that is not covered by this insurance. We have no duty to defend or continue defending after we have paid our applicable limit of liability under this insurance.

E. We Will Also Pay

We will also pay these costs, in addition to other amounts payable under this insurance, as part of any claim, proceeding, or suit we defend:

1. reasonable expenses incurred at our request, but not loss of earnings;

2. premiums for bonds to release attachments and for appeal bonds in bond amounts up to the limit of our liability under this insurance;

3. litigation costs taxed against you;

4. interest on a judgment as required by law until we offer the amount due under this insurance; and

5. expenses we incur.

3 of 6

Continued on next page

WC 00 00 00 A   WORKERS COMPENSATION AND EMPLOYERS LIABILITY INSURANCE POLICY

Standard   Effective April 1, 1992   1st Reprint

F. **Other Insurance**

We will not pay more than our share of damages and costs covered by this insurance and other insurance or self-insurance. Subject to any limits of liability that apply, all shares will be equal until the loss is paid. If any insurance or self-insurance is exhausted, the shares of all remaining insurance and self-insurance will be equal until the loss is paid.

G. **Limits of Liability**

Our liability to pay for damages is limited. Our limits of liability are shown in Item 3.B. of the Information Page. They apply as explained below.

1. Bodily Injury by Accident. The limit shown for "bodily injury by accident—each accident" is the most we will pay for all damages covered by this insurance because of bodily injury to one or more employees in any one accident.

    A disease is not bodily injury by accident unless it results directly from bodily injury by accident.

2. Bodily Injury by Disease. The limit shown for "bodily injury by disease—policy limit" is the most we will pay for all damages covered by this insurance and arising out of bodily injury by disease, regardless of the number of employees who sustain bodily injury by disease. The limit shown for "bodily injury by disease—each employee" is the most we will pay for all damages because of bodily injury by disease to any one employee.

    Bodily injury by disease does not include disease that results directly from a bodily injury by accident.

3. We will not pay any claims for damages after we have paid the applicable limit of our liability under this insurance.

H. **Recovery From Others**

We have your rights to recover our payment from anyone liable for an injury covered by this insurance. You will do everything necessary to protect those rights for us and to help us enforce them.

I. **Actions Against Us**

There will be no right of action against us under this insurance unless:

1. You have complied with all the terms of this policy; and

2. The amount you owe has been determined with our consent or by actual trial and final judgment.

    This insurance does not give anyone the right to add us as a defendant in an action against you to determine your liability. The bankruptcy or insolvency of you or your estate will not relieve us of our obligations under this Part.

PART THREE
OTHER STATES INSURANCE

A. **How This Insurance Applies**

1. This other states insurance applies only if one or more states are shown in Item 3.C. of the Information Page.

2. If you begin work in any one of those states after the effective date of this policy and are not insured or are not self-insured for such work, all provisions of the policy will apply as though that state were listed in Item 3.A. of the Information Page.

3. We will reimburse you for the benefits required by the workers compensation law of that state if we are not permitted to pay the benefits directly to persons entitled to them.

4. If you have work on the effective date of this policy in any state not listed in Item 3.A. of the Information Page, coverage will not be afforded for that state unless we are notified within thirty days.

B. **Notice**

Tell us at once if you begin work in any state listed in Item 3.C. of the Information Page.

PART FOUR
YOUR DUTIES IF INJURY OCCURS

Tell us at once if injury occurs that may be covered by this policy. Your other duties are listed here.

1. Provide for immediate medical and other services required by the workers compensation law.

2. Give us or our agent the names and addresses of the injured persons and of witnesses, and other information we may need.

3. Promptly give us all notices, demands and legal

4 of 6

WORKERS COMPENSATION AND EMPLOYERS LIABILITY INSURANCE POLICY   **WC 00 00 00 A**

1st Reprint   Effective April 1, 1992   **Standard**

papers related to the injury, claim, proceeding or suit.

4. Cooperate with us and assist us, as we may request, in the investigation, settlement or defense of any claim, proceeding or suit.

5. Do nothing after an injury occurs that would interfere with our right to recover from others.

6. Do not voluntarily make payments, assume obligations or incur expenses, except at your own cost.

PART FIVE—PREMIUM

A. Our Manuals

All premium for this policy will be determined by our manuals of rules, rates, rating plans and classifications. We may change our manuals and apply the changes to this policy if authorized by law or a governmental agency regulating this insurance.

B. Classifications

Item 4 of the Information Page shows the rate and premium basis for certain business or work classifications. These classifications were assigned based on an estimate of the exposures you would have during the policy period. If your actual exposures are not properly described by those classifications, we will assign proper classifications, rates and premium basis by endorsement to this policy.

C. Remuneration

Premium for each work classification is determined by multiplying a rate times a premium basis. Remuneration is the most common premium basis. This premium basis includes payroll and all other remuneration paid or payable during the policy period for the services of:

1. all your officers and employees engaged in work covered by this policy; and

2. all other persons engaged in work that could make us liable under Part One (Workers Compensation Insurance) of this policy. If you do not have payroll records for these persons, the contract price for their services and materials may be used as the premium basis. This paragraph 2 will not apply if you give us proof that the employers of these persons lawfully secured their workers compensation obligations.

D. Premium Payments

You will pay all premium when due. You will pay the premium even if part or all of a workers compensation law is not valid.

E. Final Premium

The premium shown on the Information Page, schedules, and endorsements is an estimate. The final premium will be determined after this policy ends by using the actual, not the estimated, premium basis and the proper classifications and rates that lawfully apply to the business and work covered by this policy. If the final premium is more than the premium you paid to us, you must pay us the balance. If it is less, we will refund the balance to you. The final premium will not be less than the highest minimum premium for the classifications covered by this policy.

If this policy is canceled, final premium will be determined in the following way unless our manuals provide otherwise:

1. If we cancel, final premium will be calculated pro rata based on the time this policy was in force. Final premium will not be less than the pro rata share of the minimum premium.

2. If you cancel, final premium will be more than pro rata; it will be based on the time this policy was in force, and increased by our short-rate cancelation table and procedure. Final premium will not be less than the minimum premium.

F. Records

You will keep records of information needed to compute premium. You will provide us with copies of those records when we ask for them.

G. Audit

You will let us examine and audit all your records that relate to this policy. These records include ledgers, journals, registers, vouchers, contracts, tax reports, payroll and disbursement records, and programs for storing and retrieving data. We may conduct the audits during regular business hours during the policy period and within three years after the policy period ends. Information developed by audit will be used to determine final premium. Insurance rate service organizations have the same rights we have under this provision.

5 of 6

Continued on next page

WC 00 00 00 A   WORKERS COMPENSATION AND EMPLOYERS LIABILITY INSURANCE POLICY

Standard   Effective April 1, 1992   **1st Reprint**

PART SIX—CONDITIONS

A. **Inspection**

We have the right, but are not obliged to inspect your workplaces at any time. Our inspections are not safety inspections. They relate only to the insurability of the workplaces and the premiums to be charged. We may give you reports on the conditions we find. We may also recommend changes. While they may help reduce losses, we do not undertake to perform the duty of any person to provide for the health or safety of your employees or the public. We do not warrant that your workplaces are safe or healthful or that they comply with laws, regulations, codes or standards. Insurance rate service organizations have the same rights we have under this provision.

B. **Long Term Policy**

If the policy period is longer than one year and sixteen days, all provisions of this policy will apply as though a new policy were issued on each annual anniversary that this policy is in force.

C. **Transfer of Your Rights and Duties**

Your rights or duties under this policy may not be transferred without our written consent.

If you die and we receive notice within thirty days after your death, we will cover your legal representative as insured.

D. **Cancelation**

1. You may cancel this policy. You must mail or deliver advance written notice to us stating when the cancelation is to take effect.

2. We may cancel this policy. We must mail or deliver to you not less than ten days advance written notice stating when the cancelation is to take effect. Mailing that notice to you at your mailing address shown in Item 1 of the Information Page will be sufficient to prove notice.

3. The policy period will end on the day and hour stated in the cancelation notice.

4. Any of these provisions that conflict with a law that controls the cancelation of the insurance in this policy is changed by this statement to comply with the law.

E. **Sole Representative**

The insured first named in Item 1 of the Information Page will act on behalf of all insureds to change this policy, receive return premium, and give or receive notice of cancelation.

6 of 6

Because the definition refers only to state or territorial laws, the policy does not include the United States Longshore and Harbor Workers' Compensation Act (LHWCA) or other federal workers' compensation or occupational disease laws.

According to Paragraph D, the term "state" means any of the fifty states and the District of Columbia. The definition does not include Puerto Rico or the U.S. territories, and coverage applies in those jurisdictions only when they are listed in Item 3.A. of the information page. The two largest U.S. territories, Puerto Rico and the Virgin Islands, have monopolistic state funds. The other territories, of which Guam is the largest, generally permit commercial insurers to write workers' compensation insurance.

The policy defines covered locations to include all workplaces listed in Item 1 or 4 of the information page and all of the insured's workplaces in states listed in Item 3.A. unless other insurance or self-insurance applies. The insurer should exclude by endorsement workplaces covered by other insurance or self-insurance.

Part One—Workers' Compensation Insurance

The coverage provided by Part One obligates the insurer to pay all benefits required of the insured by the workers' compensation law. The insured automatically receives complete protection under the workers' compensation laws of states listed in item 3.A. for all locations, operations, and employees within the designated state laws' scope even if the locations are not listed in the declarations; the insured did not disclose them to the insurer, or the insured did not anticipate them at the policy inception; and even if the insured has not yet paid the premium for the additional operations. The only exceptions to this broad grant of coverage are employer's operations otherwise insured or specifically excluded by endorsement. Workers' compensation insurance pays any designated state law's benefits without territorial limitation beyond that imposed by the compensation law itself. As discussed earlier, the extraterritorial provisions of most state workers' compensation laws can provide coverage for accidents occurring outside the state under some circumstances.

Nearly every workers' compensation law contains a provision that makes the principal employer liable for workers' compensation to employees of a contractor or subcontractor who performs work for the principal and who does not insure its employees. Because the insurer assumes all of the insured's liability under a designated workers' compensation law, it would have to pay compensation benefits to any employee of an uninsured contractor or subcontractor.

The separate paragraphs of Part One emphasize the major concepts involved in this coverage. Part One has no exclusions. Exclusions can be added by endorsement if permitted by the state law.

The coverage applies to bodily injury by accident and by disease, including resulting death. The accident must occur during the policy period; the last day of last exposure to disease in the insured's employment must occur during the policy period. The conditions of the employment must cause or aggravate the bodily injury by disease. Those stipulations clarify which policy applies when injuries arise out of the course of employment by more than one employer. The laws of many states specify a method to determine which policy must respond.

The insurer will pay the benefits required by the workers' compensation law. This term ("benefits") is broad enough to include both compensation and medical benefits. The policy shows no dollar limit for those benefits because any applicable limits would be those found in the law itself. If the benefits of the law change, the insurer does not have to endorse the policy because the exact limits are not stated in the policy.

The insurer has the right and duty to defend claims covered by the policy and the right to investigate and settle the claims, but the insurer has no obligation to defend a claim that is not covered by the policy.

The insurer also agrees to pay other additional types of costs, such as reasonable expenses that the insured incurs at the insurer's request; premiums for release of attachment or appeal bonds; litigation costs; interest on a judgment as required by law; and expenses that the insurer incurs. However, the policy does not cover the insured's loss of wages resulting from complying with the insurer's requests.

If other insurance or self-insurance also applies to a loss covered by this policy, the insurer will contribute by equal shares with such other insurance and self-insurance. This means that the insurer will pay only its proportional share of a loss when other insurance also applies.

Many states' workers' compensation laws include special provisions relating to illegal employment, violation of health and safety regulations, or improper discharge or discrimination. For example, employing minors in hazardous occupations would be an illegal employment. When an illegally employed person is injured in the course of employment or when an employee is injured because of the violation of some safety regulation, some states provide for additional compensation or for double or triple benefits. Similarly, the law may impose such penalties in discrimination cases. This policy provision provides that the insured will reimburse the insurer for any such excess benefits required under a workers' compensation law because of: (1) serious and willful misconduct, (2) illegal employment (done so knowingly by the insured), (3) failure to comply with health and safety laws and regulations, and (4) discharge, coercion, or discrimination against employees in violation of the workers' compensation law.

When the insurer pays compensation or employers' liability benefits on an insured's behalf, any recovery right the insured or the injured employee may have against a third party is transferred to the insurer to the extent of its payment. The insurer may then attempt to recover from the responsible third party. The insured must do all that is necessary to preserve those rights and to assist the insurer in enforcing them. The insured cannot waive the insurer's right to recover from others without the insurer's consent. Many contracts, particularly in the construction industry, require a waiver of subrogation because construction crews are working as a team. In this work environment, it is difficult, if not impossible, to find one party at fault because team members make collective decisions and take collective action but are insured separately. A standard endorsement, Waiver of Our Right to Recover From Others (WC 00 03 13), is available for such situations. The endorsement waives the insurer's right to recover from those firms listed in the endorsement schedule when the insured performs work for them under a written contract that requires such a waiver. Insurers generally charge either a flat dollar amount or a nominal percentage of the premium for this endorsement. Sometimes the waiver applies to a specific customer or job site. In that case, the premium auditor must obtain separate payroll for those customers or job sites, and a charge is made accordingly.

Statutory provisions incorporate various legal requirements. The requirements are preceded by the statement that they apply "where they are required by law." One requirement makes workers' compensation coverage the insurer's direct obligation to any injured employee or, in the event of death, to the employee's dependents. Because workers' compensation insurance is primarily for the benefit of employees and their dependents, they have a direct right of action against the insurer and are, in effect, insureds under the policy as if they were specifically named.

For the employee's protection, an injury notice to the employer is presumed to be notice to the insurer, insofar as any obligation rests on the injured party, and the employer's knowledge is held to be the insurer's knowledge. In addition, a default by the employer in the premium payment after an accident will not jeopardize the employee's position. Failure to give the insurer the notice required by the policy does not deprive the employee of the right to compensation, nor does the employer's debt, insolvency, bankruptcy, legal incapacity, or inability to pay the benefits deprive the employee of that right. Default, bankruptcy or insolvency of the insured does not relieve the insurer of its responsibility under the policy. All the findings or judgments rendered against the employer are binding on the insurer. All workers' compensation laws covered by the policy become a part of the contract just as if the insurer had written them into the policy, and employees have the rights to compensation defined by those laws. If the policy and the applicable workers' compensation law conflict, the policy provisions are interpreted to comply with the law.

Part Two—Employers' Liability Insurance

Although the coverage provided by compensation laws is extensive, employers could have some legal responsibility to injured employees not covered by workers' compensation laws. Part Two protects employers against suits brought against them by employees who have alleged that they sustained injury or contracted disease not covered by the workers' compensation law as a result of the employers' negligence. For example, casual laborers may not be eligible for workers' compensation benefits, but they may hold the employer liable for job-related injuries. Whereas insurers pay benefits under Part One without regard to fault, workers not entitled to protection under the workers' compensation law must prove the employer's liability for an injury to collect any damages.

Coverage applies to bodily injury by accident and to bodily injury by disease, including bodily injury that ends in death. The bodily injury must arise out of and in the course of employment. As in Part One, the accident must occur during the policy period, and employment conditions must cause or aggravate the bodily injury by disease. The last day of last exposure to the injurious conditions leading to disease must occur during the policy period. Coverage applies only to employment necessary or incidental to operations in states listed in Item 3.A. of the information page. Injured parties must bring suits for damages in the U.S., its territories or possessions, or Canada.

Third party (third-party-over) action
A legal action that arises when an injured employee sues and recovers from a negligent third party and the third party, in turn, sues the employer for at least a partial recovery based on the employer's joint negligence.

The insurer will pay damages for which the insured is legally liable for covered bodily injury to an insured's employee. The policy specifically lists four types of claims that are covered, but the coverage is not limited to those four. Those four include third-party-over claims, care and loss of services claims, consequential injuries claims, and dual capacity claims. This suit, called a **third party (third-party-over) action**, is a legal action that arises when an injured employee sues and recovers from a negligent third party and the third party, in turn, sues the employer for at least a partial recovery based on the employer's joint negligence. The employers' liability coverage would defend the suit and cover the resulting loss, subject to the limits of liability. In addition to the workers' compensation benefits, the injured employee can sue the third party for damages. However, the third party may then contend that the employer's negligence caused the accident and sue the employer on the grounds of this negligence. For example, a contractor's employee is digging a ditch to connect utility lines, and the employee's pick cracks the gas main. The contractor notifies the gas company to come and repair the leak, but the gas company is slow in responding. As a result, gas concentrates and explodes, and an employee is injured. The employee collects workers' compensation benefits but also sues the gas company, claiming it was negligent, and receives a $100,000 judgment. The gas company, in turn, sues the contractor for the $100,000 plus expenses, alleging that the contractor's negligence allowed the employee to break the gas main, thereby causing the accident.

Care and loss of services (consortium)
The loss of services, companionship, and comfort resulting from the injury or death of a spouse.

Coverage also applies to claims for **care and loss of services (consortium)**. Care and loss of services is the loss of services, companionship, and comfort resulting from the injury or death of a spouse. Often called simply consortium, it is a husband's or wife's right to his or her spouse's services, companionship, and affection, including sexual relations. Loss of consortium is regarded as actionable in many states, and injured employees' spouses have often been successful in winning substantial damages from employers in cases of this kind. Some state workers' compensation statutes bar such claims; if not barred, such a claim would be covered by the employers' liability insurance.

A **consequential bodily injury** is an indirect injury to an employee's family member caused solely by the employee's injury. A claim arises when a worker's family member suffers bodily injury solely because the worker is injured. For example, the injured employee's children may become physically ill after visiting their seriously injured parent in the hospital.

Consequential bodily injury
An indirect injury to an employee's family member caused solely by the employee's injury.

The policy specifically requires that the three types of claims just described be the direct consequence of bodily injury arising out of and in the course of the injured employee's employment by the insured.

Dual capacity is a legal doctrine that makes an employer liable in tort to an employee for additional damages as a party who has committed a wrongful or negligent act beyond its role as employer. According to this doctrine, which has been accepted by the courts in some states, the workers' compensation law only excludes suits against employers in their capacity as an employer. If the employer is also the manufacturer of the product that caused the injury, the employee can collect workers' compensation benefits and then sue the employer/manufacturer in its capacity as a manufacturer. Many employers are also the landowners, and employees may sue the employer as a landowner even if the employee has already collected under workers' compensation for the work-related injury. Because liability awards or settlements can be much larger than workers' compensation claims—liability claims can include such items as pain and suffering, which are not considered in a workers' compensation claim—injured employees often have a financial incentive to pursue such claims. Any settlement or award in the dual capacity claim would be reduced by the payments under the workers' compensation coverage.

Dual capacity
A legal doctrine that makes an employer liable in tort to an employee for additional damages as a party who has committed a wrongful or negligent act beyond its role as employer.

Other situations that may lead to employers' liability claims but that are not specifically listed in the policy (as the four above are) include claims by persons employed in exempt employments, such as certain domestic workers; persons not covered because of numerical exemptions in the workers' compensation law; or noncompensable injuries or diseases. In some jurisdictions, an illegally employed minor, or his or her parents, may be able to sue the employer rather than collect workers' compensation benefits.

Part Two contains twelve exclusions, which prevent overlapping coverage with other forms of insurance and eliminate coverage not intended by the insurer. The exclusions are as follows:

1. Liability assumed under a contract with a third party because a general liability policy more properly covers that liability.

2. Punitive or exemplary damages for any illegally employed person's injury or death.

3. Employers' liability coverage for employees employed in violation of the law with the insured's knowledge or knowledge of any executive officers of the insured.

4. Any obligation imposed by a workers' compensation, occupational disease, unemployment compensation, or disability benefits law or any similar law. For example, X, a manufacturer whose main plant is in

Illinois, sells a machine to an Ohio firm and agrees to install the machine in the Ohio plant. X sends a crew from Illinois to make the installation and also employs many Ohio workers to assist. However, X fails to obtain workers' compensation coverage from the monopolistic Ohio state fund. One Ohio worker sustains injury, and the Ohio Industrial Commission orders X to pay benefits required by the Ohio Workers' Compensation Act. In this case, the policy would consider Ohio law to be a workers' compensation or occupational disease law, and therefore no coverage would be available under Part Two of the policy. Because Ohio is a monopolistic state, the insured also would not have Part One coverage under the policy. Even with other states insurance, coverage would not extend to the monopolistic state. (The source for coverage for such a situation is the stop gap endorsement to be discussed later in this chapter.)

5. Intentional bodily injury caused or aggravated by the insured.

6. The policy restricts coverage to the U.S., its territories or possessions, and Canada (except for citizens and residents of the U.S. or Canada who are temporarily outside these countries).

7. Damages arising out of wrongful discharge from employment, coercion, discrimination, criticism, demotion, and reassignment, and similar personnel actions or omissions are excluded. This exclusion is necessary because Part One includes a reimbursement provision that applies to excess benefits payable if the insured discharges, coerces, or discriminates against an employee in violation of the workers' compensation law. If Part Two did not include a similar exclusion, some insureds may erroneously assume that it would cover those injuries.

   Claims for monetary damages arising out of alleged wrongful employment practices such as wrongful termination, discrimination, and sexual harassment have grown exponentially in the past decades. These claims are excluded because coverage is limited to claims for bodily injury.

8. The policy specifically excludes persons subject to the U.S. Longshore and Harbor Workers' Compensation Act, Nonappropriated Fund Instrumentalities Act, Outer Continental Shelf Lands Act, Defense Base Act, Federal Coal Mine Health and Safety Act, and any other similar federal workers' compensation or occupational disease law.

9. The policy excludes bodily injury to any person subject to the Federal Employers' Liability Act or a similar federal act.

10. The policy excludes bodily injury to masters or members of crew of a vessel. The Jones Act covers those persons.

11. If fines or penalties are imposed on the insured for violating a federal or state law, the policy will not respond.

12. The final exclusion eliminates coverage under the federal Migrant and Seasonal Agricultural Worker Protection Act or a similar law for awarding damages for violation of those laws or regulations under them.

As under Part One, and most other liability insurance coverage, the insurer has a right and a duty to defend the insured. This provision expressly disclaims defense of claims not covered and defense of claims after the limits of liability under employers' liability have been exhausted.

The policy also specifies the additional costs of defense assumed by the insurer. This is identical to the provision in Part One.

As in Part One, the Other Insurance Provision calls for contribution by equal shares. If more than one insurance policy or self-insurance plan applies, each insurer (or self-insurer) contributes equally with every other insurer until the loss is paid or the insurance is exhausted.

Item 3.B. of the information page shows separate limits of liability for bodily injury by accident and bodily injury by disease, and the limits of liability section explains those limits. Disease limits include a policy aggregate and a limit per each employee. This policy section defines the terms "bodily injury by accident" and "bodily injury by disease" to be mutually exclusive. This definition prevents two sets of limits (one for accident and one for disease) from applying to the same loss.

The Recovery From Others policy section is similar to the paragraph from Part One that explains the insurer's subrogation rights regarding employers' liability claims.

The insured has no right of action against the insurer under Part Two unless the insured has complied with all the policy terms and the amount of the insured's obligation has been established. No one (for example, the party bringing the lawsuit against the employer) has the right to add the insurer as a defendant in an action against an insured to determine the insured's liability.

Part Three—Other States Insurance

Some insureds unexpectedly expand operations into states after the insurer issues the policy. The policy can provide coverage for such expansion of operations through other states insurance. An appropriate entry on the information page activates other states insurance. Rather than take a chance on omitting a state, many insureds request that the policy list all states other than monopolistic fund states. However, insurers cannot provide coverage in states in which they are not licensed. Many of the largest writers of workers' compensation as well as smaller specialty insurers are licensed in only one or a very few states. Such insurers offer the lowest cost coverage or may be the only coverage available to the insured, thereby posing a problem for insureds with multi-state operations who are insured by such insurers. The solution is to find another insurer willing to provide a policy that lists those states in Item 3.A.

As Part Three explains, other states insurance applies only if Item 3.C. of the information page lists one or more states. That entry designates the states in which this coverage applies either by specifically listing them or by referring to them as "all states except…" followed by the names of those states in which the insurer cannot or does not wish to provide coverage. If the policy designates a state in Item 3.C. and the insured begins operations in that state after the policy effective date, the policy provides the same coverage as if the insurer had listed that state in Item 3.A. If the insurer cannot pay the benefits directly, it will reimburse the insured for any benefits it must pay under the workers' compensation law. This section of the policy states that if the insured has work in a state on the effective date of the policy and if the state is not listed in Item 3.A., the policy will not provide coverage in that state unless the insurer is notified within thirty days.

The policy states, "Tell us at once if you begin work in any state listed in Item 3.C. of the Information Page." Because insureds may not always remember to give such notice whenever Part Three coverage applies, premium auditors should determine the exposure and charge premiums applying to any state except monopolistic jurisdictions and the excepted states even though the insurer did not list the state in Item 3.A. of the policy declarations. The reason is that the policy provided coverage. The premium audit and resulting premium charge will be exactly the same as if the insurer had listed the state in Item 3.A. at inception or added it by endorsement midterm. The premium auditor should notify the underwriting department of premium audit findings so that an underwriter can make the proper state filings, if required, and update the policy. If the premium auditor uncovers separate workers' compensation coverage in an additional state, the premium auditor should report that fact to the underwriting department so that an underwriter can attach a proper exclusion endorsement to the policy.

Part Four—Your Duties if Injury Occurs

Part Four explains the policy conditions relating to the insured's duties. Those conditions first obligate the insured to give medical attention or services required by the workers' compensation law. The insured must give prompt notice of injury, claims, or suit to the insurer not only to protect the insured's own rights, but also to give the insurer a chance to identify and investigate claims or suits to protect its rights. Part Four also requires that the insured cooperate with the insurer and that the insured attend hearings and trials at the insurer's request. The insured must also help in securing witnesses. Insureds cannot, except at their own expense, voluntarily make any payment, assume any obligation, or incur any expenses except for the immediate medical and other services at the time of injury as required by the workers' compensation law. The insured also cannot interfere with the insurer's right of recovery from others after the injury occurs.

The insured's failure to comply with one or more of the policy conditions will not relieve the insurer of its responsibilities to the injured employee or the deceased employee's survivors under the workers' compensation law. The law's purpose is to protect the injured employee, and any coverage denial would defeat that purpose.

Part Five—Premium

Part Five of the standard provisions policy form explains how the insurer determines the premium. Because the insurer determines workers' compensation and employers' liability insurance premiums by manual rules, a single sentence incorporating the manuals into the policy contract by reference would suffice. Insureds, however, rarely have copies of the manuals, so Part Five provides a brief explanation of premium determination procedures.

All premiums are determined by the insurer's manuals. If the insurer changes its manuals during the policy period, the changes can be applied to the policy if permitted by law or by the governing authority.

The classifications paragraph tells the insured that the classifications and rates shown on the information page may change if they do not accurately describe the work covered by the policy. The laws of many states restrict the changes that can be made after a policy has been in effect for a certain number of days.

In almost all cases, remuneration is the premium basis. It includes the remuneration of the insured's employees and executive officers as well as employees of uninsured contractors and subcontractors for whom the insurer may be liable under the workers' compensation insurance portion of the policy. It also states that in the case of contractors and subcontractors and their employees, the insurer may use the contract price as remuneration if the insured does not have payroll records for such employees. No charge is made for employees of contractors or subcontractors whose employers have provided satisfactory evidence of insurance. To confirm that contractors and subcontractors carry workers' compensation insurance, insureds almost always require that their contractors and subcontractors provide certificates of insurance, and auditors usually verify that the insured has received such certificates. Certificates of insurance are discussed in the next chapter.

The insured is responsible for paying all premiums when due.

The Final Premium provision tells the insured how the insurer determines the final premium. It explains why the final premium may be different from the estimated premium. It also shows how the insurer will determine the premium on policy cancellation.

The Records paragraph obligates the insured to keep records of information needed to compute premium and to provide them when requested.

The insurer has a right to audit the insured's records during business hours at any time during the policy period and within three years after policy expiration insofar as the records relate to the policy. A premium auditor should be prepared to cite the audit provision to the insured because it leaves no doubt concerning the premium auditor's right to examine the insured's records.

Part Six—Conditions

The remaining policy conditions, further limiting or defining the rights and obligations of the parties to the insurance contract, appear in Part Six.

The inspection condition gives the insurer permission to inspect a policy-holder's workplaces and operations. Those inspections enable the insurer to determine that safe practices are in use and that the insured takes proper precautions for employees' and visitors' safety. Although this condition states that the policy permits the insurer to inspect workplaces, the policy does not obligate the insurer to perform inspections. When such inspections are performed, however, the policy indicates that this does not constitute an undertaking to warrant that any workplaces, operations, machinery, or equipment inspected are safe or healthful. They are not safety inspections, but rather underwriting inspections for the insurer's benefit. Courts generally uphold the insurer's position. However, following a disaster, insurers sometimes face lawsuits by insureds seeking settlement from insurers based on failure to detect and warn of hazardous conditions.[7]

If the insurer issues the policy for more than a one-year policy period, policy provisions consider each year to be separate, and the insurer computes the premium in accordance with the manual rules and rates in effect for that year. An exception is a three-year fixed-rate policy, which would carry an endorsement modifying this provision.

An insured cannot transfer or assign the policy to a new interest unless the insurer consents in writing. Insurers seldom consent to a transfer, preferring to underwrite the new interest. This provision also clarifies the extension of coverage to the insured's legal representative in the event of the insured's death.

The policy generally permits cancellation; however, some compensation laws restrict the insurer's cancellation right. The cancellation section of the policy outlines the insurer's and insured's cancellation right and would be subject in all cases to any workers' compensation law requirements. The insured can usually cancel the policy by mailing or by delivering to the insurer a written notice that states when the cancellation will be effective. The insurer can cancel the policy by mailing or by delivering to the insured a written notice stating when the cancellation will be effective. The policy expressly stipulates that the insurer's cancellation cannot occur fewer than ten days after delivery of the notice. If state law requires a longer period of time before cancellation takes effect, that law would prevail.

In essence, the insured can cancel the policy virtually without any notice. The insurer, however, must provide at least ten days' notice before its cancellation becomes effective. The reason for this provision is to permit the insured time to obtain a new policy. On cancellation, the insurer should make premium adjustment as soon as possible (some states set limits) in accordance with cancellation provisions—the return premium will be on a pro rata basis if the insurer cancels, and a short rate penalty will apply if the insured cancels.

When the policy lists more than one named insured, the first named insured in Item 1 of the information page is considered the sole representative and is authorized to act on the other insureds' behalf to change the policy, receive return premiums, and give or receive notice of cancellation.

Endorsements

Despite the flexibility offered by the standard workers' compensation policy, many situations require modification of standard policy provisions. Insurers may accomplish those modifications by adding an appropriate endorsement to the policy. An endorsement amends the provisions of the policy to which it is attached. Insurers and insurance advisory organizations have developed standard endorsement forms to meet special situations. Insurers may attach endorsements to the policy at the inception, or they may add them during the policy period.

Standard endorsements to workers' compensation policies are primarily of two types: those that extend or limit the coverage provided and those that incorporate special provisions affecting the premium determination. Either endorsement type may have implications for the audit, so a premium auditor must be certain to examine all the endorsements added to a policy. Particular care is necessary regarding endorsements added midterm because the premium auditor may have to segregate the exposure base for the corresponding periods.

A six-digit numbering system identifies specific workers' compensation endorsements. The Experience Rating Modification Factor Endorsement, for example, is WC 00 04 03. The "WC" establishes that the endorsement applies to workers' compensation and employers' liability insurance. The first two digits refer to the applicable state—00 indicating that the endorsement applies countrywide. Other endorsements may use a two-digit state code or "89" for miscellaneous endorsements, notices, and related transactions. A "99" indicates an insurer-specific endorsement. The middle two digits indicate the different types of endorsements, as follows:

01—Federal coverages and exclusions

02—Maritime coverages and exclusions

03—Other coverages and exclusions

04—Premium endorsements

05—Retrospective premium endorsements

06—Miscellaneous endorsements

Whenever relevant, the endorsement heading includes the word "coverage" or "exclusion." The last two digits indicate the sequence within each of those six general categories. In some cases a letter (A, B, C, etc.) follows the last digits to indicate later versions of the endorsement. If no letter is shown, there have been no revisions to the original filing. NCCI endorsements marked "standard" have been filed with the state; endorsements designated "advisory" have not been filed.

Endorsements Modifying Coverage

Endorsements modifying coverage either add forms of coverage to the standard policy or exclude certain coverages that the insured does not need or has insured elsewhere. Numerous endorsements are available; this chapter describes some common coverage and exclusion endorsements. Because both federal and maritime coverage or exclusion endorsements involve exposures that go beyond the state law, a later chapter addresses those endorsements and the associated legal concepts.

The Voluntary Compensation and Employers' Liability Coverage Endorsement (WC 00 03 11 A) allows insureds to voluntarily extend workers' compensation benefits to employees who would not be entitled to benefits under state law. Most states' workers' compensation laws exempt some types of employment from statutory workers' compensation benefits. (The most commonly exempted occupations are farm labor, domestic employment, and casual labor.) In some states, the law does not apply to employers with fewer than a minimum number of employees. Even when the law does not entitle such persons to workers' compensation benefits, the insured may want to offer the same benefits to them either as an employee benefit or in hopes of avoiding a lawsuit if the employee is injured. If state law permits, complying with all the law's provisions—including any required notification and filings—and adding the appropriate classification to the policy brings the exempted employees within the workers' compensation law's provisions.

Under the Voluntary Compensation endorsement, the insurer must segregate the remuneration of employees covered because the insurer must show such remuneration separately on audit invoices. The insurer should not show the remuneration paid to those employees as part of the remuneration developed in the states for which the policy provides statutory coverage.

The insurer can show the rates for voluntary compensation coverage under the "Designated Workers Compensation Law" section in the Voluntary Compensation endorsement schedule or on the information page. The manual stipulates that the rates charged should be those for the state shown under the "Designated Workers Compensation Law" section.

A sample Voluntary Compensation endorsement appears in Exhibit 2-5. The notes at the end of the endorsement show possible uses of the endorsement. The Voluntary Compensation endorsement amends the standard policy to include an additional coverage called voluntary compensation insurance. **Voluntary compensation insurance** is insurance coverage that provides compensation to employees who are not subject to the workers' compensation law, to an extent that would be payable if the employees had been subject to the workers' compensation law. The additional coverage does not make employees subject to the workers' compensation law. It does, however, obligate the

Voluntary compensation insurance
Insurance coverage that provides compensation to employees who are not subject to the workers' compensation law, to an extent that would be payable if the employees had been subject to the workers' compensation law.

EXHIBIT 2-5

Voluntary Compensation and Employers' Liability Coverage Endorsement (WC 00 03 11 A)

WORKERS COMPENSATION AND EMPLOYERS LIABILITY INSURANCE POLICY		WC 00 03 11 A
2nd Reprint	Effective August 1, 1991	Standard

VOLUNTARY COMPENSATION AND EMPLOYERS LIABILITY COVERAGE ENDORSEMENT

This endorsement adds Voluntary Compensation Insurance to the policy.

A. **How This Insurance Applies**

This insurance applies to bodily injury by accident or bodily injury by disease. Bodily injury includes resulting death.

1. The bodily injury must be sustained by an employee included in the group of employees described in the Schedule.
2. The bodily injury must arise out of and in the course of employment necessary or incidental to work in a state listed in the Schedule.
3. The bodily injury must occur in the United States of America, its territories or possessions, or Canada, and may occur elsewhere if the employee is a United States or Canadian citizen temporarily away from those places.
4. Bodily injury by accident must occur during the policy period.
5. Bodily injury by disease must be caused or aggravated by the conditions of your employment. The employee's last day of last exposure to the conditions causing or aggravating such bodily injury by disease must occur during the policy period.

B. **We Will Pay**

We will pay an amount equal to the benefits that would be required of you if you and your employees described in the Schedule were subject to the workers compensation law shown in the Schedule. We will pay those amounts to the Persons who would be entitled to them under the law.

C. **Exclusions**

This insurance does not cover:

1. any obligation imposed by a workers compensation or occupational disease law, or any similar law.
2. bodily injury intentionally caused or aggravated by you.

D. **Before We Pay**

Before we pay benefits to the persons entitled to them, they must:

1. Release you and us, in writing, of all responsibility for the injury or death.
2. Transfer to us their right to recover from others who may be responsible for the injury or death.
3. Cooperate with us and do everything necessary to enable us to enforce the right to recover from others.

If the persons entitled to the benefits of this insurance fail to do those things, our duty to pay ends at once. If they claim damages from you or from us for the injury or death, our duty to pay ends at once.

E. **Recovery From Others**

If we make a recovery from others, we will keep an amount equal to our expenses of recovery and the benefits we paid. We will pay the balance to the persons entitled to it. If the persons entitled to the benefits of this insurance make a recovery from others, they must reimburse us for the benefits we paid them.

F. **Employers Liability Insurance**

Part Two (Employers Liability Insurance) applies to bodily injury covered by this endorsement as though the State of Employment shown in the Schedule were shown in Item 3.A. of the Information Page.

1 of 2

Continued on next page

WC 00 03 11 A   WORKERS COMPENSATION AND EMPLOYERS LIABILITY INSURANCE POLICY

Standard   Effective August 1, 1991   2nd Reprint

Schedule

Employees	State of Employment	Designated Workers Compensation Law

Notes:

1. Use this endorsement to afford voluntary compensation coverage pursuant to Rules II and VIII of the Basic Manual.
2. Use Voluntary Compensation Maritime Endorsement to provide Voluntary Compensation Coverage under Program II of Manual Rule XIII.
3. Work in a monopolistic state fund state should not be included in the Schedule unless employers liability coverage is provided in that state by the Employers Liability Coverage Endorsement.
4. Various uses of this endorsement are illustrated below.

Schedule

Employees	State of Employment	Designated Workers Compensation Law
All officers and employees not subject to the workers compensation law.	Any state shown In Item 3.A. of the Information Page.	The state where the Injury takes place.
All domestics, farm and agricultural workers.	Utah	Utah
All partners of the insured partnership.	Kansas	Kansas

ITEM P-26— VOLUNTARY COMPENSATION AND EMPLOYERS LIABILITY
COVERAGE ENDORSEMENT—WC 00 03 11 A

EFFECTIVE DATE	August 1, 1991, on a new and renewal basis.
ANNOUNCEMENT CIRCULAR (FOR DETAILS)	NCCI-91-50, dated April 19, 1991.
TECHNICAL CONTACT	Ellen Fell Baig, Associate Counsel 407-997-4729
PENDING	MD, NM
*RECOMMENDED	HI, TX
EFFECTIVE	AK, AL, AR(4), AZ, CO, CT, DC, DE(2), FL, GA, IA, ID, IL, IN, KS, KY, LA, MA(3), ME, MN, MO, MS, MT, NC, NE, NH, NY, OK, OR, PA(1), RI, SC, SD, TN, UT, VA, VT
NOT FILED	MI, WI
NOT APPLICABLE	CA, NJ

(1) Approved a revision to this item, effective September 19, 1991. Refer to PA Comp. Rating Bureau Circular No. 1258 for more details.

(2) Effective September 23, 1991.
(3) Effective February 1, 1992.
(4) Effective March 2, 1992.

Please consider this the final status on this item.

2 of 2

insurer to pay on the insured's behalf an amount equal to the compensation and other benefits that would have been payable to the employees if they were subject to the workers' compensation law designated in the endorsement. To receive benefits under the policy, the employee must release the employer from responsibility in writing, transfer to the employer the right of recovery from any responsible parties, and cooperate with the insurer. If the employee rejects the coverage, the employee retains the right to sue the employer. Such a suit would be covered by the employers' liability coverage.

The Employers Liability Coverage Endorsement (WC 00 03 03 C), otherwise known as a stop gap endorsement, is used to close the possible gap in coverage for workers' compensation or general liability policies should the insurance provided by a monopolistic state fund not provide coverage in the event of a claim. The coverage provided is the same as that provided by the employers' liability portion of a standard workers' compensation and employers' liability policy.

Suppose an employee who ordinarily works in a monopolistic state and is covered by that state's monopolistic fund is temporarily engaged in operations in another state or the injuries do not come within the particular law's scope. In this situation, the extraterritorial features of the laws in most monopolistic states would extend compensation coverage, but some states restrict the extraterritorial coverage to operations incidental to employment within the other state. (The Washington state law is only extraterritorial regarding federal lands or property within Washington's boundaries.)

When the state fund insurance does not cover an injury because it is not work-related within the law's scope, the injured employee or his or her spouse or children may still try to hold the employer liable for the injury. Even if the claim is groundless, the employer may need employers' liability coverage to defend against the claim.

Some insurers develop their own forms and rates for stop gap coverage. The NCCI Employers Liability Coverage Endorsement provides extraterritorial coverage for the states listed in the endorsement if the state law does not. It provides just employers' liability insurance and can be used for any monopolistic fund states other than Ohio. (A different endorsement, WC 34 03 01 B, is used in Ohio to deal with special coverage situations in that state.) The endorsement can also be used for any state where the insured is not subject to the state's workers' compensation law but desires employers' liability coverage.

Some exclusion endorsements can affect the amount included in the premium base. For example, several states' workers' compensation laws allow executive officers to elect not to have the law's protection, in which case the Partners, Officers and Others Exclusion Endorsement (WC 00 03 08) can designate individuals not covered by the policy. Similarly, if the relevant state law allows, the insurer can exclude certain jobs or locations from the policy coverage by the Designated Workplaces Exclusion Endorsement (WC 00 03 02).

When these endorsements are part of the policy, the premium auditor does not include remuneration for those employees or workplaces in the premium base.

Endorsements Affecting Premiums

In contrast to endorsements that modify coverage, some endorsements affect the premium even though the coverage remains the same. These endorsements are based on anniversary date, experience rating, and premium discount considerations.

An Anniversary Rating Date Endorsement (WC 00 04 02), shown in Exhibit 2-6, is used by insurers whenever the anniversary rating date differs from the policy's effective date.

EXHIBIT 2-6

Anniversary Rating Date Endorsement

WORKERS COMPENSATION AND EMPLOYERS LIABILITY INSURANCE POLICY	WC 00 04 02
Original Printing Effective April 1, 1984	Standard

ANNIVERSARY RATING DATE ENDORSEMENT

The premium and rates for this policy, and the experience rating modification factor, if any, may change on your anniversary rating date shown in the Schedule.

Schedule

Anniversary Rating Date _____ (Month) _____ (Day)

Notes:

1. The anniversary rating date is explained in Rule I of the Basic Manual.
2. Use this endorsement to show the insured's normal anniversary rating date if different from the policy effective date.
3. The insurer may show the anniversary rating date in item 2 or item 4 of the Information Page.

Generally, the anniversary rating date is the effective date of the policy in force and each annual anniversary thereafter until the applicable rating bureau changes it. However, if an insured cancels and rewrites a policy midterm—perhaps to bring all its policies in line with its fiscal year—the two dates no longer agree. The anniversary rating date would be the effective date (and annual anniversary thereafter) of the old policy. The new policy, whether issued by the same insurer or another, must carry the classifications and rates applicable on the canceled policy until the canceled policy's normal anniversary date.

Even in most states that allow rate deviations, the new policy must carry the rates that applied for that insurer at the original policy inception date until the normal anniversary date. The new policy must be issued with the Anniversary Rating Date Endorsement, which shows the normal anniversary rating date. This endorsement indicates to the insured that rates may change during the term of the new policy. As of the anniversary rating date, any changes in rates or rules will be applied to the policy. Experience rating modification changes are also effective as of the anniversary rating date, and if the rating changes the policy, it will be endorsed accordingly.

This anniversary rating date requirement promotes uniformity in statistical reporting. When the new policy period is over (that is, one year after the insured cancels and renews coverage), the effective date of the replacing policy then becomes the new anniversary rating date.

For example, suppose an insurer writes a policy for the period June 1, 20X5, to June 1, 20X6, using rates effective on October 1, 20X4 (the latest rates effective on or before the policy's inception date). If the policy is canceled on January 1, 20X6, and replaced with a policy with a period of January 1, 20X6, to January 1, 20X7, the insurer should attach an endorsement like the one in Exhibit 2-6 to the new policy. The insurer will use rates effective October 1, 20X4, from the inception date to the normal anniversary rating date, June 1, 20X6. After the anniversary rating date, the insurer will use the latest rates in effect on or before the anniversary rating date. A rate change effective October 1, 20X5, would apply for coverage after the anniversary rating date.

Whenever an Anniversary Rating Date Endorsement applies to a policy, the premium audit procedure must take it into account. Because the unit statistical report must reflect the separate rating periods, the premium auditor must separately report the exposure base for the periods before and after the anniversary date. This is true regardless of whether a rate change or experience modification change occurred. The premium auditor must separately show the rates in effect before and after the rating date for each period even if the rates have not changed. Similarly, even if the experience rating has not changed, the premium auditor must apply the modification separately to the periods before and after the anniversary date. The premium auditor must also separate the remuneration accordingly.

Insurers are sometimes permitted to apply rate increases to all policies as of the effective date of the rate change rather than on the anniversary date. This further complicates the situation because such changes seldom coincide with the anniversary rating date. Premium auditors cannot use ratio tables in such situations because these tables apply only to the annual premium and not to partial periods. Premium auditors must apply an applicable rate increase separately to each period. Therefore, the premium auditor must split the premium base for outstanding rate increase dates.

Wrap-up policies generally involve anniversary date provisions. A **wrap-up policy** is an insurance policy or a series of policies written to cover a large construction project, including all persons and entities working on that project.

Wrap-up policy
An insurance policy or a series of policies written to cover a large construction project, including all persons and entities working on that project.

The auditor must split the exposure on all such policies to show payrolls before and after the anniversary rating date.

An Experience Rating Modification Factor Endorsement (WC 00 04 03) is used by insureds whose policies produce more than a certain amount of premium (the exact amount varies by state, with $3,000 or $5,000 per year for two years being common) and is subject to experience rating modification. Experience rating formulas compare the insured's actual and expected losses for a prior three-year period to produce either a debit or credit rating factor that is applied to the manual rates in calculating the premium for the insured's current policy. Insurers attach the Experience Rating Modification Factor Endorsement on an experience-rated policy issued before the actual experience rating modification is available. The endorsement is shown in Exhibit 2-7.

Although the insurer may endorse the policy later (showing the newly calculated modification), often the insurer does not attach a copy of the endorsement to the audit requisition. Whenever this modification is missing, the premium auditor should make certain the billing clerk or processor obtains the modification before billing the adjusted premium.

A Premium Discount Endorsement (WC 00 04 06 A) is another premium modifier that is typically attached to high-premium policies that do not fall under loss-cost rating systems. Because certain costs do not vary directly with premium size (it costs little more to process and print a policy with a $10,000 premium than one with a $100,000 premium, and while underwriting is probably more expensive for the higher-premium policy, it seldom would cost ten times as much), premiums are reduced for policies over $5,000 in states that have not adopted loss-cost rating. Under loss-cost rating, the insurance advisory organization publishes only the loss-cost portion of the rates and the insurers apply factors to cover their expenses, which can be adjusted for premium-size-related factors.

In states where the premium discount endorsement is applicable, the insurer must attach the Premium Discount Endorsement when the estimated advance policy premium exceeds $5,000. This is done to show how the insurer determined the applicable premium discount. Exhibit 2-8 shows a copy of this endorsement.

The insurer uses the premium discount shown on the endorsement in calculating the advance premium, premiums called for by subsequent endorsements, and interim audit premiums. The insurer does not revise the premium discount percentage until the final audit develops the earned premium.

The endorsement includes a list of all policies' numbers (if more than one is in effect) and the respective estimated standard premiums for all states covered by each policy. The premium discount percentage depends on the total standard premium for all policies listed on the schedule.

EXHIBIT 2-7

Experience Rating Modification Factor Endorsement (WC 00 04 03)

WORKERS COMPENSATION AND EMPLOYERS LIABILITY INSURANCE POLICY   WC 00 04 03

Original Printing	Effective April 1, 1984	Standard

EXPERIENCE RATING MODIFICATION FACTOR ENDORSEMENT

The premium for the policy will be adjusted by an experience rating modification factor. The factor was not available when the policy was issued. The factor, if any, shown on the Information Page is an estimate. We will issue an endorsement to show the proper factor, if different from the factor shown, when it is calculated.

Notes:

1. This endorsement shall be used if the insured's experience rating modification factor is not available when the policy is issued.

2. An appropriate typewritten entry may be made in the Information Page instead of using this endorsement.

Premium discount percentages vary by state. The premium auditor or reviewer should check the appropriate state exception pages in the manual. Premium discounts do not apply in California and may not apply for policies under a retrospective rating plan, a plan that increases or reduces an insured's premium for a policy period based on the insured's losses during the same period.

EXHIBIT 2-8

Premium Discount Endorsement (WC 00 04 06 A)

WORKERS COMPENSATION AND EMPLOYERS LIABILITY INSURANCE POLICY WC 00 04 06 A

Issued August 15, 1995

PREMIUM DISCOUNT ENDORSEMENT

The premium for this policy and the policies, if any, listed in Item 3 of the Schedule may be eligible for a discount. This endorsement shows your estimated discount in Items 1 or 2 of the Schedule. The final calculation of premium discount will be determined by our manuals and your premium basis as determined by audit. Premium subject to retrospective rating is not subject to premium discount.

Schedule

1. <u>State</u>   Estimated Eligible Premium

	First $10,000	Next $190,000	Next $1,550,000	Balance

2. Average percentage discount: _____ %

3. Other policies:

4. If there are no entries in Items 1, 2, and 3 of the Schedule, see the Premium Discount Endorsement attached to your policy number:

Notes:

1. Use this endorsement to show the application of Manual Rule VII, Premium Discount, or to identify the insured's policy which shows the application of the Discount Rule.
2. Do not make entries in Items 1, 2, or 3 if a policy number is to be shown in Item 4.
3. The company has the option of replacing Item 1 with the appropriate Table in use by the company. The company may also revise Item 1 to conform to Manual Rules applicable to certain states.
4. Item 2 may be used if all eligible premium is developed in one or more states using the same discount.
5. Item 3 is available to list all policies that are combined under the Discount Rule.
6. Use Item 4 if premium discount is shown on another policy issued to the insured.

THE *BASIC MANUAL FOR WORKERS COMPENSATION AND EMPLOYERS LIABILITY INSURANCE*

The *Basic Manual for Workers Compensation and Employers Liability Insurance* (the *Basic Manual*) is a manual developed by NCCI that specifies the rules and procedures for writing workers' compensation insurance. The *Basic Manual* applies in approximately thirty-five states and the District of Columbia. The independent bureau states have separate manuals. Despite their unique features, the manuals for those states follow the same general approach as the *Basic Manual*. Naturally, the *Basic Manual* also does not apply in the six states in which only the monopolistic state fund can provide workers' compensation insurance.

The *Basic Manual* and the manuals of the independent bureau states specify the rules and procedures for writing workers' compensation insurance. Uniform rules for all insurers in a state facilitate the rating process, although some states now require each insurer to file the manual independently. Because the premium section of the standard workers' compensation and employers' liability policy states that "All premium for this policy will be determined by our manuals of rules, rates, rating plans and classifications," the entire manual forms a part of the contract.

The 2001 edition of the *Basic Manual* consists of three parts:

- Part One—Rules
- Part Two—Classifications
- Part Three—Rates and State Exceptions

Pages are numbered separately in each part, and the page numbers begin with a letter indicating the part.

Part One—Rules includes pages R1 through R40 plus appendices. Exhibit 2-9 shows page R1 of the manual as a sample of this part. Exhibit 2-10 provides an outline of the manual rules 1, 2, and 3.

Part Two—Classifications includes an alphabetical list of classification descriptions (C pages) with notes or guides within the classification descriptions as to the proper classification an insurer should use. These pages also show the unique four-digit number for each classification.

Part Three—Rates and State Exceptions includes the applicable rates (or loss costs) by classification for the state as well as any special classifications, special rules, rating plans, or other exceptions that apply in a particular state. In the words of the *Basic Manual*, "Refer to Part Three for Rates, State Special Rules, and Special Classifications in conjunction with applying Parts One and Two in a specific state."[8]

EXHIBIT 2-9

Basic Manual Part One—Rules

Basic Manual—2001 Edition

PART ONE—RULES

Effective 01 Jul 2001 12:00:01

(Exceptions: <u>AZ</u>, <u>NC</u>)

This manual contains rules that have been approved by state insurance regulators. These rules cover the following topics:

- Introduction—Application of Manual Rules

- Rule 1—Classification Assignment

- Rule 2—Premium Basis and Payroll Allocation

- Rule 3—Rating Definitions and Application of Premium Elements

- Rule 4—Workers Compensation Insurance Plan Rules

INTRODUCTION—APPLICATION OF MANUAL RULES

(Additional Rules: <u>FL</u>,<u>IN</u>, <u>NC</u>) (Exceptions: <u>AK</u>, <u>AL</u>, <u>AZ</u>, <u>GA</u>, <u>IL</u>, <u>IN</u>, <u>ME</u>, <u>NC</u>, <u>VA</u>[___])

1. Rules apply separately to each policy, except as provided in the rules related to <u>premium discount</u> and executive officers.

2. This manual applies only from the anniversary rating date that occurs on or after the effective date of this manual.

3. The effective date of a change in any rule, classification, rate, or loss cost is 12:01 a.m. on the date approved for use.

4. Changes made during a policy period are effective as of the next anniversary rating date on or after the date of change, unless otherwise specified.

5. The anniversary rating date is the effective month and day of the policy in effect and each anniversary thereafter unless a different date has been established by the National Council on Compensation Insurance, Inc. (NCCI) or other licensed rating organization. *Refer to Rule 3-A-2 for more information.*

6. The National Council on Compensation Insurance, Inc. may determine the propriety of classification assignments and applicability of all **Basic Manual** rules. NCCI has the right to conduct inspections of operations, assign classifications, and determine the propriety of classification assignments.

7. NCCI has authority to conduct test audits and to require corrections in accordance with the results of the test audit.

8. Appeals involving the application of the rules or classifications of this manual may be resolved through the applicable administrative appeals process. *Refer to **User's Guide** for more information.*

9. Interpretation of state or federal laws pertaining to coverage issues is not within the jurisdiction of NCCI.

10. *Additions* will be indicated by shading of the revised text; deletions will be indicated by shading and underlining surrounded by brackets in the text, i.e. *Changes* in loss costs or rates will be reflected on Update Pages.

11. Some **Basic Manual** rules may have special assigned risk rules, notes or exceptions. In states where assigned risk markets do not exist, these rules, notes and exceptions do not apply.

EXHIBIT 2-10

Outline of Basic Manual Rules 1, 2, and 3 and Appendices

Rule 1 Classification Assignment

A. Classification System

B. Explanation of Classifications

C. Classification Wording

D. Classification Procedures

E. Miscellaneous Employees

F. Changes or Corrections in Classifications

Rule 2 Premium Basis and Payroll Allocation

A. Premium Basis

B. Payroll

C. Overtime

D. Payroll Limitations

E. Executive Officers, Members of Limited Liability Companies, Partners, and Sole Proprietors

F. Wages for Time Not Worked

G. Interchange of Labor

H. Subcontractors

I. Voluntary Compensation Insurance

J. Volunteer Workers

K. Migrant and Seasonal Agricultural Workers

Rule 3 Rating Definitions and Applications of Premium Elements

A. Explanation and Application

B. Three Year Fixed-Rate Policy Option

C. Domestic Workers--Residences

Appendix A—State Reference Chart Premium Discount Tables

Appendix B— Cancellation Tables

Appendix C—Workers' Compensation and Employers' Liability Increased Limits Percentages Appendix D—Schedule Rating Plan

---

Exhibit 2-11, an excerpt from Page S1 of the Georgia state rate pages, provides an example of this section. Because the premium computation follows the rules of the *Basic Manual*, premium auditors must be thoroughly familiar with its content and organization. They should also have it readily available for reference. The *Basic Manual* is as much a part of the insurance contract as the policy itself, and the insurer must follow it explicitly.

EXHIBIT 2-11

Georgia Rate Page

WORKERS COMPENSATION AND EMPLOYERS LIABILITY

GEORGIA
Page S1
Original Printing

Effective July 1, 2005
APPLICABLE TO ASSIGNED RISK POLICIES ONLY

CLASS CODE	RATE	MIN PREM	CLASS CODE	RATE	MIN PREM	CLASS CODE	RATE	MIN PREM	CLASS CODE	RATE	MIN PREM	CLASS CODE	RATE	MIN PREM
0005	8.47	750	1710E	12.17	750	2501	7.46	750	3111	9.09	750	3685	3.94	721
0008	8.32	750	1741E	11.58	750	2503	3.26	623	3113	5.45	750	3719	11.91	750
0016	11.11	750	1747	10.37	750	2534	8.53	750	3114	8.44	750	3724	12.03	750
0034	11.20	750	1748	9.30	750	2570	10.54	750	3118	8.77	750	3726	12.23	750
0035	5.39	750	1751X	3.14	605	2576	–	–	3119	3.08	597	3803	12.62	750
0036	13.39	750	1803D	18.87	750	2578	–	–	3122	5.86	750	3807	7.14	750
0037	11.49	750	1852D	12.41	750	2585	9.18	750	3126	10.63	750	3808	9.74	750
0042	14.28	750	1853	9.77	750	2586	6.13	750	3131	5.60	750	3821	11.11	750
0050	17.77	750	1860	5.48	750	2587	4.71	750	3132	9.39	750	3822	13.86	750
0059D	0.80	–	1924	7.23	750	2589	5.48	750	3145	6.63	750	3824	11.58	750
0065D	0.15	–	1925	12.41	750	2600	7.41	750	3146	10.31	750	3826	2.19	468
0066D	0.15	–	2001	8.89	750	2623	9.42	750	3169	7.64	750	3827	7.76	750
0067D	0.15	–	2002	11.73	750	2651	6.28	750	3175D	9.06	750	3830	2.87	566
0079	12.08	750	2003	8.18	750	2660	8.77	750	3179	10.22	750	3851	7.32	750
0083	15.28	750	2014	14.99	750	2670	5.66	750	3180	8.65	750	3865	10.04	750
0106	39.42	750	2016	4.65	750	2683	10.10	750	3188	7.73	750	3881	9.77	750
0113	11.34	750	2021	4.15	750	2688	7.49	750	3220	8.62	750	4000	19.49	750
0170	8.53	750	2039	14.60	750	2702X	65.55	750	3223	11.55	750	4021	11.58	750
0251	14.84	750	2041	7.32	750	2705X*	218.51	750	3224	14.31	750	4024E	8.77	750
0400	21.62	750	2065	10.16	750	2710	16.20	750	3227	7.73	750	4034	15.31	750
0401	27.37	A	2070	9.57	750	2714	14.78	750	3240	7.38	750	4036	9.74	750
0758NX	0.53	–	2081	15.34	750	2731	11.97	750	3241	12.03	750	4038	7.52	750
0759NX	2.84	–	2089	16.17	750	2735	14.37	750	3255	13.09	750	4053	7.55	750
0770NX	1.69	–	2095	11.14	750	2759	15.05	750	3257	9.63	750	4061	11.08	750
0773NX	5.07	–	2105	8.68	750	2790	4.15	750	3270	5.92	750	4062	6.84	750
0774NX	3.32	–	2110	9.24	750	2797X	15.46	750	3300	9.77	750	4101	7.73	750
0775NX	2.55	–	2111	9.06	750	2802	14.16	750	3303	11.91	750	4111	6.61	750
0776NX	2.96	–	2112	8.18	750	2812	10.52	750	3307	9.98	750	4112	3.44	649
0779NX	2.34	–	2114	11.31	750	2835	6.55	750	3315	8.32	750	4113	6.58	750
0799NX	10.60	–	2121	4.89	750	2836	6.78	750	3334	6.81	750	4114	6.31	750
0908P	163.00	313	2130	11.46	750	2841	18.13	750	3336	6.31	750	4130	10.93	750
0909P	195.00	345	2131	5.04	750	2881	8.44	750	3365	18.63	750	4131	9.51	750
0912P	509.00	659	2143	8.68	750	2883	9.72	750	3372	8.47	750	4133	6.96	750
0913P	456.00	606	2150	–	–	2913	9.45	750	3373	18.90	750	4150	3.47	653
0917	9.92	750	2156	11.14	750	2915	11.43	750	3383	4.03	734	4206	12.17	750
1005*	20.82	750	2157	11.14	750	2916	10.99	750	3385	3.64	678	4207	2.84	562
1016*	149.07	750	2172	2.87	566	2923	10.96	750	3400	10.40	750	4239	6.49	750
1164E	14.63	750	2174	9.45	750	2942	8.65	750	3507	7.64	750	4240	12.23	750
1165E	9.75	750	2177X	5.92	750	2960	17.62	750	3515	8.65	750	4243	5.63	750
1169X	3.44	649	2211	15.08	750	3004	12.20	750	3548	5.33	750	4244	10.25	750
1320	6.87	750	2220	5.84	750	3018	16.14	750	3559	5.75	750	4250	5.42	750
1322	34.66	750	2286	6.22	750	3022	8.92	750	3574	3.52	660	4251	8.03	750
1430	18.93	750	2288	11.70	750	3027	10.34	750	3581	3.58	669	4263	7.46	750
1438	10.37	750	2300	7.20	750	3028	12.26	750	3612	8.32	750	4273	6.40	750
1452	5.42	750	2302	6.87	750	3030	24.58	750	3620	12.32	750	4279	7.11	750
1463	28.02	750	2305	6.04	750	3040	19.31	750	3629	3.76	695	4282	9.00	750
1473X	4.12	747	2361	6.96	750	3041	11.11	750	3632	10.49	750	4283	10.57	750
1474X	11.17	750	2362	5.54	750	3042	6.93	750	3634	6.10	750	4299	5.36	750
1604EX	12.62	750	2380	7.29	750	3064	12.00	750	3635	6.40	750	4304	12.26	750
1624E	13.39	750	2386	4.95	750	3066	10.40	750	3638	3.79	700	4307	5.66	750
1642	11.43	750	2388	5.09	750	3076	8.32	750	3642	3.82	704	4308	–	–
1654	13.57	750	2402	10.78	750	3081D	9.84	750	3643	6.69	750	4351	2.10	455
1655	10.43	750	2413	6.04	750	3082D	17.30	750	3647	5.51	750	4352	2.93	575
1699	6.75	750	2416	8.41	750	3085D	8.95	750	3648	6.16	750	4360	2.19	468
1701	12.41	750	2417	11.11	750	3110	12.20	750	3681	4.27	750	4361	4.21	750

REFER TO UPDATE PAGE FOR ALL SUBSEQUENT REVISIONS TO ALL CLASS CODES
* Refer to the Footnotes Page for additional information on this class code.

SUMMARY

Premium computation for workers' compensation insurance, a line of business that constitutes a significant portion of all property-casualty insurance premium income, requires the services of premium auditors. For premium auditors to perform this task, they must have a thorough knowledge of the coverage provided, the premium basis, and the classification procedures involved in workers' compensation insurance.

Most accidents and occupational diseases are subject to state workers' compensation statutes, which require employers to provide compensation for covered injuries without regard to fault. The most common methods of meeting an employer's obligation for workers' compensation include voluntary private insurance, workers' compensation insurance plans, state funds, employers mutual insurance companies, self-insurance, and self-insured groups. Although workers' compensation statutes provide broad protection, the laws of the different states vary in modifying the common law definition of an employee to include or exclude certain occupations.

For an injury to be covered by a workers' compensation law, it must generally cause an impairment, it must result from an accident or an occupational disease, and it must be work related. The benefits provided in the event of a valid workers' compensation claim include medical benefits, disability income or death benefits to replace lost wages, and rehabilitation services to help the injured employee return to work. Disability income benefits can be temporary total disability (TTD), temporary partial disability (TPD), permanent total disability (PTD), or permanent partial disability (PPD). Because of the compulsory and social nature of workers' compensation insurance, the state supervises the payment of benefits to ensure compliance with the law.

All insurers use the standard Workers' Compensation and Employers' Liability Insurance Policy. The policy includes both the information page, which provides the necessary information to identify the insured, the policy period, the states covered, the operations, and the policy limits; and the standard provisions policy form, which defines the coverages, exclusions, premium provisions, and conditions common to all such insurance contracts unless modified by endorsement. The standard provisions policy form includes a general section and six parts. Part One defines workers' compensation insurance; Part Two defines employers' liability insurance; and Part Three defines other states insurance. Parts Four, Five, and Six explain the insured's duties in the event of an injury, the premium determination procedure, and the conditions.

Many standard endorsements are available to tailor the standard policy's coverage to insureds' needs. Most of those endorsements either modify the coverage provided or define factors in the premium computations. Premium auditors must always be alert for policy endorsements that affect the audit.

The workers' compensation policy incorporates the manual by reference in the contract. The workers' compensation manual, whether it is the NCCI *Basic Manual* or an independent state rating bureau's manual, defines the rules and classifications that insurers must use in underwriting and premium auditing workers' compensation insurance. The next two chapters describe the rules defining the premium basis and classification procedures that are particularly important to premium auditors.

CHAPTER NOTES

1. Insurance Information Institute, *The III Insurance Fact Book 2006* (New York: Insurance Information Institute), p. 33.

2. Susanne Sclafane, "You Were Expecting, Maybe, Liberty Mutual?" *National Underwriter* Property & Casualty, August 23/30, 2004, p. 12.

3. "Workers' Compensation," www.paulbalep.com/workers_compensation.htm. (accessed Sept. 20, 2005).

4. Bruce Hillman, "Positional Risk Doctrine," *National Underwriter,* August 12, 1996, p. 19.

5. "Workers Compensation Medical Losses Are More Than Half of Total Losses," NCCI study, www.state.vt.us/labind/wcomp/ ReportVIIB-PresDrugsAddendum. pdf (accessed Sept. 20, 2005).

6. Senate Republican Office of Policy, "Briefing Report Workers Compensation—Comprehensive Reform Needed not a Band-Aid," April 14, 2003, Report Number INS 03-02, www.republican.sen.ca.gov/pubs/030414_WorkersComp.pdf (accessed Sept. 20, 2005).

7. "Insurers Oppose Broadening R.I. Inspection Liability," *Insurance Journal,* November 18, 2004, www.insurancejournal.com/news/east/2004/11/18/47835. htm?print=1 (accessed Sept. 26, 2005), and "Insurer and 2 Inspection Firms Dismissed from R.I. Nightclub Trial," *Insurance Journal,* November 4, 2005, www. insurancejournal.com/news/east/2005/11/13/61844.htm (accessed Nov. 19, 2005).

8. National Council on Compensation Insurance, Inc., *Basic Manual for Workers Compensation and Employers Liability Insurance* (Boca Raton, Fla.: NCCI, 2001), Preface.

Direct Your Learning

Workers' Compensation Premium Determination—Part I

Educational Objectives

After learning the content of this chapter and completing the corresponding course guide assignment, you should be able to:

▶ Justify the use of payroll as a measure of loss exposure versus other possible measures.

▶ Given the necessary information in a workers' compensation case situation, determine the appropriate amount of payroll to include in the basis of premium.

- Describe payroll, including each of its inclusions and exclusions.

- For each possible inclusion to the definition of payroll, explain how to assign the proper value.

- Identify situations requiring a premium auditor to compute payroll and apply the proper procedures to use in such situations.

- Describe premium bases other than payroll used for some classifications in workers' compensation insurance.

▶ Explain how each of the following applies to premium determination on a workers' compensation policy.

- Rates
- Loss constant
- Expense constant
- Minimum premiums

- Experience rating plan
- Premium discount
- Cancellations
- Anniversary date effects

▶ Explain how a change in a classification may necessitate changes in the experience modification calculation.

▶ Define or describe each of the Key Words and Phrases for this chapter.

CHAPTER 3

Develop Your Perspective

What are the main topics covered in this chapter?

With only a few exceptions, the premium base for workers' compensation is payroll, or remuneration. Because businesses must maintain payroll records for tax and accounting purposes, these records are difficult for insureds to manipulate in order reduce their insurance premiums. This chapter examines premium determination for workers' compensation, including rates, loss constants, expense constants, minimum premiums, experience rating plans, premium discounts, cancellations, and anniversary date effects.

Identify what payroll is included or excluded in determining workers' compensation premium.

- What limitations are inherent in payroll?
- What payroll is imputed for officers and subcontractors?
- When are workers' compensation premiums not based on payroll?

Why is it important to learn about these topics?

Workers' compensation insurance protects employers from the losses caused by work-related injuries to or diseases of their employees. Both insurers and insureds are concerned with proper premium determination because of the large number of dollars associated with workers' compensation premiums.

Consider how accurate premium auditing can assign appropriate premium charges to each workers' compensation policy.

- How does experience rating provide timely and appropriate premium modification?
- How and why are premium discounts applied?

How can you use what you will learn?

Analyze the complex nature of workers' compensation premium determination.

- How can the information presented in this chapter serve as a good reference tool in dealing with workers' compensation premium determination?

Workers' Compensation Premium Determination—Part I

Workers' compensation insurance protects employers from the losses caused by work-related injuries to or diseases of their employees. The premium for that protection should reflect the exposure to such losses. That loss exposure varies considerably, both according to the size of the employer's work force and according to the degree of hazard of the work performed. The workers' compensation system establishes equitable premiums by relating the premium to the employer's payroll and by class-rating employers according to their business. This chapter explains the premium basis for workers' compensation insurance, and the next chapter describes classification procedures.

PAYROLL AS A LOSS EXPOSURE MEASUREMENT

With only a few exceptions, the premium base for workers' compensation insurance is payroll, or remuneration. In workers' compensation insurance, those two terms are used synonymously, which causes no confusion as long as one adheres to the explicit definition provided in the NCCI *Basic Manual for Workers Compensation and Employers Liability Insurance (Basic Manual)*. Payroll serves as an effective premium base because payroll varies directly with the loss exposure covered by the insurance, is relatively easy for the insurer to determine and verify from available records, and is not readily subject to manipulation by the insured.

Naturally, an employer's exposure to workers' compensation losses increases when the employer adds more employees to its work force. As a result, the payroll records generally provide a direct loss exposure measure: the larger the total payroll, the greater the loss exposure. Because not all employees earn the same wage rate, the number of hours worked rather than the payroll paid may seem to be an even better loss exposure measure. In fact, the Washington State Fund, the exclusive insurer for workers' compensation in Washington, uses hours worked as the premium base.[1] However, while the probability of an accident relates more directly to hours worked—the cost of workers' compensation claims does not. Benefit levels depend in part on the injured employee's wages before the accident, which is a factor not reflected in hours worked. Payroll would therefore appear to be more directly related to the actual loss exposure assumed by the insurer.[2]

Payroll records are usually available because of the accounting and tax record-keeping requirements employers must meet anyway. These requirements encourage accurate record keeping for payroll paid. The employee's interest in receiving the full amount earned and the employer's competing interest in controlling costs provide the most effective check on payroll record accuracy. Therefore, payroll provides a reliable premium base that is relatively easy for a premium auditor to determine from existing records. (Businesses often also record hours worked, but not always with the same degree of accuracy as payroll.)

Because businesses must maintain payroll records for tax and accounting purposes, these records are difficult for insureds to manipulate, which some may want to do in an effort to reduce their insurance premiums. Premium auditors can verify payrolls by reconciling them with federal and state tax returns, financial statements, and other accounting records. An insured may manipulate the payroll by paying an employee as an independent contractor or by some similar means to avoid showing the payments on the regular payroll, but as long as the employer has made some payment, an alert premium auditor should be able to locate it.

Payroll also provides a premium base responsive to changing economic conditions. The same factors that cause loss settlements to rise also cause payrolls to increase, thereby generating more premium to pay the losses. That natural adjustment process reduces the need for more frequent workers' compensation rate increases.

PREMIUM BASIS FOR WORKERS' COMPENSATION

For the reasons already mentioned, insurers almost always base workers' compensation premiums on payroll. When an insurer writes the policy, the policy defines the premium as a certain rate per $100 of payroll for the policy period. Following the conclusion of the policy period, the premium auditor determines the actual payroll to compute the final earned premium. The *Basic Manual* provides rules regarding the forms of payroll that insurers should include in determining the total. The following discussion explains those rules and describes the exceptional situations in which payroll is not the premium base.

Payroll

The *Basic Manual* stipulates, "Premium is calculated on the basis of the total payroll paid or payable by the insured for services of individuals who could receive workers compensation benefits for work-related injuries as provided by the policy."[3] Employees covered by the policy are those whom the applicable workers' compensation statute may reasonably consider employees. Consequently, premium auditors must determine whether an employer-employee relationship exists between the employer and the individuals who provide services to the employer. Payroll for services of employees covered by the policy also implies that the services occurred within the policy period, so premium auditors must establish the policy period cut-off dates for the audit. Total payroll paid by the insured is a slightly broader concept than most insureds realize. The *Basic Manual* rules, however, explain the concept and offer guidance to interpret various rules and definitions. According to the *Basic Manual*, **payroll** means money or substitutes for money. Inclusions and exclusions to payroll follow.

Payroll
Money or substitutes for money.

Inclusions

In addition to ordinary wages or salaries, payroll includes several other types of compensation.[4] Premium auditors may have to convince the insured that the workers' compensation premium base includes such items. Those inclusions generally create greater equity in the rating system. Employers may otherwise offer these alternate compensation forms along with lower wages, and therefore lower premiums. Rule 2.B.1. lists those additional items that the manual includes in the premium base. (Many states have exceptions to one or more of these items.) Premium auditors should know the specific rules for the following items in each state in which they conduct premium audits.

Payroll Inclusions

- Wages or salaries
- Commissions
- Bonuses
- Extra pay for overtime work except as provided in Rule V.E.
- Pay for holidays, vacations, or periods of sickness
- Employer payments of amounts otherwise required by law to be paid by employees to statutory insurance or pension plans
- Payment to employees on any basis other than time worked
- Payment or allowance for hand tools
- Value of apartment or housing
- Value of lodging, other than apartment or house
- Value of meals
- Substitutes for money
- Payments for salary reduction, retirement, and cafeteria (IRC 125) plans
- Davis-Bacon wages paid to employees or placed by an employer into third-party pension trusts
- Annuity plans
- Expense reimbursement to extent that records do not substantiate the expense as having been incurred as a valid business expense
- Payment for filming of commercials

In general, however, the following items shown in the preceding box are included in payroll for premium base purposes:

- *Wages or salaries.* To eliminate confusion, the definition of payroll begins by including wages or salaries, including retroactive wages or salaries.

- *Commissions.* Many employers pay employees on a commission or commission-plus-salary basis. Those employees include salespeople, chauffeurs, and drivers for laundries, bakeries, bottling companies, oil and gas distributors, and milk dealers. They may drive their own automobiles or their employers' autos.

  In a situation involving salary plus commission, the premium auditor must determine both the salary and the commission paid during the policy period. When a business hires an employee on a straight commission basis, the premium auditor must determine the full amount of commission paid. One way is to examine the insured's tax file, including IRS forms such as W-2 and 1099. Form 1099 is the form employers use to report compensation of persons whom the law does not consider employees for income tax withholding, FICA (Social Security), or FUTA (unemployment) purposes (although insurance coverages and laws may consider them employees).

  Businesses often hire salespeople under a contract providing a drawing account against commission. If the commission is less than the drawing account or if the employee earns no commission, the insurer should include the drawing account in the premium base.

Bonus
Payroll given to an employee in addition to what is usual or strictly due from an employer.

- *Bonuses.* A **bonus** is payroll given to an employee in addition to what is usual or strictly due from an employer. Many employers give year-end bonuses. Unless the bonus is awarded as a special reward for individual invention or discovery, the premium auditor should include the bonus amount as part of the total payroll. Bonuses also include stock bonus plans and the value thereof.

- *Extra pay for overtime work.* Extra pay for overtime work is included in payroll unless it falls under an exception in Rule 2.B.2., which specifies the conditions under which insurers can exclude extra pay for overtime work from the premium base. If the increased pay does not result from overtime work as defined in the *Basic Manual* or if the insured does not meet the *Basic Manual*'s record-keeping requirements, the premium auditor must include the extra pay in the premium base. In Utah, Delaware, and Pennsylvania, insurers must always include the extra pay for overtime work in the premium base.

- *Pay for holidays, vacations, or periods of sickness.* The *Basic Manual*'s premium basis rule includes pay for unworked holidays, vacations, or sick time as payroll for premium determination. Some union contracts provide pay for days not worked because of jury duty, funerals, weddings, or birthdays. Under such circumstances, the insurer must also include this pay as payroll. This pay is only the regular pay for this time. Although insureds sometimes include holiday, vacation, and sick pay in an overtime record, pay for unworked days is considered pay for straight time. The premium auditor must scan the overtime column and pick out any amounts paid for holidays, vacations, sick days, or other days of leave and include those amounts in the basis of premium. Some employers have arrangements with unions whereby the employer gives the money to the union vacation fund from which the employees receive their pay.

Sick pay provided by a party other than the employer is excluded from payroll. Also, some jurisdictions vary as to whether premium auditors should exclude vacation, sick, and holiday pay.

- *Employer payments of amounts otherwise required by law to be paid by employees to statutory insurance or pension plans.* Insurers should not deduct from an employee's payroll payments by the *employer* of contributions required by law that the *employee* would otherwise pay. For example, the employer pays the employee's portion of FICA taxes. The manual includes such payments in the premium base.

  Although not required by law, contributions by the employer to a savings plan or vacation fund as part of a union or wage contract are considered part of an employee's pay. For instance, the union contract may require an employer to contribute an amount equal to 5 percent of an employee's wage to a union-supervised savings account. All such contributions are part of the employee's wages, and a premium auditor should include the amount contributed by the employer in determining the employee's payroll.

- *Payment to employees on any basis other than time worked.* Following are some examples of alternate compensation arrangements that the *Basic Manual* considers payments under any of these arrangements as payroll: piecework, an incentive plan, and a profit-sharing plan.

  Piecework is a payroll system that compensates an employee for each output unit, subject to an agreed-on minimum amount. The premise is that an employee, working efficiently, can earn more money on a piecework basis than on an hourly wage basis. The employer usually pays increments when the employee completes established quotas.

  An **incentive plan** is a payroll plan that increases an employee's hourly pay rate after the employee has completed an established quota of work units. It works similarly to a piecework payroll system to stimulate a higher rate of production. Such a plan would increase an employee's hourly pay rate after the employee has completed an established quota of work units. The premium auditor should include both straight-time wages and the wages including the incentive increment.

  An employer can have a **profit-sharing plan,** which is an incentive plan that distributes an employer's profit among all or selected employees on a predetermined basis. Usually any profit over a certain level is distributed among employees on some fair basis, such as salary, salary grade, or years of service. Employers also designed profit-sharing plans to stimulate greater and more efficient production. The premium auditor should include income from the profit-sharing plan with other wages in determining an employee's total payroll.

Piecework
A payroll system that compensates an employee for each output unit, subject to an agreed-on minimum amount.

Incentive plan
A payroll plan that increases an employee's hourly pay rate after the employee has completed an established quota of work units.

Profit-sharing plan
An incentive plan that distributes an employer's profit among all or selected employees on a predetermined basis.

- *Payment or allowance for hand tools.* In some trades or occupations, granting a monetary tool allowance to employees who furnish their own hand tools or hand-held power tools is customary. Insurers should include such allowances with wages in determining an employee's total payroll. Premium auditors should check state exceptions relative to tool allowances.

- *Value of apartment or housing.* If an employer provides a house or an apartment to an employee, the value of such accommodations should be included as payroll. "Value" means actual value based on comparable accommodations. For clergy, and sometimes teachers, the church or school budget contains an amount for a housing allowance. Premium auditors should add the amount of the housing allowance to the payroll to obtain total payroll.

- *Value of lodging, other than apartment or house.* Some employees receive lodging other than a house or an apartment as part of their compensation. To the extent that the insured's payroll records show the value of such lodgings, the premium auditor should include it as payroll. In some states, inclusion may depend on the circumstances under which the employer provides the lodging (for example, by reducing wages).

- *Value of meals.* A common practice for hotels and restaurants is to allow employees to eat a certain amount of food from the kitchen. Other employers may provide board as part of the employee's compensation. Insurers should include as payroll the value of the meals furnished to employees as part of their pay, to the extent shown in the insured's payroll records. In some states (Wisconsin, for example), the *Basic Manual* stipulates minimum values for board and lodging that the insurer should include as payroll when the insured's records do not reveal the actual value of the furnished meals or lodgings. However, premium auditors should make every effort to determine the actual value.

- *Substitutes for money.* Some businesses award merchandise certificates to employees exceeding established quotas. Their value is subject to income taxes, and the premium auditor must include the value of the certificates in determining total payroll. The exclusions to the definition of payroll list some substitutes that are not to be included. Other substitutes for money may be merchandise or store credits, most commonly used in mercantile businesses. A premium auditor would not find those items in payroll records. The premium auditor can often establish their existence by questioning the insured, who usually maintains a separate journal or other record of merchandise or store credits to employees. Premium auditors must include the actual value of merchandise that employees receive in addition to payroll. The premium auditor must also include the value of any credits.

Cafeteria-style benefits plan
An employer-provided benefit program that allows an employee to choose benefits from a menu of available alternatives.

- *Payments for salary reduction, retirement, and cafeteria plans.* Employers often provide plans whereby employees can have part of their wages withheld and contributed toward a retirement or cafeteria-style benefits plan. A **cafeteria-style benefits plan** is an employer-provided benefit program that allows an employee to choose benefits from a menu of available alternatives. Each employee is given a certain number of benefit dollars, and the plan allows each employee to buy the benefits perceived to be most desirable. These plans typically include a salary reduction agreement through which the employer does not pay a specific percentage of the employee's salary to him or her, but instead pays it into the pension or other plan. The Internal Revenue Service must approve the plan as a bona fide pension or profit-sharing arrangement and base the employee's federal income tax on the reduced salary.

Premium auditors should include such withheld (salary reduction) sums as payroll. Cafeteria-style benefits plans come in many forms. Some insureds have established employee savings plans under which an employee diverts contributions (by way of a salary reduction agreement) for payment, by the employer, into the savings plan. These plans include 401(k) plans and flexible spending plans or accounts for medical and dependent care expenses. Those employee contributions are often a percentage of the employee's salary. The manual includes such employee salary reduction contributions made by the employer as payroll for premium computation purposes (but not for federal income tax purposes). Often under those plans, the employer also contributes based on the amount of the employee contribution. The *Basic Manual* does not consider such employer contributions to be payroll for premium computation purposes unless the employer reports the same contributions as current taxable income to the employee.

- *Davis-Bacon wages or wages from a similar prevailing wage law paid to employees or placed by an employer into third-party pension trusts.* The 1931 Davis-Bacon Act prohibits the federal government from funding any construction project on which wages are below the prevailing wage for the area. In adhering to the required wage scale, nonunion employers with federal contracts occasionally make direct payments to workers to cover the wage difference. Such payments are to be included as payroll. Similarly, if such wages are placed into a pension fund for the employees, that amount is also included as payroll. If the employer provides some form of fringe benefit, the premium auditor must look at the benefit being provided to determine whether to include it. The premium auditor should look at the payroll inclusions and exclusions in making that determination.

- *Annuity plans.* The Internal Revenue Code allows employees the option of having a portion of their compensation withheld from their pay and treating that amount as a tax-deferred annuity. If they do so, the withheld amount is included as payroll. Essentially, the employee owned the dollars and had the employer withhold them and place them in an annuity. Therefore, the premium auditor should include the amount as payroll. Premium auditors should not include contributions made by the employer.

- *Expense reimbursement to the extent that records do not substantiate the expense as having been incurred as a valid business expense.* Amounts paid to employees sometimes include reimbursements for traveling expenses in addition to compensation. The insurer should not add those expenses to the salary for premium computation purposes, provided the insured maintains a definite, verifiable record of them. If such records are not maintained, the premium auditor should include the amount of the reimbursements as payroll. However, if the insured's records are not clear, the premium auditor can exclude from total unsubstantiated reimbursements a reasonable expense allowance, if certain conditions are met. This is allowed by an exception to this inclusion that states, "When it can be verified that the employee was away from home overnight on the business of the employer, but the employer did not maintain verifiable receipts for incurred expenses, a reasonable expense allowance, limited to a maximum of $30 for each such day, will be permitted."[5]

Some insureds try to submit accounts that they prepared long after they incurred the expenses, showing expenses for several months or a full year. Because they do not meet proper accounting standards, those accounts are not acceptable. Other insureds that cannot produce proper expense accounts sometimes request that an arbitrary amount or percentage of the salesperson's earnings be deducted to represent the expenses. This procedure is also not permissible.

- *Payment for filming of commercials.* The final element of the definition of payroll is amounts paid for the filming of commercials, excluding any subsequent residuals that the participants earn in the commercial each time it is rebroadcast. Therefore, when an employer pays someone to appear in one of its commercials, that amount is to be included as payroll.

Exclusions

In addition to the seventeen specific items that the *Basic Manual* lists as included as part of payroll, the *Basic Manual* also specifically excludes eleven items, shown in the box below, from the total payroll.

Payroll Exclusions

- Tips and other gratuities
- Payments by an employer to group insurance or pension plans
- Special rewards for invention or discovery
- Dismissal or severance pay
- Payments for active military duty
- Employee discounts on goods purchased from the employee's employer
- Expense reimbursements to the extent that records substantiate the expense as having been incurred as a valid business expense
- Supper money for late work
- Work uniform allowance
- Sick pay to an employee by a third party
- Employer-provided perquisites

- *Tips and other gratuities.* Although some employees, such as waiters and waitresses, receive a large portion of their income as tips, adequate records for workers' compensation premium purposes often do not exist. The inequity that results from excluding tips in pricing workers' compensation insurance for some classifications is therefore probably smaller than that which would result from including amounts that are difficult to determine accurately. Also, tips would be a small amount compared to the total payroll paid by most employers because even in restaurants, many employees receive only an hourly wage or a salary. Further, classification, ratemaking, and experience rating balance the final premiums paid even though tipping practices vary by establishment.

  In some states, the *Basic Manual* includes gratuities as payroll. When the employer has maintained verifiable records of tips, the insurer should include the actual amounts shown in the records. If no record exists, the premium auditor must refer to the rules that apply in that state. The New Jersey manual, for example, provides that "if no such record has been kept, then the actual amount shall be fixed at $10 per week ($2 per day) for each employee receiving gratuities."[6]

- *Payments by an employer to group insurance or pension plans.* Rule 2.B.1.f. requires that total payroll include employer payments to statutory insurance or pension plans otherwise required to be paid by employees. However, total payroll does not include contributions not required by law or that are negotiated under the Davis-Bacon Act. Although such group insurance and pension plans are widespread, they are usually not a significant factor in attracting employees. Such plans typically relate the employer's contribution to the amount contributed by the employee rather than to the value of the employee's services. For those reasons, such payments by the employer do not reflect the exposure to workers' compensation losses, so the premium auditor should not include them in the premium base.

  As explained regarding employee savings plans, premium auditors should include the employees' contributions arising out of the employee's salary reduction agreement, but technically made by the employer, as payroll. However, premium auditors should exclude employer matching contributions to such plans (unless the employer includes them in the employee's taxable income) as a payment made by the employer to a group insurance or pension plan.

- *Special rewards for invention or discovery.* The *Basic Manual* also excludes from payroll "the value of special rewards for individual invention or discovery."[7] Such rewards are one-time payments that do not reflect the time worked. Therefore, they do not reflect the exposure to workers' compensation losses.

- *Dismissal or severance pay.* Premium auditors should not include as part of payroll any dismissal wages or severance payments. Severance payments are not the employee's earnings, but rather an amount the employer provides to ease the terminated employee into another position. Premium auditors should determine, however, whether a lump-sum settlement also includes any accrued vacation pay or pay for time already worked, which the premium auditor should include as payroll.

- *Payments for active military duty.* If an employer pays an employee on active military duty, the premium auditor should not include that amount as part of payroll. Premium auditors should exclude those amounts, above and beyond any accrued vacation pay, because they are voluntary and gratuitous.

- *Employee discounts on goods purchased from the employee's employer.* Many employers, to entice workers, grant employees a discount on any goods they purchase. If the employee purchases nothing, no benefit is received. Because these discounts are not part of pay and do not represent an increase in the workers' compensation loss exposure, the premium auditor does not include the value of these fringe benefits as part of payroll.

- *Expense reimbursements to the extent that records substantiate the expense as having been incurred as a valid business expense.* This exclusion is the complement to an earlier inclusion. If an employer maintains records showing that an employee did in fact incur the expense for which he was reimbursed, payroll does not include the amount of those reimbursements.

  In a note to the exclusion, the NCCI has clarified the treatment of reimbursed employee expenses and flat expense allowances as a premium basis. Insurers can exclude from payroll reimbursed expenses and flat expense allowances, except for those hand or power tools, paid to employees, provided that all three of the following conditions are met: (1) the reimbursed expenses or expenses for which allowances were paid were incurred on the business of the employer, (2) the amount of each employee's expense payments or allowances is shown separately in the records of the employer, and (3) the amount of each expense reimbursement or allowances payment approximates the actual expenses incurred by the employee in the conduct of his or her work.[8]

- *Supper money for late work.* The premium auditor should exclude from payroll any amount paid by an employer to buy supper for employees working late. These amounts are usually negligible.

- *Work uniform allowance.* Similarly, payroll does not include an allowance paid by an employer to employees to offset the cost of uniforms required by the employer to be worn at work.

- *Sick pay to an employee by a third party.* If an employer has purchased some form of disability income insurance for its employees and an employee is receiving payments under that insurance (possibly through the employer), the premium auditor should not include those amounts as payroll.

- *Employer-provided perquisites (perks).* The *Basic Manual* lists six specific perks that some employers provide to their employees that premium auditors should not include as payroll. Those perks are the following: use of automobiles, air travel, incentive vacations, discounts on property or services, club memberships, and tickets to entertainment events.

Overtime Wages

Except in Pennsylvania, Delaware, and Utah, which make no distinction between regular and overtime wages, overtime wages present a special case in calculating the premium basis. Because employees receive a higher pay rate for overtime work, their pay is not in direct proportion to the number of hours worked if some of those hours constitute overtime. Generally, the *Basic Manual* rules exclude the extra pay so that the basis of premium more directly reflects the actual loss exposure to employee injuries. However, the rules also contain specific provisions defining overtime and stipulating the records required for an insurer to exclude such extra pay from the premium base. Unless all of the *Basic Manual*'s conditions are met, the manual does not allow a premium auditor to exclude overtime pay. One exception (in addition to the states listed above) is any stevedoring classification with a classification code number followed by the letter "F." The *Basic Manual* defines overtime, as used in determining the premium basis, as those hours worked for which there is an increase in the rate of pay:[9]

- For work in any day or in any week in excess of the number of hours normally worked
- For hours worked in excess of eight hours in any day or forty hours in any week
- For work on Saturdays, Sundays, or holidays

A further restriction of the definition is, "In the case of guaranteed wage agreements, overtime means only those hours worked in excess of the number specified in such agreement."[10]

Whereas the wage and hour laws are designed to protect employees from possible abuse, the intent of the *Basic Manual* overtime rule is to identify those situations in which a higher pay rate applies because the number of hours worked in the day or week exceeds the number of hours normal and usual to the industry. If a forty-hour work week is normal for the industry, the employer probably understands what constitutes overtime. Overtime for workers' compensation insurance purposes, however, is not necessarily overtime according to the wage and hour laws.

If the normal workday is seven hours, the union contract may require one-and-one-half times the hourly wage rate for any work in excess of seven hours per day. An employer may pay an employee working eight hours $10 an hour for the first seven hours and $15 for the additional hour. Total wages for the day would be $85. In computing the basis of premium, the premium auditor would deduct the extra pay (in this case $5) so that the payroll included—$80—is the same as if only the regular rate had been paid for the entire time worked ($10 per hour × 8 hours = $80).

On the other hand, except for a guaranteed wage agreement, insurers should deduct from the premium base extra pay for overtime in excess of eight hours a day or forty hours a week, even if the longer hours are normal for the industry. Also, insurers should deduct extra pay for work on Saturdays, Sundays, or holidays even if the total hours worked during the week do not exceed the normal limit. Work on Saturdays, Sundays, and holidays has traditionally been considered overtime because those days are not part of the normal workweek.

Guaranteed wage contract
A payroll system that guarantees the employee a wage for a minimum number of hours worked per week.

In some industries, guaranteed wage contracts exist. A **guaranteed wage contract** is a payroll system that guarantees the employee a wage for a minimum number of hours worked per week. Under those contracts, employees receive a guaranteed wage for a specified number of hours per week even if the hours actually worked fall short of that number. For example, a guaranteed wage agreement may provide for a normal fifty-hour workweek with a guaranteed weekly wage of $550. That amount would be equivalent to a $10 per hour hourly wage for the first forty hours and $15 per hour for the remaining ten hours, thereby satisfying the wage and hours laws.

The payroll for an employee working fifty hours a week under such an agreement is $550 because that is a guaranteed weekly wage regardless of the hours actually worked. If such an employee works fifty-five hours, however, the weekly wage is $625. That wage includes $15 per hour for the five hours beyond the fifty hours provided in the guaranteed wage agreement. Consequently, the premium auditor would deduct $25 as extra pay for overtime ($5 per hour for the additional five hours) and include only $600 in the basis of premium.

Premium pay, or shift differential
A payroll system that increases the regular hourly wage rate for the night shift or other special conditions.

Premium pay, or **shift differential**, is a payroll system that increases the regular hourly wage rate for the night shift or other special conditions. This premium pay does not constitute extra pay for overtime because it does not involve work beyond the normal number of hours. For example, a factory may have two shifts with a $12 per hour wage rate for the day shift and $15 per hour for the night shift. Although the insured may contend that the night shift is no more hazardous than the day shift, the total payroll reflects the payroll that the insured must pay to attract the desired labor services. Because the extra pay is used as an incentive to get people to work a certain shift, some people call this incentive pay. Because the total payroll reflects the exposure to loss, there is no deduction from the premium base in this case.

Similarly, employees paid on a piecework basis may receive a higher rate after exceeding a certain production standard. As long as the employee accomplishes the increased production within the normal working hours, the insurer should not deduct the extra pay from the premium base. Insurers can treat extra pay as overtime pay only when the employee works more hours per day or per week than the normal limit.

The extra pay for overtime work as defined by the *Basic Manual* should be excluded from payroll, "provided the insured's books and records are maintained to show overtime pay separately by employee and in summary by classification."[11] If the insured does not maintain adequate records, then the insurer cannot exclude overtime pay from the total payroll.

In performing a premium audit of payroll records, (1) if the records show separately the extra pay earned for overtime, the entire extra pay should be excluded, and (2) if the records show the total pay earned for overtime (regular pay plus overtime pay) in one combined amount, and time and one-half is paid for overtime, one-third of this total pay shall be excluded. (If double time is paid for overtime and the total pay for such overtime is recorded separately, one-half of the total pay for double time shall be excluded.)[12]

An exception to this overtime rule is that it does not apply to payroll assigned to any classification under the caption "stevedoring" with a code number followed by the letter "F."

Wages for Time Not Worked

In some industries, employers pay employees for extra time not worked. For example, if employees work seven hours per day for five days a week, an employer may pay the employees for eight hours each day at the regular pay rate. If an employer does this, the insurer should not deduct the amount for the extra hour. Such pay is not overtime but part of the employees' normal payroll, which the insurer must include in the premium base.

Particularly in the construction industry, other periods exist when employees are not actually working but the employer must pay them anyway. Those periods include work suspensions or delays as a result of weather conditions, delays while waiting for materials, delays while waiting for another contractor to complete work, and delays arising from equipment breakdown. Standby time may occur when the operators of cranes, hoists, or other equipment are on the job, but the employer does not constantly require their services. In addition, employees who are not on strike may be unable to work because of a strike. The insurer should include wages paid for such idle time in total payroll and assign those wages to the same classification it would if the employee had been working in normal duties. In these instances, the payroll of these employees should be assigned to the clerical office employees classification (Code 8810), provided the employer's records clearly disclose the facts.

Similarly, if superintendents, foremen, or engineers are not doing their normal jobs when no work is in progress, the insurer should assign their pay to the classification describing the work they perform during that period. If their duties during the period are exclusively office work or drafting, or if the workers are idle, the premium auditor can assign their payroll to the clerical classification (Code 8810), except for those qualifying for the "Contractor— or Construction Superintendent" classification (Code 5606).

Payroll Limitations

For most employments, payroll is included into the exposure base without limitation. However, a payroll limitation for executive officers and for employees of athletic teams and carnivals does exist. The NCCI sets the maximum weekly payroll limitation applicable to highly-salaried individuals based on the state's average weekly wage rounded to the nearest $100. Generally, this amount automatically changes as wage levels change each year, using the NCCI's latest available semiannual call for wage data. The NCCI reviews the limitation amount at the time of each general rate revision and adjusts it by any indicated change in wage level.

The state pages (miscellaneous values page) or the Premium Audit Advisory Service's "Blue Card" shows the maximum payroll applicable for executive officers, members of athletic teams, and carnival workers. The premium base excludes the part of those employees' average weekly pay in excess of the limitation, provided that the following are true:[13]

- Books and records are maintained to show separately the total payroll earned by each employee is in excess of the weekly payroll limitation for the total time employed during the policy period.
- Separate records are maintained, in summary, by classification for such employees.[14]

This payroll limitation applies after the extra pay for overtime is deducted. In determining the average weekly wage, premium auditors should treat partial weeks as full weeks.

Imputed Payroll

In many circumstances, individuals receive no payroll at all or payroll far more modest than the actual value of their services, yet they are entitled to protection under workers' compensation laws. In such cases, premium auditors must impute the actual value of those services to arrive at a premium commensurate with the loss exposures. The *Basic Manual* stipulates the amount that insurers should include for some workers, such as executive officers. For other situations, the premium auditor must calculate the payroll that an individual would normally earn for the work performed.

Executive Officers and Owners

Special problems arise in determining the appropriate amount on which to base the premium for corporate officers and business owners. Not only is their compensation likely to be a relatively large amount, but they are also likely to receive it in many forms. It can be difficult to distinguish compensation for their labor from income on their investment in the business. A premium auditor must first determine whether the workers' compensation policy covers these persons because workers' compensation laws vary by state. If covered, the premium auditor must determine an appropriate amount to include in the premium base.

The president, vice president, secretary, treasurer, and other duly appointed corporate officers are employees of the corporation. In most states, executive officers are entitled to workers' compensation benefits. In about thirty states, however, they can elect not to be covered by the workers' compensation law.

Consequently, the insurer must endorse the policy with the **Partners, Officers and Others Exclusion Endorsement** (WC 00 03 08) for this election, which is a workers' compensation endorsement that indicates a corporation's coverage exclusion for officers. Premium auditors should include only payroll of those executive officers covered by the policy in the premium base, subject to the payroll limitation rules.

Insurers should not include executive officers' payroll in the premium base when those officers are not active in the business and therefore not exposed to its hazards. An NCCI interpretation defines two such situations:

- The executive officer is elected for the value of his or her name or because of stock holdings, has no duties and does not visit the premises, except perhaps to attend directors' meetings
- The executive officer ceases to perform any duties and does not visit the premises, except perhaps to attend directors' meetings[15]

If the officer visits the business frequently, even with no duties, the insurer should include the payroll. Sometimes an executive officer may receive little or no salary. An officer may be retired from the business or may concentrate on some other business or activity of which he or she is an employee or officer. Such officers may work only irregularly in the business insured by the policy, but they may still sustain an injury and collect workers' compensation. The *Basic Manual* therefore provides that insurers should include that officer's payroll in the premium base for each executive officer. The *Basic Manual*'s state pages (miscellaneous values page) show the minimum and maximum amount to include in the premium base for each executive officer.

A premium auditor's report should always identify the names and titles of all executive officers, including their duties, and list the amount the premium auditor included in the premium base for each so that a reviewer can later confirm that the premium auditor properly applied the minimum and maximum limitations.

The *Basic Manual* also lists four additional situations in which premium auditors must impute some payroll:

- The executive officer does not perform any duties but frequently visits the premises.
- The executive officer frequently visits the premises of the business for conferences, directors' meetings, or similar duties, even if the officer is an employee or officer of another operation in which he or she takes an active interest.
- The officer receives no salary; however, a regular salary is credited to him or her on the books. In this instance the amount credited must be included in payroll.
- The officer receives no salary, either drawn or credit, or the premium audit records fail to disclose the salary. In this instance the amount to be included in the payroll is the applicable minimum per Rule 2-D of the *Basic Manual*.

If an officer receives a bonus during the policy period, the premium auditor should prorate the amount of the bonus for the period of employment during the policy period. That is, if the person was employed for the full policy period, the premium auditor should assign the amount of the bonus divided by fifty-two to each week of the policy period.

A person may be an executive officer of more than one corporation insured under one policy, or each of the corporations may be insured under separate policies. If the same insurer issues the separate policies, the premium auditor should consider all the corporations as a unit in applying the minimum and maximum payroll limitation rules.

Subchapter S corporation
A small corporation restricted to no more than 100 stockholders that provides limited liability to its owners and is taxed like a partnership to avoid double taxation on dividends paid.

A **Subchapter S corporation** is a small corporation restricted to no more than 100 stockholders that provides limited liability to its owners and is taxed like a partnership so that its owners avoid double taxation on dividends paid. Small businesses are afforded special treatment under the Internal Revenue Code so that they can enjoy the advantages of incorporation but be taxed like a partnership. A qualifying corporation pays no federal income tax, although it must file an informational return (Form 1120 S). The corporation's profits distributed to shareowners are taxable as part of their personal income, but there is no double taxation of dividends for Subchapter S corporations.

A Subchapter S corporation's owners may find it advantageous to collect little or no salary so that they may receive larger dividends, which are not subject to payroll taxes, as are salaries. For this reason, shareowners who are active in the business often collect dividends instead of salaries. Insurers should include only amounts actually paid as salary or other payroll in the premium base, not amounts distributed as dividends.[16] If the only income to a Subchapter S corporation's officers is a share of undistributed taxable income, the insurer should include in the premium base the minimum amount specified by the state rate pages in the manual.

States have enacted laws allowing limited liability organizational forms. These organizations are sometimes known as limited liability corporations or limited liability partnerships. They are a cross between a partnership and a corporation. Premium auditors should be familiar with the law in their own states and know their state's rules regarding the payroll of the "partners" or "officers" of these organizations. In many states, the minimum and maximum premiums that apply to officers of corporations and to partners also apply to "members" and non-member officers or managers of the limited liability company.

Although they are employers rather than employees, partners and sole proprietors in over half the states can elect to be covered by the workers' compensation law. If the partner or sole proprietor has elected to be covered, insurers add fixed amounts to the premium base in most states. In 2006, those amounts range from $13,000 to $106,600 per person, depending on the state. The *Basic Manual* stipulates, "Premium for each partner or sole proprietor treated as an employee is based on the payroll amount shown on the state pages."[17]

Because they are business owners, partners and proprietors may receive a substantial portion of their income as profits rather than salary. If insurers based the premium for partners and proprietors on actual salary subject to limitations such as those applicable to executive officers, most partnerships and proprietorships would draw only a minimum amount in salary. Accordingly, a fixed premium basis provides a reasonable loss exposure measure for such individuals.

Subcontractors

Most workers' compensation laws hold a contractor responsible for workers' compensation benefits to employees of uninsured subcontractors. The standard workers' compensation policy automatically insures this responsibility. Premium auditors must therefore ascertain whether this loss exposure exists and include the proper premium charge if it does. Insureds must either furnish satisfactory evidence that the subcontractor has insured the loss exposure or pay a premium based on the subcontractor's payroll.

Additionally, there are often situations in which the subcontractor is an individual without employees. When faced with this situation, a premium auditor must determine whether the subcontractor is an independent contractor or is actually an employee. The two major tests of an employer-employee relationship are: (1) the degree of direction and control the employer has over the worker and (2) the relative nature of the work. If the use of those tests indicates that the subcontractor is actually an employee, the premium auditor should treat the subcontractor as an employee in the audit and make charges according to the *Basic Manual*.

If those tests indicate that the subcontractor is an independent contractor, the premium auditor must determine whether the subcontractor is subject to the state workers' compensation law. As explained earlier, in many states a sole proprietor must elect to be covered. Based on the available facts, if the premium auditor determines that the subcontractor is subject to the workers' compensation law, the subcontractor must furnish evidence of insurance or the premium auditor will make a charge under the insured contractor's policy.

Subcontractors may request that their insurer furnish to a third party evidence that they are covered by insurance. A **certificate of insurance** is a document issued by an insurer or an authorized representative of the insurer as evidence that a policy has been issued providing coverage in a certain amount. A certificate of insurance that is issued by the subcontractor's insurer can demonstrate that insurance covers the subcontractor's statutory workers' compensation obligation. Exhibit 3-1 shows an example of such a certificate of insurance.

A certificate of insurance should always indicate coverage for the state and preferably for the location (or locations) at which the subcontractor performs work and for the period for which coverage is in effect. Some subcontractors self-insure their workers' compensation obligation and may furnish a certificate to that effect.

Certificate of insurance
A document issued by an insurer or an authorized representative of the insurer as evidence that a policy has been issued providing coverage in a certain amount.

EXHIBIT 3-1

Certificate of Insurance

ACORD™ CERTIFICATE OF LIABILITY INSURANCE

DATE (MM/DD/YY) 11/07/19X7

PRODUCER	TEL. NO. 616-592-0711
A.M. ABLE AGENCY 250 MAIN ST. WORKINGTOWN, PA 19000 (215) 697-0000	

THIS CERTIFICATE IS ISSUED AS A MATTER OF INFORMATION ONLY AND CONFERS NO RIGHTS UPON THE CERTIFICATE HOLDER. THIS CERTIFICATE DOES NOT AMEND, EXTEND OR ALTER THE COVERAGE AFFORDED BY THE POLICIES BELOW.

INSURERS AFFORDING COVERAGE

INSURED		
BLS CONSTRUCTION 3000 INDUSTRIAL HIGHWAY WORKINGTOWN, PA 19000	INSURER A:	INSURANCE COMPANY A
	INSURER B:	INSURANCE COMPANY B
	INSURER C:	INSURANCE COMPANY C
	INSURER D:	
	INSURER E:	

COVERAGES

THE POLICIES OF INSURANCE LISTED BELOW HAVE BEEN ISSUED TO THE INSURED NAMED ABOVE FOR THE POLICY PERIOD INDICATED. NOTWITHSTANDING ANY REQUIREMENT, TERM OR CONDITION OF ANY CONTRACT OR OTHER DOCUMENT WITH RESPECT TO WHICH THIS CERTIFICATE MAY BE ISSUED OR MAY PERTAIN, THE INSURANCE AFFORDED BY THE POLICIES DESCRIBED HEREIN IS SUBJECT TO ALL THE TERMS, EXCLUSIONS AND CONDITIONS OF SUCH POLICIES. AGGREGATE LIMITS SHOWN MAY HAVE BEEN REDUCED BY PAID CLAIMS.

INSR LTR	TYPE OF INSURANCE	POLICY NUMBER	POLICY EFFECTIVE DATE (MM/DD/YY)	POLICY EXPIRATION DATE (MM/DD/YY)	LIMITS	
A	**GENERAL LIABILITY** [X] COMMERCIAL GENERAL LIABILITY [ ] CLAIMS MADE [X] OCCUR GEN'L AGGREGATE LIMIT APPLIES PER: [ ] POLICY [ ] PRO-JECT [ ] LOC	SP 0002	7/1/X7	7/1/X8	EACH OCCURRENCE FIRE DAMAGE (Any one fire) MED EXP (Any one person) PERSONAL & ADV INJURY GENERAL AGGREGATE PRODUCTS - COMP/OP AGG	$ 1,000,000 $ 50,000 $ 5,000 $ 1,000,000 $ 2,000,000 $ 2,000,000
A	**AUTOMOBILE LIABILITY** [X] ANY AUTO [ ] ALL OWNED AUTOS [ ] SCHEDULED AUTOS [ ] HIRED AUTOS [ ] NON-OWNED AUTOS	SP 0002	7/1/X7	7/1/X8	COMBINED SINGLE LIMIT (Ea accident) BODILY INJURY (Per person) BODILY INJURY (Per accident) PROPERTY DAMAGE (Per accident)	$ 1,000,000 $ -NA- $ -NA- $ -NA-
	GARAGE LIABILITY [ ] ANY AUTO				AUTO ONLY - EA ACCIDENT OTHER THAN EA ACC AUTO ONLY: AGG	$ $ $
B	**EXCESS LIABILITY** [X] OCCUR [ ] CLAIMS MADE [ ] DEDUCTIBLE [ ] RETENTION $	3XS-1522-25	7/1/X7	7/1/X8	EACH OCCURRENCE AGGREGATE	$ 5,000,000 $ 10,000,000 $ $ $
C	**WORKERS COMPENSATION AND EMPLOYERS' LIABILITY**	29984-31	7/1/X7	7/1/X8	[X] WC STATU-TORY LIMITS [ ] OTH-ER E.L. EACH ACCIDENT E.L. DISEASE - EA EMPLOYEE E.L. DISEASE - POLICY LIMIT	 $ 100,000 $ 100,000 $ 500,000
	OTHER					

DESCRIPTION OF OPERATIONS/LOCATIONS/VEHICLES/EXCLUSIONS ADDED BY ENDORSEMENT/SPECIAL PROVISIONS
BUILDING CONTRACTOR / WORK SITE AT CERTIFICATE HOLDER'S PREMISES

CERTIFICATE HOLDER	ADDITIONAL INSURED; INSURER LETTER: ___	CANCELLATION
CCC REAL ESTATE 25 2ND ST. WORKINGTOWN, PA 19000		SHOULD ANY OF THE ABOVE DESCRIBED POLICIES BE CANCELLED BEFORE THE EXPIRATION DATE THEREOF, THE ISSUING INSURER WILL ENDEAVOR TO MAIL _10_ DAYS WRITTEN NOTICE TO THE CERTIFICATE HOLDER NAMED TO THE LEFT, BUT FAILURE TO DO SO SHALL IMPOSE NO OBLIGATION OR LIABILITY OF ANY KIND UPON THE INSURER, ITS AGENTS OR REPRESENTATIVES. AUTHORIZED REPRESENTATIVE

ACORD 25-S (7/97)

© ACORD CORPORATION 1988

Without satisfactory evidence that the subcontractor has insured its obligation, the premium auditor must include the subcontractor's payroll in the basis of premium. The insurer calculates the premium the same way as if the subcontractor's employees were the insured's employees.

If the subcontractor's payroll records are not available, the premium auditor should include the full subcontract price for the work performed during the policy period in the premium basis. An exception to that rule delineates minimum amounts to charge in various situations. If investigation reveals that a definite amount of the subcontract price represents payroll, that definite amount shall be payroll for the additional premium computation. However, that amount must be at least 50 percent of the subcontract price in contracts for labor and materials and at least 90 percent of the subcontract price in contracts for labor only. If the contract is for mobile equipment with operators, the amount included must be at least $33^1/_3$ percent of the subcontract price. Exhibit 3-2 outlines the premium auditor's decision-making process in determining the basis of premium for subcontractors.

If vehicles—along with drivers, chauffeurs, and helpers—are hired under contract and no evidence of workers' compensation insurance exists, the premium auditor should include those persons' payroll in the audit under the appropriate classifications. If the premium auditor cannot determine the actual payroll, then the premium auditor should consider $33^1/_3$ percent of the total amount paid for the hire of those vehicles as the drivers' payroll. If the owner of the vehicle is also a driver, the premium auditor should still include $33^1/_3$ percent of the contract price for payroll of the owner/driver. If the contract price in those situations does not include the cost of fuel, maintenance, or other services provided to a vehicle's owner or owner-operator under contract, the premium auditor should add the value of such goods and services to the contract price before determining the $33^1/_3$ percent.[18] The premium auditor should look closely at businesses in which the use of drivers seems to be necessary but the business does not show any drivers on its payroll. The premium auditor frequently becomes aware of the potential loss exposure because a concurrent commercial auto policy provides coverage for "hired vehicles (or cars)," which requires a premium audit. Because of experience with similar operations, the premium auditor asks whether any "vehicles under contract" are present.

Unsalaried Employees

Individuals may work without receiving any payroll. If so, the workers' compensation law or a voluntary compensation endorsement may still cover them. The insurer should therefore charge some premium for this loss exposure when it occurs.

How can individuals who receive no payroll be employees in the absence of a contract of hire? They may receive some consideration for their services other than monetary compensation. Interns or apprentices may work without pay during a training period required to enter a particular occupation.

EXHIBIT 3-2

Determining the Basis of Premium for Subcontractors

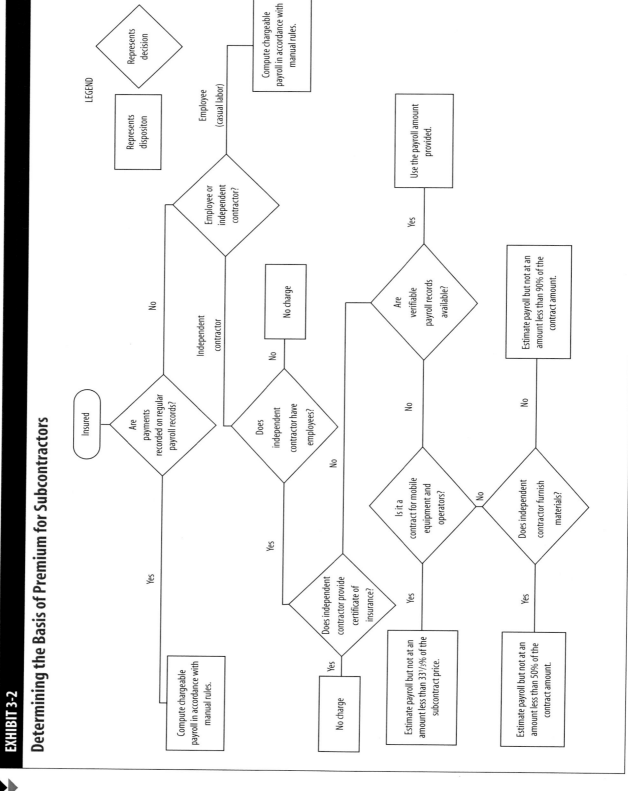

The opportunity to serve an apprenticeship would therefore be a valuable consideration that could induce a person to work without pay.

A particular state's workers' compensation statute may specifically include workers who may not otherwise qualify as employees. Premium auditors need to check the applicable state's statute and, if a loss exposure is present, include an appropriate amount in the premium base. Cases that frequently arise regarding volunteers involve relatives, student nurses, volunteer workers, and welfare workers. In all cases, the premium auditor must first determine whether the person is covered by the state workers' compensation law. If the person is not covered, insurers can provide volunteer workers with benefits equal to those under the act through the voluntary compensation endorsement. When this is done, the voluntary compensation endorsement should set forth the basis of premium.

For covered unsalaried employees, a good rule for determining their payroll is to include an amount equal to the amount that a regular employee doing the same type of work would receive. For student nurses, the premium auditor should include the actual payroll, if any, plus board and lodging. If the employer neither pays payroll nor furnishes board and lodging, the premium auditor should include an amount equal to the starting salary for a beginning trained nurse. If the student nurse receives only board and lodging, the premium auditor should include the value of the board and lodging plus an additional amount to make the total equal to the beginning salary for a trained nurse.

Premium Bases Other Than Payroll

Except in Washington, as explained, insurers base workers' compensation insurance premiums almost entirely on the total payroll to employees. Only a few cases exist in which that principle does not apply. Those cases involve classifications for which the description or footnotes appearing on the state rate pages specify the premium base.

Per Capita Premiums

Insurers charge premiums for domestic workers in residences per capita. The classifications in the *Basic Manual* for those workers are as follows:

- Domestic Workers—Inside—Code 0913
- Domestic Workers—Inside—Occasional—Code 0908
- Domestic Workers—Outside—Including Private Chauffeurs—Code 0912
- Domestic Workers—Outside—Occasional—Including Occasional Private Chauffeurs—Code 0909

Rule 3.C. of the *Basic Manual* defines those classifications. The rates shown next to those code numbers on the state rate pages are the rates per each employee falling into that classification rather than the usual rate per $100 of payroll.

If an insured employs full-time domestic workers for less than the entire policy period, the insurer can prorate the per capita charge according to the workers' employment period. However, each pro rata charge will be at least 25 percent of the per capita charge. For occasional domestic workers (Codes 0908 and 0909), a single per capita charge applies for each aggregate of employed time that is one-half of the customary full time for such workers. An additional per capita charge applies to any remainder.[19]

Upset Payroll

Upset payroll
A payroll basis applied in the pulpwood, logging, or lumbering industry based on the number of cords of wood produced.

Upset payroll applies to insureds engaged exclusively in the pulpwood, logging, or lumbering industry. The NCCI introduced this exposure base because of difficulty encountered in obtaining adequate payroll records from the employers in this industry. If the insurer cannot obtain adequate payroll records, the basis of premium for this classification is an upset payroll based on the number of cords of wood produced. Some states require that upset payroll be used even if payroll records are available.

For example, the state rate page may provide that for premium computation purposes insurers use a $16-per-cord upset payroll for logs up to eight feet long and $14-per-cord for logs longer than eight feet long. This method produces a realistic approximation of the actual payroll. This is only the payroll figure, and the insurer must multiply it by the rate.

Taxicabs

A similar situation arises for the taxicab company classification for all but garage employees (Code 7370) when no verifiable payroll records exist showing the taxicab drivers' payroll. In that case, the insurer bases the premium on the amount per vehicle per policy-year for employee-operated vehicles shown in the state pages under "Miscellaneous Values." If the owner also leases or rents such vehicles, the insurer calculates an additional premium based on the amount per vehicle per policy-year for leased or rented vehicles also shown on the state pages under "Miscellaneous Values." This amount approximates the total earnings from driving one cab.[20] The insurer must then apply the rate against this amount.

Policy Surcharge—Aircraft

If the insured uses owned or leased aircraft to transport employees, the chance of workers' compensation losses increases. The insurer can cover this additional loss exposure by using the Aircraft Premium Endorsement. Insurers base the premium for this coverage on the number of passenger seats (up to ten seats) in the aircraft. (Classifications also exist for the employees who service or fly the aircraft.) The applicable rate per passenger seat appears in the state pages under "Miscellaneous Values." If the premium auditor discovers that the insured operates aircraft for transporting personnel, the premium auditor must include the applicable surcharge and any appropriate classifications. If the policy does not already show the surcharge, the premium auditor should notify the underwriter.

Insurers must charge executive officers who are pilots or members of the aircraft crew a premium to reflect this additional loss exposure. Rule 2.E.1.c.(2) of the *Basic Manual* states that for each week during which the officer performs some flight duties, the premium auditor should assign the payroll of the officer for that entire week to Code 7421 (aircraft operation—flying crew), unless the officer's nonflight duties during the week would be subject to a higher-rated classification. For those weeks during which the officer did not perform some flight duties, the premium auditor should assign the payroll as outlined by Rule 2.E.1.c.(1) (the usual executive officer classification rules).

The premium auditor should base the flying time on the pilot's log book required by federal regulations or other verifiable records. If such records are not available to indicate when the officer performed flight duties, the premium auditor should assign the officer's payroll to the highest rated classification to which he or she is subject.

Volunteer Firefighters and First-Aid Departments

Volunteer firefighters or volunteer first-aid departments may have their own class codes and rates. The miscellaneous values page of the state pages may specify that premiums for firefighters should be based on number of volunteers, number of pieces of equipment, or even population. Volunteer first-aid departments may have similar premises bases.

PREMIUM DETERMINATION FOR WORKERS' COMPENSATION

With the exceptions already discussed, the premium base is the insured's total payroll to employees covered by the policy. The premium for the policy is essentially the premium base multiplied by the applicable rate. However, factors besides the rate can influence the premium amount, including loss constants and expense constants in some states, minimum premiums, experience modifications, and premium discounts.

Workers' Compensation Rates

The rates for workers' compensation insurance vary by classification because the losses are much greater in some classifications than in others. The rate is the premium charged for each $100 of payroll. It must be high enough to generate sufficient premium to pay the losses in that classification and to cover expenses. In most states, the NCCI develops loss costs. Insurers add an expense component to these loss costs and file the resulting rates with the state insurance regulators for approval.

Workers' compensation insurance receives special attention from regulatory authorities. Most states require that rates for workers' compensation insurance be filed and approved before use.

The manual rate is an insurance rate for a classification published in a rating manual and filed by the insurer. For NCCI states, the manual rate for each classification is shown after its code number on the *Basic Manual's* state rate pages. For independent rating bureau states, the manual rate for each classification appears on the rate pages for that state. Often the manual rate is referred to as the authorized rate. According to the *Basic Manual*, the **authorized rate** is "the manual rate or any other rate that has been authorized by the appropriate insurance regulatory authority for use by the carrier."[21]

Authorized rate
The manual rate or any other rate that has been authorized by the appropriate insurance regulatory authority for use by the carrier.

Sometimes, (a) rates may apply. An **(a) rate** is a rate that is used by an insurer that is not statistically credible because adequate data do not exist for that particular coverage or class. Such rates are based on the experience and best judgment for each individual loss exposure. The symbol "(a)" in the rate column indicates that the insurer must obtain the rate for that classification from the NCCI or the independent rating bureau or must develop the rate itself. Classifications with (a) rates generally have such unusual loss exposures that the rates do not have the same degree of statistical credibility as manual rates.

(a) rate
A rate that is used by an insurer that is not statistically credible because adequate data do not exist for that particular coverage or class. Such rates are based on the experience and best judgment for each individual loss exposure.

The loss costs or rates for a classification code number followed by the symbol "E" or "D" include a disease loading (the manual formerly used a "D" but now uses an "E"). A **disease loading** is the increased loading in the insurance rate applied to specific classification codes that reflect specific disease hazards inherent in the operations described by those classifications. Such loadings reflect specific disease hazards inherent in the operations described by those classifications. Examples of such disease hazards are silicosis and asbestosis. With approval, the insurer can add a supplemental disease loading for a manual rate. An insurer can also delete the loading when the substance is not present in the insured's operations.[22]

Disease loading
The increased loading in the insurance rate applied to specific classification codes that reflect specific disease hazards inherent in the operations described by those classifications.

Loss Constant

Experience has shown that the cost per exposure unit is higher for small employers than for large ones. In an effort to equalize the loss ratios for small and large employers, insurers in some states add a loss constant to the premium for policies with annual premiums under $500. A **loss constant** in workers' compensation is a consistent flat charge added to policies with low premiums intended to equalize the loss ratios. In some states, the loss constant may be the same for all rating classes; in other states, the loss constant may vary by industry group. For example, loss constants for three industry groups may be (1) manufacturing, $30; (2) contracting, $16; and (3) all others, $10. The loss constant for each classification appears next to its code number on the state rate pages. Certain classifications, however, do not have loss constants. The NCCI has eliminated the loss constant or combined it with the expense

Loss constant
In workers' compensation insurance, a consistent flat charge added to policies with low premiums intended to equalize the loss ratios.

constant in all but about six states. Premium auditors should check the *Basic Manual* to determine whether the loss constant applies in the state involved.

Expense Constant

The expense loading in workers' compensation rates does not provide enough premium to cover the expense of issuing and servicing policies with small premiums. The expense constant is a flat charge designed to cover administrative expenses, such as policy issuance and record keeping. The expense constant is used commonly in workers' compensation and employers' liability policies to help cover the expenses of issuing, recording, and auditing that are common to all policies regardless of size. If a state has an expense constant in effect, it applies to all policies, not merely to policies with small premiums.

The expense constant appears in the state pages under "Miscellaneous Values," and insurers should show it on the policy's information page. Because the NCCI includes the expense constant in calculating the minimum premium for each policy, insurers should not add it if the minimum premium becomes the final premium for the policy.[23] The expense constant is not subject to a premium discount, an experience rating modification, or a retrospective rating adjustment.[24] If the policy is canceled, the insurer should add the pro rata portion of the expense constant, but not less than $15.[25]

Minimum Premiums

A **minimum premium** is the lowest amount for which an insurer can write an insurance policy. The *Basic Manual* states it as the lowest total policy premium for any policy period not exceeding one year. The minimum premium for a classification provides the insurer with enough premium to cover a policy's usual issuing and servicing costs. The information page indicates the minimum premium on an estimated basis. The minimum premium for any classification includes the loss constant, if any, and the expense constant. (The minimum premium is not subject to experience rating.) However, the minimum premium is subject to prorating on short-term policies if the short-term policy is issued to replace a binder or if the short-term policy is issued solely to establish concurrence with other insurance policies.

Minimum premium
The lowest amount for which an insurer can write an insurance policy.

Amount of Minimum Premium

Unless the classification is (a) rated, the minimum premium appears on the state rate pages opposite the code number for each classification. The underwriter develops the (a) rated minimum premiums, subject to the applicable rating bureau's approval.

The code numbers for per capita classifications also provide for three-year minimum premiums. For policies issued for longer than one year (other than per capita policies), a minimum premium applies to each unit of twelve months, or a portion thereof, as if it actually constituted a separate policy.

Certain coverages have minimum premiums that the manual considers coverage minimum premiums. When those minimum premiums apply, the insurer charges them in addition to the other premium on a premium audit. Those coverages are admiralty law and Federal Employers Liability Act (FELA) operations. When a policy has increased limits under employers' liability, the increased limits table specifies the minimum premium to use.

Determining the Minimum Premium

The insurer determines the minimum premium at audit based on the classifications developing premium. If total payroll times the rate for the proper classification is less than the minimum premium shown for that classification, the insurer should charge that minimum premium.

If more than one classification is involved, the minimum premium for the policy is the highest minimum premium for any classification included in the policy. When a policy includes per capita-rated classes, the minimum premium for the policy is the highest minimum premium for any classification applying on the policy regardless of whether the classification is a per capita-rated classification or a payroll-rated classification.

If a policy includes two or more states, the premium auditor should determine the state minimum according to the minimum premium rules for each state. The minimum for the policy is the highest of the several state minimum premiums included in the policy.

Experience Rating Plan

Experience modification
A rate multiplier derived from the experience rating computation; a method of tailoring manual rates to a policyholder's experience based on the policyholder's premium and loss records.

The **experience modification** is a rate multiplier derived from the experience rating computation and is a method of tailoring manual rates to a policyholder's experience based on the policyholder's premium and loss records. This modification is then sent to the insurer. The purpose of the experience modification is to tailor the state manual rate to the policyholder's experience based on the premium and loss record of certain prior years. This modification rewards employers who are relatively successful in controlling losses and penalizes those who are not. As accidents occur less frequently or their severity diminishes, the policyholder's experience modification becomes a factor less than one and reduces the insured's overall premium for the current year.

The insurer uses the experience modification to calculate the estimated premium at policy inception and also when the insurer calculates the final premium adjustment. If the policyholder's loss record has not been favorable, the experience modification calculated will prove to be a factor greater than one and will consequently cause workers' compensation premiums to increase.

An insured qualifies for experience rating if the payroll developed during the experience period produces a stipulated minimum premium based on the manual rates in force on the date for which the rating is to be established. The minimum annual premium varies by state, from $2,200 to $5,500.

The experience modification is calculated based on a formula involving the payroll and losses for each policyholder. The experience period used in calculating an experience modification for a risk is generally three complete years of loss experience ending one year before the modification's effective date. For example, the modification for the year January 1, 20X8, to January 1, 20X9, would be calculated by using payroll and losses for the three-year period January 1, 20X4, to January 1, 20X7. The experience from the year January 1, 20X7, to January 1, 20X8, would not be used until the following year. Using payroll and losses for three consecutive years averages the results, preventing substantial fluctuations that could occur if only one year's experience were used.

When a premium auditor changes an insured's classification for its major operations, the premium auditor should be aware of the possible influence on the experience rating modification factor. If an insured has been incorrectly classified, the experience rating process has been comparing the insured's actual experience with that of businesses in a different classification. Therefore, the process has been incorrectly calculating the insured's experience rating modification (assuming that the insured's classification was incorrect during the experience period). Recalculating the modification is beyond the premium auditor's role, but the premium auditor should bring the possible incorrect modification to the attention of the underwriter.

Insurers must apply this plan to each qualified insured regardless of whether a debit or a credit modification results. The plan's intent is to rate on the normal anniversary date and not to allow an insured to alter an existing policy by cancellation or rewriting or to extend a policy term to qualify for or to avoid the plan's application.

Timely Issuance of Modifications

Problems have occurred in gathering the data necessary to issue an experience modification in a timely manner. Part of the problem has been incomplete loss data, but another part has been the inability of an insurer to conduct the final premium audit. An insured, knowing that a large additional premium would apply, may be tempted to delay the final premium audit. This situation can lead to experience modifications being made well into a policy term. If the modification was higher than that used in calculating the policy premium, insurers were asking some insureds to pay the difference at that time. This led to much policyholder dissatisfaction. If the new modification was lower and the insured was entitled to a refund, however, few complaints were voiced.

The NCCI made several changes in the manual rules in response to problems arising from modifications being determined after the policy period had begun. If it has been unsuccessful in obtaining the unit statistical plan data necessary to calculate the modification, the NCCI issues contingent modifications. After the NCCI has made at least two attempts to gather the data, it will issue a contingent rating. A **contingent rating** is a rate modification, issued by the NCCI based on data available at the time a policy is issued that

Contingent rating
A rate modification, issued by the NCCI based on data available at the time a policy is issued that allows an insurer to use a modification on the policy that should more closely approximate what the final modification will be.

allows an insurer to use a modification on the policy that should more closely approximate what the final modification will be.

In addition, the NCCI has introduced rules regarding the endorsement of "late issued" modifications on a workers' compensation policy. If the final modification is lower than the contingent modification (or the previous year's modification) used on the policy, the insurer is to apply the modification retroactively to the beginning of the policy term.

If use of the final modification would result in an increase in premium, the NCCI has established a graduated application. If the NCCI determines the final modification during the first ninety days of the policy period, the insurer can apply it retroactively to the policy inception date. If it is determined after the policy has been in force for ninety days, the insurer computes the increase in premium pro rata from the date the insurer endorses the policy. Similar rules exist when the policy is issued with the Anniversary Rating Date Endorsement.

To avoid insureds' intentionally delaying data collection when they know the new modification will be higher, the manual rules state that the preceding rules regarding an increase in premium do not apply when the modification is issued late because of failure of the insured to comply, a retroactive reclassification of a risk, or changes in ownership.

Experience Rating Issues

Because of the expense of workers' compensation insurance, employers are always looking for ways to reduce the cost of their coverage. Many employers are aware of the effect a claim has on its experience modification factor. One insurer has developed a software program that calculates the surcharges that apply if an insured reports a claim. The employer then decides whether to submit the claim to the insurer. If the amount of the claim is less than the amount by which the insured's premiums will increase, the insured would likely retain the claim and not report it to the insurer.

This practice has implications for insurers. First, insurers are not receiving the premiums due them. Second, the statistics that insurers report are inaccurate because of missing loss information. In turn, this will cause future rates to be lower than they should be. Some question exists as to whether this practice amounts to fraud on the insured's part. This practice should be monitored closely and necessary action taken to ensure that insurers receive the appropriate premiums.

Another practice affecting experience modifications and premium auditors' work is employee leasing. The NCCI *Experience Rating Plan Manual* examined the owner/employer when determining whether a change in ownership should mean a change in the experience rating modification. That is, if the owner changed, the manual stated that the insurer should discontinue the current experience modification and a new experience period should begin. This was done under the theory that the owner of the business primarily determined whether a business would have losses. If the owner was very safety conscious, the business would likely have fewer losses. If that owner sold the business, the new owner may not be as safety conscious, so the insurer should discontinue the modification earned by the previous owner.

Because of this rule, if an employer with an experience debit fired all its employees and then leased them back from an employee-leasing firm, the insurer would discontinue the experience debit. The employee-leasing firm, as a new employer, would begin a new experience rating period and therefore, in effect, earn a 1.00 modification for at least a while.

Partly because of the increasing use of employee leasing (sometimes undertaken to avoid an experience debit), the NCCI reexamined the rules regarding ownership changes. In most cases of ownership changes, the operations, the majority of employees, and the majority of the supervisors remain the same. In some cases, the day-to-day management is exactly the same; only the person owning the stock has changed. Premium auditors who work for insurers that have been sold to another organization can ask whether any changes that took place immediately as a result of the sale, in their opinion, would affect workers' compensation experience.

As a result of this review, the NCCI revised the manual rules regarding ownership changes. The experience rating modification continues to apply unless each of the following three conditions is met:

- The change must be a material change such that the:

    a. entire ownership interest after the change had no ownership interest before the change, or

    b. the collective ownership of all those having an interest in an entity both before the change and after the change amounts to either less than one-third ownership before the change or less than one-half ownership after the change.

- The material change in ownership is accompanied by a change in operations sufficient to result in reclassification of the governing classification.

- The material change in ownership is accompanied by a change in the process and hazard of the operations.[26]

If an entity undergoes a change that does not meet the preceding criteria, the experience for that entity will be transferred to the experience rating calculation of the acquiring, surviving, or new entity. Exact rules regarding ownership changes appear in Part Three of the NCCI *Experience Rating Plan Manual*. Rules regarding when the new modification applies appear on Part 2.C.10.a.

Although these changes address many of the employee-leasing transactions that are solely attempts to avoid experience debits, insurers and the NCCI continue to monitor such changes in ownership. Although the NCCI determines whether to continue a modification, premium auditors may become involved in gathering information for their companies when a change in ownership occurs.

Premium Discount

Premium discount
A credit adjustment for policies with total premiums over a certain size, recognizing that, as the premium increases, the portion required to pay certain expenses decreases.

Standard premium
A premium that is calculated by using state rating classifications, applying them to an insured's estimated exposures for the policy period, and allowing for various adjustments.

Total standard premium
The total premium charged for a workers' compensation policy that includes the premium for all states covered under the policy.

Premium discount is a credit adjustment for policies with total premiums over a certain size, recognizing that, as the premium increases, the portion required to pay certain expenses decreases. The premium discount gives an insured a credit adjustment in relation to the total earned premium. Insurers base premium discounts on the theory of graduating expenses according to the premium size. Premium discount plans have been adopted in most states, whereby an insured owing a total standard premium of $5,000 or more is entitled to a discount. The **standard premium** is a premium that is calculated by using state rating classifications, applying them to an insured's estimated exposures for the policy period, and allowing for various adjustments. The standard premium is the state premium based on the authorized rates for each classification, including surcharges, plus any appropriate additional charge, such as experience rating modification, schedule rating modification, loss constants, and minimum premiums. The insurer excludes the expense constant in determining the standard premium. The **total standard premium** is the total premium charged for a workers' compensation policy that includes the premium for all states covered under the policy. Premium discounts do not apply to standard premiums included in a retrospective rating plan.[27] Insurers can combine separate policies issued to an insured by a single insurer or by two or more insurers under the same management when applying premium discounts.[28] If a policy includes coverage in one or more states that have approved the premium discount plan and the policy develops total standard premium greater than the stipulated minimum amount, the standard premium is subject to premium discount.

Insurers show the premium discount as a credit entry on the summary sheet and invoice, usually as the last entry. Premium discount tables are in the appendix to the Rules section of the *Basic Manual*.

Without Retrospective Rating

The premium discount varies depending on whether the insurer issues the policy for a single state or multiple states. If a policy provides coverage in only one state, the insurer determines the premium discount for that state by applying the discount percentages on the state rate pages to the total standard premium.[29]

Premium discounts for policies insuring operations in more than one state are more involved than for single-state policies. The *Basic Manual* states the following: "Premium discount applies on an interstate basis. It is determined by applying the appropriate discount percentages to each state's portion of the total standard premium in excess of the authorized threshold amount."[30] Exhibit 3-3 shows the premium discount computation for multiple-state policies.

EXHIBIT 3-3

Premium Discount Computation—Multiple-State Policy

STATEMENT OF PREMIUM ADJUSTMENT					
NAME AND ADDRESS OF INSURED Hullett Furniture Company 546 Bellbrook Road Easton, MD 21601					
NAME AND ADDRESS OF AGENCY 111 Main Street Easton, MD 21603		**Policy Number** WC 5678		**Kind of Policy** Workers' Comp	
		Policy Period 5-1-X5 to 5-1-X6		**Date** 5-25-X6	
		Audit Period 5-1-X5 to 5-1-X6		**Type of Audit** Field	

Code	Description/Location	Base Amount	Rate	Premium	Previously Billed	Additional Return
	Maryland					
2881	Furniture Assembling—Wood	$2,466,289	4.85	$119,615		
2883	Furniture Mfg.	1,312,714	9.72	127,596		
8044	Furniture Store	404,218	3.25	13,137		
8810	Clerical NOC	101,222	0.30	304		
				$260,652		
	Premium Discount—MD		15.5%	(40,401)		
				$220,251		
	Virginia					
8044	Furniture Store	$601,412	3.85	$23,154		
8810	Clerical NOC	79,901	0.19	152		
				$23,306		
	Premium Discount—VA		10.9%	(2,540)		
				$20,766		
	Expense Constant			60		
	Total Premium			$241,077		
	Experience Mod			1.00		
				$241,077	$240,000 (paid year-to-date)	$1,077 additional premium due

With Retrospective Rating

As mentioned, the standard premium portion that is subject to a retrospective rating plan is not subject to premium discount. The remainder of that standard premium, however, is subject to premium discount. Insurers compute the premium discount as follows:

- Determine the discount as if none of the premium is subject to retrospective rating
- Determine the discount based on only that premium that is subject to retrospective rating
- The difference between 1 and 2 is the premium discount

Insurers should distribute the total premium discount by state in proportion to the standard premium subject to premium discount.[31]

Other Methods

Insurers can use any other method to determine the premium discount, provided that the discount does not differ from the discount produced by the methods described above by more than 0.1 percent of the standard premium.

Cancellations

Some premium adjustment factors apply to less than the normal one-year policy period. For example, the insurer or insured may have canceled the policy before expiration, or a different rate may apply to part of the policy period. In such cases, the premium auditor must carefully obtain the payroll for precisely the applicable periods and split the payroll shown on the audit report according to those requirements.

When an insurer or insured cancels a policy before its normal expiration date, the premium adjustment must reflect the shortened policy period. Two cancellation methods are available: pro rata and short rate. Insurers use the pro rata cancellation method when the insurer cancels the policy or when the insured cancels because it is going out of the business. An insurer uses the short-rate cancellation method when an insured cancels for reasons other than going out of business.

Pro Rata Cancellations

Insurers should make premium adjustments by applying authorized rates to the audited payrolls for the period during which the policy was in effect. The pro rata portion of the expense constant applies, subject to a $15 minimum. If, however, the final premium is less than the pro rata portion of the specified minimum, the insurer should charge the pro rata portion of the minimum premium.

Insurers can issue long-term policies for a period not exceeding three years, with the proviso that the insurer will treat such coverage as respects rates, rules, loss and expense constants, minimum premiums, and statistical reports exactly as though they consisted of separate annual policies (subject to all adjustments that would be made annually if one-year policies were issued). If canceled, the insurer considers the coverage as having consecutive twelve-month units, or if the coverage period is not a multiple of twelve months, the insurer considers the last unit as a short-term policy.

If an insurer cancels a policy at the insured's request before the normal expiration date for the reason that the insured has completed its work, the insurer should adjust the premium on a pro rata basis. For three-year fixed-rate policies, the insurer should adjust the premium by applying authorized rates to payroll or other premium basis and adding to it the pro rata portion of the three-year loss constant and three-year expense constant.

Short-Rate Cancellations

Premium adjustment for short-rate cancellations requires applying the appropriate short-rate percentage corresponding to the time the policy was in force to the premium on a full annual basis, determined by applying authorized rates to the audited payroll extended pro rata to a full annual basis. The insurer must add the short-rate portion of the expense constant, subject to a $15 minimum, to the short-rate premium regardless of premium size. However, if the final premium as computed is less than the specified minimum premium, the insurer should charge the minimum premium. Exhibit 3-4 illustrates how to calculate earned premium for a short-rate cancellation. Premium auditors can find the short-rate cancellation table in Appendix B of the *Basic Manual*.

EXHIBIT 3-4

Example of a Short-Rate Cancellation

A policy in effect for 185 days develops actual payroll of $55,500.

The manual rate is $0.50 per $100 of payroll.

The expense constant is $35.

The minimum premium is $73.

1. Payroll extended to annual basis = $55,500 × (365 ÷ 185) = $109,500.

2. Annual premium = $1,095.00 × $0.50 = $548.

3. Short-rate percentage for 185 days = 61%.

4. Short-rate premium for canceled policy = $548 × 0.61 = $334.

5. Short-rate portion of expense constant = $35 × 0.61 = $21.

6. Total premium for canceled policy = $334 + $21 = $355.

7. Minimum premium not applicable.

For policies covering more than one state, the insurer should apply the short-rate portion of the annual loss constant on an individual state basis for the coverage period only in each state in which the loss exposure develops.

For short-term policies that the insured cancels before their normal expiration date, the premium auditor should apply the short-rate portion of the annual loss constants, charge the short-rate portion of the expense constant, and compare the result to the full annual minimum premium.

For three-year fixed-rate policies, if the insured cancels the policy (except when retiring from business covered by the policy), the insurer should determine the earned premium by applying the authorized rates to payroll or another premium basis and adding the pro rata portion of the loss constant and expense constant charged on the policy plus a $25 cancellation charge. In no event should the premium exceed the premium extended at the pro rata basis for the full three-year period.

Anniversary Date Effects

The Anniversary Rating Date Endorsement (WC 00 04 02), shown in an earlier chapter, is a nonpremium-bearing endorsement that, when attached to a policy, affects the premium audit setup and the premium audit adjustments. Insurers use this endorsement when the normal rating date is different from the policy dates. For example, if an insurer cancels and rewrites a policy, the new policy (whether issued by the same insurer or another insurer) must carry the classifications and rates applicable to the canceled policy until the normal policy rating date. In most states that permit rate deviations, the new policy must still carry the new insurer's rates applicable at the original inception date until the anniversary date.

This requirement affects the premium audit in that whenever the insurer attaches the Anniversary Rating Date Endorsement to the policy, the premium auditor must segregate the payroll for all classes into the periods before and after the anniversary rating date. To illustrate, assume the policy dates are December 1, 20X8, to December 1, 20X9, and the anniversary rating date is May 1, 20X8. The premium audit would show payrolls from December 1, 20X8, to May 1, 20X9, and from May 1, 20X9, to December 1, 20X9.

This endorsement also affects the premium audit adjustment. In most cases, the insurer uses two different sets of rates and modifications. Using the preceding example, the rates and modifications applicable for December 1, 20X8, to May 1, 20X9, would be those in effect as of May 1, 20X8, or just before that date. For May 1, 20X9, to December 1, 20X9, the rates and modifications applicable would be those effective May 1, 20X9, or just before that date.

Statutory Premium Increases or Decreases

Included in every workers' compensation rate is an amount that the insurer allocates to pay losses. The insurer predicates this amount on what it expects to pay in workers' compensation losses based on the statutory benefits payable under the state workers' compensation law at the time the insurer issued the policy. Any increase in the statutory benefits during the policy period would render the expected loss component included in the original rates inadequate. When this occurs, all premiums for the state involved should increase on outstanding policies. Restricting or reducing benefits can similarly result in a premium decrease on existing policies. This increase or decrease, expressed as a percentage, applies to premiums earned after the effective date of the change in benefits. Insurers should add the Rate Change Endorsement (WC 00 04 07), shown in Exhibit 3-5, to existing policies to indicate the change in rates.

EXHIBIT 3-5

Rate Change Endorsement

WORKERS COMPENSATION AND EMPLOYERS LIABILITY INSURANCE POLICY	WC 00 04 04
Original Printing Effective April 1, 1984	Standard

RATE CHANGE ENDORSEMENT

Rate changes that apply to the policy have been approved by the proper regulatory authority. The changes are shown in the Schedule.

Schedule

State	Date of Change	State Coverage % Change	Longshoremen's and Harbor Workers' Act Coverage %

Notes:

1. Use this endorsement to show a change in rates for state coverage.

2. Use the first and second columns to show the state and effective date of the change.

3. Use the third column if the change is a flat percentage applicable to all classifications.

4. Use the fourth column to show the new percentage, if any, applicable to non-F classifications for work subject to the Longshoremen's and Harbor Workers' Compensation Act.

5. The company may show a fifth column (Classification Code Number and Rate) in order to show the change on a Schedule of Rate basis.

To simplify the computation, most states allow insurers to apply an average increase percentage to the total premium if little seasonal variation occurs. Other situations require insurers to separately determine premium for the periods before and after the effective date of the change.

Premium Computation—Ratio Method

When a flat increase in premium is announced, the insurance advisory organization usually provides a corresponding ratio table for adjusting the premium on outstanding policies. Exhibit 3-6 shows the ratio table for a 2.2 percent flat increase that applied to premiums on the unexpired portions of outstanding policies.

EXHIBIT 3-6

Ratio Table for Adjustment of a 2.2 Percent Flat Increase for Outstanding Policies

Portion of Policy Period to Which Outstanding Rate Change Is Applicable	Percentage Increase Applicable to Annual Premium
One Month	0.18
Two Months	0.37
Three Months	0.55
Four Months	0.73
Five Months	0.92
Six Months	1.10
Seven Months	1.28
Eight Months	1.47
Nine Months	1.65
Ten Months	1.83
Eleven Months	2.02

The procedure for using the ratio table is as follows:

- Determine the earned premium based only on the classes with payroll exposure. This earned premium excludes any additional charges or credits.
- Determine the policy's unexpired portion.
- From the ratio table, find the percentage increase applicable for the unexpired portion of the policy.
- Increase the total annual premium by the percentage charge shown next to the policy's expiration date.

Exhibit 3-7 illustrates this procedure. The earned premium without the rate increase is $260,652. Assuming the rate increase takes effect on October 1, 20X0, and the policy expires on July 1, 20X1, the rate increase applies to a nine-month period. The corresponding percentage increase in the ratio table is 1.65. Multiplying the annual premium by 1.65 percent yields $4,301 to be added because of the rate increase for a $264,953 total premium. The premium discount then applies to that amount.

EXHIBIT 3-7

Application of Rate Increase

STATEMENT OF PREMIUM ADJUSTMENT						

NAME AND ADDRESS OF INSURED

FIFI's Furniture, Inc.
Sofa, CT 06598

NAME AND ADDRESS OF COMPANY

Colonial Crafts Mutual
Hebron, CT 06248

NAME AND ADDRESS OF AGENCY

Thomas Hooker Ins. Agency
Charter Oak, CT 06499

POLICY NUMBER

81 WC 234567

KIND OF POLICY

POLICY PERIOD   MM/DD/YY TO MM/DD/YY

7/1/X0   TO   7/1/X1

DATE

AGENCY CODE

Z-1636

AUDIT PERIOD

SAME

TYPE OF AUDIT

TO   ☒ FIELD   ☐ MAIL   ☐ ESTIMATE

CODE	DESCRIPTION/LOCATION	BASE AMOUNT	RATE	PREMIUM	PREVIOUSLY BILLED	ADDITIONAL RETURN
2881	Furniture Assembling—Wood	$2,466,289	4.85%	$119,615		
2883	Furniture Mfg.—Wood	1,312,714	9.72	127,596		
8044	Furniture Store	404,218	3.25	13,137		
8810	Clerical	101,222	.30	304		
				260,652		
0998	Rate Incr. (10/1/X0)	(260,652)	1.65	4,301		
				264,953		
0063	Prem. Disc. (Table 4)	(264,953)	15.6	(41,333)		
	Total Premium			223,620	216,000	7,620
					Deposit	Additional premium due

Premium Computation for Seasonal Operations

When insurers cannot apply the average increase, premium auditors must divide payrolls and compute earned premium as follows:

- Determine the earned premium before the premium increase date
- Determine the earned premium after the increase date
- Apply the applicable rate increase to premium earned after the effective date of the increase

Exhibit 3-8 shows a premium adjustment example for this situation.

EXHIBIT 3-8

Rate Increase for Seasonal Operation

STATEMENT OF PREMIUM ADJUSTMENT						
NAME AND ADDRESS OF INSURED FIFI's Furniture, Inc. Sofa, CT 06598			**NAME AND ADDRESS OF COMPANY** Colonial Crafts Mutual Hebron, CT 06248			
NAME AND ADDRESS OF AGENCY Thomas Hooker Ins. Agency Charter Oak, CT 06499			**POLICY NUMBER** 81 WC 234567		**KIND OF POLICY**	
			POLICY PERIOD MM/DD/YY TO MM/DD/YY 7/1/X0 TO 7/1/X1		**DATE**	
		AGENCY CODE Z-1638	**AUDIT PERIOD** SAME		**TYPE OF AUDIT** TO ☒ FIELD ☐ MAIL ☐ ESTIMATE	
CODE	**DESCRIPTION/LOCATION**	**BASE AMOUNT**	**RATE**	**PREMIUM**	**PREVIOUSLY BILLED**	**ADDITIONAL RETURN**
	To 10/1/X0					
8044	Furniture Store	$30,000	3.25%	$975		
8810	Clerical	8,000	.30	24		
				999		
	After 10/1/X0					
8044	Furniture Store	131,600	3.25	4,277		
8810	Clerical	23,600	.30	71		
				4,348		
0998	Rate Incr. (10/1/X0)	4,348	2.2	96		
				4,444		
	Total Premiums			5,443	5,300	143
					Deposit	Additional premium due

A state may have more than one premium increase because of an increase in statutory benefits within a twelve-month period. In those cases, insurers should base each increase charge on the total earned from the increase's effective date to the expiration date.

Insurers can use the following example as a guideline to determine whether to apply an outstanding premium increase to a canceled policy. Assume an insurer issues a policy for January 1, 20X5, to January 1, 20X6. The state covered on the policy is New Hampshire. The insurer cancels the policy on October 18, 20X5. New Hampshire had a 6 percent premium increase effective October 1, 20X5 applicable to policies expiring on or after November 1, 20X5.

Although the insurer canceled the policy before November 1, 20X5, the premium increase does apply because the normal policy expiration date is after November 1, 20X5. In this case, the insurer must split the payroll before and after October 1, 20X5, and must apply the 6 percent premium increase to the premium developed after October 1, 20X5.

Insurers cannot use the ratio method tables on canceled policies. The insurer must split the payroll before and after the effective date of the premium increase.

The important point to remember in all cases is that the policy's normal expiration date is the determining factor when deciding whether a premium increase applies to a canceled policy.

SUMMARY

Insurers base workers' compensation insurance premiums on the insured's total payroll to employees covered by the policy. Payroll, which is the same as payroll, includes not only ordinary wages and salaries, but also commissions, bonuses, extra pay for overtime work, pay for periods not worked, required payments by employers to statutory insurance or pension plans for employees, payments based on any factor other than time worked, tool allowances, the value of housing, lodging and meals, and store certificates or other substitutes for money. According to the NCCI *Basic Manual* rules, payroll does not include tips, group insurance contributions, special awards, or dismissal pay. To exclude extra pay for overtime work, the overtime work must meet the *Basic Manual* definition and must be supported by adequate records. For executive officers, members of athletic teams, and carnival workers, the payroll to be included may be subject to an average weekly limitation.

Sometimes individuals covered by the policy do not receive payroll for their services. In those situations, the premium auditor must impute the value of their services and include it in the premium basis. The *Basic Manual* rules specify minimum amounts that insurers should include for executive officers and for partners or sole proprietors. Unless the insured furnishes certificates of insurance covering subcontractors, the premium auditor must include either their total payroll or the percentage (up to 100 percent) of the total contract price stipulated by the manual in the premium base. When individuals such as relatives, student nurses, volunteers, or welfare recipients work without pay, the premium auditor should include the amount earned by employees performing comparable tasks or work.

The classification definitions and footnotes in the NCCI *Basic Manual* explain the exceptions for which the manual does not base workers' compensation premiums on payroll. Examples include per capita charges for domestic workers, upset payrolls for logging operations, annual values for taxicab operations, and policy surcharges for aircraft.

Determining the final earned premium requires multiplying the premium base by the applicable rate. Depending on the state, the insurer may have to add a loss constant if the premium is less than $500. The expense constant is a premium charge that insurers add to every policy. For policies with small premiums, the minimum premium stipulated in the manual rate pages may apply instead. If the premium is large enough for the insured to qualify, the insurer modifies the premium according to an experience rating plan.

Premium discount plans are available in most states. The discount reflects the lower proportion of expenses to premium as premium size increases. Insurers discount the premium by applying the percentage given in the manual for the state. If the policy covers more than one state, the insurer must determine the standard premium separately for each state and apply the appropriate percentage in each case. If retrospective rating plans are involved, the standard premiums included in such plans are not subject to premium discount.

Premium adjustments must also reflect the actual coverage period, which is not necessarily one year. Insurers adjust premiums on policies canceled before normal expiration either pro rata or by the short-rate table, depending on the cancellation terms. For a pro rata cancellation, the premium equals the rate times the premium base for the period the policy was in effect plus prorated loss and expense constants, if applicable. A short-rate cancellation requires the insurer to apply the appropriate percentage from the short-rate table to the premium extended to an annual basis from the payroll for the actual policy period. Other cases require the insurer to split the premium base into portions of one year because of a rate change. Such rate changes can occur in the middle of the policy term because of an anniversary rating date different from the policy inception date or because of a rate change on existing policies resulting from a change in the benefits provided by the workers' compensation law.

After determining the insured's total payroll to employees covered by the policy, the premium auditor must also classify the operations to find the appropriate rates. A correct premium adjustment results from methodically applying the steps explained in this chapter together with a careful and logical classification assignment. The next chapter explains classification procedures for workers' compensation insurance.

CHAPTER NOTES

1. One exception to the hours worked is the wallboard classifications, which use square footage as the premium base. This change was made in the mid-1990s.
2. National Council on Compensation Insurance, Inc., *Workers Compensation Insurance Basis of Premium—Payrolls vs. Manhours* (Boca Raton, Fla.: NCCI, June 19, 1978).
3. National Council on Compensation Insurance, Inc., *Basic Manual for Workers Compensation and Employers Liability Insurance* (Boca Raton, Fla.: NCCI, 2001), Part 1, Rule 2.A.

4. In the previous version of the *Basic Manual*, the underwriting guide pages explained that auditors should include as payroll compensation paid to employees for time spent traveling to or from work or to or from a specific job site. Although not referenced in the new version of the manual, the intent remains to include such compensation.

5. *Basic Manual*, Part 1, Rule 2.B.2.

6. Compensation Rating and Inspection Bureau, comp., *New Jersey Workers' Compensation and Employers' Liability Insurance Manual 2006* (Newark, N.J., 2006), Part Three, Section Three, p. 7.

7. *Basic Manual*, Part 1, Rule 2.B.2.d.

8. *Basic Manual*, Part 1, Rules 2.B.2.h.(1), (2), (3).

9. *Basic Manual*, Part 1, Rule 2.C.1.

10. *Basic Manual*, Part 1, Rule 2.C.1.

11. *Basic Manual*, Part 1, Rule 2.C.2.a.

12. *Basic Manual*, Part 1, Rule 2.D.2.a.

13. Some states may use something other than weekly wage, such as monthly wage.

14. *Basic Manual*, Part One, Rule 2.D.2.

15. *Basic Manual*, Rule 2.E.1.b.(5).

16. National Council on Compensation Insurance, Inc., *Workers Compensation Insurance Premium Audit Reference Book* (Boca Raton, Fla.: NCCI, 1983), Section V, p. 28a. This book is no longer in print, but the treatment of such amounts is still the same. Readers can also refer to the 1985 PAAS Educational Bulletin on the topic.

17. *Basic Manual*, Rule 2.E.3.

18. *Basic Manual*, Rule 2.H.3.

19. *Basic Manual*, Part 1, Rule 3.C.5.b.

20. *Basic Manual*, note to Taxicab Co. classification, Part 2 Taxicab Co. Class 7370, eff. July 2001.

21. *Basic Manual*, Part 1, Rule 3.A.

22. *Basic Manual*, Rule 3.A.7.c.

23. *Basic Manual*, Rule 3.A.11.a.

24. *Basic Manual*, Rule 3.A.11.a.

25. *Basic Manual*, Rule 3.A.11.f.

26. National Council on Compensation Insurance, Inc., *Experience Rating Plan Manual for Workers Compensation and Employers Liability Insurance* (Boca Raton, Fla.: NCCI, 1984), Part Three, B.2, p. 8 (second reprint, effective July 1, 1990).

27. *Basic Manual*, Part 1, Rule 3.A.19.

28. *Basic Manual*, Part 1, Rule 3.I.9.b.

29. *Basic Manual*, Part 1, Rule 3.I.9.a.(1).

30. *Basic Manual*, Part 1, Rule 3.I.9.a.(1).

31. *Basic Manual*, Part 1, Rule 3.I.9.a.(2).

Direct Your Learning

Workers' Compensation Premium Determination—Part II

Educational Objectives

After learning the content of this chapter and completing the corresponding course guide assignment, you should be able to:

▶ Explain what is contained in the *Basic Manual for Workers Compensation and Employers Liability Insurance* and how it is used.

▶ Describe the content and use of classification references other than the *Basic Manual* used to determine workers' compensation exposures.

▶ Given a case and the appropriate references, apply the classification rules in assigning the correct workers' compensation exposure amounts to the proper classification(s), with justifications for the assignments made.

  • Apply the rules of basic classifications, standard exception classifications, general exclusions, and general inclusions in assigning the correct exposure amounts to a workers' compensation audit.

  • Apply workers' compensation classification captions, notes, words, and phrases to a workers' compensation audit.

  • Assign classifications and payroll for separate legal entities insured on the same policy, businesses not described by a classification, secondary businesses, miscellaneous employees, and employees involved in an interchange of labor.

▶ Describe the various techniques available to premium auditors for determining the proper classification.

▶ Define or describe each of the Key Words and Phrases for this chapter.

Outline

Classification References

Classification Rules

Classification Techniques

Summary

CHAPTER 4

Develop Your Perspective

What are the main topics covered in the chapter?

Checking to see that payroll is assigned to the proper classifications is an important part in the premium audit dealing with workers' compensation insurance policies. To classify payroll, a premium auditor must access appropriate references; analyze appropriate classification rules as they apply to the employment circumstances; and apply techniques for classifying jobs by activity, description, or cross reference.

Describe the classification reference a premium auditor accesses in assigning the appropriate workers' compensation classification codes.

▶   Why is the *Basic Manual* always the ultimately defining resource?

▶   When would the *Scopes Manual* be more useful than the Premium Audit Advisory Service (PAAS) *Classification Guide*?

Why is it important to learn about these topics?

Payroll assignment is necessary because the rates for workers' compensation insurance vary considerably by classification. Accurately assigning classifications is important so that each class of business is assigned the proper rate for the loss exposure.

Consider how the references, rules, and techniques improve the accuracy of classification assignment by a premium auditor.

▶   Why are so many different references useful in augmenting the information presented in the *Basic Manual*?

▶   How do the classification rules make the choice of classifications more specific?

How can you use what you will learn?

Analyze the references available, classification rules, and classification techniques necessary to assign proper workers' compensation classifications.

▶   What are the most useful resources for the types of accounts you work with?

▶   What is the most effective way for you to summarize the rules you must apply regularly?

Workers' Compensation Premium Determination—Part II

Workers' compensation insurance policies require a premium audit that involves not only determining the total payroll reflecting the loss exposures covered by the policy but also assigning the payroll to appropriate classifications. Payroll assignment is necessary because the rates for workers' compensation insurance vary considerably according to the classification. As explained in Chapter 1, class rating isolates the potential causes of loss associated with a particular business and its environment. Therefore, employers in hazardous businesses pay higher rates for workers' compensation insurance. The benefits provided to all workers are the same. In theory, therefore, each class of business bears its own share of the losses from work-related injuries and occupational diseases. To achieve that result, however, premium auditors must accurately and consistently assign both premiums and losses to the proper classes.

The rules and classification definitions explained in the workers' compensation manuals were designed to facilitate consistency in classification assignments. In assigning classifications, premium auditors must be consistent and follow those rules and definitions logically. This chapter describes the workers' compensation manuals and other helpful classification references, the rules regarding classification procedures, and techniques for logically analyzing information to achieve appropriate classification assignments.

CLASSIFICATION REFERENCES

Although experience familiarizes premium auditors with workers' compensation classifications, even the most experienced premium auditors must frequently refer to standard sources to ensure correct classification assignments in every case. State exceptions and other subtle variations (for example, an insurer may have made a special filing to meet the needs of its insureds) as well as continual revisions prevent memorization of classifications. The only way to be certain of a classification is to reread the printed phraseology.

Classification references fall into two groups. The main reference is the workers' compensation manual that applies in the particular jurisdiction; many other references are available that supplement the manual with alternative data formats as well as additional explanations and interpretations.

The *Basic Manual*

The *Basic Manual for Workers Compensation and Employers Liability Insurance*, published by the NCCI, is used in the majority of states (thirty-seven) as well as the District of Columbia. It is not used in the five monopolistic state funds or by certain independent state bureaus. The remaining eight independent bureau states use workers' compensation manuals similar to the *Basic Manual*, but they are issued by the independent state bureaus. Manuals can be purchased in paper or electronic format. Some independent state manuals are available online for no charge. Exhibit 4-1 shows the names of workers' compensation basic manuals currently in use and the Web site address for the bureau or agency that issues each manual. Manuals for monopolistic states are not covered in this discussion.

EXHIBIT 4-1	

The NCCI and Eight Independent Bureau States That Issue Workers' Compensation Manuals

NCCI	*Basic Manual for Workers Compensation and Employers Liability Insurance* www.ncci.com
CA	*California Workers Compensation Uniform Statistical Reporting Plan* www.wcirbonline.org
DE	*Delaware Workers Compensation Manual* www.dcrb.com
MA	*Massachusetts Workers Compensation and Employers Liability Insurance Manual* www.wcribma.org
MI	*Michigan Workers Compensation Placement Facility Manual* www.caomrisk.com
NJ	*New Jersey Workers Compensation and Employers Liability Insurance Manual* www.njcrib.com
NY	*New York Manual for Workers Compensation and Employers Liability Insurance* www.nycirb.org
PA	*Pennsylvania Workers Compensation Manual* www.pcrb.com
TX	*Texas Workers' Compensation and Employers' Liability Manual* www.tdi.state.tx.us/wc/regulation

Many rules and classifications in the independent manuals (as well as state exceptions to the *Basic Manual*) vary from the *Basic Manual*. Premium auditors handling multi-state risks must be knowledgeable enough to know that variations exist and how to research them to ensure correct application of rules. However, this chapter presents workers' compensation rules and procedures in the context of the *Basic Manual*.

Part One—Rules

Part One of the *Basic Manual* is the Rules Section (R pages), which contains four broad rules applicable to workers' compensation. These rules include the following:

1. Classification Assignment
2. Premium Basis and Payroll Allocation
3. Rating Definitions and Application of Premium Elements
4. Workers Compensation Insurance Plan Rules (applicable to assigned risk policies only)

Each rule has numerous subcategories. Premium auditors must understand the rules section to classify a risk properly. In addition to explaining how to assign classifications properly, the Rules Section explains the differences among the classes, the intended scope of the classes, and abbreviations used in classification wording.

Part Two—Classifications

Part Two of the manual includes the pages often referred to as C pages. These pages contain an alphabetical classifications listing established by the NCCI. Exhibit 4-2 shows one of those classifications. The descriptions that the *Basic Manual* uses for each classification listed are phrases perceived as most applicable for the operation. The specific classification code number is in the margin or sidebar directly to the left of the phraseology. The classification phraseology frequently coincides with the job title assigned to workers by insureds in that business. The job title is usually a descriptive term readily recognizable by both the insured and insurer as conveying the exposure assumed.

The entire boldface typed phrase and the classification code number identify the classification. Importantly, the same classification code number will often apply to more than one classification wording. For example, Code 9586, as shown in Exhibit 4-2, applies to the classification, "Barber Shop, Beauty Shop, or Hair Styling Salon."

EXHIBIT 4-2

BARBER SHOP, BEAUTY SHOP, OR HAIR STYLING SALON

9586   BARBER SHOP, BEAUTY SHOP, OR HAIR STYLING SALON

Classification wording
The description within the Classification Section of the *Basic Manual* that includes the businesses and activities within a classification.

Notes
The explanatory descriptions within the Classification Section of the *Basic Manual* that identify, explain, extend, or limit the classification's scope and supercede general manual rules.

Any reference to a classification on the information page, premium audit work sheets, or premium billings should include words appearing in boldface type. Any part of the classification description appearing in lighter face type and any notes immediately following the classification description form part of the classification wording. **Classification wording** includes the description within the Classification Section of the *Basic Manual* that includes the businesses and activities within a classification. Notes are an integral part of the overall classification. **Notes** are the explanatory descriptions within the Classification Section of the *Basic Manual* that identify, explain, extend, or limit the classification's scope and supercede general manual rules. Some examples follow.

Notes often identify an activity that is not readily apparent in the job description or job title. The "Chain Mfg.: Formed or welded" classification (Code 3257) contains a note that the classification includes manufacturing chains from wire.

Notes can also explain how to classify other closely related operations. The "Paper: Mfg." classification (Code 4239) contains a note that premium auditors should rate wood pulp manufacturing as Codes 4206 or 4207—pulp manufacturing.

Notes can extend the classification definition by identifying an activity that may appear to go beyond the basic classification but that is in reality an important segment of that particular business. The "Concrete: Construction NOC" classification (Code 5213) includes a note that specifies that the classification includes the making, setting up, or taking down of forms. Without this note, someone may argue that such operations would be carpentry work.

Notes can limit the classification by specifically excluding operations that appear to be an integral part of the exposure being defined, but that the premium auditor must separately rate. The "Cement Mfg." classification (Code 1701) contains a note that premium auditors should separately rate excavation or digging, dredging, mining, or quarrying.

The classification pages list classifications in alphabetical order. However, classification phraseologies occasionally begin with a different word than the premium auditor anticipates, so they do not always appear in the expected place. The other classification guides available can help to overcome that problem.

Part Three—Loss Costs, Rates and State Exceptions

Part Three, the last manual section, contains the state rate and exception pages. Those pages vary in specific content by the states for which they apply. Their format is similar in that they contain both the special classifications and rules that apply in that state and the workers' compensation rates or loss costs for each classification code. Part Three may also provide procedural notes, interpretations, rulings, miscellaneous values, and administrative data relevant to the particular state's workers' compensation law. Exhibit 4-3 shows that, in Georgia, classifications exist for kaolin milling and mining (a process not found in many states and therefore without a specific classification in the *Basic Manual* classifications section). Obviously, premium auditors must know the state pages for the states in which they work.

EXHIBIT 4-3
Special Georgia State Pages Classification

	KAOLIN
1751	**Milling & Drivers**
	Digging, mining or quarrying to be separately rated.
1169	**Mining Surface & Drivers**
	Includes construction, repair and maintenance of all buildings, structures or equipment, and installation of machinery.

Although the *Basic Manual* or the corresponding manual for a jurisdiction is the fundamental reference for classifications, additional references are often useful in determining the proper classification for a particular operation. The NCCI issues many of those references. Others come from various sources. Even though they may be less authoritative, they have other advantages that make them useful to premium auditors. The following sections describe some of the most common classification references.

Scopes Manual

The **Scopes Manual** is an NCCI publication designed as an aid to understanding and assigning workers' compensation classifications. It begins with a numerical index that lists all classification code numbers included in the *Scopes Manual*. Although insurers use the information in the *Scopes Manual* to classify risks, the provisions of *Basic Manual* take precedence. It is updated several times per year to include new interpretations or amendments as required. Symbols appear next to certain types of classifications. These include circles ("●") next to construction or erection classifications, squares ("■") next to farm classifications, and diamonds ("◆") next to mercantile classifications. No symbols appear next to other classifications. These symbols are important when determining proper classification, as special rules apply depending on the type of insured.

The next section in the *Scopes Manual* is an alphabetical reference section that simply lists the classes in alphabetical order with the corresponding code number, including many alternate wordings. The next section is an industrial reference section listing industry groups of classifications, such as all classifications related to aircraft operation, amusements, masonry and plastering, machine shops, etc.

Scopes Manual
An NCCI publication designed as an aid to understanding and assigning workers' compensation classifications.

The main section, "National Scopes," of the *Scopes Manual* follows, providing information in classification code number sequence. In addition to listing the code number, each section for a code number shows the correct phraseology for the classification; cross-referenced phraseology for the classification; state specific phraseologies; a detailed description of the classification's "scope"; the date the code was established; the date the code was discontinued (if applicable); the code and its replacement code (if applicable); the states that retained the scope (if applicable); the NCCI schedule or group; the NAICS (North American Industry Classification System), a six-digit number used to identify a particular industry in the hierarchical structure of the classification system for the Census Bureau; analogy assignments; equipment and materials used; additional applications and information; special conditions, related operations not classified to that code; and State Addendums.

State Addendums allow independent bureau states to enter their interpretations and applications of a particular scope that differs from NCCI's interpretation of that scope. It should be noted that, although many independent bureau states are not governed by the *Basic Manual*, they have opted to provide classification scope information in the *Scopes Manual*. The last two sections of the Scopes Manual pertain to state special exceptions to the national scopes and state special classifications. Premium auditors and underwriters find the *Scopes Manual* to be helpful in determining the operations included within a certain classification's scope.

Exhibit 4-4 shows an anatomy of a scope from the *Scopes Manual*. It is included to help the user understand the composition of a typical scope.

Classification Codes Book

Classification Codes and Statistical Codes Manual (Classification Codes Book)
A reference published by the NCCI providing two arrangements of workers' compensation classification codes in one manual.

The NCCI's **Classification Codes and Statistical Codes Manual** (hereafter referred to as the **Classification Codes Book**) is a reference published by the NCCI providing two arrangements of workers' compensation classification codes in one manual. The NCCI printed the first section, "Classification Codes by Numerical Sequence," on white paper. Readers can readily differentiate the second section, "Classification Codes by Schedules and Groups," by its yellow paper.

Classification Codes by Numerical Sequence

The classification codes by numerical sequence section lists the same classifications shown in the *Basic Manual;* however, this section of the *Classifications Codes Book* arranges the listings in numerical sequence by code number. Exhibit 4-5 shows an excerpt from a selected page.

Premium auditors can find two columns of statistical numbers to the left of the listed classifications. The first column shows the workers' compensation and employers' liability (WC&EL) code number listing. Those numbers determine the order of the listing of the classifications in the book and enable a premium auditor to find the classification phraseology corresponding to a

EXHIBIT 4-4

Anatomy of a Scope

SCOPES® MANUAL	*Issued January 2006*	Anatomy of a Scope—xiii

ANATOMY OF A SCOPE

> This portion of *Scopes® Manual* is intended to help the user understand the composition of a typical scope. A scopes entry actually consists of several individual components. When these components are combined, the result is the scope of a classification, the most comprehensive compilation of information regarding a particular classification code available.

CLASSIFICATION CODE
A four-digit number assigned to an insured that identifies all or a portion of an insured's operation for rating purposes.

PHRASEOLOGY
The classification code's description. These descriptions have been filed with and approved by regulators in states where they are effective.

STATE SPECIAL
Certain states may opt to use a national classification code and modify its definition to accommodate a special industry within the state's jurisdiction. State special phraseologies used for national codes such as these should not be confused with state special codes found in the State Special section of this manual.

N/A means this code is not available in the states indicated (Oklahoma in this example). One should review the indices or the State Special section of this manual and the OK state special pages in the *Basic Manual* to find an alternative classification.

CROSS-REF.
These are additional definitions that have been assigned the same code number as the initial definition indicated in the scope. One classification code may have several definitions assigned or referenced to it.

SCOPE
The narrative that explains the intent of the classification code.

STATE ADDENDUM
Independent states may use this area to enter their interpretation(s) and application(s) of a particular scope that differ from NCCI's interpretation of that scope.

6504   **N/A—OK**

PHRASEOLOGY FOOD SUNDRIES MFG. NOC—NO CEREAL MILLING. Includes cleaning, grinding, sorting or mixing of coffee, sugars, confections, pastry flours, spices or nuts.

CROSS-REF. *Baking Powder Mfg.*—mfg. of ingredients to be separately rated. Assign to the appropriate chemical Code 4828 or 4829. Can mfg. to be separately rated as 3220; *Coconut Shredding or Drying; Coffee Cleaning, Roasting or Grinding; Flour Mixing and Blending—No Milling; Malted Milk Mfg.—From Powdered Milk, Sugar, Malt, Cocoa; Mayonnaise Mfg.; Nut Cleaning or Shelling; Popcorn Mfg.; Potato Chip Mfg.; Spice Mills; Yeast Mfg.*
State Special: Hawaii—Miso Mfg.; **Hawaii**—Poi Mfg.

SCOPE Code 6504 applies to a wide variety of foodstuff manufacturing which is not otherwise classified (NOC). It is a heterogeneous class, the scope of which may be measured in part by its phraseology and the phraseologies of its cross-references. The class is not restricted to the particular products specified in its phraseology or this scope and contemplates simple preparation or packaging of already manufactured products.

   State Addendum
   Name of state—in this state potato chip manufacturing is assigned to Code 2003.

NOTE: The above scope is for illustrative purposes only. Please see *Scopes® Manual* to review Scope 6504 in its entirety.

> Please be aware when utilizing *Scopes® Manual* for classification assistance, that the object of the classification system is to group similar employers so that each classification reflects exposures common to them. Subject to certain exceptions discussed in the *Basic Manual for Workers Compensation and Employers Liability Insurance*, it is the business of the employer within a state that is classified, and not the separate employments, occupations, or operations of individual employees within the business.

Continued on next page

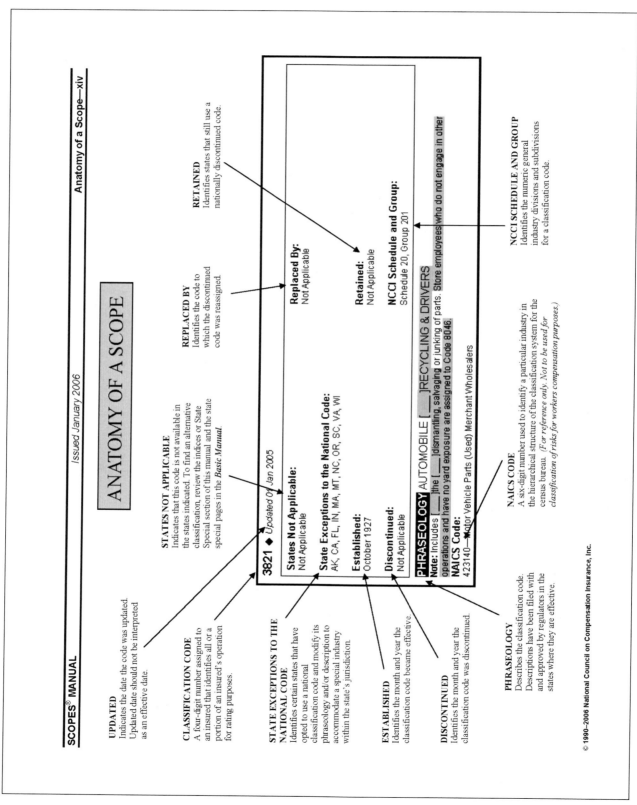

ANATOMY OF A SCOPE

UPDATED
Indicates the date the code was updated. Updated date should not be interpreted as an effective date.

CLASSIFICATION CODE
A four-digit number assigned to an insured that identifies all or a portion of an insured's operation for rating purposes.

STATE EXCEPTIONS TO THE NATIONAL CODE
Identifies certain states that have opted to use a national classification code and modify its phraseology and/or description to accommodate a special industry within the state's jurisdiction.

ESTABLISHED
Identifies the month and year the classification code became effective.

DISCONTINUED
Identifies the month and year the classification code was discontinued.

PHRASEOLOGY
Describes the classification code. Descriptions have been filed with and approved by regulators in the states where they are effective.

STATES NOT APPLICABLE
Indicates that this code is not available in the states indicated. To find an alternative classification, review the indices or State Special section of this manual and the state special pages in the *Basic Manual*.

3821 ◆ *Updated as of Jan 2005*

States Not Applicable:
Not Applicable

State Exceptions to the National Code:
AK, CA, FL, IN, MA, MT, NC, OR, SC, VA, WI

Established:
October 1927

Discontinued:
Not Applicable

PHRASEOLOGY AUTOMOBILE [____]the [____]dismantling, salvaging or junking of parts. Store employees who do not engage in other operations and have no yard exposure are assigned to Code 8046.
NAICS Code:
423140—Motor Vehicle Parts (Used) Merchant Wholesalers

REPLACED BY
Identifies the code to which the discontinued code was reassigned

Replaced By:
Not Applicable

Retained:
Not Applicable

NCCI Schedule and Group:
Schedule 20, Group 201

RETAINED
Identifies states that still use a nationally discontinued code.

NCCI SCHEDULE AND GROUP
Identifies the numeric general industry divisions and subdivisions for a classification code.

NAICS CODE
A six-digit number used to identify a particular industry in the hierarchical structure of the classification system for the census bureau. *(For reference only. Not to be used for classification of risks for workers compensation purposes.)*

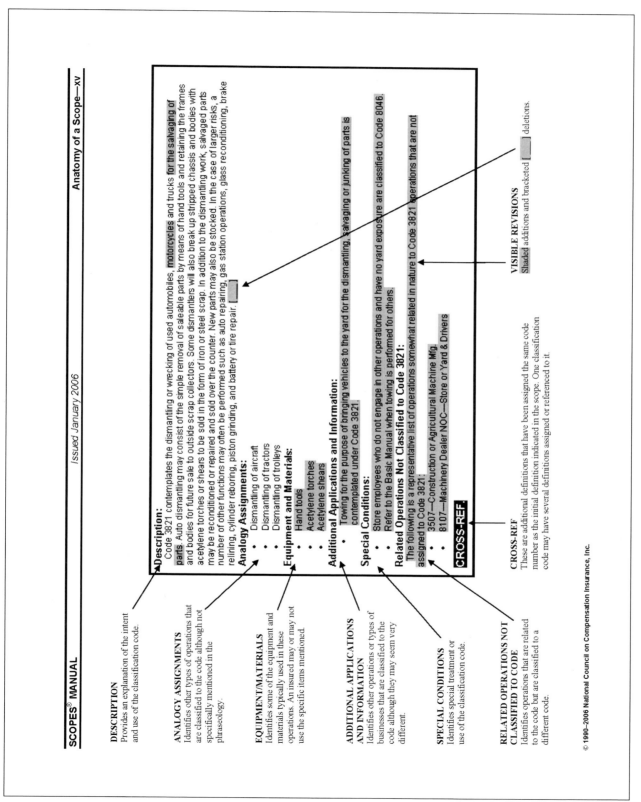

Description:

Code 3821 contemplates the dismantling or wrecking of used automobiles, motorcycles and trucks for the salvaging of parts. Auto dismantling may consist of the simple removal of saleable parts by means of hand tools and retaining the frames and bodies for future sale to outside scrap collectors. Some dismantlers will also break up stripped chassis and bodies with acetylene torches or shears to be sold in the form of iron or steel scrap. In addition to the dismantling work, salvaged parts may be reconditioned or repaired and sold over the counter. New parts may also be stocked. In the case of larger risks, a number of other functions may often be performed such as auto repairing, gas station operations, glass reconditioning, brake relining, cylinder reboring, piston grinding, and battery or tire repair. [ ]

Analogy Assignments:
- Dismantling of aircraft
- Dismantling of tractors
- Dismantling of trolleys

Equipment and Materials:
- Hand tools
- Acetylene torches
- Acetylene shears

Additional Applications and Information:
- Towing for the purpose of bringing vehicles to the yard for the dismantling, salvaging or junking of parts is contemplated under Code 3821

Special Conditions:
- Store employees who do not engage in other operations and have no yard exposure are classified to Code 8046
- Refer to the Basic Manual when towing is performed for others

Related Operations Not Classified to Code 3821:
The following is a representative list of operations somewhat related in nature to Code 3821 operations that are not assigned to Code 3821:
- 3507—Construction or Agricultural Machine Mfg.
- 8107—Machinery Dealer NOC—Store or Yard & Drivers

CROSS-REF.

DESCRIPTION
Provides an explanation of the intent and use of the classification code.

ANALOGY ASSIGNMENTS
Identifies other types of operations that are classified to the code although not specifically mentioned in the phraseology.

EQUIPMENT/MATERIALS
Identifies some of the equipment and materials typically used in these operations. An insured may or may not use the specific items mentioned.

ADDITIONAL APPLICATIONS AND INFORMATION
Identifies other operations or types of businesses that are classified to the code although they may seem very different.

SPECIAL CONDITIONS
Identifies special treatment or use of the classification code.

RELATED OPERATIONS NOT CLASSIFIED TO CODE
Identifies operations that are related to the code but are classified to a different code.

CROSS-REF
These are additional definitions that have been assigned the same code number as the initial definition indicated in the scope. One classification code may have several definitions assigned or referenced to it.

VISIBLE REVISIONS
Shaded additions and bracketed [ ] deletions.

Continued on next page ▶▶

Classification Assignment Example

As a further guide to selecting the correct classification, the following example is provided.

Assume that the insured is a window cleaning contractor based in Alabama. The starting point for selecting a classification would be to look up "window cleaning" in the **Alphabetical Index** to *Scopes*® *Manual.* This index lists hundreds of additional cross-references not found in the filed phraseologies listed in *Basic Manual.* In this case, although several window-related businesses are listed, window cleaning is not one of them.

As a next step, the underwriter would reference the **Industrial Index** to *Scopes*® *Manual.* This index lists scopes based upon industrial groupings of scopes with similar characteristics. In searching through this index, two appear to be candidates: "Laundering, Cleaning and Dyeing" and "Building Operation—Miscellaneous." After scanning the phraseologies provided for each of the class codes listed in the industrial grouping, the "Laundering, Cleaning and Dyeing" category is ruled out.

"Building Operation—Miscellaneous" yields these potential candidates:

9014   Buildings—operation by contractors
9170   Buildings—operation by contractors: includes window cleaning above one story (CO)
9014   Janitorial service by contractor
9001   Janitorial service by contractor: includes window cleaning (FL)

Classifications in bold print indicate that the classifications are state specials, and are therefore only applicable in one or a few states. Although the two in bold look promising, the state abbreviations in parentheses show that these state special codes are only applicable in Colorado and Florida. Since the insured is based in Alabama, neither of the state special codes would apply.

Looking at the two that are left, we can see that both are national codes because they are not in bold type and do not have a state listed in parentheses. Another interesting observation is that both phraseologies are listed under Code 9014. This is an example of the cross-referencing feature incorporated in this manual, which offers additional reference points to simplify finding the correct classification.

Since the class code is national, we turn to the **National Scopes** section, which lists scopes in numerical order by class code.

In reading through the definition for Code 9014, this code clearly applies to window cleaners, and the search is complete.

EXHIBIT 4-5

Excerpt From *Classification Codes Book* (Numerical Sequence—White Pages)

WC&EL CODE	SCHED & GRP	P&O CODE	Phraseology
7228	320	42133 99793	Trucking—local hauling only—& drivers (MO) (E:12-33) (MI) (E:12-48) (D:8-79) (7219)
7229	320	42133 99793	Trucking—long distance hauling—& drivers (MO) (E:12-33) (MI) (E:12-48) (D:8-79)
7230	320	42133 99793	Trucking: Parcel or package delivery—all employees & drivers (E:12-44) (Not available in CA and NY)
7230D	320	—	Trucking—hauling exclusively for retail stores (WI) (E:11-37) (D:10-54)
231	320	42133 94099	Trucking: Mail parcel or package delivery—all employees & drivers (E:4-81) (Not available in CA, NJ and TX)
7231	320	—	Luggage Delivery—all employees & drivers (HI) (E:2-84)
7232	320	—	Trucking: Mail, Parcel or Package Delivery—Under Contract with the U.S. Postal Service—all employees & drivers (E:9-91) (Not available in DE, HI, MA, MI, NH, NJ, NY, PA and TX)
7236D	300	—	Coal Dock Operation (state coverage where payrolls for state exposure are segregated) (CA) (D:1-47) (7244)
7241D	280	—	Boat Building—pleasure type (State coverage where payrolls for state exposure are not segregated) (CA) (D:10-73)
7242	320	—	Bicycle Delivery of Envelopes, Parcels or Packages (NY) (E:10-94)
7248	353	—	Marine Appraisers or Surveyors (CA)
7250D	320	—	Trucking—hauling of explosives—& drivers (E:5-45) (Not available in CA, GA, MA, MN and TX) (D:6-79) (7219) (Retained in AZ, MO and NJ)
7270D	320	—	Truckmen—NOC—incl. drivers (TX) (E:2-49) (D:12-70)
7271D	320	—	Truckmen—petroleum products, liquefied gases—incl. drivers (TX) (E:2-49) (D:12-70)
7272	320	—	Water Truck Service Companies—all operations (CA) (E:10-74)
7309F	300	44637 99222	Stevedoring NOC (E:7-27)

Reprinted with permission from *Classification Codes and Statistical Codes Manual, 2001 Edition* (Boca Raton, Fla.: National Council on Compensation Insurance, Inc., 2001), p. 27.

particular code number when the premium auditor knows only the workers' compensation code number. Because some of the code numbers apply to multiple classification phraseologies, the listing by code number also helps to define the range of operations included within a particular classification. Although in most instances the initial code number and corresponding classification description are appropriate for the operation, occasionally the section may list a more appropriate classification description as an alternative under the same code number.

If NCCI has discontinued a classification, a capital "D" follows the code number. When NCCI assigns experience from the discontinued classification to a new classification, this section shows that new class code in parentheses after the classification description. If this section does not show a new code number, premium auditors must individually classify risks according to the specific operations involved. Also shown in parentheses for many classes are the dates the bureau created and discontinued (if applicable) the classification. Premium auditors should consult the *Basic Manual* for the exact classification wording that they should use on the policy because this manual abbreviates the classification phraseologies.

The second column contains the schedules and group codes that appear in the "Classification Codes by Schedules and Groups" (yellow pages). Those numbers relate to the different levels into which the classification system segregates occupations. The first and second digits indicate the schedule, and the three-digit combination represents the group.

Classification Codes by Schedules and Groups

The "Classification Codes by Schedules and Groups" section of the *Classification Codes Book* arranges classifications by main industry divisions called *schedules*—a two-digit number. The section further subdivides those into three-digit classification *groups* having similar or related characteristics.[1] The first two digits of the three-digit group number correspond to the schedule code. The third digit signifies the group within that schedule.

The index to this section lists thirty-seven schedules. The schedule numbers do *not* correlate to the U.S. Department of Labor's "work field" numbering system or to other more prominent numbering designation symbols. They stem from the system devised by NCCI. The thirty-seven separate schedules represent distinct and recognizable industries. Subdividing the schedules into groups combines businesses that use similar technology or perform similar operations.

As stated, the schedule is a two-digit number, and the group is a three-digit number combining the two-digit schedule code with an additional digit to identify the specific group within that schedule. Groups are usually referred to by the entire three-digit number. For example, Group 241 refers to Gases and Miscellaneous Inorganic Chemicals, which is a subset of Schedule 24, Chemicals. Schedule 24 shows the following seven groups:

240—Chemical and Dyestuff Rating Plan

241—Gases and Miscellaneous Inorganic Chemicals

242—Extracts, Drugs and Medicine

243—Paints, Ink and Polishes

244—Vegetable Oils and Animal By-Products

245—Coal, Wood and Petroleum Products and Distillation

246—Explosives and Ammunition

Within each group, the active classes, state specials, and discontinued classes are shown with classifications within each in alphabetical order.

A capital "D" indicates discontinued classes in this section as well. The classification to which the bureau assigned the discontinued classification's experience is shown in parentheses. This section also abbreviates classification phraseologies. Exhibit 4-6 shows an excerpt of a page from this *Classification Codes Book* section.

The *Classification Codes Book* can help a premium auditor find the appropriate classification when the only starting point is the general nature of the activity. After narrowing the possibilities to the probable schedule and group, the premium auditor can then scan all the classifications within the group and study the definitions of those that seem likely to apply.

PAAS Classification Guide, Database, and Services

The Premium Audit Advisory Service (PAAS) provides a classification guide and database, industry classification publications, classification consultation service, and educational bulletins for the benefit of those involved in classifying employment categories.

Classification Guide and Database

The Premium Audit Advisory Service (PAAS) publishes more than 40,000 workers' compensation classifications guides on NCCI codes and state exception codes, as well as 1,100 ISO general liability codes. The guides are distributed in two formats: as a PAASbase CD or through the ISOnet Web site. The PAAS classification guides provide detailed descriptions of all workers' compensation and general liability codes except monopolistic states. The guides include extensive interpretations on the intent and proper application of each classification.

Each guide includes (1) contemplated operations—a description of the operations, suboperations, and processes used in a business with the classification code and, if applicable, a description of the products sold or serviced by such a business; (2) operations assigned by analogy—the widest possible range of descriptions applicable to the classification code; and (3) related codes—a broad list of codes for operations usually not considered within the scope of

EXHIBIT 4-6

Excerpt From *Classification Codes Book* (Schedules and Groups—Yellow Pages)

Group 246—Explosives and Ammunition

Explosives or Ammunition Mfg.:			
Bag Loading—propellant charges—& drivers			4770
Black Powder Mfg. & Drivers			4799
Cap, Primer, Fuse, Booster or Detonator Assembly & Drivers			4779
Fireworks Mfg.—& drivers			4779
Cartridge Charging or Loading & Drivers			4775
Shell Case Loading & Drivers			4775
High Explosives Mfg. & Drivers			4773
Projectile, Bomb, Mine or Grenade Loading & Drivers			4776
Smokeless Powder Mfg.—single base—& drivers			4774
Explosives Distributors & Drivers			4777
Blasting Agents—preparation or distribution—& drivers			4777

State Specials

Explosives Mfg. (CA)			4771
Explosives or Ammunition Mfg.: Cartridge charging or loading— all operations—& drivers (AL, AZ, ID, IN, NJ and TX)			4766
Explosives or Ammunition Mfg.: Cartridge mfg. or assembly—& drivers (CT, MN and NY)			4767
Fireworks Mfg.—& drivers (CO, NJ, NY, OK and TN)			4761
Rocket Engine Ignitor Mfg. & Drivers (GA and UT State Fund)			4759
Rocket Engine Mfg.—solid propellant & drivers (GA and UT State Fund)			4758

Discontinued

Cartridge Charging or Loading—all operations—& drivers		4766D	(4775)
Cartridge Component Mfg.—small arms		3154D	(3574)
Cartridge Mfg. or Assembly—& drivers		4767D	(3574)
Fiberloid Mfg.	4441D	4440D	(4459)
Fireworks Mfg.—& drivers		4761D	(4779)
Pyroxylin Mfg.		4440D	(4459)
Pyroxylin Plastic Mfg.		443D	(4440)
Viscoloid Mfg.	4442D	4440D	(4459)

Reprinted with permission from *Classification Codes and Statistical Codes Manual, 2001 Edition* (Boca Raton, Fla: National Council on Compensation Insurance, Inc., 2001), p. 14 (yellow pages).

the classification. When classifying a risk, the premium auditor or underwriter needs to consider such operations separately.

The classification guides provide interpretations and are based on NCCI guidelines and industry interpretation. PAAS panels review each classification guide for adherence to manual and state rules. A cross-reference link is provided on most of the guides between workers' compensation and general liability. References to NAICS and SIC (the old Standard Industrial Classification System) are also provided in most guides.

Three PAAS subcommittees developed the guides. The NCCI, ISO, and independent bureaus have reviewed the guides to ensure that the guides are authoritative sources.

The **PAAS Database** is an electronic version of the *Classification Guide*, a comprehensive PAAS classification database and published guide describing operations contemplated by workers' compensation classifications and general liability codes. The database allows searches using different criteria. Premium auditors can easily find related classifications.

PAAS Database
A comprehensive PAAS classification database and published guide describing operations contemplated by workers' compensation classifications and general liability codes.

Industry Classification Publications

PAAS also publishes industry classification publications that provide in-depth information on the classifications appropriate for each operation and suboperation associated with the following specific topics or industries:

- Basis of premium
- Commercial building construction
- Contractors—executive supervisors
- Governmental subdivisions
- Heating, ventilating, and air conditioning
- Oil and gas
- Residential building construction
- Standard exceptions and businessowners
- Street and road construction

The industry guides are provided as part of the PAASbase CD or PAAS on ISOnet. They make extensive use of illustrations and provide guidelines for both workers' compensation and employers' liability insurance.

Classification Consultation Service

The PAAS classification consultation service allows subscribing insurers to tap the expertise of the PAAS staff, reference materials, and contacts with the NCCI, independent rating bureaus, regulators, and industry associations to resolve specific problems or establish a procedure.

Educational Bulletins

The PAAS Educational Bulletins can also help in resolving classification problems. Those bulletins address an issue and provide guidelines and interpretation for classes used, industry practices, and so on. The bulletins often address rules that premium auditors commonly misunderstand or misapply. Given a particular set of options, the premium auditor can then identify the recommended course of action. The bulletins offer advice on topics ranging from clarification of basic rules and procedures to interpreting the effect of evolving technologies on the premium audit function.

Other Classification References

Other classification references include the *Commercial Lines Manual*; circular letters, manual amendment bulletins, and revised manual pages; insurer-specific resources; and association educational papers/resources.

Commercial Lines Manual

Commercial Lines Manual (CLM)
An ISO publication that includes rules and rating procedures for nine major lines of commercial insurance.

The **Commercial Lines Manual (CLM)** is an ISO publication that includes rules and rating procedures for nine major lines of commercial insurance. The *CLM* is described in detail in a subsequent chapter. The *CLM* can offer some insight into workers' compensation classifications.

The *CLM*'s advantages stem in many instances from the correlation of workers' compensation and general liability classification descriptions of exposures. That correlation exists because if two businesses have similar exposures, the classifications describing those businesses are likely to be similar.

The aid obtained from the *CLM* is primarily that of a second opinion. The premium auditor searching for the most applicable classification often finds that second opinion a stimulus for thought. For example, following the workers' compensation manual, the premium auditor may have reached a classification assignment about which there is some doubt. Through cross-referencing the workers' compensation classification to the *CLM* classification, the premium auditor may perceive a distinction or an interpretation in the classification terminology or attendant notes leading either to a different, more relevant classification or to confirming the original assignment.

Circular Letters, Manual Amendment Bulletins, and Revised Manual Pages

Circular letters
Bulletins issued by the NCCI and independent state rating bureaus providing information regarding changes, pending law amendments, changes in procedures, or changes of classification codes.

Circular letters are bulletins issued by the NCCI and independent state rating bureaus providing information regarding changes, pending law amendments, changes in procedures, or changes of classification codes. Circular letters inform subscribers of rate increases or decreases and their consideration or pending implementation. Circular letters also outline pending law amendments. Circular letters sometimes report changes in procedures that are under consideration or that have been submitted to authoritative government bodies for approval. They also provide notice of classification code changes and explain the reasons for such changes. The NCCI also issues notices called "Status of Item Filings," which update insurers as to the status in each state of NCCI filings.

A **manual amendment bulletin** is a bulletin issued by the NCCI and independent state rating bureaus informing the user of workers' compensation manuals of pending changes in the manual. When a bulletin is issued, the pending amendments described await a final decision on implementation.

The follow-up to manual amendment bulletins is the revised manual page. The revised manual page is an amended page that replaces a page currently incorporated within the manual. Premium auditors should study the new page and contrast it with the old page to understand the application and rationale of the changes.

Recognizing the information that has changed is easy because the amended information is either underlined (new text) or in brackets (deleted text). Generally, insurers recommend that premium auditors retain the prior version of the pages for three years, because policy conditions could require a premium audit of a policy up to three years after it has expired. Premium auditors should check with their own insurers to determine their guidelines.

Manual amendment bulletin
A bulletin issued by the NCCI and independent state rating bureaus informing the user of workers' compensation manuals of pending changes in the manual.

Insurer-Specific Resources

Each insurer employing premium auditors or reviewers usually has its own premium auditor's (or reviewer's) manual and related insurer manuals. Many insurers have also compiled excellent classification interpretation manuals that further explain classification assignment methods. Those manuals may carry the weight of final authority for that insurer. Premium auditors, reviewers, and even underwriters should study those insurer manuals and know how to use them properly. Insurer procedures vary within the insurance industry, so premium auditors and reviewers should be thoroughly grounded in the procedures preferred by a particular insurer.

To augment their manuals, many insurers issue internal bulletins applicable to the operations and procedures of each insurer's premium auditing department. Premium auditors should be aware of all such bulletins because they can assist the classification process. The premium auditor's employer determines their applicability.

Association Educational Papers/Resources

An often overlooked reference source is the premium auditor's association. Practically all states or metropolitan areas large enough to support an insurer home office or large branch office have such an association. The local chapter usually belongs to a larger regional association, and many members belong to the National Society of Insurance Premium Auditors (NSIPA). All of those associations develop and release educational papers on specific premium auditing topics. The NSIPA also maintains a library of premium audit reference materials.

A local association may release an educational paper because of a need perceived by the membership for a consensus on a topic. The papers draw from a broad spectrum of input from members from several different insurers and backgrounds. That consensus and decision, although not binding on its membership, assist in consistently approaching classification problems. That consistency not only promotes the professional image of premium auditing but also enhances the individual premium auditor's professional image.

Most, if not all, reference sources are now available electronically as well as in paper format, including the comprehensive NCCI manuals and the independent rating bureau manuals. Many other commonly used reference sources exist, including the *Classification Cross-Reference* by International Risk Management Institute, Inc. (IRMI), which cross-references workers' compensation codes from NCCI, California, Delaware, Pennsylvania, Michigan, New Jersey, New York, Texas, and ISO, NAICS, and SIC codes. SilverPlume is a provider of electronic insurance information in the property-casualty industry. One of its products—Sage Property & Casualty—is a comprehensive online reference library. Individuals or insurers can subscribe to the library and select different tiers of the product. For a fee, information from NCCI, ISO, PAAS, IRMI, ODEN, independent rating bureaus, ACORD, A.M. Best, and numerous other publishers can be accessible in one place.

CLASSIFICATION RULES

Part One—Rules of the *Basic Manual* states the rules that premium auditors should follow in assigning classifications. Any business can involve many different operations in widely varying combinations. Some of those operations may be extremely hazardous, although others are not. Some may be minor and incidental to other operations. Equity may require the premium auditor to rate some of the insured's operations separately from the others. The classification rules attempt to delineate classification procedures that are both equitable and simple to apply.

Classifications Explained

The first step in classifying a workers' compensation exposure is to determine the type of business being classified. Classification treatment depends on whether the type of business being classified is a mercantile, construction, farm, employee leasing/temporary agency, or other type of business. For typical businesses, the object of the classification procedure is to assign the one code that best describes the business in a state.

As Rule I-A. of the NCCI *Basic Manual* explains,

> The purpose of the classification system is to group employers with similar operations into classifications so that:
>
> - The assigned classification reflects the exposures common to those employers
> - The rate charged reflects the exposure to loss common to those employers

There are certain exceptions, such as separate classification of standard exception employments and general exclusions. It is important to determine whether a standard exception code is already included in the wording of the classification code before applying the standard exception classifications. Additionally, some classifications require that a separate classification be assigned, while some project classifications direct that separate classification cannot be assigned. There are general inclusions that do not allow for separate classification treatment of certain aspects of the business.

Basic Classification of Typical Businesses

It is essential to determine the basic classification (for businesses without special classification symbols) and then determine whether any employees or operations can be separately rated. In general, therefore, as Rule I.A.2. of the *Basic Manual* states, "Subject to certain exceptions, it is the business of the employer within a state that is classified, not separate employments, occupations, or operations within the business." Additional details are provided on classification procedures for businesses later in this chapter.

Standard Exception Classifications

Once the basic classification is determined, it is necessary to determine whether standard exception classifications may be separately rated. Examples of standard exception classifications include Code 8810—Clerical Office Employees NOC; Code 8871—Clerical Office or Drafting Telecommuter Employees; Code 7380—Drivers; Chauffeurs and Their Helpers NOC-Commercial; Code 8742—Salespersons or Collectors—Outside; and Code 8748—Automobile Salespersons. Codes 8810 and 7380 include "NOC," which stands for "not otherwise classified."

Many classification codes already include clerical and driving exposures. For instance, Code 8832—Physician & Clerical prohibits the use of Code 8810 to clerical office employees of physicians or dentists. Code 8044—Store: Furniture & Drivers already includes the driving exposure; therefore, Code 7380 cannot apply to these businesses. Code 4361—Photographer—All Employees & Clerical, Salespersons, Drivers, includes all exposures including all standard exception exposures. It should be noted that the phraseology "All Employees" does not, in itself, prohibit the assignment of standard exception codes; it is the fact that "clerical, salespersons, drivers" are included in that wording.

In addition to determining whether the classification wording allows for a standard exception classification, it is necessary to determine whether the employees whom the business owner considers "clerical" or "outside sales" may actually qualify for these classification codes. It is common for business owners to consider supervisors of employees "clerical" because they are not directly performing physical labor. In factories, for instance, supervisors are included in the governing code, as they do not qualify for Code 8810. It is important to consider the type of work the employee is performing as well as the site at which the work is performed. Additionally, the employee must

Clerical employees
Employees defined in the *Basic Manual* as having clerical office duties within a clerical office.

Clerical office duties
According to the *Basic Manual*, include "creation or maintenance of employer records, correspondence, computer programs, files drafting, telephone duties, including telephone sales, data entry or word processing, copy or fax machine operations, unless the insured is in the business of making copies or faxing for the public, and general office work similar in nature to the above."

Clerical office
According to the *Basic Manual*, a workplace for clerical employees; a work area physically separated from an employer's workplace hazards.

Residence office
A clerical work area located in the clerical employee's dwelling.

be physically separated. To qualify for code 8810, the employee(s) must be performing clerical/drafting work in a clerical environment.

Clerical employees are employees defined in the *Basic Manual* as having clerical office duties within a clerical office. The *Basic Manual* further defines clerical employees as those meeting the manual requirements for both the definition of clerical office duties and the definition of a clerical office. According to *Basic Manual* Rule I.B.2.a.(1), **clerical office duties** include "creation or maintenance of employer records, correspondence, computer programs, files drafting, telephone duties, including telephone sales, data entry or word processing, copy or fax machine operations, unless the insured is in the business of making copies or faxing for the public, and general office work similar in nature to the above."

Rule I.B.2.a.(2) further explains that clerical office exposures do not include anyone exposed to the operative hazards of the business or duties incidental or related to the business but not of a clerical office nature. Rule I.B.2.a.(3)(a) and (b) states that the classification continues to apply when a qualified clerical office employee performs a duty outside the qualified office area, as long as that duty does not involve direct supervision or physical labor and is related to the duties in the office. Therefore, an employee can deposit funds at a bank, purchase office supplies, and pick up or deliver mail, provided that doing these jobs is incidental to the employee's duties in the office.

Rule I.B.2.a.(2)(a) and (b) further states that a **clerical office** is, according to the *Basic Manual*, a workplace for clerical employees; a work area physically separated from an employer's workplace hazards. It must "be physically separated by: floors, walls, partitions, counters, or other physical barriers that protect the clerical employee from the operating hazards of the business." It does not include "work or service areas, areas where inventory is located, areas where products are displayed for sale, or areas to which the purchaser customarily brings the product from another area for payment." If the specified walls or partitions do not physically separate an employee from other operations or the employee has any other duty in addition to clerical functions, the premium auditor cannot include that employee within the clerical classification. Instead, the premium auditor must assign that employee's total payroll to the highest rated classification of the operations to which the employee is exposed.

An employee must meet two requirements to qualify for the Clerical Telecommuter Employees classification. The employee must meet the definition of clerical telecommuter duties and work in an area that falls within the definition of a residence office.

Most of the definition of clerical telecommuter duties is the same as that for clerical office employees except that it refers to a qualified residence office rather than a qualified clerical office.

The manual defines a **residence office** as a clerical work area located in the clerical employee's dwelling. The dwelling must be separate and distinct from the employer's location.

The **Drafting Employees** classification applies only to "employees engaged exclusively in drafting and confined to office work" as described in the clerical employees definition. Premium auditors must assign the entire payroll of employees exposed to any other operations to the highest rated classification of operations to which they are exposed.

Following the logic of the two clerical employee definitions, the Telecommuting Drafting Employees standard exception classification is confined to persons performing drafting and working in a residence office as described in the Clerical Telecommuter Employee rule.

Executives often do not meet the definition of clerical office employees because their responsibilities may require them to leave the office and their duties are not exclusively clerical. Rule II.E.1.a. specifies that premium auditors should assign the payroll of executive officers to the classification that applies to the principal operations in which the executive officer is engaged. If the officer regularly engages in duties that are ordinarily performed by a superintendent or foreperson, the premium auditor should assign the officer's payroll to the governing classification. If the officer performs construction, erection, or stevedoring operations, his or her payroll must be divided in and assigned to the classifications that apply to the different operations subject to Rule II.G.

Code 8742—Salespersons Collectors—Outside applies to employees who perform these duties away from the employer's premises. It does not apply to employees engaged in delivery or pickup of merchandise; however, an occasional courtesy delivery would not preclude the assignment of Code 8742. It is not uncommon for business owners to request that route salespeople or supervisors be included in Code 8742. However, these salespeople are delivering and stocking goods and are subject to the governing code and/or drivers (depending on the phraseology). For instance, Code 2003—Bakers & Drivers, Route Supervisors and Code 20.70, Creamery or Dairy Route Supervisors, Drivers (as well as several other classifications) include these exposures. The route supervisors or salespeople cannot qualify for code 8742.

Code 8742 applies to other employees or operations by analogy. For example, the classification applies to bank or trust company employees such as special officers and armed or unarmed attendants, ushers, door attendants, appraisers, field premium auditors, runners or messengers; to claim representatives or special agents of insurers; to outside salespersons and collectors of real estate agencies; to outside social case or welfare workers employed by homemaker services; and to scouts who recruit players for professional sports teams.

The *Basic Manual* includes automobile salespersons as standard exceptions. These employees may perform these duties on or away from the employer's premises. Automobile salespersons are employed by sales and service agencies that are engaged in the selling or long-term leasing of new or used automobiles, vans, trucks, motorcycles, and mobile homes. Demonstration or delivery operations may be a normal part of their duties.

The Drivers, Chauffeurs, Messengers and Their Helpers NOC—Commercial (Code 7380) classification includes employees engaged in such duties on or in connection with a vehicle, garage, or bicycle. The classification applies to persons delivering the insured's own goods, products, or services. This classification also includes garage employees and employees using bicycles in their operations.[2] Drivers, chauffeurs, and helpers are not standard exceptions in every state.

Premium auditors can divide the payroll of an employee who is a part-time driver with any other basic classification, provided the insured maintains proper payroll records to disclose the actual payroll by classification and such a division does not go against the classification phraseology, notes, or manual rules. A later section of this chapter describes this interchange of labor situation in detail.

A common request by business owners is to classify each employee based on his or her actual duties. This idea goes against *Basic Manual* rules and would present difficulties in performing a premium audit. The important thing to understand is that each basic classification code includes the higher-end and lower-end exposures. If all of these exposures were not included in one classification code, then there would be a considerable rate disparity between the multiple classification codes for the same type of business. For instance, Code 8044—Store: Furniture & Drivers includes store employees, warehouse employees, and delivery drivers. The business owner/controller will often request that the store employees be rated to Code 8810 or Code 8742. The argument made is that the store employees' exposures are not as high as the exposures of the warehouse, especially the delivery people. However, if the store exposures (the lower-end exposures) were not included in Code 8044, then the warehouse rate and delivery rate would be considerably higher.

Another example is an automobile body shop. Estimators are expressly included within the scope of 8393—Automobile Body Repair. The business owner may argue that the estimators are not cutting or welding metal and should be subject to Code 8810 or 8742. However, if the estimators were not included in the basic classification, then the overall rate would be substantially higher.

General Exclusions

General exclusion
A category of business operations that is so unusual that the *Basic Manual* excludes it from the basic classifications for rating workers' compensation insurance.

A **general exclusion** is a category of business operations that is so unusual that the *Basic Manual* excludes it from the basic classifications for rating workers' compensation insurance. Exclusions usually involve hazards much more severe than the business's normal operations. Premium auditors separately classify general exclusions and standard exceptions unless the basic classification's wording specifically includes them.[3] If the classification definition merely refers to "all employees," premium auditors must still exclude those operations. General exclusions are the following:[4]

- *Aviation*—Includes all operations of the flying and ground crews. Premium auditors must separately classify anyone piloting a plane, serving as a member of the crew, or servicing the plane on the ground.

- *New construction or alterations*—Includes both erection of new buildings and additions to existing buildings. Alterations may include structural changes or the erection or removal of store fronts or permanent interior partitions. This exclusion also applies to extraordinary repairs, such as replacement of heating and cooling systems, plumbing, or electrical wiring. If no one has previously occupied the premises, new construction also includes installation of machinery, equipment, and fixtures. Painting in connection with any of these activities also belongs in this general exclusion.

- *Stevedoring*—Premium auditors would include any tallying or checking clerks in warehousing or freight-handling operations connected with stevedoring. This situation may occur when an insured is located on navigable waters. Such businesses may load their products on ships or unload raw materials or finished goods from ships. Premium auditors would treat any tallying or checking done during the stevedoring process as a general exclusion. They would not consider it a general exclusion operation if the tallying or checking was done in conjunction with the warehouse activities.

- *Sawmill operations*—If the insured operates a pallet mill and also has a sawmill operation at the same location that saws logs into lumber for use by the pallet mill, the premium auditor will separately rate the sawmill operations from the basic classification by assigning the sawmill payroll to the sawmill classification.

- *Employer-operated daycare service*—Some large employers operate daycare centers on their premises for the convenience of employees. In those cases, the payroll of the daycare employees is not included within the employer's basic classification.

General Inclusions

A **general inclusion** is a category of business operations that is common in many businesses and is, therefore, included in the scope of the basic classification in the *Basic Manual* for rating workers' compensation insurance. Some operations are a normal and necessary part of a business even though they at first seem to be distinct from the business itself. For example, an onsite cafeteria involves processes and skills different from those of a manufacturing operation, but the cafeteria employees are probably few, and they encounter many of the same hazards as everyone else in the plant. The rules provide that premium auditors include such employees' payroll in the basic classification. Those operations are general inclusions and are as follows:

- *Restaurants or cafeterias operated by the insured for employee use*—Premium auditors should include the cafeteria employees at the factory in the

General inclusion
A category of business operations that is common in many businesses and is, therefore, included in the scope of the basic classification in the *Basic Manual* for rating workers' compensation insurance.

factory classification. Such operations receive a separate classification when conducted in connection with construction, erection, lumbering, or mining.

- *Manufacture of containers by the insured, such as bags, barrels, bottles, boxes, cans, cartons, or packing cases for sole use by the operations insured by the policy*—This provision may include the insured's shipping department or other operations necessary for the distribution of the insured's product. Premium auditors would separately classify only a distinct enterprise supplying containers to other firms.

- *Hospitals or medical facilities operated by the insured for its employees*[5]—The basic classification includes plant doctors, nurses, and first-aid attendants.

- *Maintenance or repair of the insured's building or equipment by the insured's employees*[6]—Premium auditors should include a janitor's remuneration in the basic classification.

- *Printing or lithographing by the insured on its own products.*[7]

Unless the insured performs construction, erection, lumbering, or mining work, the rules allow only three situations in which a premium auditor can separately classify a general inclusion operation. One is if the operation constitutes a separate and distinct business of the insured as provided in Rule I.D.3. (Assignment of Classifications). Also, the premium auditor must separately classify an operation if the basic classification's wording specifically excludes it. Finally, if a standard exception classification describes the insured's principal business, then the premium auditor must separately classify the operation that would otherwise be a general inclusion. The rules for general inclusions and for general exclusions apply to all classifications. Construction or erection operations constitute their own specialized handling.

Classification Wording

The question often arises regarding the range of operations included in established classifications. Rule I.C. provides specific guidance in interpreting the classification's intent.

Captions and Notes

Caption
The information preceding related classifications in the *Basic Manual* that forms a part of all of the classification's definition.

When either captions or notes appear, they form part of the classification wording. A **caption** is the information preceding related classifications in the *Basic Manual* that forms a part of all of the classification's definition. Captions precede related classifications and apply to all of them. Notes are the information following classification descriptions in the *Basic Manual* that restrict the classification's definition and control its use.

Words and Phrases

When the manual uses ordinary words in classification phraseology, insurers and premium auditors should give them their ordinary meanings. The *Basic Manual's* Rule I-C. defines the following common classification words and phrases:

- All Employees, All Other Employees, All Operations, or All Operations to Completion
- Clerical
- Drivers
- Includes or &
- Local Manager
- No or Not
- NOC
- "Or" or "And"
- Salespersons
- Stories in Height
- To Be Separately Rated

If any classification includes the phrase "all employees," "all other employees," "all operations," or "all operations to completion," the premium auditor should not assign any other classification to that operation unless specifically indicated by the classification wording. Three exceptions exist to this rule. The standard exception and general exclusions rules still apply. Also, if some of the operations fall within the Construction or Erection Permanent Yard (Code 8227) or Contractor—Project Manager, Construction Executive, Construction Manager or Construction Superintendent (Code 5606) classifications, the premium auditor can assign those operations to those classifications. Finally, a premium auditor can assign different classifications if some operations constitute a separate and distinct business as defined by the manual (Rule I.C.2.).

"Clerical" means clerical office employees and drafting employees as defined by the manual in Rules I.B.2.a. as described previously.

"Drivers" is also defined by the rule regarding standard exception classifications (Rule I.B.2.b.).

Either "includes" or "&" means that the classification contains the operations or employees specifically designated. Premium auditors should not assign employees or operations included in such a classification to any other classification, even if separate classification descriptions may apply. A classification phrase occasionally reads "includes clerical" or "& drivers." In those instances, the standard exception classifications do not apply.

When used as part of classification wording, the term "local manager" means the person who is in charge of an operation in a yard but who is not normally subject to the hazards of the governing classification. Premium auditors should assign the payroll of local managers to the governing classification. An example of this classification is "Hay, grain or feed dealer & local managers, drivers" (Code 8215).

"No" or "not" preclude applying a classification to an insured with operations described by the phrase following the word "no" or "not"—for example, "Store: Agriculture Implement—not farm machinery." The note to this classification indicates that the premium auditor should not use it for an insured engaged in the rental or sale of farm machinery.

Two exceptions exist to this rule. First, the rule applies to each location for mercantile and mining businesses. Second, the rule applies to each job or location for construction operations.

"NOC" stands for "not otherwise classified." Premium auditors should use any classification designated as NOC only when no other classification more specifically or accurately describes the insured's business.

NOC classifications can fit many operations to which no other classification applies. Those classifications can also be a problem if the premium auditor discovers such a classification early in the process and fails to look further. Whenever classification assignments seem questionable, premium auditors should consider NOC classifications a last resort. A classification containing NOC is frequently the most appropriate, but the premium auditor should make certain that the business is indeed "not otherwise classified."

For example, premium auditors should classify a carpentry contractor engaged in remodeling work and room additions on houses as "Carpentry: Detached one- or two-family dwellings" (Code 5645). However, one could argue that "Carpentry: NOC" (Code 5403) is a more accurate classification. The crux of the argument is that because no carpentry code exists for remodeling, the carpenter is engaged in carpentry operations that are not otherwise classified. However, the classification system's objective is that the "rate for each classification reflects the exposures common to those employers." Exposures implicit in building a house, in building a room addition, or in doing remodeling work on a residential dwelling are common to both a general carpentry contractor working on residences and to a remodeling carpentry contractor working on a residence. Therefore, in that example, "Carpentry: Detached one- or two-family dwellings" (Code 5645) adequately describes the insured's exposures. On the other hand, "Carpentry: NOC" (Code 5403) contemplates the different exposures faced by commercial contractors. That example demonstrates the misleading reasoning that can result in accepting an NOC classification too quickly.

The word "or" in classifications also means "and." Although at first this may seem confusing, an example is provided in the *Basic Manual* to demonstrate the intent. The classification "Cleaning or Dyeing" (Code 2586) would apply to a business engaged in cleaning *and* dyeing.

"Salespersons" means the standard exception classification defined in Rule I.B.2.c.

Several classifications in the manual refer to "stories in height." Carpentry and painting are two. The manual defines a story as fifteen feet in height. It is measured from the lowest point above ground to the highest point above ground.

If a classification requires operations or employees "to be separately rated," premium auditors should separately classify all such operations or employees according to Rule I.C.2.k. That phrase usually appears in the notes that accompany the basic classification description.

Assigning Classifications and Payroll

As mentioned, premium auditors try to assign the one basic classification that best describes the employer's business within a state. With certain exceptions, each classification includes all the labor types found in a business. Therefore, "it is the business that is classified, not the individual employments, occupations, or operations within a business."[8]

Classifying Separate Legal Entities, Business Not Described by a Classification, and Other Classification Assignment Rules

A business to be classified is normally a separate legal entity. If a policy covers more than one legal entity, the premium auditor should assign each separate legal entity to the basic classification that describes the legal entity's entire business within a state. That procedure applies even if the insured conducts the business at more than one location. If no classification exists that describes the business, the premium auditor should assign the classification that most closely describes the business. Rule I.D.2. explains how a premium auditor should do this. Exhibit 4-7 shows the specific wording. The premium auditor should show wording that describes the business and then show the code number of the classification that most closely describes the business. For instance, the scope of Code 3821—Automobile Dismantling & Drivers gives examples of some types of analogy assignments. These examples are "Dismantling of Aircraft, Dismantling of Tractors, and Dismantling of Trolleys." The rules of the assigned classification apply to the business.

EXHIBIT 4-7

Rule I.D.2. of *Basic Manual*

Business Not Described by Any Classification

If no basic classification clearly describes the business, the classification that most closely describes the business must be assigned. For a business not described by any classification, show the wording that describes the business in Item 4 of the Information page of the policy. With this wording, show the code number of the classification that most closely describes the business. All the rules pertaining to the assigned basic classification apply to this operation.

In general, how many separate operations or locations are involved makes no difference as long as a single manual classification describes the total business. That one classification applies to the total business. Exceptions to this include standard exceptions, general exclusions, classifications requiring certain operations to be separately rated, mercantile businesses, farm operations, repair operations, construction and erection operations, and when the insured operates more than one business in a state. Except in those cases, the premium auditor must assign a single classification that most accurately describes the insured's entire operations. Premium auditors cannot assign another classification to any portion of the business's operations even if another classification specifically describes the operation in question, or if the operation in question is at another location within the state, unless one of the exceptions named is appropriate.

Standard exception and general exclusion classifications best describe some businesses. For a bank or an insurer, for example, the greatest amount of payroll, but not all, would fall into the clerical employee classification. In that case, "the operations of all employees not included in the definition of the standard exception classification shall be assigned to the separate basic classification that most closely describes their operations."[9] Therefore, the premium auditor should assign a bank's cafeteria employees to Code 9082 or 9083 "Restaurant NOC or Restaurant Fast Food" depending on whether wait service is provided. Even if the classification wording says "all employees," premium auditors should separately classify standard exception and general exclusion operations.

Finally, some insureds are involved in repair operations not described by a basic classification. In those cases, the premium auditor should assign the operations to the classification that applies to the manufacture of the product, unless the repair work is described by the phraseology of some other classification.

Assigning Additional Basic Classifications to Secondary Businesses

If a classification requires premium auditors to separately rate operations or employees, or if an employer operates a secondary business within a state, a premium auditor can assign an additional basic classification under certain conditions. The *Basic Manual* specifies that the insured is considered to be operating more than one business in the state "if portions of the insured's operations in that state are not encompassed by the classification applicable to the insured's principal business."[10]

Rule I.D.3. of the *Basic Manual* lists the following necessary conditions for a portion of an insured's business to qualify as a separate undertaking or enterprise and therefore be eligible for separate rating:

a. The insured's principal business is described by a basic classification that requires certain operations or employees to be separately rated.

b. The insured conducts one or more of the following operations:
- Construction or erection
- Farming

- Employee leasing, labor contracting, temporary labor services
- Mercantile business

c. The insured conducts more than one operation in a state.

(1) For purposes of this rule, an insured is conducting more than one operation in a state if portions of the insured's operations in that state are not encompassed by the classification applicable to the insured's principal business. To qualify for a separate classification, the insured's additional operation must meet all of the following conditions:

a. Be able to exist as a separate business if the insured's principal business in the state ceased to exist.

b. Be located in a separate building, or on a separate floor in the same building, or on the same floor physically separated from the principal business by structural partitions. Employees engaged in the principal business must be protected from the operating hazards of the separate additional operations.

c. Maintain proper payroll records. Refer to Rule 2-G. for the description of proper payroll records.

(2) If the separate additional operation is not encompassed in the classification applicable to the insured's principal business and meets all the conditions listed above in c(1), the insured is considered to be engaged in an additional operation. If this is the case, a separate basic classification may be assigned to each operation that qualifies as a separate additional operation.

(3) If the additional operation does not meet all conditions listed above in c(1) and is not encompassed in the classification applicable to the insured's principal business and has a rate:

Lower than the insured's principal business, assign the additional operation to the same classification as the insured's principal business.

Higher than or equal to the insured's principal business, assign the additional operation to the classification that describes the additional operation.

(4) Policies with more than one classification may include employees working under several classifications. Payroll assignment for these employees is subject to the Interchange of Labor rule. Refer to Rule 2-G.[11]

The intent of this rule is to scrutinize the operations, occupations, or employments within an insured's business that are not normal or usual to such an enterprise. Premium auditors classify the insured's business, but if the insured's business includes an operation that is unusual for such a venture, the premium auditor can consider that operation's exposures and the classifications applicable separately if the required tests are met.

According to Rule I.D.3.g., if the business is a mercantile risk, it is classified according to the majority of the gross receipts by location. If two different types of products are sold and these products would be subject to different classification codes, then the gross receipts will determine the applicable classification code. For example, if a retail store sells TVs, VCRs, DVDs, stereo equipment, etc. (subject to classification code 8017), as well as appliances such as washers/dryers, refrigerators, and other large appliances (subject to classification code 8044), it is necessary to determine the gross receipts for the items sold, subject to each classification. If, for instance, 58 percent of the gross receipts are from large appliances, code 8044 will apply. It should be noted that mercantile classifications can change from year to year depending on the gross receipts. Two mercantile codes cannot apply to the same entity at the same location (unless directed to do so in the classification wording; that is, 8232/8058). However, if a mercantile risk has more than one location, then separate classification codes can be applied. For instance, if a store sells TVs at one location and large appliances at another location, then codes 8017 and 8044 may apply to the same store. For some types of mercantile risks, the premium auditor must assign more than one classification code as directed. For instance, Code 8232 directs that Code 8058 be applied to store employees. These classification codes are sister codes that apply to building material dealers.

Rule I.D.3.d. states that, when classifying construction risks, several different classifications may apply to the same entity. These different classifications are due to the fact that construction businesses' exposures vary depending on the type of work being done. Again, it is important to note that if work subject to more than one classification code (if done separately) is done at the same job or location, then the premium auditor must ensure that the exposures of the different work are not already encompassed by one classification code. For instance, several construction codes are project codes. This means that some work that may appear to be subject to different classification codes is already encompassed in the main classification. Code 5645—Carpentry-Detached One- or Two-Family Dwellings encompasses all carpentry work performed in connection with building a one- or two-family residence by a particular contractor. Without realizing this, the premium auditor may mistakenly include Code 5437—Carpentry-Installation of Cabinetry Work or Interior Trim for the trim work/cabinetry when the *Basic Manual* prohibits the use of Code 5437 when another carpentry operation was performed at the same job or location by the same contractor. Code 5437 could apply, however, to a contractor that specialized only in cabinetry work and/or trim work. Another project code, for example, is Code 6306—Sewer Construction-All Operations and Drivers. This code encompasses concrete work, filling and backfilling, fencing, etc. If this were not a project code, then the premium auditor may have assigned the filling and backfilling to Code 6217, the concrete work to Code 5213, the fencing erection to 6400, etc. Additionally, the setting up of forms is expressly included in the concrete classification codes, as they are an integral part of the concrete work. If this was not included in the wording, then the premium auditor may assign a carpentry code in error. A contractor has to take special care in hiring subcontractors. If for instance, a trim contractor subject to code 5437 hires a framing contractor to perform work on a single-family residence and the framing contractor does not carry the proper coverage, all employees engaged in any type of carpentry work would be subject to Code 5645, including the insured's trim workers.

Rule I.D.3.e. states that separate classification codes may be applied to farm operations in the event that proper division of payroll is maintained. If separate payroll records are not maintained, then the classification would be based on proportional acreage. Outside domestic employees at farm locations are subject to the farm classification(s), while inside domestic workers are excluded. Separate classification treatment is applied to inside domestic workers. Domestic workers of non-farm risks are separately rated regardless of whether they are indoor or outdoor domestic workers.

Rule I.D.3.f. states that employees of these types of risks are assignable to the classification code(s) that would be applied if they were the clients' employees.

Miscellaneous Employees

The *Basic Manual* states, "**Miscellaneous employees** are those who perform duties conducted in common for separate operations that are subject to more than one basic classification. The remuneration of any miscellaneous employees shall be assigned to the governing classification."[12] Miscellaneous employees include the following:

- General superintendents other than construction executives that meet the requirements of Code 5606—Contractor-Project manager, Construction Executive, Construction Manager or Construction Superintendent
- Maintenance or power plant employees
- Shipping or receiving clerks
- Yard workers other than construction yard employees properly assigned to Code 8227—Construction or Erection Permanent Yard

Consider, for example, a four-story factory with two floors devoted to a general job machine shop and two floors devoted to plastic goods manufacturing. "Machine Shop NOC" (Code 3632) applies to the machine shop. One of the three plastics manufacturing classes applies to the plastic goods manufacturing. A premium auditor would assign the porters and cleaners serving all four floors to the governing classification, which could be either Code 3632 or the plastics manufacturing classification, depending on which produces the larger payroll amount. Refer to Rule I.B.5. for the definition of the governing classification.

Interchange of Labor

Some employees who would not be considered miscellaneous employees may also perform duties directly related to more than one basic classification. An example is an employee who occasionally interchanges between operations subject to more than one basic classification. Suppose, for example, that one of the machine shop employees works for the plastic goods manufacturer two days

Miscellaneous employees
Employees who perform duties that are commonly conducted for several operations that are subject to more than one basic classification code and are assigned to the governing classification.

a week. Assuming the manual allows the two classifications on the policy, a premium auditor may divide the payroll between the two classes, provided that the employer maintains payroll records showing the actual payroll by classification for each employee. If payroll records do not exist, the premium auditor should assign all of the employer's payroll to the classification with the higher rate.[13]

An exception to Rule II.G. is that employees in the Clerical Office Employees (Code 8810), Clerical Telecommuter Employees (Code 8871), or the Salespersons, Collectors, or Messengers—Outside (Code 8742) classifications are not eligible for payroll division. However, if the interchange of labor occurs between Codes 8810 and 8871, the premium auditor should assign Code 8871 when the employee spends the majority of his or her time in that job. Otherwise, Code 8810 applies.

CLASSIFICATION TECHNIQUES

The "Classifications" section of "Part Two—Classifications" in the *Basic Manual* alphabetically lists the specific classifications and the corresponding code numbers. Premium auditors continually refer to those pages to find the correct classifications applying to the insured's business. As Chapter 1 explains, workers' compensation insurance rating works on the theory that each class of business should bear its own losses. Therefore, the correct classification assignment is essential for the equitable treatment of insureds and for the credibility of the rating system.

Most premium audits do not require extensive investigation to find the correct classifications. In many instances, classifications are obvious. The occasional challenge, which arrives usually as a troublesome surprise, requires careful, logical analysis to determine the most appropriate classification.

Classification assignments should reflect the operations as they were during the audited period. Classifications assigned in previous premium audits or at the policy's inception naturally reflect exposures that existed at that time. That assignment often applies throughout the entire policy if it was initially the correct classification. However, changes occasionally necessitate altering the assigned classification. Those changes can occur within the jobs themselves or within the insured's business.

Premium auditors must be aware of the *Basic Manual* rules (or state rules, if different) regarding a change in classifications after policy inception. According to Rule I.F.1., if the insured's operations change, no problem results from changing the classifications to reflect that change in operations as of the date of the change. However, if a classification change is needed because the insurer incorrectly issued the policy initially, the *Basic Manual* Rules I.F.2. and 3. specify when that change may take place. If the change results in a decrease in premium, the premium auditor should apply the change as of the policy's inception date.

If the change results in an increase in premium, different rules apply depending on when the determination is made. If the premium auditor determines that a change to a higher rated classification is necessary during the first 120 days of the policy period, the insurer can endorse the current policy as of the inception date. If the premium auditor discovers the error after the current policy has been in force for 120 days but before the final 90 days of the policy period, the insurer can endorse the policy as of the date the premium auditor determines the need for the change. If the premium auditor determines the need for a change within the last 90 days of the policy period, or at final premium audit, the insurer cannot endorse the expiring policy. The change can only be reflected on the renewal policy, if at all.[14] Because of the differences in state laws on this topic, premium auditors must be aware of the laws in the states in which they conduct premium audits.

Perhaps a chance remark or an incidental bit of information calls a previously assigned classification into question. A conscientious premium auditor cultivates the habit of challenging every classification scheduled in the policy declaration. Such a challenge may entail no more than a momentary pause to consider whether an application applies. The challenge may occasionally expand to investigating the manuals and additional sources available to verify which classification does apply.

Useful ways to analyze the insured's operations for classification purposes are by job activity, by job description, by analogy, and by cross-reference. The following sections explain each of these techniques. Although, as in some of the following examples, considering the number of employees involved in analyzing the appropriate classification is occasionally useful, premium auditors must ultimately determine the dollar amount of payroll, not merely a head count. Thus, premium auditors should view those references to the number of employees as shorthand for the payroll amount.

By Job Activity

One of the most frequent methods by which premium auditors determine the appropriate classification is by analyzing the job activity itself. Knowing how to analyze a job's activities can enable the premium auditor to judge whether standardized job descriptions accurately describe the work exposures. Although correlations between job descriptions and classification definitions are often warranted, a premium auditor should maintain a healthy skepticism.

Consider, for example, the following case. The premium auditor visits the Master Machine Shop to make the workers' compensation premium audit. From the name and conversation with the owner, the premium auditor determines that the business is a job-shop machine shop. The firm makes parts and other items to customer specifications. The shop employs twenty-two persons full time: eighteen machinists, one clerical worker, one salesperson, one driver, and one janitor.

The company name includes the words "machine shop." The *Basic Manual* contains a classification "Machine Shop NOC" (Code 3632). Because both the insured's name and the work performed by most of the employees suggest a machine shop operation, the premium auditor assigns Code 3632 as the governing classification. The clerical worker, salesperson, and driver are all subject to the standard exceptions rulings. The janitor is a miscellaneous employee whose exposure is close to that of a general inclusion; therefore, the premium auditor includes the janitor's payroll in the governing classification.

The premium auditor's classification breakdown is the following:

Machine Shop (Code 3632)	For nineteen employees
Clerical (Code 8810)	For one employee
Salespersons (Code 8742)	For one employee
Drivers (Code 7380)	For one employee

It would seem that the premium auditor has accurately classified the business operation and followed the rules regarding classification divisions.

A year later, the premium auditor returns to the Master Machine Shop for another workers' compensation premium audit. The owner says the firm still machines items as before, turning out machined tools to customer specifications. The firm has added only one new employee, a patternmaker.

However, the insured in this case does not conduct the patternmaking as a separate and distinct business. The original classification assigned, "Machine Shop NOC" (Code 3632), still seems to apply and to preclude any payroll division for the patternmaker.

The owner's explanation that the firm is "still involved in machining items as before, turning out machined tools to customer specifications" reveals another possibility. Perhaps the premium auditor stopped one question shy of the correct exposure last year. The *Basic Manual* contains another classification: "Tool Mfg.: Drop or machine forged NOC: Machining or finishing of tools or die making operations" (Code 3114). The premium auditor must now determine whether producing custom-made machine tools is the insured's principal business. If so, then Code 3114, rather than "Machine Shop NOC" (Code 3632), is the appropriate classification. The pattern-maker's presence alerted the premium auditor to the emphasis on tools in the machine shop.

This example demonstrates one of the challenges that premium auditors often face. The premium auditor had been there the year before, and the business had not noticeably changed. It looked like a routine premium audit. Instead, the premium audit became more complex than anticipated. The change in operations was not dramatic, but rather a natural development within the boundaries of that business type. This example should also remind premium auditors and underwriters not to classify individual occupations or operations within a business.

A business's normal evolution may change the operations enough to make another classification more appropriate. The premium auditor must recognize when such changes occur. The best way for a premium auditor to do this is by questioning the insured, the job description, and even the apparently accurate classification itself every year to ensure that the classification code is correct.

The Master Machine Shop example demonstrates how important understanding the job activity can be. The apparent "Machine Shop NOC" classification assignment seems inappropriate because the job activity has changed from what the premium auditor observed during the first visit.

Consider another example of classification by activity. The premium auditor calls on Watson and Stephens Enterprises for a premium audit under a workers' compensation policy. The office is located in an office complex. The policy information page lists clerical employees and drivers. Both are standard exceptions, so the principal business is not identified. The policy shows the following:

Clerical (Code 8810)	For three employees
Drivers (Code 7380)	For twelve employees

The premium auditor inquires about the line of business and learns that it is an auto livery service furnishing chauffeured limousines for hire. The driver employees' exposure is consistent with the standard exception classification phrasing, "Drivers, Chauffeurs Messengers and their Helpers NOC Commercial" (Code 7380). That classification would include garage employees.

The Drivers classification (Code 7380) seems appropriate for that operation. No classification exists specifically for auto livery. Classifications for automobile leasing and automobile rental are in the *Basic Manual*, but the clients of Watson and Stephens do not rent cars; they hire chauffeured limousines. Therefore, the premium auditor must search further to find an appropriate basic classification. A classification for a livery company does not exist, but a notation in the *Basic Manual* reads "Livery Co.—see Limousine Co." That classification is not under Automobile, but under Livery. That reference leads to the following classification:

Limousine Co.:
Garage employees	Code 8385
All other employees & drivers:	
Nonscheduled	Code 7370
Scheduled	Code 7382

After duly considering those definitions, the premium auditor would obtain the pertinent figures and supportive data and complete the premium audit worksheet, which should indicate the following:

Clerical (Code 8810)	For three employees

Limousine Co.:
All other employees & drivers:	
Nonscheduled (Code 7370)	For eleven employees
Garage employees (Code 8385)	For one employee

In that case, correctly classifying the insured's operation resulted directly from the premium auditor's questions concerning the business's primary activity. Although the clerical and drivers classifications listed on the information page appeared to define the employees' work exposure, the object is to assign the classification that reflects the exposures common to the business. By concentrating on the insured's operations, the premium auditor discovered the classification that most accurately defined both the business operations and the employees' work exposures.

The insured's company name, the employees' job descriptions, and the apparent activities can obscure the correct assignment. All three elements may seem to be in perfect agreement, only to be the incorrect classification when the premium auditor analyzes the operations of the business. The premium auditor must continually analyze and question to determine the most appropriate classification.

By Job Description

Workers' compensation classifications group insureds by industry, not by employment types. The intent is to compare "like to like" so that each class of business bears its own losses. Any one employer's actual operations and principal business should be essentially the same as that of any other employer within the applicable industrial classification grouping. Therefore, the job descriptions or job titles for the various occupations, employments, and operations within those grouped industries should also be similar. Employers continually refine job descriptions to accurately reflect the job substance. The standard exceptions are good examples of concise, widely accepted job descriptions. If the insured has designated an employee work function as clerical, the employer, the employee, and the premium auditor share an idea about certain work activities implied by that description. The employee must actually engage in clerical activities to justify that designated description.

Job Titles

The job descriptions or job titles of the insured's employees provide an immediate clue regarding classifications. The company name or title together with the job descriptions of the largest group of employees often indicate the basic classification applying to the insured. Such correlations between standard industrial job definitions and the *Basic Manual* classifications make many classification assignments simple.

Company Name and Advertising

The insured has often carefully chosen the company name to convey the nature of the business to the general public. Useful questions, therefore, would include the following:

- Which classification does the insured's name suggest?
- What business does the name imply, and which classification correlates to that business?

Another initial clue is the insured's advertising. If the insured has advertising brochures and handouts available, the premium auditor should use them. Brochures not only tell exactly what the firm does, but also how it does it better than anyone else. If no such brochures are available, the premium auditor could use the telephone book Yellow Pages or the insured's Web site. Many times, signs on the insured's trucks or vehicles provide additional detail into what services are offered.

By Analogy

Although the classification process strives to group operations with similar hazards, adherence to the wording of job descriptions or business operations does not always lead to that result. Classification by analogy represents an alternative that may help to establish a classification appropriate for the hazards involved.

Manufacturing wooden shoes of the type worn in Holland illustrates that approach. The manual contains the classification "Boot or shoe: Mfg. NOC" (Code 2660). The rules permit applying this classification to manufacturing any shoe type for which the manual provides no more specific classification. The only other boot or shoe classification is "Boot or shoe: Mfg.—rubber" (Code 4410). Therefore, manufacturing wooden shoes falls within Code 2660 if considered strictly according to the product's name.

However, analyzing the operation reveals that the insured shapes wooden blocks in automatic lathes. This analysis suggests another manual classification, "Wood: Turned products mfg. NOC" (Code 2841). Because no wood turning classification exists specifically for wooden shoes, the premium auditor may assign Code 2841. However, neither of those classifications describes manufacturing wooden shoes. A premium auditor looking for a classification whose normal operational hazards are most similar to the wooden shoe manufacturer may find the classification "Last or Shoe form mfg." (Code 2790). The normal process in this operation is shaping wooden blocks into the form of shoes by turning on automatic lathes. The hazards normally found in that operation are almost identical to the wooden shoe manufacturer. Therefore, an equitable solution would be to assign the classification "Wooden shoe mfg." (Code 2790). This procedure for assigning classifications is controlled by Rule I.D. in the *Basic Manual*, described earlier.

The "Classification Codes by Schedules and Groups" section of the *Classification Codes Book* can greatly assist classification by analogy. The classifications listed within a particular industry group can include some operations similar to the insured's. Even the discontinued classifications shown in those pages may suggest analogous operations.

When classifying by analogy, the premium auditor should consider all aspects of the situation and try to describe it without reference to that business's normal terminology. The premium auditor may also ask the insured to describe the business in nontechnical terms. Such an explanation may compare the operation to other businesses, which may suggest another classification contemplating similar operations and hazards. Assigning classifications through the use of analogy requires frequent reference to the *Basic Manual*, the *Classification Codes Book*, and the *CLM*. Premium auditors use the last two primarily for cross-reference.

By Cross-Reference

Premium auditors may find cross-referencing a useful tool. The concept of comparing "like to like" for ratemaking purposes applies to general liability and to workers' compensation rates. A premium auditor may find that a corresponding general liability classification definition is more precise. That definition's terminology may then point to a different workers' compensation classification.

Cross-referencing may apply to a premium auditor calling on the Solar-Powered Razor Company. The company manufactures a solar-powered, hand-held razor similar to solar-powered items such as hand-held calculators. The workers' compensation *Basic Manual* contains the classification "Razor Mfg.: NOC" (Code 3122). Yet that classification does not seem appropriate. The *Classification Codes Book* correlates Code 3122 to general liability Code 51999, which the *CLM* defines as "Cutlery (not powered) and Flatware Mfg." Because the razor is powered, that classification does not apply. The *CLM* also shows a classification "Razors or Razor Blades Mfg." (Code 58575). The classification notes state that electric razors should be separately classified and rated. That phrase leads to the consideration that this solar-powered razor may be more akin to an electric razor than to cutlery or blade razors.

The classification assigned at the policy's inception, "Razor Mfg.: NOC" (Code 3122) may seem reasonable at first. In this example, however, the premium auditor questions its applicability and more thoroughly researches the classifications. The thought that electric razor manufacturing may be classified differently for workers' compensation leads to a review of the workers' compensation classifications to find "Electrical Apparatus: Mfg. NOC" (Code 3179), which includes electrical fixtures or appliances. In this example, the terminology "not electric" within the general liability classification inspires the chain of thought leading to the correct classification.

SUMMARY

The theory of workers' compensation ratemaking is that each class of business should pay for its own losses. For that theory to work, premium auditors must accurately assign classifications. Premium auditors must precisely follow the workers' compensation *Basic Manual*'s rules applying to the particular jurisdiction. The more premium auditors understand the classification system's logic, the better they can apply those rules to difficult situations. Therefore, they must know the *Basic Manual* thoroughly and refer to it continually.

In addition to the *Basic Manual*, several other references can provide guidance for classification decisions. Those references include the *Scopes Manual*, *Classification Codes Book*, the *Commercial Lines Manual*, circular letters, insurer manuals and bulletins, many references from PAAS, and educational papers of premium auditors' associations.

The objective of the classification procedure is to assign the basic classification that best describes the business. Premium auditors must assign all employees' payroll to that basic classification unless the rules provide an explicit reason to do otherwise. The *Basic Manual* separately lists standard exceptions—clerical workers, drafting employees, drivers, and salespeople. Premium auditors do not assign the payroll of workers included within the standard exceptions to the classification unless the description of the basic classification includes the standard exception. The payroll of seemingly distinct but incidental operations defined in the rules under general inclusions remains with that of other operations falling within the basic classification. However, the rules also provide for premium auditors to separately classify certain unusual and hazardous operations listed under general exclusions unless the description of the basic classification specifically includes those operations. The premium auditor must keep in mind the general inclusions, the general exclusions, and the words and phrases defined in the rules when applying a particular classification description.

The *Basic Manual* clearly specifies the circumstances that permit using any classifications other than the one that best describes the business, the standard exceptions, and the general exclusions. It should be noted that each entity within the state is classified in accordance with the activities of that entity. If all employees are under one entity, premium auditors can assign the insured's secondary business an additional basic classification if the insured's additional operation meets all of the following conditions: (1) it could exist as a separate business if the insured's principal business in the state ceased to exist, (2) it is located in a separate building, or on a separate floor in the same building, or on the same floor physically separated from the principal business by structural partitions, and (3) it maintains proper payroll records. The separate operation must not be encompassed in the classification applicable to the insured principal business and must meet all of the preceding conditions. If the conditions cannot be met, a secondary business may be assigned a separate classification only when its classification carries a higher rate than the principal business. If the premium auditor classifies the business to more than one basic classification code, then he or she should assign the payroll of miscellaneous employees to the governing classification, but divide the payroll of employees who interchange between assigned classifications, subject to the limitations of the interchange of labor rule in the *Basic Manual* Rule 2.G.1. The next chapter describes the rules for assigning separate classifications for construction or erection operations.

Assigning the proper classification to the insured's business may require analysis. Useful analysis techniques include classification by job activity, by job description, by analogy, and by cross-reference. Each of these approaches can provide insights to help solve obscure or ambiguous classification problems. Although such analytical techniques may require additional time, they increase the premium auditor's confidence that he or she has correctly assigned classifications and thus improve the accuracy of the rating process.

CHAPTER NOTES

1. National Council on Compensation Insurance, Inc., *Classification Codes for Workers' Compensation and Employers Liability Insurance* (Boca Raton, Fla.: National Council on Compensation Insurance, Inc., 1987), "Classification Codes by Schedules and Groups," p. i.
2. *Basic Manual*, Rule I.B.2.b.
3. *Basic Manual*, Rule I.B.4.
4. *Basic Manual*, Rule I.B.4.
5. *Basic Manual*, Rule I.B.3.
6. *Basic Manual*, Rule I.B.3.
7. *Basic Manual*, Rule I.B.3.
8. *Basic Manual*, Rule I.D.
9. *Basic Manual*, Rule I.D.5.
10. *Basic Manual*, Rule I.D.3.c.(1).
11. *Basic Manual*, Rule I.D.3.
12. *Basic Manual*, Rule I.E.1.
13. *Basic Manual*, Rule II.G.2.
14. *Basic Manual*, Rule I.F.3.

Direct Your Learning

Workers' Compensation—Construction Operations

Educational Objectives

After learning the content of this chapter and completing the corresponding course guide assignment, you should be able to:

▶ Explain how each of the following affects the assignment of workers' compensation classifications in construction:

- Distinct operations classification
- Separate payroll records
- Scope of classifications
- Subcontractors
- Division of an employee's payroll
- Executive supervisors
- Common laborers

▶ Explain how construction industry practices, personnel, and the construction process create challenges regarding a premium auditor's determination of employer/employee relationships.

▶ Describe the residential construction process and the NCCI *Basic Manual* rules for classification at each stage in the process.

▶ Describe the commercial construction process and the NCCI *Basic Manual* rules for classification at each stage in the process.

▶ Describe the NCCI *Basic Manual* rules for classification of operations involved in highway construction, utility line construction, and irrigation or drainage system construction.

▶ Describe the NCCI *Basic Manual* rules for classification of operations involved in construction or erection of permanent yards and shops.

▶ Define or describe each of the Key Words and Phrases for this chapter.

Develop Your Perspective

What are the main topics covered in the chapter?

Construction premium audits generally are complicated when compared to premium audits of other businesses, particularly regarding assigning the proper classifications for workers' compensation coverage. This chapter describes construction classifications and the nature of construction, including the residential and commercial construction processes.

Describe the procedures for assigning workers' compensation classifications in construction.

- ▶ For what construction operations are distinct workers' compensation classifications provided?

- ▶ How can an employer separately classify its distinct operations?

Why is it important to learn these topics?

Proper assignment of workers' compensation classifications ensures that insureds as well as premium auditors are treated equitably. This information provides a background to premium auditors to better understand the construction industry so that construction workers can be properly classified.

Examine the consequences of improper assignment of workers' compensation classifications.

- ▶ What is the potential outcome for the policyholder?

How can you use what you will learn?

Evaluate the types of contractors and subcontractors that would have been involved in constructing a grocery store.

- ▶ What specialized activities are involved in site preparation, setting the foundation, and building the superstructure?

- ▶ When are specialized contractors normally involved in these processes?

- ▶ How can these activities be properly classified by the premium auditor?

Workers' Compensation— Construction Operations

The nature of the construction industry, combined with the special rules for classifying construction or erection operations, makes construction firm premium audits far more complicated than most other premium audits. Although the classification procedure for workers' compensation generally strives to assign the one basic classification that best describes the insured's business for construction operations, the NCCI *Basic Manual for Workers Compensation and Employers Liability Insurance (Basic Manual)* stipulates that, "Each distinct type of construction or erection operation must be assigned to the class that specifically describes the operation only if separate payroll records are maintained for each operation."[1]

Assigning distinct operations to the proper construction classifications requires a detailed payroll records analysis. It also requires considerable familiarity with the construction industry's practices. In addition to explaining the special rules for classifying construction or erection operations, this chapter describes the residential and commercial construction process. Although identifying every classification and every state exception that may apply to the construction process is not possible, a general description should assist a premium auditor in recognizing the specific construction operation described by a particular classification. Premium auditors involved in auditing contractors can serve as the eyes and ears of the insurer, and may be a source of information for underwriting and claim decisions. It is helpful to understand the terminology of construction operations as well as industry practices.

In construction operations and in this chapter, the terms "contractor," "builder," and "developer" are used interchangeably.

CONSTRUCTION CLASSIFICATIONS

The *Basic Manual* includes approximately 80 classification code numbers and 140 classification phrases describing construction operations. The diverse nature of construction operations and the related hazards justify a multitude of classifications despite the resulting complications for premium auditors. Classifications group insureds with similar loss exposures so that each group pays its share of workers' compensation losses. To do otherwise would be unequitable for construction businesses that are not engaged in hazardous operations.

The general rule for classifying workers' compensation insurance is to rate the entire operation by the highest rated classification, but there is a significant exception for workers' compensation. The *Basic Manual* supports the need for separate rating of distinct operations. Rule IV.D.8. provides that, as long as the insured maintains separate payroll records for each operation, construction or erection operations can be separately classified and rated.

The wide variation in rates among construction operations can be illustrated by a review of advisory loss costs in Georgia. Advisory loss costs range from $7.99 per $100 of payroll for "Painting or Paperhanging NOC & Shop Operations, Drivers" (Code 5474) to $33.09 for "Iron or Steel: Erection: Construction of Dwellings Not Over Two Stories in Height" (Code 5069). In contrast, the advisory loss costs for clerical workers is $0.24 per $100 of payroll. Therefore, loss costs and rates for construction classifications not only tend to be much higher than rates for most businesses, but also they tend to vary widely by classification within the construction field.

Distinct Operations Classification

Construction projects involve many phases and require the services of several skilled building trades. Subcontractors specializing in certain construction types often complete separate project parts. Even when the general contractor hires and directly supervises workers, building codes and union contracts often require the members of a particular building trade to exclusively perform certain operations. As long as payroll records show which employees did the work and what their wages were, the premium auditor should assign each distinct operation to the classification that specifically describes it.

The usual physical separation by structural partitions requirement for nonconstruction operations does not apply to assigning additional basic classifications for construction operations. Executing different operations simultaneously on a construction project is common. Masons, electricians, carpenters, and plumbers often work on the same building at the same time. These workers perform distinct operations that the premium auditor should assign to separate classifications.

In fact, union jurisdictions and wage scales can provide clues to the proper classifications. A laborer engaged in pouring concrete, for example, may have a different pay rate from that of a laborer assisting in installing electrical wiring. Union jurisdictions, however, vary by locality, so premium auditors must not rely exclusively on union reports for proper classifications.

Separate Payroll Records

Premium auditors can separately classify distinct operations only if the insured maintains separate payroll records for each operation. Those records must show the actual time worked. Under no circumstances can a premium auditor allocate payroll to workers' compensation classifications on a percentage basis. The *Basic Manual* stipulates that "If separate payroll records are not maintained for any construction or erection operation, the highest rated classification that applies to the job or location where the operation is performed must be assigned."[2]

Assigning separate classifications requires the contractor's payroll records to show more detail than would be necessary in other businesses because the records must show the time worked on and payroll amounts for each distinct operation. Premium auditors should suggest suitable accounting procedures to the insured when appropriate and explain how adequate records may reduce the total premium charged.

Scope of Classifications

Although premium auditors should assign distinct construction operations to separate classifications, each classification can include incidental operations within its scope. Consequently, the *Basic Manual* rules state, "If a construction or erection operation is included in the scope of another classification, a separate code must not be assigned."[3] For example, concrete construction normally requires carpenters to build wooden forms for the concrete. Although essentially carpentry work, building forms is an integral part of concrete construction. The workers building the forms are exposed to the same hazards and subject to the same supervision as those pouring the concrete.

Such incidental operations can also involve frequent interchange of labor. The supervisor may switch workers among various incidental tasks as the need arises. Maintaining separate time and payroll records in such situations would be impractical. The rating bureau therefore designs classifications to include within their scope any incidental operations.

For example, a contractor building a house employs carpenters to erect the frame. Premium auditors should assign their payroll to "Carpentry: Detached One- or Two-Family Dwellings" (Code 5645). When it is time to install the finished floors in the house, the contractor may direct those same carpenters to lay the floor. In this case, laying the floor comes within the scope of the carpentry classification. The carpenters may work on the rough frame one day or the finished floor the next, as directed by the supervisor. All of this work is part of the project. Regardless of whether the employees lay floors part of the time, premium auditors should assign the entire payroll of the contractor's employees to the carpentry classification. Even if the general contractor had separate crews for the framing and finishing work, the premium auditor should assign both crews to the carpentry classification because all that work is within the scope of the carpentry activities that are contemplated when building the house. The premium auditors would still treat other noncarpentry activities as operations subject to separate classifications.

Subcontractors

Separately classifying distinct construction operations creates an additional complication with subcontractors. Any subcontractor with the workers' compensation obligation adequately insured qualifies for separate classification as a distinct operation under the subcontractor's own policy. Specifically, the *Basic Manual* says that a premium auditor should classify an insured subcontractor who performs one type of work on a construction project on the basis of the classification describing the particular work involved.[4] If the insured uses insured subcontractors, the premium auditor does not pick up any payroll for those subcontractors on the insured general contractor's policy.

The previous example assumes that a contractor hired an insured subcontractor who specializes in flooring to perform the flooring work. The insured subcontractor's employees specialize in laying floors and perform no other carpentry operations for the general contractor at that location. As previously noted, because the general contractor gave the premium auditor the general contractor's insurance policy with evidence that the subcontractor had workers' compensation insurance in force, the premium auditor would make no premium charge. However, because the classification pertains to the premium audit on the subcontractor's policy, premium auditors should separately classify the subcontractor's payroll as "Carpentry: Installation of Finished Wooden Flooring" (Code 5437). This illustrates the *Basic Manual* rule that directs the premium auditor to classify the insured subcontractor on the basis of the classification that describes the specific work involved. This is true even though the premium auditor would classify differently the same work performed by the general contractor's employees.

Classification differs if the subcontractor does not have insurance. In that case, the principal contractor may be held liable for any workers' compensation benefits for the subcontractor's employees just as if they were the principal contractor's employees. Because the principal contractor is responsible for the payment of benefits to employees of uninsured subcontractors, the *Basic Manual* provides that premium auditors should charge an additional premium on the policy that insures the contractor. The premium auditor should therefore assign the payroll of the subcontractor's employees to the same classification as if they were the principal contractor's employees.[5]

Division of Employee's Payroll

Some employees are involved in what is called interchange of labor—that is, they perform duties directly related to more than one classification shown on the policy. Separately classifying distinct construction operations raises this possibility with construction operations. If an employee does work related to two different classifications shown on the policy, the premium auditor can divide that employee's payroll between those two classifications, provided the entries on the insured's original records disclose an allocation of each individual employee's payroll. The records must show the time actually worked in each operation. However, if the work is like that previously described (one type of work is included within the scope of another), the premium auditor cannot divide the payroll. All payroll would go into the "project" classification.

Executive Supervisors

A classification that sometimes causes confusion is "Contractor—Executive Supervisor or Construction Superintendent" (Code 5606), which applies to supervisors or superintendents who have administrative or managerial responsibility for construction or erection projects and who exercise "operational control indirectly through full-time job supervisors or foremen of the employer."[6] The classification "does not apply to any person who is directly in charge of or who is performing any degree of actual construction work."[7] The supervision by an executive supervisor is a full-time job that requires work in the office as well as at the construction site. In fact, the classification contemplates all of those activities. Therefore, such an employee's payroll cannot be divided between two classifications. A premium auditor cannot place an individual who spends time directly supervising or actually performing any operation other than office or sales work in this executive supervisor classification. The premium auditor must place that individual in the classification describing the specific operation over which the person is exercising supervision, provided the insured maintains separate payroll records for each operation. Otherwise, the premium auditor must assign the supervisor to the highest rated classification applying to the job or location where the operation is performed.[8]

Common Laborers

Misunderstandings can also occur regarding common laborers. Insureds may assign common laborers to assist with various construction operations as needed at different project stages. If adequate records exist, the premium auditor should assign a laborer's payroll to the classifications describing the operations involved. If the records do not show the time devoted to each operation, the premium auditor should assign the laborer's payroll to the highest rated classification, not the governing classification. The exception is when common laborers qualify as miscellaneous employees according to Rule IV.E.1. For example, premium auditors can assign the payroll of yard workers engaged in cleanup activities to the governing classification because cleanup duties are common to all the operations at the construction site. Other miscellaneous employees include general superintendents, maintenance or power plant employees, shipping or receiving clerks, and elevator operators.

CONSTRUCTION INDUSTRY PROJECTS, PERSONNEL, AND PROCESS

To properly audit any account, a premium auditor must understand the nature of its operations. The same holds true for construction accounts. A premium auditor who is familiar with the operations common to a construction project is better qualified to determine that all expected operations can be accounted for, either by employees of the principal contractor or of subcontractors. Unfortunately, the varied nature of construction work makes understanding all types of construction difficult.

Construction Projects

"Building a building is like setting up a temporary company," according to an executive of one of the nation's largest construction firms. For a large office building, "you're managing about $100 million in resources. There may be 700 men working at the peak. You have to set up a staff that is probably going to be together for three years. That team is going to operate as a pretty independent entity and go through a lot together."[9]

Each construction project is an independent undertaking, with workers assembling the materials and building the structure at a particular site. Consequently, a premium auditor is likely to find extreme fluctuations in the volume of a contractor's business as the contractor completes some projects and begins others. The payroll will rise and fall accordingly. Moreover, the inability to work at certain times because of weather conditions or other complications further contributes to the irregular pattern of construction payrolls.

Construction projects are also likely to involve many separate entities. Even small firms can manage large-scale projects because they can subcontract portions of the work. It is not unusual for a general contractor with only a few employees to build an entire housing development by bringing in subcontractors. Using subcontractors requires considerable effort in scheduling and coordinating the subcontractors' work. It also presents the premium auditor with the considerable challenge of untangling the employment relationships involved.

Construction Personnel

Construction workers may be skilled or unskilled. Construction workers include many skilled craftspeople who learned their crafts only after long training periods. For each construction project, the contractor must recruit workers with the needed skills. Whereas long-term employment with the same employer may be normal in other industries, construction workers often move among employers. Many relocate when jobs are scarce in an area because of bad weather or economic downturns. Recruiting personnel can be a constant problem for a contractor as well as for employee-leasing firms.

One way to address the problem of recruiting personnel is to negotiate union contracts. The union and the employer usually specify in such contracts the procedures for recruiting workers. The union sponsors a hiring hall, or a pool of skilled construction workers. The contractor notifies the union of the number of workers needed, and the union refers workers to the contractor. The wages and working conditions conform to those stipulated in the existing collective bargaining agreement.

Not all contractors employ union labor, and the percentage of those who do varies considerably by locality. Small firms may be able to count on the services of a few friends, relatives, or others with strong attachments for a skilled labor supply that the firm must occasionally supplement with casual workers. Those firms may pay lower wages than the union scale, but the 1931 **Davis-Bacon Act** prohibits the federal government from funding any construction project on which wages are below the prevailing wage for the area. Familiarity with union procedures and other personnel practices can help a premium auditor evaluate the payroll records and properly determine the payroll.

Davis-Bacon Act
A 1931 federal act that prohibits the federal government from funding any construction project on which wages are below the prevailing wage for the area.

Most construction workers' unions are affiliated with the American Federation of Labor–Congress of Industrial Organizations (AFL–CIO). The AFL–CIO Building and Construction Trades Department includes member unions, such as iron workers, boilermakers, carpenters, and granite cutters. Each of those national and international unions includes many local unions that refer members to those contractors who have entered collective bargaining agreements. Being familiar with the local unions and the scope of their duties can help premium auditors in evaluating the work being done on a construction site.

Because of the variety of skills involved, construction workers must be able to work independently while cooperating with other workers. The **general contractor** is the person or organization responsible for work quality and the timely completion of a construction project. Therefore, the contractor often establishes a temporary office at the construction site to supervise the entire project.

General contractor
The person or organization responsible for work quality and the timely completion of a construction project.

The contractor exercises that supervision through a definite hierarchy. On top is the general contractor, who may appoint separate project managers if the firm is large enough to execute several projects simultaneously. A **project manager** is the individual who manages the resources of a construction project to complete the task.

Project manager
The individual who manages the resources of a construction project to complete the task.

Next in the hierarchy is the **project superintendent**, the individual who organizes the subcontractors' work as well as the general contractor's employees to accomplish the goals of the construction project. Each operation may include supervisors, forepersons, and assistants. Under them are the skilled laborers, and at the bottom are apprentices who assist and learn from the skilled laborers.

Project superintendent
The individual who organizes the subcontractors' work as well as the general contractor's employees to accomplish the goals of the construction project.

General Construction Process

Unlike manufacturing, the nature of construction operations is not always immediately apparent. Visiting construction sites presents an opportunity to observe firsthand the construction process, including what operations the insured performs as well as what machinery the insured uses and for what purpose. An occasional field visit with an engineer-inspector can also increase the premium auditor's knowledge. When calling on a contracting firm, the premium auditor may spend time in a waiting area in which engineering or construction publications are available. Those technical publications can help the premium auditor learn about new machinery and new techniques that contractors use in the construction field.

To understand the nature of construction operations, premium auditors must understand the construction process. The premium auditor should not be reluctant to ask questions when confronted with unfamiliar terms or conditions. Obtaining an explanation of a term will help avoid mistakes that could result in misclassifying the payroll involved. Regardless of the type of structure, the construction process is essentially the same. That process includes the following seven distinct stages:

1. Preparing the site
2. Setting the foundation
3. Building the superstructure
4. Installing utilities
5. Enclosing the superstructure
6. Finishing the surfaces
7. Landscaping the site

Although differences exist between residential and commercial construction, both use the same process. The remainder of this chapter explains both residential and commercial construction stages to help premium auditors identify specific operations and correctly classify them according to the manual rules that apply. Notice, however, that this text does not completely define classifications or state exceptions, which a premium auditor must always obtain from the *Basic Manual*.

RESIDENTIAL CONSTRUCTION PROCESS

Although both residential construction and commercial construction involve the same process, most residential construction is generally on a smaller scale. A general contractor with only three or four employees may build a private development with between 50 and 100 homes by subcontracting much of the work to specialty contractors. The premium auditor's primary concern in such a situation may be to identify all the subcontractors involved, determine whether an employment relationship is present, and review the certificates of insurance, if necessary. A proper premium audit may require investigating possible employer-employee relationships. If a specialty contractor depends on one general contractor for a substantial share of overall income, an employer-employee relationship may technically exist based on the relative nature of the work test. Premium auditors should therefore analyze the contractor's activities from the beginning of the process to the end—not only to classify the operations properly, but also to ensure that they have included all operations.

Preparing the Site

Any construction project begins with preparing the site. The preparation includes clearing the land, locating the structures, and moving the earth as needed to build on the site. For building single-family houses, the contractor can perform most of those operations with bulldozers and dump trucks. A larger scale project or an unusual site may require heavier, more specialized equipment, as well. Exhibit 5-1 illustrates many of the types of construction equipment that a premium auditor may encounter.

EXHIBIT 5-1

Examples of Construction Equipment

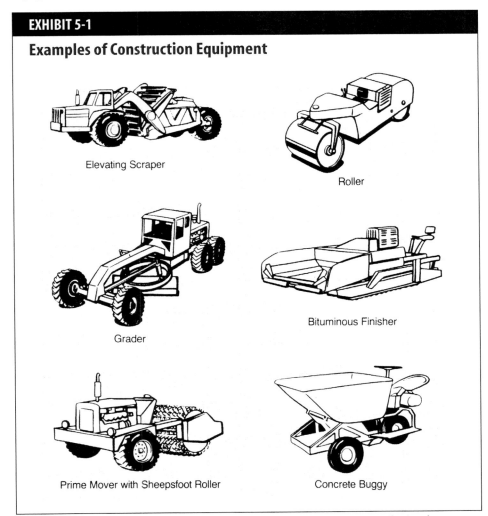

Elevating Scraper

Roller

Grader

Bituminous Finisher

Prime Mover with Sheepsfoot Roller

Concrete Buggy

Continued on next page

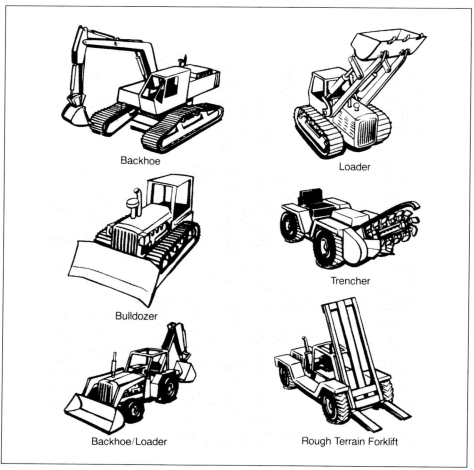

Backhoe

Loader

Bulldozer

Trencher

Backhoe/Loader

Rough Terrain Forklift

Reprinted with permission of Associated Equipment Dealers.

Clearing the Site

The contractor must remove all major obstacles from the site before any other work can begin. Clearing operations may include demolishing old structures, breaking up large rocks and boulders, cutting trees, burning underbrush, and scraping away rocks and remaining vegetation. Unless the obstacles are exceptional, bulldozers such as the one in Exhibit 5-1 can remove the brush and small trees and perform the general site clearing. In that case, the clearing operations come within the scope of the "Excavation & Drivers" (Code 6217) classification. If blasting or specialized heavy equipment is necessary to clear the site, the premium auditor must separately classify those operations.

In other situations, the developer tries to preserve as many trees as possible. In that case, the first operation consists of laying out, clearing, and grading roads to provide access to each lot. Premium auditors should assign such excavating, grading, and paving for roads to the appropriate street or road construction classification even though the individual lot grading belongs to the classification "Grading of Land NOC & Drivers" (also Code 6217).

Grading the site often includes stripping the topsoil from the intended foundation area. The contractor keeps the topsoil and, after completing the foundation backfilling, spreads the topsoil over the backfilled area. Premium auditors must be able to distinguish between grading and excavation loss exposures even though the workers' compensation classification code is the same for both (Code 6217). Generally, grading involves work on the ground level, and excavation involves work below ground level. The two loss exposures are different, and premium auditors separately classify and rate them on general liability policies.

Marking the Foundation

Once the contractor has cleared the site, the next step is to mark the exact foundation corners according to the plans or blueprints for the structure. The general contractor, a specialty foundation contractor, an excavation contractor, a general carpentry contractor, or an engineering or architectural firm may mark the foundation. The appropriate classification follows according to which parties do the work because those parties usually mark the foundation in conjunction with other duties found within one of those classifications.

Completing the Excavation

If the dwelling will not have a basement, any necessary excavation can be done by backhoe equipment or sometimes by hand. However, if the dwelling will have a basement, a bulldozer usually does the excavation. The builder should then dig trenches for footings or piers to a predetermined depth either by hand or with backhoe equipment. The required depth depends on soil conditions and climate because the excavation's bottom must be deeper than the local frost line. Those operations usually come within the excavation classification.

Occasionally, contractors need explosives or air hammers to remove rock formations. The premium auditor should ascertain whether blasting permits are necessary or whether the contractor uses compressors. In either case, manual rules deem this rock excavation. In some areas, because of rock, low elevation, or other reasons, contractors place footings on the surface and bring in earth and backfill around the footings and basement walls. If the operation is by that method and the contractor does not excavate, the premium auditor would assign the filling to the grading classification.

Contractors transfer spoil—the dirt and gravel removed from an excavation—in dump trucks. The contractor may store the spoil for possible reuse on the site or at other nearby sites. If the contractor does not need the spoil, dump trucks haul it away and dispose of it elsewhere.

Setting the Foundation

All structures include both a substructure, which supports the building's weight, and a superstructure, which rests on top. The substructure or foundation

Foundation
All of a building below the first floor level, including the masonry substructure that extends below ground level.

rests on some part of the earth and spreads the superstructure's weight over that bearing surface so that it does not sink. A **foundation** is all of a building below the first floor level, including the masonry substructure that extends below ground level. Part of the foundation is often visible above the ground.

Foundation Footings

A foundation must have sufficient ground-bearing area to support a structure's weight without settling. The footing's function is to spread the weight over the bearing surface. Footings are made of concrete poured to a depth and width sufficient to support the structural design load. The proper footing type depends on soil conditions and climate.

If the dwelling is in an area in which the ground freezes, the footings' bottom must be deeper than the local frost line. Otherwise, water may freeze underneath the concrete, causing upheaval and cracking and great damage to the house. Contractors can dig trenches or spaces for footings by hand or with backhoe equipment. The contractor then places a wood or metal form in the desired position, pours concrete into the form, and levels the concrete. Exhibit 5-2 shows examples of footings designed to support freestanding piers.

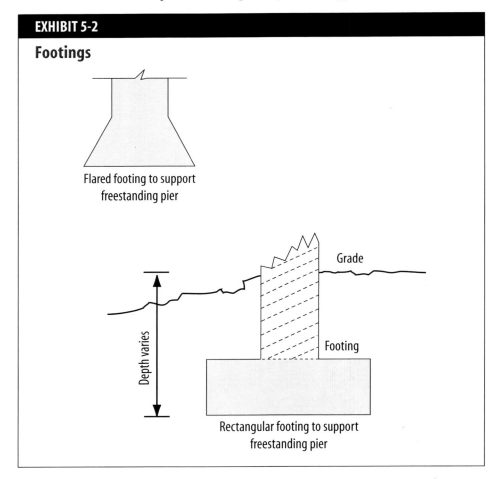

EXHIBIT 5-2

Footings

Flared footing to support freestanding pier

Grade

Depth varies

Footing

Rectangular footing to support freestanding pier

Premium auditors should classify excavating footing trenches as excavation work. The private residence concrete class "Concrete: Work—Incidental to the Construction of Private Residence" (Code 5215) applies to all concrete work if one contractor erects footings, walls, floors, and driveways. That classification also includes concrete work incidental to private garages constructed in connection with a private residence. If a subcontractor does only the sidewalks, floors, or driveways (including grading by hand or with light power equipment), the proper classification on the subcontractor's policy would be "Concrete or Cement: Work—Floors, Driveways, Yards or Sidewalks & Drivers" (Code 5221). Premium auditors cannot use the "Concrete: Work—Incidental to the Construction of Private Residence" (Code 5215) at the same job or location where Code 5221 applies. State exceptions do exist.

If the soil at the footing level cannot bear the weight of a home or if the contractor cannot find such soils at a depth that can be economically reached by lowering the level of the walls and footings, the contractor must use piles. A pile-driving rig places piles into the ground to a considerable depth. Using piles to support private residences constructed on wet, swampy land such as low-lying coastal areas is necessary if the structure's walls are to remain completely vertical. In such areas, using piles to support all types of dwelling foundations is common.

Foundation Types

Contractors commonly use three foundation types: the continuous wall, the pier, and the slab.

If the dwelling will have a basement, it must have a continuous wall foundation. Basements are not common in all geographic areas. They are found mostly in areas where the frost line is three or four feet below ground level (that is, as much as the top three or four feet of the ground freeze during winter). Because the foundations must be below frost line, the added excavation for a basement costs comparatively little. In warmer climates, however, in which the frost line is less than one foot below ground level, basements are less common because of the additional excavation cost required. Whether or not a house has a basement, the contractor may use a continuous wall foundation. As the name implies, a **continuous wall foundation** is a masonry wall resting on footings that run all the way around the perimeter of a house. Contractors may make continuous wall foundations of cement block, natural stone, or solid concrete. If the wall foundation does not enclose a basement, it should still provide a crawl space under the house.

Continuous wall foundation
A masonry wall resting on footings that run all the way around the perimeter of a house.

Premium auditors should classify constructing a foundation wall from cement block or natural stone as "Masonry NOC" (Code 5022). The "Concrete: Construction—Private Residences—Not Monolithic" (Code 5215) classification includes constructing a foundation wall from poured reinforced concrete.

A **pier foundation** is a series of posts that support the weight of a structure's superstructure. Piers are usually made of masonry, often concrete poured

Pier foundation
A series of posts that support the weight of a structure's superstructure.

into wooden forms. Piers, like continuous wall foundations, must have footings at their base. The size and spacing of the piers and footings required vary in accordance with design load. The piers' height above the footings varies according to soil conditions. Piers are usually between eighteen and thirty inches high to provide a crawl space under the house. Constructing poured-concrete piers also comes within the residential concrete classification.

Slab foundation
A poured concrete slab resting partly on compacted fill and partly on a foundation wall or beam extending into undisturbed soil.

The concrete slab is suitable for dwellings in areas where the ground does not freeze or freezes only a few inches below ground level. A **slab foundation** is a poured concrete slab resting partly on compacted fill and partly on a foundation wall or beam extending into undisturbed soil. The slab serves also as the house's first floor, frequently with ductwork, heating coils, and other piping imbedded in it when the contractor lays the slab. In preparing the site for a slab foundation, the contractor removes all vegetation and topsoil and then excavates the area to proper depth with mechanical equipment or by hand. The excavation depth varies depending on soil conditions and slab type. The contractor fills the excavation with clean sand, gravel, or clay and then compacts it. To control moisture, the contractor installs a plastic membrane, or vapor barrier, before pouring the concrete.

Beams and moderately compacted soil support the structural slab at its edges and through the center, as shown in Exhibit 5-3. Beams extend down into undisturbed soil. The structural slab supports heavy masonry structures.

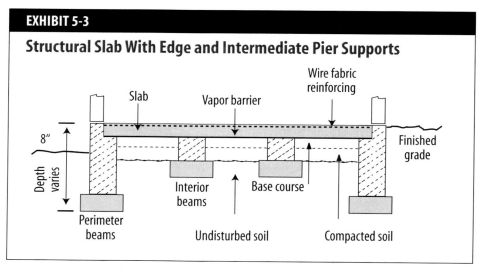

EXHIBIT 5-3

Structural Slab With Edge and Intermediate Pier Supports

Removing vegetation and topsoil and excavating to the proper depth for a slab foundation come within the excavation classification. Premium auditors should classify compacting the sand or gravel, adding base course material when required, building forms, and pouring and leveling cement for a slab foundation all as concrete work.

Foundation Walls

Exhibit 5-4 illustrates various types of foundation walls. If a dwelling has a basement or is on a hillside, the foundation walls may be as high as five or six feet above the footings, as in the illustration. Local building codes, of course, usually govern the foundation types permitted and their specifications. The illustration also portrays the various methods and materials builders use to construct foundation walls. Although the facing side illustrates a wood form used in connection with constructing a poured reinforced-concrete foundation wall, sometimes builders use metal forms for that purpose. Building wooden forms is incidental concrete construction and, consequently, is included in the concrete construction classification.

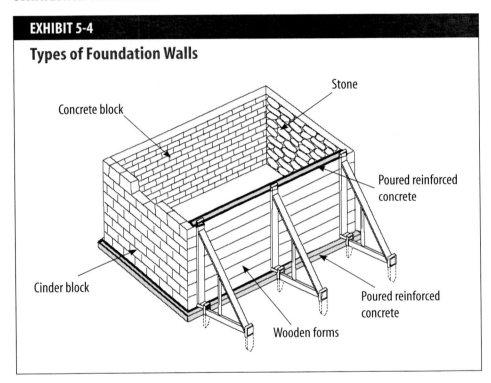

EXHIBIT 5-4

Types of Foundation Walls

Stone

Concrete block

Poured reinforced concrete

Cinder block

Poured reinforced concrete

Wooden forms

The "Masonry NOC" (Code 5022) classification covers constructing foundation walls from cinder block, concrete block, brick, preformed slab I-beam construction, or natural stone, as well as stucco finishing of foundation walls. Constructing poured reinforced concrete foundation walls comes within the concrete work classification.

Foundation Forms

Home foundation construction also depends on forms that serve as molds for poured concrete. Constructing forms is a special carpentry skill that calls for considerable experience. The foundation of an average small house requires twenty to thirty yards of concrete, weighing from forty to sixty tons. To hold that weight without shifting, forms must be well built. Prefabricated wood, aluminum, and steel forms are increasingly common because of the ease with which a contractor can set them up and take them down. Exhibit 5-5 shows constructing a wood form for a foundation wall. For all the various foundation construction types described, premium auditors must assign the payroll developed from constructing, setting up, or taking down forms to the appropriate concrete classification (Concrete: Work—Incidental to the Construction of Private Residence [Code 5215]).

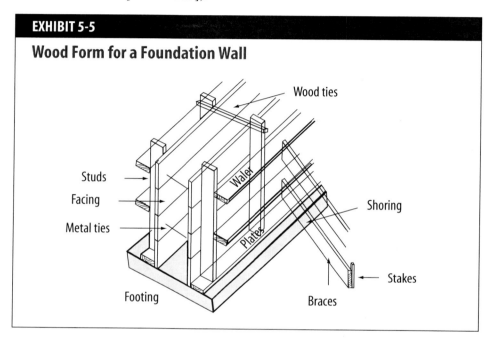

EXHIBIT 5-5

Wood Form for a Foundation Wall

Foundation Waterproofing

Premium auditors do not separately rate waterproofing done by the foundation contractor. Premium auditors assign waterproofing to the appropriate foundation construction code. When a specialty contractor does the waterproofing, however, the premium auditor should assign the operation to the appropriate classification according to the application method. The *Basic Manual* has separate classifications for each of the following methods:

- Application by brush or hand-pressured caulking gun (5474—"Painting or Paperhanging NOC & Shop Operations, Drivers")

- Application by trowel—Interior (5480—"Plastering NOC & Drivers")

- Application by trowel—Exterior (5022—"Masonry NOC")

- Application by spray gun, cement gun, concrete gun, or other pressure apparatus (5213—"Guniting—Not Chimneys—All Operations," except as provided below)

- Application to exterior walls of foundations or subterranean structures by apparatus inserted into the ground (9014—"Waterproofing—Subterranean Work Only—Application of Waterproofing Material by Means of Apparatus Inserted in the Ground")

Premium auditors should separately classify excavation incidental to water-proofing operations as excavation (Code 6217). Therefore, only one of the methods actually carries the waterproofing classification wording.

Girder Erection

The foundation also includes supports, called girders. **Girders** are the horizontal foundation supports for a structure's upper floors. Girders can be made of wood or steel. They are usually supported by the exterior concrete or masonry wall and by interior iron columns filled with concrete (called Lally columns). When the residence does not exceed two stories in height, premium auditors should classify erecting steel girders and Lally columns as "Iron or Steel: Erection: Construction of Dwellings Not Over Two Stories in Height" (Code 5069). When a contractor performs that type of iron work on a private residence exceeding two stories in height, the appropriate classification should be "Iron or Steel: Erection: NOC" (Code 5057). If a contractor builds a large private residence exceeding two stories in height with steel framing, the appropriate classification should be "Iron or Steel: Erection: Frame Structures" (Code 5040).

When contractors use wood girders, carpenters install the Lally columns. For practical purposes and because of the small amount of labor involved, premium auditors should assign that work to the appropriate carpentry classification.

Girder
The horizontal foundation supports for a structure's upper floors.

Backfilling

Backfilling is the process of putting earth back against the foundation after the foundation is completed. First, the foundation wall should be completely cured (properly dried), which can require two to four weeks for poured concrete. The contractor can then scoop earth into the space around the foundation a little at a time. The contractor must backfill carefully because a large rock or sudden jolt may cause a crack in the foundation. Backfilling comes within the scope of the grading classification.

Backfilling
The process of putting earth back against the foundation after the foundation is completed.

Building the Frame

Once the contractor completes the foundation, the next step is to erect the house's frame. The frame members are columns or posts with beams connecting one to another. When they are properly assembled, those members provide a rigid skeleton to support the house's walls, floors, and roof. Frameworks are made from steel, reinforced concrete, or wood, but builders almost always use wood for framing houses because working with wood is easier and less expensive. Therefore, carpenters do most of the work.

Generally, the frames for houses have three major parts: floor framing, wall framing, and roof framing. Most floor framing is done with joists. **Joists** are the horizontal members of floor framing to which the planks of the floor are nailed. Most wall framing uses studs. **Studs** are the vertical members of wall framing. Most houses have sloped roofs. Therefore, they use **rafters**, which are the sloping supports of a roofing frame.

Joists
The horizontal members of floor framing to which the planks of the floor are nailed.

Studs
The vertical members of wall framing.

Rafters
The sloping supports of a roofing frame.

Exhibit 5-6 illustrates the frame for a sloped roof.

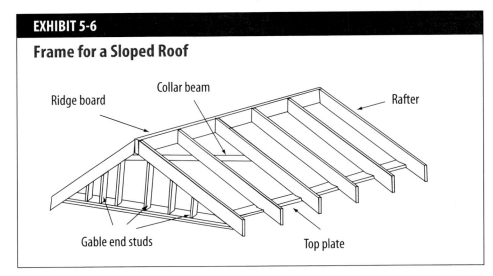

EXHIBIT 5-6

Frame for a Sloped Roof

Ridge board

Collar beam

Rafter

Gable end studs

Top plate

The major steps in erecting wood frames at the building site are the following:

- Laying out and marking the locations and positions of the framing members according to the blueprint
- Marking the lengths of lumber
- Sawing the lumber
- Assembling the parts
- Leveling and plumbing the frame

When all carpentry work in connection with constructing a dwelling is performed by the same carpentry contractor, premium auditors should assign it to the appropriate carpentry classification, depending on whether the building is a detached private residence for one or two families or a multifamily dwelling not over three stories high. Those classifications are "Carpentry: Detached One- and Two-Family Dwellings" (Code 5645) and "Carpentry: Dwellings—Three Stories or Less" (Code 5651). That work may include constructing and erecting the sill, rough framework, rough floor, studs, joists, rafters, roof deck, roof shingles (including incidental flashing), sidewall sheathing, siding (except metal), doors, wallboard installation, windows, stairs, finished floor, cabinet installation, and all interior wood trim. If an insured specialty contractor does the roofing or installs cabinets, wallboard, finished flooring, or any other interior trim, that work can be separately classified in most states. Premium auditors should consider the work that carpentry contractors perform while installing metal railings on wooden porches, patios, or stairs as incidental to carpentry operations and assign those operations accordingly to the appropriate carpentry classification.

Installing Utilities

After the frame of a structure is complete, but before the contractor can finish the interior, workers from the appropriate building trades install the necessary utilities. Because of the skills involved, building code requirements, licensing procedures, and sometimes union jurisdictions, subcontractors generally perform most of that work. The installation order depends on the size and flexibility of the parts that the subcontractors must place between the walls. The heating and air conditioning system normally is installed first, followed by the plumbing and electrical wiring.

Heating and Air Conditioning

Installing heating and air conditioning systems generally requires the services of one or more specialty contractors. The appropriate classification depends on the system type and the nature of the installation work required.

Forced-air systems allow central air conditioning to be combined with heating. Central units generate cool air in the summer and hot air in the winter, and air ducts convey the cooled or heated air to all the rooms of the house. Such a system therefore involves essentially two installation operations. The first one is fabricating and installing the necessary ductwork between the walls. A premium auditor should classify that operation as "Heating and Air-Conditioning Ductwork—Shop and Outside & Drivers" (Code 5536), provided that no operations occur at the job site for which "Sheet Metal Work" (Code 5538) would apply. If the insured conducts any other sheet metal work at the same job, the premium auditor should assign all payroll to "Sheet Metal Work" (Code 5538).

The other step required to complete the system is installing the central heating unit and cooling unit if plans call for one. Those units can be either gas or electric. Premium auditors should classify the contractor who installs the sheet metal-type hot air unit as "Sheet Metal Work: Shop and Outside NOC & Drivers" (Code 5538). The premium auditor should classify the contractor who installs the air conditioning compressor as "Air-Conditioning Systems: Non-Portable: Machinery Installation or Repair of Compressors, Motors or Other Machinery & Drivers" (Code 3724). Premium auditors can separately classify incidental plumbing (Code 5183) and incidental electrical wiring (Code 5190) if the insured maintains properly segregated payroll records. A concrete classification may be appropriate if a concrete slab is necessary for the unit.

Hot water or steam heat systems use radiators in each room and connecting pipes carrying hot water to spread heat throughout the house. Boilers heat the water in the pipes using coal, oil, or gas as fuel for the burner. Plumbers generally install the pipes, radiators, and boilers. Premium auditors classify those operations as "Plumbing NOC & Drivers" (Code 5183).

Using electric heat may be preferable in some situations. Although electric heat pumps are installed in the same fashion as other forced-air systems, electricians usually perform all the assembly, installation, and wiring work. Premium auditors can classify those operations as "Electrical Wiring—Within Buildings & Drivers" (Code 5190).

If cooling the entire house is not practical, builders may place individual room air conditioning units in the windows of selected rooms. Premium auditors should classify the installation work as "Air Conditioning Systems: Portable Units—Installation, Service or Repair & Drivers" (Code 9519).

Plumbing

A house requires two completely separate plumbing systems, one for fresh water and the other for sewage. Pipes can be copper, steel, lead, cast iron, or plastic. Plumbers cut the pipes to fit the design specifications, including the necessary joints and fittings. In addition to doing considerable pipe cutting, threading, and fitting, plumbers install bathroom fixtures and kitchen sinks and make connections to the water and sewer mains.

The "Plumbing NOC & Drivers" (Code 5183) classification encompasses all piping inside the building as well as all connections to sewers, water mains, septic tanks, and cesspools. This classification includes ditching from the house to the mains or property lines if done by the plumbing contractor. If a specialty contractor does ditching, the premium auditor can separately classify it as "Sewer: Construction—All Operations & Drivers" (Code 6306), "Gas: Main or Connection Construction & Drivers" (Code 6319), "Water Main or Connection Construction & Drivers" (Code 6319), or "Well Drilling—Water & Drivers" (Code 6204).

Electrical Wiring

Electricians usually install the electrical wiring after the heating ducts and plumbing because the wiring is the most flexible of those. The electricians string the insulated conduits—usually either Romex or BX cables—through the floors, walls, and attics throughout the house. In addition to wiring lights and electrical outlets, the electrician must wire the major electrical appliances in the house, such as the range, furnace, water heater, clothes dryer, garbage disposal, dishwasher, fans, and air conditioners.

Because of strict electrical code requirements, general contractors usually subcontract such work to an electrical contractor. However, for classification purposes, it does not matter whether a specialist contractor or the employees of the general contractor perform the work. The classification "Electrical Wiring—Within Buildings & Drivers" (Code 5190) includes all inside wiring and incidental electrical fixtures and installation or repair of appliances. Incidental wiring of outside lights at low elevations or lantern posts should also come within that classification.

Enclosing the House

Having completed the framework, the contractor generally encloses the frame as quickly as possible to protect it from the weather. Enclosing the frame also makes it possible to work on the interior when weather conditions do not permit outside work. The enclosure includes the roof, the exterior walls, and the floor. Those components protect the structure from the weather even though the contractor must add many more features to the interior. The contractor can enclose the frame on the interior, however, only after roughing in the utilities.

Roofing

The contractor generally puts the roof on to cover the structure before starting the walls or floors. After framing the roof and covering it with shiplap (wooden sheathing), square cut boards, or plywood sheets, the builder can install roofing material on that roof structure.

Roofing materials commonly used on one- and two-family dwellings include asphalt shingles, wood shingles, asbestos cement shingles, tile, slate, sheet metal, and aluminum. Asphalt roll material is available but is seldom used on small houses.

In most areas, roofing is commonly included with the general carpentry contract, especially if the roofing material is wood shingles. If the roofing material is slate, tile, or sheet metal, a roofing specialist is more likely to do the roofing.

Premium auditors should assign specialist contractors in all roofing types, including work on either flat or sloped roofs, metal, shingle, slate, tile, or other roofing types such as new roof installation or repair to "Roofing: All Kinds & Yard Employees, Drivers" (Code 5551) on the roofing contractor's policy. The only exception is when carpentry contractors engaged in constructing an entire house also construct the roof. In such instances, the appropriate carpentry classification applies to all house construction work, including roofing. Roofing activities are integral to the overall dwelling construction when performed by the contractor's own employees. In that case, roofing comes within the scope of carpentry operations at that site, and the premium auditor cannot assign a separate classification.

For commercial buildings, contractors use the **built-up roof**, a roof composed of three to five alternate layers of tar and gravel (asphalt). A detached private dwelling is not likely to have such a roof, but a builder may use it on a two- or three-story multi-family building. Such a roof contains alternate courses of impregnated felt, lapped and cemented together with either asphalt or coaltar pitch coatings applied hot to the roof deck. The deck could be wood, steel, or pre-cast gypsum or concrete slabs. The contractor usually surfaces the roof with a slag or gravel coating. Premium auditors should separately classify a specialty roofing contractor installing pre-cast slabs for roof decks.

Built-up roof
A roof composed of three to five alternate layers of tar and gravel (asphalt).

Builders construct chimneys and fireplaces with brick, cinder block, natural stone, or concrete block. Premium auditors should classify chimney construction, including ornamental work around fireplaces, as masonry. Fireplaces usually have a fire brick lining and dampers inserted by masons. Instead of fire brick, using a metal form that contains vents for more efficient heating is possible. Masons set that form in place. The masonry classification therefore covers constructing either type of fireplace. That classification is "Masonry NOC" (Code 5022).

Some residential building codes require brick and mortar fire stops under the roof between wall studs to prevent fire from spreading up through the hollow space inside the walls. Masons normally install fire stops. **Flashings** are material strips sealing the joints where the roof meets vertical surfaces such as chimneys, parapet walls, and skylights. Masons can install flashings while constructing chimney or parapet walls. Premium auditors should assign roof flashing work performed by a roofing or carpentry contractor to the appropriate roofing or carpentry classification to which it is incidental.

Metal gutters and downspouts are necessary for roof drainage. When a specialty contractor installs gutters and incidental flashing, the sheet metal work erection classification applies. If a roofing contractor or carpentry contractor installs metal gutters and downspouts, the insured general contractor must maintain separate time and payroll records. Otherwise, the appropriate roofing or carpentry code applies.

Exterior Walls

The frame supporting the house's weight is covered by a curtain (non-load-bearing) wall erected around it. That method of building houses is generally far more economical than using load-bearing walls to support the house's weight. Because it does not support the house, the contractors can construct the curtain wall from materials selected for their appearance and cost. Constructing exterior walls may involve many different crafts depending on the materials involved. Materials for covering walls are generally one of three types: masonry; siding; or other materials applied directly to the wall, such as poured concrete or stucco.

Masonry is a building material that includes brick, concrete block, clay tile, stone, and glass block. Masons carefully lay out the walls to ensure that they are straight and that they intersect properly. Then they lay the brick, block, or stone one layer at a time, placing mortar in the joints to hold the wall materials together. Bricklayers or stone masons usually place the materials in the wall while mason tenders or helpers mix the mortar and keep the mason supplied with materials. The masonry classification covers constructing exterior walls from any masonry materials. Metal railings installed by masonry contractors while building brick or concrete block porches, patios, or stairs are considered incidental to masonry operations, and premium auditors assign them accordingly to the masonry classification.

Flashings
The material strips sealing the joints where the roof meets vertical surfaces such as chimneys, parapet walls, and skylights.

Masonry
A building material that includes brick, concrete block, clay tile, stone, and glass block.

Wooden frame houses can also be enclosed with wood, metal, or vinyl siding. The three layers are usually sheathing, a vapor barrier, and siding. Sheathing can be wood boards, plywood, or gypsum or insulating board panels. Builders nail sheathing directly on the framework to provide a base for the finished siding. Builders put the windows, doors, and attic louvers in place after they complete the sheathing. The vapor barrier can be roofing felt, aluminum foil, or polyethylene film installed to prevent the passage of water vapor through the wall. The siding then forms the final layer, as illustrated in Exhibit 5-7. Siding materials include many wood products and other specially manufactured materials.

EXHIBIT 5-7

Exterior Siding Installation

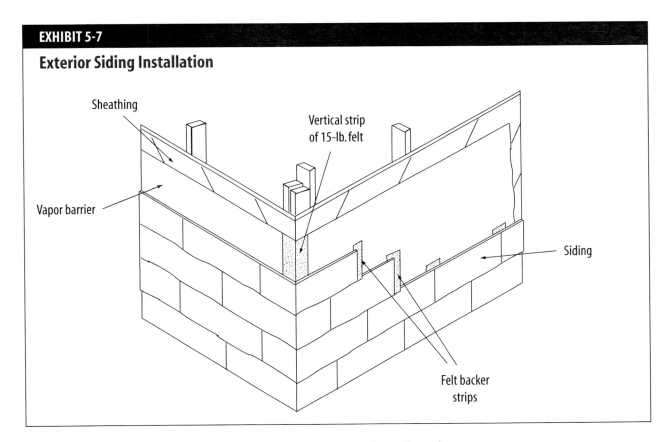

Builders can use exterior grade lumber, plywood, or pressed wood products as shingles to cover the sides of a house. Lapped board lumber can also serve as siding. In either case, the builder nails the wood siding material directly into the wall in an overlapping arrangement to shed water. Carpenters usually place wood siding on the house, and premium auditors should assign such work to the appropriate carpentry classification.

Builders use vinyl, aluminum, and steel siding on many houses. They also use manufactured siding materials with stone or similar facings. Although the manufactured siding materials resemble masonry walls, they must be assembled like siding. The specific assembly procedures depend on a manufacturer's instructions. When a specialty contractor installs metal or vinyl siding on a house, the premium auditor should classify the operation as carpentry because carpentry classifications include siding installation.

Builders may mix stucco or similar materials at the construction site and apply them over the frame. When dry, these materials form a solid, waterproof wall. Premium auditors classify stucco work or plastering on building exteriors as masonry (Code 5022).

Floors

Floors are actually at least two layers: the subfloor and the finished floor. The subfloor is a rough wooden floor joined to the frame. The carpenters who build the frame also usually install the subfloor to support all the subsequent interior work. The builder may install the finished floor later as part of finishing the interior. That sequence prevents damage to the finished floor from the remaining construction work inside the house. The appropriate carpentry classification applies.

Finishing the Interior

The builder must carefully enclose the surfaces that will show on the inside so that errors do not detract from the house's appearance. Several trades may be involved in those finishing operations. The necessary steps include placing insulation in the walls and attic, finishing the interior walls, adding the interior trim, and installing the desired flooring.

Insulation

Insulation comes in many forms and types. Two types of insulation are blanket and loose fill insulation, which are installed between the attic and floor joists. Builders often use batts (blanket thermal insulation) to insulate framed walls. Often the carpenters building the house add the insulation. The "Insulation: Work NOC & Drivers" (Code 5479) classification applies only to insulation work performed as a separate operation, not part of any other construction operation performed by the same contractor at the same job or location.

Interior Walls

In wood frame buildings, the builder usually erects the framework for the inner partitions along with that for the exterior walls. The builder then fastens the wall material to the studs to enclose the wall. The wall materials most often used in houses are plaster and wallboard or paneling, although a builder may use tile for bathroom or kitchen walls. Depending on the material used, wall construction may involve carpenters, plasterers, masons, tile setters, or painters.

Plaster over lath was once the most commonly used inside wall and ceiling finish. Constructing plaster walls requires considerable time because the builder must first erect the lath, which serves as a base for the plaster, and the builder must also allow the plaster to dry between coats.

Builders usually apply plaster not to the wall itself, but to a lath framework to which it can adhere. **Lath framework** is a lattice of narrow strips of wood or corrugated metal strips for the purpose of supporting tiles and plastering. The builder generally secures the lath framework by nailing it to the studs, which must be strong enough to support three plaster layers, often as much as $^3/_4$ to $^7/_8$ inches thick in total.

Builders use several types of lath, each adapted to a particular kind of wall. Most types have perforations or openings. As the wet plaster oozes through those openings and mushrooms out behind them, it forms "plaster rivets," which, when dry and hard, secure the plaster to the lath. Exhibit 5-8 shows three types of lath: plaster board, metal wire mesh, and wood lath. All three are nailed onto the wall studs. The plaster board comes in panels ranging in size from 16 inches by 32 inches to 24 inches by 64 inches and is about $^3/_8$ inch thick. The wire lath generally comes in 2-foot by 8-foot panels. The wood laths are rough wood strips about $^1/_3$ inch thick by 1$^5/_8$ inches wide and up to 4 feet long. Builders apply laths horizontally, leaving joints open over the studs' centers.

Lath framework
A lattice of narrow strips of wood or corrugated metal strips for the purpose of supporting tiles and plastering.

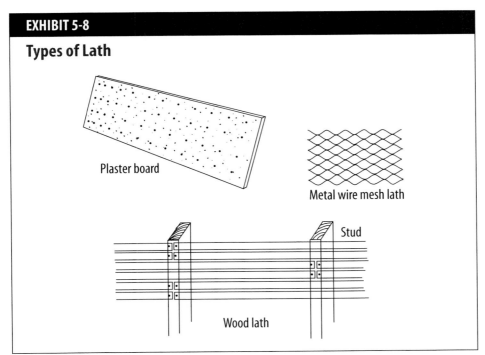

EXHIBIT 5-8

Types of Lath

Plaster board

Metal wire mesh lath

Stud

Wood lath

If the carpentry contractor building the dwelling does the lathing, the work belongs in the carpentry classification. If a specialty contractor does the lathing, the "Lathing & Drivers" (Code 5443) classification applies.

A builder applies at least two and often three coats of plaster to a wall, including a scratch coat, a brown coat, and the finish coat. Each coat performs a different structural function and aids in properly bonding the wall. Specialists usually perform the plastering, and premium auditors should classify them on their own policy as "Plastering NOC & Drivers" (Code 5480).

Wallboard
A sheet material composed of a gypsum filler and faced with paper.

Wallboard or sheet rock is a more economical substitute for plaster. **Wallboard** is a sheet material composed of a gypsum filler and faced with paper. Wallboard sheets vary in thickness and are generally four feet wide. They are available in several lengths up to twelve feet long. The edges along the wallboard's length are recessed to receive joint cement and tape. When the taping is completed, no seam is visible where the wallboards join.

Builders nail or screw dry wallboard sheets directly to the studs to cover the wall. If the carpenters building the house install the wallboard, the work belongs in the carpentry classification. If a specialty subcontractor does the work, the premium auditor for the subcontractor's policy assigns the operation to "Wallboard Installation Within Buildings & Drivers" (Code 5445). The same classification assignments apply to installing plywood or pine paneling or similar wall coverings nailed directly into the studs.

To hide where the separate sheets intersect, the builder applies a special cement to the joints with a wide putty knife. Next, the builder centers a perforated paper tape with feathered edges over the channel between the two wallboards being joined. With the putty knife, the builder presses the tape into the cement, forcing the cement through the tape perforations. After that has dried, other cement applications conceal the tape. A final light sanding of each joint leaves a smooth finish.

If done by the carpentry contractor building the dwelling, taping comes within the carpentry classification. If an insured subcontractor is doing the taping only, the plastering classification applies. When incidental finishing operations are conducted, Code 5480 (Plastering) applies. If the taping is done by an insured painting contractor doing both painting and taping, the premium auditor should assign the work on the painting contractor's policy to "Painting or Paperhanging NOC & Shop Operations, Drivers" (Code 5474). A wallboard installation contractor may also tape as an incidental part of the installation (Code 5445).

Builders often use plastic, ceramic, masonry, or glass tile on kitchen and bathroom walls as well as on bathroom floors. The builder must apply that tile over a plywood or plasterboard base with adhesive. Grouting fills the joints between tile pieces. The classification "Tile, Stone, Mosaic or Terrazzo Work—Inside" (Code 5348) covers that operation when it is performed separately from other construction activities at the same site.

Interior Trim

Finishing the inside of a house requires much additional carpentry work. Stairways and door units may be made from stock parts, but they can require much cutting and fitting. The inside trim usually includes baseboards where the walls meet the floor and casings around doors and windows. Usually, that work is incidental to the other carpentry operations involved in constructing a house. If a house has elaborate trim or cabinet work, however, the builder may use a specialty contractor. In that case, the premium auditor of the specialty contractor would assign the operation to the classification "Carpentry: Installation of Cabinet Work or Interior Trim" (Code 5437). The premium auditor cannot use that classification for a contractor who performs any other carpentry operations at the same job or location. If the contractor does such operations, the carpentry classification applies.

Flooring

Flooring materials include hardwoods, resilient flooring, tile, and carpeting. A specialty contractor usually installs the flooring, and premium auditors use separate classifications for each when the contractor performs the installation as a separate operation.

Painting and Decorating

Painting and decorating add a protective coating to the walls as well as make them more attractive. Before painting, builders should condition surfaces so that the surfaces are smooth and clean. Builders can apply paint by brush or roller, but large surfaces are usually spray-painted. Builders may also cover walls with wallpaper. When a builder performs those operations separately from other construction activities at the site, the premium auditor should assign them to the painting or paperhanging classification. A separate "Paperhanging & Drivers" (Code 5491) classification is available only if the contractor is engaged exclusively in paperhanging. Premium auditors cannot assign that code at the same job or location where the contractor also performs painting.

Finishing the Site

After building each house, the contractor must add building accesses and special features. The contractor must also remove debris and clean the site. The project is not completed until the contractor landscapes the lot. The contractor's own employees usually perform the cleanup, but the contractor may hire a landscape contractor to plant trees and shrubs and lay the lawn.

Building Accesses and Features

Accesses and features added to a house may include sidewalks, driveways, patios, or similar concrete work. Premium auditors assign each of the above to the appropriate concrete construction classification. A separate classification exists for swimming pool construction (Code 5223).

Landscaping

The contractor may have to grade the lot after completing the house to provide the desired slope to the lot. The contractor can then spread the topsoil removed earlier. A landscaper then plants the trees and shrubs in the locations marked on the landscape plan. Finally, either sodding or seeding produces a lawn. The classification "Landscape Gardening & Drivers" (Code 0042) includes most of those operations. However, if the operations include changing the contour of the ground, landscaping no longer applies. The notes for the landscaping classification state that premium auditors should separately rate excavation, filling, or backfilling as "Excavation & Drivers" (Code 6217). As mentioned, the code for "Grading of Land NOC & Drivers" is also 6217, but grading and excavation are differentiated in general liability insurance.

Cleanup

After they have planted the trees, shrubs, and lawn, the contractor and landscaper remove their equipment and temporary facilities. The contractor must haul away any debris. The general contractor's employees clean up the site and make certain the house is ready for occupancy. That operation comes within the governing classification unless the payrolls of the cleaners, watch-guards, and timekeepers exceed that of all other construction or erection employees at the same job or location. In that case, the "Cleaner—Debris Removal" (Code 5610) classification applies. Likewise, if the insured hires a specialty contractor to provide cleaning, watch-guard, or timekeeping services, classification Code 5610 would apply.

COMMERCIAL CONSTRUCTION PROCESS

Although commercial construction follows essentially the same process, commercial projects tend to be larger, more complex, and more hazardous than residential construction. The construction of an office building or a shopping center may involve dozens of subcontractors and require months or even years to complete. As with all premium audits involving subcontracted operations, the insurer expects the premium auditor to ascertain that the insured has certificates of insurance available so that workers' compensation coverage is evident. Wrap-up programs are increasingly common and may necessitate considerable time to complete a premium audit. Wrap-up policies are designed to reduce insurance costs on major construction projects. All parties in a construction project are covered under one umbrella policy. Following the stages of the construction process helps in determining the correct construction classifications.

Preparing the Site

As with residential construction, commercial construction requires preparing the site before a builder can start building. Preparation includes clearing the site, bringing in the necessary equipment and facilities, locating the foundation, excavating, and dewatering. Previous sections of this chapter describe many of those operations. The following sections describe additional considerations for commercial structures.

Clearing the Site

Removing unwanted objects from the site may only require bulldozers. On the other hand, builders often erect a commercial structure on the site of an older structure that the builder must first demolish. The specific classification depends on the building to be demolished. Even without wrecking, there may be a salvage operation.

Temporary Facilities

Because many people will be working at the construction site for some time, the contractor normally erects temporary facilities at the site. Those facilities may include shelters for equipment, storage spaces for tools and materials, and offices for supervisors and timekeepers, as well as sanitary facilities. The contractor also usually erects a barricade around the construction site to protect the general public from danger. Those activities come within the "Carpentry—NOC" (Code 5403) classification.

Excavating

Although much of the site preparation and surveying occurs as in residential construction, a commercial building frequently requires far more excavation. For example, it may involve blasting and power machinery.

The contractor usually hauls away excavated material in dump trucks. Excavation contractors frequently employ trucks and operators on a sub-contract basis. Premium auditors should include drivers of trucks belonging to an uninsured hauling subcontractor in the excavation classification in accordance with the *Basic Manual* rules regarding standard exceptions. If subcontractors have insurance, the premium auditor can classify them separately under trucking. The premium auditor uses the appropriate trucking classification because the hauler is carrying goods of others, which is the nature of the trucking business. If a road contractor hauls excavated materials from the site for use on a road, then the appropriate street or road construction classification applies.

Other work incidental to excavation may include testing soil, pumping water, and installing bracing to prevent cave-ins, except when the work is under existing buildings.

Dewatering

Another specialized operation often necessary in commercial construction is dewatering. **Dewatering** is the process of removing accumulated water from an excavation or a trench, usually accomplished using pumping equipment and hoses. A heavy rain, snow, or thaw at a construction site may cause water to accumulate in an excavation or a trench.

Dewatering
The process of removing accumulated water from an excavation or a trench, usually accomplished using pumping equipment and hoses.

Well point
A perforated pipe on a construction site that is driven into the earth to collect underground water.

In some areas, underground water seeps into excavations or trenches. To counteract that seepage, builders use well points combined with pumping equipment and hoses. A **well point** is a perforated pipe on a construction site that is driven into the earth to collect underground water. Pumping equipment draws out water seeping into the pipe. That operation usually continues until the contractor completes the excavation and concrete or other work below ground level.

Unions usually require an engineer to be present while the builder operates such pumping equipment. Premium auditors should assign the engineer's payroll to the classification with which the work is associated. For example, if the dewatering enables the foundation excavation work to go on, the classification would be "Excavation & Drivers" (Code 6217). If the builder has completed the excavation and the dewatering is necessary so that the builder can perform concrete work, the work would fall within the appropriate concrete construction classification. If a specialty contractor having no other operation on the job performs the dewatering, the applicable classification is "Millwright Work NOC & Drivers" (Code 3724) because the bulk of the operation involves installing the pump.

Setting the Foundation

Because commercial structures tend to be much larger than residential structures, the foundations are more elaborate. Although the foundation footings also spread the weight over the bearing surface, the weight is much greater. The foundation work is therefore often much more extensive for a commercial building, and the work is more likely to involve specialized subcontractors.

Foundation Footings

Commercial structures often require pile footings. The premium auditor should therefore expect to find work included in the "Pile Driving" (Code 6003) classification in most large commercial construction projects. When the contractor manufactures concrete piles at the job site or pours concrete into the hollow steel piles, the concrete construction classification applies. The same classification encompasses the drilling of pier holes and pouring of concrete by the foundation contractor. Premium auditors should assign a specialty contractor drilling pier holes for foundations and encasing them to the "Drilling NOC and Drivers" (Code 6204) classification on the specialty contractor's policy.

Foundation Forms

The number of foundation forms required by a commercial building may justify a temporary carpentry shop on the site. If the shop makes forms for concrete construction, the premium auditor should assign its payroll to the concrete classification. If the shop prepares rough and finished carpentry work only, the "Carpentry NOC" (Code 5403) classification applies. If the builder uses the shop for various operations with no payroll division, the premium auditor should assign its payroll to the governing class of the operations using the shop.

Sometimes contractors assemble forms in a temporary shop located away from the job site. Even so, the concrete classification still applies to the operation. If the contractor assembles the forms away from the job site in a qualifying permanent carpentry shop, the premium auditor can assign the operation to the carpentry shop classification if the contractor conducts this as a separate and distinct business.

Foundation Walls

The foundation walls in commercial structures are usually reinforced concrete. All the operations involved in constructing them—including making and erecting forms, placing steel reinforcing rods, pouring the concrete, and stripping the forms, come within the concrete construction classification. Occasionally, brick or cement block foundations require the masonry classification.

As in residential construction, the *Basic Manual* considers waterproofing foundation walls incidental when the contractor who erected the walls performs that operation. When waterproofing is performed by an insured specialty contractor, a premium auditor should separately classify waterproofing according to the application method described earlier.

Building the Superstructure

Houses almost always have wood frames to support their weight; however, larger buildings use many load-bearing techniques. Buildings that require vast interior spaces, such as churches or auditoriums, usually have load-bearing walls. When the outside walls carry the building's weight, less need exists for interior columns or partitions. Although builders used stone walls that way in the past, they now usually construct load-bearing walls from poured reinforced concrete. The most common technique, especially for large office buildings, uses a structural steel skeleton as the building's frame. The steel skeleton is essentially the same as a house's wood frame, except that it is much larger and stronger.

Iron or Steel Erection

A steel erector is usually a subcontractor rather than a general contractor. Contractors normally establish two separate contracts, one for structural steel and another for miscellaneous steel, including such nonstructural items as staircases, railings, and door and window lintels.

Builders use two principal methods to erect structural steel in constructing a building. One involves erecting an entirely steel frame structure. The other uses concrete or masonry walls to support the structural steel. Local building codes usually restrict the latter construction type, depending on the height of the building. The payroll sequence on a job usually indicates which construction type a contractor is using. When steel frame buildings are built, the operation usually continues without pause until completion. When concrete or masonry walls are used to support structural steel, payrolls are usually intermittent because after placing the steel for one floor, the steel erector must wait for the mason to complete the next story before it can place more structural steel. Blueprints and specifications also indicate construction type. For classification purposes, the manual divides steel frame buildings into two categories: "Iron or Steel: Erection: Frame Structures Not Over Two Stories in Height" (Code 5059) and "Iron or Steel: Erection: Frame Structures" (Code 5040). A premium auditor cannot assign both classes to the same job or location.

One-story buildings such as airplane hangars, churches, and gymnasiums exceed the height normally contemplated for a two-story structure. For that reason and to clarify the terms "story in height" and "stories in height," the *Basic Manual* defines a story as being fifteen feet in height.[10] As previously mentioned, the *Basic Manual* does not permit division of payroll between Codes 5059 and 5040 at the same job or location. If part of a building is over two stories, the premium auditor should assign the entire payroll for the steel frame erection to Code 5040. For example, for a school that is two stories in height except for one wing that is forty-six feet high (a story is fifteen feet), the premium auditor should classify the entire payroll for the steel frame erection as Code 5040.

Contractors use concrete or masonry walls supporting steel joists or beams to construct buildings. If the structure's size requires additional support, interior steel columns may support those joists. Because that operation is neither steel frame construction nor described by any other class, the premium auditor should assign it to the "Iron or Steel: Erection: NOC" (Code 5057) classification. The manual treats interior iron or steel staircases as nonstructural iron and assigns them to the classification "Iron or Steel: Erection: Iron, Brass or Bronze—Nonstructural—Interior" (Code 5102). With few exceptions, premium auditors classify iron work on a building's outside as "Iron or Steel: Erection: Iron—Exterior" (Code 5040).

All iron or steel erection classes include installation by bolting, riveting, or welding if the same contractor performs the entire operation. Premium auditors would use the classification "Welding or Cutting NOC & Drivers" (Code 3365) for a specialist contractor who is not engaged in other construction operations at the job.

Iron and steel erection also includes constructing elevated tanks, radio and TV towers, smokestacks, gas holders, metal bridges, fire escapes, and all ironwork on a building's outside such as balconies and fireproof shutters. If a steel erector not casting the beams or girders installs precast concrete beams or girders, that operation also comes within the appropriate iron or steel classification. If a concrete contractor casting the beams installs precast concrete beams or girders, premium auditors should classify that operation as concrete construction.

Scaffolds, Cranes, and Hoists

When building a structure several stories high, a builder must lift both workers and materials to the upper floors. A scaffold on the outside of a building normally gives workers a place to walk at the level at which they are working. A hoist or portable elevator raises workers and materials to the appropriate floor. A builder may also need a tower or climber crane to lift heavy materials to the building's higher levels. Exhibit 5-9 illustrates those methods in constructing a multi-story building.

EXHIBIT 5-9

Construction of a Multi-Story Building

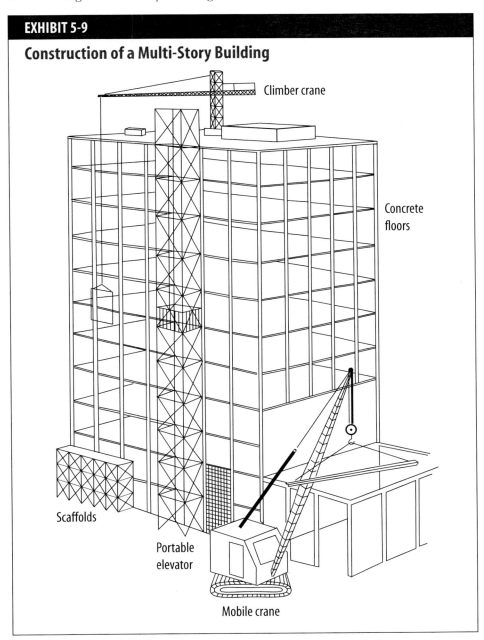

The payroll of a climber crane's operator is assignable to the specific operation classification for which the builder uses the crane. When a general contractor's employees operate a climber crane to hoist miscellaneous material as needed for numerous operations and subcontractors on the job, the premium auditor should assign the operators' payroll to the general contractor's governing classification.

If the steel erector hires cranes along with operators from other contractors, and certificates of insurance indicate that the owner of the equipment has met the workers' compensation obligation, the premium auditor should not charge the steel erector a workers' compensation premium for those crane operators. In that situation, the owner of the cranes would be responsible for the operators' workers' compensation coverage. When auditing such an insured hoisting specialist in NCCI states, premium auditors would classify the payroll of the operators of a climber crane rented to others as "Mobile Crane and Hoisting Service Contractors—NOC—All Operations & Drivers" (Code 9534).

Similarly, when the general contractor erects and operates scaffolds, portable elevators, or hod hoists, the governing classification applies. When an insured specialty hoist or scaffold contractor installs, repairs, or removes hoists, elevators, or scaffolds, the premium auditor should classify that operation as Code 9534.

Installing Utilities

As in residential construction, specialty contractors usually install the utilities in commercial buildings. Although there may also be specialized communications systems and other utilities not found in private residences, the principal utilities in commercial buildings are the same heating, plumbing, and electrical systems required in houses.

Air Conditioning and Heating

Because of the size of commercial buildings, heating and ventilating systems usually have to be much larger and more elaborate than in private homes. They are almost always forced-air systems with central air conditioning included. The buildings usually include considerable duct work, which the premium auditor should classify as "Sheet Metal Work: Shop and Outside NOC & Drivers" (Code 5538) when a contractor fabricates and installs the ducts as a separate operation. A specialty contractor normally installs the compressors and motors. That operation is described as "Air-Conditioning Systems: Non-Portable: Machinery Installation or Repair of Compressors, Motors or Other Machinery & Drivers" (Code 3724). Premium auditors should separately classify steam boiler installation or repair when performed by a specialty contractor.

Plumbing

The plumbing classification includes installing gas, water, steam, hot water, or other pipe fittings and any necessary connections. It also includes servicing and repairing gas, water, steam, and sanitation systems. It does not include constructing sewers, water mains, or gas mains.

Electrical Wiring

The classification "Electrical Wiring—Within Buildings & Drivers" (Code 5190) covers installing and repairing wiring and fixtures within buildings. It includes installing or connecting any electrical machinery or apparatus that can operate from an ordinary outlet. Premium auditors should separately classify installation of heavier electrical machinery or auxiliary apparatus. Premium auditors should classify electrical wiring outside, such as erecting poles, stringing wires, and installing transformers, as "Electric Light or Power: Line Construction & Drivers" (Code 7538).

Automatic Sprinkler Installation

Many buildings now include automatic sprinkler systems for added fire protection. Specialty contractors often perform the installation, in which case the "Automatic Sprinkler: Installation & Drivers" (Code 5188) classification applies.

Enclosing the Superstructure

Builders may use certain specialized techniques for constructing commercial buildings in addition to the methods this chapter has already described for enclosing residential structures. Some of those techniques require special classification treatment. Premium auditors should therefore investigate which workers actually build the roofs, walls, and floors and which methods they use.

Roofing

Conventional felt and bitumen built-up roofs make up most flat roofing on commercial buildings, but contractors may use silicone and plastic materials. Contractors often use corrugated metal for pitched roofs. Unless the roof includes insulation panels placed by a different contractor before roofing, the roofing classification covers all the operations involved in installing either roof type. Separate roofing contractors usually perform that work, and they may provide a roof guarantee.

Exterior Walls

Builders can construct the outside walls of commercial buildings by one of the methods already described for houses, but concrete construction is most common. Contractors frequently use metal siding for the walls of commercial buildings. Other exterior wall materials include marble slabs, slate, glass, stainless steel, and aluminum.

One technique for constructing the walls of commercial buildings involves casting concrete wall panels on the ground and then raising them into place. Exhibit 5-10 illustrates that method, called tilt-up panel wall construction, at the ground level. Constructing the high-rise building in Exhibit 5-9 would also employ this technique.

Premium auditors should classify pouring and casting prefabricated concrete tilt-up panels for walls or floors, when performed on the ground, as concrete construction. The particular concrete classification that applies to constructing tilt-up panels depends on the building type. All operations required to attach concrete tilt-up panels—in place, including raising, placing, bolting, and welding—come within the concrete construction classification. Some jurisdictions even allow that classification to cover casting panels at a permanent location.

Exhibit 5-10 shows a mobile crane lifting the finished concrete panels into place. In most states, premium auditors classify the payroll for operators of mobile cranes rented to others as "Mobile Crane and Hoisting Service Contractors—NOC—All Operations & Drivers" (Code 9534).

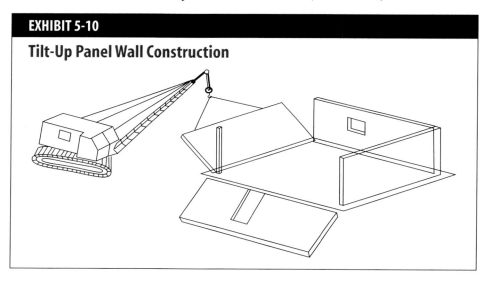

EXHIBIT 5-10

Tilt-Up Panel Wall Construction

Premium auditors should classify a general contractor or a subcontractor applying sheet metal siding as "Sheet Metal Work: Shop and Outside NOC & Drivers" (Code 5538). If welding is required to attach metal walls to the frame, the welding classification applies when others have previously erected the steel frame and an insured subcontractor performs the welding as a separate operation. If the welding is not a distinct operation, the iron or steel erection classification applies.

Premium auditors should classify a contractor constructing exterior walls from cement blocks, bricks, or brick veneer as masonry. Installing masonry wall materials such as marble slabs or slate also comes within the masonry classification. Lifting slabs into place with mobile cranes resembles constructing tilt-up panel walls. The entire operation, including the crane operators, belongs in the masonry classification.

Some buildings have glass exterior panels. A specialty contractor usually performs the installation, and premium auditors should classify that work as "Glazier—Away From Shop & Drivers" (Code 5462).

When builders use stainless steel or aluminum panels for the exterior walls, the sheet metal work classification (Code 5538) applies to the erection of the walls.

Floors

Commercial buildings usually have concrete floors. For floors not on the ground, all operations including forming, reinforcing, pouring, and stripping forms come within the "Concrete: Construction NOC" (Code 5213) classification. Premium auditors should classify constructing a ground-supported concrete floor for a commercial building—including forming, pouring, and finishing—as "Concrete or Cement: Work—Floors, Driveways, Yards, or Sidewalks & Drivers" (Code 5221). Because premium auditors can use both classifications at a job or location, separate payroll records are necessary. If the insured does not provide them, the premium auditor would assign all payroll to the higher rated of those two classifications.

Finishing the Interior Surfaces

Finishing a commercial building's interior involves most of the operations described for residential construction and may include additional ones. Finishing the internal surfaces includes installing insulation; constructing interior walls; plastering, painting, and decorating; installing elevators, escalators, and stairways; and installing doors and windows.

Insulation

Premium auditors should separately classify any insulation work by an insured specialty contractor. When a builder installs insulation as a part of or incidental to any other construction operation, premium auditors should assign the payroll involved to the classification of the operation to which it is incidental. For example, the plumbing classification would apply if the plumbing contractor who installed the piping also installed the insulation around the piping. When the general contractor installs insulation, the governing classification applies.

Interior Walls

Constructing interior walls usually requires carpenters. Premium auditors should assign carpentry work for a commercial structure, including framing and interior trim, when performed by the general contractor as "Carpentry: NOC" (Code 5403). Premium auditors can separately rate wallboard installation, provided that the insured maintains proper payroll records. Premium auditors should separately classify installing cabinet work, interior trim, or parquet or wooden flooring by insured specialists.

The applicable classification for specialty contractors installing portable office partitions, whether metal or wood, is "Furniture or Fixtures Installation— Portable NOC" (Code 5146).

Plastering, Painting, and Decorating

Any inside plastering or stucco work comes within the plastering classification. The painting classification includes painting both interior and exterior surfaces and painting any equipment. A separate classification exists for painting metal structures over two stories in height (Code 5037). Premium auditors should classify other decorating work according to the materials used.

Elevators, Escalators, and Stairways

Elevator erection or repair is a distinct operation that premium auditors should separately classify. Escalator installation comes within the classification "Electrical Apparatus: Installation or Repair & Drivers" (Code 3724).

Doors and Windows

When a contractor uses metal door frames or window frames, the premium auditor should separately classify their installation. The "Door, Door Frame, or Sash: Erection—Metal or Metal Covered" (Code 5102) classification also covers installing metal frames and sashes for skylights. Erecting wood door or window frames and sashes comes within the appropriate carpentry classification.

Landscaping

A specialty landscaping contractor usually landscapes the grounds around a commercial building. Such a contractor may also perform other operations such as masonry or concrete work for walkways, courtyards, or other exterior features.

NONBUILDING CONSTRUCTION PROJECTS

In addition to residential and commercial structures, many other projects involve construction operations. For examples, some of the major nonstructural construction types include highways, utility lines, and irrigation or drainage systems.

Highway Construction

Highways require extensive construction operations. Firms specializing in that construction type and owning the necessary equipment usually perform highway projects. The classifications for street or road construction and bridge or culvert construction cover most of the operations involved.

Street or Road Construction

In the construction of a new road, the first step is clearing the right of way. That involves felling and disposing of trees, removing stumps and roots, and cutting brush. The workers doing the clearing usually use power saws to fell trees and bulldozers, shovels, or other mechanical means to remove stumps and roots. Excavating the roadbed follows. Roadbed excavation often necessitates cutting into slopes or filling depressions to modify the grade or alignment. Excavating and moving earth and boulders require power-operated equipment. Next comes grading by bulldozers, graders, and earth-compacting machinery. The contractor must provide for roadbed drainage during excavation and grading. Catch basins and piping often perform those tasks, although in rural areas open ditches may suffice. Many roads require cribwork (to prevent erosion), including stone, masonry, and concrete embankment retaining walls.

Premium auditors should classify all of the preceding operations up to and including the graded earth foundation on which the road is to be built as "Street or Road Construction: Subsurface Work & Drivers" (Code 5507).

The classification "Street or Road Construction: Rock Excavation & Drivers" (Code 5508) applies to excavating mass rock and includes all drilling, blasting, and removal operations plus any blasting in connection with removing large stones or boulders. Contractors place large mats over the section or boulder they are blasting to prevent damage or injury by flying rock. The payroll of all employees involved in those operations (drillers, blasters, machine operators, laborers, and drivers) belongs in this classification. On sizable jobs in which stone is available, contractors usually obtain stone for the roadbed by quarrying or stonecrushing operations. The road contractor generally performs those operations, and premium auditors should classify them separately. The street or road construction rock excavation classification includes incidental quarrying or stone crushing, but not tunneling.

The "Street or Road Construction: Paving or Repaving & Drivers" (Code 5506) classification covers most of the remaining operations. The contractor places a small stone or gravel subbase on top of the graded earth foundation and compresses it with rollers. For an asphalt road surface, a course of asphalt and stone—also compacted by rollers—follows. Over that comes the finish course of sand, fine stone, or gravel and asphalt, which a road-paving machine lays while hot. Hot rollers compact that material until the surface is smooth.

For a concrete road, the contractor places surface forms over the subbase, adds reinforcing mesh or rods, and pours concrete into one section at a time from ready-mix concrete trucks. The contractor levels off the surface and allows the section to set, after which the contractor removes the forms.

The paving or repaving classification also includes the following operations:

- Trimming and finishing shoulders
- Installing curbing

- Erecting guard rails or fences
- Painting safety lines or center stripes
- Spraying roads with liquid asphalt or other material
- Scraping and maintaining existing dirt roads
- Paving bridges or culverts with spans that qualify for assigning Code 5507 (clearance at any point is less than ten feet, and the span between terminal abutments is less than twenty feet)
- Repaving roads and bridges, including removing old surfaces
- Maintaining asphalt or concrete mix plants (temporary only)

Premium auditors should separately classify beautification work by a road contractor, including spreading top soil (no grading), sodding, seeding, and planting trees and shrubs, as "Street or Road Construction: Beautification Work & Drivers" (Code 0042). This is the same code as "Landscape Gardening & Drivers."

Bridge or Culvert Construction

Culverts allow water to pass under a road. Contractors usually use steel or concrete pipes as culverts to provide drainage or a passageway for a small brook or stream. Larger streams, valleys, roads, or railroads require a bridge structure. If the bridge or culvert has a span between terminal abutments of less than twenty feet and clearance of less than ten feet at any point, "Street or Road Construction: Subsurface Work & Drivers" (Code 5507) applies. If the span between terminal abutments is more than twenty feet or clearance is more than ten feet, the premium auditor must instead classify the bridge construction operations into the classification or classifications that describe the bridge's construction type. That is, premium auditors would classify concrete bridges as "Concrete: Construction in Connection With Bridges or Culverts" (Code 5222), and they would classify steel bridges as "Iron or Steel: Erection: Metal Bridges" (Code 5040). "Carpentry NOC" (Code 5403) would apply if a bridge is constructed of wood.

Building a bridge usually involves the following operations:

- Excavation
- Pile driving
- Pouring concrete into hollow steel piles
- Constructing abutments—concrete or stone
- Steel (other than reinforcing) erection
- Installing guard rails—steel
- Painting steel bridges
- Concrete paving—deck, sidewalks, and curbing

Except for operations that are considered within the scope of concrete construction or steel erection, premium auditors should separately classify all operations.

Piers at various intervals normally support a bridge over a large body of water. Those piers usually require using caissons or cofferdams. A **caisson** is a hollow, cylindrical, or rectangular object, usually made of steel or concrete, used to prevent water or soft soil from entering an excavation or construction under water. Caissons can be sunk in land or in water. When on land, the contractor sinks them to the required depth, plugs the bottom with concrete, and then fills the caisson with sand. The contractor caps off the top with concrete to provide a base for a pier or bridge. A **cofferdam** is a temporary watertight enclosure from that is pumped dry to expose the bed of a body of water. Concrete is then poured into the cofferdam to form the foundation.

If the caisson is to be used in water, it may be precast on land and floated out to the proper place for sinking. Premium auditors should classify such caisson work as "Caisson work—All Operations to Completion" (Code 6252). That classification includes all operations up to the high-water mark, including pile driving, excavation, masonry, or concrete work. The high-water mark separates the substructure from the bridge construction work above it. Those classifications apply only when the contractor performs that work in open water. When a bridge constructed over navigable water requires using barges, floats, or any boat or vessel type, the Longshore and Harbor Workers' Compensation Act or admiralty law may apply. A similar classification with the same code number exists for cofferdam work: "Cofferdam Work—Not Pneumatic—All Operations to Completion." It also includes pile driving, excavation, and masonry or concrete work up to the substructure completion.

Utility Line Construction

For individual buildings to have utility service, builders must construct utility lines to connect with the main system. When a new development is built, the builder constructs the utility lines usually serving that development when it lays out the streets. Sometimes, however, a particular utility may not serve an existing development, and the builder may install lines to add the existing buildings to the system. Often the contractor must place the lines underground.

Sewer Construction

The "Sewer: Construction—All Operations & Drivers" (Code 6306) classification encompasses all sewer construction operations, including tunneling at street crossings, except when performed under air pressure. Premium auditors should separately classify all other tunneling and surface restoration.

Contractors install sewer lines deep enough to place the pipe below the lines of other utilities, such as water or gas pipes. If the terrain permits, the sewage flows by gravity. If the terrain does not permit a continuous flow, the contractor or municipality must install pumping stations to lift the sewage or force its flow through the main. A sewer system is normally a main or trunk line in one street and smaller side pipes called laterals running from that main through side streets. Connections from those laterals receive sewage

Caisson
A hollow, cylindrical, or rectangular object, usually made of steel or concrete, used to prevent water or soft soil from entering an excavation or construction under water.

Cofferdam
A temporary watertight enclosure that is pumped dry to expose the bed of a body of water.

from houses or other buildings. Exhibit 5-11 diagrams a sewer system in a residential neighborhood.

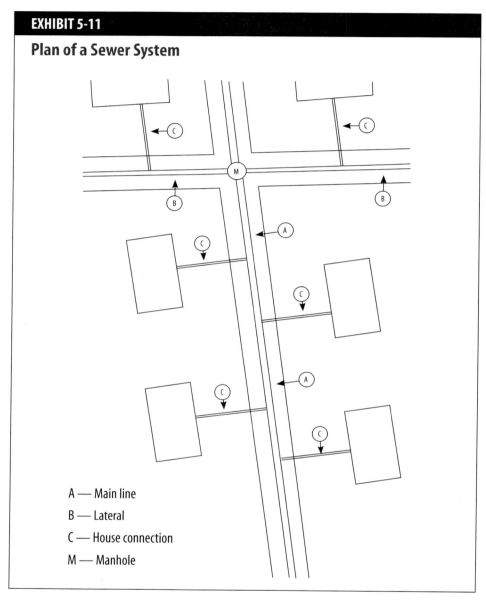

EXHIBIT 5-11

Plan of a Sewer System

A — Main line
B — Lateral
C — House connection
M — Manhole

Building or house connections are usually four-inch pipes. The laterals are four-inch pipes or larger, depending on the housing density. The pipe is normally clay or concrete, although a builder may use composition pipe where the codes permit it. Brick or concrete manholes permit access to the sewer lines. If the sewer line passes through a swampy area, it may be necessary to support the pipe by piles or concrete supports.

Although not a regular procedure, a contractor may set up a temporary plant on the job site to manufacture concrete pipe. Premium auditors should classify pipe manufacturing at such a plant by the sewer contractor as sewer construction.

Where the earth's composition permits, builders use a trench digger to excavate the trench. When it encounters rock, a builder may use a backhoe. Removing the rock may also require blasting. Because of the depth to which they must dig sewer trenches, builders must frequently shore the sides to prevent their collapse. At railroad crossings and busy street intersections where the builder cannot interrupt the traffic flow, builders dig tunnels and push the pipe through them.

The builder places large pipe in the trench by mechanical means. The equipment type that the builder uses for lowering it depends on the size of the pipe and the depth of the trench. After the builder places clay pipe in position, the builder must caulk the joints. Concrete or composition pipe is usually self-locking. After builders have placed and sealed the pipe, they remove the shoring and backfill the trench. Watering the earth usually makes it settle faster. As it completes backfilling, the builder makes temporary repairs to the road surface. The *Basic Manual* considers all those operations, when performed by the same contractor, to be incidental to the sewer construction and therefore included in the sewer construction classification.

After the temporary repairs, the contractor makes the final repairs to the street or ground where it dug the trench. If the trench was in the street, the entire street may need to be repaved. If the builder dug the trench in a grassy area such as a park, such final repairs may include laying sod or seeding and possibly replanting trees. The *Basic Manual* considers those operations surface restoration, which, according to the manual, the premium auditor must rate separately.

Premium auditors classify drainage systems for roads, when installed by the road contractor, as street or road construction.

In addition, when specialist contractors perform certain of those operations, the premium auditor assigns each contractor's payrolls based on the specific operation performed. Such situations may include the following:

- Excavation and/or backfill
- Manholes—brick or concrete
- Pile driving
- Mass rock excavation or blasting of boulders
- Laying and sealing pipe
- Temporary street repaving
- Connecting building or house plumbing performed by a plumber doing other work within the structure
- Connecting building or house plumbing performed by a specialist performing only that operation
- Sewer cleaning
- Cleaning building or house connections with portable equipment

The premium auditor should assign any of the preceding operations performed by the contractor laying or sealing the pipe to sewer construction.

Water Mains

Unlike the sewer construction classification, the "Water Main or Connection Construction & Drivers" (Code 6319) classification description does not include the phrase "all operations." However, most premium auditors have interpreted that classification similarly to encompass related operations, including tunneling at street crossings, except when performed under air pressure. Premium auditors should separately rate tunneling other than at street crossings. The manual considers excavating mass rock or boulders, with or without blasting, as incidental except when performed as a separate operation.

Installing water mains and building connections resembles sewer construction except for the kind of pipe used and the depth of the trench. Water mains are usually cast iron or concrete. When the builder uses concrete pipe, the pipe must be waterproof, and the contractor must securely seal all joints. Water mains vary in size from six, eight, or ten inches in diameter or larger, depending on the needs of the area served. Laterals may be as small as four inches, and house connections are frequently small copper pipes or tubing.

Contractors lay water mains in trenches below the frost line to prevent freezing. If freezing is not a hazard, the mains must still be deep enough to prevent damage by traffic. Digging the trenches and shoring, when required, are incidental to the water mains classification.

Premium auditors separately classify the following operations when performed by specialist contractors:

- Trench excavation and backfill
- Mass rock excavation of boulders requiring blasting
- Temporary repaving of a trench
- Connecting building or house plumbing performed by a plumber contractor doing other work in the building
- Connecting building or house plumbing performed by a specialist doing no other work

Premium auditors should assign any of the preceding operations performed by the contractor laying or sealing the pipe to the water main classification. The water main classification does not apply to installations by a municipal water authority that operates a waterworks (Code 7520), constructing aqueducts involving tunneling (Code 6251 or 6260), and any shaft-sinking in connection with aqueducts (Code 6252).

Gas Mains

Contractors construct gas mains in essentially the same manner as water mains. The only differences are the pipe type and size and the required trench's depth.

Gas mains use cast iron, wrought iron, steel, or plastic pipe varying in size from $2^{1}/_{2}$ inches to 12 inches or larger in diameter. As with water mains, contractors must securely seal joints, usually by coupling, although they frequently weld steel pipe. Because freezing is not a hazard, the depth of the gas lines may be as little as $2^{1}/_{2}$ feet. Otherwise, the operations are the same as for installing water mains.

The "Gas: Main or Connection Construction & Drivers" (Code 6319) classification excludes gas main installation by gas companies and gas pipeline construction between natural gas-producing fields and connection points with local distribution systems. Premium auditors must separately classify those operations.

Irrigation or Drainage System Construction

The NCCI originally established the classification "Irrigation or Drainage System Construction & Drivers" (Code 6229) to apply to open ditch irrigation or drainage systems not using pipe. Interpretations have broadened that classification's scope to include drainage systems that do involve piping. For example, a contractor may lay perforated tile or composition pipe around foundations or footings or buildings to carry off excess water. A contractor may also lay it below the surface of an athletic field to carry water away from the area.

Premium auditors should assign installing metal or concrete septic tanks with perforated piping leaching fields to the irrigation or drainage systems classification when the installation involves no other plumbing operations. The classification wording is "Septic Tank Installation & Drivers" with the same code, Code 6229. If a contractor installing a septic tank with a leaching field also performs other plumbing operations in the building to which the system is connected, the manual considers the installation as plumbing. Cesspool construction by a specialist contractor performing no other plumbing operations may involve excavation and brick, block, or stone masonry classifications.

The irrigation or drainage systems classification excludes any operation involved in sewer construction, tunneling or dam construction, pile driving, and dredging.

CONSTRUCTION OR ERECTION OF PERMANENT YARDS AND SHOPS

A special classification, "Construction or Erection Permanent Yard" (Code 8227), is available for contractors maintaining a **permanent yard**, which is a maintenance yard used for the storage of material and construction equipment and for the maintenance of equipment. Contractors can also use them for downtime because of inclement weather or when no jobs are in progress and they have assigned employees yard duties. To qualify, such yards must be permanent locations. If a yard meets that requirement, the payroll for employees' time spent in the yard belongs in that classification. Premium auditors must assign payrolls for work away from the yard to that operation's

Permanent yard
A maintenance yard used for the storage of material and construction equipment and for the maintenance of equipment.

classification. For example, a contractor may send a master mechanic who normally works in such a yard to a sewer job site to repair equipment. The premium auditor should assign the payroll for that time, including time going to and from the job, to the sewer classification.

On large projects, a contractor usually sets up a yard at or adjacent to the job site. The *Basic Manual* considers such a yard temporary, and the contractor's permanent yard classification does not apply. A **temporary yard** is a temporary maintenance yard established at a construction site for the storage of material and equipment and the maintenance of equipment used on that site. A temporary yard can become a permanent yard if the contractor continues to use it after the contractor completes the project for which it established the yard. For example, a road contractor may secure a job several hundred miles away. The contractor may lease land adjacent to the job site for the storing, repairing, and maintaining equipment to be used on the job. As long as that job is in progress, the *Basic Manual* considers the yard temporary, and premium auditors should assign the payroll of yard employees to the appropriate street and road construction classification. After the contractor completes the original job, the contractor may obtain another job in the same area. If the contractor uses the same yard for the second job, it may qualify as a permanent yard. In addition to supplying a location for storing, maintaining, and repairing equipment, a contractor's permanent yard also provides storage for material such as sand, brick, lumber, and concrete forms.

Temporary yard
A temporary maintenance yard established at a construction site for the storage of material and equipment and the maintenance of equipment used on that site.

That classification does not include fabrication or mill operations. Premium auditors should assign iron or steel fabrication at a permanent yard location to the appropriate iron works shop classification depending on whether the material fabricated is structural, ornamental, or decorative. Although the cleaning and reconditioning of forms in a permanent yard do come within the permanent yard classification, premium auditors should classify the manufacturing of wooden forms at a permanent location as "Carpentry: Shop Only & Drivers" (Code 2802).

Under normal conditions the payroll assigned to the permanent yard should be only a small percentage (under 10 percent) of a contractor's total payroll. If payroll for the yard operation is more than 10 percent, a thorough analysis is in order.

Contractors occasionally include pay for time not worked (rainy days, holidays, or vacations) as yard payroll. This payroll is not considered downtime. A premium auditor should properly assign such payroll to the classification applicable to the operation usually performed by those employees.[11]

Premium auditors should separately classify employees performing the normal drivers' duties. For example, premium auditors classify the operator of a truck or tractor-trailer unit transporting equipment or supplies from the yard to a job site in accordance with the rules applying to drivers. The *Basic Manual* does not intend Code 8227 to apply to any operation away from the permanent yard.

SUMMARY

The manual requirement that premium auditors separately classify each distinct operation complicates classifying construction or erection operations. That requirement stems from the widely varying degrees of hazard involved in various construction operations. Although separately classifying distinct construction operations results in more equitable treatment of insureds, it also requires much more effort for premium auditors. The mobility and seasonal fluctuation of construction activity further complicate the task.

To correctly classify construction operations, analyzing the construction process stages is helpful. Those stages are preparing the site, setting the foundation, building the superstructure, installing the utilities, enclosing the structure, finishing the interior, and landscaping the site. Although each may involve different techniques, both residential and commercial construction follow that process. Although premium auditors must always refer to the appropriate manual to determine the exact classification that applies, that analysis of the construction process helps to identify particular operations and to locate the correct classification. Reviewing the general contractor's overall operations is important. That analysis clarifies incidental operations and leads to assigning construction operations to their proper classifications.

CHAPTER NOTES

1. National Council on Compensation Insurance, Inc., *Basic Manual for Workers Compensation and Employers Liability Insurance* (Boca Raton, Fla.: NCCI, 2001), Rule I.D.3.d., https://www.ncci.com/Manuals/basic2001/national/Basic2001-National-f00022.htm (accessed Aug. 7, 2006).

2. *Basic Manual*, Rule I.D.3.d.

3. *Basic Manual*, Rule I.D.3.d.

4. *Basic Manual*, Rule I.D.3.d.(1).

5. *Basic Manual*, Rule I.D.3.d.(2).

6. *Basic Manual* (effective July 1, 2006), note 1 to Code 5606.

7. *Basic Manual* (effective July 1, 2006), note 3 to Code 5606.

8. *Basic Manual* (effective July 1, 2006), note 2 to Code 5606.

9. N. R. Kleinfeld, "Boom Times for the Builders of New York," *The New York Times*, July 26, 1981, Sec. 3, p. 1.

10. *Basic Manual*, Rule 2.F.1.

11. *Basic Manual*, Rule 2.F.1.

Direct Your Learning

Maritime Workers' Compensation Insurance and Premium Determination

Educational Objectives

After learning the content of this chapter and completing the corresponding course guide assignment, you should be able to:

▶ Given a case involving a work-related injury, determine which workers' compensation law would apply and what legal remedies and benefits would be available to the worker.

- Distinguish among the federal laws applicable to employee injury cases.

- Apply the tests used to determine under which federal act an employee will be covered.

▶ Describe the major provisions of the United States Longshore and Harbor Workers' Compensation Act (LHWCA) and its extensions.

▶ Describe the coverage provided by and the process of premium determination for LHWCA exposures, including the distinction between *F* and non-*F* classifications.

▶ Describe the coverage provided by and the process of premium determination for admiralty law and Federal Employers' Liability Act exposures.

▶ Define or describe each of the Key Words and Phrases for this chapter.

CHAPTER 6

Develop Your Perspective

What are the main topics covered in the chapter?

Some federal laws entitle certain employees to compensation without regard to fault. These laws change the employees' benefits and rights from those provided under state workers' compensation laws.

Identify those employees who are entitled to benefits under federal laws.

▶ What persons and employments are covered by the United States Longshore and Harbor Workers' Compensation Act (LHWCA)?

▶ How does the LHWCA differ from admiralty law acts?

Why is it important to learn these topics?

It is important for premium auditors, particularly those dealing with maritime exposures, to know the various laws and acts relating to workers' compensation exposures for maritime workers. This information is necessary for a premium auditor to determine the jurisdiction when dealing with maritime compensation exposures.

Consider employees covered by the LHWCA and its extensions.

▶ What persons and employments are included?

▶ What activities and occupations are specifically excluded?

How can you use what you will learn?

Evaluate the activities of a contractor who is engaged in many varied types of construction and renovation projects.

▶ What federal act may be involved in the reconstruction of a marina?

▶ What question should the premium auditor ask to determine the application of federal acts?

Maritime Workers' Compensation Insurance and Premium Determination

The discussion in this text so far has centered on insurance for an employer's liability under state workers' compensation laws. In many situations, however, potential employee injury claims come within federal rather than state jurisdiction. Federal laws entitle certain employee groups to compensation for work-related injuries without regard to fault. In such cases, the principle is the same as under state workers' compensation laws, but the benefits schedule, and therefore the applicable rates, differ from those of state laws. Employees in groups under exclusive federal jurisdiction may sue employers for damages resulting from work-related injuries.

Because different rates apply to the different insurance coverages in situations that come under federal jurisdiction, premium auditors must understand the laws and coverages involved to adjust the premium. Premium auditing is complicated by the fact that most of those situations concern maritime employments in which distinctions between land and water areas and between crew members and harbor workers are especially difficult to draw.

Maritime compensation exposures often appear unexpectedly when the policy does not indicate such an exposure. Those surprises may result from the underwriter's limited familiarity with the nature of the insured operations, from insufficient underwriting information when the insurer wrote the coverage, or from the insured's venture into a new operation with a maritime exposure after the policy's inception. In any case, premium auditors must ascertain all the exposures not only to determine the premium correctly, but also to verify that the policy shows the proper coverages.

FEDERAL JURISDICTION

Although insurers settle most workers' compensation claims according to a particular state's law, certain cases come within federal jurisdiction. Under the United States Constitution, federal jurisdiction over workers' compensation cases can arise in two ways. One way is by the powers granted to Congress to enact specific legislation. The other involves cases of admiralty and maritime jurisdiction, which the Constitution assigns to the federal judiciary.

Article I, Section VIII of the Constitution empowers Congress to make laws for several specific purposes, such as to collect taxes, to regulate interstate and foreign commerce, to coin money, to raise armies, and to perform other stipulated functions of the federal government. It also allows Congress "to make all laws which shall be necessary and proper for carrying into execution" those powers. Beyond those express and implied powers, Congress left all other legislative matters to the states. Amendment X formalized this principle: "The powers not delegated to the United States by the Constitution, nor prohibited by it to the States, are reserved to the States respectively, or to the people." Therefore, the states legislate most matters relating to public safety, education, domestic relations, and property, as well as numerous other matters. Courts, however, have broadly interpreted the power of Congress to regulate commerce so that a great many federal laws cover areas that may otherwise come under state jurisdiction. Such is the case with the United States Longshore and Harbor Workers' Compensation Act (LHWCA) and other federal laws governing the compensation of work-related injuries.

Article III of the Constitution, which establishes the federal judiciary, stipulates in Section II that the federal "judicial power shall extend. . . to all cases of admiralty and maritime jurisdiction. . . ." Although the Constitution provides no further definition of that jurisdiction, courts have generally understood it to encompass the customary laws of the sea, such as applied in the admiralty courts of England. The Constitution's framers evidently believed federal jurisdiction was necessary to preserve uniformity in applying those laws of the sea. Because historically maritime customs provided sailors one of the earliest forms of compensation for work-related injuries, federal courts presided over those compensation claims from the beginning.

Admiralty Law

In the phrase "admiralty and maritime jurisdiction," the Constitution implies a broader scope than the jurisdiction exercised in the admiralty courts of England. Those courts arose in medieval times to deal with acts of piracy and other crimes on the high seas that were beyond the reach of local authorities. Trade expansion in the sixteenth century increased the number of maritime disputes, and in England the Royal Council delegated to the admiralty courts matters concerning salvage, spoil, wreck, piracy, privateering, prize, and mercantile cases. The revival of the common law, however, limited the admiralty courts' jurisdiction solely to "things done upon the sea."

Admiralty law
The traditional body of rules and practices relating to commerce transacted at sea, navigation, and general maritime affairs.

Like the common law, admiralty law developed over time through custom and precedent. **Admiralty law** is the traditional body of rules and practices relating to commerce transacted at sea, navigation, and general maritime affairs. Statutes have modified admiralty law when necessary, but it remains essentially a distinct body of legal doctrines and procedures handed down in the opinions of judges and legal scholars of all seafaring nations. According to one authority,

The "general" maritime law in the United States, insofar as it remains unmodified by statute, contains, then, two parts. First is the corpus of traditional rules and concepts found by our courts in the European authorities, and applied here with no more variation than is normal when purportedly identical bodies of law are applied in decision by courts in different cultural ambients without common appellate review. . . . Second are rules and concepts improvised to fit the needs of this country, including, of course, modifications of the first component.[1]

A fundamental principle of U.S. maritime law is its uniformity throughout the country. That principle justifies the exclusive federal jurisdiction over maritime matters. States may legislate on maritime matters that are of local concern only. State legislation may not interfere with the uniform application of the maritime law.

The uniformity principle underlay a landmark Supreme Court decision in 1917. The case involved the longshoreman Jensen, who died while unloading a steamship in New York harbor. When the accident occurred, Jensen was working on the gangplank connecting the ship with the pier. Jensen's widow filed a claim under the New York Workmen's Compensation Act and received an award. The employer, however, appealed the case to the Supreme Court, which ruled that because the accident occurred in navigable waters and because Jensen's employment was maritime in nature, "the rights and liabilities of the parties were matters clearly within the admiralty jurisdiction." Therefore, the New York compensation statute did not apply, and the court revoked the award. As the Court explained, "No such legislation is valid if it contravenes the essential purpose expressed by an act of Congress, or works material prejudice to the characteristic features of the general maritime law, or interferes with the proper harmony and uniformity of that law in its international and interstate relations."[2]

Because Jensen's maritime employment brought him within admiralty jurisdiction, the New York law did not apply. Had he worked a short distance away on land, the decision would have been different. The geographic extent of admiralty jurisdiction can therefore be of prime concern. Whereas in England admiralty jurisdiction was limited to the water within the ebb and flow of the tides, in the U.S. it extends to all navigable waters. Chief Justice Roger Taney explained the difference by pointing out that in England "there was no navigable stream in the country beyond the ebb and flow of the tide; nor any place where a port could be established to carry on trade with a foreign nation." In contrast, Taney observed, "We have thousands of miles of public navigable water, including lakes and rivers in which there is no tide. And certainly there can be no reason for admiralty power over a public tide water, which does not apply with equal force to any other public water used for commercial purposes and foreign trade."[3] Admiralty jurisdiction therefore extends to all rivers and lakes that form part of a "continued highway over which commerce is or may be carried on with other States or foreign countries."[4]

Because of its separate origins, admiralty law involves unique vocabulary and procedures. The most significant procedural distinction of admiralty law is the action *in rem* against a vessel. In ordinary civil procedure, a complaint must name the person or legal entity obligated to respond to the suit, but an admiralty proceeding may begin with a petition stating the facts of the case and naming the ship. A maritime lien then attaches the ship until the parties settle the case.

Liability insurance policies written to cover maritime operations usually have an *in rem* endorsement attached. An **in rem endorsement** is an endorsement to a maritime operations liability insurance policy that extends the policy to cover liability claims when the defendant named in a lawsuit is a vessel belonging to the insured, rather than the named insured. When the insurer adds this endorsement, the insurer will not deny claims because the lawsuit does not name the insured.

Admiralty law significantly affects injured maritime workers' compensation because it may come within the law's jurisdiction. The customary law of the sea essentially provides two remedies for injured sailors or crew members: maintenance and cure, and damages for injuries resulting from unseaworthy vessels. Legislation regarding those matters has added to the available remedies and to the potential for confusion. Two applicable laws are the Jones Act and the Death on the High Seas Act.

Maintenance and Cure

With the hazards of sea voyages, the traditional rights of sailors included the right to maintenance and cure at least for the duration of the voyage. **Maintenance** is a remedy for injured sailors and crew members to receive food and lodging. The responsible party may pay maintenance in the form of a dollar amount of compensation. **Cure** is a remedy for injured sailors and crew members to receive medical care, encompassing a broad array of hospital and related medical costs, including rehabilitation. In addition to maintenance and cure, the injured sailor is entitled to unearned wages for the contract period for which he or she signed on. Justice Joseph Story summarized this principle over a century and a half ago when he declared that a "seaman, who is taken sick or is injured or disabled in the service of the ship, without any fault on his own part, is by the maritime law entitled to be healed at the expense of the ship."[5] In addition, the right to maintenance and cure exists irrespective of the vessel owner's or employer's fault. Furthermore, injured sailors are entitled to full wages for the voyage, transportation back to the home port, food and quarters to the end of the voyage, and medical treatment both during the voyage and after for as long as is necessary and effective. Those rights expire, however, with a sailor's death. Except for funeral expenses, the employer has no further obligation to the deceased sailor's estate or heirs. Therefore, for a period of time under general maritime law, an injured seaman received benefits much in excess of those received by the dependents of seamen who were killed. That was the result of the Harrisburg decision

In rem endorsement
An endorsement to a maritime operations liability insurance policy that extends the policy to cover liability claims when the defendant named in a lawsuit is a vessel belonging to the insured, rather than the named insured.

Maintenance
A remedy for injured sailors and crew members to receive food and lodging at least for the duration of the voyage.

Cure
A remedy for injured sailors and crew members to receive medical care, encompassing a broad array of hospital and related medical costs, including rehabilitation.

in which the U.S. Supreme Court ruled that general maritime law did not provide a cause of action for wrongful death.[6] The only option to the heirs was to file suit under the wrongful death statutes of the various states, some of which did not include unseaworthiness as a basis for a wrongful death suit. The *Moragne* decision in 1970 (described later in this chapter) changed that.

To be eligible for maintenance and cure, the injured person must not only be a seaman, but must also prove that the illness or injury manifested itself as a consequence of being in service of the ship. The courts have broadly interpreted "seaman"; realistically, it includes anyone who is on board the ship and in service of the ship. That includes cooks, laundry employees, and the masters of the ship.

"In service of the ship" means that a contract of employment with the ship should exist. The person must be subject to the call of duty and earning wages as such. The injury need not be work-related, nor must it occur on the ship. It may occur, for example, during shore leave. Shore leave is an integral and necessary part of a crew member's duties.

A vessel owner has few defenses against maintenance and cure claims. If the crew member intentionally concealed an illness or injury at the voyage's beginning or if the cause of the injury or illness was the crew member's own willful misbehavior, deliberate act, or indiscretion, an insurer may deny liability. A crew member can enforce the maintenance and cure remedy against the vessel owner or against the vessel (*in rem*).

Damages Resulting From Unseaworthy Vessel

Under the maritime law, a sailor contracting to serve on a ship during a voyage relies on an implied warranty that the ship is seaworthy. That warranty is absolute, continuing, and nondelegable.[7] It extends not only to the vessel's structure, but also to its provisions, including competent officers and crew, good condition of all requisite equipment, sufficient food, water, and fuel, and other necessary stores and implements for the voyage. The lack of any of those items makes a ship unseaworthy. A sailor sustaining an injury because the ship proves to be unseaworthy may sue for damages. The suit must be brought within three years as outlined by the Uniform Statute of Limitations for Maritime Torts. Both the vessel and its owner are liable for damages when the injury results from unseaworthiness.

In order to claim the benefit of the seaworthiness warranty, the injured person must prove seaman status. The injured seaman need not prove negligence. The vessel, however, need not be perfect. It must only be reasonably fit for its intended use.

Federal Compensation and Employers' Liability Laws

Federal involvement in the laws governing workers' compensation claims predated the first state workers' compensation statutes. In 1908, Congress passed two laws concerning the compensation claims of specific employee groups. Since then, Congress has enacted several additional compensation statutes, of which the most significant is the United States Longshore and Harbor Workers' Compensation Act (LHWCA). Before describing the intricacies of the LHWCA and its extensions, this chapter reviews the other federal legislation.

Federal Employees' Compensation Act

Congress first ventured into the compensation field to provide benefits to federal government employees sustaining work-related injuries. Subsequent legislation broadened the coverage and liberalized the benefits provided by the Federal Employees' Compensation Act (FECA). The Federal Employees' Compensation Division within the Department of Labor administers claim settlements. Because the federal government retains this exposure, no insurance is involved. Federal employees therefore constitute a substantial group of workers whose job-related injuries do not affect the work of premium auditors.

Federal Employers' Liability Act

The Federal Employers' Liability Act (FELA), on the other hand, defines a legal liability exposure that premium auditors may encounter. FELA applies solely to employees of interstate railroads and assures them of the same rights to compensation regardless of the state in which an injury occurs. Unlike workers' compensation statutes, FELA does not provide compensation without regard to fault. Rather, the doctrine of comparative negligence applies. The doctrine of **comparative negligence** is a defense to negligence that apportions damages to the respective degree of fault when both the plaintiff and the defendant are at fault. The doctrine states that the employer cannot defeat the claim by arguing that the employee's negligence contributed to the injury. Rather, the employee must prove some negligence by the employer. The award's size then varies in proportion to the amount of each party's negligence.

Comparative negligence
A defense to negligence that apportions damages to the respective degree of fault when both the plaintiff and the defendant are at fault.

By enacting FELA, Congress preempted the legislative interest in compensating injured interstate railroad workers. Therefore, state workers' compensation laws do not apply to workers covered by FELA. Employees of other interstate carriers such as bus lines and truckers, however, are subject to state workers' compensation laws because Congress has not mentioned them in any legislation.

As a result of a 1939 amendment and subsequent judicial interpretation, FELA's original restriction to railroad workers employed in interstate transportation duties has nearly evaporated. In one case, the Supreme Court allowed an office clerk to bring suit against her railroad employer under FELA for an injury resulting from a window breaking in the office. The court ruled that because the plaintiff's duties included filing the drawings for designs of engines, cars, parts, and bridges, those duties substantially furthered interstate commerce.[8] By that line of reasoning, virtually any railroad employee may have the right to seek compensation under FELA.

The trend in FELA cases has also been toward weakening the burden of proof of the employer's negligence. That trend led one authority to suggest that railroad workers sustaining injuries on the job have "the best of both worlds" under FELA.[9] That is, they stand an excellent chance of recovering damages, and instead of being limited to the benefits schedule provided by the workers' compensation law, the jury may award them sizable judgments. Of course, cases still exist involving injured railroad workers who cannot prove the employer's negligence and therefore receive no compensation for their injuries.

Death on the High Seas Act

Congress also responded to the inadequacy of maritime law in responding to death claims. Enacted in 1920 (just before the Jones Act), the Death on the High Seas Act (DOHSA) allows recovery for death of a person (not just a seaman) "caused by wrongful act, neglect or default occurring on the high seas beyond a marine league from the shore of any State." Survivors of nonseamen have about the same recovery rights as under the Jones Act (described in the next section). Nonseamen's survivors can only bring claims for ordinary negligence. The damages recoverable under this law are about the same as under the Jones Act. The two acts are inconsistent with each other, and courts have spent much time trying to reconcile those differences.

The maintenance and cure remedy and the seaworthiness doctrine were intended for seamen. Nonseamen relied on the state statutes for remedies. Congress and the courts did not like the uneven results that arose from some persons relying on state statutes and their diversity, and from others relying on maintenance and cure and the seaworthiness doctrine.

DOHSA applies only to death occurring more than three nautical miles (a nautical mile is 6,080 feet) from the shore of any state. Therefore, this law left those who were killed in what many refer to as territorial waters (within three miles of land) still relying on state law. The Jones Act responded to that gap regarding seamen killed in territorial waters.

Jones Act

In 1920, Congress amended the general maritime law by permitting sailors to bring a direct negligence action against their employer and by creating the possibility of an action for wrongful death. The Merchant Marine Act of that year, commonly called the Jones Act, provided the following:

> . . . any seaman who shall suffer personal injury in the course of his employment may, at his election, maintain an action for damages at law with the right of trial by jury, and in such action all statutes of the United States modifying or extending the common law right or remedy in cases of personal injury to railway employees shall apply.[10]

Therefore, the Jones Act placed sailors in the same "best of both worlds" situation that interstate railroad workers achieved with the passage of FELA. Besides the remedies of maintenance and cure and damages for unseaworthiness, injured sailors have the additional recourse under the Jones Act of suing the shipowner for damages caused by negligence in operating the ship. Realistically, before the Jones Act, maintenance and cure was the only other recovery possible. Previously, the courts barred an injured American crew member from suing his or her employer for injury caused by the negligence of the master or member of the crew. Although the seaworthiness warranty was available, unseaworthiness was hard to prove, and the courts did not consider operational negligence to be unseaworthy.

As under FELA, the comparative negligence principle applies with the Jones Act, and that act guarantees the right to a jury trial. Although the injured sailor must prove negligence to establish the employer's liability, the potential for a large jury award is great. Moreover, the courts have so broadly interpreted the proof of negligence requirement that violating a safety regulation, for example, suffices.[11] Therefore, the prospects for recovery under the Jones Act are excellent, although by no means certain, and the limitations contained in workers' compensation statutes regarding both benefit schedules and the exclusion of other remedies do not apply.

The Jones Act provision for a wrongful death action follows the same principles. It also incorporates the FELA provisions and guarantees the right to trial by jury. Because the only obligation to survivors or heirs of a seaman who died from injuries had previously been for funeral expenses, the Jones Act added significantly to the potential employer's liability in such cases. The heirs can only bring the suit for wrongful death against the employer, even if the employer was not the vessel owner.

Although the Jones Act covers "any seaman" injured in the course of employment, it does not define the term "seaman." Subsequent legislation, the United States Longshore and Harbor Workers' Compensation Act (LHWCA), restricted the application of the Jones Act, however, by its definition of covered employees. The **United States Longshore and Harbor Workers' Compensation Act (LHWCA)** is a federal statute that eliminates the right of maritime workers (other than masters or crew members of vessels) to sue their employers; it requires such employers to provide injured or ill workers with benefits like those provided by state workers' compensation statutes for work-related injury or illness. The LHWCA provides an exclusive remedy for injured maritime employees but does not include "a master or member of a crew of any vessel." In effect, this legislation divides maritime workers into two categories. Because masters and members of the crew are excluded from LHWCA coverage, they can seek the remedies the Jones Act provides for seamen.[12]

Despite this differentiation, cases arise in which an employee injured aboard a floating object in the navigable waters claims benefits under the LHWCA rather than asking for seamen's benefits. To recover seamen's benefits, the employee must prove that he or she is a seaman. Then, the employee will be limited to recovering only maintenance and cure unless he or she can prove that the injury resulted from either unseaworthiness or negligence. Lacking such proof, the employee stands to recover a greater amount under

United States Longshore and Harbor Workers' Compensation Act (LHWCA)
A federal statute that eliminates the right of maritime workers (other than masters or crew members of vessels) to sue their employers; it requires such employers to provide injured or ill workers with benefits like those provided by state workers' compensation statutes for work-related injury or illness.

the LHWCA, which provides benefits without regard to fault or negligence. Because the LHWCA gives the employer the burden of proving that the employee is not entitled to benefits, the employee often wins an award under the LHWCA. Employees working on floating construction equipment and floating oil drilling rigs can frequently choose between seamen's benefits and compensation benefits according to which will give them the higher award for their injuries. An employee can even accept compensation benefits under the LHWCA and then claim seaman status to sue for a larger award under the Jones Act.[13]

The traditional legal test of seaman status included four elements. First, the vessel must be in navigation. A vessel capable of movement, even if it is at anchor or under repair, is **in navigation**. If the structure is affixed to the sea bottom (for example, an oil well), the courts would not consider it a vessel in navigation. Second, the worker must have been employed as a master or member of the crew. The employment must call for service on a vessel. Third, the employee must have a more or less permanent connection with the vessel, although that does not require living on board. Fourth, the worker's duties must contribute to the function of the vessel or accomplishment of its mission. Some authorities and courts had said that the person's duties must be primarily to aid in navigation.[14] The 1991 Wilander case stated that the seaman does not have to aid in navigation but only be on board in furtherance of its purpose. That case also questioned the "member of the crew" requirement. It said it was a question for the jury and that juries could differ.[15]

In navigation
A vessel capable of movement, even if it is at anchor or under repair.

The courts have interpreted those four tests in many different ways. Some have combined them into three requirements. In *Reeves v. Mobile Dredging and Pumping Company, Inc.*, the Third Circuit Court relied on Wilander in abandoning the member of the crew and aid in navigation tests and used an employment-related connection to a vessel in navigation test. It stated that the seaman must have maintained a more or less permanent connection to a vessel, the vessel must be in navigation, and the seaman's employment must contribute to the function of the vessel or the accomplishment of its mission.

In 1995 in *Chandris v. Latsis*, the Supreme Court reduced the seaman requirements to two (albeit virtually the same as the three listed previously).[16] In this case, the court held that, for an employee to be a seaman, the employee's duties must contribute to the vessel's function or the accomplishment of its mission, and the employee must have a connection to a vessel (or an identifiable group of vessels) in navigation that is substantial in duration and nature. (The lower court had said the seaman had to be "either permanently assigned to a vessel or performed a substantial part of his work on a vessel.") Probably most important are the instructions from the Supreme Court, which state that those working on a vessel for the duration of a voyage are not automatically considered seamen. The court said "a 'voyage test' would conflict with our prior understanding of the Jones Act as fundamentally status-based, granting the negligence cause of action to those maritime workers who form the ship's company."[17] The court also said that where the injury occurred is not the crucial issue. The crucial issues are the nature of the seaman's service, his or her status as a member of the vessel, and his or her relationship to the vessel and its operation in navigable waters. Also, the court found that land-based workers do not become seamen just because they are working on a vessel when injured, and seamen do not lose their seaman status just because they are on land when injured. When deciding a case, a court should consider both the duration of a worker's connection to a vessel and the nature of a worker's activities in determining whether the worker is a seaman. As a general rule, the courts and juries should not find an employee to be a seaman if the employee spends less than 30 percent of his or her time in the service of a vessel in navigation.

Adding to the confusion regarding who is and who is not a seaman, courts or juries must also decide what is "in navigation" and what is a "vessel." The Supreme Court has held that a body of water is "navigable" for federal admiralty jurisdiction purposes if it, by itself or by uniting with other waterways, forms a continuous highway capable of sustaining interstate or foreign commerce.[18]

The term "vessel" encompasses most types of man-made floating objects as well as ships transporting passengers or cargo and fishing boats. The courts have held several kinds of construction equipment, for example, to be vessels. These include barges, dredges, and the like.[19] Therefore, the insured's ownership, lease, or charter of any floating equipment, or the use of such equipment by subcontractors, should alert premium auditors to the potential of maritime exposures.

An injured worker can recover for all damages attributable to his or her injury. They include medical expenses (but not if paid under maintenance and cure), pain and suffering, lost earnings, mental anguish, past and future economic loss, and impaired enjoyment of life. The worker cannot recover for loss of consortium (love, companionship, and affection). Damages also include, in the event of death, funeral expenses, loss of financial support, and loss of services (value of nurture, guidance, and education provided to children). The Jones Act specifies the beneficiaries entitled to recovery. The act ranks those beneficiaries and, if a more highly ranked beneficiary recovers, none of the lower ranked beneficiaries can recover. The rankings are spouse and children, the decedent's parents, and next of kin dependents.

Even with the passage of the Jones Act and the DOHSA, discrepancies remained in maritime law regarding death claims. Within territorial waters (that is, those not covered under DOHSA), an injury to a seaman from an unseaworthy vessel created liability, but death to a seaman from the same cause did not. Similarly, an unseaworthy vessel that caused death outside the territorial limit resulted in liability, whereas the same vessel and same death within territorial waters did not. Finally, because the courts had extended the unseaworthiness doctrine to longshoremen, death to a seaman caused by unseaworthiness within territorial waters produced no liability, yet death to a longshoreman (to whom the courts extended the benefit because he does the same work as a seaman) would have a remedy if allowed by state statute.

This last discrepancy arose because the Supreme Court ruled in the *Gillespie* case that the Jones Act (which provides a negligence-based claim for wrongful death of a seaman) precludes state remedy. The survivors of a longshoreman killed in the territorial waters of a state that allows wrongful death suits based on unseaworthiness, however, could sue under that theory. The survivors of a seaman killed in exactly the same way could not sue.

The *Moragne v. States Marine Lines* decision in 1970 reflected the general displeasure of the courts with these discrepancies. Many courts had been allowing suits for the death of seamen under the unseaworthiness doctrine. The Supreme Court ruled in the *Moragne* case that an action did lie "under general maritime law for death caused by violation of maritime duties."[20] The Court therefore allowed maritime law to apply, but did not displace the ability of the survivors to also file suits under state law.

THE LHWCA AND ITS EXTENSIONS

Because admiralty jurisdiction barred applying state workers' compensation laws to most maritime workers working on board vessels in navigable waters, Congress filled the gap by enacting a federal compensation law. The LHWCA, passed in 1927, applied the principle of the workers' compensation laws to certain maritime workers.

As other gaps in compensation coverage appeared, Congress extended the LHWCA provisions to those situations. The most significant legislative development, however, was the 1972 amendment of the act redefining its coverage of maritime workers and substantially increasing the benefits under the original act and its extensions. As part of those amendments, Congress also removed the extension of the unseaworthiness doctrine to longshore workers that the courts had granted. Judicial decisions have clarified many of the troublesome issues involved, but the courts have not resolved all ambiguities.

The United States Longshore and Harbor Workers' Compensation Act (LHWCA)

Because Congress modeled it after the New York Workmen's Compensation Law, the LHWCA applies essentially the same compensation principles to workers excluded from the protection of state laws according to the Supreme Court's ruling in the Jensen case. The LHWCA provides compensation without regard to fault for eligible maritime workers injured in the course of employment. Congress initially intended the act to be the exclusive remedy for such injuries. Because in practice, however, it did not serve as the exclusive remedy, Congress extensively amended the 1927 act in 1972. The 1972 amendments removed some legal problems and introduced others, prompting further amendments in 1984, including a change in the law's title to a nonsexist form (*Longshore*, rather than Longshoremen's, and Harbor Workers' Compensation Act).

Although injured longshore and harbor workers could not directly sue their employers, third-party-over actions had become common. Before 1972, an employee of a stevedoring firm injured while loading or unloading a vessel could sue the vessel's owner on the grounds that the injury resulted from the vessel's unseaworthy condition or on the grounds of negligence. An unseaworthiness claim was easier to prove and was therefore the most frequent basis for suit. The vessel owner may then recover any damages awarded to the employee from the employer because of the implied indemnity covering the stevedoring work on the vessel. This third-party-over action produced the same result as if the employer paid damages in excess of the LHWCA benefits directly to the employee. However, proving that the stevedoring company's negligence was responsible for the unseaworthy condition was difficult. Also important is that, in some cases, the vessel owner and employer were the same.

The 1972 amendments to the LHWCA eliminated the right of maritime workers to sue shipowners under the unseaworthiness doctrine and the shipowner's right to bring a third-party-over action against the employer. To make this restriction more palatable to maritime workers, the amendments also significantly increased the benefits and extended the act's jurisdiction.

The provision of the 1972 amendments addressing those issues was Section 905(b). That section involved employees who were employed by an entity other than the vessel owner. Often this meant that a stevedore employed the employee. Usually, a vessel owner brings the vessel into port and then turns over the vessel to the stevedore to unload. The stevedore's employees then unload the vessel. Section 905(b) states that a longshore employee injured while unloading cargo of a vessel cannot sue his or her stevedore-employer for negligence. The exclusive remedy available to the injured worker was compensation benefits under the LHWCA. The employee could sue the vessel owner for negligence, and the section provided that if found negligent, the vessel owner could not then seek reimbursement from the stevedore. The act barred all indemnification agreements to that effect. To appease the vessel owners, it also made them liable on no grounds other than their own negligence—that is, unseaworthiness was removed.

The 1984 amendments clarified the definition of covered employees and many benefit provisions. The next section analyzes the amended act in terms of the employer's obligation, the persons eligible for benefits, the injuries covered, and the benefits provided.

Employer's Obligation

Every employer under the LHWCA must secure compensation payment in one of two ways. One way is to obtain insurance coverage from any insurer authorized to write workers' compensation insurance and approved by the Secretary of Labor. The other way is to become a self-insured employer by furnishing to the Secretary of Labor satisfactory proof of the financial ability to pay compensation directly and to receive the authorization to do so. This authorization normally requires the deposit of a surety bond or other suitable guarantee. Employers who have failed to secure compensation required under the act face fines of up to $10,000 and prison terms of up to one year.

Compliance with the act must also be certified for a stevedoring firm to be eligible to conduct business at a port. As the act states, "No stevedoring firm shall be employed in any compensation district by a vessel or by hull owners until it presents to such vessel or hull owners a certificate issued by a deputy commissioner assigned to such district that it has complied with the provisions of this chapter requiring the securing of compensation to its employees."[21] Therefore, unless the firm qualifies under the act as a self-insurer, insurance coverage for LHWCA exposures is a necessary condition for business.

Persons and Employments Covered

The LHWCA substantially covers all maritime employment. **Maritime employment** includes those employees engaged in longshoring, harbor work, ship repair, shipbuilding, and ship-breaking in navigable waters of the U.S. except the master or members of the crew of a vessel. Like workers' compensation statutes, the act defines the term "employee" for purposes of the act. When used in the LHWCA:

> The term "employee" means any person engaged in maritime employment, including any longshoreman or other person engaged in longshoring operations, and any harbor-worker including a ship repairman, shipbuilder, and ship-breaker, but such term does not include:
>
> (A) individuals employed exclusively to perform office clerical, secretarial, security, or data processing work;
>
> (B) individuals employed by a club, camp, recreational operation, restaurant, museum, or retail outlet;
>
> (C) individuals employed by a marina and who are not engaged in construction, replacement, or expansion of such marina (except for routine maintenance);
>
> (D) individuals who (i) are employed by suppliers, transporters, or vendors, (ii) are temporarily doing business on the premises of an employer described in paragraph (4), and (iii) are not engaged in work normally performed by employees of that employer under the Act;
>
> (E) aquaculture workers;
>
> (F) individuals employed to build, repair, or dismantle any recreational vessel under sixty-five feet in length;
>
> (G) a master or member of a crew of any vessel; or
>
> (H) any person engaged by a master to load or unload or repair any small vessel under eighteen tons net;
>
> if individuals described in clauses (A) through (F) are subject to coverage under a State workers' compensation law.[22]

Maritime employment
Those employees engaged in longshoring, harbor work, ship repair, shipbuilding, and ship-breaking in navigable waters of the U.S. except the master or members of the crew of a vessel.

Paragraph 4, as referenced in (D), says:

> The term "employer" means an employer any of whose employees are employed in maritime employment, in whole or in part, upon the navigable waters of the United States (including any adjoining pier, wharf, dry dock, terminal, building way, marine railway, or other adjoining area customarily used by an employer in loading, unloading, repairing, or building a vessel).[23]

The act also excludes from coverage "an officer or employee of the United States or any agency thereof or of any State or foreign government or of any political subdivision thereof."[24]

The act otherwise provides compensation benefits in employee disability or death cases, but only if the disability or death results from an injury occurring on the navigable waters of the United States (including any adjoining pier, wharf, dry dock, terminal, building way, marine railway, or other adjoining area customarily used by an employer in loading, unloading, repairing, dismantling, or building a vessel).[25]

Therefore, the question that most often arises is whether the LHWCA or a state workers' compensation law applies. An employee can be engaged in maritime operations (such as building a marina) on nonnavigable waters wholly within one state and therefore be covered by the state rather than the federal act. Frequently, an employee can also be engaged in operations related to loading or unloading a ship, but executed on land rather than on water. Consequently, the problem is where to draw the line between land and water, and thereby between state and federal jurisdiction. Before 1972, federal jurisdiction stopped at the water's edge. The LHWCA applied at one end of the gangplank, but not at the other. Although the line was clear, employees loading or unloading ships crossed into and out of federal jurisdiction several times a day. In addition, as a result of the advent of containerized operations, more of the work of transferring cargo takes place on shoreside areas than had been the case. Therefore, longshore workers once protected by the LHWCA were no longer under its jurisdiction merely because of the modernization of operations.

The 1972 amended act expanded federal jurisdiction landward to correct those problems. So as not to extend unintended coverage to any worker who happened to come into the dock area, however, the amended act limited coverage to maritime employment. For the act to apply, the worker must meet two criteria. The injured worker must be an employee according to the act's definition, and the injury must have occurred on navigable waters. These two requirements can be summarized as tests of status and situs (descriptions of which follow). However, the intent of the 1972 amendments was to expand coverage, not restrict it. Therefore, several court cases have held that if a person would have been covered before the 1972 amendments, that person should be covered after the amendments.[26]

The LHWCA expressly includes as a "person engaged in maritime employment" any member of several classes of workers, the first of which is "any longshoreman or other person engaged in longshoring operations." A worker who can be characterized as a "longshoreman" within that term's ordinary meaning, employed as such at the time of the injury, has the status required by the act without further inquiry concerning particular duties.[27] The worker's union affiliation may indicate the longshoreman's status, but the affiliation is not conclusive proof that the worker is a longshoreman.

The act even covers a worker not employed as a longshoreman if "engaged in longshoring operations." Such operations include two subcategories: **stevedoring operations**, which is the immediate loading and unloading of vessels, and **terminal operations**, which are the cargo-handling activities associated with stevedoring operations. Longshoring operations are all operations necessary to transfer cargo between land and water, including transportation modes that are performed by workers associated with that transfer rather than with the transportation itself. The test is essentially whether the employee's work relates directly to the cargo or to the equipment or premises used to handle it. The act does not exclude as "office clerical" stevedoring cargo checkers, talliers, and clerks who document cargo movement.

> **Stevedoring operations**
> The immediate loading and unloading of vessels.

> **Terminal operations**
> The cargo-handling activities associated with stevedoring operations.

The definition of employees covered by the LHWCA also specifically mentions ship repairers and shipbuilders. Those terms include the many trades or crafts represented within a shipyard's labor force. Therefore, all shipyard workers—welders, burners, machinists, carpenters, electricians, painters, sandblasters, crane operators, and their assistants, and many others—are shipbuilders or ship repairers. Premium auditors should consider all functions that contribute to the enterprise shipbuilding or ship repairing and therefore regard employees who perform those functions as covered harbor workers.[28] As with longshoremen, a shipbuilder or ship repairer retains that status even while temporarily assigned to nonmaritime work. The general occupation, rather than the precise duties at the time of injury, establishes the maritime employment status.

Although constructing and repairing commercial vessels generally meets the status requirement, the Secretary of Labor issues certificates of exemption from coverage under the LHWCA when state act coverage is available and when the entity works on small vessels only. The act defines **small vessels** as commercial barges under 900 lightship displacement tons and tugboats, towboats, crew boats, supply boats, fishing vessels, or other work vessels if they are less than 1,600 tons gross. The exempt vessels definition does not include military vessels, Corps of Engineers dredges, and U.S. Coast Guard vessels. **Displacement** is the empty vessel's weight measured in long tons (2,240 pounds); **gross tons (long tons)** is the measurement of the volume of a vessel's enclosed spaces, counting each 100 cubic feet as one gross ton. If the facility receives federal maritime subsidies or the employee is not subject to a state workers' compensation law, the LHWCA covers the employee.

> **Small vessels**
> Commercial barges under 900 lightship displacement tons and tugboats, towboats, crew boats, supply boats, fishing vessels, or other work vessels if they are less than 1,600 tons gross.

> **Displacement**
> The empty vessel's weight measured in long tons (2,240 pounds).

> **Gross tons,** or **long tons**
> The measurement of the volume of a vessel's enclosed spaces, counting each 100 cubic feet as one gross ton.

Shipbreaking
All facets of scrapping a vessel, from striping nonferrous fittings and parts from the hull to reducing the hull to pieces of a convenient size, and the associated functions of moving and piling the scrap and loading it for shipment out of the waterfront scrapyard.

The LHWCA also lists shipbreakers among covered harborworkers. **Shipbreaking** includes all facets of scrapping a vessel, from striping nonferrous fittings and parts from the hull to reducing the hull to pieces of a convenient size, and the associated functions of moving and piling the scrap and loading it for shipment out of the waterfront scrapyard. Premium auditors should consider all workers in this industry as covered employees.

The act includes all harbor workers, whether expressly mentioned in the act or not, unless they are masters or members of the crew of vessels or engaged by the master to load, unload, or repair a vessel under eighteen tons net. For example, maritime employees within the act's coverage include linesmen, vessel watchmen, gangplank attendants, marine inspectors and surveyors, divers, marine construction workers, ship cleaners and chandlers, and others whose employment is clearly identified with the water or the waterfront but who are not members of the crews of vessels.

Workers who load or unload small vessels that cannot be considered ships are also maritime employees. Performing such operations is just as much maritime when it relates to small vessels as when it relates to large ones. The act's specific exclusion of "any person engaged by the master to load or unload or repair any small vessel under eighteen tons net" should dispel any doubt concerning this conclusion. The specification that the exclusion applies only to those "engaged by the master" clearly indicates that those engaged by others—the owner or, far more often, a marina operator, a boat repair yard, or another employer performing such services for the owner under contract—are covered employees.

The 1984 amendments specifically exclude building, repairing, or dismantling recreational vessels less than sixty-five feet long from coverage under the LHWCA (Section F). The factories are normally at inland locations, and the repair facilities are usually at inland boat dealers or on inland lakes or rivers that are not navigable, so that exclusion is logical.

However, a few recreational vessel construction and repair facilities are located on or near navigable waters. Those operations may continue to be under the LHWCA for that part of the work done on vessels while floating in navigable waters or on dry docks, building ways, or marine railways adjacent to those waters. Those workers would be deemed to fall under the admiralty jurisdiction and would not be covered by a state act as would those workers at inland locations. Building or repairing pleasure craft more than sixty-five feet long usually does meet the status test for coverage under the LHWCA.

The definition of "employee" in the amended LHWCA limited the persons protected by the act who were at the newly covered shoreside areas, but Congress did not intend to withdraw the act's previous coverage of other maritime employees.[29] The Supreme Court used that reasoning to conclude that a sewer construction worker directing the unloading of materials from a supply barge in the Hudson River was a maritime employee.[30] Therefore, auditors should regard all employment actually performed on the navigable waters of the U.S. as maritime employment, whether or not the employment bears an immediate relation to commercial shipping operations.

Two tests that are used to determine whether a person is covered under the LHWCA are a status test and a situs test. A **status test** is a requirement under the LHWCA that the employee be engaged in maritime employment. The status test's significance appears most readily in longshoring operations that extend some distance from the water. Any worker performing cargo-handling duties on the water is an employee within the act's terms while doing so. Whether such an employee retains the act's protection while ashore depends on the facts of each case. The premium auditor should determine whether the worker meets the status test in such a case based on the degree to which the worker's shoreside presence is merely incidental to the work on the water. If it is, the worker retains employee status while ashore.

A **situs test** is a requirement under the LHWCA that the claimant's location at the time of injury be on navigable waters or certain adjoining areas. In determining situs eligibility, the premium auditor needs to understand how the situs test is applied. Extending the LHWCA's jurisdiction landward to areas adjoining navigable waters provides full protection to workers engaged in maritime operations, whether they are on land or water at the time of injury.

In general, a premium auditor can readily identify the locations at which an entity conducts longshoring operations as piers or marine terminals. Because of the large scale on which modern shipping is conducted and particularly because of the large holding areas required for handling containerized cargo, marine terminals covering many hundreds of acres are not uncommon. Such terminals come within the jurisdiction of the LHWCA. The precise location where an injury occurred does not have to be one used for loading or unloading operations, nor must it immediately adjoin the water. If the overall area that includes the location is part of a terminal adjoining the water, the location meets the situs test.[31]

In areas where additional space is not available immediately adjacent to the previously established boundaries of a waterfront pier or terminal and where many stevedoring companies work at the same terminal, facilities such as gear lockers (buildings in which stevedoring equipment is maintained and stored) may be located outside a terminal's fenced boundaries. Because such facilities exist solely for loading and discharging ships, premium auditors should regard them as extensions of the terminals. Hence, although they do not adjoin the water, they are parts of terminal complexes that do and are therefore within the act's jurisdiction.

The LHWCA expressly includes any dry dock, building way, or marine railway within its jurisdiction. A **dry dock** is a dock from which water can be pumped out and that is used for building ships or for repairing ships below their waterline. It includes both a floating dock and a graving dock, and the cranes, scaffolds, and appurtenant structures with them. A **building way** or **marine railway** includes the land adjacent to the incline or track system

Status test
A requirement under the LHWCA that the employee be engaged in maritime employment.

Situs test
A requirement under the LHWCA that the claimant's location at the time of injury be on navigable waters or certain adjoining areas.

Dry dock
A dock from which water can be pumped out and that is used for building ships or for repairing ships below their waterline.

Building way, or **marine railway**
The land adjacent to the incline or track system that is devoted to constructing or repairing vessels on the ways.

that is devoted to constructing or repairing vessels on the ways. Some ship-yards have lateral-transfer tracks on which workers can shift vessels removed from the water around the yard; the entire area covered by such a system is a marine railway within the act's scope. Similarly, premium auditors should not limit the area for shipbuilding or repairing to a particular location or locations but should regard it as the entire, overall facility devoted to covered activities. The relevant area is the entire shipyard or other facility customarily used in loading, unloading, repairing, or building a vessel. Such facilities include nearby locations functioning as part of the same facility even if they are separated from the main facility by roads or fences.

Constructing and repairing commercial vessels always meet the situs test for coverage under the LHWCA. A commercial shipyard must be located on a navigable waterway because commercial vessels move in and out; any waterway that supports commercial vessel traffic is navigable by definition. Similarly, constructing and repairing recreational vessels more than sixty-five feet long also usually meet the situs test. Because few large yachts are used on nonnavigable waters, virtually all of those operations are on navigable waters and are therefore covered by the federal act.

Extending the jurisdiction of the LHWCA to land areas adjoining the U.S.'s navigable waters created a gray area in which either state or federal law may apply. The Supreme Court has ruled that this is concurrent jurisdiction area. According to the Court, injured shipyard workers are not barred from compensation under the state law merely because the LHWCA may also apply,[32] nor does an award under one law exclude possible compensation under the other law as long as the courts consider proper credit for the first award.[33]

In doubtful situations, premium auditors should assume that jurisdiction of the LHWCA may apply. As long as its benefit levels are higher, injured workers will tend to seek compensation under the LHWCA. Moreover, the act provides that, in adjudicating a claim, "it shall be presumed, in the absence of substantial evidence to the contrary. . .that the claim comes within the provisions of the chapter."[34] Therefore, the burden is on the employer to demonstrate that coverage clearly does not exist rather than on the claimant to demonstrate that coverage applies.

Injuries and Diseases Covered

The definition of "injury" used in the LHWCA represents an amalgamation of the corresponding sections of the New York Workmen's Compensation Law. According to the LHWCA, "The term 'injury' means accidental injury or death arising out of and in the course of employment, and such occupational disease or infection as arises naturally out of such employment or as naturally or unavoidably results from such accidental injury, and includes an injury caused by the willful act of a third person directed against an employee because of his employment."[35]

Therefore, any work-related accident and virtually any disease associated with the employment qualify for compensation if the employee has suffered any impairment as a result.

Benefits

LHWCA benefits are essentially the same as state workers' compensation benefits, only usually higher. Following the 1972 amendments, however, LHWCA benefits tended to be more liberal than those provided in many states. Consequently, when a jurisdiction question arises, injured workers have been more inclined to seek LHWCA benefits.

Like other compensation laws, the LHWCA provides medical, disability, death, and rehabilitation benefits. The act authorizes all necessary medical care for an injury's effects. The employee has an initial free choice of physicians, although the Secretary of Labor can disqualify physicians, and there is no limit to the cost or period of treatment.

For temporary disability, insurers pay LHWCA benefits during the disability period, subject to a three-day waiting period. If disability lasts longer than fourteen days, payment is retroactive to day one. Insurers base compensation for permanent partial disability on one of two factors: (1) a statutory schedule for the loss, or loss of use, of specified body parts and for disfigurement or (2) the employee's loss in wage-earning capacity. In permanent total disability cases, compensation based on the employee's weekly wage is paid for life. The act does place a minimum and maximum on those amounts.

LHWCA benefits also cover burial expenses up to $3,000 as well as payments to dependents based on the deceased employee's weekly wage. Those benefits apply either when the injury causes death or when an employee sustaining permanent total disability because of the injury subsequently dies from other causes.

The LHWCA also provides vocational rehabilitation through appropriate state agencies and payments not exceeding $25 per week for maintenance while the employee is undergoing such vocational training.

The compensation for disability is two-thirds of the employee's weekly wage. The maximum compensation, however, is 200 percent of the national average weekly wage. The minimum is 50 percent of the national average weekly wage or the employee's actual weekly wage, whichever is less. The Department of Labor calculates the national average weekly wage and revises the amount every October 1.

The LHWCA is administered by the Division of Longshore and Harbor Workers' Compensation, Office of Workers' Compensation Programs, of the U.S. Department of Labor through district directors appointed to sixteen compensation districts. The district director or an administrative law judge settles claims. Parties first appeal disputed claims to a three-person panel of the Benefits Review Board of the U.S. Department of Labor. The full board can review its decision, and the parties can appeal to the U.S. Court of Appeals.

LHWCA Extensions

In addition to covering maritime workers, federal law has also covered other groups of employees outside of the jurisdiction of state workers' compensation laws. Those include employees of government contractors at overseas installations, civilian employees of the armed forces, and workers on offshore drilling rigs on the outer continental shelf. In each case, Congress extended the LHWCA's provisions to apply to those workers.

Defense Base Act

Many civilians work at American military installations around the world. State workers' compensation laws do not apply outside the U.S., and the Federal Employees' Compensation Act (FECA) covers only direct employees of the federal government. The Defense Base Act applies to the employees of government contractors outside the continental U.S. A waiver can exempt employees who are not U.S. citizens if the Secretary of Labor approves it. The Defense Base Act extends the LHWCA's provisions to these overseas employees of government contractors. The act precisely states its jurisdiction, and few legal questions have arisen in its application.

Civilian Employees of Nonappropriated Fund Instrumentalities Act

Civilian Employees of Nonappropriated Fund Instrumentalities Act
An act that excludes post exchange employees from the civil service laws and from FECA.

A 1942 Supreme Court decision held that an army exchange was an integral part of the War Department, subject to the same legal immunities and therefore exempt from a state gasoline tax.[36] This decision raised the possibility that post exchange employees may come under the civil service laws. The **Civilian Employees of Nonappropriated Fund Instrumentalities Act**, an act that excludes post exchange employees from the civil service laws and from FECA, clarified this question.[37] The act provides instead for compensating injured employees of nonappropriated fund instrumentalities according to the terms of the LHWCA. Employees covered by this law are those who are not compensated from funds appropriated by Congress, but who are employed by instrumentalities of the U.S. (Under the Defense Base Act, the covered employees work for a contractor under contract with a U.S. government agency.) For the most part, these are civilian employees of the armed forces who are U.S. citizens working in post exchanges, ship service stores, service clubs, daycare centers, and similar ancillary operations at air, naval, and military bases outside the continental U.S.

Outer Continental Shelf Lands Act

The outer continental shelf is an active area for petroleum exploration and production. Outer continental shelf lands are beyond the boundaries of the continental U.S. and therefore come under federal jurisdiction. The outer continental shelf consists of all submerged lands lying seaward and outside the area of lands beneath navigable waters as defined in Section 1301 of 43 U.S. Code Annotated. Essentially, it includes all submerged lands extending seaward from the three-mile territorial limit. Along the Atlantic Coast, the average distance from the shore to the continental shelf's outer edge is about seventy miles. In some places it reaches nearly 250 miles.

The Outer Continental Shelf Lands Act extends the LHWCA's provisions to employees conducting operations on the outer continental shelf under a federal lease or another authorization relating to exploring for, developing, removing, or transporting by pipeline natural resources. It does not apply to masters or members of a crew of any vessel or to federal, state, or any foreign government's employees.

INSURANCE FOR LHWCA EXPOSURES

With appropriate endorsements, the workers' compensation and employers' liability policy can provide coverage for all of the LHWCA loss exposures. Rule XII of the NCCI's *Basic Manual* delineates the procedures for insuring exposures under the LHWCA and its extensions.

LHWCA Coverage

The LHWCA uses the same principles as the state workers' compensation laws. A complication arises because an employer may be subject to both the LHWCA and the state workers' compensation law at the same time. Although both of those exposures can be insured, insurers must separately cover and hence separately rate them. The same is true of the various extensions of the LHWCA.

Although the LHWCA is a workers' compensation law, an insurer cannot enter it in Item 3.A. of the information page on a workers' compensation policy. Instead, insurers provide LHWCA coverage by adding the standard Longshore and Harbor Workers' Compensation Act Coverage Endorsement (WC 00 01 06 A) to the standard workers' compensation policy. Exhibit 6-1 shows this endorsement. The endorsement amends the definition of "workers' compensation law" to include the LHWCA regarding operations in any state in the endorsement's schedule. The policy then applies to those operations as though the insurer listed the state in Item 3.A. of the information page. An insurer can even list a monopolistic fund state, for example, on the endorsement to provide LHWCA coverage for operations in that state. The manual applicable in the state named in the information page governs the policy, but the insurer must also agree to abide by the rules and regulations of the Labor Department's Office of Workers' Compensation Programs.

EXHIBIT 6-1

Longshore and Harbor Workers' Compensation Act Coverage Endorsement

WORKERS' COMPENSATION AND EMPLOYERS' LIABILITY INSURANCE POLICY	WC 00 01 06 A
1st Reprint Effective April 1, 1992	**Standard**

LONGSHORE AND HARBOR WORKERS' COMPENSATION ACT COVERAGE ENDORSEMENT

This endorsement applies only to work subject to the Longshore and Harbor Workers' Compensation Act in a state shown in the Schedule. The policy applies to that work as though that state were listed in Item 3.A. of the Information Page.

General Section C. **Workers' Compensation Law** is replaced by the following:

C.   **Workers' Compensation Law**

Workers' Compensation Law means the workers' or workmen's compensation law and occupational disease law of each state or territory named in Item 3.A. of the Information Page and the Longshore and Harbor Workers' Compensation Act (33 USC Sections 901 950). It includes any amendments to those laws that are in effect during the policy period. It does not include any other federal workers' or workmen's compensation law, other federal occupational disease law or the provisions of any law that provide nonoccupational disability benefits.

Part Two (Employers' Liability Insurance), C. Exclusions., exclusion 8, does not apply to work subject to the Longshore and Harbor Workers' Compensation Act.

This endorsement does not apply to work subject to the Defense Base Act, the Outer Continental Shelf Lands Act, or the Nonappropriated Fund Instrumentalities Act.

Schedule

State	Longshore and Harbor Workers' Compensation Act Coverage Percentage

The rates for classifications with code numbers not followed by the letter "F" are rates for work not ordinarily subject to the Longshore and Harbor Workers' Compensation Act. If this policy covers work under such classifications, and if the work is subject to the Longshore and Harbor Workers' Compensation Act, those non F classification rates will be increased by the Longshore and Harbor Workers' Compensation Act Coverage Percentage shown in the Schedule.

Notes:

1.   The Longshore and Harbor Workers' Compensation Act is a federal workers' compensation law that applies to workers in maritime employments, including longshore, harborworkers, shipbuilders, shipbreakers and ship repairers. It does not apply to masters or crews of vessels. See Rule XII of the Basic Manual for additional details.

2.   Use this endorsement to provide workers' compensation insurance and employers' liability insurance for work subject to the Longshore and Harbor Workers' Compensation Act in any state, including a monopolistic state fund state.

3.   Coverage is provided in a state by naming the state in the Schedule.

4.   The following entry may be typed or printed in the Schedule to provide coverage in Item 3.A. states: "Each state named in Item 3.A. of the Information Page."

5.   The following entry may be typed or printed in the Schedule to provide coverage in Item 3.A. and 3.C. states: "Each state named in Item 3.A. or 3.C. of the Information Page."

The endorsement broadens the standard workers' compensation policy's coverage to apply to a similar, but separate, statutory obligation of the employer. Part one of the policy, in which the insurer promises to "pay promptly when due the benefits required" of the insured by the workers' compensation law, includes LHWCA benefits by virtue of this endorsement. When the insurer endorses the policy to provide LHWCA coverage for the insured's operations, the insurer pays any benefits awarded under the LHWCA regardless of where the injury took place.

Premium auditors must remember that the LHWCA does not necessarily cover the same persons as the state workers' compensation law. For example, if the state act excludes an executive officer, that exclusion has no bearing on LHWCA coverage. For an insured subject to both the state compensation law and the LHWCA, premium auditors would have to include in the basis of premium the payroll of an executive officer performing maritime work even though the state act may exclude the officer from state act coverage.

LHWCA coverage requires premium charges additional to and/or different from those for state workers' compensation exposures. A later section of this chapter, titled "Premium Determination," describes those different charges and the different rules for longshore coverage. If an insurer intends to provide LHWCA coverage and to collect the additional premium, the policy should include the Longshore and Harbor Workers' Compensation Act Coverage Endorsement. Otherwise, the basic policy does not cover the exposure under the workers' compensation insurance section or under the employers' liability section. If a premium auditor discovers LHWCA exposures with no coverage, he or she should report the situation immediately to the underwriter for rectification.

Coverage for LHWCA Extensions

Coverage for the LHWCA's extensions requires the appropriate endorsement in each case.

Defense Base Act Coverage Endorsement (WC 00 01 01 A)

To provide coverage for exposures under the Defense Base Act, the standard workers' compensation policy should include the Defense Base Act Coverage Endorsement, such as the one in Exhibit 6-2. This endorsement amends the policy to include the Defense Base Act within the definition of workers' compensation law as used in the policy.

Outer Continental Shelf Lands Act Coverage Endorsement (WC 00 01 09 A)

Insurers can provide coverage for operations on the outer continental shelf by adding the endorsement shown in Exhibit 6-3 to the standard policy. This endorsement includes a precise description of the operations and their locations, including the name of the state whose boundaries, if extended to the outer continental shelf, would include the location of the work.

EXHIBIT 6-2

Defense Base Act Coverage Endorsement

WORKERS' COMPENSATION AND EMPLOYERS' LIABILITY INSURANCE POLICY   WC 00 01 01 A

1st Reprint   Effective April 1, 1992   Standard

DEFENSE BASE ACT COVERAGE ENDORSEMENT

This endorsement applies only to the work described in the Schedule or described on the Information Page as subject to the Defense Base Act. The policy applies to that work as though the location included in the description of the work were a state named in Item 3.A. of the Information Page.

General Section C. **Workers' Compensation Law** is replaced by the following:

C. **Workers' Compensation Law**

Workers' Compensation Law means the workers' or workmen's compensation law and occupational disease law of each state or territory named in Item 3.A. of the Information Page and the Defense Base Act (42 USC Sections 1651 1654). It includes any amendments to those laws that are in effect during the policy period. It does not include any other federal workers' or workmen's compensation law, other federal occupational disease law or the provisions of any law that provide nonoccupational disability benefits.

Part Two (Employers Liability Insurance), C. Exclusions., exclusion 8, does not apply to work subject to the Defense Base Act.

Schedule

Description of Work

Notes:

1. The Defense Base Act makes the Longshore and Harbor Workers' Compensation Act apply to contractors performing work at overseas military bases, whether in a territory or possession of the United States or in a foreign country, and to various public works contracts performed outside the continental United States.

2. Use this endorsement to provide workers' compensation insurance and employers' liability insurance for work subject to the Defense Base Act extension of the Longshore and Harbor Workers' Compensation Act.

3. The description of the work must include the location where the work is to be performed.

This endorsement broadens the coverage to include LHWCA benefits payable under the Outer Continental Shelf Lands Act. It does not provide coverage for injuries to the master or members of the crew of a vessel. They are subject to the Jones Act or admiralty law. Therefore, for workers on an offshore drilling platform, coverage depends on whether the platform is a floating structure or a permanent structure.

EXHIBIT 6-3

Outer Continental Shelf Lands Act Coverage Endorsement

WORKERS' COMPENSATION AND EMPLOYERS' LIABILITY INSURANCE POLICY   WC 00 01 09 A

1st Reprint   Effective April 1, 1992   Standard

OUTER CONTINENTAL SHELF LANDS ACT COVERAGE ENDORSEMENT

This endorsement applies only to the work described in Item 4 of the Information Page or in the Schedule as subject to the Outer Continental Shelf Lands Act. The policy will apply to that work as though the location shown in the Schedule were a state named in Item 3.A. of the Information Page.

General Section C. **Workers' Compensation Law** is replaced by the following:

C.   **Workers' Compensation Law**

Workers' Compensation Law means the workers' or workmen's compensation law and occupational disease law of each state or territory named in Item 3.A. of the Information Page and the Outer Continental Shelf Lands Act (43 USC Sections 1331 1356). It includes any amendments to those laws that are in effect during the policy period. It does not include any other federal workers' or workmen's compensation law, other federal occupational disease law or the provisions of any law that provide nonoccupational disability benefits.

Part Two (Employers' Liability Insurance), C. Exclusions., exclusion 8, does not apply to work subject to the Outer Continental Shelf Lands Act.

Schedule

Description and Location of Work

Notes:

1.   The Outer Continental Shelf Lands Act makes the Longshore and Harbor Workers' Compensation Act apply to work involving the development from fixed platforms of the natural resources of the Outer Continental Shelf. Use this endorsement to provide workers' compensation insurance and employers' liability insurance for work on the Outer Continental Shelf subject to the Longshore and Harbor Workers' Compensation Act.

2.   The description of the work must show the state whose boundaries, if extended to the Outer Continental Shelf, would include the location of the work.

3.   Use the Maritime Exclusion Endorsement or Maritime Coverage Endorsement to exclude or cover the exposure for masters and members of the crews of vessels.

Nonappropriated Fund Instrumentalities Act Coverage Endorsement (WC 00 01 08 A)

Insurers can attach the endorsement shown in Exhibit 6-4 to a standard workers' compensation policy to afford coverage under the act providing LHWCA benefits for civilian employees of the Army and Air Force Exchange Service,

Army and Air Force Motion Picture Service, Navy Ship's Stores Ashore, Navy Exchanges, Marine Corps Exchanges, Coast Guard Exchanges, and other instrumentalities of the U.S. Such instrumentalities are under the jurisdiction of the armed forces and are conducted for the pleasure and improvement of the personnel of the armed forces.

EXHIBIT 6-4

Nonappropriated Fund Instrumentalities Act Coverage Endorsement

WORKERS' COMPENSATION AND EMPLOYERS' LIABILITY INSURANCE POLICY   WC 00 01 08 A

1st Reprint   **Effective April 1, 1992**   **Standard**

NONAPPROPRIATED FUND INSTRUMENTALITIES ACT COVERAGE ENDORSEMENT

This endorsement applies only to the work described in the Schedule or described on the Information Page as subject to the Nonappropriated Fund Instrumentalities Act. The policy applies to that work as though the location shown in the Schedule were a state named in Item 3.A. of the Information Page.

General Section C. **Workers' Compensation Law** is replaced by the following:

C. **Workers' Compensation Law**

Workers' Compensation Law means the workers' or workmen's compensation law and occupational disease law of each state or territory named in Item 3.A. of the Information Page and the Nonappropriated Fund Instrumentalities Act (5 USC Sections 8171 8173). It includes any amendments to those laws that are in effect during the policy period. It does not include any other federal workers' or workmen's compensation law, other federal occupational disease law or the provisions of any law that provide nonoccupational disability benefits.

Part Two (Employers' Liability Insurance), C. Exclusions., exclusion 8, does not apply to work subject to the Nonappropriated Fund Instrumentalities Act.

Schedule

Description and Location of Work

Notes:

1. The Nonappropriated Fund Instrumentalities Act makes the Longshore and Harbor Workers' Compensation Act apply to civilian employees of certain instrumentalities such as the Army and Air Force Exchange Service, Army and Air Force Motion Picture Service, Navy Ship's Stores Ashore, Navy, Marine and Coast Guard Exchanges and other instrumentalities of the United States under jurisdiction of the Armed Forces conducted for the pleasure and improvement of Armed Forces personnel.

2. Use this endorsement to provide workers' compensation insurance and employers' liability insurance for work subject to the Nonappropriated Fund Instrumentalities Act.

Premium Determination

Insurers base premiums for coverage under the LHWCA or its extensions on payroll. Therefore, premium determination follows essentially the same procedure for LHWCA coverage as for state workers' compensation act coverage. However, certain additional considerations are involved in both the basis of premium and the classifications and rates for LHWCA coverage. Premium auditors should consult the state manuals and rules for exceptions. The following discussions do not mention all state exceptions.

Basis of Premium

The stevedoring industry's unique payroll practices affect the premium auditor's task of determining the basis of premium. With one significant exception, the basis of premium rules in the workers' compensation manual are the same for LHWCA coverage. That exception involves overtime pay for stevedores (not for all maritime work). Stevedoring contractors also commonly employ some other unusual payroll procedures that can complicate a premium audit.

The stevedoring industry records the hours on the clock during which the employees did a particular job and the type of cargo handled. Applicable wage rates, or cargo rates, vary according to the cargo type. The prescribed wage rate structure contains penalty rates for handling offensive materials such as raw hides, soda ash, old bones, acids, ammunition, and explosives. A copy of the prevailing wage rate schedule can assist the premium auditor in interpreting payroll records. Because of this long-established pay practice, excluding extra pay for overtime would be both cumbersome and unrealistic. Therefore, the *Basic Manual* stipulates the following exception:

> Exclusion of overtime pay does not apply to payroll assigned to any classification under the caption "Stevedoring" with a code number followed by the letter F.[38]

Virtually all employers seeking stevedoring personnel use the union hiring hall dispatcher. Because the demand varies according to the number of ships in port, the union members may work for several different employers. Therefore, stevedoring firms may maintain a central pay office so that employees receive a single weekly paycheck regardless of how many firms they worked for during the week. Each firm prepares payroll sheets in duplicate and calculates the payroll taxes due. The firm sends a copy to the central pay office along with a check for the total net payroll. The central office then combines all the payroll sheets and issues paychecks to each employee.

Each employer also contributes to a trustee account established for disbursing fringe benefits such as health insurance and retirement benefits. This practice requires a careful accounting of hours worked for each employer. The employee receives benefits based on the total hours worked for all employers. Vacation pay is included in the basis of premium. Therefore the premium auditor must investigate the nature of "vacation payments" that the central office charges back to the employer. This allows the employer to record annual taxable wages for state and federal payroll tax return reporting and payment of the employer's and employee's taxes thereon. If individual employee tax returns include those vacation wages, the premium auditor should include those vacation wages in the premium base.

Classifications and Rates

Although the same payroll serves as the premium base whether LHWCA coverage or state coverage applies, the classification and rating system structure provides the basis for each insurer collecting the additional premium for broadening the coverage to include LHWCA benefits. The bureau bases rates or loss costs for certain classes designated by the letter F following the classification code number on LHWCA loss experience. For the remaining classifications, insurers apply a percentage increase factor to the state-coverage-only rate to increase it to reflect the LHWCA exposure.

F **classifications**
Classifications that describe freight handling, stevedoring, or other operations inherently subject to LHWCA jurisdiction.

Certain classifications (called **F classifications**) describe freight handling, stevedoring, or other operations inherently subject to LHWCA jurisdiction. The manual indicates those classifications by the letter *F* following the classification code number. An example is the classification "Freight Handling NOC" (Code 7350F). The manual rates for these *F* classifications apply to coverages under either the LHWCA or a combination of the LHWCA and the state act, and have been calculated accordingly. Therefore, the manual rate for an *F* classification multiplied by the premium base produces the premium required for LHWCA coverage or the premium required for a combination of LHWCA and state act coverage.

F classifications describe operations inherently subject to LHWCA jurisdiction. The existence of those classifications eliminates the need to divide payroll between operations subject to the LHWCA and those subject only to the state workers' compensation law. The nature of stevedoring operations at most ports would make an accurate payroll division on that basis virtually impossible.

Some freight-handling operations, however, may be performed at railroad yards, airports, or warehouses in locations not adjoining navigable waters of the U.S. For coverage under the state compensation law only, non-*F* classifications describe the same operations as *F* classifications but carry a rate appropriate for state coverage only. For example, the classification "Freight Handling NOC" (Code 7360) describes the same operation as the Code 7350F classification, but it contemplates coverage only under state law.

The NCCI has stated that because the scope of the LHWCA is subject to court interpretation based on the facts of the situations, whether to use the *F* classification or the non-*F* classification is best left to the discretion of the insured and insurer. The insured and the insurer can make that decision based on their knowledge of the facts or with the assistance of their legal representatives.[39]

The NCCI calculates the statistical experience for *F* classifications independently of other classifications to provide adequate rates to pay both state and

LHWCA benefits. Therefore, when a statutory rate change occurs because of a change in state benefits, a premium auditor cannot use the ratio method of computing the resulting premium change for policies including F classifications. The premium auditor must split the premium base into the periods before and after the rate change and compute the premium for each period separately.

The modernization of cargo-handling techniques has transformed the nature of stevedoring operations. In particular, ocean-bound cargoes are now commonly shipped in steel containers that the shipper or carrier seals before leaving the port. Trucks deliver the containers to the dock where dockside gantries or mobile cranes place them aboard ship. Exhibit 6-5 illustrates an on-ship gantry hoisting containers onto a containership. A separate stevedoring classification for containerized freight operations (Code 7327F) exists. It does not include any work in the ship's holds or over-the-road trucking operations, which premium auditors should separately classify as trucking local or trucking long haul (Codes 7228 and 7229, respectively).[40]

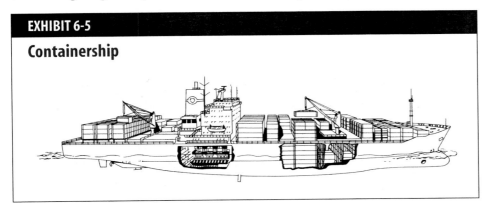

EXHIBIT 6-5

Containership

Exhibit 6-6 shows another technique, called the "roll on-roll off" (Ro-Ro) method. Trucks hauling cargo trailers enter side openings of the ship and proceed directly to the appropriate space for stowing the loaded trailer. At the destination port, other trucks enter the ship to hook up the trailers and roll off.

Still another technique is called "LASH," for "lighters aboard ship." **Lighters** are small steel barges that carry the cargo through a harbor. Specially designed ocean cargo ships use their own traveler cranes to lift the lighters out of the water and place them aboard the ship. At the destination port, the crane places the lighters in the harbor waters, and tug boats tow them to the dock for unloading.

Lighters
Small steel barges that carry cargo through a harbor.

When traditional cargo-handling methods are involved, insurers must classify the operation according to whether the cargo transfer between vessels and the pier requires hoisting equipment (Code 7309F—an NOC classification) or whether it can be entirely performed by hand or hand trucks (Code 7317F). However, the manual does not permit payroll division between those classes in connection with loading or unloading any one vessel. In either case, the stevedoring classification includes all loading or unloading, stowing, shifting, and trimming of cargo on board vessels; the transfer of cargoes between vessels

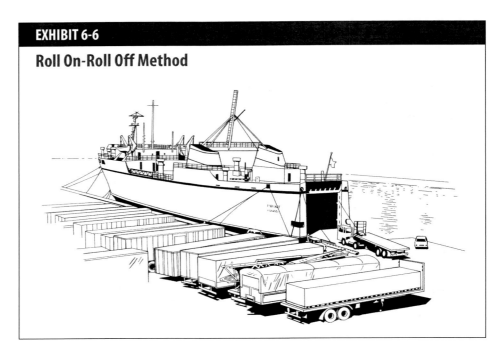

EXHIBIT 6-6

Roll On-Roll Off Method

and the pier; and the transfer of cargo from the pier's apron to the point of deposit or warehouse and any necessary tiering, sorting, or breaking down as well as operating any mechanical equipment used in the process.

Premium auditors should separately classify drivers not conducting stevedoring operations as described above as either trucking local or trucking long haul (Codes 7228 and 7229, respectively). Insurers should separately classify talliers and checking clerks under Code 8709F or 8719.

Constructing and repairing commercial vessels always meet the situs test for coverage under the LHWCA. Constructing and repairing commercial vessels always meets the status test regarding work on board the vessels while afloat and work on piers, docks, building ways, dry docks, and marine railways. Other commercial shipyard work also meets the status test unless the employer has secured a certificate of exemption from the Secretary of Labor.

Because the rates for LHWCA coverage are traditionally higher than for state act coverage, premium auditors must be careful when auditing a shipyard with a certificate of exemption. The LHWCA may continue to cover some portions of the operation, as noted above. In addition, the premium auditor should examine the certificate itself because it may apply only to a specific part of the operation.

An interchange of labor between covered and exempt parts of the operation is possible. The manual permits division of payroll, provided the insured maintains the proper payroll records. Finally, the exemption automatically terminates if a nonexempt vessel is being built or repaired. The premium auditor should examine both the allocation of payrolls to state act and federal act classes as well as the specifications of the vessels being built or repaired.

When a shipyard is not subject to exemption, one occasional cause of controversy occurs when a shop is located outside the yard area, perhaps even several miles away from the waterfront. Although case law on that point is far from conclusive, the act's administrators have consistently held that all of the facilities involved in constructing or repairing a vessel meet the situs test regardless of their physical location as long as the area in question is part of the overall maritime facility.[41] Some shipyard operators have located their machine shops and other operations away from the waterfront, trying to escape liability under the act, but the act still covers those locations.

Some shipyards, particularly those specializing in fishing vessels, are small operations. Most, however, are large enterprises. Constructing an ocean-going vessel is comparable to erecting a major building in terms of the amount of labor involved. Repair, overhaul, or conversion jobs may require almost as much labor as the initial construction. The large payrolls, combined with high rates, subject shipyards to considerable insurance premiums. The premium auditor should therefore plan such a premium audit carefully so that those insureds receive attention commensurate with their size. As with most large enterprises, shipyards usually have excellent records. Many maintain job cost accounting systems, and their books of account closely resemble building contractors' books.

The major premium audit problem encountered with shipyards concerns *F* classes. In most states, constructing or repairing ocean-going vessels and river craft comes under one or more of those classifications. The *F* classes include both employees subject to the LHWCA and employees subject only to the state act. Insureds often protest including employees whom the LHWCA does not cover in the same rate as the yard employees subject to the federal law. Including all employees described by the classification phraseology is mandatory because the bureau promulgated the rates or loss costs on the assumption that insurers would include employees regardless of their coverage status. Because the *F* class rates are usually high, employers may seek to use lower-rated classifications for some of their operation. Such payroll divisions are valid only if allowed by the classification phraseology.

Shipyards also resemble building contractors in that they may engage many kinds of specialist subcontractors. Sublet operations may include welding, painting, pipe fitting, boiler making, diesel engine work, machinery installation or repair, air conditioning and refrigeration equipment servicing, and many other operations. Dealers in electronic equipment may install or repair radios, televisions, or radar or navigation systems on board vessels. Those subcontracted operations concern premium auditors in two ways. First, the premium auditor should check certificates of insurance to verify the subcontractor's LHWCA coverage because the general contractor is liable for compensation to the uninsured subcontractor's employees.[42] Second, when auditing firms that may have done work for a shipyard or on board a ship, the premium auditor should carefully review sales invoices and similar documents. An unsuspected exposure under the LHWCA may be disclosed if the insured billed shipyards or ships' agents for installed goods or completed repairs.

The few recreational vessel construction and repair facilities (generally excluded from coverage under the LHWCA) located on or near navigable waters present a challenge to premium auditors. Those operations may continue to be under the LHWCA for the part of the work done on vessels while floating in navigable waters or on dry docks, building ways, or marine railways adjacent to those waters. Coverage also usually applies to constructing or repairing pleasure craft more than sixty-five feet long.

A premium auditor may be uncertain about whether the navigable waters of the U.S. include a particular inland lake or river. Premium auditors can resolve that question by consulting the underwriter, the legal department, or the LHWCA's administrator.

Non-F classifications require more attention from the premium auditor. Employees could conceivably perform any operation listed in the *Basic Manual* classification section on the navigable waters of the U.S. and therefore be subject to the LHWCA. Although painting ship hulls is a distinct operation, painting an ocean liner's cabin walls is the same operation as painting the rooms of a house. However, painters on an ocean liner would be under LHWCA jurisdiction. If any of the insured's operations described by a non-F classification involve some employees subject to the LHWCA, the *Basic Manual* rates and minimum premiums for those classifications must be increased by the United States Longshore and Harbor Workers' Compensation Coverage Percentage. The **United States Longshore and Harbor Workers' Compensation Coverage Percentage** is the fixed percentages set in each state that specify the increase in rates charged in the *Basic Manual* for workers' compensation and employers' liability coverages for those employees subject to the LHWCA. That coverage percentage is found under "Miscellaneous Values" or "Advisory Miscellaneous Values" on the state rate pages. That section of the Georgia state pages appears in Exhibit 6-7.

United States Longshore and Harbor Workers' Compensation Coverage Percentage
The fixed percentages set in each state that specify the increase in rates charged in the *Basic Manual* for workers' compensation and employers' liability coverages for those employees subject to the LHWCA.

EXHIBIT 6-7

LHWCA Coverage Percentage Workers' Compensation and Employers' Liability—Georgia, Effective May 1, 1996

United States Longshore and Harbor Workers' Compensation Coverage Percentage applicable only in connection with Rule XII-D.3.—U.S. Longshore and Harbor Workers' Compensation Act of the *Basic Manual*   113%

Multiply a Non-F classification rate by a factor of 2.13

Adapted with permission of National Council on Compensation Insurance, *Basic Manual*, Georgia, p. S4 (original printing, effective May 1, 1996).

Suppose, for example, an insured with LHWCA coverage endorsed on the policy redecorates ocean liner interiors while the ships are docked at Savannah, Georgia. The premium auditor discovers payroll of $50,000 assigned to "Painting or Paper Hanging NOC & shop operations, drivers" (Code 5474). The rate for this classification is $17.84, and the minimum premium is $750. To calculate the premium adjustment in this case, the premium auditor must first increase the rate by the LHWCA Coverage Percentage ($17.84 per $100 × 2.13 = $38.00 per $100). The premium auditor then uses this increased rate to determine the premium ($50,000 payroll × $38.00 per $100 = $19,000).

The premium auditor should also increase the minimum premium by the LHWCA Coverage Percentage ($750 × 2.13 = $1,598), but in this case the minimum premium would not apply. The LHWCA coverage percentage increase does not apply to loss and expense constants.

When a statutory rate change occurs, a change may also occur in the LHWCA Coverage Percentage for the state. If the change applies to outstanding policies, the premium auditor must segregate the premium base into the periods before and after the change's effective date. The premium auditor must then separately compute the appropriate premium for each period.

A premium auditor may discover LHWCA exposures in many types of construction or erection operations. Construction work on land is not subject to maritime jurisdiction even if such work occurs in a shoreside area where vessels are loaded, unloaded, built, or repaired. However, all construction work involving structures over navigable waters or in navigable waters is maritime employment.

Employers may permanently mount construction equipment on a vessel or temporarily place it on a barge, scow, or lighter. In either case, the vessel's operators and the equipment on the vessel become subject to maritime jurisdiction. The insured may also use rowboats or small power boats in the construction work, and work from these boats is also maritime employment.

Employees working on board floating construction equipment may qualify as seamen, and, if so, the premium auditor should assign their payroll to the appropriate admiralty classification for the vessel type involved. For any marine construction work not assigned to an admiralty or an *F* classification, the premium auditor should use the LHWCA Coverage Percentage.

Builders may drive piling to support structures, piers, and bridges into place, or they may make them of concrete and pour the concrete into forms installed in drilled or excavated holes. As long as the pile driver and other equipment are located on land, no maritime exposure exists. If the employer mounts any of this equipment on a vessel, then the work is maritime in nature.

Many kinds of containment and diversion structures extend into the water. They include dams, sea walls, levees, jetties, and breakwaters. Bulkheads are installed to prevent the water from eroding the adjoining land. Bridges, docks, and piers actually extend over the water, as do certain buildings. Those structures are often a source of confusion as to jurisdiction because they are situated in or over the water and are often associated with shipyard or stevedoring operations subject to the LHWCA. In one case, the court considered a worker building a bridge over navigable waters to be in maritime employment.[43] Telephone and telegraph cables, electric transmission lines, and various kinds of pipelines must often cross navigable waters and may also involve maritime employment.

Although constructing buildings or structures on shore is not usually subject to maritime jurisdiction, when erecting a structure next to navigable waters, the contractor may use equipment on board a vessel moored in the waters adjacent to the building site. The operators of such equipment would be engaged in maritime employment.

One maritime exposure that premium auditors often overlook is the rental to others of construction equipment with operators, especially cranes or hoisting equipment. The contractor may use that equipment aboard a vessel or barge for various kinds of marine construction. It may be used in a ship-yard to build or repair vessels. A contractor's mobile crane can be particularly useful to a stevedoring contractor needing extra hoisting equipment to move cargo during a peak period or when the stevedore's own equipment is out of service for repair. A contractor may welcome the rental income for otherwise idle equipment, but the maritime usage may create liability for seamen's or LHWCA benefits if the operator is injured.

When auditing a contractor with potential maritime exposures, the premium auditor should ask the following questions about the insured's operations:

- What was each job site's location? Was it adjacent to navigable waters?
- What type of structure was erected at each job site?
- Does the insured own, lease, or charter vessels or floating equipment?
- Was the work of the type in which vessels would be used?
- Does the construction method indicate that vessels were required to complete the work?
- Did the insured rent or lease equipment to others? If so, what type of equipment was rented, to whom was it rented, and for what purpose? Did the insured furnish the operators?

The premium auditor may find it helpful to review the contracts, estimates, bidding documents, engineering or architectural designs and specifications, job cost records, superintendents' or foremen's progress reports, equipment lists, depreciation schedules, subcontracts, and payments to subcontractors. The premium auditor should also review invoices for equipment rented to the insured and for equipment rented by the insured to others.

Another important source of information is the insured's insurance policy file. If the insured owns or rents vessels, the insured may have secured ocean marine hull or protection and indemnity insurance to cover them. When reviewing the certificates of insurance for the subcontractors, premium auditors must note whether those subcontractors have LHWCA coverage, because otherwise the general contractor becomes liable for LHWCA benefits to the subcontractor's employees. If a premium auditor discovers a maritime exposure, he or she should gather as much information as possible about the operations (including a payroll breakdown) and send that information to the underwriter. The underwriter should make the necessary changes in rates and classifications.

Premium auditors can divide payrolls between maritime and nonmaritime work provided the proper records exist to support this division. The premium auditor should carefully examine such records. Few insureds have sufficient knowledge of maritime rules to keep those records accurately. Furthermore, accounting systems rarely supply the data necessary to make this payroll segregation. Because the rates for maritime work are usually much higher, considerable potential for abuse exists in making the division. LHWCA benefits may apply even to construction workers on shore if the operation is incidental to work done from a vessel. The premium auditor should therefore disallow dividing an individual employee's payroll between maritime and nonmaritime work unless the records clearly disclose the amount of the employee's time worked in each operation and unless the nonmaritime work is clearly not connected with the maritime operation.

INSURANCE FOR ADMIRALTY LAW AND FELA EXPOSURES

Neither state workers' compensation laws nor the LHWCA cover masters and members of the crews of vessels. They are subject instead to admiralty law. If injured, they have the right to maintenance and cure and the right to sue the employer for damages.

Similarly, interstate railroad employees are not subject to state workers' compensation laws by virtue of FELA. This act gives injured employees the right to sue the employer for damages.

Additionally, some workers fall under the Migrant and Seasonal Agricultural Worker Protection Act (MSPA). That act makes the employers of such workers liable for bodily injury sustained by an employee caused by an intentional violation of the act or its regulations.

Therefore, any of those situations may give rise to an employer's liability outside both the state and federal compensation laws that provide exclusive remedies in other employee injury cases. The standard workers' compensation policy can provide coverage for such liability up to a stated limit. Insurers can exclude certain coverages and increase the limits, however. Therefore, a premium auditor must analyze the insured's exposures and coverages to determine when coverage applies and the correct premium for coverage of admiralty law, FELA, and MSPA exposures.

Providing the Coverage

Rule XIII of the *Basic Manual* states the rules for covering, excluding, or limiting exposures under admiralty law, FELA, or MSPA. Although Part Two of the standard policy can apply to those cases of employers' liability, the insurer must tailor the coverage to the insured's needs by attaching appropriate endorsements. Otherwise, the exclusions of Part Two of the policy prevent the policy from applying.

MSPA Coverage

To provide coverage under MSPA, an insurer should attach the Migrant and Seasonal Agricultural Worker Protection Act Coverage Endorsement (WC 00 01 11) to the policy. On that endorsement, the insurer lists the location of the work to be covered and a description of that work. The insurer bases the premium for this coverage on its evaluation of the exposures presented by the particular risk.

Coverage Programs

The *Basic Manual* allows two different approaches to insuring liability under admiralty law or FELA. The insurer uses the standard policy in either case and adds the appropriate endorsements.

Program I provides Part One coverage (workers' compensation insurance) for statutory liability under the workers' compensation law of any state designated on the information page and Part Two coverage (employers' liability insurance) for damages under admiralty law or FELA subject to a $25,000 standard limit. The insurer must attach the standard Maritime Coverage Endorsement (WC 00 02 01 A) to policies to cover masters and members of crews under admiralty law. On the endorsement, the insurer must enter a description of the work and limits for Part Two coverage.

To provide Program I coverage for an interstate railroad, an insurer should attach the standard Federal Employers' Liability Act Coverage Endorsement (WC 00 01 04) to the policy, indicating the applicable limits of liability and the state. Naming a state does not mean that Part One coverage applies in that state. The insurer would have to list that state in Item 3.A.

Program II provides the same coverage as Program I, with the addition of voluntary compensation coverage. Under this coverage, the insurer offers to settle a claim strictly in accord with the designated workers' compensation law as if the claim were subject to that law instead of the laws of negligence. The designated law is either a particular state's workers' compensation statute or the LHWCA. If the injured employee rejects the settlement offer, then employers' liability coverage applies to the employee's claim or suit, with the same standard limit of liability as for Program I.

To provide Program II for operations subject to admiralty law, the insurer should include both the standard Maritime Coverage Endorsement and the standard Voluntary Compensation Maritime Coverage Endorsement (WC 00 02 03), indicating on the latter endorsement the name of the vessel, a description of the work, and the applicable workers' compensation law. Taken together, those endorsements provide voluntary compensation coverage for masters and members of crews, define the territorial limits, and clarify the applicable limits of liability. The rates stated in the policy on the declarations or information page for maritime voluntary compensation must reflect the limits of liability stated in the Maritime Coverage Endorsement's schedule.

To provide Program II for employments subject to FELA, the insurer attaches the standard Federal Employers' Liability Act Endorsement as it did to provide Program I. In addition, it attaches the standard Voluntary Compensation and Employers' Liability Coverage Endorsement (WC 00 03 11 A) designating the employees, the state(s), and the applicable workers' compensation law.

Admiralty Law Coverage Option

The Maritime Coverage Endorsement excludes from coverage the insured's liability to provide transportation, wages, maintenance, and cure to injured sailors. However, insurers can include such coverage by entering a premium charge on the endorsement. The insurer computes the additional premium for this optional coverage by using an (a) rate.

Premium Determination

Insurers determine premium charges for admiralty law and FELA exposures by using the special classifications established for these operations. The rates for those classifications assume that the standard limit of liability applies. If increased limits of liability apply, the insurer adjusts the premium according to the manual rules. If the insured's operations are not under admiralty or FELA jurisdiction, the insurer can still use the special classifications, subject to the applicable state rules.

Classifications and Rates

Rule XIII.E. of the *Basic Manual* defines the classifications for maritime and railroad operations. The "Classifications" section of the *Basic Manual* also shows the descriptions of those classifications. For each operation described, three separate classification codes are available. One corresponds to Program I coverage for the operation. The other two are for Program II coverage with either state law or the LHWCA benefits designated. The rates for those classifications appear in the latter part of the state rate pages or among the state rates, but with an "M" after them.

When maritime operations may create a LHWCA Act exposure, the policy should include the standard Longshore and Harbor Worker's Compensation Act Coverage Endorsement (WC 00 01 06 A) to provide the coverage. As long as the insurer receives a sufficient premium for the coverage, it would normally cover a claim under state or federal compensation laws, should an employer be found to be subject to such a law.

Excavation and dredging often come under maritime jurisdiction. An employer may engage excavation or dredging contractors to dig drainage or navigation channels, or to maintain existing channels at the proper depth. The contractor may dredge material from existing waterways for use as fill at construction sites. Dredging often produces sand, gravel, or seashells for use as building materials or in making concrete. Dredging equipment may be of the bucket or suction types. The contractor may permanently mount it on a vessel or pontoon designed for holding the equipment, or it may consist of conventional excavation equipment, such as a crane with dragline, temporarily placed on a barge. As long as the equipment remains on shore, even if it is dredging a navigable waterway, no maritime exposure exists. When the contractor mounts the equipment on a vessel in navigable waters, however, the operating crew becomes subject to admiralty jurisdiction.

Constructing underwater foundations and tunnels may involve caissons to hold back mud and water while excavation and construction proceeds. Work in the caisson itself is not maritime. However, caissons often require using vessels as tenders, and the employees manning the tenders in navigable waters are subject to admiralty law. Therefore, premium auditors should always be alert for any construction operations that may involve an admiralty classification. Because of the possibility of LHWCA exposure, premium auditors should assign payrolls to the highest rated classification (whether it is an admiralty classification or a construction classification surcharged for the LHWCA exposure) that is applicable.

Limits of Liability

The standard limit of liability for covering admiralty law or FELA exposures is $25,000. To determine the additional premium for increased limits, premium auditors apply the factor found in Rule 3.A.14.b.(1). Exhibit 6-8 shows the table for increased limits. The premium auditor applies the factor to the total premium for admiralty or FELA classifications before applying an expense constant, an experience rating modification, or premium discount or retrospective rating adjustments. The additional premium for increased limits is subject to an experience rating modification.

Waters Not Under Admiralty Jurisdiction

An insured may conduct operations described by an admiralty classification on waters not under admiralty jurisdiction. For example, employees of fishing or boating operations on inland lakes would be subject to the state workers' compensation law. A standard policy without endorsements for maritime operations covers this exposure. The rules are those that apply to statutory workers' compensation coverage.

In NCCI states, the appropriate classification for such operations is the admiralty classification describing the operation corresponding to Program II coverage for the location involved and for state act benefits. LHWCA coverage can be included by applying the percentage increase factor to the rate for

EXHIBIT 6-8

Table for Increased Limits (Admiralty or FELA)

Limit per Accident	Factor		Minimum Premium	
	Program I	Program II	Program I	Program II
$100,000	1.00	1.00	$115	$230
150,000	1.17	1.15	119	238
200,000	1.30	1.28	123	246
300,000	1.51	1.48	129	258
400,000	1.68	1.63	134	268
500,000	1.80	1.75	138	276

* Refer to Appendix C for additional limits values.
(Exceptions: AK, AZ, FL, HI, LA, VA)

Adapted with permission from National Council on Compensation Insurance, *Basic Manual for Workers Compensation and Employers Liability.*

the admiralty classification or using the appropriate *F* classification. Insurers can provide admiralty coverage for dredging operations under the same policy, however, only if the separate classifications and rates for the operations subject to state and admiralty jurisdictions are clearly subdivided and the insured maintains proper records.

SUMMARY

The U.S. places most maritime workers as well as interstate railroad employees and certain other workers outside the jurisdiction of state workers' compensation laws. Federal jurisdiction over those workers arises either as a result of specific federal laws or because the location comes within the admiralty jurisdiction exercised by the federal courts. Some federal laws, such as the Federal Employers' Liability Act and the Jones Act, define the injured workers' rights in bringing negligence suits against their employers without restricting the other legal recourses available to them.

The LHWCA, however, provides an exclusive remedy to injured workers who are subject to it. As with state workers' compensation laws, the LHWCA eliminates the injured workers' right to sue their employers but guarantees compensation for work-related injuries without regard to fault. The 1972 amendments to the act expanded its jurisdiction to include maritime workers even while they are on shore and within the jurisdiction of state laws. In this concurrent jurisdiction area, either the state compensation law or the LHWCA may apply. The LHWCA applies when the employee meets both the status and situs tests, although the 1984 amendments specify certain excluded occupations. Congress has also extended the LHWCA to cover employees of government contractors at defense bases and other overseas installations, workers engaged in operations on the outer continental shelf, and the civilian employees of nonappropriated fund instrumentalities of the armed forces.

Insurers can provide insurance for LHWCA exposures by adding the Longshore and Harbor Workers' Compensation Act Endorsement to a standard workers' compensation policy. Appropriate endorsements are also available for the LHWCA extensions. Because exposures may change after the policy inception, the premium auditor should be certain that the policy has the proper endorsements. Determining the premium for LHWCA coverage follows the procedures for state workers' compensation coverage, with some modifications. Insurers base the premium on payroll, but no exclusion of extra pay exists for overtime in stevedoring operations, and the premium auditor may have to deal with a payroll system that combines several employers' payrolls. For *F* classifications, the additional premium required for LHWCA coverage is incorporated into the *Basic Manual* rates. For all other classifications, the insurer must increase the *Basic Manual* rate by the LHWCA Coverage Percentage to provide the additional premium required for LHWCA coverage.

Insurers can provide insurance for employee injury exposures under the Migrant and Seasonal Agricultural Worker Protection Act, under admiralty law, or under the Federal Employers' Liability Act by Part Two of the standard workers' compensation policy with the proper endorsements. When the insurer provides coverage for the latter two of those exposures, the policy should contain the appropriate endorsements to provide coverage under either Program I or Program II and to specify the limits of liability. The *Basic Manual* defines the classifications involving operations subject to admiralty law or FELA, and the rates for those classifications appear in a separate section on the state rate pages. The *Basic Manual* rules also explain the increased limit factor and the minimum premiums applicable to admiralty and FELA coverage.

The maze of jurisdictions complicates the compensation system for work-related injuries and creates conflict of law problems for premium auditors. With some understanding of the laws involved, however, premium auditors should be able to solve most problems. As long as a potential liability under admiralty law exists, the insurer should apply the relevant *Basic Manual* rules to collect a premium commensurate with this exposure. When a potential LHWCA exposure exists that is not covered by the policy, the premium auditor should bring this gap to the underwriter's attention.

CHAPTER NOTES

1. Grant Gilmore and Charles L. Black, Jr., *Law of Admiralty* (Mineola, N.Y.: Foundation Press, 1975), p. 47.

2. *Southern Pacific Co. v. Jensen*, 244 U.S. 205, 37 S. Ct. 524 (1917), and Albert J. Millus and Joseph F. Manes, *The Longshoremen's and Harbor Workers' Compensation Act and its Extensions* (New York: The Roberts Publishing Corp., 1978), pp. 4–8.

3. *The Genesee Chief v. Fitzhugh*, 53 U.S. 443 (12 How.) (1851).

4. *The Steamer Daniel Ball*, 77 U.S. 557 (10 Wall. 557) (1871).

5. *Reed v. Canfield*, 20 Fed. Cas. 426, 427, Case No. 11,641 (C.C.D. Mass. 1832).

6. 119 U.S. 199 (1886).

7. The case of *Mahnich v. Southern S.S. Co.*, 321 U.S. 96 (1944) was the case in which the Supreme Court realistically turned the seaworthiness doctrine (many courts refer to it as the unseaworthiness doctrine) into a strict liability rule. That case used the terms "absolute" and "nondelegable." The case referred to the doctrine as a "species of liability without fault."

8. *Reed v. Pennsylvania Railroad Company*, 351 U.S. 502, 76 S. Ct. 958 (1956).

9. Arthur Larson, *Workmen's Compensation for Occupational Injuries and Death*, Desk Edition (New York: Matthew Bender & Company, 1981), §91.70.

10. Merchant Marine Act, 41 Stat. 1007 (1920), 46 U.S.C. §688 (1975).

11. *Kernan v. American Dredging Co.*, 355 U.S. 426, 78 S. Ct. 394 (1958), and Millus and Manes, *Longshoremen's Act*, 53–54.

12. Technically, the courts did not view the Jones Act and Longshore Acts as being mutually exclusive until 1946 and the case of *Swanson v. Marra Bros., Inc.*, 328 U.S. 1,7 (1946).

13. Gilmore and Black, *Law of Admiralty*, pp. 434–436.

14. Larson, *Workmen's Compensation* §90.21, and Gilmore and Black, *Law of Admiralty*, pp. 331–334.

15. *McDermott Int'l v. Wilander*, 498 U.S. 337, 111 S. Ct. 807 (1991).

16. *Chandris v. Latsis*, 515 U.S. 347, 115 S. Ct. 2172 (1995).

17. *Chandris v. Latsis*, at 2184-2186.

18. *The Steamer Daniel Ball*.

19. Gilmore and Black, *Law of Admiralty*, p. 47, and Larson, *Workmen's Compensation*, §90.23.

20. *Moragne v. States Marine Lines, Inc.*, 398 U.S. 375, 90 S. Ct. 1772 (1970).

21. United States Longshore and Harbor Workers' Compensation Act, as amended, §937.

22. LHWCA, § 902. Definitions.

23. LHWCA, § 902. Definitions.

24. LHWCA, §3(a).

25. LHWCA, §3(a).

26. *Weyerhaeuser Co. v. Gilmore*, 528 F.2d 957 (9th Cir. 1975), *cert. denied*, 429 U.S. 868 (1976).

27. *Northeast Marine Terminal Co. v. Caputo*, 432 U.S. 429, 97 S. Ct. 2348 (1977).

28. *Alabama Dry Dock & Shipbuilding Co. v. Kininess*, 554 F.2d 176 (5th Cir. 1977) *cert. denied*, 434 U.S. 903 (1977).

29. U.S. Department of Labor, Office of Workers Compensation Programs, *Guidelines for Determination of Claims under Amended Longshoremen's Act*, Program Memorandum No. 58 (August 5, 1977).

30. *Director, OWCP v. Perini North River Associates*, 459 U.S. 297, 103 S. Ct. 634 (1983).

31. *Dravo Corp. v. Maxin*, 545 F. 2d 374 (3d Cir. 1976) (*cert. later denied*), and Larson, *Workmen's Compensation*, §89.30.

32. *Sun Ship, Inc. v. Pennsylvania*, 447 U.S. 715, 100 S. Ct. 2432 (1980).

33. Larson, *Workmen's Compensation*, §89.50.

34. LHWCA, §20.

35. LHWCA, §902(2).

36. *Standard Oil Company v. Johnson*, 316 U.S. 481, 62 S. Ct. 1168 (1942).

37. Millus and Manes, *Longshoremen's Act*, pp. 222–224. The Act is U.S. Code (1970) title 5, Sections 8171-8173 (Public Law 85-538, 85th Congress).

38. National Council on Compensation Insurance, Inc., *Basic Manual for Workers Compensation and Employers Liability Insurance* (Boca Raton, Fla.: NCCI, Inc., 1995), exception to Rule V.E.2.a., p. R21.

39. National Council on Compensation Insurance, Inc., *Scopes of Basic Manual Classifications*, January 1997 edition (Boca Raton, Fla.: NCCI, Inc., 1997), note to Code 7350F, Section 1, p. 113.

40. Some states have filed to replace the former code 7219 with two separate codes for local hauling and long-distance hauling (Codes 7228 and 7229, respectively). Some states still use the single Code 7219, Trucking NOC classification.

41. U.S. Department of Labor, *Guidelines*, pp. 13–14.

42. LHWCA, §4(a).

43. *Lemelle v. B. F. Diamond Construction Co.*, 674 F.2d 296 (4th Cir. 1982), *cert. denied*, 459 U.S. 1177 (1983).

Direct Your Learning

Commercial General Liability Insurance

Educational Objectives

After learning the content of this chapter and completing the corresponding course guide assignment, you should be able to:

▶ Describe the following aspects of commercial lines insurance:

- Monoline and package policies
- *Commercial Lines Manual (CLM)* classification table
- *Commercial Lines Manual (CLM)* divisions of insurance
- Common policy conditions for a commercial package policy
- Common declarations for a commercial package policy

▶ Describe the legal basis of liability and possible sources of liability.

▶ Describe the contents of the following components of the Commercial General Liability (CGL) policy:

- Declarations
- Coverage form
- Endorsements

▶ Given a case involving a general liability policy, determine the following:

- Major business group and premium bases applicable
- Exposure bases for premium determination and any inclusions or exclusions
- Amount of exposures to include in calculating the premium

▶ Define or describe each of the Key Words and Phrases for this chapter.

Outline

Develop Your Perspective

What are the main topics covered in the chapter?

Insurance Services Office (ISO) is a principal insurance advisory organization for commercial general liability insurance. As such, there is uniformity in the way commercial lines policies are packaged, the contents of those policies, and the exposures bases used to calculate premiums.

Identify the sections of the commercial package policy.

▶ How do common elements, such as declarations and conditions, eliminate redundancy and confusion?

▶ How do package policies help to eliminate overlap or gaps in coverages?

Why is it important to learn about these topics?

Because the ISO *Commercial Lines Manual* standardizes the business groups and exposures bases for commercial general liability, knowledge about the inclusions and exclusions stated in the manual will also help to standardize premium audits and policy premiums.

Examine the various exposures bases upon which commercial liability premiums are developed.

▶ How do the exposure bases create logical measurements of liability loss exposures?

▶ How do the exposures bases reflect increases and decreases in a policyholder's business and, therefore, their exposure to loss?

How can you use what you will learn?

Examine your own company's commercial liability loss exposures.

▶ What exposures bases would be appropriate to measure those loss exposures?

Commercial General Liability Insurance

Next to workers' compensation insurance, general liability insurance is most often subject to premium audits. General liability insurance may be sold as a standalone policy or as apart of a package with other insurance coverages. Premium auditors may therefore be working with a commercial package policy even though they are determining the premium for the general liability coverage. Other commercial coverages, however, may also be subject to premium audit, and packaging those coverages in a common policy can increase the opportunities for premium auditors to contribute to the underwriting and premium billing of those commercial coverages.

The policy forms and manual rules filed by Insurance Services Office (ISO) serve as the basis for the discussion in this chapter because they are the most prevalent. This chapter explains ISO's commercial lines policies and *Commercial Lines Manual (CLM)* as the foundation for explaining premium audits for general liability and other commercial lines. The chapter then moves specifically into general liability by explaining the possible premium bases for general liability coverage.

ISO'S APPROACH TO COMMERCIAL LINES INSURANCE

Most commercial insurance coverage forms are not as uniform as are those for workers' compensation insurance. ISO recommends to its members the coverage and policy forms to use. Each insurer then decides either to follow ISO and use those forms or to deviate in the wording and file its own forms with state insurance regulators. While most insurers use policy forms that resemble, if not duplicate, ISO forms, problems can arise because not all forms are identical. The differences between insurer forms may mean that a prior insurer's premium auditor could have audited different loss exposures than those that the current premium audit includes.

Although premium auditors should refer obscure coverage questions to underwriters, they should understand coverages and manual rules well enough to recognize additional exposures and to include the appropriate premium charges. Premium auditors should therefore be familiar with the coverage terms provided by each major commercial lines policy. Maintaining a set of forms their insurer uses can be beneficial for premium auditors.

Monoline Policies Compared to Package Policies

Monoline policy
A policy that provides coverage for just one line of insurance.

Package policy
A policy that covers two or more lines of insurance.

Insurers can write commercial lines policies as monoline policies or package policies. A policy that provides coverage for just one line of insurance—for example, liability coverage—is called a **monoline policy**. A **package policy** covers two or more lines of insurance. A package policy can meet the insurance needs of a typical business. Combining coverages greatly simplifies obtaining the necessary insurance. Package policies can include property, liability, and inland marine coverages. Premium auditors must understand the coverages that the policy offers and how various endorsements or schedules may modify the package policy to broaden or limit coverage. Package policies do not necessarily show all coverages on the premium auditor's copy. To determine the proper exposures on audit in those instances, the premium auditor may have to check the file. Some policies show classification exposures, rates, or premiums only on a separate rating worksheet, not on the premium auditor's copy of the policy. Monoline policies of all types are still issued because, among other reasons, not all insurers want or are able to write all lines of insurance and insureds sometimes split up their coverages to obtain better pricing or policy wording.

Umbrella liability policy
A policy that provides excess coverage over several primary policies (typically CGL, auto, and employers' liability) and may also provide drop-down coverage.

Excess liability policy
A policy that covers liability claims in excess of the limits of an underlying policy or a stated retention amount.

Although umbrella liability or excess liability policies are, in a sense, monoline policies, they are seldom included in package policies. An **umbrella liability policy** is a policy that provides excess coverage over several primary policies (typically CGL, auto, and employers' liability) and may also provide drop-down coverage to insure exposures not covered under any primary policy. An **excess liability policy** is a policy that covers liability claims in excess of the limits of an underlying policy or a stated retention amount. In some cases, the umbrella policies provide broader coverage than the primary policies. The broader coverage is usually subject to a self-insured retention, in effect a deductible, of $10,000 or more. The premium may be calculated as a flat charge or a percentage of the premium developed on the primary policy. However, the premium base is often payroll, gross sales, or a unit count, in which case the policy may be subject to a premium audit.

Commercial Lines Manual

The *Commercial Lines Manual* (CLM) provides uniformity in format and language for the insurance lines within its scope. That uniformity simplifies the multi-line account rating task and eliminates much of the confusion caused by variations in the manuals that insurers previously used. The *CLM* also facilitates uniform treatment across state lines. In addition to combining the rules and rates for commercial lines other than workers' compensation into one manual, the *CLM* also states the rules in modern, simplified language. The main parts of the *CLM* are the Classification Table and the separate divisions containing the special rules for the various lines of insurance. Most of the manual rules and rates apply throughout the country; however, because conditions and laws vary from state to state, ISO also distributes pages that show state loss costs (or rates) and state exceptions to the general *CLM* rules.

Classification Table

The **Classification Table** is a table that provides the necessary rating and classification information for general liability, fire, crime/fidelity, and package policy classification in the *CLM*. Each classification in the *CLM* has a unique code that applies to these lines of business. The entry for code number 91130, used for alarm and security systems monitoring, is shown in Exhibit 7-1. The Classification Table does not apply to the other insurance lines included in the *CLM* because they involve unique approaches to classification. Chapter 8 describes rules for using the Classification Table in connection with general liability classifications.

Classification Table
A table that provides the necessary rating and classification information for general liability, fire, crime/fidelity, and package policy classification in the *CLM*.

EXHIBIT 7-1

Example of *CLM* Code

91130 Alarms – security systems – monitoring

GENERAL LIABILITY	CRIME/FIDELITY
Class Code: 91130 **(8)**	Class Code: 5616
Premium Base: Payroll,	
Products/Completed Operations Incl.	
(8) This classification applies to those insureds who monitor or respond to alarms. Personal and Advertising Injury are excluded. Use Exclusion – Personal And Advertising Injury Endorsement CG 21 38. Alarms installation, servicing or repair shall be separately classified and rated.	
FIRE	**COMMERCIAL PACKAGE POLICY**
Class Code: 0702	PMA: Service
CONTENTS, FIRE	
Rate Group: Refer to State Rates Section of CLM Division Five – Fire and Allied Lines.	

Copyright, ISO Properties, Inc., 2001.

Divisions for Lines of Insurance

The remaining part of the *CLM* is broken into eighteen divisions pertaining to the various lines of insurance incorporated into the *CLM*. The divisions represent the major categories of commercial lines loss exposures, the coverages available for those exposures, and the rules and rates for those coverages. Because the loss exposures and coverages for each of these commercial lines are distinctly different, each requires individual treatment. Therefore, each division has its own rules and rates. Those divisions are as follows:

- Division One: Commercial Automobile (CA)
- Division Two: Boiler and Machinery (BM)
- Division Three: Crime and Fidelity (CR)
- Division Four: Farm (FR)
- Division Five: Commercial Fire and Allied Lines(CF)
- Division Six: General Liability (GL)
- Division Seven: Professional Liability (PR)
- Division Eight: Inland Marine (CM)
- Division Nine: Multiple Line—Commercial Package Policy (MLCP)
- Division Ten: Businessowners (MLBP) and Special Trade Contractors (MLTC)
- Division Eleven: Employment-Related Practices Liability (EP)
- Division Twelve: Market Segments—

    Apartment Building Owners (MSAB); Auto Service Risks (MSAS); Dry Cleaning and Laundry Facilities (MSDC); Florists (MSFL); Hardware and Home Improvement Stores (MSHI); Hotels, Motels and Inns (MSHM); Janitorial Services (MSJS); Landscapers (MSLS); Plumbing and HVAC Contractors (MSPC); Restaurants (MSRS); Self Storage Facilities (MSSF); Supermarkets (MSSM); Staffing Firms (MSST)

- Division Thirteen: Commercial Liability Umbrella (CU)
- Division Fourteen: Capital Assets Program (Output Policy) (OP)
- Division Fifteen: Management Protection (MP)
- Division Sixteen: Reserved for Future Use
- Division Seventeen: E-Commerce (EC)
- Division Eighteen: Financial Institutions (FI)

Each division has a separate explanatory memorandum, applicable forms and endorsements general index, table of contents, rates, state exceptions, and rules and procedures related to the specific insurance line detailed therein.

The *CLM* comes in a traditional loose-leaf binder and an online version. When using the paper manual, many premium auditors rearrange the placement of the divisions. Because premium auditors refer most frequently to divisions six, General Liability (GL); one, Commercial Auto (CA); and nine, Multiple Line—Commercial Package Policy (MLCP), they sometimes arrange their manuals in that order with the remaining divisions inserted afterward. Because of the size of the manual, some premium auditors do not carry all sections of the manual to all premium audits; others have the manual loaded into their laptop computer to have it easily available while working at an insured's premises.

In the paper manual, dates shown at the bottom of each page are printing dates and are not necessarily the effective dates. The manual revision notice accompanying a new or revised page states the effective date. Effective dates can vary when each insurer must file rates and rules in that particular state or when the insurer chooses to make an independent filing. In the online version of the manual, double-clicking on an information icon shows the effective date for the provision.

Commercial Lines Policies

The uniform format of ISO policies eliminates redundant information and makes locating important information in the policy easier. All the forms and endorsements for a particular line of business compose a coverage part. Each line has one set of forms and one set of manual rules. As noted, a monoline policy includes only one coverage part along with the common policy conditions and common policy declarations. A commercial package policy contains two or more coverage parts. In either case, the same forms and the same rules apply.

Exhibit 7-2 shows some of the coverage parts that may be included in a commercial package policy. The common policy conditions and the common declarations appear in every policy along with at least one coverage part. A **coverage part** is a commercial package policy component in a line of insurance (such as commercial property or commercial general liability) that comprises the declarations page, one or more coverage forms, applicable endorsements, and in some cases a general provisions form. A coverage part consists of the following: one or more line of business declarations, one or more coverage forms, any applicable endorsements, and sometimes a separate conditions or general provisions form (conditions are included in the auto and general liability coverage forms).

A monoline policy (see Exhibit 7-5) consists of a coverage part with attachment of common policy declarations (which insurers may combine with the line of business declarations to make one form) and common policy conditions.

The coverage part may become part of a package policy in combination with the following: one or more other coverage parts, common policy declarations, and common policy conditions.

Common Policy Conditions

The common policy conditions (IL 00 17) apply to all coverage parts included in the policy. Those conditions relate to cancellation, changes, examination of books and records, inspections and surveys, premiums, and transfer of rights and duties. The most important ones for premium auditors are those affecting the first named insured and the examination of books and records condition.

Coverage part
A commercial package policy component in a line of insurance (such as commercial property or commercial general liability) that comprises the declarations page, one or more coverage forms, applicable endorsements, and in some cases a general provisions form.

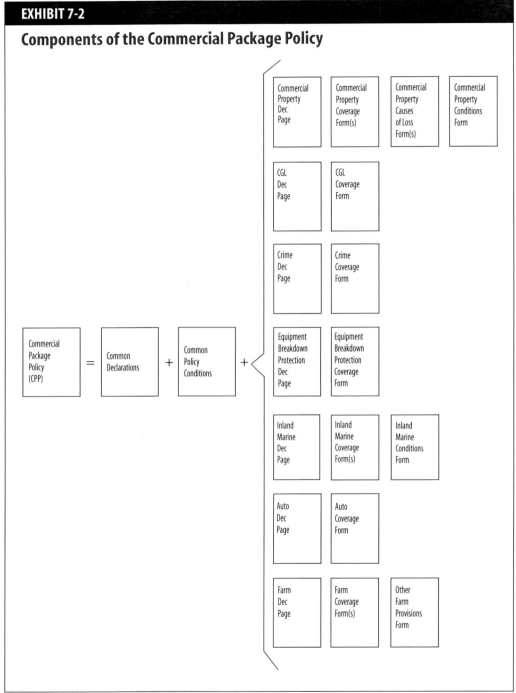

EXHIBIT 7-2

Components of the Commercial Package Policy

Copyright, ISO Properties, Inc., 1982, 1988.

The **first named insured** is the person or organization whose name appears first as the named insured on an insurance policy and who pays premiums, receives any returned premiums, cancels the policy, and receives the notice of cancellation or nonrenewal. It is not unusual for commercial policies to have several and even a dozen or more named insureds. To simplify administration of the policy, the common policy conditions emphasize that for policies with more than one named insured, the first named insured has the following rights and duties:

- Responsibility for premium payment.
- Authority to make changes to the policy with the consent of the insurer.
- The right to cancel the policy.
- The right to receive cancellation notice from the insurer. The insurer may send the notice to the address shown in the policy for the first named insured.
- The right to receive any return premiums from the insurer.

The examination of books and records condition explicitly states the insurer's right to audit the insured's books and records during the policy period and within three years thereafter. Premium auditors should be especially familiar with this condition so that they can cite it verbatim when necessary. The exact wording is:

> C. Examination Of Your Books And Records
>
> We may examine and audit your books and records as they relate to this policy at any time during the policy period and up to three years afterward.

Common Declarations

Exhibit 7-3 shows a sample common declarations page (IL DS 00).

The common declarations page gives the policy number and the specific information identifying the insured and the coverage. The first item specifies the named insured, the insured's mailing address, the exact policy period, and a brief description of the insured's type of business. Insurers indicate the coverage parts included in the policy by showing the advance premium charges for each coverage. The words "this premium may be subject to adjustment" appear prominently above that coverages list. The common policy declarations page also lists by number all forms included in the policy. Within this framework for ISO's approach to commercial lines insurance, a discussion of commercial general liability insurance follows.

First named insured
The person or organization whose name appears first as the named insured on an insurance policy and who pays premiums, receives any returned premiums, cancels the policy, and receives the notice of cancellation or nonrenewal.

EXHIBIT 7-3

Common Policy Declarations

POLICY NUMBER:

IL DS 00 07 02

COMMON POLICY DECLARATIONS

COMPANY NAME AREA	PRODUCER NAME AREA

NAMED INSURED: _____

MAILING ADDRESS: _____

_____

POLICY PERIOD: FROM _____ TO _____ AT 12:01 A.M. STANDARD
TIME AT YOUR MAILING ADDRESS SHOWN ABOVE.

BUSINESS DESCRIPTION	

IN RETURN FOR THE PAYMENT OF THE PREMIUM, AND SUBJECT TO ALL THE TERMS OF THIS POLICY, WE AGREE WITH YOU TO PROVIDE THE INSURANCE AS STATED IN THIS POLICY.

THIS POLICY CONSISTS OF THE FOLLOWING COVERAGE PARTS FOR WHICH A PREMIUM IS INDICATED. THIS PREMIUM MAY BE SUBJECT TO ADJUSTMENT.

	PREMIUM
BOILER AND MACHINERY COVERAGE PART	$ _____
CAPITAL ASSETS PROGRAM (OUTPUT POLICY) COVERAGE PART	$ _____
COMMERCIAL AUTOMOBILE COVERAGE PART	$ _____
COMMERCIAL GENERAL LIABILITY COVERAGE PART	$ _____
COMMERCIAL INLAND MARINE COVERAGE PART	$ _____
COMMERCIAL PROPERTY COVERAGE PART	$ _____
CRIME AND FIDELITY COVERAGE PART	$ _____
EMPLOYMENT-RELATED PRACTICES LIABILITY COVERAGE PART	$ _____
FARM COVERAGE PART	$ _____
LIQUOR LIABILITY COVERAGE PART	$ _____
POLLUTION LIABILITY COVERAGE PART	$ _____
PROFESSIONAL LIABILITY COVERAGE PART	$ _____
_____	$ _____
	TOTAL: $ _____

Premium shown is payable: $_____ at inception. $ _____

FORMS APPLICABLE TO ALL COVERAGE PARTS (SHOW NUMBERS):

Countersigned:	By:
(Date)	(Authorized Representative)

NOTE

OFFICERS' FACSIMILE SIGNATURES MAY BE INSERTED HERE, ON THE POLICY COVER OR ELSE-WHERE AT THE COMPANY'S OPTION.

COMMERCIAL GENERAL LIABILITY INSURANCE

Organizations of all types purchase general liability insurance for covering premises and operations liability loss exposures and products and completed operations liability loss exposures. Because general liability insurance covers a wide range of liability loss exposures faced by most organizations, it is the foundation for most organizations' liability insurance programs.

General liability insurance for small enterprises is now generally provided by businessowners policies. The coverage is similar to that described next, but of significance to premium auditors is that such policies are generally rated based on property loss exposures, although some classes, such as construction, have auditable premium bases.

Commercial general liability insurance provides protection against claims arising from bodily injury to others or damage to property of others. The following discussion is an overview of commercial general liability insurance coverage.

Legal Basis of Liability

Legal liability can be based on either criminal or civil law, but insurance can treat only claims based on civil law. However, the same incident may have both civil and criminal aspects. For example, a drunk driver who injures a pedestrian may face both criminal penalties and a civil lawsuit by the injured party. Civil claims can be based on tort law; contractual obligations; or federal, state, or local statutes, as illustrated in Exhibit 7-4.

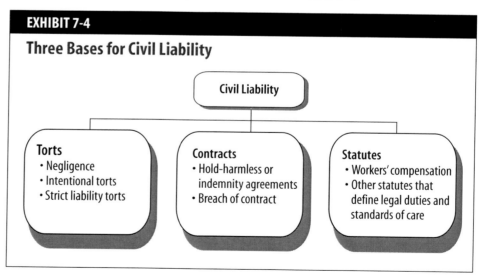

EXHIBIT 7-4

Three Bases for Civil Liability

Civil Liability

Torts
- Negligence
- Intentional torts
- Strict liability torts

Contracts
- Hold-harmless or indemnity agreements
- Breach of contract

Statutes
- Workers' compensation
- Other statutes that define legal duties and standards of care

Tort law consists of a body of precedents and equity principles. A tort can be defined as a civil wrong, other than breach of contract, for which the law provides a remedy in the form of an action for damages. A tort can be either an act or omission. The three elements of a tort are: a legally protected right, a wrongful invasion of that right, and damages that are a proximate result.

The most common tort involved in insurance is the tort of negligence. In brief, to establish a claim based on negligence, the plaintiff must prove the following:

- The defendant owed the plaintiff a duty.
- The defendant breached that duty.
- The breach was the proximate cause of the injuries.
- The plaintiff suffered actual loss or damage.

The law also recognizes intentional torts and absolute liability torts. These torts do not require that the plaintiff prove negligence on the part of the tortfeasor. A tortfeasor is the one who is alleged to have committed the tort. A wrongdoer is a broader term that includes tortfeasors as well as those who have committed criminal offenses.

Legal liability can also be imposed on an insured contractually. Leases, construction agreement, easements, and maintenance agreements are among the types of contracts that frequently impose liability on an insured and that can be covered by commercial general liability insurance. However, not all contractually assumed liability is covered by commercial general liability insurance.

Finally, liability can be imposed by statute. The most common are workers' compensation and no-fault auto insurance statutes. These exposures are excluded from the CGL policy, but other laws can affect liability claims under general liability coverages.

Sources of Liability

Premises liability and operations liability arises from the ownership, maintenance, or use of property and from an insured's activities. **Premises liability** is the exposure to liability for bodily injury or property damage due to the ownership, occupancy, or use of the premises. **Operations liability** is the exposure to liability for bodily injury or property damage resulting from the insured's activities. The possessor of land or buildings owes certain common-law duties to others for their safety. Similarly, anyone conducting business operations has a duty to conduct the operations with reasonable care to avoid bodily injury to others or damage to the property of others. Certain highly hazardous activities impose absolute liability on the tortfeasor: for example, blasting, or keeping wild animals. Under absolute liability, the tortfeasor is responsible for the damages even if the tortfeasor took all possible precautions.

Premises liability
The exposure to liability for bodily injury or property damage due to the ownership, occupancy, or use of the premises.

Operations liability
The exposure to liability for bodily injury or property damage resulting from the insured's activities.

The degree of control exercised by the insured over the premises affects the potential extent of liability, and the insurer should reflect the extent of liability in the premium charged. An absentee owner presumably has less exposure because occupants assume the liability arising out of their activities on the premises. If the owner occupies the entire premises, the owner is entirely responsible for the property's occupancy, use, control, and maintenance. If the insured leases some or all of the property to others, or from others, the premium auditor should verify the extent of the insured's interest.

As a general rule, a party is not liable for its independent contractor's wrongful acts. However, several well-established exceptions exist that are often categorized as nondelegable duties. Included within those are highly hazardous activities, work close to public ways in which the nature of the act is likely to result in harm if due care is not used, action that is illegal unless licensed, and the first party's negligence in selecting an independent contractor. Furthermore, the laws in some states impose a duty on the property owner to provide a safe place to work for the employees of a contractor. Although the possibility of becoming liable for an independent contractor's acts is sometimes difficult for the insured to imagine, coverage for that exposure is important if for no other reason than to provide legal defense in case a lawsuit names the insured.

Products liability and completed operations liability loss exposures are other major loss exposures for many firms. **Products liability** is the exposure to liability for bodily injury or property damage due to products sold or distributed by the exposed party. **Completed operations liability** is the exposure to liability for bodily injury or property damage due to work completed by the exposed party.

Products liability claims can be based on allegations of injury arising from products claimed to have been improperly designed or manufactured, improperly labeled, or improperly packaged. Because the potential claims resulting from defective products can be staggering, equity demands that the premium auditor be certain that the premium developed fully reflects the volume of the sales of the insured's product and the proper classification of the insured's product.

The completed operations loss exposure arises when the insured renders a service, such as constructing a building or installing a heating system. Such insureds are not in the business of manufacturing, selling, distributing, or handling goods as such. Liability for completed operations arises if bodily injury or property damage occurs after the insured has completed or abandoned such operations, and away from premises owned by or rented to the named insured. Operations include materials and parts or equipment furnished in connection with the insured's business.

Contractual liability is the liability expressly assumed under a written contract or agreement. Often those contracts are called hold-harmless or indemnification agreements. Contractual liability does not include liability under a warranty of fitness or quality of the insured's products or under a warranty that work performed by or on the named insured's behalf is done properly.

Other important sources of liability encompassed by commercial general liability insurance are personal and advertising liability. These include claims for damages due to libel, slander, false arrest, unlawful detention, and others. These claims do not involve bodily injury or damage to the property of others.

Products liability
The exposure to liability for bodily injury or property damage due to products sold or distributed by the exposed party.

Completed operations liability
The exposure to liability for bodily injury or property damage due to work completed by the exposed party.

Contractual liability
The liability expressly assumed under a written contract or agreement.

Commercial General Liability Policy

Insureds can obtain coverage for liability loss exposures with the commercial general liability policy. In addition to the common policy declarations and common policy conditions, a complete commercial general liability policy includes the Commercial General Liability Declarations (CG DS 01), Commercial General Liability Coverage Form either CG 00 01 or CG 00 02 (the first being the occurrence version and the second the claims-made one). The alternative versions of the coverage forms differ in that one applies to events occurring within the policy period, whereas the other applies only to claims first made within the policy period. The distinction between occurrence forms and claims-made forms is an important one. Claims-made forms are usually written on forms developed by individual insurers; it is one of the few areas in which ISO forms do not dominate the market. Detailed comments on the differences are, however, beyond the scope of this text. The Broad Form Nuclear Exclusion Endorsement (IL 00 21) and any other endorsements that may apply are also part of the policy.

Exhibit 7-5 illustrates the components of a monoline commercial general liability policy.

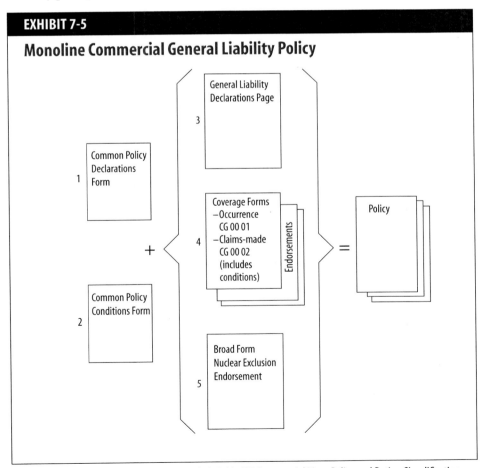

EXHIBIT 7-5

Monoline Commercial General Liability Policy

Adapted with permission from *Workshop Leader's Guide,* ISO Commercial Lines Policy and Rating Simplification Project © Insurance Services Office, Inc., 1985, p. 52.

Commercial General Liability Declarations Page

Commercial general liability insurance requires additional information beyond what appears in the common policy declarations page. Exhibit 7-6 shows a sample Commercial General Liability declarations page. Like the common policy declarations page, the Commercial General Liability declarations page shows the policy number, the insured's name and address, and the policy period.

The declarations page shows the applicable limits for general liability insurance. Separate limits apply to each occurrence and to personal and advertising injury coverage. As part of the occurrence limit, sublimits apply per premises to damage to premises rented to the insured and per person for medical expense. Furthermore, two aggregate limits exist. (An aggregate limit is the most that the insurer will pay for losses during the policy period.) One aggregate limit applies to products-completed operations coverage; the other, the general aggregate, applies to all other coverages combined. The policy stipulates that the limits shown in the commercial general liability declarations page are the maximum that will be paid regardless of the number of insureds, claims, or claimants.

If the policy uses the claims-made coverage form, the declarations state the retroactive date that applies. The policy does not cover claims arising from events occurring before the retroactive date. It is therefore an important condition in defining the extent of coverage provided.

The declarations page also shows, by a check in the appropriate box, whether the insured is an individual, a partnership, a joint venture, a trust, a limited liability company, or other type of organization including a corporation. A brief description of the business is shown along with the location of all premises owned, rented, or occupied by the insured.

The advance premium calculation is detailed in columns showing the classification, code number, premium basis, rate, and premium. A parenthetical note below the total premium line states that the policy is subject to audit. Finally, the declarations page lists, usually by number, all endorsements attached.

Commercial General Liability Coverage Form

The Commercial General Liability Coverage Form occurrence version has five sections, and the claims-made version has six sections. In the following discussion of those sections, the explanations apply to both the occurrence and the claims-made versions, except as noted.

In both versions, Section I describes the three kinds of coverage provided. Coverage A provides bodily injury and property damage liability coverage. It obligates the insurer to "pay those sums that the insured becomes legally obligated to pay as damages because of 'bodily injury' or 'property damage' to which this insurance applies." The two versions differ only regarding the coverage trigger—in other words, what must happen during the policy

EXHIBIT 7-6

Commercial General Lability Declarations

POLICY NUMBER: _____

COMMERCIAL GENERAL LIABILITY
CG DS 01 10 01

COMMERCIAL GENERAL LIABILITY DECLARATIONS

COMPANY NAME AREA	PRODUCER NAME AREA

NAMED INSURED: _____

MAILING ADDRESS: _____

_____

POLICY PERIOD: FROM _____ TO _____ AT 12:01 A.M. TIME AT
YOUR MAILING ADDRESS SHOWN ABOVE

IN RETURN FOR THE PAYMENT OF THE PREMIUM, AND SUBJECT TO ALL THE TERMS OF THIS POLICY, WE AGREE WITH YOU TO PROVIDE THE INSURANCE AS STATED IN THIS POLICY.

LIMITS OF INSURANCE		
EACH OCCURRENCE LIMIT	$ _____	
DAMAGE TO PREMISES RENTED TO YOU LIMIT	$ _____	Any one premises
MEDICAL EXPENSE LIMIT	$ _____	Any one person
PERSONAL & ADVERTISING INJURY LIMIT	$ _____	Any one person or organization
GENERAL AGGREGATE LIMIT	$ _____	
PRODUCTS/COMPLETED OPERATIONS AGGREGATE LIMIT	$ _____	

RETROACTIVE DATE (CG 00 02 ONLY)
THIS INSURANCE DOES NOT APPLY TO "BODILY INJURY", "PROPERTY DAMAGE" OR "PERSONAL AND ADVERTISING INJURY" WHICH OCCURS BEFORE THE RETROACTIVE DATE, IF ANY, SHOWN BELOW.
RETROACTIVE DATE: _____
(ENTER DATE OR "NONE" IF NO RETROACTIVE DATE APPLIES)

DESCRIPTION OF BUSINESS
FORM OF BUSINESS:
□ INDIVIDUAL   □ PARTNERSHIP   □ JOINT VENTURE   □ TRUST
□ LIMITED LIABILITY COMPANY   □ ORGANIZATION, INCLUDING A CORPORATION (BUT NOT IN-CLUDING A PARTNERSHIP, JOINT VENTURE OR LIMITED LIABILITY COMPANY)
BUSINESS DESCRIPTION: _____

CG DS 01 10 01   © ISO Properties, Inc., 2000   Page 1 of 2   □

Continued on next page
▶▶

ALL PREMISES YOU OWN, RENT OR OCCUPY	
LOCATION NUMBER	ADDRESS OF ALL PREMISES YOU OWN, RENT OR OCCUPY

CLASSIFICATION AND PREMIUM							
LOCATION NUMBER	CLASSIFICATION	CODE NO.	PREMIUM BASE	RATE		ADVANCE PREMIUM	
				Prem/ Ops	Prod/Comp Ops	Prem/ Ops	Prod/Comp Ops
			$	$	$	$	$

PREMIUM SHOWN IS PAYABLE:

STATE TAX OR OTHER (if applicable) $ _____

TOTAL PREMIUM (SUBJECT TO AUDIT) $ _____

AT INCEPTION $ _____

AT EACH ANNIVERSARY $ _____

(IF POLICY PERIOD IS MORE THAN ONE YEAR AND PREMIUM IS PAID IN ANNUAL INSTALLMENTS)

AUDIT PERIOD (IF APPLICABLE)	☐ ANNUALLY	☐ SEMI-ANNUALLY	☐ QUARTERLY	☐ MONTHLY

ENDORSEMENTS
ENDORSEMENTS ATTACHED TO THIS POLICY:

THESE DECLARATIONS, TOGETHER WITH THE COMMON POLICY CONDITIONS AND COVERAGE FORM(S) AND ANY ENDORSEMENT(S), COMPLETE THE ABOVE NUMBERED POLICY.

Countersigned:	By:
(Date)	(Authorized Representative)

NOTE

OFFICERS' FACSIMILE SIGNATURES MAY BE INSERTED HERE, ON THE POLICY COVER OR ELSEWHERE AT THE COMPANY'S OPTION.

period for coverage to apply to a particular instance of bodily injury or property damage. The **occurrence coverage form** provides coverage for bodily injury or property damage that occurs during the policy period. The **claims-made coverage form** provides coverage for bodily injury or property damage that is claimed during the policy period.

Coverage B applies to personal and advertising injury liability arising in the course of the insured's business. It covers damages for offenses, such as libel or slander, committed during the policy period. Coverages A and B apply on either a claims-made or an occurrence basis, depending on the form used.

Coverage C provides medical payments coverage. It covers certain medical expenses for injuries suffered on premises owned by the insured or suffered because of the insured's operations if the accident occurs during the policy period. For Coverage C, therefore, the trigger is the same in both policy versions. Only Coverages A and B are available on a claims-made basis.

Exclusions are vital to understanding the scope of any insurance coverage. The primary purpose of exclusions is to clarify coverage. Not every loss exposure is commercially insurable—for example, war risks to fixed property. Certain loss exposures are better handled in specialized policies, such as workers' compensation or auto insurance. The CGL policy contains three detailed sections dealing with what is not covered. Separate exclusions apply to Coverage A, bodily injury and property damage liability; Coverage B, personal and advertising liability; and Coverage C, medical payments. Exhibit 7-7 lists the exclusions for Coverages A, B, and C. In some cases, exceptions to the exclusions result in coverage that would appear to be excluded by the title of the exclusion. For example, contractually assumed liability is excluded but an exception to that exclusion restores coverage for liability arising from certain types of contracts. In addition, policy provisions other than those labeled as exclusions can operate to eliminate coverage. For example, the definition of "property damage" states that, for the purposes of the CGL policy, electronic data are not tangible property.

Section II of the Commercial General Liability Coverage Form clarifies who is an insured under the policy. If the declarations page designates the insured as an individual, the owner of the business and the owner's spouse are insureds, but only regarding the conduct of the business. If the declarations page indicates that the business is a partnership or a joint venture, all members and partners plus their spouses are also insureds, but only regarding the conduct of the business. For a limited liability company, members are insureds regarding their conduct of the business, and managers are insureds, but only regarding their duties as a manager. If the policy designates any other organization form, the entity is insured, the executive officers and directors are insured regarding their duties as officers or directors, and the stockholders are insured regarding their liability as stockholders. In the case of a trust, the trust is an insured and the trustees are also insureds, but only regarding their duties as trustees. The policy does not cover partners or parties to joint ventures with the insured unless the policy shows the partnership or joint venture as a named insured in the declarations page.

Occurrence coverage form
A coverage form that provides coverage for bodily injury or property damage that occurs during the policy period.

Claims-made coverage form
A coverage form that provides coverage for bodily injury or property damage that is claimed during the policy period.

EXHIBIT 7-7

Exclusions Applicable to Commercial General Liability Insurance

CGL Coverage A Bodily Injury and Property Damage Liability Exclusions

a. Expected or Intended Injury

b. Contractual Liability

c. Liquor Liability

d. Workers' Compensation and Similar Laws

e. Employer's Liability

f. Pollution

g. Aircraft, Auto, or Watercraft

h. Mobile Equipment

i. War

j. Damage to Property

k. Damage to Your Product

l. Damage to Your Work

m. Damage to Impaired Property or Property Not Physically Injured

n. Recall of Products, Work, or Impaired Property

o. Personal and Advertising Injury

p. Electronic Data*

*By endorsement: Violation of Statutes That Govern E-Mails, Fax, Phone Calls or Other Methods of Sending Material or Information.

CGL Coverage B Personal and Advertising Liability Exclusions

a. Knowing Violation of Rights of Another

b. Material Published With Knowledge of Falsity

c. Material Published Prior to Policy Period

d. Criminal Acts

e. Contractual Liability

f. Breach of Contract

g. Quality or Performance of Goods — Failure to Conform to Statements

h. Wrong Description of Prices

i. Infringement of Copyright, Patent, Trademark or Trade Secret

j. Insureds in Media and Internet Type Businesses

k. Electronic Chatrooms or Bulletin Boards

l. Unauthorized Use of Another's Name or Product

m. Pollution

n. Pollution-Related

o. War

CGL Coverage C Medical Payments Exclusions

a. Any Insured

b. Hired Person

c. Injury on Normally Occupied Premises

d. Workers' Compensation and Similar Laws

e. Athletics Activities

f. Products-Completed Operations Hazard

g. Coverage A Exclusions

Subject to certain limitations, the policy also insures volunteers while performing duties related to the business; employees acting within the scope of their employment; persons acting as the insured's real estate manager; and, if the insured dies, temporary custodians of the insured's property and the insured's legal representatives. The policy automatically covers for ninety days any newly acquired or formed organization, other than a partnership, joint venture, or limited liability company, for any insured events occurring after the acquisition date, provided that the insured has ownership or majority control.

In both CGL versions, Section IV stipulates conditions regarding bankruptcy; the insured's duties in the event of an occurrence, a claim, or a suit; the right of legal action against the insurer; other insurance; premium audit; representations; separation of insureds; the transfer of recovery rights against others to the insurer; and what happens when the insurer does not renew. In the claims-made version, the other insurance condition makes the policy excess over any applicable insurance not on a claims-made basis. When the policy does not show a retroactive date in the declarations pages or when a retroactive date applies, the other insurance continues in effect after the retroactive date. In addition, the claims-made version has a condition relating to the insured's right to claim and occurrence information. Otherwise, the conditions in both versions are identical.

The most important condition from the premium auditor's point of view is obviously the premium audit condition. It stipulates that the insurer will calculate the premium "in accordance with our rules and rates" and explains the premium audit procedure. That explanation states the following:

> Premium shown in this Coverage Part as advance premium is a deposit premium only. At the close of each audit period we will compute the earned premium for that period and send notice to the first Named Insured. The due date for audit and retrospective premiums is the date shown as the due date on the bill. If the sum of the advance and audit premiums paid for the policy period is greater than the earned premium, we will return the excess to the first Named Insured.[1]

The premium audit condition also requires the first named insured to keep records of the information needed for premium calculation and to send copies to the insurer when requested.

Section V in the claims-made version provides an extended reporting period to remedy coverage gaps. Those coverage gaps could occur when the insured or insurer cancels or does not renew claims-made coverage, the insured renews or replaces the policy with a claims-made policy with a later retroactive date, or the insured replaces the claims-made policy with an occurrence policy. If bodily injury or property damage occurs before the policy period's end, but the resulting claim is first made after the policy period's end, a coverage gap could exist. Under certain circumstances, the extended reporting period treats the claim as though it had been first made during the expiring policy period.

The occurrence version's Section V and the claims-made version's Section VI definition sections are identical. They define terms used in the policy: advertisement, auto, bodily injury, coverage territory, employee, executive officer, hostile fire, impaired property, insured contract, leased worker, loading or unloading, mobile equipment, occurrence, personal and advertising injury, pollutants, products-completed operations hazard, property damage, suit, temporary worker; volunteer worker; your product; and your work. Each of those terms has a special meaning when used in the policy.

Those terms' exact meanings affect the coverage provided and may also affect the premium audit. For example, a premium auditor should be able to determine whether particular mobile cranes, tractors, trucks, and other construction equipment come within the auto or mobile equipment definition. Insurers base the insurance rate for mobile equipment operation on the payroll of the equipment operators or the income derived from the rental of such equipment to others, whereas the insurance rate for autos is per auto. In 2004, the new ISO CGL forms amended the definition of mobile equipment by eliminating, from the definition of mobile equipment, land vehicles that are subject to motor vehicle insurance requirements in the state where the equipment is licensed or principally garaged. Such equipment is considered autos. The commercial auto policy was amended to provide coverage for such items. Premium auditors must be aware of this change to ensure that automobile premiums are correctly calculated.

Although the CGL eliminates the need for many endorsements, endorsements can still be used to limit or broaden coverage. In addition, insurers attach the broad form nuclear exclusion endorsement to all policies. The nuclear exclusion appears in a separate endorsement because of the complexity of its language and because it applies to other insurance lines as well as commercial general liability insurance.

If the insured does not need or the insurer does not want to provide all the coverages included in the CGL, endorsements are available to eliminate products-completed operations coverage, personal and advertising injury coverage, advertising injury coverage only, medical payments coverage, or damage to premises rented to the insured coverage. On the other hand, endorsements are available to broaden the coverage to meet the needs of certain insureds—for example, electronic data liability and coverage for additional insureds.

Several specialized endorsements are available to modify a claims-made policy. One of those endorsements excludes specific accidents, products, work, or locations. That endorsement may make insurance more readily available in long-term exposure cases. For an additional premium, however, the insured can purchase an endorsement that extends the reporting period for specific accidents, products, work, or locations. Other endorsements significantly limit a claims-made policy's coverage.

PREMIUM BASES

Insurers base premiums for commercial general liability insurance on many measures. The uniformity arising from the strict regulation of workers' compensation insurance does not exist for general liability coverages. Insurers have more discretion in choosing a premium base that reflects the loss exposure assumed for classes of business other than workers' compensation.

As far as possible, the *CLM* uses inflation-sensitive exposure bases.[2] Those bases measure the exposure in dollars so that a change in the dollar's value does not automatically require an adjustment in rates. Exhibit 7-8 shows the exposure base for each major business group.

EXHIBIT 7-8

General Liability Premium Bases

Major Business Group	Premium Base
Mercantile	Gross Sales
Manufacturing	Gross Sales
Contracting/Servicing	Payroll
Buildings/Premises	
Apartments	Units
Hotels	Gross Sales
Offices	Area
Lessors	Area
Miscellaneous	Various

General Liability Rule 24 in the *CLM* defines premium bases used in the manual and the exposure units for each. The following sections explain those premium bases.

Admissions

A major potential liability facing theaters, shows, or sports events is the possibility of bodily injury to a spectator. That exposure is the same whether the ticket price is $80 or $10. Therefore insurers write policies covering such operations with the premium based on the number of admissions.

According to the *CLM*, **admissions** is a premium base that includes the total number of persons, other than employees of the named insured, admitted to an insured event. This applies to events conducted on the premises, whether with paid admissions, tickets, complimentary tickets, or passes. When that premium base applies, the manual shows the rates per 1,000 admissions.

Admissions
A premium base that includes the total number of persons, other than employees of the insured, admitted to an insured event.

Most theaters keep a ticket count as a check on dollar amounts received. The tickets are usually numbered sequentially, and the difference between the numbers of the first and last tickets sold that day provides a count against which the premium auditor can verify receipts. In some instances, the insured may record only the dollar amount of ticket receipts. The premium auditor would then have to divide the total amount by the ticket price to obtain the number of admissions. If the insured has given any complimentary admissions, the premium auditor must add them to the total.

Area

Area is a common method of measuring public liability loss exposures for commercial general liability insurance purposes. A building's or property's physical existence encompasses a measurable area. Because the amount or size of area is rarely disputable, it has been a standard coverage and exposure determination measure. Insurers have not generally considered area to be a premium audit difficulty. Manual rates apply per 1,000 square feet of area.

Area
The total number of square feet of floor space at the insured premises.

The *CLM* defines **area** as "the total number of square feet of floor space at the insured premises" calculated by first multiplying horizontal dimensions of the outside of the outer building walls (length times width) and then multiplying that result by the number of floors, including basements. Area for premium computation excludes the area of the following:

- Courts and mezzanine-type floor openings
- Portions of basements or floors if 50 percent or more of the area is used for shop or storage for building maintenance, dwelling by building maintenance employees, heating units, power plants, or air conditioning equipment

Exhibit 7-9 shows a three-story building that may require a premium auditor to measure the area to verify the premium base. The first floor dimensions are 160 feet long by 80 feet wide—multiplying 160 feet times 80 feet equals 12,800 square feet. Because the building has three floors, the total for the building is three times 12,800 square feet each, which equals 38,400 square feet. The basement area houses the furnace and maintenance facilities, so the insurer does not include it in the calculation. An open-court design light-well pierces the top floor; it has an area of 40 feet times 40 feet, which equals 1,600 square feet. In compliance with the manual definition, insurers should deduct the area of the open-space court from the overall total. The total for the three floors is 38,400 square feet, minus the 1,600 square feet of the top floor, equals 36,800 square feet. In this example, therefore, the chargeable area for premium purposes is 36,800 square feet.

Each

Sometimes a more convenient measure than area may be the actual number of items involved in the insured's business. The classification footnotes in the *CLM* indicate and define the unit, such as per person, per 100 tons, per 10,000 fillings, or per 1,000,000 gallons.

EXHIBIT 7-9

Illustration of Area Measurement

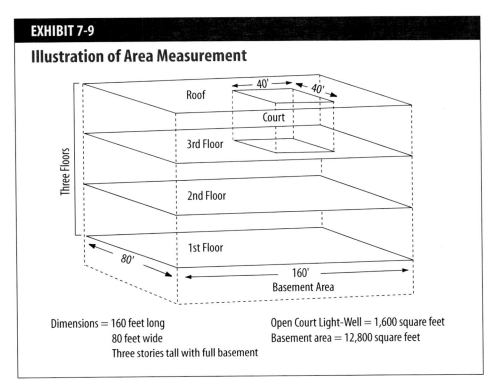

Dimensions = 160 feet long
80 feet wide
Three stories tall with full basement

Open Court Light-Well = 1,600 square feet
Basement area = 12,800 square feet

Premium auditors can sometimes determine the actual number by physical inspection. In other cases, the premium auditor must gather the information from production reports or the insured's other records. When auditing a club or trade association with a CGL policy defining the premium as a certain rate per member, the premium auditor must only determine the number of members that the organization has. Schools may pay premiums that are a certain rate per pupil or per faculty member. Premium auditors can frequently obtain the number of pupils from the average daily attendance reports that the insured makes to the state board of education. Premium auditors can obtain the number of faculty members from the payroll records.

Some premium bases offer more of a challenge. For example, insurers base premiums for camps on each camper day. One camper camping for one day equals one camper day. One camper camping for ten days equals ten camper days. The insured may not have adequate records of camper days, and the premium auditor may have to reconstruct camper days from receipts or lot allocations. If the camp fee is $25 per day and total receipts for the policy period are $250,000, then the premium basis is 10,000 camper days. Because the receipts may include additional charges but exclude uncollected fees, an estimate is the most a premium auditor can expect in such situations.

Gross Sales

For many loss exposures, gross sales may be the best exposure measure. For example, consider two identical stores. They have the same area in square feet, but one does much more business than the other. Using area, they would be charged the same premium. However, gross sales may be a better exposure measure because it reflects the number of customers actually entering the store. Insurers state rates per $1,000 of gross sales.

Gross sales is a premium base that is the gross amount of money charged by the named insured for all goods or products sold or distributed, operations performed, or rentals made. For clubs rated on a gross sales basis, insurers do not include a one-time initiation fee in determining gross sales.

In accounting terminology, gross sales include transactions occurring when a buyer and a seller agree on a product's sale. In contrast, receipts are the cash received by the seller from the buyer. Receipts are rarely identical to gross sales because of deductions for returns and allowances, cash discounts for prompt payment, and uncollectible accounts. Premium auditors can normally obtain the gross sales directly from the general ledger, but insureds often suggest that the premium auditor deduct certain items as not relevant to the loss exposure. Although premium auditors often have to disagree and explain why such items should be included in the premium base, CLM rules stipulate that the insurer can legitimately exclude a few items, such as sales and excise taxes.

Gross sales
A premium base that is the gross amount of money charged by the named insured for all goods or products sold or distributed, operations performed, or rentals made.

Gross Sales Inclusions

The insured's sales accounts may show several categories reflecting a reduction in profits from the sale of merchandise, but this is not necessarily a reduction in the liability exposure. The premium base should include the full sales price even if the insured does not collect the full amount. According to the CLM, insurers should not deduct the following items from gross sales in determining liability premiums:

- *Foreign exchange discounts.* The foreign exchange discount is the liability exposure based on the values in U.S. currency. As such, any discount based on foreign exchange is not deductible.

- *Freight allowances.* Premium auditors can consider freight allowances as part of the sale because they reflect usual steps to expand sales volume. They do not reflect a reduction in the insured's liability exposure.

- *Goods on consignment and warehouse receipts.* Premium auditors should include the total sales of consigned merchandise and warehouse receipts, not the value of the consigned merchandise or the value shown on the receipt, in the premium base.

- *Trade or cash discounts.* In some industries, it is established practice to allow discounts to distributors. The discount may vary depending on the number of units purchased. For example, a publisher may allow a 40 percent discount when a bookstore purchases one copy of a book, but 50 percent if the store buys ten or more copies. The number of books sold and the probable exposure, however, have not changed. Therefore, discounts are not deducted in calculating gross sales.

Insureds may allow the customer to deduct a certain agreed-on percentage for cash payment or payment before a specified date. Again, such cash discounts do not alter the liability arising from the sale. Insurers should base the premium on the purchase price notwithstanding the fact that the insured accepted a lesser amount in return for prompt payment.

- *Bad debts.* With regard to bad debt, the liability loss exposure arises from the merchandise's physical existence after the insured relinquishes possession of it. Whether the insured receives the full sum for the product or writes off a sum is irrelevant because the price paid for the item is the established potential liability measure. Payment in full for a product is not a prerequisite to legal recourse against the seller.

- *Installment sales repossessions.* Installment sales repossessions are included in gross sales totals. Insurers should include only the amounts actually collected by the insured, provided the insured's records actually disclose such amounts. Insurers include the amount that the insured has collected, but exclude the credit against sales for the amount not collected. That may not be a perfect measure of the exposure while the product was in the buyer's hands, but it does reflect that some exposure did exist during that period and that the exposure was less than if the merchandise had remained with the buyer for the product's entire life. This may appear to conflict with the treatment of bad debts; bad debts are not deducted because the goods remain in circulation. Note that while the uncollected portion of the selling price on goods repossessed is excluded, collections before repossession are included.

Gross Sales Exclusions

Excludable items that insurers can deduct from gross sales include the following:

- Sales or excise taxes that are collected and submitted to a government division
- Credits for repossessed merchandise and products returned
- Allowances for damaged and spoiled goods
- Finance charges for items sold on installments
- Freight charges on sales if freight is charged as a separate item on the customer's invoice
- Royalty income from patent rights or copyrights that are not product sales
- Rental receipts for products liability coverage only

Sales taxes are imposed on the purchaser and collected by the seller. The insured (seller) should separately list sales taxes on the sales invoices and maintain a separate account for sales tax payable. Such taxes in no way reflect the liability assumed by the insurer and would therefore be inappropriate to include. The question has arisen as to whether the gross sales amount of lottery tickets should be included since in many cases this is a sizable sum and represents a premises exposure to the insured because persons come in to buy the tickets. It is generally agreed that such proceeds would come under this category, and the only amount that should be included is the small percentage of the sales that the retailer is allowed to keep.

Also, buyers may return for credit merchandise that is defective or otherwise unsatisfactory. If only a partial shipment is damaged, the seller may allow a credit without the return of the merchandise. In either case, sales revenues are reduced when calculating gross sales for premium audit purposes because potential liability is reduced by the return of the goods or, if goods remain in circulation, the agreement that they are damaged in effect cancels the seller's warranty. When the insured repossesses merchandise that it sold on installments, the uncollected portion of the selling price is deducted.

Likewise, whether the customer pays cash or buys on installment does not affect the loss exposure arising from the product's sale. Therefore, insurers exclude finance charges from the premium base, provided the insured separately shows them in its records.

Freight charges on sales are excluded if the charge is a separate item on the customer's invoice. If the customer pays for the delivery of merchandise, the insurer should deduct that amount from the premium base as long as the insured's records actually disclose the amount. Regardless of who pays for the delivery, the insured's exposure is the same.

Another exclusion is the royalty revenues from patents or copyrights. These are normally small, and the associated loss exposures are minimal. Insurers accordingly exclude those amounts from the premium base.

The definition of the insured product for the purposes of products liability does not include vending machines or other property rented to or located for the use of others but not sold. Therefore, rental receipts for such property are not included in the premium basis for products liability coverage.

Foreign Sales

The CGL policy defines coverage territory to mean the U.S. (including its territories and possessions), Puerto Rico, and Canada. However, other parts of the world are also included in the definition. Coverage for foreign sales applies in all other parts of the world if the bodily injury or property damage arises out of goods or products made or sold by the insured in the coverage territory and if the insured's responsibility to pay damages is based on a suit in the coverage territory or in a settlement the insurer agrees to.

Foreign sales can result in claims under the policy. In fact, the more serious the claim, the more likely that the original suit will be brought in the U.S. because U.S. courts are usually more favorable to claimants and the damage awards are usually higher. Therefore, insurers include all sales, foreign or domestic, in the premium base.

Some specialty insurers provide separate policies covering only foreign sales, which could result in their exclusion from the primary (standard) insurer's policy. Premium auditors should consult insurer underwriting departments for their specific interpretation when they encounter such situations.

Intercompany Sales

Intercompany sales are the sale of goods between two or more separate legal entities that are named insureds on the same policy. Such sales are usually between a parent corporation and its subsidiary or between two subsidiaries of the same parent corporation. An example is a parent manufacturer or processor and its subsidiary supplier(s) or retailer(s).

Different insurers view the inclusion or exclusion of intercompany sales differently, but ISO's intent is to include intercompany sales in gross sales. Covered claims between named insureds on the same policy can also arise. The insurer can be faced with a claim between a parent and subsidiary or two subsidiaries due to the separation of insureds condition. This condition provides that, except for limits of liability, the insurance applies as if each named insured were the only named insured and separately to each insured against whom a claim is made or a suit is brought. Therefore, a suit by one named insured against another is covered just as if they were totally unrelated and insured by separate policies.

The CLM rules include all sales of goods or products from one company to another, including those sales from one named insured to another. However, goods transferred to a subsidiary or parent retail operation are included at wholesale value.

Another reason to include intercompany sales is that the potential for third-party claims are the same for parent companies and subsidiaries as for any other insured. Visiting salespeople, repair workers, inspectors, and so forth can make liability claims against the owners of any premises. If intercompany sales are eliminated and all the sales of the subsidiary were to the parent or other subsidiaries, the insurer would receive no premium at all for this exposure.

Therefore, the premium auditor should treat each named insured as separate in all respects. If the insured desires to eliminate the premium charge for products-completed operations coverage on intercompany sales, the Exclusion—Intercompany Products Suits Endorsement (CG 21 41) can be attached to the policy. If the exclusion endorsement is attached to the policy, the premium base for the premises-completed operations exposure would still include the intercompany sales figure because the endorsement applies only to products-completed operations suits.

Cost Plus Contracts

Insureds may undertake some projects on a cost plus basis. For example, a construction firm may contract to build a chemical plant for an amount equal to all the costs plus a certain percentage. If the construction firm is the

Intercompany sales
The sale of goods between two or more separate legal entities that are named insureds on the same policy.

insured, the premium auditor should determine how the firm's accounting procedures treat the revenues from that contract. The insured may report the gross contract price as revenue, or it may consider the cost portion of the contract as merely a purchasing service for the customer and report only the fees under the contract as revenue. In the latter case, the receipts shown would reflect only a small portion of the actual liability loss exposure. The premium auditor should report both the cost expenditures and the fee as the premium base.

Payroll

Payroll serves as the premium base for contracting or servicing operations. In those cases, it provides a good exposure measure. Payroll also has the advantage of requiring no additional burdensome recordkeeping by the insured because federal tax laws already require the insured to keep such records. Moreover, because the insured and others use the payroll records for other purposes, such records present less of a problem regarding verification. Payroll also reflects the degree of direct control over operations. Employees are involved in most of the activities that create potential liability.

Because payroll also serves as the premium base for workers' compensation insurance, the premium auditor's task is simplified if the auditor can concurrently perform the premium audits for commercial general liability and workers' compensation insurance. The commercial general liability insurance inclusions are similar to the workers' compensation insurance inclusions with the exceptions that are discussed below. Some items are included in workers' compensation payrolls but not in the general liability calculations. These items include payments for retirement or cafeteria plans made through employee-authorized deductions from the employee's gross pay; Davis-Bacon wages paid to employees' annuity plans; and expense reimbursement to the extent that the records do not substantiate that the expense was incurred.

Exclusions are also similar except that under commercial general liability insurance, the payroll for the standard exception classifications (clerical, salespersons, and drivers) and aircraft pilots and copilots are excluded. The commercial general liability insurance exclusions also specify that insurers should separately classify drafting employees. Workers' compensation payroll exclusions not excluded from the commercial general liability insurance premium base include military duty payments, employee discounts, expense reimbursement to the extent that the employer's records substantiate that the expense was incurred, supper money for late work, work uniform allowance, sick pay paid by a third party, and several employer-provided perquisites such as employer contributions to a savings plan.

Payroll Inclusions

Specific items are included as payroll, according to the *CLM*. For example, salespeople, chauffeurs, and drivers for laundries, bakeries, and milk dealers often receive a straight commission or a commission plus salary. The premium auditor should determine the full amount of commissions paid, including reviewing the insured's tax reports such as W-2 and 1099 forms. If an employee, such as a salesperson, is hired under a contract providing a drawing account against commission, the premium auditor should include the drawing account when it exceeds the commissions.

Bonuses are also considered payroll inclusions. A bonus is an amount given that is over and above regular earnings, often for superior job performance. Insurers include bonuses as part of an employee's compensation.

Generally premium auditors do not include the extra amount paid for overtime work. Overtime is defined as hours worked for which there is an increase in the rate of pay, including the following: work in any day or week in excess of the number of hours normally worked; hours worked in excess of eight hours in any day or forty hours in any week; and work on Saturdays, Sundays, or holidays.

Overtime can be excluded if the insured keeps specific records separately showing overtime pay by employee and in summary by classification. Premium auditors calculate the overtime exclusion by one of the following methods:

- If the records break down the pay between regular and overtime, the premium auditor excludes the entire extra pay for overtime work.

- If the records show only one amount for the total pay earned for overtime (that is, one amount for both regular pay and overtime pay), the premium auditor calculates overtime by excluding one-third of the total amount when the employer pays the worker time-and-a-half for overtime. If the employer pays the worker double time for overtime, then the premium auditor excludes half of the total amount.

The manual rule's intent on overtime is that the insurer should deduct overtime pay from payroll only if the number of hours actually worked in the day or week exceeds the number of hours normal and usual to the particular business or industry. Regardless of the normal workday or workweek, overtime pay will be deductible for the number of hours actually worked in excess of eight hours per day or forty hours per week. Only the portion of the overtime pay that is in excess of the straight time pay is deductible. Overtime exclusion does not apply to any payroll assigned to stevedoring.

In addition to pay for holidays, vacations, and sick days, insurers should also include pay for other time not worked, such as for jury duty, funerals, or weddings if the employee is paid for those days. Insurers include mandatory payments by employers on employees' behalf to statutory insurance or pension plans, such as Social Security, in the premium basis. Similarly, employer contributions to a savings plan, a vacation fund, or an individual retirement account are considered part of an employee's pay. A salary reduction agreement may provide an employer's contribution to a savings plan instead of a certain amount of salary. Insurers also include that amount in the premium base, although the employer's matching contribution is not included (unless the employer includes that amount in the employee's taxable income).

As explained previously, employers may base wages on piecework, incentive plans, or profit-sharing plans. Insurers still include those wages.

Also included in the premium base are any allowances made to employees for tools the employees furnish. The employees must use the tools in their work or operations for the insured.

If the employer provides housing, the insurer should include the actual value in the employee's compensation. A premium auditor can determine the actual value by examining the rental price of comparable accommodations in the vicinity. As with workers' compensation insurance, the premium auditor can add to the amount shown in the insured's records if necessary to reach the housing's actual value. The premium auditor should include in the premium base the value of any other form of lodging furnished by the employer, to the extent that the insured's records disclose that value.

To the extent shown in the insured's records, the insurer should include the value of employer-furnished meals in the premium base. Premium auditors also should include the value of store certificates, merchandise, credits, or any other substitute for money received by employees as part of their pay in the premium base.

The premium auditor includes the payroll of mobile equipment operators and their helpers, whether or not the operators are designated or licensed to operate automobiles. Determining this amount can be difficult when the operators and their helpers are provided to the insured along with equipment hired under contract.

If mobile equipment is hired with operators, the insurer includes the operator's payroll and assigns it to the appropriate classification. That *CLM* rule also applies to employees who move the equipment, provided the equipment moves under its own power. The payroll amount is often based on the number of hours used, and the insured usually knows the normal rate paid to operators—both union and nonunion rates. When that information is available, the premium auditor must multiply hours by the rate to obtain the payroll. If the premium auditor cannot obtain actual payrolls, then the manual stipulates that the insurer use one-third of the total amount paid for the hire of the equipment as wages.

That premium charge covers the liability arising out of the insured's direction and control of the equipment and operator. The equipment owner's insurance covering its operations has no bearing on the potential liability.

When the insured hires mobile equipment without operators, the premium base should include the payroll of the insured's regular employees who operate the equipment. That payroll is found in the insured's normal payroll records. As mentioned previously, land vehicles that are subject to a compulsory or financial responsibility law or another motor vehicle insurance law in the state where they are licensed or principally garaged are rated as autos in the ISO CGL and commercial auto forms. The payroll for the operators of such equipment is excluded from the CGL premium base because such operators are insured under automobile policies.

Insurers can use flat amounts as the payroll for sole proprietors, partners, and a corporation's executive officers. The premium auditor should refer to the manual's state rate pages for the specific amounts. Managers of limited liability companies (LLCs) are considered executive officers. Members of LLCs are considered co-partners.

The manual's intent is to assign the flat amount payroll of the officers, partners, and individual insureds to the classification in which they are primarily engaged. However, if they are principally engaged in clerical or outside sales operations, their payroll would be excluded for premium calculation purposes.

Premium auditors can reduce the payroll amount of officers or co-partners of temporary or seasonal businesses by 2 percent for each full calendar week in excess of twelve weeks during which the insured business does not operate.

This inclusion recognizes the employment-leasing practice whereby a labor-leasing firm furnishes workers to the named insured. The premium auditor should classify the employees as if they were direct employees. If payroll is not available, the premium auditor should use the full contract price as the payroll. If a definite amount of the contract is for payroll, a premium auditor should use that amount. If an insured pays an employment agency for temporary personnel, the premium auditor should consider the entire fee payroll.

Payroll Exclusions

According to the *CLM*, payroll does not include certain items. For example, partially because of the difficulty of documenting the amounts, tips are excluded from payroll.

Payroll also excludes voluntary payments to a group insurance or pension plan by the insured at the insured's expense other than, as mentioned previously, payment by an employer of amounts otherwise required by law to be paid by employees to statutory insurance or pension plans, such as Social Security. Payroll does include an employee's contribution, even if paid by the insured on the employee's behalf.

If an employee receives a cash reward for a discovery or invention, a premium auditor does not include that amount as part of payroll. Likewise, if an employee receives income as part of a severance package, the premium auditor does not include that amount as payroll. However, if part of the income received represents pay for time worked or accrued vacation, the premium auditor should include that amount.

Insurers always exclude the payroll of clerical office employees except when the classification wording or footnote specifically stipulates inclusion. To meet the manual definition, clerical office employees must work in areas physically separated by walls, floors, or partitions from all other work areas of the insured and have duties strictly limited to keeping the insured's books or records or conducting correspondence.

Insurers treat the payroll of salespersons, collectors, and messengers the same as clerical payroll, but the payroll of employees whose duties include the delivery of any merchandise handled, treated, or sold is not excluded. The manual also states that these persons should work principally away from the insured's premises. If the principal duties of a driver or a driver's helper are to work on or in connection with autos (that is, the driving duties are not just an inconsequential part of another job), premium auditors should not include the payroll of such employees as part of payroll. Similarly, if the principal duties of an aircraft pilot or copilot involve working on or in connection with an aircraft, the premium auditor should not include the payroll of those employees.

In determining the payroll amount for the one classification that best describes the insured's operations, insurers exclude drafting employees' payroll if the drafting employees' duties are limited to office work and if they are engaged as drafting employees in such a manner as not to be exposed to the hazards of the operations of the business. Premium auditors should assign that payroll to a separate drafting employees classification (Code 91805). Engineers and architects are rated separately from drafting employees.

In addition to the exclusions listed in the manual, premium auditors generally regard payments for expense reimbursement or expense allowances except for tools as exclusions, even though not explicitly mentioned in the manual. When payroll is the premium base, the manual states that the rates apply per $1,000 of payroll.

Total Cost

Total cost
A premium base that reflects the insured's liability loss exposure based on the total cost of the job.

According to the *CLM*, **total cost** is a premium base that reflects the insured's liability loss exposure based on the total cost of the job. Total cost includes the cost of all labor, materials, and equipment furnished, used, or delivered for use in the execution of the work; and all fees, bonuses, or commissions made, paid, or due. However, it does not include the cost of finished equipment installed but not furnished by the subcontractor if the subcontractor does no other work on or in connection with such equipment. The manual rates are stated per $1,000 of total cost.

Total Operating Expenditures

Total operating expenditures are the total expenditures by the insured during the policy period. Total operating expenditures are the rating base used for rating governmental entities. Accounts payable, grants, entitlements, and shared revenue are included, as are expenditures for independent contractors' operations when the contractor does not carry adequate insurance. Also included are any federal or state funds for the sole purpose of training employees.

This occurs unless a separate policy with adequate coverage and limits has been issued in the name of the governing body granting such funds, with the governmental entity named as an additional insured or a hold-harmless agreement in favor of the governmental subdivision.

Capital improvements are excluded from the total operating expenditures. These are any purchase or improvement of any individual item of personal or real property that is bonded or financed, including interest thereon, or that exceeds 5 percent of total operating expenditures. However, expenditures for work performed by the named insured in connection with such capital improvements is included. Other exclusions include the following: expenditures for independent contractors' operations when the contractor carries adequate insurance; welfare benefits (not administrative costs), including expenditures for activities designed to provide public assistance and institutional care; expenditures from the Intragovernmental Service Fund if funding is budgeted for and received from other funds; and expenditures on those exposures which are separately rated.

Rule 24. G. 4 in the manual provides a detailed explanation of governmental accounting terms that is helpful to premium auditors auditing such entities.

Rates apply per $1,000 of total operating expenditures.

Units

The units premium base is simply an exposure count, such as apartment units. Insurers normally use units as an exposure base with dwelling classifications. A **unit** is a premium base that reflects the insured's liability loss exposure based on the number of units the insured owns. The CLM describes a unit as "a single room or group of rooms intended for occupancy as separate living quarters by a family, by a group of unrelated persons living together, or by a person living alone."

Unit
A premium base that reflects the insured's liability loss exposure based on the number of units the insured owns.

SUMMARY

General liability is one of the insurance lines for which Insurance Services Office (ISO) is the principal rating organization. ISO develops policy forms, publishes rules manuals for writing those lines of insurance, collects statistics, calculates and files rates, and performs other advisory and research functions for its subscribers. ISO publishes the *Commercial Lines Manual (CLM)*, which combines the rules and classifications for nine lines of insurance into one manual. That combination facilitates uniformity in treating those lines of insurance. The General Liability section of the CLM presents the rules for general liability insurance, which involves premium auditing more frequently than do the other lines in the *CLM*. General liability coverages are often combined with other coverage forms in package policies, which the uniform format of the simplified commercial lines policy facilitates.

Insurers usually assemble general liability policies by adding the declarations and the desired coverage parts to a policy jacket. The declarations identify the insured and summarize the coverages and the corresponding limits of liability, premium base, and rates. The coverage parts are standard forms defining particular types of coverage provided.

Liability exposures are pervasive. Liability can be either civil or criminal, but insurance can deal only with civil liability. Civil liability can be based on tort law; contractual obligations; and federal, state, or local statutes.

Most businesses require premises and operations coverage to protect them from the liability exposures arising from the business's existence. For businesses offering goods or services for sale, products-completed operations coverage provides protection for the liability exposures arising from a product or an operation after the insured has relinquished control.

Insurers can write commercial general liability coverage on either an occurrence basis or a claims-made basis, and different rates apply to each. Both versions of the CGL form incorporate three coverages: Coverage A, bodily injury and property damage liability; Coverage B, personal and advertising injury liability; and Coverage C, medical payments. They differ primarily based on how coverage is triggered. The forms include numerous conditions, exclusions, and definitions that have to be carefully reviewed when analyzing coverage.

Insurers base premiums for general liability insurance on any one of several measures of the exposures insured. The premium bases are indicated in the *CLM Classification Table*. The general rules in the *CLM* explicitly define the bases, which are admissions, area, each, gross sales, payroll, total cost, total operating expenditures, and units. Premium auditors should be familiar with the definitions of each of these premium bases to extract the correct information from the insured's records.

In addition to determining the premium base amount for the policy period, the premium auditor must assign the correct classification for the exposure and apply any other premium development factors that are involved. The next chapter discusses those procedures.

CHAPTER NOTES

1. ISO Commercial General Liability Form (CG 00 01 12 04), Section IV.5.b. Copyright, ISO Properties, Inc., 2003.
2. Premium charges for most insurance policies are determined by multiplying the rate times the exposure. Insurance practitioners use the term "exposure base" to describe the loss exposures used in the calculation, such as square feet of a building or sales receipts of a store. This same exposure base is also called a "premium base" because it is the basis for premium determination. Most persons in the insurance industry use the terms interchangeably.

Direct Your Learning

Commercial General Liability Premium Determination

Educational Objectives

After learning the content of this chapter and completing the corresponding course guide assignment, you should be able to:

▶ Given a general liability insurance case, assign the correct exposure amounts to the proper classification(s) and give reasons for the assignments made.

- Classify general liability loss exposures according to *Commercial Lines Manual* (CLM) rules.

- Explain the general and business-group-specific classification procedures.

▶ Explain how general liability premiums are determined, including the application of general liability rates, premium modifications, and minimum premiums.

▶ Describe composite rating as it is applied to pricing a package policy.

▶ Describe the classifications, rating structure, and audit procedures applied to governmental subdivisions.

▶ Describe the premium audit procedures applied to the following categories of professional liability insurance:

- Hospital professional liability insurance

- Physicians, surgeons, and dentists professional liability insurance

- Blood banks professional liability insurance

▶ Define or describe each of the Key Words and Phrases for this chapter.

CHAPTER 8

Develop Your Perspective

What are the main topics covered in the chapter?

General liability classification is based on the procedures for classification assignment in the Insurance Services Office's *Commercial Lines Manual* (*CLM*). This chapter addresses the detailed process for assigning classifications, including exceptions and modifications. Additional procedures necessary for performing premium audits for governmental subdivisions and specific types of professional liability insurance are also included.

Compare the general and business-group-specific classification procedures.

- How would a premium auditor know which rules are to be applied?
- What rules apply based on an insured's major business group?

Why is it important to learn these topics?

Premium auditors are expected to understand the accurate use of the *CLM* and classification of general liability loss exposures to ensure accurate rates are applied. Such application is a basic competency within the premium auditors' profession.

Consider how a premium auditor makes rating classification decisions based on the *CLM*.

- Explain how the explanatory rule listings guide a premium auditor in understanding the loss exposures defined and included within the rates for each classification.
- Describe the general and specific classification procedures that guide the premium auditor in grouping similar operations into rating classifications.

How can you use what you will learn?

Evaluate the extensive and detailed *CLM* content that a premium auditor must apply in reviewing a complex general liability policy.

- How can the auditor organize the information needed as a reference to apply it to the account?

Commercial General Liability Premium Determination

This chapter continues the description of premium audit procedures for general liability insurance. The last chapter outlined general liability coverages and premium bases, and this chapter concentrates on classification assignment and other premium determination procedures. Properly assigning classifications can make a substantial difference in earned premium. Preserving equity in the rating system is also essential.

GENERAL LIABILITY CLASSIFICATION

As with workers' compensation, premium auditors must classify general liability exposures so that each type of business operation pays its share of insured losses. In fact, the classification system for general liability insurance has much in common with the workers' compensation classification system. Workers' compensation classification concepts also have considerable relevance for general liability insurance, but premium auditors should not disregard the differences.

The Insurance Services Office (ISO) *Commercial Lines Manual* (CLM) lists the classifications and stipulates the procedures for assigning classifications to insureds with general liability policies. The classifications list appears in the Classification Table, which is a separate *CLM* section.

Commercial Lines Manual Classification Table

The *CLM* Classification Table pages, paginated with a CS letter code, list alphabetically the classifications applicable to general liability insurance, as well as to crime, commercial fire and allied lines, and multiple-lines insurance. The Classification Table is a compilation of the various classifications used in the lines of insurance to which the *CLM* applies. The total number of classifications in the table therefore exceeds the number used in the past. The compilation reduces the need for classification by analogy and encourages more uniform coding and rating. The Classification Table section has two parts: the explanatory rules and the classifications listing.

Exhibit 8-1 shows a sample page from the classifications listing that also illustrates explanatory rules.

EXHIBIT 8-1

Classification Table Listing

Description	Fire and Allied Lines	Multiple Line				General Liability		Crime	Crime and Contents, Fire		For Company Use
	Class Code	CPP PMA	BP Class Code	BP Rate No.	BP Rate Group	Class Code	Premium Base	Class Code	Rate Group	Class Limit	
Carpentry—construction of residential property not exceeding three stories in height	(1)	(1)		NA	NA	91340 (2)	p				
Carpentry	(1)(3)	(1) (3)		NA	NA	91342 NOC	p				
Carpentry—interior	(1)	(1)		NA	NA	91341 (4)	p				
Carpentry—shop only	3959	IP		NA	NA	91343 (5)	p	1751	1	5,000	
Carpet or Rug Mfg.	(6)	(6)		NA	NA	51777	s	2201	2	15,000	
Carpet, Rug, Furniture or Upholstery Cleaning—on customers' premises	(7)	C,S		NA	NA	91405	p+		NA		
Carpet, Rug or Upholstery Cleaning—shop only	(8)	(8)		NA	NA	11007	s+	7217	2	5,000	
Catalog or Premium Coupon Redemption Stores	0567	M	73905	6	2	11020	s				
Caterers	0542	S		NA	NA	11039 (9)	s	5810	3	5,000	
Caulking Compounds, Putty or Similar Products Mfg.	5000	IP		NA	NA	51790	s	2891	1	5,000	

Notes:

(1) Contractors equipment storage, use code 0567 and CPP PMA C.

Equipment in the open, use code 1190 and CPP PMA C.

Office, use code 0702 and CPP PMA C or O.

Vehicle Storage or repair, refer to "Automobile" classifications.

(2) This classification includes construction of private garages in connection with such residential property.

(3) Carpentry shop, use code 3959 and CPP PMA IP.

(4) This classification includes the installation of doors, floors, windows, cabinets and hardwood or parquet flooring.

This classification is not applicable to contractors engaged in any other carpentry operations at the same job or location.

(5) The following shall be separately classified and rated:
- lumberyards
- building material dealers
- Home Improvement stores.

(6) Use code 2800 and CPP PMA IP for carpet or rug manufacturing. Carpet sales, use code 0520 and CPP PMA M.

(7) For storage of cleaning equipment and supplies, use code 0567.

(8) Refer to "Laundries and Dry Cleaning" classifications.

(9) This classification applies to risks serving food away from the insured's premises only. Concessionaires selling beverages or food at exhibitions, parks, shows, sports contests or theaters and store operations shall be separately classified and rated

CS-37

3rd Edition 2-91

Explanatory Rules

The **explanatory rules** orient users to the Classification Table, including definitions, symbols, and abbreviations appearing in the table. The rules describe the general content of the Classification Table, outline the column headings, and explain the use of certain general symbols. For general liability insurance, the most important rules are those explaining the symbols used in the corresponding columns and the definitions and abbreviations used in the classification descriptions.

The exposure base column in the Classification Table uses certain symbols to indicate the applicable basis of premium. These symbols are as follows:

a   Area

c   Total cost

m   Admissions

p   Payroll

o   Total operating expenses

s   Gross sales

u   Units

The classification listing explains all other premium bases (the letter *t* refers the reader to the classification notes). The definitions of those premium bases appear in the coverage rules of "Division Six—General Liability" in the *CLM*. All exposures are on a per thousand basis unless otherwise indicated.

A dagger or plus sign symbol († or +) in the premium base column in the Classification Table indicates that products and/or completed operations coverage is included within the rate for premises/operations coverage at no additional charge. In those cases, the policy declarations should show that the products-completed operations are subject to the policy's general aggregate limit.

The explanatory rules also define certain standardized words or abbreviations that have the same meaning whenever they appear in a classification description. Several of these terms provide classification guidance—for example, the following:

- If the classification description contains the word "including," premium auditors should not assign the operations so designated to a separate classification even though another classification describes such operations or the insured conducts such operations at a separate location.
- "NOC" means not otherwise classified. An NOC classification applies only if no other classification more specifically describes the insured's business.
- "NPD" means no payroll division. Premium auditors cannot divide the payroll with another classification. Either that particular classification applies solely or it does not apply at all. However, premium auditors

Explanatory rules
The definitions, symbols, and abbreviations appearing in the Classification Table of the *Commercial Lines Manual* that orient the user to the content.

can use an NPD classification for division of payroll under the following circumstances: (1) the activity constitutes a separate and distinct enterprise having no connection with the operations covered by any classification specified in the restrictions and (2) if the other classification has no connection with the operations covered by any other classification in the policy. For classifications applicable to construction or erection operations, those two provisions apply only to the operations that each separate job or location comprises.

- A distributor is a merchant or broker that sells products mainly for resale or business use and that chiefly sells to dealers or stores; other merchants; and industrial, institutional, and commercial users.

- Dealers or stores include all merchants or mercantile establishments that sell products directly to the ultimate consumer and that are not distributors.

Classifications Listing

The first column at the left side of each page in the classifications listings (see Exhibit 8-1) lists the classifications that concisely describe the insured's operations or line of business. The description uses terms common to retailing, wholesaling, manufacturing, servicing, contracting, or professional business. Classification descriptions avoid unusual or highly technical terminology that may obscure the application of the classification.

In many instances, the wording parallels the wording that the NCCI *Basic Manual* uses. Cross-referencing the two manuals' classification sections sometimes facilitates classification assignment.

The first column under the heading "General Liability" shows the code number for each classification. The same classification and code number apply to both premises/operations and products-completed operations coverages. The arrangement of those code numbers reflects the five major business groups defined in the *CLM*. The code number's first digit always indicates the business group into which the classification falls, as follows:

Business Group	Code Number
Mercantile	10000-19999
Miscellaneous	40000-49999
Manufacturing or Processing	50000-59999
Buildings or Premises—office or residential occupancy or leased to others	60000-69999
Contracting or Servicing	90000-99999

The second column under the heading "General Liability" contains symbols identifying the premium applicable for each classification. A *p* in this column, for example, indicates that the premium base used with this classification is payroll. The footnote to classifications, indicated by a *t*, describes the classifications' premium bases.

General Classification Procedures

"Division Six—General Liability" of the *CLM* states the rules for assigning classifications to insureds with general liability policies. Rules 25 and 26 present general classification assignment concepts and define the general classification inclusions and exclusions. Rules 27, 28, 29, 31, and 32 describe the classification procedures for the five major business groups.

General liability classification procedures closely resemble the workers' compensation classification procedures. In both cases, the object is to group like operations into the same rating classification. Insurers should classify the business, not individual employments, occupations, or operations within a business. The premium auditor must therefore distinguish between single and multiple business operations. The *CLM* "Division Six—General Liability" rules stipulate how insurers should do that in a uniform and consistent manner.

The first rule a premium auditor should follow in general liability classification procedures is to assign the single classification that best describes the insured's operation. This rule applies whenever the insured's operation or operations normally fall within one business type. For example, a rubber tire manufacturer may conduct the following operations: tire casing manufacturing, tire manufacturing packaging, storage warehouse, and shipping. In addition, the insured may maintain a maintenance department, a security force, grounds-keepers, and a cafeteria. Several of the tire manufacturer's operations have nothing to do with tire manufacturing. Nevertheless, premium auditors should classify the total operation as "Tire Mfg. – auto, bus or truck" (Code 59750).

If the insured conducts two or more separate and distinct business operations or types of businesses, the premium auditor may divide the total exposure between appropriate classifications. The *CLM* provides some guidelines within each of the rules relating to each major business group.

General liability classifications encompass the operations common to the specific business described. Certain incidental operations are expected in a business; other operations present a profoundly different exposure that insurers must separately rate. Rule 26 defines the normal inclusions and exclusions for classifications in general. (Classification wording and footnotes take precedence over any general or coverage rules.)

In addition to the following general classification inclusions and exclusions, the *CLM* also lists several "special" inclusions and exclusions that are specific to a particular type of loss exposure. The Business Group Specific Procedures section following the general sections describes those special inclusions and exclusions.

Included Operations and Hazards

The scope of all classifications includes certain incidental operations. Insurers must not separately classify those operations unless the insured conducts them as separate and distinct enterprises. The following box lists operations or hazards included within the scope of all classifications.

Operations Included Within the Scope of All Classifications

- Advertising signs
- Athletic games
- Booths, exhibits, and other displays of the insured's merchandise
- Elevators and escalators
- Electronic games located on the insured's premises
- Greenhouses
- Maintenance, repair, or alteration of insured's buildings or equipment
- Medical facilities operated by the insured for employees
- Parking areas operated in connection with the insured's business
- Pickup and delivery
- Printing or lithographing on insured's own products
- Restaurants and commissaries
- Sale of used or second-hand goods
- Social gatherings
- Swimming pools or other athletic facilities not commercially operated
- Vending machines
- Workshops and workyards

Excluded Operations and Hazards

Unless the classification footnotes state otherwise, the following operations do not come within the scope of other classifications, and the premium auditor must separately classify them. The following box lists the operations or hazards excluded from the scope of all classifications.

Operations Excluded From the Scope of All Classifications

- Amusement centers
- Amusement devices (other than electronic games located on the insured's premises) or amusement parks
- Draft or saddle animals
- Machinery or equipment rented to others
- New construction or demolition operations
- Sawmill operations
- Stevedoring, including tallyers or checking clerks
- Swimming pools or other athletic facilities if commercially operated
- Vehicles or carts from which goods are sold

Business-Group-Specific Classification Procedures

Each of the preceding inclusions or exclusions applies to all classifications, regardless of the business group involved. Rules 27, 28, 29, 31, and 32 provide the rules specific to the various major business groups, including some additional business-group-specific inclusions and exclusions (Rule 30 describes the transition program).

Manufacturing and Processing

As Exhibit 8-2 indicates, specific classification procedures differ depending on the business group involved. Rule 27 states the classification rules for manufacturing and processing operations. Insurers should use the rates of the territory in which the insured produces or assembles the products as classified or in which the processing as classified occurs. The three important principles involved in classifying such operations include separately classifying and applying the rules to each named insured; classifying by final product or process, not by component part or interim process; and separately classifying and rating retail operations of the manufacturer selling its own products.

Insurers should independently classify each named insured listed on the declarations page. Named insureds are generally separate legal entities, and as such they can sue other named insureds. According to the Commercial General Liability Coverage Form, coverage applies "as if each Named Insured were the only Named Insured." The premium auditor must therefore separately classify each named insured to compute an appropriate premium.

As previously discussed, the *CLM* in Rule 27.B.2. specifies that for premium computation purposes in determining gross sales, the premium auditor should include all sales of goods or products from one company to another, including those sales from one named insured to another.

Rule 27 also prohibits premium auditors from separately classifying and rating the manufacturing of component parts or interim processes conducted by the named insured. Therefore, the premium auditor should not include in gross sales the value of any transfers of component parts or interim processes within the same named insured. That rule applies if the named insured incorporates such parts or processes into a final product produced by the named insured, and such component parts are normally manufactured by or interim processes conducted by businesses in producing that type of product. In such cases, the premium auditor classifies the final product.

The proper classification is the one that best describes the intended use of the insured's products or operations. The intended use is important because the policy covers damages arising out of the use of the product after the insured relinquishes control. Paper filters sold to a pharmaceutical firm, for example, may lead to enormous losses resulting from the contamination of drugs because of the filters' failure. That exposure is considerably greater than one arising from selling paper filters for use in home coffee makers. Classification by intended use also applies separately to each named insured. Insurers do not separately classify divisions or departments of a single named insured even if they are all located in different states.

EXHIBIT 8-2

How to Classify a Risk

1.   Determine the insured's business occupation (from application).

2.   Check classification:
— Inclusions
— Exclusions
— Specific classification footnotes to determine whether additional classifications are necessary.

3. For Manufacturing risks:

— Classify by final product/process, not by component part or interim process. (For example, if the insured makes parts for a motorcycle in separate plants, incorporating these parts into the motorcycle, classify as motorcycle mfg., rather than as seats, engines, etc., mfg.)

— Separately classify each named insured. (Each insured is a separate entity and may be sued as such. If, however, the policy is amended to exclude inter-company suits, it is *not* necessary to separately classify each named insured and gross sales between named insureds should not be included.)

3. For Contracting risks:

— If one classification description covers the operation, use it.

— If there is more than one operation, determine whether these similar separate operations are customarily part of the overall operation; if not, classify separately. (For example, in dam construction, ditchdigging should not be classified separately if ditchdigging operations are commonly performed by dam construction contractors.)

— If no one classification fits, classify every separate operation within the contracting operation separately. (For example, in building construction, separately classify and rate each operation [carpentry, electrical, concrete construction, etc.])

3. For Mercantile risks:

— Classify by the type of goods sold.

— Determine whether insured is a dealer or distributor in accordance with the definition.

— For combined dealer/distributor operations, use classification of higher rate operation unless separate records for each operation are kept.

3. For Building/Premises risks:

— If owned and completely occupied by insured, classify according to occupancy.

— If owned and partially occupied by insured, classify portion occupied by insured according to occupancy, and remainder as lessor's risk.

— If owned or sublet but not occupied by insured, classify under appropriate lessor's risk classification.

— If occupied but not owned by insured, classify according to occupancy.

Copyright, ISO Properties, Inc., 1985.

Also, if the named insured is a manufacturer and it sells its products through its own retail operations, insurers should separately classify and rate the retail operations and the manufacturing operations. The retail and the manufacturing exposures are different, and the insurer should collect a premium for each. The premium auditor should classify and rate the retail operations according to the rules for mercantile risks (Rule 29). In such cases the wholesale value of the goods transferred to the retail operation should be the amount included within gross sales.

Multiple classifications may also apply to a manufacturer for a different reason, provided the premium auditor observes rules regarding classification by named insured and classification by final product. Suppose, for example, that Acme Motorcycle Company has a subsidiary, Acme Engine Company, and that both entities are named insureds. Acme Engine Company not only supplies motorcycle engines to Acme Motorcycle Company, but also sells them to other manufacturers. In that case, the following two classifications apply to Acme Engine Company:

- Engines sold to others: "Engine or Turbine Mfg.—not aircraft—NOC" (Code 52619)
- Engines sold to Acme Motorcycle Company: "Motorcycle, Moped or Motor Scooter Mfg." (Code 57202).

Code 52619 applies in addition to the motorcycle manufacturing class because the manual considers engines final products when sold to outside businesses.

In addition to the classification inclusions and exclusions discussed earlier, special business group inclusions apply to manufacturers and processors. Special classification inclusions, or operations that should not be separately classified and rated, for manufacturers are as follows:

- For manufacturing of containers such as bags, barrels, bottles, boxes, cans, cartons, or packing cases unless sold to others, including other named insureds, the manual considers manufacturing containers for the insured's products incidental to the product manufacturing.
- Installing, servicing, or repairing the named insured's products is a special inclusion that applies even when the installing or servicing does not normally prevail in this business. This inclusion is an important exception to the principle of separately classifying distinct operations. However, if a separate named insured listed on the policy installs and services products other than those manufactured by the named insured, separate classifications would apply.

The special business group exclusion for manufacturers is office operations located away from the premises where the insured conducts manufacturing, processing, or assembling operations. Premium auditors should separately classify any location or premises operated by a manufacturer used solely for an office.

Contracting or Servicing

Rule 28 stipulates the procedures for classifying contracting or servicing loss exposures. In general, if the insured has a single operation, or many separate operations that normally prevail in the business described by a single classification, the single manual classification that best describes the single enterprise applies. If those separate operations do not normally prevail in a business described by a single classification, the premium auditor should separately classify and rate each operation.

By their nature, construction operations preclude physical separation and often involve some labor interchange. Even so, Rule 28 requires (when the manual allows more than one classification) dividing the insured's payroll among the separate classifications that apply at each job or location, provided that the insured's payroll records reflect this division. The premium auditor should use the rates that are applicable in the territory in which the job is located.

However, insurers cannot separately classify any particular part of an operation that could otherwise qualify for a classification if it is an integral part of the total operation. For example, "Concrete Construction" (Code 91560) includes making, setting up, and taking down concrete forms. Therefore, a premium auditor would classify a carpenter involved with constructing forms under Code 91560 rather than a carpentry code.

Premium auditors should assign any operation for which the insured does not maintain separate payroll records to the highest rated classification applicable to the job or location. The insured's records must show a breakdown in payroll between the applicable classifications; the payroll division must be in dollar terms and not hours. Premium auditors should not use estimates or percentage splits.

If the insured has drafting employees who are exposed to any operative hazards of the business, the premium auditor should assign the payroll of those drafting employees to the highest rated classification of work to which the employees are exposed.

At a job site, a miscellaneous employee performs various functions in contracting or servicing related to the entire job. Such miscellaneous employees include job superintendents, timekeepers or guards, workers performing general cleanup or snow removal, and workers performing similar incidental tasks. Premium auditors should assign miscellaneous employees to the classification carrying the largest amount of payroll (not the one with the highest rate) at a job or location during the policy period.

Labor interchange
Employees involved in several classifications but not the overall job.

Confusion sometimes arises between miscellaneous employees and labor interchange. **Labor interchange** refers to employees involved in several classifications but not the overall job. Premium auditors assign the payroll of workers involved in labor interchange to the highest rated classification if the insured does not provide an acceptable breakdown of payroll.

If an employee's work involves more than one classification with different exposure bases, the premium auditor should assign the employee's entire payroll to the classification in which payroll is the exposure base. For example, an employee may normally work at a plumbing supply store (mercantile business group). Under normal circumstances, the premium base used to measure the store's exposure would be gross sales. However, if the employee's work also includes installation or repair activities not related to the goods sold from the store, it can be established that part of this work is of a contracting nature, which carries a different exposure base—payroll. Although the premium auditor could separately classify the store or shop operation, the installation classification includes the employee's entire payroll.

In addition to using the general classification exclusions, premium auditors must separately classify the following operations:

- Blasting operations performed by the insured as "Blasting Operations" (Code 91210)
- Restaurant or commissary operations in connection with construction, erection, lumbering, or mining operations

Contracting and servicing risks have no special business group inclusions.

Contractors often hire subcontractors to complete a portion of the job. When an insured hires a subcontractor to perform a construction operation, premium auditors must separately classify that operation. The presence of subcontractors on a construction site creates additional hazards. For this reason, premium auditors must separately classify the subcontractors and develop the appropriate premium. The "Contractor-subcontracted work" classifications do not extend coverage to the subcontractor. They are only a measure of the insured's increased exposure. The subcontractors must still purchase their own Commercial General Liability (CGL) policy to cover losses for which they are held responsible.

Properly classifying subcontractors involved in construction operations depends on two major factors: type of work performed and adequate insurance.

If a subcontractor is adequately insured, the type of construction work the general contractor performs on that project determines the classification assignment. The possible classifications appear in the Classification Table under the heading "Contractors-subcontracted work." The basis of premium for those classifications is the total cost of the work.

Each of those classifications carries the following important note: "This classification applies to that portion of the operations performed by adequately insured subcontractors of the insured. Operations performed by subcontractors without adequate insurance shall be classified and rated under the specific classification description for each operation."[1]

Insurers and their employees have interpreted the term "adequately insured subcontractor" in several ways, including the following:

- The subcontractor carries limits of insurance equal to or greater than the limits of insurance of the contractor (probably the most widely used definition).
- The subcontractor carries limits of insurance at least equal to the amount that is specified by each insurer.
- The subcontractor carries the limits as specified by the contractor.
- Some combination of these interpretations exists, such as that specified by the contractor, but in no case less than a certain amount.

included w/o ins

When the subcontractor does not have insurance or the insurance is inadequate, the premium auditor must assign the subcontractor to the specific classification that describes the operation performed. In other words, premium auditors should classify subcontractors with inadequate insurance as though they were employees.

The *CLM* does not explicitly define what amount premium auditors should include for inadequately insured subcontractors assigned to the payroll-based classifications. Instead of a specific insurer interpretation, premium auditors could use the subcontractor rule in the NCCI *Basic Manual*.

Mercantile

gross sales

Rule 29 describes specific procedures for classifying stores or other mercantile operations. Insurers rate mercantile classifications on a gross sales basis and use the rates applicable in the territory for each location of the insured's operations.

Stores vary considerably in the particular goods they carry, often making it difficult to apply the rule that stores should be assigned to the store classification that best describes the risk.

When the insured is a combined dealer and distributor, the premium auditor should assign the insured to the higher rated classification unless the insured maintains separate records. Assigning both a dealer and a distributor code requires that the insured's records clearly show a separation in the sales between the two operations. Premium auditors should not accept an estimate or percentage allocation.

Unless specified in a classification footnote, insurers need not separately classify installing, servicing, and repairing merchandise sold by the insured. For example, a carpet store usually installs the carpets it sells. A premium auditor should not add a separate classification for carpet installation even though that classification exists. Installing the carpet obviously creates some exposure for the insured for which the insurer desires some premium. The premium is generated in a somewhat roundabout way. The premium base for mercantile risks is gross sales. If a merchant does install, service, or repair its carpets, a cost is involved. Most merchants charge more for their carpet rather than absorb this additional cost. By charging more, gross sales increase, and the premium therefore increases. Mercantile establishments have no special business group exclusion.

Building or Premises

Rule 31 applies to offices, residences, or space leased to others. Classification in such situations depends on the ownership or occupancy of the building or premises because different ownerships and uses create differing degrees of potential loss.

Insurers rate apartments, residential condominiums, and similar buildings on a units basis. If the entire building is used for residential purposes, a premium auditor need only find the single appropriate classification and count the number of units. That applies regardless of whether the premises or building is owned, occupied, or operated by the insured or someone else.

Insurers must separately classify and rate the portion of the premises rented to others that is not on a units basis under one of the "lessor's risk only" classifications. If the building's owner operates a business enterprise that is not residential and occupies a portion of the building not rated on a units basis, premium auditors must separately classify and rate that portion of the premises based on the operation being performed.

Insurers rate other buildings or premises on an area basis. Classification then depends on whether the insured owns the building and the degree to which the insured occupies the building.

If the insured owns and entirely occupies the building or premises, the nature of the occupancy determines the classification. For example, insurers would classify a building owned by a group of physicians and containing their offices only as "Medical Offices" (Code 66561).

The premium auditor bases classification for any portion of the premises occupied by the insured on that occupancy, as described above. If the insured occupies 90 percent or more of the premises, that classification applies to the entire premises. Otherwise the premium auditor should classify the remainder of the premises according to the appropriate "lessor's risk only" classifications. If the physicians in the previous example rent more than 10 percent of their building to an accountant and if the physicians are not responsible for building maintenance, an additional classification, "Building or Premises—bank or office—mercantile or manufacturing (lessor's risk only)—Other than Not-For-Profit" (Code 61212) applies. If the physicians are responsible for maintenance, Code 61217 applies.

If the insured does not occupy the building, a "lessor's risk only" classification applies to the entire building or premises. Again, separate classifications apply

[handwritten margin note: Lessor's risk unless
- fully occupied + unowned
- " " + owned
- partially occupied by owner rest is LR]

[handwritten margin note: LR diff codes depending on maintenance respons.]

LR
- diff. codes for maint. respons.
- diff. codes for profit or non prof.

depending on whether the insured is responsible for building maintenance and whether the business to which the building is rented is for profit or not-for-profit. If the physicians moved out and rented their entire building to lawyers and accountants, the proper classification of their entire building would again be Code 61212 or 61217 for the physicians' general liability insurance.

If the insured occupies but does not own the building or premises, the insurer bases the classification on the occupancy. If the group of physicians moved to rented space in an office building, the appropriate classification for their offices would be "Medical Offices" (Code 66561).

Miscellaneous

Rule 32 assists in properly classifying an insured that does not clearly fall into one of the previous specific business groups.

As with the other business groups, the premium auditor should use the classification and the premium base that best describes the insured's operations. The classification rules to be used with miscellaneous classifications depend on the premium base for the classification selected.

Premium Base	Classification Rule
Gross sales	Rule 29—Mercantile risks
Payroll	Rule 28—Contracting or servicing risks
Area	Rule 31—Building or premises
Other (such as professional associations)	See the footnotes for the class for premium base and rating instructions

PREMIUM DETERMINATION

As for other kinds of insurance, the premium for a general liability policy equals the applicable rate times the measured exposure. The premium computation, however, also requires adjusting for premium modifications and applying minimum premiums. The *CLM* Premium Determination Rule (Rule 35) gives step-by-step instructions for premium computation. Exhibit 8-3 summarizes the Premium Determination Rule. The first two steps in this process—determining the classification and determining the premium base—have already been covered.

Rates

Premium auditors can find in the manual rates that insurers have filed and insurance regulators have approved for use in a particular state. Those are the basic limits rates, which the premium auditor may need to adjust for coverage changes on a particular policy.

EXHIBIT 8-3

Rule 35: Premium Determination

A. Determine the applicable classification

Which Rule #

— Determine the insured's business operation and find an appropriate classification. Only one classification applies for both premises/operations and products/completed operations.

— Use the "Classification Table" to determine the code number.

— Check the classification footnotes to determine whether any operations need to be separately classified and rated. Multiple classifications may be necessary when footnotes indicate that certain operations need to be separately classified.

B. Determine the premium base applicable to the classification(s). Use the premium base column in the "Classification Table." The same premium base applies to both premises/operations and products/completed operations.

C. Select the basic limits rate(s) for the classification(s) from the appropriate "Company State Rate" section for both premises/operations and products/completed operations.

— Determine the basic limits rate applicable to the classification(s) (either "occurrence" or "claims-made") for the appropriate territory. In other words, determine the policy version desired and then find the code.

— For manufacturing or processing risks, use the territory where the products as classified are produced or assembled, or where the processing as classified takes place.

— For contracting or servicing risks, use the territory where the job is located.

— If "claims-made" coverage is chosen, adjust the occurrence rate by the appropriate claims-made multiplier.

D. Adjust the basic limits rate(s) to reflect any coverages (other than deductibles).

— Adjust the rate(s) for any coverages deleted or restricted except those required by classification footnotes.

— Adjust the rate(s) for any coverages being bought back—that is, those deleted by classification footnotes. Underwriters must consider the hazards of the particular risk in determining whether to provide the excluded coverage and, if so, the appropriate price. Example: medical payments for pupils in schools.

Continued on next page

Rule 35:
Premium Determination
10 steps

E. Adjust the resulting basic limits rate(s) by the appropriate increased limits factors and any other applicable rate modification(s). Then adjust for coverage written on a deductible basis according to Rule 15.

— Determine which increased Limits Table applies. Use the indicator in the State Rate pages.

— Determine the appropriate increased limits factors (separately for each subline) for the limits selected. The increased limits factors are found in the "Increased Limits" section of the manual or in the "State Exceptions" section.

— If a deductible is purchased, determine the deductible discount. Subtract it from the appropriate increased limits factors. Note that this is a shortcut procedure. Since the deductible applies only to the basic limits rates, subtracting the discount from the increased limits factors gives the same result as performing the entire standard calculation.

— Apply any applicable experience and schedule rating modification (debit or credit).

— Multiply the basic limits rate(s) by the increased limits factors.

F. Multiply the number of units of exposure developed under the premium base for each classification by the corresponding adjusted rate(s) developed in Item E.

— For manufacturing risks, include gross sales from one named insured to another.

Because manufacturers' retail operations are separately rated, include as gross sales of the manufacturer the wholesale value of goods transferred to his or her own retail operation.

If the policy is amended to exclude inter-company products suits (that is, one named insured suing another), the value of goods transferred from one named insured to another should not be included in determining the exposure for products/completed operations.

G. Determine the minimum premium.

— For contracting or servicing risks, use the entire payroll developed when rating a single operation. If more than one classification applies, however, divide the payroll for each distinct type of operation.

— For subject classifications, apply the Transition Program, if applicable.

— Determine the minimum premium(s) based on the increased limits assignment.

— Refer to the "Countrywide Rates" section for the minimum premium table.

— Determine whether a special storekeepers minimum premium applies.

H. Determine any other additional premiums.

— If you identified more than one classification in Step A of this rule, repeat Steps B through G as many times as necessary to determine the premium for each classification.

I. Add the premium determined in Step F or G, whichever is greater, to the premium(s) determined in Step H to obtain the total policy premium.

J. Charge the premium developed in Step I or the policy writing minimum premium, whichever is greater.

— The policy writing minimum premium is $100.00. This minimum is the least you can charge for a policy, which may include general liability and other coverage parts.

Basic Limits Rates

Rates appear on the state rate pages opposite the classifications' code numbers. Next to the classification code numbers are the basic limits rates for general liability coverage. Separate rate pages exist for claims-made and for occurrence coverage. The CLM shows rates for both premises/operations and products-completed operations. Sometimes the CLM breaks down the premises/operations rates by territory. Exhibit 8-4 shows an example of a state rate page.

The rates on an insurer's state rate pages apply to the premium base indicated for the classification in the Classification Table. The insurer must use the premium base listed next to any particular classification in the Classification Table.

If the symbol (a) appears on the rate pages or loss cost pages instead of a specific rate, then that classification is (a) rated. The (a) rated symbol means that underwriters must specially rate such classifications. An **(a) rated classification** usually describes operations with unique characteristics or for which inadequate statistical experience exists. The underwriter attempts to base rates for such unusual exposures on an analogous classification's experience. The underwriter, at his or her discretion but within insurer guidelines, may use a rate for a similar operation or assign another rate.

If claims-made coverage applies, the next step is to adjust the occurrence rate by the factor for the appropriate year in the claims-made multiplier table for the specific class and coverage.

(a) rated classification
The rate classifications provided by the ISO *Commercial Lines Manual* that describe operations with unique characteristics or for which inadequate statistical experience exists.

EXHIBIT 8-4

CLM General Liability State Loss Cost Page

FLORIDA (09)

COMMERCIAL LINES MANUAL
DIVISION SIX—GENERAL LIABILITY
LOSS COST PAGE

OCCURRENCE—$100,000/200,000 BASIC LIMIT
   Prem./Ops.   (Subline Code 334)
   Products   (Subline Code 336)

Premises/Operations

Code No.	Limit I.D.	Territory 001	Territory 002	Territory 004	Territory 005	Territory 006	Territory	Territory Prod/ Comp Ops
12797	2B	.178	.192	.122	.118	.162		.206
12805	1B	1.18	1.28	.80	.80	1.06		.31
12841	2–	2.56	2.74	1.53	1.49	1.90		–
12927	2–	1.58	1.69	1.08	1.05	1.40		–
13049	2B	.18	.179	.119	.119	.162		.096
13111	1B	3.44	4.14	1.97	2.03	2.12		.36
13112	2B	.185	.189	.126	.123	.167		.071
13201	2B	2.26	2.23	1.49	1.78	1.47		.35
13204	2B	1.09	1.09	.93	.93	.93		.43
13205	2B	.33	.33	.28	.28	.28		.33
13314	1B	.241	.231	.153	.149	.19		.43
13351	1B	1.18	1.28	.68	.66	.84		.31
13352	1B	1.18	1.28	.68	.66	.84		.31
13410	3C	2.03	2.03	1.39	1.54	1.38		2.43
13411	3C	(a)	(a)	(a)	(a)	(a)		(a)
13412	3C	2.34	2.01	1.40	1.60	1.40		1.13
13453	2B	1.76	1.76	1.11	1.11	1.11		(a)
13454	2B	1.88	1.68	1.08	1.29	1.07		(a)
13455	2B	2.29	2.29	1.44	1.44	1.44		(a)
13506	2C	2.56	2.74	1.74	1.69	2.26		.43
13507	2C	2.56	2.74	1.74	1.69	2.26		.43
13590	2A	1.99	1.99	1.52	1.52	1.52		1.01
13621	3B	.82	.82	.63	.63	.63		1.01
13670	2B	.185	.189	.126	.123	.167		.071

13673	1B	3.44	3.89	1.85	2.01	1.99		.38
13715	3B	.226	.227	.158	.145	.185		.87
13716	1B	2.47	2.54	1.28	1.26	1.68		.87
13759	1C	2.47	2.26	1.58	1.53	2.09		1.08
13930	2C	.178	.192	.122	.118	.162		1.88
14068	2B	.124	.13	.082	.081	.109		.43
14101	2C	2.56	2.74	1.42	1.38	1.76		1.24
14279	2B	1.14	1.14	.77	.77	.77		.43
14401	1A	5.87	6.54	3.12	3.38	3.34		.62
14405	3–	2.06	2.06	1.50	1.50	1.50		–
14527	2B	.178	.192	.122	.118	.162		1.59

CLAIMS-MADE MULTIPLIERS—To convert from occurrence to claims-made, multiply the occurrence rates by the following:

Year in Claims-Made	Premises/Operations Codes 50000-59999 90000-99999	Premises/Operations All Other	Prod/Comp Ops All Codes
1	.80	.85	.75
2	.88	.91	.80
3	.93	.95	.86
4	.95	.96	.87
5 or more	.97	.96	.89

CG-LC-004
Copyright, Insurance Services Office, Inc., 1996.

Coverage Change Adjustments

Sometimes insureds want to delete a coverage or add a different coverage because of their particular exposures. Such coverage changes often mean a change in the premium to be charged. Premium auditors should carefully study the policy to determine when such coverage modifications are made. An informed premium auditor will perform premium audits with a greater degree of accuracy and fairness.

Other Premium Modifications

Other factors may also affect the premium computation for general liability insurance. The *CLM* "Division Six—General Liability" rules provide for modifications for increased limits, deductibles, and experience or schedule rating modifications.

Increased Limits

Insurers may increase or otherwise alter liability limits by endorsement. The endorsement may specify a particular job or location as being subject to those altered limits. Consequently, the premium auditor should audit the exposure as a separate entity. If the insurer or insured changes the overall limits of liability for the policy during the policy period, the premium auditor should separate the periods affected and show them as two separate audit periods. That procedure facilitates properly applying the higher rates that reflect the higher limits of liability. Premium auditors calculate those rates using the increased limits factor tables provided in the *CLM*.

Two sets of increased limits factor tables exist. For premises/operations coverage, Tables 1, 2, and 3 display the increased limits factor corresponding to various levels of aggregate and per occurrence limits. Table 1 applies to the least hazardous operations, and Table 3, shown in Exhibit 8-5, applies to the most hazardous. Similarly, for products-completed operations, Tables A, B, and C show the increased limits factors. Table A applies to the least hazardous operations and Table C, to the most hazardous. The state rate pages indicate which table applies for each classification. The *CLM* specifically identifies some increased limits factors as guide (a) rates.

Deductibles

When a deductible applies, the insured agrees to contribute up to a certain sum, either per claim or per accident, toward settling any claim. Depending on the deductible's size, a corresponding reduction of rates follows. Because the deductible amount influences the loss experience, insurers use a separate statistical code to indicate the deductible amount.

Insurers develop tables to show the amount of the premium reduction for various deductible amounts. Each subline normally has its own deductible table.

Experience or Schedule Rating Modifications

Experience rating modification
A method of tailoring manual rates to a policyholder's experience based on the policyholder's premium and loss record.

Insureds with good loss experience may warrant a lower rate, and insureds with unfavorable loss experience, a higher rate. An **experience rating modification** is a method of tailoring manual rates to a policyholder's experience based on the policyholder's premium and loss record. For general liability insurance, an experience rating modification applies directly to the manual rate rather than to the premium. An insurer would calculate a 15 percent credit, for example, by multiplying the manual rate times 0.85. The insurer would then use the result as the applicable rate. Such an experience rating modification applies after the insurer has adjusted the base rate for increased limits and deductibles.

A **schedule rating modification** is a rating plan that awards debits and credits based on specific categories—such as the care and condition of the premises or the training and selection of employees—to modify the final premium to reflect factors that the class rate does not include. Schedule rating modifications can apply in addition to or instead of experience rating modifications. Schedule rating modifications recognize factors that should directly affect losses but that the experience modification does not reflect. Underwriters give the schedule credits or debits based on their experience and judgment.

Schedule rating modification A rating plan that awards debits and credits based on specific categories—such as the care and condition of the premises or the training and selection of employees—to modify the final premium to reflect factors that the class rate does not include.

EXHIBIT 8-5

Increased Limits Table

FLORIDA (09)   COMMERCIAL LINES MANUAL
                                       DIVISION SIX
                                    GENERAL LIABILITY
                                    EXCEPTION PAGES

RULE 56.
INCREASED LIMITS TABLES (Cont'd)

3. Premises/Operations (Subline Code 334) Table 3—$100/200 Basic Limit

Aggregate $	Per Occurrence 25	50	100	200	300	500	1,000
$ 50	0.69 (46)	0.79 (51)					
100	0.70 (48)	0.82 (49)	0.96 (55)				
200	0.71 (48)	0.83 (51)	1.00 (55)	1.17 (60)			
300	0.72 (48)	0.84 (51)	1.01 (52)	1.18 (60)	1.31 (66)		
500		0.86 (51)	1.03 (53)	1.20 (57)	1.33 (66)	1.50 (67)	
600		0.87 (51)	1.04 (55)	1.21 (58)	1.34 (64)	1.51 (70)	
1,000			1.05 (54)	1.22 (59)	1.35 (66)	1.52 (68)	1.78 (71)
1,500				1.23 (60)	1.36 (66)	1.53 (69)	1.79 (73)
2,000				1.24 (60)	1.37 (66)	1.54 (70)	1.80 (73)
2,500					1.38 (66)	1.55 (70)	1.81 (73)
3,000					1.39 (66)	1.56 (70)	1.82 (72)

Continued on next page

The following factors MUST be referred to company before using.

Aggregate	Per Occurrence							
	$ 500	1,000	1,500	2,000	3,000	4,000	5,000	10,000
$ 1,500			1.97 (74)					
2,000			1.98 (74)	2.12 (75)				
2,500			1.99 (74)	2.13 (75)				
3,000			2.00 (74)	2.14 (75)	2.37 (77)			
4,000	1.57 (70)	1.83 (73)	2.01 (74)	2.15 (75)	2.38 (77)	2.59 (79)		
5,000	1.58 (70)	1.84 (73)	2.02 (74)	2.16 (75)	2.39 (77)	2.60 (79)	2.78 (79)	
10,000		1.85 (73)	2.03 (74)	2.17 (75)	2.40 (77)	2.61 (79)	2.80 (79)	3.54 (85)
20,000								3.55 (85)

Table 56 B.3. Premises/Operations (Subline Code 334) Table 3—$100/200 Basic Limit

CG-E-1 2

Copyright, Insurance Services Office, Inc., 1996.

1ST EDITION 09-96
CLM/CLEMS

Minimum Premiums

Subline
A subcategory of classifications within a *CLM* class code that applies to various types of general liability exposures.

The minimum premium is the lowest annual amount for which an insurer can write insurance for each full year of coverage for a particular **subline** of insurance. A subline is a subcategory of classifications within a *CLM* class code that applies to various types of general liability exposures. Issuing and servicing expenses for a policy require collecting the minimum amount even if the insured operation is small or if the insured or insurer cancels the policy soon after inception.

To determine the minimum premium, underwriters must first determine the applicable increased limits tables from the state rate pages for both the premises/operations and products-completed operations sublines for each classification shown on the policy. Next, the underwriter must find the minimum premium for the classification. An insurer's rate pages show the minimum premium, which the insurer bases on the increased limits table that is applicable for each subline. A different minimum premium exists for each of the three increased limits factor tables for premises/operations and for each of the three increased limits factor tables for products-completed operations. The underwriter must then multiply the minimum premium by the increased limits factor.

Minimum premiums apply separately to each subline for which the insurer charges a premium. Both a premises/operations minimum and a products-completed operations minimum exist when the insurer provides coverage for both sublines. When more than one classification for an insurance subline exists, the insurer chooses the highest minimum premium for each subline.

If an insurer writes an exposure on an "if any" basis, the insurer does not apply a minimum premium for that classification unless an exposure develops during the policy period and the premium auditor discovers the exposure at an audit. All minimum premiums, except the policy writing minimum, are subject to adjustment for additional interests and increased limits.

Policy Writing Minimum Premiums

The policy writing minimum premium is the lowest amount per year for which an insurer may write a policy. It applies when the total minimum premium for a subline is less than the policy writing minimum. Although the amount varies, a typical policy writing minimum premium is $100.

Special Combined Minimum Premiums

Minimum premium Rule 14 also lists about thirty classifications for which a special combined basic limits minimum premium applies for both the premises/operations and products-completed operations sublines. Those classifications are those that previously qualified for a storekeepers program. The intent of applying one minimum to both sublines was to avoid sudden premium increases for those loss exposures because insurers write many of them for the minimum premium.

Composite Rating

Composite rating is an optional insurance pricing approach that uses a premium base other than the one specified in the rating manual to price an entire account. Composite rating simplifies pricing a package of coverages. An insurer can use any form or format of measurable base as long as the insurer indicates the base on the policy.

Premium audit procedures are relatively simple inasmuch as the insurer usually combines all coverages under one common premium base. The procedure can simplify a potentially complex audit. However, defining the premium base can sometimes be difficult.

Composite rating
An optional insurance pricing approach that uses a premium base other than the one specified in the rating manual to price an entire account.

The composite rating endorsement should precisely identify the premium base. Because no manual rules exist to follow, the underwriter must explain the composite rating base in that endorsement. The underwriter should strive to select a base that reflects the insured exposures and that is convenient to measure.

Assume, for example, that the underwriter wishes to insure the RWR Barrel Company. The underwriter estimates the premium necessary to insure the exposure and defines the premium as a certain rate "per barrel." The RWR Barrel Company estimates sales of 10,000 barrels in the coming year. Because the underwriter requires $20,000 in premium to grant coverage, the underwriter would specify the rate as $2 per barrel. The insurer issues the policy with a composite rating endorsement to this effect. The premium auditor must determine the number of barrels sold during the policy period to calculate the earned premium. If the insured records the dollar sales amount and not a unit count of barrels sold, the price per barrel may vary considerably, and an accurate premium audit may be practically impossible.

Some states require that the estimated premiums be calculate using standard rates and premium bases. The insurer then divides the resulting premium by the estimated number of composite rating units, yielding the composite rate that will apply. With this method of making composite rates, the premium auditor may have to complete the audit showing both the standard premium base and the composite rated premium base. Although the insurer uses the latter data to make the premium adjustment, the former data verify the accuracy of the composite rating procedure.

Composite rating offers a useful approach to pricing a package of insurance coverages for a single account. Premium auditors should discuss any problem arising with a composite rated policy with the underwriter involved.

GOVERNMENTAL SUBDIVISION AUDITS

The premium audit for a municipality, county, township, or other governmental subdivision presents a particular challenge to the premium auditor. The multitude of possible loss exposures, the variety of premium bases used for those loss exposures, the profusion of records and sources needed for completion, and the many offices or locations that the premium auditor may have to visit to obtain the necessary data make this type of premium audit especially complicated.

A municipality is a unique insured for a premium auditor. A large municipality involves many varied exposures. A municipality's operations resemble a conglomeration of many and varied small businesses. In fact, either governmental authorities or private businesses may perform many of the operations. The possibility of a significant difference in the loss experience of public and private insureds, together with the complexity of governmental operations, led insurers to develop procedures for governmental subdivisions.

Classification and Rating Structure for Governmental Subdivisions

The *CLM* uses total operating expenditures as the exposure base for governmental subdivisions. The *CLM* defines total operating expenditures as "total expenditures (including grants, entitlements and shared revenue) without regard to source of revenue during the policy period, including accounts payable" but excluding certain items (which are described later in this chapter).[2] The exposure base provides a measure of all the diverse exposures presented in governmental subdivisions. In addition, it reduces the complexity of determining the overall premium charge.

The classification coding groups all governmental subdivisions as either municipalities—including boroughs, cities, towns, townships, and villages— or counties or parishes. Within each category, separate classification codes exist according to the population. Exhibit 8-6 shows those classifications. The premium auditor must obtain accurate population figures to assign the correct classification. The figures should include the resident student population of towns with colleges and boarding schools. Because state and federal funding and revenue sharing programs allocate funds according to population, most governmental entities have population information readily available. If not, the premium auditor can obtain it directly from the U.S. Census Bureau.

EXHIBIT 8-6

Governmental Subdivisions Population Codes

Municipalities—Boroughs, Cities, Towns, Townships, Villages, etc.

Population	Takes Code Number
under 2,500	44100
2,501 – 10,000	44101
10,001 – 25,000	44102
25,001 – 50,000	44103
50,001 – 100,000	44104
100,001 – 250,000	44105
over 250,000	44106

Counties or Parishes

Population	Takes Code Number
under 10,000	44108
10,001 – 25,000	44109
25,001 – 50,000	44110
50,001 – 100,000	44111
100,001 – 250,000	44112
over 250,000	44113

Other classifications are applicable for operations that could be provided to the private sector. The intent is to include in one classification all operations normal for governmental subdivisions unless specifically designated as separately rated or classified. For example, insurers should separately classify and rate zoos because they are not usual to most governmental subdivisions.

In most instances, for example, fire departments and sewage disposal plants are governmental subdivision operations. Even though classifications listed separately in the manual describe such operations, the CLM still includes classifications in the overall coverage of governmental operations unless specifically designated as requiring separate rating or classification. Therefore, some classifications appear in the CLM classification pages that would seem appropriate for municipal activities, but they are actually available only for use by and assignment to private sector operations.

Premium Audit Procedures

In auditing a governmental subdivision, the premium auditor first obtains knowledge of the insured governmental subdivision's operations and then begins deducting items or exposures.

Total Operating Expenditures

The premium auditor can obtain the total operating expenditures from a ledger of receipts, disbursements, and balances or a report the insured makes to a higher governmental subdivision or similar source. A government entity's expenditures are a matter of public record and must be available as needed.

Exclusions

Having obtained the total operating expenditures, the premium auditor then determines the various exclusions and subtracts those numbers from the total operating expenses. The CLM sets out the exclusions discussed in this section.

Capital Improvements

The first exclusion is "any purchase or improvement of any individual item of personal or real property which is bonded or financed, including interest thereon or that exceeds 5 percent of 'Total Operating Expenditures'; however, work performed by the named insured in connection with such purchase or improvement shall be included with 'Total Operating Expenditures.'"[3]

Bondable items and the interest thereon are self-explanatory, and the records should readily indicate the totals and explanations necessary to support the excluded amounts. The premium auditor can likewise easily document improvements and new construction. If the named insured's employees are active in the procedures performed, the premium auditor should not exclude the amount attributable to employee involvement.

The phrase "or exceeds 5 percent of 'Total Operating Expenditures'" requires further clarification. The operative expression in this rule is "individual item of personal or real property." Volume buying of supplies would not apply unless one of those items' cost alone exceeded 5 percent of total operating expenditures. The premium auditor should note any amounts exceeding 5 percent of revenues when reviewing the records for excludable items. A rule a premium auditor may use could be the item's probable life. For example, $270,000 worth of paving equipment would obviously be a major item because the insured would expect it to last for several years. Purchasing a major item of this sort could well exceed 5 percent of a municipality's total operating expenditures. The premium auditor should also note any other items in the capital accounts that relate to possible exclusions.

Premium auditors should exclude interdepartmental transfers of funds from the transferor's expenditures, because the auditor will include them in the recipient's expenditures. Premium auditors should also exclude expenditures from an intragovernmental service fund (formerly called a working capital fund) from the premium basis if that funding is budgeted and received from other funds. That step is necessary to prevent double counting certain expenditures.[4] The insured may record an amount used for investment purposes, such as purchasing a certificate of deposit, as an expenditure even though it is not actually an expenditure (and therefore should not be included), but merely a change in the type of assets held. Insureds usually place temporary surpluses with a bank or financial institution to generate interest income. Because the insured could move such amounts around between such institutions to take advantage of varying interest rates, those apparent expenditures could seem to be in total a large amount when in fact they are only a small amount recycled several times. Such investment transactions could appear in any fund account.

Independent Contractors

The second exclusion is the following:

> Expenditures for independent contractors operations—where the contractor carries adequate insurance. When the contractor does not carry adequate insurance, the cost of the contract will be included in "Total Operating Expenditures."[5]

Because most governmental subdivisions require contractors bidding for work to have insurance coverage matching their own, most independent contractors encountered in a premium audit have adequate insurance (at least according to one possible definition of adequate). The premium auditor should nevertheless request certificates of insurance for each contractor to verify insurance coverage with limits of liability equaling those on the governmental subdivision's policy. In the event of inadequate insurance coverage, the premium auditor should not exclude the amount paid to that contractor from the overall premium base.

Welfare Benefits

The *CLM* explains the **welfare benefits exclusion** as follows:

> The expenditure for public assistance and institutional care excluded from a governmental entity's "total operating expenditures" premium base.

> Welfare benefits (not administrative costs)—including expenditures for activities designed to provide public assistance and institutional care (for example, old age assistance, aid to dependent children, aid to blind, social security payments).[6]

Benefits to welfare recipients do not constitute an operating expenditure because they are not a mandatory expenditure to perform or continue a public service.

Insurers should include Comprehensive Employment and Training Act (CETA) funds unless a separate policy or hold-harmless agreement exists between the CETA program's prime sponsor and the governmental entity. If some of the CETA fund payments are for services relating to exclusions or separately rated exposures, the premium auditor needs to segregate them. The premium auditor may indicate that keeping such fund expenditures separate may aid the governmental subdivision. If that entity can specify the insurance cost for such activities, the premium auditor can charge back that cost against the distributed CETA funds.

Separately Rated Operations

Insurers must still separately rate and classify certain governmental operations not common or usual to most governmental subdivisions. Therefore, premium auditors should exclude expenditures, if any, for those operations from total operating expenditures. Premium auditors should separately classify and rate the following operations:

- Amusement parks
- Exhibition or convention buildings
- Dams, levees, or dikes
- Golf courses
- Housing projects
- Lakes or reservoirs
- Medical care facilities and services
- Penal institutions and jails
- Schools and colleges
- Ski facilities
- Stadiums, bleachers, or grandstands
- Streets, roads, highways, or bridges—existence and maintenance hazards
- Street, road, highway, or bridge construction
- Transportation systems, facilities, and services
- Utilities

- Wharves, piers, docks, marinas, and watercraft
- Zoos

In many instances, the separately rated operations require the premium auditor to examine records other than those indicating the operating expenditures. The premium auditor may have to turn to the receipts or revenues accounts to obtain necessary data for some of those operations.

The worksheet in Exhibit 8-7 provides a guide for doing a premium audit for a governmental subdivision. Terminology is important in providing premium audits for governmental subdivisions. Many of the terms have specific accounting meanings.

EXHIBIT 8-7

Rating Worksheet for Governmental Subdivisions

Name and State of Municipality or County _____

Population _____ Year of Census _____ Class Code _____

A. Determination of Rateable Exposures for Classes Not Separately Rated
The basic exposure basis for these classes is per $1000 of "Total Operating Expenditures." As defined, "Total Operating Expenditures" means the total operating costs (expenditures without regard to source of revenue) of the insured during the policy period, subject to the four types of deductions set forth below in 2(a) through 2(d). Rateable exposure is determined as follows:

    (1) Total Operating Costs $ _____

    (2) Deductions:

        (a) capital improvements (bondable items incl. interest thereon, new construction, major improvements and purchase of major items) $ _____

        (b) expenditures for independent contractor operations $ _____

        (c) welfare benefits (not administrative costs) $ _____

        (d) expenditures on exposures that are separately rated—See Item B below $ _____

        (e) Total Deductions, (a) + (b) + (c) + (d) $ _____

    (3) Operating expenditures, (1) – (2) (e)
(enter on rating worksheet in Item C) $ _____

B. Classifications that are Separately Rated
Determination of Deduction for Item A. (2) (d):

                      Separately Rated Classifications
                (See Manual for Regular Exposure Basis)   Total Expenditures

        (a) amusement parks $ _____

        (b) arenas, exhibition or convention buildings $ _____

        (c) dams and dikes $ _____

        (d) golf courses $ _____

Continued on next page

(e)	housing projects		$ _____
(f)	lakes or reservoirs		$ _____
(g)	medical care facilities (separately budgeted)		$ _____
(h)	penal institutions (separately budgeted)		$ _____
(i)	schools and colleges		$ _____
(j)	ski facilities		$ _____
(k)	stadiums, bleachers or grandstands with seating capacity in excess of 5,000		$ _____
(l)	streets or roads—existence and maintenance hazard		$ _____
(m)	streets or roads—new construction		$ _____
(n)	transportation systems and facilities including airports, bus systems, or other mass transit facilities, such as subways and aircraft		$ _____
(o)	utilities—electric, gas, water, steam		$ _____
(p)	wharves, piers, docks, marinas, and watercraft		$ _____
(q)	zoos		$ _____
Total of (a) through (q); show In A.(2) (d)			$ _____

Copyright, ISO Properties, Inc., 1979. Adapted with permission.

Exhibit 8-8 defines many of the accounting terms found in doing premium audits for governmental subdivisions.

EXHIBIT 8-8

Accounting Terms Used in Auditing Governmental Subdivisions

Grant
A contribution or gift by one governmental unit to another unit. It can be cash or other assets. The contribution is usually made to aid in the support of a specific function.

For example, education, but it is sometimes for general purposes. Capital grants are restricted for the acquisition and/or construction of fixed (capital) assets. All other grants are operating grants.

Entitlement
The amount of payment to which a political subdivision is entitled as determined by the federal government.

For example, revenue sharing.

Shared Revenue
A revenue levied by one government but shared on a predetermined basis, often in proportion to the amount collected at the local level with another government or class of government.

Fund
An independent fiscal and accounting entity with a self-balancing set of accounts recording cash and/or other resources together with all related liabilities, reserves, and equities. Transfer of funds should be excluded from the expenditures of the transferor (and included in the expenditure of the recipient).

General Fund	Used to account for all financial resources except those required to be accounted for in another fund. It would be used for all general government operations such as administration, public works, parks, recreation, etc. Also included under this general heading would be education. In situations of this nature you would have a general government fund and an education fund. The General Fund is used to account for the ordinary operations of a governmental unit that is financed from taxes and other general revenues.
Special Revenue Funds	Used to account for the proceeds of specific revenue sources (other than special assessments, expendable trusts, or for major capital projects) that are legally restricted to expenditure for specified purposes. An example is a motor fuel tax fund used to finance highway and road construction.
Capital Projects Funds (Bond Funds)	Used to account for financial resources to be used for the acquisition or construction of major capital facilities (other than those financed by Propriety Funds, Special Assessment Funds, and Trust Funds).
Debt Service Fund	A fund established to account for the accumulation of resources for and the payment of general long term debt principal and interest. Formerly called a sinking fund.
Special Assessment Fund	A fund set up to finance and account for the construction of improvements or provision of services that are to be paid for, wholly or in part, from special assessments levied against the benefited property. An example would be the construction of sewer lines.
Enterprise Fund	A fund established to finance and account for the acquisition, operation and maintenance of governmental facilities and services that are entirely or predominantly self supported by user charges. Examples of enterprise funds are those for water, gas and electric utilities, swimming pools, airports, parking garages, and transit systems.
Intra-Governmental Service Fund	A fund established to finance and account for services and commodities furnished by a designated department or agency to other departments and agencies within a single governmental unit. Amounts expended by the fund are restored thereto either from operating earnings or by transfers from other funds, so that the original fund capital is kept intact. Formerly called a Working Capital Fund.

Copyright, ISO Properties, Inc., 1990, 1992. Adapted with permission.

PROFESSIONAL LIABILITY INSURANCE

Professional liability insurance is another liability insurance area occasionally requiring special premium audit procedures in insurance coverage for varied and wide-ranging professional exposures. The public expects a high standard of competence from individuals in a profession. Failure to meet that standard may render a professional person liable for any resulting damages. To provide protection for such eventualities, insurers developed professional liability insurance.

For all professional liability coverage parts, this insurance covers only professional liability exposures. Insureds must obtain coverage for related nonprofessional exposures separately, and the insurer must separately compute the corresponding premium.

The *CLM* covers twelve professional liability coverages in "Division Seven— Professional Liability." Insurers write other professional coverages on an individual basis. The following sections describe the professional coverages a premium auditor is most likely to encounter.

Hospital Professional Liability Coverage

Hospital professional liability coverage provides protection against claims by any patient for injury arising out of a medical incident involving rendering or failing to render professional services. A standard coverage part contains the coverage provisions, exclusions, and other conditions of the hospital professional liability policy. Most insurers write the professional liability together with premises and operations liability to avoid a question as to which coverage applies in certain situations.

Hospitals and other healthcare facilities are among the most regulated industries in terms of recordkeeping. Local, state, and federal authorities require numerous reports and data relevant to their operations. To determine the professional liability exposure, a premium auditor will extract information from the daily census, which all hospitals maintain for their own use. The daily census contains such necessary information as the number of outpatient visits and average daily bed occupancy.

Exposure Bases

Insurers base premiums for hospital professional liability insurance on beds or on outpatient visits, depending on the facility type. The *CLM* defines beds as "the daily average number of beds, cribs and bassinets occupied during the policy period. The rates apply per bed."[7] One patient for one day equals one bed day. One patient for thirty days is thirty bed days. The premium auditor should record the number of beds occupied, not the total number of beds in the facility. The premium should reflect only the number of beds actually in use. Hospitals, clinics, and homes keep a monthly total of bed days (or patient days), which the premium auditor can obtain on request. Under Medicare and Medicaid rules and regulations, hospitals must file a monthly report to collect amounts due to them. The report shows patient days or bed days.

Hospitals may use either an admissions basis or a dismissal basis method of recording patient days. A small hospital using a dismissal basis may have days showing a zero count. That does not mean that it had no patients on that day, but rather that it had no dismissals.

Hospitals frequently keep bassinet occupancy totals separate from the bed days. In some instances, they may also maintain separate records of children's beds or special therapy beds. The premium auditor must obtain the totals for all occupancies. Premium auditors should not accept a summary the hospital has prepared for the premium audit. They should obtain the monthly reports for the premium audit period, determine from them the total bed days for the month, and add those figures to determine the total bed days for the policy period. The premium auditor should then divide the total by the number of days in the policy to determine the exact average bed occupancy. Remember, the rate is based on the daily average number of beds occupied, not the number of bed days. Because the rate "per bed" is a significant figure, both hospitals and insurers should ensure that those figures are as accurate as possible.

The premium auditor should also calculate the average bed occupancy as a percentage of bed capacity. That calculation is a test of the reasonableness of the data. If the data are correct but indicate a low occupancy rate, the hospital may have financial difficulties. An abnormally high occupancy rate suggests overcrowding, which increases the hazards of professional losses. In either case, the premium auditor should notify the underwriter.

When patients do not stay overnight, insurers may base premiums for medical professional liability on outpatient visits. The CLM defines this premium base as "the total number of visits made during the policy period by patients who do not receive bed and board service. The rates apply per 100 outpatient visits."[8]

A patient who comes to a hospital on ten separate occasions either for the same treatment each time or for different treatments accumulates ten outpatient visits. However, during one day, a patient may receive, for example, emergency, X-ray, and pharmaceutic treatment. Consequently, the hospital may record three outpatient visits. If so, the premium auditor should count outpatient visits in the same manner as the hospital and should not adjust the total merely because the same patient received three separate treatments.

Hospitals keep records for outpatient visits in the reports mentioned earlier. The premium auditor should obtain the cumulative total of such visits to compute the premium.

Classifications

The manual rules list the classifications for hospital professional liability insurance. This is the liability insurance that provides coverage to a hospital against claims of negligence resulting from malpractice, professional errors, or mistakes by hospital staff. Six types of facilities exist, as follows:

1. Outpatient clinics
2. Convalescent or nursing homes
3. Hospitals
4. Mental-psychopathic institutions
5. Outpatient surgical facilities
6. Sanatoriums or other health institutions

The rules distinguish the classifications and code numbers that apply to each type of facility depending on the status (for-profit, not-for-profit, governmental, or osteopathic) and premium base.

Physicians, Surgeons, and Dentists Professional Liability Insurance

Physicians, surgeons, and dentists professional liability insurance protects these professionals against claims asserting malpractice arising out of their professional acts or omissions. This insurance also protects individuals for whom those professionals are responsible (nurses, for example). Insurers can cover individual liability, partnership liability, or both. Individual professional liability policies cover individuals specifically named as an insured. Partnership liability policies cover the described partnership and any members of it regarding acts or omissions of others.

The premium base is on an "each" basis and per year. The insurer assigns each single physician, surgeon, or dentist to a separate classification based on the various types of medical professional exposures.

Blood Banks Professional Liability Coverage

A special endorsement to hospital professional liability insurance provides coverage for claims against blood banks arising out of rendering or failing to render, during the policy period, professional services in connection with donating blood under the insured's supervision; injury that occurs during the policy period and arises out of any blood products handled or distributed by the named insured; or reliance in which any representation or warranty is made at any time regarding such products. The premium base for this coverage is "donations," which the *CLM* defines as "the total of all blood donations administered by the named insured during the policy period. The rates apply per donation."[9] For insurance purposes and for regulatory purposes, the blood bank keeps cumulative daily and monthly totals of all blood donations received.

SUMMARY

Liability insurance requires premium auditors to measure the exposure and to assign the proper classifications. The *Commercial Lines Manual* lists the available classifications for common coverages in a special section called the Classification Table. The rules defining general liability classification procedures appear in the *CLM*'s "Division Six—General Liability."

The classification depends on the nature of the operation; the manual allows additional classifications only under certain conditions. The rules also specify operations that are generally included within and generally excluded from the scope of a classification description. Specific classification assignment rules apply to each of the five major business groups. As with workers' compensation, job descriptions, activity, analogy, cross-reference, and terminology can assist the premium auditor in assigning the proper classifications.

Premium computation requires multiplying the measured premium base by the applicable rate. The *CLM* rules explain minimum premiums and other premium modifications.

General liability insurance for governmental subdivisions may require a premium auditor to take a different approach. The classification and rating structure for governmental subdivisions provides coverage for all operations except certain specified, separately rated operations based on the governmental entity's total operating expenditures. The program requires the premium auditor to ascertain total expenditures and to deduct defined exclusions to determine the premium basis. Classification depends on the type and population of the governmental subdivision.

Liability insurance for professionals may also require special premium audit procedures. Hospital professional liability insurance requires a premium auditor to determine the average number of beds occupied, the number of outpatient visits, or the number of blood donations. Physicians, surgeons, and dentists professional liability insurance is designed to protect those professionals from malpractice claims arising out of their professional acts or omissions. Insurers may cover other professional liability exposures for a flat charge on a per capita basis or on some other basis that reflects the exposure's magnitude. Premium audits for those policies are less common, but if circumstances require an audit, it is a situation that the premium auditor should treat carefully.

CHAPTER NOTES

1. Insurance Services Office, *Commercial Lines Manual*, Classification Table, Code 91588, http://info.iso.com (ISOnet, accessed Aug. 17, 2006).
2. *Commercial Lines Manual*, (ISO) SIM-GL-MU, Rule 24.G.1.
3. *Commercial Lines Manual*, (ISO) SIM-GL-MU, Rule 24.G.3.a.
4. *Commercial Lines Manua*, (ISO) SIM-GL-MU, Rule 24.G.3.d.
5. *Commercial Lines Manual*, (ISO) SIM-GL-MU, Rule 24.G.3.e.
6. *Commercial Lines Manual*, (ISO) SIM-GL-MU, Rule 24.G.3.c.
7. *Commercial Lines Manual*, "Division Seven—Professional Liability," (ISO) SIM-PR-MU, Rule 33.C.1.
8. *Commercial Lines Manual*, "Division Seven—Professional Liability," (ISO) SIM-PR-MU, Rule 33.C.3.
9. *Commercial Lines Manual*, "Division Seven—Professional Liability," (ISO) SIM-PR-MU, Rule 33.C.2.

Direct Your Learning

Business Auto Insurance and Premium Determination

Educational Objectives

After learning the content of this chapter and completing the corresponding course guide assignment, you should be able to:

▶ Summarize the content of "Division One—Automobile" of the ISO *Commercial Lines Manual* (CLM).

▶ Given a case, determine the coverage provided by the business auto coverage part.

   • Describe the contents of the Business Auto Coverage Form Declarations.

   • Describe the system of covered auto symbols used with business auto coverage, and describe each symbol.

   • Describe each type of coverage included in the Business Auto Coverage Form.

▶ Explain how the following endorsements modify the coverage provided by the Business Auto Coverage Form: Drive-Other-Car Coverage; Nonownership Liability; Hired Autos; Individual as the Named Insured; Medical Payments; No-Fault Coverages; Rental Reimbursement; Audio, Visual, and Data Electronic Equipment; Tapes, Records, and Discs; and Uninsured and Underinsured Motorists.

▶ Given a case, classify trucks, tractors, and trailers according to *CLM* rules for primary and secondary classifications.

▶ Describe the premium audit procedures for commercial auto insurance for each of the following:

   • Perpetual inventory schedules

   • Composite rated policies

   • Coverage symbols

   • Fleet and nonfleet designations

▶ Define or describe each of the Key Words and Phrases for this chapter.

▶▶ 9.1

CHAPTER 9

Develop Your Perspective

What are the main topics covered in the chapter?

Automobile insurance includes coverage for liability and property loss exposures. Insurers can incorporate a wide range of vehicles and coverages under a business auto policy. The ISO *Commercial Lines Manual* and the policy forms provide the information needed to determine the coverages provided by the policy.

Identify the loss exposures that can be insured under a commercial auto policy.

- How does "Division One—Automobile" of the *Commercial Lines Manual* (*CLM*) classify auto types?
- Why are state pages important in reviewing this section of the CLM?

Why is it important to learn these topics?

Business auto insurance creates a challenging premium basis for premium auditors to verify.

Consider how a premium auditor can effectively and efficiently gather information about an organization's commercial autos.

- What questions should a premium auditor ask and of whom?
- What records should a premium auditor examine?

How can you use what you will learn?

Analyze the actions required if you were the premium auditor for a commercial fleet policy.

- What would your focus be in preparing a premium audit for a fleet with a perpetual inventory schedule?
- How would your focus change for a policy that is composite rated?

Business Auto Insurance and Premium Determination

Because of the frequency of auto accidents and their potential for causing both bodily injury and property damage, anyone owning or operating an auto may be faced with a staggering financial liability. Commercial auto insurance is the primary risk management treatment for this liability loss exposure. Even though commercial auto insurance totaled approximately $29 billion in written premiums[1] in 2004, commercial auto insurance is not particularly important to premium auditors because most commercial auto insurance policies are not audited. Nevertheless, those commercial auto insurance policies that are audited present premium auditors with interesting challenges and an opportunity to add value.

Commercial auto policies have a premium base that is difficult to verify. Sometimes discovering a vehicle's existence is difficult for the premium auditor. Skilled questioning and observation are vital skills for auto premium adjustments because verifiable records are less readily available for autos than records of payroll and sales. Even when records are available, they rarely show all the information necessary for proper classification. In some cases, the premium auditor may have to see the vehicle in person, but a careful and precise premium audit can be worth the effort because the premium developed from a single auto can be substantial, and the difference in premium between alternate classifications of just one vehicle can be hundreds of dollars. An experienced premium auditor can spot many such classification errors by scrutinizing the schedule of commercial autos.

Commercial auto policies use the term "auto" to mean a land motor vehicle, trailer, or semi-trailer and some mobile equipment designed for travel on public roads. Because the exposure arises from the insured's use of autos, the premium depends on the number of autos insured and their characteristics. Rating private passenger autos is relatively straightforward. However, businesses may own a fleet of autos that includes cars and trucks. Trucks range in size from a small pickup truck to a truck and semitrailer that can be 110 feet long and weigh over 100,000 pounds, as well as other equipment that is insured with a commercial auto policy.

Even if an insurer correctly classifies an insured's auto or autos when the policy is issued, the insured's ownership and use of these autos may change during the policy term. For example, if a vehicle is not needed for its original purpose, an insured may relocate it to where it can be used. Such a change may result in a much higher rated territory or use for purposes that carry a much higher rate. Because coverage applies automatically, whether the insurer charges the proper premium or not, the premium auditor plays a vital role in enabling the insurer to collect the proper premium.

COMMERCIAL LINES MANUAL "DIVISION ONE— AUTOMOBILE"

The Insurance Services Office (ISO) *Commercial Lines Manual* (CLM) "Division One—Automobile" is the manual approved for use in all but a few states. Where approved, each insurer decides whether it will use the *CLM*.

The ISO commercial auto program has four distinct coverage forms—Business Auto Coverage Form, Truckers Coverage Form, Motor Carrier Coverage Form, and Garage Coverage Form. A fifth form exists for business auto physical damage coverage when written without liability coverage. The rules for writing, rating, and auditing these coverage forms appear in the *CLM*'s "Division One—Automobile."

The *CLM*'s state pages contain any exceptions to the *CLM* rules as well as the applicable rates. ISO calculates only the loss cost portion of the rates, and insurers must add their own expense component to determine the final rate they will use.

Division One Sections

"Division One—Automobile" of the *CLM* has seven sections.

Section I—General Rules (Rules 1–16)

Section I explains how premium auditors should apply "Division One– Automobile" rules and the general procedures for premium determination. It also explains how to classify autos by type, as shown in Exhibit 9-1.

Section II—Trucks, Tractors, and Trailers (Rules 21–25)

Section II describes the eligibility and premium development procedures for trucks, tractors, and trailers, plus any rules that are specific to that vehicle type. This section includes information on truckers and motor carriers, a specialized group. Because the premium determination and premium auditing procedures for truckers are among the most complex rules within the automobile division, a later chapter is devoted to truckers.

EXHIBIT 9-1

How to Classify Autos

A. If an auto has more than one use, use the highest rated classification, unless 80% of the use is in a lower rated activity. In that case, use the lower rated classification.

B. Classify and rate autos of the truck type that transport property or are used in business according to the Trucks, Tractors and Trailers Subsection.

C. Classify and rate autos of the private passenger type according to the Private Passenger Types Subsection.

D. Classify and rate buses, taxicabs and other autos that are used in the business of transporting people according to the Public Transportation Subsection.

E. Classify and rate new and used auto dealers according to the Garage Subsection.

F. Classify and rate autos that do not fit into these categories according to the Special Types Subsection.

G. When a risk is required by law to have or is eligible for a coverage that is not available in the territory of principal garaging, use the registration address to determine the territory for that coverage.

Source: *Commercial Lines Manual,* "Division One—Automobile," Section I, Rule 16. Copyright, ISO Properties, Inc., 2006.

Section III—Private Passenger Types (Rules 31–34)

The rating classification for private passenger vehicles includes four-wheeled private passenger and station wagon types, and nonbusiness usage pickups, panel trucks, and vans insured under a Business Auto, Truckers, or Motor Carrier Form. Vehicles in this classification also have either of the following characteristics: they are owned by a corporation, a partnership, an unincorporated association, or a government agency, or they are rated as part of a fleet (five or more self-propelled vehicles under common ownership). This section also includes farmers' autos.

Section IV—Public Transportation (Rules 38–43)

The public transportation section applies to autos registered or used for transporting members of the public, such as taxis, limousine services, buses, and van pools (transportation arrangements for employees for a single employer).

Section V—Garages (Rules 48–55)

The garage section applies to franchised and nonfranchised auto, motorcycle, truck and trailer dealers; and to garagekeepers liability. Section V does not apply to other auto-related businesses, such as gas stations and auto repair shops even though the title of this section is garages. These loss exposures are insured with the Commercial General Liability Coverage Form and the Business Auto Coverage Form. Garagekeepers liability (also called garagekeepers legal liability) is used to cover the bailment exposure of any business with customers' autos in its care, not just those that are obviously auto-related. For example, a restaurant that provides valet parking has this loss exposure and this coverage need. A garagekeepers endorsement can be added to the business auto policy for insureds not eligible for the garage policy.

Section VI—Special Types (Rules 62–83)

The *CLM* separately handles some special operations and vehicles. Examples include motor homes and campers that are not individually owned, ambulances, antique autos, driver training programs, fire departments, funeral directors, law enforcement vehicles, leasing or rental companies, and motorcycles.

Section VII—Common Coverages and Rating Procedures (Rules 88–113)

Section VII includes common endorsements that insurers can use to modify the coverages and the rating procedures common to all states.

State Pages

The *CLM* also contains specific pages for each state. State pages may indicate that certain rules or procedures do not apply in a certain state or that certain procedures or rules that do not apply countrywide do apply in a certain state. The state rate pages give the applicable rates for the state in question. Finally, the state pages indicate the appropriate territory for the different areas of the state.

BUSINESS AUTO COVERAGE PART

Business Auto Coverage Form
A coverage form filed by ISO that indemnifies the insured for liability arising out of the ownership, maintenance, or use of autos and physical damage to autos owned, leased, or hired by the named insured.

The **Business Auto Coverage Form** is a coverage form filed by ISO that indemnifies the insured for liability arising out of the ownership, maintenance, or use of autos and physical damage to autos owned, leased, or hired by the named insured. Business auto coverage forms have the flexibility to meet the needs of most businesses except truckers and auto dealers. Insurers can include business auto coverage as part of a commercial package policy or issue it as a monoline policy. A complete business auto policy includes the Common Policy Conditions and Common Policy Declarations Forms, the Business Auto Coverage Form Declarations (CA DS 03), the Business Auto Coverage Form (CA 00 01), and any applicable endorsements. The Business Auto Coverage Part consists of the Business Auto Coverage Form Declarations, the Business Auto Coverage Form, and any applicable endorsements.

The following discussion describes the business auto coverage portions most relevant to properly determining earned premium.

Common Policy Conditions and Declarations

The business auto coverage is not complete without the Common Policy Conditions. Those conditions are common to all coverages, and the insurer must include them if it writes coverage as a monoline policy or part of a package policy. The cancellation, changes, inspection, transfer of interest, and right to examine the insured's books and records conditions are in the Common Policy Conditions. The Common Policy Declarations page gives the information necessary to identify the named insured, address, policy period, and coverages purchased.

Business Auto Coverage Form Declarations

In addition to the usual information contained in the declarations, the Business Auto Declarations page (CA DS 03) indicates the particular coverages that apply to all the vehicles insured by the policy. Premium auditors must therefore understand the covered auto symbols system used to trigger coverage and shown on the declarations page. The Business Auto Coverage Form Declarations contains six items. Exhibit 9-2 shows the first two items.

Item One—Information on Insured

Item One identifies the named insured, named insured's address, business form (partnership, corporation, limited liability company, individual or other), policy period, premium, audit period (if applicable), and the endorsements attached to the policy at inception. The names of the insurer and producer as well as the policy number are shown above Item One.

Item Two—Schedule of Coverages and Covered Autos

Item Two is a four-column schedule indicating the coverages provided, the autos to which each coverage applies, the limit(s) of liability, and the premiums for each coverage and the total premium for all coverages and endorsements. A note at the bottom of Item Two states that the policy may be subject to final premium audit.

The first column lists the possible coverages under the Business Auto Coverage Form. The second column has space for a numeric symbol that is used to trigger coverage. These symbols and how they are used are discussed later. The third column is used for coverage limits and deductibles when coverage is provided. The final column shows the premium for each coverage. Coverage is provided only if the symbol, limits, deductible, and premium are shown.

EXHIBIT 9-2

Business Auto Coverage Form Declarations—Items One and Two

POLICY NUMBER:

COMMERCIAL AUTO
CA DS 03 03 06

BUSINESS AUTO DECLARATIONS

COMPANY NAME AREA	PRODUCER NAME AREA

ITEM ONE

Named Insured:

Mailing Address:

Policy Period

From:

To: At 12:01 A.M. Standard Time at your mailing address.

Previous Policy Number:

Form Of Business:

☐ Corporation   ☐ Limited Liability Company   ☐ Individual
☐ Partnership   ☐ Other:

In return for the payment of the premium, and subject to all the terms of this policy, we agree with you to provide the insurance as stated in this policy.

Premium shown is payable at inception: $

Audit Period (If Applicable): ☐ Annually   ☐ Semi-Annually   ☐ Quarterly   ☐ Monthly

Endorsements Attached To This Policy:

IL 00 17 – Common Policy Conditions (**IL 01 46** in Washington)
IL 00 21 – Broad Form Nuclear Exclusion (Not applicable in New York)

CA DS 03 03 06   © ISO Properties, Inc., 2005   **Page 1 of 11**

<table>
<tr><td colspan="4" align="center">**Countersignature Of Authorized Representative**</td></tr>
<tr><td colspan="4">**Name:**</td></tr>
<tr><td colspan="4">**Title:**</td></tr>
<tr><td colspan="4">**Signature:**</td></tr>
<tr><td colspan="4">**Date:**</td></tr>
</table>

Note

Officers' facsimile signatures may be inserted here, on the policy cover or elsewhere at the company's option.

ITEM TWO

Schedule Of Coverages And Covered Autos

This policy provides only those coverages where a charge is shown in the premium column below. Each of these coverages will apply only to those "autos" shown as covered "autos". **"Autos" are shown as covered "autos" for a particular coverage by the entry of one or more of the symbols from the Covered Autos Section of the Business Auto Coverage Form next to the name of the coverage.**

Coverages	Covered Autos	Limit	Premium
Liability		$	$
Personal Injury Protection (Or Equivalent No-Fault Coverage)		Separately Stated In Each Personal Injury Protection Endorsement Minus $ Deductible.	$
Added Personal Injury Protection (Or Equivalent Added No-Fault Coverage)		Separately Stated In Each Added Personal Injury Protection Endorsement.	$
Property Protection Insurance (Michigan Only)		Separately Stated In The Property Protection Insurance Endorsement Minus $ Deductible For Each Accident.	$
Auto Medical Payments		$	$
Medical Expense And Income Loss Benefits (Virginia Only)		Separately Stated In Each Medical Expense And Income Loss Benefits Endorsement.	$
Uninsured Motorists		$	$
Underinsured Motorists (When Not Included In Uninsured Motorists Coverage)		$	$

© ISO Properties, Inc., 2005 CA DS 03 03 06

Continued on next page

ITEM TWO
Schedule Of Coverages And Covered Autos (Cont'd)

Coverages	Covered Autos	Limit		Premium
Physical Damage Comprehensive Coverage		Actual Cash Value Or Cost Of Repair, Whichever Is Less, Minus		$
		$	Deductible For Each Covered Auto, But No Deductible Applies To Loss Caused By Fire Or Lightning. See Item Four For Hired Or Borrowed Autos.	
Physical Damage Specified Causes Of Loss Coverage		Actual Cash Value Or Cost Of Repair, Whichever Is Less, Minus		$
		$	Deductible For Each Covered Auto For Loss Caused By Mischief Or Vandalism. See Item Four For Hired Or Borrowed Autos.	
Physical Damage Collision Coverage		Actual Cash Value Or Cost Of Repair, Whichever Is Less, Minus		$
		$	Deductible For Each Covered Auto. See Item Four For Hired Or Borrowed "Autos".	
Physical Damage Towing And Labor		$	For Each Disable-ment Of A Private Passenger Auto.	$.
				$
Premium For Endorsements				$
Estimated Total Premium*				$

*This Policy May Be Subject To Final Audit.

CA DS 03 03 06	© ISO Properties, Inc., 2005	Page 3 of 11

Item Three—Schedule of Covered Autos You Own

Item Three, shown in Exhibit 9-3, is the schedule showing the covered autos owned by the named insured at policy inception. The schedule describes each auto and shows the premiums for each coverage. The schedule also includes the necessary classification and rating information. Item Three includes a section to indicate limits and deductibles if different limits apply to different autos. If that schedule is not completed, the limits and deductibles shown in Item Two apply.

EXHIBIT 9-3

Business Auto Coverage Form Declarations—Item Three

ITEM THREE
Schedule Of Covered Autos You Own

Covered Auto Number:	
Town And State Where The Covered Auto Will Be Principally Garaged	
Description (Year, Model, Trade Name, Body Type, Serial Number (S), Vehicle Identification Number (VIN))	

| Purchased: | Original Cost New | $ |
| | Actual Cost New (N) Or Used (U) | $ |

Classification

Radius Of Operation	Business Use s=service r=retail c=commercial	Size GVW, GCW Or Vehicle Seating Capacity	Age Group	Primary Rating Factor Liab.	Primary Rating Factor Phy. Dam.	Secondary Rating Factor	Code

Except For Towing, All Physical Damage Loss Is Payable To You And The Loss Payee Named To The Right As Interests May Appear At the Time Of The Loss.

Coverages – Premiums, Limits And Deductibles
(Absence of a deductible or limit entry in any column below means that the limit or deductible entry in the corresponding Item Two column applies instead.)

Coverages	Limit	Premium
Liability	$	$
Personal Injury Protection	Stated In Each Personal Injury Protection Endorsement Minus $ Deductible Shown	$
Added Personal Injury Protection	Stated In Each Added Personal Injury Protection Endorsement	$
Property Protection Insurance (Michigan Only)	Stated In The Property Protection Insurance Endorsement Minus $ Deductible Shown	$
Auto Medical Payments	$	$
Medical Expense And Income Loss Benefits (Virginia Only)	Stated In Each Medical Expense And Income Loss Benefits Endorsement For Each Person	$
Comprehensive	Stated In Item Two Minus $ Deductible Shown	$
Specified Causes Of Loss	Stated In Item Two Minus $ Deductible Shown	$
Collision	Stated In Item Two Minus $ Deductible Shown	$
Towing And Labor	$ Per Disablement	$

Page 4 of 11   © ISO Properties, Inc., 2005   CA DS 03 03 06

Copyright, ISO Properties, Inc., 2005.

Item Four—Schedule of Hired or Borrowed Covered Auto Coverages and Premiums

Hired or borrowed auto information appears on Item Four's schedule (see Exhibit 9-4). The schedule shows by state the estimated cost of hire, rates, and premium for hired or borrowed autos.

EXHIBIT 9-4

Business Auto Coverage Form Declarations—Item Four

ITEM FOUR
Schedule Of Hired Or Borrowed Covered Auto Coverage And Premiums

	Liability Coverage – Rating Basis, Cost Of Hire			
State	Estimated Cost Of Hire For Each State	Rate Per Each $100 Cost Of Hire	Factor (If Liability Coverage Is Primary)	Premium
	$	$		$

	Liability Coverage – Rating Basis, Number Of Days – (For Mobile Or Farm Equipment – Rental Period Basis)			
State	Estimated Number Of Days Equipment Will Be Rented	Base Premium	Factor	Premium
	$		$	
			Total Premium	$

Cost of hire means the total amount you incur for the hire of "autos" you don't own (not including "autos" you borrow or rent from your partners or "employees" or their family members). Cost of hire does not include charges for services performed by motor carriers of property or passengers.

Physical Damage Coverage

Coverages	Limit Of Insurance		
Comprehensive	Actual Cash Value Or Cost Of Repair, Whichever Is Less, Minus $ Deductible For Each Covered Auto, But No Deductible Applies To Loss Caused By Fire Or Lightning.		
	Estimated Annual Cost Of Hire	Rate Per Each $100 Annual Cost Of Hire	Premium
	$	$	$
Specified Causes Of Loss	Actual Cash Value Or Cost Of Repair, Whichever Is Less, Minus $ Deductible For Each Covered Auto For Loss Caused By Mischief Or Vandalism.		
	Estimated Annual Cost Of Hire	Rate Per Each $100 Annual Cost Of Hire	Premium
	$	$	$
Collision	Actual Cash Value Or Cost Of Repair, Whichever Is Less, Minus $ Deductible For Each Covered Auto.		
	Estimated Annual Cost Of Hire	Rate Per Each $100 Annual Cost Of Hire	Premium
	$	$	$

Total Premium:	$

CA DS 03 03 06   © ISO Properties, Inc., 2005

Item Five—Schedule for Nonownership Liability

Item Five, shown in Exhibit 9-5, is a schedule for nonownership liability. Because of the differing rating bases, the schedule is divided into three subsections: garage service operations, social service agencies, and all other insureds. There is space to indicate the number of employees, the number of partners, the number of employees whose principal duty involves the operation of autos, the number of volunteers, and the total premiums.

EXHIBIT 9-5

Business Auto Coverage Form Declarations—Item Five

ITEM FIVE
Schedule For Non-Ownership Liability

Named Insured's Business	Rating Basis	Number	Premium
Other Than Garage Service Operations And Other Than Social Service Agencies	Number Of Employees		$
	Number Of Partners		$
Garage Service Operations	Number Of Employees Whose Principal Duty Involves The Operation Of Autos		$
Social Service Agencies	Number Of Employees		$
	Number Of Volunteers		$
	Total Premiums		$

© ISO Properties, Inc., 2005   CA DS 03 03 06

Copyright, ISO Properties, Inc., 2005.

Item Six—Schedule for Gross Receipts or Mileage Basis—Liability Coverage—Public Auto or Leasing Rental Concerns

Item Six (see Exhibit 9-6) is a schedule of the estimated exposures, rates, and premiums for a public auto or leasing rental concerns written on either a gross receipts or mileage basis. When applicable, the insurer uses Item Six in place of Item Three.

Business Auto Coverage Form

The Business Auto Coverage Form (CA 00 01) contains the description of the symbols and the coverages provided and exclusions applicable to each, coverage conditions, and the business auto coverage definitions. The coverage form contains the following five sections:

- Section I—Covered Autos
- Section II—Liability Coverage
- Section III—Physical Damage Coverage
- Section IV—Business Auto Conditions
- Section V—Definitions

EXHIBIT 9-6

Business Auto Coverage Form Declarations—Item Six

ITEM SIX

Schedule For Gross Receipts Or Mileage Basis – Liability Coverage – Public Auto Or Leasing Rental
Concerns

Location No:				
(Check One)		Gross Receipts (Per $100)		Mileage (Per Mile)
Estimated Yearly:				
		Rates		
Liability		$		
Auto Medical Payments		$		
Medical Expense Benefits (VA Only)		$		
Income Loss Benefits (VA Only)		$		
		Premiums		
Liability		$		
Auto Medical Payments		$		
Medical Expense Benefits (VA Only)		$		
Income Loss Benefits (VA Only)		$		

Location No:				
(Check One)		Gross Receipts (Per $100)		Mileage (Per Mile)
Estimated Yearly:				
		Rates		
Liability		$		
Auto Medical Payments		$		
Medical Expense Benefits (VA Only)		$		
Income Loss Benefits (VA Only)		$		
		Premiums		
Liability		$		
Auto Medical Payments		$		
Medical Expense Benefits (VA Only)		$		
Income Loss Benefits (VA Only)		$		

CA DS 03 03 06   © ISO Properties, Inc., 2005   Page 9 of 11   □

Section I—Covered Autos

Section I contains the "Description of Covered Auto Designation Symbols," which Exhibit 9-7 shows. The covered auto symbols allow the underwriter flexibility to tailor policy coverages to specific business auto exposures. Each of ten symbols represents a particular relationship between the insured and the covered auto, and also indicates the coverage the policy will provide for autos the insured acquires after the policy's inception. The premium auditor must know what each of the symbols means.

EXHIBIT 9-7

Section I—Business Auto Coverage Form

COMMERCIAL AUTO
CA 00 01 03 06

BUSINESS AUTO COVERAGE FORM

Various provisions in this policy restrict coverage. Read the entire policy carefully to determine rights, duties and what is and is not covered.

Throughout this policy the words "you" and "your" refer to the Named Insured shown in the Declarations. The words "we", "us" and "our" refer to the Company providing this insurance.

Other words and phrases that appear in quotation marks have special meaning. Refer to Section **V** – Definitions.

SECTION I – COVERED AUTOS

Item Two of the Declarations shows the "autos" that are covered "autos" for each of your coverages. The following numerical symbols describe the "autos" that may be covered "autos". The symbols entered next to a coverage on the Declarations designate the only "autos" that are covered "autos".

A. Description Of Covered Auto Designation Symbols

Symbol		Description Of Covered Auto Designation Symbols
1	Any "Auto"	
2	Owned "Autos" Only	Only those "autos" you own (and for Liability Coverage any "trailers" you don't own while attached to power units you own). This includes those "autos" you acquire ownership of after the policy begins.
3	Owned Private Passenger "Autos" Only	Only the private passenger "autos" you own. This includes those private passenger "autos" you acquire ownership of after the policy begins.
4	Owned "Autos" Other Than Private Passenger "Autos" Only	Only those "autos" you own that are not of the private passenger type (and for Liability Coverage any "trailers" you don't own while attached to power units you own). This includes those "autos" not of the private passenger type you acquire ownership of after the policy begins.
5	Owned "Autos" Subject To No-Fault	Only those "autos" you own that are required to have No-Fault benefits in the state where they are licensed or principally garaged. This includes those "autos" you acquire ownership of after the policy begins provided they are required to have No-Fault benefits in the state where they are licensed or principally garaged.
6	Owned "Autos" Subject To A Compulsory Uninsured Motorists Law	Only those "autos" you own that because of the law in the state where they are licensed or principally garaged are required to have and cannot reject Uninsured Motorists Coverage. This includes those "autos" you acquire ownership of after the policy begins provided they are subject to the same state uninsured motorists requirement.
7	Specifically Described "Autos"	Only those "autos" described in Item Three of the Declarations for which a premium charge is shown (and for Liability Coverage any "trailers" you don't own while attached to any power unit described in Item Three).
8	Hired "Autos" Only	Only those "autos" you lease, hire, rent or borrow. This does not include any "auto" you lease, hire, rent, or borrow from any of your "employees", partners (if you are a partnership), members (if you are a limited liability company) or members of their households.
9	Nonowned "Autos" Only	Only those "autos" you do not own, lease, hire, rent or borrow that are used in connection with your business. This includes "autos" owned by your "employees", partners (if you are a partnership), members (if you are a limited liability company), or members of their households but only while used in your business or your personal affairs.
19	Mobile Equipment Subject To Compulsory Or Financial Responsibility Or Other Motor Vehicle Insurance Law Only	Only those "autos" that are land vehicles and that would qualify under the definition of "mobile equipment" under this policy if they were not subject to a compulsory or financial responsibility law or other motor vehicle insurance law where they are licensed or principally garaged.

Owned auto
An auto defined by the ISO Business Auto Coverage Form as owned by the insured, including trailers that are not owned while attached to owned vehicles.

Hired auto
An auto that the insured leases, hires, rents, or borrows, excluding autos leased, hired, rented, or borrowed from employees, partners, LLC members, or members of their households.

Nonowned auto
An auto defined by the ISO Business Auto Coverage Form as not owned, leased, hired, rented, or borrowed and that is used in connection with an insured's business.

Exhibit 9-8 shows an overview of how autos may be covered by the Business Auto Coverage Form. "Any auto" can be subdivided into autos owned by the insured and all other autos. An **owned auto** is an auto defined by the ISO Business Auto Coverage Form as owned by the insured, including trailers that are not owned while attached to owned vehicles. Owned autos, for policy purposes, are either private passenger types or types other than private passenger, owned by the insured, including trailers that are not attached to owned vehicles. Insured autos that the insured does not own are either hired autos or nonowned autos. A **hired auto** is an auto that the insured leases, hires, rents, or borrows, excluding autos leased, hired, rented, or borrowed from employees, partners, LLC members, or members of their households. A **nonowned auto** is an auto defined by the ISO Business Auto Coverage Form as not owned, leased, hired, rented, or borrowed and that is used in connection with an insured's business.

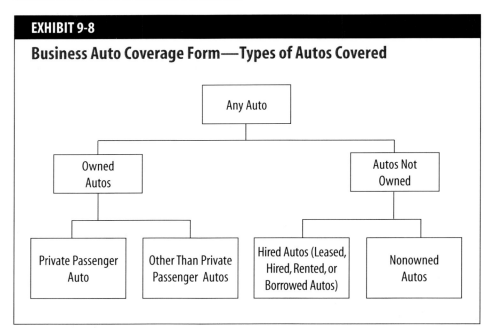

EXHIBIT 9-8

Business Auto Coverage Form—Types of Autos Covered

The symbols are as follows:

- Symbol 1—Any Auto. Insurers use Symbol 1 only for liability coverage because it makes any auto that the named insured owns, hires, borrows, or uses a covered auto.

- Symbol 2—Owned Autos Only. Symbol 2 provides automatic coverage for any type of owned auto. This symbol can be used for liability, auto medical payments, uninsured motorists, or any of the physical damage coverages (other than towing). The policy extends liability coverage to trailers or semitrailers while attached to owned power units.

- Symbol 3—Owned Private Passenger Autos Only. Symbol 3 provides automatic coverage only for owned private passenger autos. An auto that the insured leases for longer than six months is considered an owned auto. This symbol can be used for liability, medical payments, uninsured motorists, and physical damage coverages. Insurers can also use it for towing coverage, whereas they cannot use Symbol 4 for that purpose (because insurers are willing to provide towing coverage to only private passenger autos).

Towing

- Symbol 4—Owned Autos Other Than Private Passenger Autos Only. Symbol 4 serves the same purpose as Symbol 3 except that it is for owned autos other than private passenger-type vehicles. The liability coverage extends to trailers or semitrailers while attached to owned power units. This symbol covers trucks, truck-tractors, buses, taxis, motorcycles, trailers, and emergency vehicles. Unlike Symbol 3, it cannot be used for trailer coverage because insurers provide towing coverage only to private passenger autos.

No Towing

- Symbol 5—Owned Autos Subject to No-Fault. Symbol 5 provides automatic no-fault coverage on owned autos when the state in which the insured licenses or principally garages the auto requires such coverage. The insurer must attach an endorsement to the policy when using this symbol. This symbol can be used only for the personal injury protection (PIP) and added PIP coverages (and also property protection insurance in Michigan).

End.

- Symbol 6—Owned Autos Subject to a Compulsory Uninsured Motorists Law. Insurers use Symbol 6 to provide automatic uninsured and underinsured motorists coverage when the state in which the insured licenses or principally garages the owned auto requires (the state does not permit rejection of) such coverage. An endorsement must be attached to the policy when this symbol is used.

End.

- Symbol 7—Specifically Described Autos. Symbol 7 provides coverage only for autos that the insurer lists in Item Three of the declarations and for which the policy shows a premium charge. The policy covers trailers and semitrailers for liability when attached to a power unit described in Item Three. Insurers can use Symbol 7 for all coverages.

All coverages

- Symbol 8—Hired Autos Only. Symbol 8 provides coverage for the insured's interest in any auto the named insured leases, hires, rents, or borrows, except those owned by any of the named insured's employees, partners, or family member. Symbol 8 can be used by itself or in conjunction with Symbol 2, 3, 4, 7, or 9 for liability or physical damage. However, if the insured leases or hires a vehicle with a driver, physical damage coverage is on a refer-to-company basis. This symbol cannot be used for no-fault, uninsured motorists, or medical payments (except for funeral directors) coverages.

Used with 2,3,4,7,9

- Symbol 9—Nonowned Autos Only. Symbol 9 extends coverage to autos owned by employees, partners, LLC members, or anyone else as long as it is used in the insured's business and the named insured does not own, lease, hire, rent, or borrow the vehicle. If the insured borrows the vehicle, it is in the insured's care, custody, or control and therefore is considered a hired auto. If the insured's employee uses his or her own vehicle as a matter of convenience, perhaps to go to the bank or to run an errand for the insured, the vehicle is a nonowned auto. Insurers use this coverage only for liability coverage.

- Symbol 19—Mobile Equipment Subject To Compulsory or Financial Responsibility or Other Motor Vehicle Law Only. Symbol 19 is used to cover land vehicles that would qualify under the definition of mobile equipment under this policy if they were not subject to a compulsory or financial responsibility or other motor vehicle insurance law where they are licensed or principally garaged. This symbol can be used for liability, medical payments, uninsured motorists, and physical damage coverages.

Exhibit 9-9 summarizes how covered auto symbols can be used to cover differently defined auto exposures for each of the major coverages under the policy.

EXHIBIT 9-9

Business Auto Coverage—Use of Covered Auto Symbols

Coverage	Covered Auto Symbol									
	1	2	3	4	5	6	7	8	9	19
Liability	X	X	X	X			X	X	X	X
PIP		X	X	X	X		X			X
Medical payments		X	X	X		X				X
UM		X	X	X		X	X			X
Physical damage*		X	X	X			X	X		X
Towing			X				X			

* except towing

When Symbol 1 (Any auto) is used to designate liability coverage, the policy provides automatic coverage for hired and nonowned autos and mobile equipment included in Symbol 19. Symbols 8, 9, and 19 are not needed for liability coverage when Symbol 1 is used for liability; Symbol 1 includes the coverage that would be provided by Symbols 8, 9, and 19.

The policy explicitly states that "the symbols entered next to a coverage on the Declarations designate the only 'autos' that are covered 'autos,'" except that Symbols 1, 2, 3, 4, 5, 6, and 19 provide automatic coverage for

Symbol 1 includes 8, 9, 19

autos (of the type described by the symbol) that are acquired by the insured during the policy period. The policy also states the following:

> But, if Symbol 7 is entered next to a coverage in ITEM TWO of the Declarations, an "auto" you acquire will be a covered "auto" for that coverage only if:
>
> a. We already cover all "autos" that you own for that coverage or it replaces an "auto" you previously owned that had that coverage; and
>
> b. You tell us within 30 days after you acquire it that you want us to cover it for that coverage.

The policy also covers service trailers for liability insurance. A **service trailer** is a trailer with a load capacity of 2,000 pounds or less that is primarily designed for travel on public roads while it is attached to any power unit that the insured owns. Service trailers do not need to be listed in the policy for liability coverage, but they must be listed for physical damage coverage.

Coverage for mobile equipment is coordinated by complementary coverage wording in the Business Auto Coverage Form and the general liability coverage form. The Business Auto Coverage Form provides liability insurance for mobile equipment while it is being carried or towed by a covered auto, or unless the mobile equipment is classified as an auto in accordance with Symbol 19. The general liability coverage form insures mobile equipment except when the equipment is being carried or towed by a covered auto or when the use of the mobile equipment is subject to compulsory, financial responsibility, or other motor vehicle laws.

The Business Auto Coverage Form automatically provides liability coverage on an auto temporarily substituted for a covered auto if the coverage part provides liability insurance. The covered auto must be out of service because of its breakdown, repair, servicing, loss, or destruction. Coverage is excess over any other applicable insurance.

> **Service trailer**
> A trailer with a load capacity of 2,000 pounds or less that is primarily designed for travel on public roads while is it attached to any power unit that the insured owns.

Section II—Liability Coverage

The Business Auto Coverage Form will respond to a claim when all of the following are true:

- The insured must have a legal obligation to pay damages.
- The obligation must result from bodily injury or property damage.
- The injuries must be caused by an accident as defined by the policy.
- The accident must result from the ownership, maintenance, or use of a covered auto.

In addition to paying claimants for liability claims, the Business Auto Coverage Form covers the legal defense expenses for those claims. This duty to defend is provided only for claims covered by the policy. The insurer has the right to investigate, defend, and settle claims as it deems appropriate.

The Business Auto Coverage Form provides the following supplementary payments for defense expenses:

- Expenses that it incurs in the defense of claims
- Expenses incurred by the insured at the insurer's request, including up to $250 a day because of time off from work
- Court costs in any suit
- Up to $2,000 for the cost of bail bonds
- The cost of release of attachment bonds
- Post-judgment interest

These payments do not reduce the limits of insurance. However, the insurer's duty to defend or settle ends when the liability coverage limit of insurance has been exhausted by payment of judgments or settlements.

The liability coverage provided by the Business Auto Coverage Form protects not only the named insured but also permissive users and others responsible for the insured's conduct. The Business Auto Coverage Form's liability coverage does not extend to the owner of hired or borrowed autos unless the vehicle is a trailer. Also, the policy does not cover someone using a covered auto in selling, servicing, repairing, parking, or storing autos unless that is the insured's business.

The out-of-state coverage extension is a provision of the Business Auto Coverage Form that increases the policy limit to meet the compulsory, financial responsibility, and no-fault laws in a state in which the covered auto is being used. Under this provision, the insurer agrees to increase the policy limits to meet the requirements of any compulsory or financial responsibility law in a state in which a covered auto is being used. The out-of-state coverage extension does not apply to motor carriers who carry passengers or the property of others.

Unless otherwise endorsed, the Business Auto Coverage Form provides coverage on a single limit basis. One limit applies for all bodily injury and property damage claims arising from a single accident. In most jurisdictions, the minimum limit in the CLM is $25,000.

Section III—Physical Damage Coverage

Physical damage coverages for covered autos is an option available to insureds under the Business Auto Coverage Form. Physical damage coverage can be categorized as collision and other than collision, with other than collision having two versions: specified causes of loss coverage and comprehensive coverage.

Collision coverage is coverage for physical loss to a covered auto or its equipment caused by collision of a covered auto with another object or by overturn of the covered auto. **Specified causes of loss coverage** is coverage for physical loss to a covered auto or its equipment caused by fire, lightning, explosion, theft, windstorm, hail, earthquake, flood, mischief, or vandalism, or resulting from the sinking, burning, collision, or derailment of any conveyance

Collision coverage
Coverage for physical loss to a covered auto or its equipment caused by collision of a covered auto with another object or by overturn of the covered auto.

Specified causes of loss coverage
Coverage for physical loss to a covered auto or its equipment caused by fire, lightning, explosion, theft, windstorm, hail, earthquake, flood, mischief, or vandalism; or resulting from the sinking, burning, collision, or derailment of any conveyance transporting the covered auto.

transporting the covered auto. **Comprehensive coverage** is coverage, subject to certain exclusions, for physical loss to a covered auto or its equipment resulting from any cause except collision or overturn.

The most the insurer will pay for physical damage loss is the covered auto's actual cash value or the cost to repair or replace the auto, whichever is less—minus the applicable deductible.

Section IV—Business Auto Conditions

Section IV of the Business Auto Coverage Form states the conditions applicable to the policy in addition to the common policy conditions. The common policy conditions state that the insured's books and records are subject to examination by the insurer. Such an examination may result in a premium adjustment so that the premium charged reflects actual loss exposures insured.

Section V—Definitions

Words or phrases in the policy that are given a particular definition include accident, auto, bodily injury, insured, contract, loss, mobile equipment, property damage, suit, and trailer. Premium auditors should be familiar with these definitions, especially the auto and mobile equipment definitions because they directly affect the premium audit.

Auto has a broad definition that is limited primarily by what individual states choose not to register or license for public highway use. The Business Auto Coverage Form defines **auto** as a land motor vehicle, trailer, or semitrailer designed for travel on public roads, including attached machinery or equipment, but excluding mobile equipment that is not subject to compulsory, financial responsibility, or other motor vehicle insurance laws. This definition of auto includes mopeds, motorcycles, three-wheeled vehicles, motor homes, cars, trucks, tractor-trailer combinations, forklift trucks, and backhoes. This will vary from state to state. State motor vehicle insurance laws apply.

The Business Auto Coverage Form defines "mobile equipment" to include various types of vehicles generally not designed for use on public roads and that are excluded from state motor vehicle insurance laws. **Mobile equipment** may include any of the following types of equipment: bulldozers, farm machinery, forklifts, cranes, and road construction or resurfacing equipment. The Business Auto Coverage Form does not provide liability insurance for mobile equipment unless it is being carried or towed by a covered auto or is subject to compulsory, financial responsibility, or other motor vehicle insurance laws. General liability policies cover mobile equipment except while being carried or towed by an auto or when subject to compulsory, financial responsibility, or other motor vehicle insurance laws. Insurers ordinarily insure physical damage to mobile equipment of any type in an inland marine policy such as a contractors' equipment floater. However, mobile equipment that must be insured for liability insurance on a Business Auto Coverage Form can also be insured for physical damage on a Business Auto Coverage Form as well.

Comprehensive coverage
Coverage, subject to certain exclusions, for physical loss to a covered auto or its equipment resulting from any cause except collision or overturn.

Auto
A land motor vehicle, trailer, or semitrailer designed for travel on public roads, including attached machinery or equipment, but excluding mobile equipment that is not subject to compulsory, financial responsibility, or other motor vehicle insurance laws.

Mobile equipment
Various types of vehicles generally not designed for use on public roads and that are excluded from state motor vehicle insurance laws.

Endorsements

Endorsements are often added to the Business Auto Coverage Form to meet the insurance needs of the insured. Frequently used endorsements include drive-other-car coverage, nonownership liability, hired autos, individual as the named insured, medical payments, and no-fault coverages.

Drive-Other-Car Coverage (Rule 88)

Insurers can endorse the Business Auto Coverage Form to provide coverage for use (by individuals named in the endorsement and their spouses) of autos not owned by either the named insured or by the named individual. By attaching the Drive-Other-Car Coverage—Broadened Coverage for Named Individuals Endorsement (CA 99 10), any individual named in the endorsement (and his or her spouse) can be covered for liability, medical payments, uninsured motorists, comprehensive, and collision. The policy provides only those coverages for which a premium is shown in the endorsement schedule or in the declarations. A spouse who resides with the named individual receives the same coverage without being specifically named in the endorsement. The rates for this coverage are shown in the state rate pages.

Nonownership Liability (Rule 89)

Employers have a liability exposure for employees using autos in the course of their employment even though the employer does not own such autos. For example, an employee may use his or her own auto to pick up supplies or run errands for the employer. Although the employee's own personal auto insurance would normally cover the employer as an additional interest, the employer cannot be certain that such coverage is adequate in every situation. For example, a personal auto policy may not cover the particular auto driven by the employee at the time of the loss. Also, the employee may not have high enough liability limits. Likewise, some action of the employee may void the employee's coverage. The premium auditor should always question employees' use of their own vehicles and specify the use of those vehicles.

Symbols 1 and 9 of the Business Auto Coverage Form allow the employer to protect against that exposure. However, this does not protect the employee unless the employer has endorsed its policy (using the Employees as Insureds Endorsement—CA 99 33). Without that endorsement, the employee must rely on his or her own personal policy for protection.

The insurer determines the premium by the insured's total number of employees. If the insured is a partnership, the insurer bases the premium on the number of active employees and partners and the insurer's private passenger-type rates in the CLM. Nonownership liability also covers the insured's liability arising from vehicles owned by the named insured's partners. This coverage protects only the partnership, not the individual partners. There is no standard endorsement to provide coverage for the partners in such a situation; they must rely on their own policies.

If the insured is a social service agency, the insurer determines the advance premium charge for the use of autos based on the number of employees. To cover the exposure created by the volunteers, the insurer bases the premium on the total number of volunteers who regularly use their own autos to transport social service clients in connection with the agency's programs. Similar to the absence of coverage for employees when operating their own vehicles, there is no coverage for the volunteers for social service agencies unless the policy is so endorsed; if that coverage is desired, Social Service Agencies—Volunteers as Insureds Endorsement (CA 99 34) can be attached to the policy.

The insurer considers the advance premium for that coverage the earned premium unless a substantial change in exposure occurs during the policy period. The premium brackets in terms of number of employees are broad (0-25; 26-100; 101-500; 501-1,000; and over 1,000). Because a substantial change in exposure (number of employees) does not occur frequently, few insurers require a premium audit for this exposure.

If the insured has nonownership liability coverage and the premium auditor discovers (possibly when auditing a different coverage) that the majority of the insured's employees regularly use their own vehicles in the employer's business, the premium auditor should notify the underwriter because Rule 89 does not apply when more than 50 percent of the insured's employees regularly operate their autos in the insured's business. Rating in that case is on a refer-to-company basis. Nonownership coverage is included in the garage liability form, so the rule does not apply to garage loss exposures.

Hired Autos (Rule 90)

The Business Auto Coverage Form, Symbols 1 and 8, include coverage for liability arising from all autos leased, hired, rented, or borrowed except autos leased, hired, rented, or borrowed from any employee, partner, LLC member, or members of their households. The long-term leasing of autos is a popular alternative to ownership for many firms. In those situations, the lessee (the vehicle's renter) frequently chooses or is required to provide primary coverage for both the lessor and the lessee. Different rating instructions apply depending on which party is responsible for the primary insurance.

If the insured (lessee) is responsible for providing the primary insurance covering the auto, the rule states that autos leased for six months or more are rated as owned autos. In this situation, the Lessor—Additional Insured And Loss Payee (CA 20 01) is available, and it identifies the lessor (vehicle owner and leasing company) as an additional insured and loss payee under the policy. The lessor usually requires a copy of the endorsement because it describes the coverage and the policy limits that apply, and stipulates that the insurer will notify the lessor if the policy is canceled, and that the lessor will receive payment, as its interest may appear, together with the insured in the event of a loss. The insurer increases the otherwise applicable liability rate for an owned auto by a factor stated in the *CLM*. If the insured leases the auto for less than six months, the rating is on a refer-to-company basis.

An alternative endorsement—the Hired Autos Specified as Covered Autos You Own Endorsement (CA 99 16)—is available. It states that the policy will consider hired autos described in the endorsement as owned autos and that the policy will cover such autos' owners as insureds under the policy for liability insurance with respect to that car only. The Additional Insured—Lessor Endorsement provides broader coverage to the lessor than does the Hired Autos Specified as Covered Autos You Own Endorsement. The latter does not require the insurer to give notice of cancellation to the lessor and does not make the lessor a loss payee.

Another situation in which a leased vehicle will be treated as an owned vehicle is with the Employee as Lessor Endorsement (CA 99 47). Insurers use this endorsement when an employee leases his or her auto to the employer. It designates the leased auto as an owned auto under the employer's auto coverage. The employee is also added as an insured. Such a leasing arrangement is usually a fringe benefit for the employee because the employer pays the cost to insure the vehicle under its Business Auto Coverage Form. Under such a plan, the employer leases the vehicle from the employee or officer for a nominal sum (such as $1 or $10 per year). The vehicle is rated as an owned vehicle on the employer's policy.

Otherwise, the vehicle owner's insurance is normally primary, so hired auto coverage is excess. The Business Auto Coverage Form states in the "other insurance" provision that "for any covered 'auto' you do not own, the insurance provided by this Coverage Form is excess over any other collectible insurance."[2] Separate rating rules apply if the insured is a common or contract carrier (trucker). Public transportation autos, moving van associations, and freight forwarding operations are all on a refer-to-company basis.

Cost-of-hire basis
The premium basis for hired autos on a business auto policy. It is an estimate of the amount an insured will spend on hiring autos, excluding charges for truckers; autos owned by the named insured; employees', partners', or members' autos; and public autos.

For all other hired autos, the basis of premium for liability coverage is the cost-of-hire. The **cost-of-hire basis** is the premium basis for hired autos on a business auto policy. It is an estimate of the amount an insured will spend on hiring autos, excluding charges for truckers; autos owned by the named insured; employees', partners', or members' autos; and public autos. The policy covers borrowed vehicles at no charge because there is no cost of hire. Cost of hire does not include the following:

- Charges for vehicles that are not covered or are rated under a different method
- Charges for a driver when the vehicle is hired without a driver
- Charges for services provided by a trucker (The *CLM* defines a trucker as follows: "a person or organization in the business of transporting goods, materials or commodities for another.")[3]

When the insurer provides hired auto coverage (by using Symbol 1 or 8 on the declarations), the premium auditor should charge the actual exposure premium or the minimum premium, whichever is higher. The premium auditor must charge at least the minimum if it provides the coverage and no exposure develops. The minimum charge for hired autos is separate from the amount charged for nonownership coverage. As with nonownership liability, the advance premium is the earned premium unless a substantial change in exposures occurs during the policy period.

When developing the premium for hired auto coverage, the premium auditor should remember that cost-of-hire does not apply to any of the following:

- Truckers
- Autos owned or registered in the named insured's name
- Autos leased, hired, rented, or borrowed from any of the named insured's employees or partners or members of their households
- Public autos (other than social service agencies), moving van associations, and freight forwarding operations
- Autos hired, loaned, leased, or furnished to the named insured and for which the named insured is responsible for the primary insurance

Insurers can provide physical damage coverage for hired autos if they are hired, leased, rented, or borrowed without drivers. The premium is also based on total cost of hire. If the vehicles are leased, rented, hired, or borrowed with drivers, the insurer can provide coverage by attaching the Autos Leased, Hired, Rented or Borrowed With Drivers—Physical Damage Coverage Endorsement (CA 20 33). Physical damage coverage for vehicles leased, rented, hired, or borrowed with drivers is on a refer-to-company basis.

Individual as the Named Insured (Rule 91)

When the named insured under a Business Auto Coverage Form is an individual, the CLM requires that the insurer attach the Individual Named Insured Endorsement (CA 99 17). The endorsement's main effect is to provide the insured with coverage equivalent to that of a personal auto policy if the insured owns a private passenger-type auto (including a nonbusiness usage pickup truck or van). Therefore, when a person owns a business as a sole proprietor and owns both private passenger and commercial vehicles, the insurer does not have to issue separate policies to provide the insured and family members with personal auto coverage. Because the personal auto policy provides several additional coverages automatically, coverage should be carefully reviewed to ensure that no desired coverages are missing when the vehicle is insured under the Business Auto Coverage Form.

Medical Payments (Rule 92)

Both insureds and insurers regard medical payments as a useful optional coverage. The insurer's paying medical bills often assists in controlling bodily injury claims that would otherwise be difficult to handle. Some insureds do not desire medical payments coverage because their vehicles are occupied only by employees for business purposes; medical payments coverage excludes bodily injury to any of the insured's employees arising out of their employment. Although workers' compensation does cover such cases, insurers encourage medical payments coverage when an insured's vehicles are available for personal use or when nonemployees may be exposed to accidents as passengers. In states that have no-fault laws, discussed later, medical payments are a much less important coverage.

Medical payments coverage is triggered by entering the symbol next to Auto Medical Payments in Item Two of the declarations page. The Auto Medical Payments Coverage Endorsement (CA 99 03), shown in Exhibit 9-10, must also be added to the policy. Medical payments is less a classification problem than an issue of identifying vehicles covered and premiums charged.

No-Fault Coverages (Rule 93)

No-fault automobile insurance
A first-party automobile coverage that pays benefits, regardless of who is at fault, for medical expenses, loss of income, loss of services, and funeral expenses resulting from bodily injury to occupants of a covered auto because of an auto accident.

For premium audit purposes, **no-fault automobile insurance** is a first-party automobile coverage that pays benefits, regardless of who is at fault, for medical expenses, loss of income, loss of services, and funeral expenses resulting from bodily injury to occupants of a covered auto because of an auto accident. The symbol next to "Personal Injury Protection" (or equivalent no-fault coverage) in Item Two of the declarations page triggers this coverage. The insurer must attach an endorsement to the policy for each state no-fault act. Usually, when no-fault acts are in force, the coverage becomes mandatory for prescribed vehicle types. No-fault coverages are a state exception in all cases. Vehicles to which a particular no-fault law may apply include all motor vehicles, private passenger types only, all vehicles except motorcycles, or all vehicles except government-owned vehicles. The no-fault rules in the *CLM* "Division One—Automobile" and in the state pages for applicable states give details.

Normally, insurers charge no-fault premiums only for applicable vehicles principally garaged or registered in the no-fault state. Policy provisions extend the minimum amounts and types of no-fault coverage required by the jurisdiction for out-of-state vehicles being used in the state at no extra charge. When the premium auditor finds a vehicle subject to no-fault laws that was not listed on the policy as such, he or she should notify the underwriter.

Rental Reimbursement (Rule 94)

The Business Auto Coverage Form's comprehensive and specified causes-of-loss coverages include transportation expenses when a covered private passenger auto is stolen. The insurer can extend the policy by attaching the Rental Reimbursement Coverage Endorsement (CA 99 23) to cover costs for renting a substitute auto when a covered auto is damaged by a physical damage peril.

The insured can select any limit per day and any number of days for coverage to apply, except that the minimums are $15 per day and thirty days. The premium is the number of automobiles multiplied by the maximum daily reimbursement multiplied by the maximum number of days multiplied by the rate listed in the state rate pages.

EXHIBIT 9-10

Auto Medical Payments Coverage Endorsement

COMMERCIAL AUTO
CA 99 03 07 97

THIS ENDORSEMENT CHANGES THE POLICY. PLEASE READ IT CAREFULLY.

AUTO MEDICAL PAYMENTS COVERAGE

This endorsement modifies insurance provided under the following:

BUSINESS AUTO COVERAGE FORM
GARAGE COVERAGE FORM
MOTOR CARRIER COVERAGE FORM
TRUCKERS COVERAGE FORM

With respect to coverage provided by this endorsement, the provisions of the Coverage Form apply unless modified by the endorsement.

A. Coverage

We will pay reasonable expenses incurred for necessary medical and funeral services to or for an "insured" who sustains "bodily injury" caused by "accident". We will pay only those expenses incurred, for services rendered within three years from the date of the "accident".

B. Who Is An Insured

1. You while "occupying" or, while a pedestrian, when struck by any "auto".

2. If you are an individual, any "family member" while "occupying" or, while a pedestrian, when struck by any "auto".

3. Anyone else "occupying" a covered "auto" or a temporary substitute for a covered "auto". The covered "auto" must be out of service because of its breakdown, repair, servicing, loss or destruction.

C. Exclusions

This insurance does not apply to any of the following:

1. "Bodily injury" sustained by an "insured" while "occupying" a vehicle located for use as a premises.

2. "Bodily injury" sustained by you or any "family member" while "occupying" or struck by any vehicle (other than a covered "auto") owned by you or furnished or available for your regular use.

3. "Bodily injury" sustained by any "family member" while "occupying" or struck by any vehicle (other than a covered "auto") owned by or furnished or available for the regular use of any "family member".

4. "Bodily injury" to your "employee" arising out of and in the course of employment by you. However, we will cover "bodily injury" to your domestic "employees" if not entitled to workers' compensation benefits. For the purposes of this endorsement, a domestic "employee" is a person engaged in household or domestic work performed principally in connection with a residence premises.

5. "Bodily injury" to an "insured" while working in a business of selling, servicing, repairing or parking "autos" unless that business is yours.

6. "Bodily injury" caused by declared or undeclared war or insurrection or any of their consequences.

7. "Bodily injury" to anyone using a vehicle without a reasonable belief that the person is entitled to do so.

8. "Bodily Injury" sustained by an "insured" while "occupying" any covered "auto" while used in any professional racing or demolition contest or stunting activity, or while practicing for such contest or activity. This insurance also does not apply to any "bodily injury" sustained by an "insured" while the "auto" is being prepared for such a contest or activity.

D. Limit Of Insurance

Regardless of the number of covered "autos", "insureds", premiums paid, claims made or vehicles involved in the "accident", the most we will pay for "bodily injury" for each "insured" injured in any one "accident" is the Limit Of Insurance for Auto Medical Payments Coverage shown in the Declarations.

No one will be entitled to receive duplicate payments for the same elements of "loss" under this coverage and any Liability Coverage Form, Uninsured Motorists Coverage Endorsement or Underinsured Motorists Coverage Endorsement attached to this Coverage Part.

CA 99 03 07 97   Copyright, Insurance Services Office, Inc., 1996   Page 1 of 2   ☐

Continued on next page

E. Changes In Conditions

The Conditions are changed for Auto Medical Payments Coverage as follows:

1. The Transfer Of Rights Of Recovery Against Others To Us Condition does not apply.

2. The reference in Other Insurance in the Business Auto and Garage Coverage Forms and Other Insurance – Primary And Excess Insurance Provisions in the Truckers and Motor Carrier Coverage Forms to "other collectible insurance" applies only to other collectible auto medical payments insurance.

F. Additional Definitions

As used in this endorsement:

1. "Family member" means a person related to you by blood, marriage or adoption who is a resident of your household, including a ward or foster child.

2. "Occupying" means in, upon, getting in, on, out or off.

Page 2 of 2 Copyright, Insurance Services Office, Inc., 1996 **CA 99 03 07 97** ☐

Audio, Visual, and Data Electronic Equipment (Rule 95)

Physical damage coverages exclude loss of or damage to a variety of audio, visual, and electronic equipment. The Business Auto Coverage Form excludes the following: (1) tapes, records, discs, or other similar audio, visual, or data electronic devices designed for use with audio, visual, or data electronic equipment; (2) radar detectors; (3) all electronic equipment, permanently installed or not, that receives or transmits audio and visual or data signals and that is not designed solely for reproduction of sound; and (4) any accessories for the equipment in (3). The policy gives an exception to the exclusions in (3) and (4) relating to permanently installed equipment with some other qualifications. Because cars also use computers in their operation, the policy clarifies that it does cover such equipment.

The insurer can add coverage for some of the excluded equipment by using the Audio, Visual And Data Electronic Equipment Coverage Endorsement (CA 99 60). The state rate pages base the charge for this coverage on the equipment's cost new. Insurers can use a different endorsement (at no premium charge) to remove the exclusion for emergency vehicles such as fire and police.

Tapes, Records, and Discs (Rule 96)

As noted, the Business Auto Coverage Form excludes loss to tapes, records, discs, and similar devices even when used with permanently installed equipment. The insurer can add coverage by attaching the Tapes, Records, and Discs Coverage Endorsement (CA 99 30) for a flat charge per auto.

Uninsured and Underinsured Motorists Insurance (Rule 97)

Protection against uninsured motorists enables an insured and any passengers to recover damages, normally for bodily injury only, due the insured because of the negligence of an uninsured motor vehicle's owner or driver. An **uninsured motor vehicle** is any type of land motor vehicle or trailer that is not insured for bodily injury liability, that is insured for less than the financial responsibility limits, that is a hit-and-run vehicle, or whose insurer denies coverage or becomes insolvent.

Uninsured motor vehicle
Any type of land motor vehicle or trailer that is not insured for bodily injury liability, that is insured for less than the financial responsibility limits, that is a hit-and-run vehicle, or whose insurer denies coverage or becomes insolvent.

Coverage can also be provided for damages from an underinsured motor vehicle. An **underinsured motor vehicle** is any type of land motor vehicle or trailer that is insured for bodily injury liability but at limits that are lower than the underinsured limit the insured has selected in its policy. This coverage applies when the insured is involved in a not-at-fault accident with a vehicle that is insured for bodily injury liability but at limits that are lower than the underinsured limit the insured has selected in its policy. The selected limit is the maximum that the insured can collect. In some states, uninsured and underinsured coverages are combined in one endorsement. Other states require separate endorsements for each coverage.

Uninsured motorists insurance is compulsory in most states and subject to rejection by the insured in some states. Some states require uninsured motorists coverage equal to the bodily injury limits on the policy unless the insured signs a rejection form and the insurer has that form in its files.

The uninsured motorists bodily injury limits are normally only those required by the financial responsibility law of the state in which the insured vehicle is principally garaged. Certain states have provided for optional increased limits for bodily injury liability. A few states have additionally provided for property damage liability coverage on a deductible basis. The CLM "Division One—Automobile" rules make uninsured motorists coverage a state exception in every case. State pages for the state in which the vehicle is principally garaged provide coverage details and rates.

Uninsured motorists coverage provides coverage for officers, partners, and employees who use a company vehicle for personal purposes. They may be able to collect benefits greater than those available through workers' compensation; the policy reduces benefits payable under this endorsement by any benefits a covered person collects under workers' compensation.

The uninsured motorists charge is a set amount per covered vehicle or set of dealer or transporter plates. A set of plates is the number required for legal vehicle operation in the state of registration. The symbol typed next to "Uninsured Motorists" in Item Two of the declarations page indicates those vehicles with uninsured motorists coverage.

> **Underinsured motor vehicle**
> Any type of land motor vehicle or trailer that is insured for bodily injury liability but at limits that are lower than the underinsured limit the insured has selected in its policy.

TRUCKS, TRACTORS, AND TRAILERS CLASSIFICATION

The CLM classifies trucks, tractors, and trailers using a multi-phase classification system. This classification system results in a five-digit classification code. The elements of this classification system are as follows:

- Primary classification
  - Weight class
  - Business use
  - Radius class
- Secondary classification

Primary Classification

The primary classification incorporates vehicle weight, business use, and radius class. Although the same rules apply for primary classification selection, the CLM uses different digits and rates for nonfleet versus fleet vehicles.

Weight Class

The first step in determining a vehicle's primary classification is to determine the vehicle's weight class. The CLM provides for nine weight classes that coincide with general vehicle types. These weight classes are described next; however, they depend on a specific means of measuring vehicle weight that precludes the insurer's need to weigh each vehicle insured. The two measures of vehicle weight are gross vehicle weight and gross combinations weight. **Gross vehicle weight (GVW)** is the maximum loaded weight for which a single vehicle is designed, as specified by the manufacturer. **Gross combination weight (GCW)** is the maximum loaded weight for a combination truck-tractor and semitrailer or trailer for which the truck-tractor is designed, as specified by the manufacturer. Because truck-tractors (the power unit) can be used with semitrailers and trailers of various weights, the CLM provides that the GCW be determined with the weight of the heaviest semitrailer or trailer that the tractor could pull.

Because GVW and GCW are fundamental to determining a vehicle's weight class and consequently the primary classification, insurers usually rely on reference publications or the manufacturer's specifications to determine a vehicle's weight class. The VIN number is often used by reference publications to identify the specifications, including GVW and GCW, of a particular vehicle.

Light truck is a CLM vehicle size classification for trucks with a gross vehicle weight (GVW) of 10,000 pounds or less. Most vehicles in this group are of the pickup or light van type, but some pickups or light vans may have a GVW up to 17,000 pounds, depending on model size, so the premium auditor should check the GVW.

Medium truck is a CLM vehicle size classification for trucks with a gross vehicle weight (GVW) of 10,001 pounds to 20,000 pounds. Premium auditors must use particular care to determine the manufacturer's GVW on the vehicles that fit into this group. Registered weights are often unrelated to the GVW for the 1 1/2-ton or 2-ton trucks that are common in this category. Insureds usually buy the truck for the volume it can carry rather than for the weight it can carry. Premium auditors often find a truck with GVW over 10,001 pounds registered below 10,000 pounds, or a vehicle with GVW over 20,000 pounds registered below 20,000 pounds. This class includes crawler-type trucks.

Heavy truck is a CLM vehicle size classification used for trucks with a GVW of 20,001 pounds to 45,000 pounds. Manufacturers frequently refer to these as "2 1/2-ton" to "5-ton" trucks, although the "5-ton" truck usually has a GVW in excess of 45,000 pounds. Premium auditors must use the manufacturer's specified GVW, not the registered weight.

Gross vehicle weight (GVW)
The maximum loaded weight for which a single vehicle is designed, as specified by the manufacturer.

Gross combination weight (GCW)
The maximum loaded weight for a combination truck-tractor and semitrailer or trailer for which the truck-tractor is designed, as specified by the manufacturer.

Light truck
A CLM vehicle size classification for trucks with a gross vehicle weight (GVW) of 10,000 pounds or less.

Medium truck
A CLM vehicle size classification for trucks with a gross vehicle weight (GVW) of 10,001 pounds to 20,000 pounds.

Heavy truck
A CLM vehicle size classification for trucks with a gross vehicle weight (GVW) of 20,001 pounds to 45,000 pounds.

Extra-heavy truck is a *CLM* vehicle size classification for trucks with a GVW of over 45,000 pounds. Most of the trucks falling into this division have dual rear axles, but the premium auditor must still use the manufacturer's specified GVW to determine size. Large dump trucks and ready-mix (mix-in-transit) trucks are almost always in this category.

Heavy truck-tractor is a *CLM* vehicle size classification used for truck-tractors with a GCW of 45,000 pounds or less. Motorized autos equipped with a fifth-wheel coupling device for semitrailers sometimes fall into this weight size. Shuttle truck-tractors and a few truck-tractors used for intracity deliveries may fit into this size group. Pickup trucks with a fifth-wheel coupling device for pulling semitrailers belong in this category.

Extra-heavy truck-tractor is a *CLM* vehicle size classification for truck-tractors with a gross vehicle weight (GVW) of over 45,000 pounds.

Semitrailer is a *CLM* vehicle size classification for trailers equipped with a fifth-wheel coupling device for use with a truck-tractor and a load capacity of over 2,000 pounds. Premium auditors classify semitrailers strictly by load capacity and coupling device. This category includes containers that are converted into semitrailers.

Trailer is a *CLM* vehicle size classification for trailers with a load capacity over 2,000 pounds. Any trailer with a load capacity of over 2,000 pounds (other than a semitrailer) is classified as a trailer.

Service or utility trailer is a *CLM* vehicle size classification for trailers and semitrailers with a load capacity of 2,000 pounds or less. All trailers and semitrailers with a load capacity of 2,000 pounds or less are classified as service or utility trailers.

Determining the weight classification must be repeated for each vehicle listed in the policy. The next step in determining the primary classification is to determine the business use of each vehicle.

Business Use

Business use classifications reflect a vehicle's road exposure and are the second step in determining a vehicle's primary classification. Often, vehicles serve more than one purpose, thereby making business use classification problematic. However, the *CLM* provides that the highest rated (most costly) classification be used unless 80 percent or more of the vehicle's use is in a lower rated classification. The three business use classifications are service, retail, and commercial. However, the *CLM* does not have a business use classification for extra-heavy trucks (over 45,000 pounds GVW) and extra-heavy truck-tractors (over 45,000 pounds GCW).

Service use is a *CLM* commercial vehicle use classification that applies to vehicles used for transporting the insured's personnel, tools, equipment, and incidental supplies to or from a job location. The *CLM* confines this classification to autos the insured principally parks at job locations for the

Extra-heavy truck
A *CLM* vehicle size classification for trucks with a gross vehicle weight (GVW) of over 45,000 pounds.

Heavy truck-tractor
A *CLM* vehicle size classification for trucks with a gross combined weight (GCW) of 45,000 pounds or less.

Extra-heavy truck-tractor
A *CLM* vehicle size classification for truck-tractors with a gross vehicle weight (GVW) of over 45,000 pounds.

Semitrailer
A *CLM* vehicle size classification for trailers equipped with a fifth-wheel coupling device for use with a truck-tractor and a load capacity of over 2,000 pounds.

Trailer
A *CLM* vehicle size classification for trailers with a load capacity of over 2,000 pounds.

Service or utility trailer
A *CLM* vehicle size classification for trailers and semitrailers with a load capacity of 2,000 pounds or less.

Service use
A *CLM* commercial vehicle use classification that applies to vehicles used for transporting the insured's personnel, tools, equipment, and incidental supplies to or from a job location.

Retail use
A *CLM* commercial vehicle use classification that applies to vehicles used to pick up property from or deliver property to individual households.

Commercial use
A *CLM* commercial vehicle use classification that applies to vehicles used to transport property other than those vehicles defined as either service use or retail use.

Local radius
A radius class rating classification for vehicles operating within a 50-mile radius of the principal garaging location.

Intermediate radius
A radius class rating classification for vehicles regularly operating beyond a 50- to a 200-mile radius of the principal garaging location.

Long-distance radius
A radius class rating classification for vehicles regularly operating over a 200-mile radius of the principal garaging location.

Zone rating
A *CLM* commercial vehicle measurement of exposure that applies to trucks, truck-tractors, and trailers, other than light trucks and trailers used with light trucks, regularly operated beyond a 200-mile radius of the principal garaging location.

majority of the working day or uses to transport supervisory personnel between job locations. Examples of vehicles properly categorized as service use include those used by electricians and plumbers, as well as other artisan contractors, who make one or more service calls during the day. Vehicles classified as service use are considered to have less road exposure than other business use classifications.

Service use also includes product delivery as long as delivery is incidental to the installation of the product. However, if installation is incidental to the delivery of the product, the business use classification that should be applied is retail use.

Retail use is a CLM commercial vehicle use classification that applies to vehicles used to pick up property from or deliver property to individual households. Examples of vehicles properly categorized as retail use include furniture delivery, fuel oil, medical perscriptions, parcel delivery, and garbage collection. All these vehicles make periodic stops and have a relatively greater road exposure than service-use-classified vehicles and relatively less road exposure than commercial vehicles.

Commercial use is a CLM commercial vehicle use classification that applies to vehicles used to transport property other than those vehicles defined as either service use or retail use. Vehicles classified as commercial use typically have a significant road exposure, and the insurance premium for them is likewise greater than the other business use classifications.

Radius Class

The third step in determining a vehicle's primary classification is determining the applicable radius class. Radius class is measured on a straight line from the street address of principal garaging to the limit of the vehicle's regular operation. The three radius classes are local, intermediate, and long distance. **Local radius** is a radius class rating classification for vehicles operating within a 50-mile radius of the principal garaging location. **Intermediate radius** is a radius class rating classification for vehicles regularly operating beyond a 50- to a 200-mile radius of the principal garaging location. **Long-distance radius** is a radius class rating classification for vehicles regularly operating over a 200-mile radius of the principal garaging location. Exhibit 9-11 shows the three radius classes.

Another approach used in the CLM to develop an insurance premium for vehicles operating great distances is zone rating. **Zone rating** is a CLM commercial vehicle measurement of exposure that applies to trucks, truck-tractors, and trailers, other than light trucks and trailers used with light trucks, regularly operated beyond a 200-mile radius of the principal garaging location. The CLM divides the country into thirty-seven metropolitan zones and eleven regional zones. Zone determination depends on the terminal's location. A terminal is any point at which an auto regularly loads or unloads. The insured does not have to own or operate the terminal.

EXHIBIT 9-11

Radius Classes

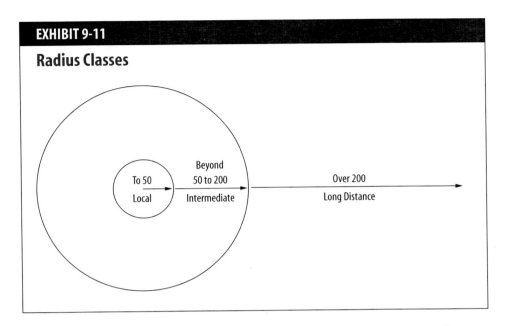

When a vehicle qualifies for zone rating, rating is based on the principal garaging zone and the zone of the terminal farthest from that point included in the auto's regular operations. For a vehicle garaged in a regional zone and operating from terminals in that zone plus terminals in one or more metropolitan zones, the proper zone combination is the regional zone and the farthest metropolitan zone.

Secondary Classification—Special Industry Classification

After the primary classification has been determined, the secondary classification is determined for each vehicle. The secondary classification is used to reflect the increased hazard associated with particular industries. Secondary classifications do not apply to zone-rated autos but do apply to zone-rated trucks, tractors, and trailers.

In addition to the main secondary classifications, the CLM has subclassifications for each secondary classification. The secondary classifications are as follows:

- Truckers
- Food delivery
- Specialized delivery
- Waste disposal
- Farmers
- Dump and transit mix
- Contractors
- Not otherwise specified

Truckers

The trucker secondary classification—special industry classification includes "a person or organization in the business of transporting goods, materials or commodities for another."[4] The CLM points out that an insured engaged in operations that meet this definition is assigned to the truckers secondary classification even if they advertise or describe themselves as a contractor, building contractor, building material dealer, or sand and gravel hauler.

To be classified as a trucker, goods, materials, or commodities transported must belong to another person or organization. Movers are classified as truckers, but they are not subject to the truckers secondary rating factors. Moving operations are the hauling of household goods, office furniture, and store fixtures and supplies for those not engaged in the manufacture, distribution, or sale of these items.

Trucker subclassifications are common carriers; contract carriers (other than iron or steel haulers); contract carriers hauling chemicals; contract carriers hauling iron and steel; exempt carriers (other than livestock haulers); exempt carriers hauling livestock; carriers engaged in both private carriage and transporting goods, materials, or commodities for others; tow trucks for hire; and all other.

Food Delivery

The food delivery secondary classification—special industry classification includes "autos used by food manufacturers to transport raw and finished products or used in wholesale distribution of food."[5] This definition covers food manufacturers when the vehicle is used to transport raw and finished products, and wholesale food distributors.

Food delivery includes beverages within the definition of food. It therefore applies to vehicles used by manufacturers, bottlers, or distributors to transport their products. Food delivery excludes trucks hauling exclusively nonedible products, but the classification wording does not limit food to that prepared for human consumption. Food delivery subclassifications include canneries and packing plants, fish and seafood, fruit and vegetable, meat and poultry, and all other.

Specialized Delivery

The specialized delivery secondary classification—special industry classification includes "autos used in deliveries subject to time and similar constraints."[6] Specialized delivery subclassifications include armored cars, film delivery, magazines or newspapers, mail and parcel post, and all other.

Waste Disposal

The waste disposal secondary classification—special industry classification includes "autos transporting salvage and waste material for disposal or resale."[7]

Waste disposal subclassifications include auto dismantlers, building wrecking operators, garbage, junk dealers, and all other.

Farmers

The farmers secondary classification—special industry classification includes "autos owned by a farmer, used in connection with the operation of his or her own farm and occasionally used to haul commodities for other farmers."[8] For this classification to apply, a farmer must own the vehicle, the farmer must use the vehicle in the operation of the farm, and the farmer may occasionally use the vehicle to haul for other farmers.

This classification also applies to ranchers. Delivery of produce to market comes within this use, but delivery to stores or homes involves the food delivery secondary classification. Farmers subclassifications include individually owned or family corporation (other than livestock hauling), livestock hauling, and all other.

Dump and Transit Mix

The dump and transit mix secondary classification—special industry classification applies only when no other secondary classification applies. Many garbage trucks, for instance, have a dumping hoist. The waste disposal secondary classification applies to those vehicles. The fundamental exposure of such trucks is the multi-stop pickup of quantities of garbage with a limited number of trips per day to a dump for disposal of the load. In this instance, the dumping operation is incidental to the vehicle's main purpose. The dump and transit mix secondary classification applies to vehicles of this type owned by contractors (even though the contractors classification is a separate secondary classification) because the contractors secondary class specifically excludes dump trucks. Dump trucks hauling for others should be classified as truckers. Special "used in dumping operations" collision rates shown on state rate pages should be used for dumping operation trucks (including ready-mix and mix-in-transit trucks), regardless of the secondary classification used. Normal rates apply to hopper-type transporters of dry commodities that unload through the bottom by gravity. Dump and transit mix subclassifications include excavating, sand and gravel (other than quarrying), mining, quarrying, and all other.

Contractors

The contractors classification applies to vehicles (other than dump trucks) used by contractors. Contractors subclassifications include building commercial; building private dwelling; electrical, plumbing, masonry, plastering, and other repair or service; excavating; street and road; and all other.

Not Otherwise Specified

The final secondary classification—special industry classification applies to vehicles not otherwise specified. "Not otherwise specified" subclassifications include logging and lumbering, and all other.

Fleet and Nonfleet

Fleet
A *CLM* commercial auto classification that applies to a policy that insures five or more self-propelled autos under one ownership.

A **fleet** is a *CLM* commercial auto classification that applies to a policy that insures five or more self-propelled autos under one ownership. This includes autos owned by allied or subsidiary interests in which the insured holds a majority financial interest. When counting self-propelled vehicles, the insurer does not include mobile equipment insured on a general liability policy. The premium auditor does not count trailers in determining fleet or nonfleet status, although the premium auditor classifies and rates them as either fleet or nonfleet according to the classification of the rest of the insured's operations. The premium auditor should not change fleet or nonfleet classification because of mid-term changes in the number of eligible self-propelled vehicles. In such situations, if the insured requests it, the insurer must cancel and rewrite the policy to comply with the *CLM* premium change rules governing change from fleet to nonfleet or vice versa. Although the rating procedure is the same, state rate pages shows factors that apply to the base rates for fleets.

PREMIUM AUDIT PROCEDURES

The objective of a commercial auto insurance premium audit should be to inventory owned autos. Before the audit visit, the premium auditor should review the policy, including any endorsements that have been attached, and prepare a vehicle inventory. An advance telephone call to the insured outlining the information needed is also a good practice.

During the audit, the premium auditor should review the insured's records (registration, invoices, bills of sale, and so on) and note the following information regarding vehicles other than private passenger-type vehicles on the prepared inventory:

- Acquisitions—Date acquired, year manufactured, make, model, type (such as pickup, stake, or tri-axle dump), garaging location, GVW or GCW, use, radius of operations, original cost new, and vehicle identification number.

- Deletions—Date sold, given away, junked, not licensed (or registered), or suspended. Laws and regulations do not permit suspension of insurance for insureds subject to financial responsibility laws, state or federal regulations pertaining to motor carriers (truckers or bus companies), or other compulsory insurance laws.

- Garaging location, radius class, size class, business use class, and secondary class.

For private passenger-type vehicles, the premium auditor must also gather the acquisition and disposal dates for those cars added or deleted during the year. In addition, the premium auditor must gather information regarding the age, use, operator experience, ownership, garaging location, and original cost new of each of the private passenger-type vehicles.

The state territory pages list the rating territories. The premium auditor determines the rating territory based on the street address of principal garaging. For any auto garaged at an employee's home, the premium auditor uses the employee's street address. This is common in sales or service operations such as marketing firms and appliance repair companies. If a street divides two rating territories, then the lower rated territory applies. For registration plates not issued for specific automobiles (dealer, repairer, or transporter plates), the premium auditor should consult the state exception pages. Some take the business's territory, while others take the territory of the auto using the plates.

Physical damage rating requires determining the **age group**, which is a classification of vehicles based on the vehicle's model year. Exhibit 9-12 shows the available age group codes. The current model year changes October 1 regardless of the actual model introduction date. Premium auditors use the age of the chassis to determine the age group of rebuilt or structurally altered automobiles.

Age group
A classification of vehicles based on the vehicle's model year.

EXHIBIT 9-12

Age Group Determination

Age Group Code	Model Year
1	Current model year
2	First preceding model year
3	Second preceding model year
4	Third preceding model year
5	Fourth preceding model year
6	All other model years

In determining the vehicle's original cost new for physical damage rating, the premium auditor must understand what the *CLM* means by that term. **Original cost new** is a valuation method for property based on the retail cost the original purchaser paid for the auto and its equipment. This valuation includes the cost before trade-in allowance; any federal, state, and local sales taxes or any other taxes charged in place of sales taxes; cost of any special equipment attached to the vehicle; and cost of special bodies or modification.

Original cost new
A valuation method for property based on the retail cost the original purchaser paid for the auto and its equipment.

Insureds can insure automobiles on a stated amount basis instead of on the original cost new basis. To do so, the Stated Amount Insurance Endorsement (CA 99 28) is attached to the policy. **Stated amount** is a valuation method that limits the insured's recovery after a loss to no more than the stipulated amount. This method of valuing property modifies the limit of insurance provision in the Business Auto Coverage Form so that the insurer's payment for a physical damage loss will be the least of the actual cash value of the damaged or stolen property, the cost of repairing or replacing the damaged or stolen property with property of like kind and quality, or the amount of insurance shown for the auto in the endorsement's schedule. It does not mean

Stated amount
A valuation method that limits the insured's recovery after a loss to no more than the stipulated amount.

that the insurer will pay that amount in case of a total loss. The payment is limited to the least of the stated amount, ACV, or the cost to repair or replace. Many insurers will write some vehicles, such as antique autos and other hard-to-value vehicles, only on a stated amount basis.

PERPETUAL INVENTORY SCHEDULES

Large, constantly changing auto fleets rated on a specified vehicle basis require special handling by the premium auditor. The insured should set up its records on a perpetual inventory basis.

The premium auditor should assist the insured in listing every owned automobile (or long-term leased vehicle the insured wants to cover on a primary basis) as of the policy effective date. The list should include the following information: description (year, make, model, and vehicle type), vehicle identification number (VIN), garaging location (city or town and state), manufacturer's gross weight (GVW or GCW), vehicle use, radius of operations, original cost new, date acquired (original autos—show policy effective date), and date deleted and reason.

As the insured acquires vehicles, the insured fills in the applicable columns. As vehicles are deleted, the insured completes the date deleted column with the date sold, junked, not registered, and so on. The premium auditor should advise the insured to obtain gross weights from the vehicle identification plates attached to the vehicle.

Composite Rated Policies

Composite rating is an optional pricing approach in which a premium base other than the one specified in the CLM is used to price an entire account. Composite rating can be more convenient for the insurer and the insured. For example, instead of using the various premium bases for a fuel oil dealer's account, the underwriter and the insured may agree to use gallons delivered as the premium base for the entire account. Gallons delivered is the premium basis for general liability coverage, which is simple for a premium audit and means that the premium audit for CGL can also be used for auto. In this example, the insured knows the auto and general liability insurance costs associated with every gallon of fuel oil delivered and can adjust the retail price accordingly. Many accounts want to have a consolidated premium base that enables them to readily determine costs when setting prices.

Insurers do not have to perform mid-term premium adjustments when, for example, vehicles are added or deleted on composite-rated accounts because changes in exposure (for example, gallons delivered in the preceding example) will be determined by premium audit at the end of the policy term. While a fuel oil dealer would usually be required to submit information on any autos added during the policy term, the underwriter will not have to have these autos rated to determine a premium for the remainder of the policy term. Rather, the increased exposure these autos present will be rated at the end of the policy term when the total amount of fuel oil delivered is known.

Composite rating differs from other pricing plans in that the insured receives—in theory, at least—no price advantage by being composite rated. If the estimated composite-rate base is overestimated at policy inception, the effect will be to give the insured a hidden premium reduction. In soft markets, low prices have led to abuses of composite rating. An account's premium under composite rating normally should not be substantially different than if it were determined without composite rating. Exhibit 9-13 shows how the premium for the fuel oil dealer may be determined using composite rating.

EXHIBIT 9-13

Composite Rating Example

Step 1—Calculate the premium for each individual coverage under the plan, using the class rates, premium basis, and experience and schedule rating plans for that coverage.

Coverage	Premium Base	Premium
Auto liability	Specified auto	$46,000
General liability	1,000 gallons	30,000
Total		$76,000

Step 2—Determine the new premium base.

Fuel Oil Dealer and Underwriter agreed to each use 1,000 gallons of fuel oil delivered as the premium basis for the entire account. Last year, Fuel Oil Dealer delivered 1,200,000 gallons of oil.

$1,200,000 \div 1,000 = 1,200$.

Step 3—Calculate the composite rate.

$\$76,000 \div 1,200 = \$63.33$ per 1,000 gallons of fuel oil delivered.

The composite rate can be adjusted. The composite rate is normally recalculated annually. The insurer or the insured, however, can request that the composite rate be recalculated if the class rates change or if the mix of the insured's exposures changes significantly.

Not all insureds are eligible for composite rating. Most insurers require eligible accounts to meet a specified minimum premium and that there be a practical or competitive justification for using this approach.

Coverage Symbols

The symbols on the declarations page designate which autos the policy covers. The premium auditor must follow the limitations or restrictions as specified by these symbols.

For Symbols 1 through 6, the premium auditor can handle additions or deletions of the designated autos at the premium audit. With Symbol 7, if the insured has not complied with the thirty-day reporting provision or the insurer does not insure all vehicles that an insured owns and the new vehicle does not replace an insured vehicle, there is no automatic coverage for newly acquired vehicles. The premium auditor should notify the underwriter, who can decide whether to endorse any additions or deletions. The premium auditor's responsibility is to provide the underwriter with all the information necessary to accomplish this. Regardless of symbol, the premium auditor should always correct classification errors.

Fleet and Nonfleet Designations

An earlier section explained the definition of fleet. The rule regarding not changing the fleet/nonfleet designation midterm applies when an insured acquires or eliminates autos after policy inception. The CLM does not intend this rule to apply when the insurer rates the insured incorrectly because of erroneous information. For example, the premium auditor should re-rate as a fleet an insured that had twenty-five autos at inception but was classified as nonfleet because the insured disclosed only four autos. The premium auditor should also notify the underwriter. The primary rating factors for fleet and nonfleet classification are the same, but the base rates can differ significantly.

SUMMARY

"Division One—Automobile" of the CLM gives the rules for commercial auto insurance. This line of insurance includes both liability and physical damage coverages for various land motor vehicles designed for travel on public roads. Separate sections within this division treat different types of motor vehicle operations: truckers, private passenger types, public transportation, garages and dealers, and special types and operations.

Insurers can write insurance for the many vehicles in this division on a business auto policy, a truckers policy, or a garage policy. The flexibility of those policies stems in large part from using covered auto symbols in the coverage form. Those symbols designate which coverages apply to which vehicles insured under the policy. Those policies can provide both liability and physical damage coverages, no-fault, medical payments, uninsured motorists, and other coverages by endorsement.

For hired autos, the basis of premium is cost-of-hire by state. For nonowned auto liability coverage, the basis of premium is the total number of the insured's employees.

If the insurer writes coverage on a truck on a specified-vehicle basis, the premium auditor must verify the covered vehicles schedule. Insurers base physical damage coverage limits on each vehicle's actual cash value or occasionally on a stated amount for each vehicle. The classification depends on several factors.

The primary classification represents a combination of the size, business use, and radius of operations of each vehicle. The secondary classification distinguishes various special industry classes.

Truckers as well as garages and dealers have special insurance needs and different premium computation rules. Accordingly, the next two chapters cover the sections of the *CLM* that deal with those lines.

CHAPTER NOTES

1. A.M. Best Company, *Best's Aggregates & Averages* (Oldwick, N.J.: A.M. Best Co., 2005), p. 605.

2. ISO Business Auto Coverage Form (CA 00 01 03 06), Section IV B.5.a. Copyright, ISO Properties, Inc., 2005.

3. Insurance Services Office, *Commercial Lines Manual*, "Division One—Automobile," Section II, Rule 24.A.1, http://info.iso.com (ISOnet, SIM–CA–MU; accessed Aug. 17, 2006).

4. *Commercial Lines Manual*, "Division One—Automobile," Section II, Rule 24.A.1.

5. *Commercial Lines Manual*, "Division One—Automobile," Section II, Rule 23.C.5.

6. *Commercial Lines Manual*, "Division One—Automobile," Section II, Rule 23.C.6.

7. *Commercial Lines Manual*, "Division One—Automobile," Section II, Rule 23.C.7.

8. *Commercial Lines Manual*, "Division One—Automobile," Section II, Rule 23.C.8.

Direct Your Learning

Motor Carrier Insurance and Premium Determination

Educational Objectives

After learning the content of this chapter and completing the corresponding course guide assignment, you should be able to:

▶ Describe the coverage provided by the Truckers Coverage Form, including the following:

- Seven items of the Truckers Coverage Form declarations page

- System of covered auto symbols used in the Truckers Coverage Form declarations

- Sections of the Truckers Coverage Form

▶ Describe the coverage provided by the Motor Carrier Coverage Form.

▶ Describe the premium audit implications of the MCS 90 Endorsement.

▶ Explain how the Motor Carrier Coverage Form addresses the issue of other insurance covering motor carriers' business auto loss exposures.

▶ Apply the ISO *Commercial Lines Manual* (CLM) rules applicable to each of the premium bases for the Truckers Coverage Form.

▶ Describe the CLM rules for rating private passenger-type vehicles written on business auto policies.

▶ Describe the premium bases, rating factors, and CLM rules for rating and classifying public autos.

▶ Describe the CLM rules for classifying and rating special vehicle types described in this chapter.

▶ Given a truckers or motor carrier case, classify an insured's auto loss exposures.

▶ Define or describe each of the Key Words and Phrases for this chapter.

CHAPTER

Develop Your Perspective

What are the main topics covered in the chapter?

Truckers have unique loss exposures as carriers exchange vehicle use and services to conduct commerce. Truckers and Motor Carrier Coverage Forms are designed to provide the flexible coverage required for these loss exposures. Unique premium bases are required to rate these loss exposures as well as those for private passenger-type vehicles, public vehicles, and special-use vehicles under the ISO *Commercial Lines Manual* (CLM).

Identify the loss exposures that are unique to truckers and special-use vehicles and methods for reflecting the loss exposures in the rates charged.

▶ How can loss exposures for public autos be determined when many drivers operate the vehicles?

▶ How can rates reflect the extent of a business's hired auto exposure that fluctuates every year?

Why is it important to learn about these topics?

Understanding how coverage is provided for a variety of exposures unique to truckers and special-use vehicles is fundamental to determining the proper rates.

Consider how coverage is provided for truckers during various types of exchanges.

▶ How is liability insurance provided when a truck bobtails or deadheads, and who provides it?

▶ How is liability and physical damage coverage provided during a trailer interchange, and who provides it?

How can you use what you will learn?

Evaluate methods for determining how carriers use their vehicles so that the appropriate rates can be charged for the loss exposures.

▶ How will you identify the extent of hauling done for others?

▶ How can you tell whether trucks have been rented to others?

Motor Carrier Insurance and Premium Determination

Commercial auto insurance is considerably more complicated when the insured is a trucker or motor carrier. In place of the Business Auto Coverage Form, the Truckers Coverage Form (CA 00 12) and the Motor Carrier Coverage Form (CA 00 20) provide auto insurance coverage for truckers and motor carriers and eliminate the need for special endorsements. Section II (Rule 24 specifically) of the *Commercial Lines Manual* (CLM) "Division One—Automobile" contains the rating and classification rules that apply to truckers and motor carriers, although the state exception pages also contain important information.

Insurers can rate truckers and motor carriers on a specified auto basis, a cost-of-hire basis, or a gross receipts basis. The specified auto basis requires the premium auditor to investigate changes in a fleet's composition during the policy period and to apply to each auto the rules concerning rating territories, vehicle class sizes, business use, and possibly zone rating. The premium determination is according to the rules for other trucks, tractors, and trailers. Insurers write trucks, tractors, and trailers hired by the insured on a cost-of-hire basis. Premium auditors must thoroughly understand the costs they should include when determining cost of hire. Truckers and motor carriers pose a special problem because they often rent their operating permits to others. The gross receipts basis requires the premium auditor to develop the premium base from the insured's records. Gross receipts rating is on a refer-to-company basis.

The Motor Carrier Coverage Form is similar to the Truckers Coverage Form in many respects. This chapter reviews the coverage for truckers, describes how that coverage differs from the motor carrier coverage, and explains the premium basis for truckers.

TRUCKERS COVERAGE FORM

Truckers are commonly subject to various intrastate and interstate regulations and to complex loss exposures that require special treatment. ISO devised truckers coverage (and later, motor carrier coverage) to meet the trucking industry's needs. One loss exposure that requires special treatment is truckers who must provide insurance coverage, on a primary basis, to any other trucker hauling for them. The Business Auto Coverage Form insures this type of loss exposure (hired auto) on an excess basis only. The frequent interchange of trailers between truckers and the practice of one trucker hiring another to operate under its permit are two other exposures that require special treatment. Truckers coverage eliminates the need to attach many special endorsements to provide the coverage truckers needed.

Not all truckers need or are even eligible for truckers coverage. Only those who fall within the *CLM* definition of trucker are eligible. Rule 24 of "Division One—Automobile" of the *CLM* defines **trucker** as "a person or organization in the business of transporting goods, materials or commodities for another." This definition is broad enough to encompass common and contract carriers subject to federal and state regulations; furniture movers; contractors; and building supply dealers who haul sand, gravel, and materials for others.

Some definitions pertaining to the trucking industry are important in understanding the coverages. A **carrier** is a person or an organization that has custody of property in transit. Three legal types of carriers exist. A **private carrier** is an organization carrying its own goods. A **contract carrier** carries goods of others under individually negotiated contracts of carriage. Finally, a **common carrier** is a carrier who carries persons or cargo of all persons from the general public. Truckers can be common or contract carriers. Private carriers (those who haul their own goods, materials, or commodities) and public or private passenger liveries (for example, buses, taxis, and limousines, called public autos in insurance terminology) are not eligible for the Truckers Coverage Form. Private carriers are not truckers according to the *CLM* definition, but are motor carriers. Insurance coverage for motor truck carriers can be written for private, contract, and common carriers. Private carriers can also be insured under the Business Auto Coverage Form. Coverage for public autos is provided by endorsement to the Business Auto Coverage Form, but it is discussed later.

One other important term in understanding trucking is "owner-operator." An **owner-operator** is a person who owns and operates his or her own truck or tractor. Trucking companies often contract with owner-operators to haul some goods using the owner-operators' truck-tractors and a trailer owned either by the owner-operator or by a trucking firm. Owner-operators play a major role in the trucking industry.

Owner-operators of trucks or truck-tractors who hire out their services to other truckers do not need truckers coverage even though these owner-operators come within the definition of a trucker. This exception exists because the truckers coverage of the trucking firms that engage them covers those owner-operators as insureds on a primary basis. However, when those owner-operators are not transporting goods for another, they are without insurance. For example, a trucker owning a truck-tractor may make a one-way trip hauling a firm's products using that firm's semitrailer. Once making the delivery, the trucker

Trucker
A person or organization in the business of transporting goods, materials or commodities for another.

Carrier
A person or an organization that has custody of property in transit.

Private carrier
An organization carrying its own goods.

Contract carrier
A carrier that carries goods of others under individually negotiated contracts of carriage.

Common carrier
A carrier who carries persons or cargo of all persons from the general public.

Owner-operator
A person who owns and operates his or her own truck or tractor.

may return home without the semitrailer attached. This situation is a bobtail operation. A **bobtail** is a truck-tractor operating without its trailer. The Truckers Coverage Form of the firm for which the trucker was hauling no longer covers the trucker (the truck-tractor's owner) because the trucker is not hauling for the firm while returning home. Insurers can arrange liability coverage for the exposure created by the nontrucking use of the vehicle (and for this loss exposure only). Insurers provide nontrucking coverage by attaching the Truckers—Insurance for Nontrucking Use endorsement (CA 23 09) to the Business Auto Coverage Form. The endorsement excludes a covered auto while used to carry property in any business and used in the business of anyone to whom the auto is rented.

Bobtail
A truck-tractor operating without its trailer.

A similar loss exposure exists when a trucking firm leases its combined truck-tractor and trailer to haul goods exclusively for another firm. While the truck is under lease, the policy of the firm for which the hauling is being performed covers the trucker. However, if the agreement is a one-way lease, the contract may cease when the trailer is unloaded. The insurance coverage also stops at this point. After unloading, the truck-tractor and trailer may return empty to its base location. This situation is called **deadheading**, which is operating a truck-tractor with a trailer that is empty. In insurance terminology, deadheading generally refers to an owner-operator's use of his or her tractor with an empty trailer while not under lease to a motor carrier (and therefore not covered under the motor carrier's auto policy). Insurers can use the same endorsement used with bobtailing (Truckers—Insurance for Nontrucking Use) to provide protection for deadheading.

Deadheading
Operating a truck-tractor with a trailer that is empty.

The Truckers Coverage Form is similar to the Business Auto Coverage Form. With the Business Auto Coverage Form, two declarations are available. One is used when the Common Policy Declarations are also attached, and one is used when Common Policy Declarations are not attached. The Truckers Coverage Form Declarations page (CA 00 13 or CA 00 14) also uses a set of covered auto symbols to designate the coverages that apply to each vehicle. The insurer can then combine the declarations with the Truckers Coverage Form, the necessary endorsements, the Common Policy Conditions, and the Common Policy Declarations page to form a complete policy. Insurers can include truckers coverage as part of a commercial package policy or issue it as a monoline policy.

Truckers Declarations (CA 00 13)

The Truckers Declarations (CA 00 13) is in nearly the same format as the Business Auto Declarations. The form has seven items, as follows:

- Item One—Insured Information
- Item Two—Schedule of Coverages and Covered Autos
- Item Three—Schedule of Covered Autos You Own
- Item Four—Schedule of Hired or Borrowed Covered Auto Coverage and Premiums

- Item Five—Schedule for Non-Ownership Liability
- Item Six—Trailer Interchange Coverage
- Item Seven—Schedule for Gross Receipts Rating Basis—Liability Coverage

Item One—Insured Information

Exhibit 10-1 shows the first two pages of the declarations, which include Item One and Item Two. Item One is identical to Item One of the Business Auto Coverage Form Declarations, listing the named insured, the policy number, and the named insured's form of business.

Item Two—Schedule of Coverages and Covered Autos

Item Two is similar to Item Two of the Business Auto Coverage Form Declarations, but it has some additional coverages, most of which deal with trailer interchange agreements. The mechanics of using the numerical symbols and entering the premium are the same as in the Business Auto Coverage Form. The symbols' descriptions, which are different from the business auto symbols, are located in the Truckers Coverage Form. Not shown in Exhibit 10-1 is the top of page 3 of the declarations page, which is also a part of Item Two and which lists the endorsements attached to the coverage form.

Item Three—Schedule of Covered Autos You Own

Item Three lists the vehicles owned at inception, with classification information, rates, and premiums. Exhibit 10-2 shows Item Three.

Item Four—Schedule of Hired or Borrowed Covered Auto Coverage and Premiums

Item Four is identical to the schedule in Item Four of the Business Auto Coverage Form Declarations page.

Item Five—Schedule for Non-Ownership Liability

Item Five shows the number of employees, the number of partners, and the premium for this coverage. Unlike the Business Auto Coverage Form, no separation is necessary for social service agencies. Exhibit 10-3 shows Item Five.

Item Six—Trailer Interchange Coverage

Item Six, shown in Exhibit 10-4, relates to the insured's liability for physical damage coverages on trailers not owned by the insured but in the insured's possession. A written trailer interchange agreement creates this liability. Using Symbol 48 next to one of the trailer interchange physical damage coverages in Item Two triggers this coverage. The schedule specifies the daily rate according to the coverage type shown in Item Two. A later section describes trailer interchange in more detail.

EXHIBIT 10-1

Commercial Auto Truckers Declarations

POLICY NUMBER:

COMMERCIAL AUTO
CA DS 14 03 06

TRUCKERS DECLARATIONS

COMPANY NAME AREA	PRODUCER NAME AREA

ITEM ONE

Named Insured:
Mailing Address:

Policy Period	
From:	
To:	At 12:01 A.M. Standard Time at your mailing address
Previous Policy Number:	

Form Of Business:

☐ Corporation   ☐ Limited Liability Company   ☐ Individual
☐ Partnership   ☐ Other:

In return for the payment of the premium, and subject to all the terms of this policy, we agree with you to provide the insurance as stated in this policy.

Premium shown is payable at inception: $

Audit Period (If Applicable): ☐ Annually   ☐ Semi-Annually   ☐ Quarterly   ☐ Monthly

Endorsements Attached To This Policy:
IL 00 17 – Common Policy Conditions (**IL 01 46** in Washington)
IL 00 21 – Broad Form Nuclear Exclusion (Not Applicable in New York)

Continued on next page

Countersignature Of Authorized Representative	
Name:	
Title:	
Signature:	
Date:	

Note

Officers' facsimile signatures may be inserted here, on the policy cover or elsewhere at the company's option.

ITEM TWO

Schedule Of Coverages And Covered Autos

This policy provides only those coverages where a charge is shown in the premium column below. Each of these coverages will apply only to those "autos" shown as covered "autos". **"Autos" are shown as covered "autos" for a particular coverage by the entry of one or more of the symbols from the Covered Autos Section of the Truckers Coverage Form next to the name of the coverage.**

Coverages	Covered Autos	Limit	Premium
Liability		$	$
Personal Injury Protection (Or Equivalent No-Fault Coverage)		Separately Stated In Each Personal Injury Protection Endorsement Minus $ _____ Deductible.	$
Added Personal Injury Protection (Or Equivalent Added No-Fault Coverage)		Separately Stated In Each Added Personal Injury Protection Endorsement.	$
Property Protection Insurance (Michigan Only)		Separately Stated In The Property Protection Insurance Endorsement Minus $ _____ Deductible For Each Accident.	$
Auto Medical Payments		$	$
Medical Expense And Income Loss Benefits (Virginia Only)		Separately Stated In Each Medical Expense And Income Loss Benefits Endorsement.	$
Uninsured Motorists		$	$
Underinsured Motorists (When Not Included In Uninsured Motorists Coverage)		$	$

Page 2 of 10   © ISO Properties, Inc., 2005   CA DS 14 03 06   □

EXHIBIT 10-2

Truckers Coverage Form Declarations—Item Three CA DS 14 03 06

ITEM THREE
Schedule Of Covered Autos You Own

Covered Auto Number:	
Town And State Where The Covered Auto Will Be Principally Garaged	
Description (Year, Model, Trade Name, Body Type, Serial Number (S), Vehicle Identification Number (VIN))	

Purchased:	Original Cost New	$	
	Actual Cost New (N) Or Used (U)	$	

Classification

Radius Of Operation	Business Use s=service r=retail c=commercial	Size GVW, GCW Or Vehicle Seating Capacity	Age Group	Primary Rating Factor Liab.	Primary Rating Factor Phy. Dam.	Secondary Rating Factor	Code

Except For Towing, All Physical Damage Loss Is Payable To You And The Loss Payee Named To The Right As Interests May Appear At the Time Of The Loss.

Coverages – Premiums, Limits And Deductibles
(Absence of a deductible or limit entry in any column below means that the limit or deductible entry in the corresponding Item Two column applies instead.)

Coverages	Limit	Premium
Liability	$	$
Personal Injury Protection	Stated In Each Personal Injury Protection Endorsement Minus $ Deductible Shown	$
Added Personal Injury Protection	Stated In Each Added Personal Injury Protection Endorsement	$
Property Protection Insurance (Michigan Only)	Stated In The Property Protection Insurance Endorsement Minus $ Deductible Shown	$
Auto Medical Payments	$	$
Medical Expense And Income Loss Benefits (Virginia Only)	Stated In Each Medical Expense And Income Loss Benefits Endorsement For Each Person	$
Comprehensive	Stated In Item Two Minus $ Deductible Shown	$
Specified Causes Of Loss	Stated In Item Two Minus $ Deductible Shown	$
Collision	Stated In Item Two Minus $ Deductible Shown	$
Towing And Labor	$ Per Disablement	$

EXHIBIT 10-3

Truckers Coverage Form Declarations—Item Five

ITEM FIVE
Schedule For Non-Ownership Liability

Rating Basis	Number	Premium
Number Of Employees		$
Number Of Partners		$
	Total Premiums	$

EXHIBIT 10-4

Truckers Coverage Form Declarations—Item Six

ITEM SIX
Trailer Interchange Coverage

Coverages	Limit Of Insurance	Daily Rate	Estimated Premium
Comprehensive	Stated In Item Two	$	$
Specified Causes Of Loss		$	$
Collision		$	$
		Total Premium	$

Item Seven—Schedule for Gross Receipts Rating Basis— Liability Coverage

Item Seven is a schedule for truckers coverage written on the gross receipts basis. The *CLM* does not allow the mileage basis for truckers. Item Seven includes a definition of gross receipts. Exhibit 10-5 shows Item Seven.

Truckers Coverage Form (CA 00 12)

The Truckers Coverage Form contains the following six sections:

- Section I—Covered Autos
- Section II—Liability Coverage
- Section III—Trailer Interchange Coverage
- Section IV—Physical Damage Coverage
- Section V—Truckers Conditions
- Section VI—Definitions

EXHIBIT 10-5

Truckers Coverage Form Declarations—Item Seven

Schedule for Gross Receipts Rating Basis—Liability Coverage

Location No:	
Estimated Yearly:	
Rates (Gross Receipts/Per $100)	
Liability	
Auto Medical Payments	
Medical Expense Benefits (VA Only)	
Income Loss Benefits (VA Only)	
Premiums	
Liability	$
Auto Medical Payments	$
Medical Expense Benefits (VA Only)	$
Income Loss Benefits (VA Only)	$

Location No:	
Estimated Yearly:	
Rates (Gross Receipts/Per $100)	
Liability	$
Auto Medical Payments	$
Medical Expense Benefits (VA Only)	$
Income Loss Benefits (VA Only)	$
Premiums	
Liability	$
Auto Medical Payments	$
Medical Expense Benefits (VA Only)	$
Income Loss Benefits (VA Only)	$

Location No:	
Estimated Yearly:	
Rates (Gross Receipts/Per $100)	
Liability	$
Auto Medical Payments	$
Medical Expense Benefits (VA Only)	$
Income Loss Benefits (VA Only)	$

Continued on next page

Premiums	
Liability	$
Auto Medical Payments	$
Medical Expense Benefits (VA Only)	$
Income Loss Benefits (VA Only)	$

Total Premiums	
Minimum Liability	$
Minimum Auto Medical Payments	$
Minimum Medical Expense Benefits (VA Only)	$
Minimum Income Loss Benefits (VA Only)	$
Liability	$
Auto Medical Payments	$
Medical Expense Benefits (VA Only)	$
Income Loss Benefits (VA Only)	$
Income Loss Benefits (VA Only)	$

When used as a premium basis:

Gross Receipts means the total amount to which you are entitled for shipping or transporting property during the policy period regardless of whether you or any other carrier originate the shipment or transportation. Gross Receipts includes the total amount received from renting equipment, with or without drivers, to anyone who is not a "trucker" and 15% of the total amount received from renting any equipment to any "trucker". Gross Receipts does not include:

A. Amounts you pay to railroads, steamship lines, airlines and other motor carriers operating under their own ICC or PUC permits.

B. Advertising Revenue.

C. Taxes which you collect as a separate item and remit directly to a governmental division.

D. C.O.D. collections for cost of mail or merchandise including collection fees.

E. Warehouse storage fees.

Most of the protection offered by the Truckers Coverage Form corresponds to the Business Auto Coverage Form, but certain provisions are modified and others added to meet unique truckers' loss exposures. The Truckers Coverage Form's insuring agreement, defense provisions, supplementary payments, and exclusions are identical to those of the Business Auto Coverage Form. The next sections concentrate on the differences between the two coverage forms.

Section I—Covered Autos

Section I lists the "Description of Covered Auto Designation Symbols." The symbols are not the same as in the Business Auto Coverage Form, but some correspond to those used with the Business Auto Coverage Form. Exhibit 10-6 summarizes the definitions of the symbols that insurers use in Item Two of the declarations page to designate the coverages provided.

Symbol 41 is used only for liability. This symbol, like Symbol 1 in the Business Auto Coverage Form, indicates automatic coverage for any auto that the insured owns, maintains, or uses during the policy period, including autos that are acquired, borrowed, or hired.

Symbol 42 indicates automatic coverages for owned autos of any type. It can be used for liability, auto medical payments, uninsured motorists, and physical damage coverages. This symbol corresponds to Symbol 2 in the Business Auto Coverage Form.

Symbol 43 indicates automatic coverage for other than private passenger-type autos. This symbol corresponds to Symbol 4 in the Business Auto Coverage Form. The Truckers Coverage Form does not include a counterpart to Business Auto Coverage Form's Symbol 3, private passenger autos only.

Symbol 44 corresponds to Symbol 5 in the Business Auto Coverage Form. The coverage form provides automatic coverage for all the insured's owned autos that require no-fault coverage in the state in which they are licensed or principally garaged. The insurer must attach an endorsement to the policy to provide the specific state's no-fault coverage.

Using Symbol 45 designates automatic uninsured motorists coverage only for those states that have mandatory uninsured motorists laws that do not permit rejection. This symbol corresponds to Symbol 6 in the Business Auto Coverage Form.

EXHIBIT 10-6

Description of Covered Auto Designation Symbols for the Truckers Coverage Form

COMMERCIAL AUTO
CA 00 12 03 06

TRUCKERS COVERAGE FORM

Various provisions in this policy restrict coverage. Read the entire policy carefully to determine rights, duties and what is and is not covered.

Throughout this policy the words "you" and "your" refer to the Named Insured shown in the Declarations. The words "we", "us" and "our" refer to the Company providing this insurance.

Other words and phrases that appear in quotation marks have special meaning. Refer to Section **VI** – Definitions.

SECTION I – COVERED AUTOS

Item Two of the Declarations shows the "autos" that are covered "autos" for each of your coverages. The following numerical symbols describe the "autos" that may be covered "autos". The symbols entered next to a coverage on the Declarations designate the only "autos" that are covered "autos".

A. Description Of Covered Auto Designation Symbols

Symbol		Description Of Covered Auto Designation Symbols
41	Any "Autos"	
42	Owned "Autos" Only	Only the "autos" you own (and for Liability Coverage any "trailers" you don't own while connected to a power unit you own). This includes those "autos" you acquire ownership of after the policy begins.
43	Owned Commercial "Autos" Only	Only those trucks, tractors and "trailers" you own (and for Liability Coverage any "trailers" you don't own while connected to a power unit you own). This includes those trucks, tractors and "trailers" you acquire ownership of after the policy begins.
44	Owned "Autos" Subject To No-Fault	Only those "autos" you own that are required to have No-Fault benefits in the state where they are licensed or principally garaged. This includes those "autos" you acquire ownership of after the policy begins provided they are subject to the No-Fault law in the state where they are licensed or principally garaged.
45	Owned "Autos" Subject To A Compulsory Uninsured Motorists Law	Only those "autos" you own that, because of the law in the state where they are licensed or principally garaged, are required to have and cannot reject Uninsured Motorists Coverage. This includes those "autos" you acquire ownership of after the policy begins provided they are subject to the same state uninsured motorists requirement.
46	Specifically Described "Autos"	Only those "autos" described in Item Three of the Declarations for which a premium charge is shown (and for Liability Coverage any "trailers" you don't own while attached to any power unit described in Item Three).
47	Hired "Autos" Only	Only those "autos" you lease, hire, rent or borrow. This does not include any "private passenger type auto" you lease, hire, rent or borrow from any member of your household, any of your "employees", partners (if you are a partnership), members (if you are a limited liability company), or agents or members of their households.
48	"Trailers" In Your Possession Under A Written Trailer Or Equipment Interchange Agreement	Only those "trailers" you do not own while in your possession under a written "trailer" or equipment interchange agreement in which you assume liability for "loss" to the "trailers" while in your possession.

Symbol		Description Of Covered Auto Designation Symbols
49	Your "Trailers" In The Possession Of Anyone Else Under A Written Trailer Interchange Agreement	Only those "trailers" you own or hire while in the possession of anyone else under a written "trailer" interchange agreement. When Symbol "49" is entered next to a Physical Damage Coverage in Item Two of the Declarations, the Physical Damage Coverage exclusion relating to "loss" to a "trailer" in the possession of anyone else does not apply to that coverage.
50	Nonowned "Autos" Only	Only those "autos" you do not own, lease, hire, rent or borrow that are used in connection with your business. This includes "private passenger type autos" owned by your "employees", partners (if you are a partnership), members (if you are a limited liability company), or members of their households but only while used in your business or your personal affairs.
59	Mobile Equipment Subject To Compulsory Or Financial Responsibility Or Other Motor Vehicle Insurance Law Only	Only those "autos" that are land vehicles and that would qualify under the definition of "mobile equipment" under this policy if they were not subject to a compulsory or financial responsibility law or other motor vehicle insurance law where they are licensed or principally garaged.

Again, the insurer must attach an endorsement to the policy to provide the specific state's uninsured motorists coverage.

Symbol 46 provides coverage only for autos that the insurer lists in Item Three of the declarations page. This symbol provides coverage identical to that provided by Symbol 7 in the Business Auto Coverage Form.

Symbol 47 provides primary coverage for any auto the insured hires, leases, borrows, or rents, except for any private passenger-type owned by any member of the named insured's household, or the named insured's employees, partners, or agents, or members of their household. Liability coverage is excess for autos not used in the insured's trucking operations. Physical damage coverage is excess. This symbol can be used alone or in conjunction with Symbol 42, 43, or 46 for liability or physical damage. It cannot be used for no-fault, uninsured motorists, medical payments, or the trailer interchange coverages. Symbol 47 corresponds to Symbol 8 in the Business Auto Coverage Form.

Symbol 48 triggers trailer interchange coverage. A **trailer interchange agreement** is a contract under which two motor carriers agree to swap trailers and to indemnify each other for any damage that occurs to the other's trailer while it is in the borrowing motor carrier's possession. Ordinary wear and tear is excluded. This symbol provides the primary coverage needed on trailers owned by others and used by the insured under a written trailer agreement.

If the truckers have an even interchange of nonowned trailers and owned trailers under the agreement, with coverage ceasing when the owned trailers are in the other party's possession, the premium auditor makes no additional charge for this coverage. For example, if Trucker A and Trucker B each has five trailers covered by an interchange agreement, the premium auditor makes

Trailer interchange agreement
A contract under which two motor carriers agree to swap trailers and to indemnify each other for any damage that occurs to the other's trailer while it is in the borrowing motor carrier's possession.

no additional charge. Because Trucker A is liable for Trucker B's five trailers, and Trucker B is liable for Trucker A's five trailers, the insurers' (both A's and B's insurers) total liability remains the same.

When entered next to one of the physical damage coverages (comprehensive, collision, or specified causes of loss) in Item Two, Symbol 49 removes the exclusion in the physical damage coverage for the insured's trailers while they are in another trucker's possession under a trailer interchange agreement. This symbol should not be entered next to the trailer interchange physical damage coverages because those coverages apply only to nonowned trailers. Only Symbol 48 is appropriate there. Symbol 49 should be entered next to one of the physical damage coverages. When Symbol 49 is used, the insurer is providing primary coverage on owned trailers even when these trailers are in another trucker's possession.

Symbol 50 provides excess coverage for autos the insured uses in its business that the insured does not own, lease, hire, rent, or borrow. Symbol 50 coverage applies to private passenger-type autos owned by the named insured's employees, partners, or members of their household, but only while used in the named insured's business or personal affairs. This symbol is similar to Symbol 9 of the Business Auto Coverage Form, except that in the case of Symbol 50, coverage applies only to private passenger-type autos. Symbol 47 (hired autos) covers the commercial autos owned by the named insured's employees, partners, or members of their household.

Symbol 59 is identical to Symbol 19. It provides coverage for mobile equipment that is now excluded from coverage under the Commercial General Liability Coverage Form. As the new coverage forms are phased in, premium auditors will have to be alert to the added items that are subject to coverage.

Exhibit 10-7 summarizes the various covered auto symbols used with truckers coverage.

Section II—Liability Coverage

The major difference in the liability coverage between the business auto form and the truckers form pertains to coverages involving vehicles of others. The Business Auto Coverage Form excludes the owner or anyone else from whom the named insured leases, hires, rents, or borrows a covered auto. The Truckers Coverage Form excludes only the owner or anyone else from whom the named insured leases, hires, rents, or borrows a covered private passenger-type auto.

Like the Business Auto Coverage Form, the Truckers Coverage Form protects the hired or borrowed trailer's owner while the trailer is connected to an insured's tractor. However, the Truckers Coverage Form also provides coverage for the owner of a hired or borrowed auto while such a vehicle is used exclusively in the named insured's business as a trucker pursuant to operating rights granted to the named insured by a public authority.

EXHIBIT 10-7

Application of Symbols for Truckers Coverage Form

Coverage	Covered Auto Symbol										
	41	42	43	44	45	46	47	48	49	50	59
Liability	X	X	X			X	X			X	X
PIP					X						
Medical payments		X	X			X					
UM		X	X		X	X					X
Trailer interchange								X	X		
Physical damage*		X	X			X	X				X
Towing†		X				X					

* except towing
† private passenger vehicles only

Specifically excluded from insured status on the truckers form is any other trucker who is subject to motor carrier insurance requirements and who meets these requirements by a means other than auto liability insurance. This exclusion applies to truckers who are self-insured or bonded in compliance with federal regulations. Without this exclusion, the liability coverage provided by the insured's truckers coverage would remain primary (rather than excess) when the insured loans or rents (hires) the vehicle to another.

Also excluded is any other trucker who does not have hired auto liability coverage that covers on a primary basis the hired autos' owners (and their agents and employees) while the autos are being used exclusively in the truckers business pursuant to operating rights granted to the trucker by a public authority.

Likewise excluded is any rail, water, or air carrier or its employees or agents with respect to a detached trailer being transported by the carrier or being loaded or unloaded from the carrier's transportation unit.

Section III—Trailer Interchange Coverage

Using Symbol 48 in Item Two of the declarations page triggers trailer interchange coverage. The same options as physical damage coverage are available—comprehensive, specified causes of loss, and collision. Trailer interchange coverage applies only to trailers the insured does not own.

Section IV—Physical Damage Coverage

The physical damage coverage in the Truckers Coverage Form specifically excludes losses to covered autos in another's possession under a written trailer interchange agreement. This exclusion does not apply to a loss payee. However, if the insurer pays the loss payee, the insured must reimburse the insurer for the payment.

The trucker who has possession of the trailer usually provides the coverage for damage to trailers being used in a written trailer interchange agreement. If the insured desires, the policy can provide coverage while the insured's trailers are being used under a written trailer interchange agreement by selecting Symbol 49, which removes the exclusion and extends the insured's coverage to owned trailers while possessed by others under a written trailer interchange agreement.

Section V—Truckers Conditions

The Business Auto Coverage Form excludes the owner or anyone else from whom the named insured hires or borrows a covered auto. In contrast, the Truckers Coverage Form, in many cases, covers owners and lessors of autos hired or borrowed by the named insured.

The truckers liability coverage is primary for covered autos hired or borrowed while the auto is used exclusively in the named insured's business as a trucker and pursuant to operating rights granted to the named insured by a public authority. The coverage is excess when another trucker hires or borrows a covered auto from the named insured.

The Truckers Coverage Form provides excess insurance for a covered trailer while connected to a power unit that is not a covered auto. If the power unit is a covered auto, the coverage for the trailer is on the same basis (primary or excess) as for the power unit.

For hired auto physical damage coverage, any covered auto the insured leases, hires, rents, or borrows is deemed to be a covered auto the insured owns. However, if the auto is leased, hired, rented, or borrowed with a driver, it is not a covered auto.

In all cases, coverage is primary for any liability assumed under an insured contract. (An insured contract is that part of any other contract or agreement pertaining to the insured's business under which the insured assumes the tort liability of another.)

Trailer interchange coverage is primary for any covered auto. The coverage provided by the Truckers Coverage Form is primary for any covered auto the named insured owns and excess for any covered auto the named insured does not own.

Section VI—Definitions

The Truckers Coverage Form contains two definitions not contained in the Business Auto Coverage Form and expands on a third. The truckers form defines **private passenger type** as "a private passenger or station wagon type 'auto' and includes an 'auto' of the pickup or van type if not used for business purposes." The form defines trucker as "any person or organization engaged in the business of transporting property by 'auto' for hire." (This is not the same definition used in the *CLM* in describing eligibility for trucker and motor carrier coverages.) The Business Auto Coverage Form specifies that semitrailers are included in the definition of trailer, but otherwise does not precisely define trailer or semitrailer. In trucking industry parlance, a trailer is a motorless wheeled vehicle designed for hauling, and a semitrailer is a trailer supported at the forward end by a truck tractor. The Business Auto Coverage Form defines trailer as including semitrailer. The Truckers Coverage Form expands on this by saying trailer "includes a semitrailer or a dolly used to convert a semitrailer into a trailer. But for Trailer Interchange Coverage only, 'trailer' also includes a container."

Private passenger type
A private passenger or station wagon type "auto"; includes an "auto" of the pickup or van type if not used for business purposes.

Endorsements

Although ISO designed the Truckers Coverage Form to reduce the need for endorsements, insurers can use nearly all the endorsements for the Business Auto Coverage Form with the Truckers Coverage Form. The Truckers endorsement (CA 23 20) and the Truckers—Insurance for Non-trucking Use endorsement (CA 23 09) are exceptions. Insurers can use those only with the Business Auto Coverage Form.

Some endorsements affect premium determination. When leased vehicles are involved, the insurer should attach one of two endorsements: the Truckers—Excess Coverage for the Named Insured and Named Lessors for Leased Autos endorsement (CA 23 08), which makes the liability coverage excess over any other collectible insurance, or the Truckers—Named Lessee as Insured endorsement (CA 23 12), which makes coverage primary for the lessee. Exhibits 10-8 and 10-9, respectively, show those two endorsements.

An example of the need for those endorsements may be when Trucker A (lessee) leases a covered auto from Owner B (lessor). In most cases, the lessee would provide the primary insurance for the lessor. However, if a hold-harmless agreement in the contract shifts the responsibility for the primary insurance to Owner B, the lessor, attaching the Truckers—Named Lessee as Insured endorsement to the lessor's policy names the lessee as an additional insured and amends the policy to provide the primary coverage for both parties. Attaching the Truckers—Excess Coverage for the Named Insured and Named Lessors for Leased Autos endorsement to the lessee's policy amends it to apply only on an excess basis. Subsequent sections in this chapter explain the different premium determination procedures for each endorsement.

EXHIBIT 10-8

Truckers—Excess Coverage for the Named Insured and Named Lessors for Leased Autos Endorsement

POLICY NUMBER:

COMMERCIAL AUTO
CA 23 08 12 93

THIS ENDORSEMENT CHANGES THE POLICY. PLEASE READ IT CAREFULLY.

TRUCKERS – EXCESS COVERAGE FOR THE NAMED INSURED AND NAMED LESSORS FOR LEASED AUTOS

This endorsement modifies insurance provided under the following:

BUSINESS AUTO COVERAGE FORM
MOTOR CARRIER COVERAGE FORM
TRUCKERS COVERAGE FORM

With respect to coverage provided by this endorsement, the provisions of the Coverage Form apply unless modified by the endorsement.

This endorsement changes the policy effective on the inception date of the policy unless another date is indicated below.

Endorsement Effective	
Named Insured	Countersigned By

(Authorized Representative)

SCHEDULE

Name of Lessor:

(If no entry appears above, information required to complete this endorsement will be shown in the Declarations as applicable to this endorsement.)

A. For a covered "auto" leased to you by the lessor named in the Schedule, LIABILITY COVERAGE is excess over any other collectible insurance while:

    1. The covered "auto" is leased to you in writing and in accordance with a written hold harmless agreement; and

    2. The covered "auto" is used pursuant to operating rights granted to you by a public authority.

B. If the Coverage Form is written on a gross receipts basis, the term "gross receipts" in the Declarations is changed to include 15% of the amount to which you are entitled for transporting property by the "auto" leased to you by the lessor.

CA 23 08 12 93   Copyright, Insurance Services Office, Inc., 1993   Page 1 of 1   □

EXHIBIT 10-9

Truckers—Named Lessee as Insured Endorsement

POLICY NUMBER:

COMMERCIAL AUTO
CA 23 12 12 93

THIS ENDORSEMENT CHANGES THE POLICY. PLEASE READ IT CAREFULLY.

TRUCKERS – NAMED LESSEE AS INSURED

This endorsement modifies insurance provided under the following:

BUSINESS AUTO COVERAGE FORM
MOTOR CARRIER COVERAGE FORM
TRUCKERS COVERAGE FORM

With respect to coverage provided by this endorsement, the provisions of the Coverage Form apply unless modified by the endorsement.

This endorsement changes the policy effective on the inception date of the policy unless another date is indicated below.

Endorsement Effective	
Named Insured	Countersigned By

(Authorized Representative)

SCHEDULE

Name of Lessee: **Address:**

(If no entry appears above, information required to complete this endorsement will be shown in the Declarations as applicable to this endorsement.)

The Lessee named in the Schedule is an "insured" for the use of a covered "auto" you own or hire, subject to the following provisions:

1. Covered "auto" must be used pursuant to operating rights granted to the lessee by a public authority.

2. The covered "auto" must be leased in writing and in accordance with a written hold harmless agreement between you and the lessee.

3. The LIABILITY COVERAGE CONTRACTUAL Exclusion does not apply to the lease agreement between you and the lessee.

4. LIABILITY COVERAGE is primary for the lessee.

5. If the Coverage Form is written on a gross receipts basis, the term "gross receipts" in the Declarations is changed to include the actual remuneration received from leasing the covered "autos" to the lessee.

6. If we cancel the policy or reduce the LIABILITY COVERAGE LIMIT OF INSURANCE we will give the lessee 30 days advance notice.

CA 23 12 12 93   Copyright, Insurance Services Office, Inc., 1993   Page 1 of 1   □

MCS 90 Endorsement

The Motor Carrier Act of 1980 establishes minimum levels of financial responsibility for both private and for-hire carriers of certain hazardous materials. The requirements of the act relating to financial responsibility for hazardous transportation are shown in Exhibit 10-10.

EXHIBIT 10-10

Financial Responsibility for Hazardous Transportation

Type of Coverage	Vehicle Size	Commodity	Insurance Amount
For-hire and private for intrastate, interstate, or international commerce	Gross vehicle weight (GVW) of 10,000 lbs. or greater	Reportable quantity of an EPA CERCLA-listed hazardous substance in cargo tanks, portable tanks, or hopper-type vehicles with rated capacity in excess of 3,500 water gallons; bulk shipments of Class 1.1, 1.2, & 1.2 & 1.3 explosives; any quantity of class 2 gas; all shipments of highway route controlled quantities of radioactive materials as defined in 49 CFR 173.403	$5,000,000
For-hire and private for interstate and international commerce	Gross vehicle weight (GVW) of less than 10,000 lbs.	Any quantity of Class 1.1, 1.2, 1.3 explosives; any quantity of Class 2.3 poison gas; all shipments of highway route controlled quantities of radioactive materials	$5,000,000
For-hire and private for interstate or international commerce in any quantity, or in intrastate commerce in bulk only	Gross vehicle weight (GVW) of 10,000 lbs. or greater	Oil listed in 49 CFR 172.101; any hazardous waste, hazardous materials, or hazardous substances defined in 49 CFR 171.8 and 49 CFR 172.101 but not mentioned above	$1,000,000
For-hire for interstate or international commerce	Any	Nonhazardous property	$750,000

What constitutes hazardous cargo can be determined by obtaining a list from the U.S. Department of Labor, Occupational Safety and Health Administration (www.osha.gov). The list contains thousands of substances considered hazardous.

One insurance mechanism to comply with the Motor Carrier Act of 1980 is the Endorsement for Motor Carrier Policy of Insurance for Public Liability under Sections 29 and 30 of the Motor Carrier Act of 1980, or the **MCS 90 Endorsement**. This endorsement is required whenever a motor carrier is subject to the Motor Carrier Act of 1980.

When the MCS 90 Endorsement is attached to a commercial auto policy, the insurer agrees to pay, up to the limits shown in the endorsement, damages that the insured becomes liable for resulting from negligence in the operation, maintenance, or use of any motor vehicle subject to this law, whether

MCS 90 Endorsement
An endorsement that is required whenever a motor carrier is subject to the Motor Carrier Act of 1980.

described in the policy or not. No provisions of the applicable auto coverage form can relieve the insurer from payment. In effect, the insurer is a surety up to the limits specified in the endorsement. As a surety, the insurer has the right to proceed against its own insured for reimbursement of damages paid solely because of the endorsement, a most likely scenario because claims under the MCS 90 Endorsement usually involve pollution that is excluded by the policy. To provide pollution coverage, insurers can add the Pollution Liability— Broadened Coverage For Covered Autos, Business Auto, Motor Carrier And Truckers Coverage Forms endorsement (CA 99 48). This endorsement can be added to business auto, trucker, and motor carrier policies.

MOTOR CARRIER COVERAGE FORM

As defined in the *Commercial Lines Manual* (CLM), a **motor carrier** is "a person or organization providing transportation by auto in the furtherance of a commercial enterprise." This definition is broader than that of "trucker" and therefore includes a wider variety of risks.

Motor carrier
A person or organization providing transportation by auto in the furtherance of a commercial enterprise.

The trucking industry underwent tremendous changes and deregulation in the 1980s and 1990s. In response to those changes, ISO introduced the Motor Carrier Coverage Form in 1994 as a more flexible alternative to the Truckers Coverage Form. ISO did not intend the motor carrier form to replace the truckers form, but only to supplement it.

In most respects, the Motor Carrier Coverage Form is identical to the Truckers Coverage Form. The remainder of this section examines the major differences between the Business Auto Coverage Form, the Truckers Coverage Form, and the Motor Carrier Coverage Form.

Covered Autos

Covered autos for the Motor Carrier Coverage Form are designated in the same way as in the business auto and truckers coverage forms: the appropriate numerical symbol or symbols are inserted in the policy declarations beside each coverage desired. Exhibit 10-11 shows the symbols.

Symbols 61 through 68 basically duplicate Symbols 1 through 8 of the Business Auto Coverage Form. Symbol 71 matches Symbol 9, and Symbol 79 matches Symbol 19. Symbols 69 and 70, which cover trailer interchange, have no corresponding symbols in the business auto policy.

The correspondence to the truckers form is even greater. Symbols 61, 62, and 64 through 71 basically duplicate Symbols 41 through 50 of the truckers form. The one exception is that the Truckers Coverage Form has no symbol for covering only owned private passenger-type autos, whereas Symbol 63 makes that option available in the motor carrier form.

EXHIBIT 10-11

Description of Covered Auto Designation Symbols for the Motor Carrier Coverage Form

COMMERCIAL AUTO
CA 00 20 03 06

MOTOR CARRIER COVERAGE FORM

Various provisions in this policy restrict coverage. Read the entire policy carefully to determine rights, duties and what is and is not covered.

Throughout this policy the words "you" and "your" refer to the Named Insured shown in the Declarations. The words "we", "us" and "our" refer to the Company providing this insurance.

Other words and phrases that appear in quotation marks have special meaning. Refer to Section **VI** – Definitions.

SECTION I – COVERED AUTOS

Item Two of the Declarations shows the "autos" that are covered "autos" for each of your coverages. The following numerical symbols describe the "autos" that may be covered "autos". The symbols entered next to a coverage on the Declarations designate the only "autos" that are covered "autos".

A. Description Of Covered Auto Designation Symbols

Symbol	Description Of Covered Auto Designation Symbols	
61	Any "Auto"	
62	Owned "Autos" Only	Only the "autos" you own (and for Liability Coverage any "trailers" you don't own while connected to a power unit you own). This includes those "autos" you acquire ownership of after the policy begins.
63	Owned Private Passenger Type "Autos" Only	Only the "private passenger type" "autos" you own. This includes those "private passenger type" "autos" that you acquire ownership of after the policy begins.
64	Owned Commercial "Autos" Only	Only those trucks, tractors and "trailers" you own (and for Liability Coverage any "trailers" you don't own while connected to a power unit you own). This includes those trucks, tractors and "trailers" you acquire ownership of after the policy begins.
65	Owned "Autos" Subject To No-Fault	Only those "autos" you own that are required to have No-Fault benefits in the state where they are licensed or principally garaged. This includes those "autos" you acquire ownership of after the policy begins provided they are subject to the No-Fault law in the state where they are licensed or principally garaged.
66	Owned "Autos" Subject To A Compulsory Uninsured Motorists Law	Only those "autos" you own that, because of the law in the state where they are licensed or principally garaged, are required to have and cannot reject Uninsured Motorists Coverage. This includes those "autos" you acquire ownership of after the policy begins provided they are subject to the same state uninsured motorists requirement.
67	Specifically Described "Autos"	Only those "autos" described in Item Three of the Declarations for which a premium charge is shown (and for Liability Coverage any "trailers" you don't own while attached to any power unit described in Item Three).
68	Hired "Autos" Only	Only those "autos" you lease, hire, rent or borrow. This does not include any "private passenger type" "auto" you lease, hire, rent or borrow from any member of your household, any of your "employees", partners (if you are a partnership), members (if you are a limited liability company), or agents or members of their households.
69	"Trailers" In Your Possession Under A Written Trailer Or Equipment Interchange Agreement	Only those "trailers" you do not own while in your possession under a written "trailer" or equipment interchange agreement in which you assume liability for "loss" to the "trailers" while in your possession.

CA 00 20 03 06   © ISO Properties, Inc., 2005   Page 1 of 14   □

Symbol		Description Of Covered Auto Designation Symbols
70	Your "Trailers" In The Possession Of Anyone Else Under A Written Trailer Inter-change Agree-ment	Only those "trailers" you own or hire while in the possession of anyone else under a written "trailer" interchange agreement. When Symbol "70" is entered next to a Physical Damage Coverage in Item Two of the Declarations, the Physical Damage Coverage exclusion relating to "loss" to a "trailer" in the possession of anyone else does not apply to that coverage.
71	Nonowned "Autos" Only	Only those "autos" you do not own, lease, hire, rent or borrow that are used in connection with your business. This includes "private passenger type" "autos" owned by your "employees" or partners (if you are a partnership), members (if you are a limited liability company), or members of their households but only while used in your business or your personal affairs.
79	Mobile Equip-ment Subject To Compulsory Or Financial Re-sponsibility or Other Motor Vehicle Insur-ance Law Only	Only those "autos" that are land vehicles and that would qualify under the defini-tion of "mobile equipment" under this policy if they were not subject to a compul-sory or financial responsibility law or other motor vehicle insurance law where they are licensed or principally garaged.

Persons Insured for Liability Coverage

The motor carrier form covers (and excludes) essentially the same classes of persons as the Truckers Coverage Form, with the following exceptions.

Owners and Lessors of Hired or Borrowed Autos

The other insurance provisions of the Motor Carrier Coverage Form are similar to the conditions in the Truckers Coverage Form, although the exact wording is somewhat different. The Motor Carrier Coverage Form places more emphasis on the contract between the parties because the question of who will be responsible for insurance, the lessor or lessee, is usually addressed in such a contract. The Motor Carrier Coverage Form does not require that a public authority grant operating rights because, unlike a trucker, a motor carrier does not necessarily need operating authority.

Persons Not Insured

The "Who Is an Insured" provisions of the Motor Carrier Coverage Form contain some exclusions that are similar to exclusions in the Truckers Coverage Form. These exclusions eliminate coverage for the following persons and organizations:

- Motor carriers for hire, including their employees and agents. Such motor carriers are subject to motor carrier insurance requirements and meet these requirements by means other than insurance.

- Motor carriers for hire, including their employees and agents, that do not carry auto insurance providing the same type of liability coverage that the motor carrier form provides for owners and lessors of autos the named insured hired.

However, neither of these two exclusions applies if the named insured leases an auto to the motor carrier under a written lease agreement in which the named insured holds the motor carrier harmless.

The Motor Carrier Coverage Form contains the same exclusion of any rail, water, or air carrier (including its employees and agents) regarding liability arising out of a detached trailer being transported by the carrier or being loaded on or unloaded from any unit of transportation. The carrier must be found in the Truckers Coverage Form.

Other Insurance

The other insurance provision of the Motor Carrier Coverage Form is similar to that of the Truckers Coverage Form. Whether coverage applies on a primary or an excess basis depends on the coverage in question.

For motor carrier liability coverage, coordination with other insurance depends on whether the covered auto is hired from the named insured or hired by the named insured, and on the terms of the written agreement between the two parties.

While another motor carrier hires or borrows a covered auto from the named insured, coverage under the named insured's policy is primary if a written agreement between the named insured (lessor) and the other motor carrier (lessee) requires the named insured to hold the lessee harmless. Coverage is excess if a written contract between the named insured (lessor) and the other motor carrier (lessee) does not require the named insured to hold the lessee harmless.

While a covered auto is hired or borrowed by the named insured from another motor carrier, coverage under the named insured's policy is primary if a written agreement between the other motor carrier (lessor) and the named insured (lessee) does not require the lessor to hold the named insured harmless. However, this provision applies only while the covered auto is being used exclusively in the named insured's business as a motor carrier for hire. The named insured's coverage is excess if a written agreement between the other motor carrier (lessor) and the named insured (lessee) requires the lessor to hold the named insured harmless. The other insurance provisions for trailer interchange and physical damage coverage in the Motor Carrier Coverage Form match those in the Truckers Coverage Form.

PREMIUM BASES FOR TRUCKERS COVERAGE FORM

Determining the premium for truckers and motor carriers is more involved than for other types of motor vehicle operations. When auditing a truckers or motor carriers policy, the premium auditor may face a lengthy investigation both to ascertain the actual exposures and to verify the classification assignments. (When the text uses the term "truckers," it means truckers or motor carriers, unless otherwise specified.) Insurers can write insurance for truckers on a specified auto basis, a cost-of-hire basis, or a gross receipts basis.

Rule 24C. of the *CLM* specifies that insurers should rate autos transporting exclusively for one firm on the same basis as those owned by that firm for both territory and classification. When this rule applies, the insurer does not need to endorse the policy, but the premium auditor should check for any state exceptions. The existence of a written contract or the insured auto permanently marked with the conspicuous trademark, name, or insignia of the firm for which the exclusive hauling is performed, is valid evidence that the auto is used exclusively for one firm. (Valid [prima facie] evidence does not necessarily dictate a final determination. It can be rebutted by controverting evidence.) Rule 24C. applies on a per-auto basis because there is no requirement that all autos owned by the insured be used exclusively for one firm. If applying this rule causes reclassification, the premium auditor should notify the underwriter because the reclassification has direct bearing on underwriting considerations.

Specified Auto Basis

When insurers write truckers coverage on a specified auto basis, the same primary classification rules regarding weight, use, and radius class for other commercial vehicles apply. The difference in premiums is a result of the secondary rating factor.

The topics of bobtailing and deadheading operations, trailer interchange agreement, and physical damage related specifically to the Truckers Coverage Form are addressed next.

Bobtailing and Deadheading Operations

An owner-operator who operates exclusively for hire by other trucking firms has no need for truckers coverage if the firms that are hiring the owner-operator provide primary coverage. The owner-operator will still need coverage for non-trucking use (bobtailing or deadheading coverage). The Truckers—Insurance for Non-trucking Use endorsement (CA 23 09) provides this coverage. Insurers use this endorsement only with a Business Auto Coverage Form. Insurers cannot use it with a Truckers Coverage Form or the Motor Carrier Coverage Form. Premium auditors determine the premium for liability coverage by multiplying the truck, tractor, and trailer base premium by a rating factor of 1.50 per unit or combined unit. No secondary rating factor applies to the units. Premium auditors calculate the no-fault and physical damage premiums according to the appropriate classifications for the risk.

Trailer Interchange Agreement

When the insurer extends coverage to include the insured's liability for non-owned trailers in the insured's possession under a written trailer or equipment interchange agreement, the insurer determines the premium by the number of owned and nonowned trailers involved.

If an even interchange of nonowned trailers and owned trailers exists, and the insurance ceases when the owned trailers are in others' possession, the premium auditor makes no additional premium charge because the insurer's total liability remains constant. For example, Trucker A and Trucker B agree in writing to exchange each of their five trailers, and each agrees to provide coverage while having possession of the other's trailers. Therefore, each insurer for Trucker A and Trucker B is providing coverage for five trailers. The exposure remains the same.

If the insurance on the owned trailers remains in force when in others' possession, the premium auditor calculates the premiums for the coverage on nonowned trailers by the following operations:

- Determining the radius class of the trailer while in the insured's possession
- Determining the daily per-trailer rate according to the radius class, coverage, and limit in the trailer interchange rate table
- Multiplying the daily per-trailer rate by the physical damage factors from the zone rating tables
- Multiplying this physical damage factor by the number of days for which the insurer provided coverage (this is the premium for only one trailer)

If an uneven interchange exists (for example, Trucker A possesses seven of Trucker B's trailers, and Trucker B possesses five of Trucker A's trailers; or Trucker A possesses three of Trucker B's trailers and Trucker B has none of Trucker A's trailers), and the insurance on the owned trailers ceases when they are in others' possession, the premium auditor calculates the premium on the difference between the number of nonowned and owned trailers.

The CLM does not explain how to determine the premium charge for Symbol 49 coverage (the named insured's trailers in anyone else's possession under a written trailer interchange agreement). The premium auditor should check with the underwriter when the underwriter uses this symbol.

Physical Damage

Additional information needed for physical damage coverage is either actual cash value or the stated amount value of each covered vehicle, depending on how the coverage is written.

Insurers base actual cash value on the vehicle's age and original cost new. The insurer determines age by the model year. The current model year changes October 1 regardless of the actual model introduction date. The age of the chassis determines the age of rebuilt or structurally altered autos. Original cost new, as discussed previously, is the retail cost the original purchaser paid for the auto and its equipment.

Stated amount modifies the limit of insurance provision in the Truckers Coverage Form so that the insurer's payment for a physical damage loss is the least of the following: (1) the actual cash value of the damaged or stolen property, (2) the cost of repairing or replacing the damaged or stolen property with property of like kind and quality, or (3) the amount of insurance shown for the auto in the endorsement's schedule.

Cost-of-Hire Basis—Hired Auto

Generally, any auto operated under a motor carrier's authority is that carrier's responsibility. The public authority with whom the motor carrier makes the filing requires that the motor carrier's insurance be primary regardless of who owns the vehicle, who is operating the vehicle, or whose goods are being transported. Consequently, liability coverage under the Truckers Coverage Form is primary for hired or borrowed autos used exclusively in the insured's trucking operations and pursuant to operating rights granted to the named insured by a public authority. As previously noted, if the insured hires an auto for some other use, the hired auto coverage is excess.

As explained, whether coverage is primary or excess under the Motor Carrier Coverage Form depends on whether a written hold-harmless agreement exists between the named insured and the other party. The Motor Carrier Coverage Form and the Truckers Coverage Form have similar provisions in this regard. When the insured hires an auto from someone else, the covered auto must be used exclusively in the named insured's business as a motor carrier for hire.

When a motor carrier for hire is the named insured lessee, this change means that in addition to determining cost of hire by state, the premium auditor must verify all of the following:

- The insurer has a copy of the lease.
- The lease has the hold-harmless agreement in the insured's favor.
- The insured has a certificate of insurance or a copy of the other party's declarations page indicating liability coverage at least in the amount of the insured's coverage.
- The insured's policy has the Truckers—Excess Coverage For the Named Insured And Named Lessors endorsement (CA 23 08) or the lessor's policy has the Truckers—Named Lessee As Insured endorsement (CA 23 12) listing the insured.

CLM Rule 24 states: "Due to variation in exposure from risk to risk it is impractical to establish uniform requirements for satisfactory insurance and written lease and hold-harmless agreements between the insured lessee and the lessor. The company should establish its own requirements."[1] Therefore, the Motor Carrier Coverage Form for lessors or lessees with hold-harmless agreements is on a refer-to-company basis.

Even if the insurer writes the insurance for a trucker on a specified auto basis, it writes the hired auto coverage on a cost-of-hire basis. The Truckers Coverage Form declarations page and the Motor Carrier Coverage Form declarations page separate the hired auto coverage into two parts—hired auto coverage for autos used in the named insured's trucking operations and for autos not used in the named insured's trucking operations. Truckers occasionally hire autos from others (with or without drivers) to transport goods under the lessee's permit and control. Truckers often rent their operating permits or certificates to others rather than hiring additional vehicles. Revenue derived from permit rental constitutes cost of hire under the permit holder's policy.

When a trucker hires a vehicle, the total cost of hire must include the wages paid to the driver. If the insured hires the auto without a driver, the premium auditor must add wages of the driver that the named insured provides to the cost of hire. Wages include salary, overtime, bonuses, commission, and any other compensation. The policy excludes cost of hire of autos under a long-term lease and for which the insurer has made a specified auto charge.

To calculate the premium when coverage is written on a cost-of-hire basis and when no hold-harmless agreements are in place requires first determining the total cost of hire. Second, the premium auditor determines the **average specified auto rate**, a calculation in the development of hired auto premium under the Motor Carrier Coverage Form that represents the average premium for all owned and leased autos. The average specified auto rate is determined by calculating the premium for all autos that the insured owns and leases and that the insured uses in trucking operations and dividing the result by the number of trucks and truck-tractors the insured owns and leases. The premium auditor determines the **cost-of-hire**, an estimate of the amount an insured will spend on hiring autos, excluding charges for (1) vehicles that are not covered, (2) drivers, and (3) services performed by common or contract motor carriers subject to any public authority's insurance requirement. The cost-of-hire rate is determined by multiplying the average specified factor given in the *CLM*.

The insurer calculates the advance premium by multiplying each $100 of the total amount estimated for the cost of hire during the policy period by the cost-of-hire rate. The insurer does this for each state in which the insured operates.

The *CLM* rules provide that "unless there is a substantial change in exposure during the policy period, the advance premium computed at the beginning of the policy term is the earned premium."[2] Therefore, a final premium adjustment is at the insurer's discretion (that is, in determining whether a "substantial" change in loss exposure occurred). Many insurers adjust the premium at audit in almost every case because experience has shown that actual cost of hire, especially for truckers, varies considerably from initial estimates. Premium auditors determine the nonowned auto premium the same way for truckers and motor carrier coverage as for business auto coverage.

Average specified auto rate
A calculation in the development of hired auto premium under a Motor Carrier Coverage Form that represents the average premium for all owned and leased autos.

Cost-of-hire
An estimate of the amount an insured will spend on hiring autos, excluding charges for (1) vehicles that are not covered, (2) drivers, and (3) services performed by common or contract motor carriers subject to any public authority's insurance requirement.

Gross Receipts Basis

Insurers can also price truckers and motor carrier insurance on a gross receipts basis. If so, the policy must cover the insured for all owned and hired, rented, leased, and borrowed trucks, tractors, and trailers used in the insured's trucking business. A policy for an applicant that operates principally trip-leased equipment must be submitted to the insurer for rating. The policy can also cover private passenger and nonownership liability. Many insurers develop a rate per $100 of gross receipts by dividing the premium that would have developed on a specified auto basis by the estimated receipts. For other insurers, the actual rate development is more sophisticated, but it still follows this procedure. CLM Rule 24. C. 3. a. limits gross receipts basis coverage to firms that have been in business for at least fifteen months and comprise ten or more trucks, tractors, or trailers used for local trucking or five or more trucks or tractors used for intermediate or long-distance trucking.[3]

The premium auditor does not calculate the rate, nor does the insurer recalculate it at audit adjustment time. The premium auditor does, however, develop the insured's actual gross receipts by performing a premium audit at the policy period's conclusion.

The Truckers Coverage Form declarations page and the Motor Carrier Coverage Form declarations page define **gross receipts** as "the total amount earned by the named insured for shipping or transporting property, whether or not collected, during the policy period." It does not matter whether the shipment originates with the insured or another motor carrier. The premium auditor need not be concerned with hired autos as a separate item because statutes require that permit holders bill for all shipments under their permit.

Gross receipts
The total amount earned by the named insured for shipping or transporting property, whether or not collected, during the policy period.

Inclusions

Gross receipts for trucking include the following: the total amount received from renting equipment, with or without drivers, to anyone who is not a trucker; and 15 percent of the total amount received from renting equipment, with or without drivers, to anyone who is a trucker.

The Motor Carrier Coverage Form declarations page has the same provision as the Truckers Coverage Form except that it uses the term "motor carrier" instead of "trucker."

Exclusions

Both forms state that gross receipts for trucking do not include the following: amounts the insured paid to railroads, steamship lines, airlines, or other motor carriers operating under their own federal or Public Utility Commission (PUC) permit; taxes the insured collected as a separate item and paid directly to the government; C.O.D. collections for cost of mail or merchandise, including collection fees; warehouse storage charges; and advertising revenue.

Verification of Gross Receipts

In many cases, state PUC or federal rules require regulated carriers to file annual reports. If available, those reports are a matter of public record and make excellent verification records.

Truckers—Excess Coverage for the Named Insured and Named Lessors for Leased Autos Endorsement (CA 23 08)

When the insurer attaches the Truckers—Excess Coverage for the Named Insured and Named Lessors for Leased Autos endorsement (CA 23 08) to the insured's policy, the insured is providing excess insurance only, and the lessor is providing the primary coverage. The premium auditor includes in the gross receipts only 15 percent of the receipts earned under the insured's certificate or permit from transporting property in a vehicle owned by a lessor described in the "name of lessor" section of the endorsement. The premium auditor must search supplementary support records for this information because the insured does not normally segregate those amounts. Exhibit 10-8 shows the Truckers—Excess Coverage for the Named Insured and Named Lessors for Leased Autos endorsement.

Truckers—Named Lessee as Insured Endorsement (CA 23 12)

If the insurer attaches the Truckers—Named Lessee as Insured endorsement (CA 23 12) to the insured's policy, the insured (lessor owner-operator) agrees to provide primary insurance when vehicles owned by the insured are operating under the filing authority of a lessee named on the endorsement. In this case, the premium auditor should include 100 percent of the amounts received for using those vehicles. Exhibit 10-9 shows the Truckers—Named Lessee as Insured endorsement.

PRIVATE PASSENGER TYPES (SECTION III)

The *CLM* defines a private passenger auto as a four-wheel auto of the private passenger or station wagon type. Consequently, pickup trucks, panel trucks, or vans that are not used for business are classified and rated as private passenger autos.

The rates shown in the state rate pages are for private passenger autos that are owned by corporations, partnerships, unincorporated associations, or government agencies, or that the insurer rates as part of a fleet. For liability insurance purposes, the rates are a flat charge for each territory for the desired limit of liability. For physical damage coverage, the rates are a flat charge based on the territory, deductible, original cost new, and age. Those rates are modified by factors found in the *CLM* for private passenger autos that are furnished to an individual by a corporation, a partnership, or an unincorporated association owning fewer than five autos and not used for business purposes; or owned by a family partnership or family corporation and garaged on a farm, not rated as part of a fleet, and not used in any occupation other than farming or ranching. Those factors vary depending on the operator's experience and the vehicle's use.

If a premium auditor can identify fleet-rated private passenger autos, pickup trucks, panel trucks, and vans as farmers' autos, the *CLM* allows a reduced rate for those vehicles. To be considered a farmer's auto, the vehicle must meet all the following qualifications:[4]

- Principally garaged on farm or ranch
- Owned by an individual or a husband and a wife resident in the same household, or by a family partnership or a family corporation
- Not used in any occupation other than farming or ranching
- Not used in going to and from work other than farming or ranching

PUBLIC TRANSPORTATION (SECTION IV)

Section IV—Public Transportation of the *CLM* applies to autos registered or used for transporting members of the public. Specialty insurers, assigned risk pools, or joint underwriting associations cover many vehicles or businesses in this section. However, the premium auditor frequently finds van pools and some other vehicles in this section on policies issued to regular nontransportation-oriented commercial insureds. These vehicles are insured on a Business Auto Coverage Form, but the insurer attaches the Public Transportation Autos Endorsement (CA 24 02) when insuring public autos. That endorsement changes the care, custody, or control exclusion so that it does not exclude property damage to or covered pollution cost or expense involving property of the insured's passengers while such property is carried by the covered auto.

Insurers can rate liability coverage for public autos on a gross receipts basis, a mileage basis, or a specified car basis. Gross receipts rating basis and the mileage rating basis are not available for school buses owned by political subdivisions or school districts, van pools, and vehicles used for transportation of employees other than van pools.

Gross Receipts Basis

Gross receipts relating to public transportation are the total amount earned by the insured for transporting passengers, mail, and merchandise. Gross receipts do not include the following: amounts paid to air, sea, or land carriers operating under their own permits; taxes collected as a separate item and paid directly to the government; C.O.D. collections for cost of mail or merchandise, including collections fees; and advertising revenues.

Rates for both the gross receipts basis and the mileage basis are determined by calculating an estimated premium and dividing it by the gross receipts or mileage during the twelve-month period ending three months before the effective date of the policy. (For complete details, see *CLM* Rule 42. C. in Section IV of the Public Auto Classification rules.)

Mileage Basis

Mileage basis
The rate basis for private passenger-type vehicles written on the Business Auto Coverage Form that equals the total miles driven by all revenue-producing autos during the policy period.

Mileage basis is the rate basis for private passenger-type vehicles written on the Business Auto Coverage Form that equals the total miles driven by all revenue-producing autos during the policy period. It does not matter whether a vehicle was actually under hire; the premium auditor includes all miles driven. Some motor carriers use mileage for depreciating vehicles, which means that a source record may be available in those instances. For this premium basis to be effective, the premium auditor or others within the insurer must establish a clear understanding regarding acceptable records at policy inception. The insured, producer, underwriter, and premium auditor must all understand and agree on the mileage determination method used, whether it is inspection, odometer reading (including axle odometer devices), or some other accurate method. All those parties must also consider (before policy inception and at the time of the premium audit) the use of substitute and borrowed or hired vehicles by the insured, and the premium auditor's measuring their mileage as revenue vehicles. Fuel tax reports are an excellent source of information. Regulated truckers must file tax reports with each state or with a regional tax authority. The numbers reported include miles driven during the month in each state in which the insured operates.

Specified Car Basis

Insurers write many public autos on a specified car basis according to the *CLM* rules. The two major divisions within this basis are as follows: zone rated and other-than-zone rated.

Zone-rated basis
An approach to pricing insurance for commercial vehicles that are larger than light trucks and are operated more than 200 miles in distance from the garage location.

The **zone-rated basis** is an approach to pricing insurance for commercial vehicles that are larger than light trucks and are operated more than 200 miles in distance from the garage location. The insurer bases the premium on various factors. A table in the state rate pages shows the premiums to which these factors apply. The table is divided according to the place of principal garaging and the terminal (the place where the vehicle loads and unloads) farthest from that point. Zone rating does not apply to taxis, limousines, school buses, church buses, urban buses, or van pools.

For public autos written on a basis other than a zone-rated basis (and for all taxis, limousines, school buses, church buses, urban buses, and van pools), the insurer bases the premium on whether the auto is part of a fleet and on the primary and secondary classifications. Those classifications determine a rating factor, which the insurer then applies to a base rate found on the state rate pages. The base rate varies according to the limits and territory. Physical damage rates also vary according to original cost new and age group.

Primary Classification

The primary classification of a public vehicle depends on its radius class and its use class. The radius class is divided into three parts: local (up to 50 miles), intermediate (beyond 50 miles to 200 miles), and long distance (over 200 miles). These are the same as the radius classes used for other commercial vehicles. Rates also vary according to whether the auto is part of a fleet. For van pools, the primary classification depends on the seating capacity of each van and whether the vehicle is employer furnished.

A three- or four-digit code indicates the primary classification. The primary classification is four digits for public autos for which a secondary classification does not apply—taxicabs, limousines (except airport limousines), van pools, and zone-rated autos. For all other public autos, the primary classification code is three digits, with the fourth digit being determined by the secondary classification based on the seating capacity.

Seating capacity, used to determine both the primary classification of van pool vehicles and the secondary classification of public vehicles, is the seating capacity specified by the manufacturer unless a public authority legislates otherwise. In the latter case, premium auditors should use the legislated seating capacity. The driver's seat does not count as part of the seating capacity. The definitions of some use classes also refer to the vehicle's seating capacity.

Fourteen use classes exist for the primary classification of public transportation autos (the fourteenth is a not-otherwise-classified classification). When a vehicle has more than one use, the highest rated classification applies unless 80 percent or more of the use is in the lower rated classification. In that case, the lower rated classification applies. The use classes are as follows:

1. Taxicab
2. Limousine
3. School bus
4. Church bus
5. Inter-city bus
6. Urban bus
7. Airport bus or airport limousine
8. Charter bus
9. Sightseeing bus
10. Transportation of athletes or entertainers
11. Van pools
12. Transportation of employees—other than van pools
13. Social service agency auto
14. Public auto not otherwise classified

Secondary Classification

The secondary classification is based on seating capacity. The factor to be applied in rating such autos also varies according to the vehicle type. Exhibit 10-12 shows the secondary codes for the various seating-capacity categories. If the insured has converted a truck, tractor, or trailer for use as a public auto, the *CLM* states that seating capacity is on a refer-to-company basis. Secondary classifications do not apply to taxicabs, limousines (except airport limousines), van pools, and zone-rated autos.

EXHIBIT 10-12

Secondary Classifications for Public Autos by Seating Capacity

Seating Capacity	Secondary Code
1–8	1
9–20	2
21–60	3
Over 60	4
All other (not secondary rated)	9

SPECIAL VEHICLE TYPES

The *CLM*'s special types section addresses the premium determination of unique groups of vehicles that are not otherwise included in other sections. For example, vehicles used by fire departments, ambulance services, and funeral homes present atypical loss exposures. Exhibit 10-13 shows a complete listing of loss exposures and circumstances encapsulated in this catch-all category. Because of their distinct loss attributes, each type has its own rating method. In some instances, the premium for a special vehicle type is a function of another type of vehicle. For example, the ISO Georgia state exception pages specify that the premium for an ambulance is a factor (1.75) of the premium for a truck.

Mobile equipment is included in special vehicle types and includes equipment owned by many businesses. Consequently, mobile equipment deserves further explanation. As mentioned, mobile equipment that is subject to state auto insurance laws is insured as autos. The *CLM*'s Rule 81 provides premium determination rules.

Mobile equipment must be insured with a Commercial General Liability Coverage Form as well because the commercial auto coverage does not apply when the mobile equipment is not operating as a vehicle. For example, a bucket truck used by utilities to repair and install cables is insured under the commercial auto policy while traveling on the road, but is insured by the General Liability Coverage Form when parked and when the bucket is in operation.

EXHIBIT 10-13

Categories of Special Vehicle Types

- Ambulance Services (Rule 64)
- Amphibious Equipment (Rule 65)
- Antique Autos (Rule 66)
- Auto Body Manufacturers and Installers (Rule 67)
- Driver Training Programs (Rule 68)
- Drive-Away Contractors (Rule 69)
- Financed Autos (Rule 70)
- Fire Departments (Rule 71)
- Funeral Directors (Rule 72)
- Golfmobiles (Rule 73)
- Law Enforcement Agencies (Rule 74)
- Leasing or Rental Concerns (Rule 75)
- Mobile or Farm Equipment (Rule 81)
- Mobile Homes (Rule 76)
- Motorcycles (Rule 77)
- Registration Plates Not Issued For A Specific Auto (Rule 78)
- Repossessed Autos (Rule 79)
- Snowmobiles (Rule 80)

Farm equipment such as harvesting combines, power-driven lawn mowers, and other self-propelled farm equipment used for farming purposes can also be covered under this rule. Insurers determine coverage premiums by applying a factor to the base premium for trucks, tractors and trailers.

SUMMARY

Although business auto coverage has the flexibility to meet most insureds' needs, truckers coverage and motor carrier coverage serve the unique needs of truckers required to insure, on a primary basis, other truckers hauling for them—a common practice in the trucking industry. Truckers and motor carrier coverage can provide liability, physical damage, no-fault, medical payments, and uninsured motorists coverages, and the insurer can add other coverages by endorsement. The motor carrier form is the more flexible of the two policies for truckers—it is not limited to those transporting property of others.

Of all the motor vehicle operations that insurers may cover, truckers and motor carriers are the most likely to require a premium audit. Insurers can cover truckers and motor carriers on a specified auto, a cost-of-hire, or a gross receipts basis. If the insurer bases premium on gross receipts, the premium auditor must examine the insured's operating revenue and lease accounts to extract this information. Premium auditors are sometimes involved with audits of policies written on a specified car basis.

Insurers can base the premium for vehicles used for public transportation on a specified auto basis or on a gross receipts or mileage basis. The classification system resembles trucking classifications. The primary classification depends on the use, the radius of operations, and, for van pools, the seating capacity. The secondary classification reflects the seating capacity for most classes.

Special types and operations of motor vehicles not previously described involve specific rules for each special type indicating percentage factors or other procedures to relate the general rules to the situation.

CHAPTER NOTES

1. Insurance Services Office, Inc., *Commercial Lines Manual*, "Division One—Automobile," Rule 24B.3.b.(1)., http://info.iso.com (ISOnet SIM-CA-MU, accessed Aug. 9, 2006).

2. *Commercial Lines Manual*, "Division One—Automobile," Section II, Rule 24C.2.e.

3. *Commercial Lines Manual*, "Division One—Automobile," Section II, Rule 24C.3.a.

4. *Commercial Lines Manual*, "Division One—Automobile," Section II, Rule 33A.

Direct Your Learning

Garage Insurance and Premium Determination

Educational Objectives

After learning the content of this chapter and completing the corresponding course guide assignment, you should be able to:

▶ Explain how the exposures facing an auto dealer or service operation justify a special policy.

▶ Explain the coverage provided by the Garage Coverage Form and common endorsements that can be attached.

▶ Describe the covered auto designation symbols used for garage coverage and their relationship to the supplementary schedules.

▶ Given a case involving a garage loss exposure, assign the proper classifications and number of rating units, amount of payroll, or other applicable exposure base.

• Define the rating units and enumerate the categories of operators included and the rating factor for each.

• Explain how to verify an insured's report of values for physical damage coverage.

• Define payroll for the purpose of determining the premium for an auto service operation.

▶ Define or describe each of the Key Words and Phrases for this chapter.

Outline

Garage Coverage

Premium Determination for Auto Dealers

Summary

CHAPTER

Develop Your Perspective

What are the main topics covered in this chapter?

The Garage Coverage Form is a package of general liability and auto coverages designed to meet the combination of loss exposures in various auto-related businesses. Rather than distinguishing general liability and auto liability loss exposures, the garage coverage includes both.

Identify the activities and operations of a typical auto dealer that generate loss exposures.

▶ How does the Garage Coverage Form address these various loss exposures?

▶ How do the supplementary schedules help tailor coverages for these exposures?

Why is it important to learn about these topics?

By understanding the nature of garage operations and the typical loss exposures common to them, it is easier to match the coverages to those exposures. Premium auditors can then ensure that adequate premiums are charged for these loss exposures.

Describe the loss exposures of a typical auto dealer and the coverages available for them.

▶ How is coverage provided for the business-owned vehicles or employee-owned vehicles used occasionally for business purposes?

▶ What are the premises exposures at the dealership, and how are they covered?

How can you use what you will learn?

One of your commercial insurance customers has acquired a franchised auto dealership. You are performing the first premium audit since the acquisition.

Analyze the customer's loss exposures to determine whether the appropriate premium has been charged to the coverage provided.

▶ How is coverage provided for automobiles left with the dealer under consignment, and how are the exposures for these vehicles measured?

▶ How are a franchised manufacturer's automobiles provided to the dealership for sale covered, and how are the exposures for these vehicles measured?

Garage Insurance and Premium Determination

As with the business auto form, the truckers form, and the motor carriers form, the Garage Coverage Form uses simplified language and covered auto symbols. Insurance Services Office (ISO) originally designed garage coverage to provide protection for auto dealers, repair shops, service stations, public storage garages, parking lots, trailer dealers, mobile home trailer dealers, and tow truck operators. In 2002, however, as noted in previous chapters, ISO restricted garage form eligibility to franchised and nonfranchised vehicle dealers.

Garage coverage is actually a combination of coverages: general liability, auto liability and physical damage, and garagekeepers insurance in one insurance policy. However, some of the coverages that are part of the CGL form, such as personal and advertising injury, must be added by endorsement if the insured desires the coverage.

For premium auditors, garage coverage introduces two different premium determination procedures: rating units and values. Insurers base premiums for auto dealers on rating units for liability coverage and values for physical damage coverage. Therefore, garage coverage requires unique premium audit procedures. This chapter outlines the garage form's format and coverage and explains the premium determination procedures.

GARAGE COVERAGE

With most businesses, classifying a given loss exposure as a general liability exposure or an auto exposure is possible. General liability insurance covers the former, and business auto coverage insures the latter. Those coverages attempt to define precisely where auto liability stops and general liability begins in areas in which coverages may overlap, such as for loading and unloading or for mobile equipment.

With auto dealers, however, it is difficult to separate auto exposures from the general liability exposures. For example, an auto dealer has premises and products liability loss exposures similar to those of many other businesses, such as a retail store. An auto dealer also typically owns one or more pickup trucks or private passenger vehicles. In this respect, it also resembles other nondealer businesses. However, the dealer's business directly involves such activities as towing, test driving, and performing repairs on a varying number of customer-owned autos in its custody. Defective work in an auto repair job or a defect in a car that the dealer sold could cause a customer to have an auto accident.

In addition, a dealer owns an ever-changing number of new or used cars for which it needs liability and physical damage coverage. Most autos in a dealer's inventory are in a showroom or lot awaiting sale, but an employee or prospective customer may drive them at any time. Other autos are constantly in use, such as executive autos, service vehicles, customer loaners, or even driver-training autos loaned to the local high school. The dealer may furnish demonstrators to sales representatives, and the vehicles used as demonstrators can change at any time. For auto dealers, garage coverage provides an appropriate coverage combination.

Auto dealer
An insured in the business of selling new or used vehicles.

Franchised auto dealer
An auto dealer that is authorized by one or more auto manufacturers to sell their autos under the manufacturers' names and trademarks.

Nonfranchised dealer
A used car dealer that has no franchise agreement with an auto manufacturer.

An **auto dealer** is an insured that is in the business of selling new or used vehicles. It may be either a franchised or nonfranchised dealer. A **franchised auto dealer** is an auto dealer that is authorized by one or more auto manufacturers to sell their autos under the manufacturers' names and trademarks. A franchised dealer may also sell used autos as part of its operation. A **nonfranchised dealer** is a used car dealer that has no franchise agreement with an auto manufacturer. In addition, franchised and nonfranchised residential mobile home or commercial trailer dealers come within the nondealer category according to ISO *Commercial Lines Manual* (CLM) rules.

Insurers can write garage coverage on the commercial package policy much like business auto coverage and truckers coverage. A complete policy consists of the Common Policy Conditions, the Common Policy Declarations, the Garage Coverage Form Declarations, a supplementary schedule, the Garage Coverage Form, and any applicable endorsements.

Garage Coverage Form Declarations (CA DS 06)

The Garage Coverage Form Declarations identifies the insured and presents other specific information concerning the particular policy. Some of the information usually located in the declarations, however, appears instead on a supplementary schedule that the insurer must attach to the Garage Coverage Form Declarations; Garage Coverage Form—Auto Dealers' Supplementary Schedule (CA DS 07).[1]

Item One—Information on Insured

Item One indicates the policy number, the named insured and the legal form of the insured's business. (The insured's mailing address and the policy term are shown on the common policy declarations.)

Item Two—Schedule of Coverage and Covered Autos

Item Two consists of a schedule of coverages and covered autos similar to those used for the business auto form, the truckers form, and the motor carriers form. Next to each of the possible coverages are spaces to indicate the symbol that specifies the autos covered, the insurer's limit of liability, and the estimated premium. If no premium charge appears opposite a coverage, then the policy does not provide that coverage. Item Two also allows space for the insurer to list the numbers of the forms and endorsements included in the policy, the premium charge for the endorsements, and the estimated total premium. Item Two of the Garage Coverage Form Declarations controls what coverages the policy affords and the auto types the policy covers. The declarations become complete by attaching a supplementary schedule.

Garage Coverage Form—Auto Dealers' Supplementary Schedule (CA DS 07)

The Auto Dealers' Supplementary Schedule lists the locations at which the insured operates, the premium computation for each applicable coverage, and some specifics related to the autos covered for physical damage and the extent of that coverage. Because the schedule is part of the declarations, the numbering of each item continues from the declarations.

Item Three—Locations

Item Three lists the locations where the named insured conducts garage operations. Location 1 is the address of the named insured's main business location.

Item Four—Liability Coverage Premiums

For each location and operator class, Item Four shows the rating factors, the number of persons, and the rating units. It also shows the total rating units and the resulting premium charges for liability, personal injury protection, and property protection. However, it does not necessarily show the rate. In this case, the premium auditor must determine the rate either by recalculating it or by obtaining the original rating worksheet. This item also states the definitions of the two major classes of operators. The insurer separately schedules any other liability premiums, such as those for furnished autos or pickup and delivery. Exhibit 11-1 shows Items Three and Four.

EXHIBIT 11-1

Auto Dealers' Supplementary Schedule—Items Three and Four

COMMERCIAL AUTO
CA DS 07 02 03

GARAGE COVERAGE FORM – AUTO DEALERS' SUPPLEMENTARY SCHEDULE

POLICY NUMBER: _____

ITEM THREE
LOCATIONS WHERE YOU CONDUCT GARAGE OPERATIONS

LOCATION NO.	ADDRESS State Your Main Business Location As Location No. 1.
1	
2	
3	

POLICY NUMBER: _____

ITEM FOUR
LIABILITY COVERAGE – PREMIUMS

Location No.	Classes Of Operators	Rating Factor	Number Of Persons	Rating Units	Total Rating Units	Liability Prem.	P.I.P. Prem.	Prop. Prot. Prem. (MI Only)	Med. Exp. Ben. Prem. (VA Only)	Inc. Loss Ben. Prem. (VA Only)
1	Class I – Employees Regular Operators					$	$	$	$	$
	Class I – Employees All Others									
	Class II – Non-Employees Under Age 25									
	Class II – Non-Employees Age 25 Or Over									
2	Class I – Employees Regular Operators					$	$	$	$	$
	Class I – Employees All Others									
	Class II – Non-Employees Under Age 25									
	Class II – Non-Employees Age 25 Or Over									
3	Class I – Employees Regular Operators					$	$	$	$	$
	Class I – Employees All Others									
	Class II – Non-Employees Under Age 25									
	Class II – Non-Employees Age 25 Or Over									
	TOTAL PREMIUMS					$	$	$	$	$

Definitions
Class I – Employees

Regular Operator – Proprietors, partners and officers active in the "garage operations", salespersons, general managers, service managers, any "employee" whose principal duty involves the operation of covered "autos" or who is furnished a covered "auto".

All Others – All other "employees".

Note

1. Part-time "employees" working an average of 20 hours or more a week for the number of weeks worked are to be counted as 1 rating unit each.

2. Part-time "employees" working an average of less than 20 hours a week for the number of weeks worked are to be counted as 1/2 rating unit each.

Class II – Non-Employees

Any of the following persons who are regularly furnished with a covered "auto": Inactive proprietors, partners or officers and their relatives and the relatives of any person described in Class I.

▶▶

Item Five—Broader Liability Coverage for Customers

The box in Item Five allows the option for broader liability coverage for the insured's customers. Checking the box changes the definition of who is insured by nullifying the paragraph in the "Who Is Insured" section of the coverage form that otherwise restricts coverage for customers with other available insurance. This is explained in more detail below.

Item Six—Garagekeepers Coverages

Item Six shows limits and premium by location as well as coverage option selections for garagekeepers coverage. Exhibit 11-2 shows Items Five and Six.

Item Seven—Physical Damage Coverage

Item Seven indicates the physical damage coverages for new and used autos. It also indicates the interests protected, the limits of liability for each location, the rates for each coverage, and the estimated premium charges.

As can be seen in Exhibit 11-3, there are two possible choices as to the types of autos covered and four possible choices as to interests covered. They are new autos, used autos, demonstrators, and service vehicles. Interests covered are the following: your interest in covered autos you own, your interest only in financed covered autos, your interest and the interest of any creditor named as a loss payee, and all interests in any auto not owned by you or any creditor while in your possession on consignment for sale.

When the insurer provides coverage under the creditor option, the coverage is for all creditors, not just the creditor shown under the loss payable clause. Therefore, if a finance company provides some coverages for autos under a floor plan, the policy should be specifically endorsed to exclude such floor plan autos. Otherwise, the premium auditor should charge a premium on such autos.

Item Seven also indicates whether the policy is on a reporting or nonreporting basis. Dealers reporting is similar in concept to the reporting used in property insurance. Because of fluctuating values at one or more locations, insurers initially write coverage for a provisional amount. Insurers base premiums on monthly or quarterly reports of values the insured submits to the insurer. If the insurer checks the reporting basis box, the insurer must also check another box in Item Seven to indicate whether the reporting basis is quarterly or monthly. Exhibit 11-3 shows Item Seven.

EXHIBIT 11-2

Auto Dealers' Supplementary Schedule—Items Five and Six

POLICY NUMBER: _____

ITEM FIVE

LIABILITY COVERAGE FOR YOUR CUSTOMERS

In accordance with Paragraph **a.(2)(d)** of Who Is An Insured under Section **II** – Liability Coverage, Liability Coverage for your customers is limited unless indicated below by "X".

☐ If this box is checked Paragraph **a.(2)(d)** of Who Is An Insured under Section **II** – Liability Coverage does not apply.

ITEM SIX

GARAGEKEEPERS COVERAGES AND PREMIUMS

Location No.	Coverages	Limit Of Insurance For Each Location (Absence of a limit or deductible below means that the corresponding ITEM TWO limit or deductible applies.)
1	Comprehensive	$ MINUS $ DEDUCTIBLE FOR EACH CUSTOMER'S AUTO FOR LOSS CAUSED BY THEFT OR MISCHIEF OR VANDALISM SUBJECT TO $ MAXIMUM DEDUCTIBLE FOR ALL SUCH LOSS IN ANY ONE EVENT; OR
	Specified Causes Of Loss	$ MINUS $ DEDUCTIBLE FOR ALL PERILS SUBJECT TO $ MAXIMUM DEDUCTIBLE FOR ALL SUCH LOSS IN ANY ONE EVENT.
	Collision	$ MINUS $ DEDUCTIBLE FOR EACH CUSTOMER'S AUTO.
2	Comprehensive	$ MINUS $ DEDUCTIBLE FOR EACH CUSTOMER'S AUTO FOR LOSS CAUSED BY THEFT OR MISCHIEF OR VANDALISM SUBJECT TO $ MAXIMUM DEDUCTIBLE FOR ALL SUCH LOSS IN ANY ONE EVENT; OR
	Specified Causes Of Loss	$ MINUS $ DEDUCTIBLE FOR ALL PERILS SUBJECT TO $ MAXIMUM DEDUCTIBLE FOR ALL SUCH LOSS IN ANY ONE EVENT.
	Collision	$ MINUS $ DEDUCTIBLE FOR EACH CUSTOMER'S AUTO.
3	Comprehensive	$ MINUS $ DEDUCTIBLE FOR EACH CUSTOMER'S AUTO FOR LOSS CAUSED BY THEFT OR MISCHIEF OR VANDALISM SUBJECT TO $ MAXIMUM DEDUCTIBLE FOR ALL SUCH LOSS IN ANY ONE EVENT; OR
	Specified Causes Of Loss	$ MINUS $ DEDUCTIBLE FOR ALL PERILS SUBJECT TO $ MAXIMUM DEDUCTIBLE FOR ALL SUCH LOSS IN ANY ONE EVENT.
	Collision	$ MINUS $ DEDUCTIBLE FOR EACH CUSTOMER'S AUTO.

PREMIUM FOR ALL LOCATIONS

Comprehensive	$
Specified Causes Of Loss	$
Collision	$

DIRECT COVERAGE OPTIONS

Indicate below with an "X" which, if any, Direct Coverage Option is selected.

☐ **EXCESS INSURANCE**

If this box is checked, Garagekeepers Coverage remains applicable on a legal liability basis. However, coverage also applies without regard to your or any other "insured's" legal liability for "loss" to a "customer's auto" on an excess basis over any other collectible insurance regardless of whether the other insurance covers your or any other "insured's" interest or the interest of the "customer's auto's" owner.

☐ **PRIMARY INSURANCE**

If this box is checked, Garagekeepers Coverage is changed to apply without regard to your or any other "insured's" legal liability for "loss" to a "customer's auto" and is primary insurance.

EXHIBIT 11-3

Auto Dealers' Supplementary Schedule—Item Seven

POLICY NUMBER: _____

ITEM SEVEN

PHYSICAL DAMAGE COVERAGE – TYPES OF COVERED AUTOS AND INTERESTS IN THESE AUTOS – PREMIUMS – REPORTING OR NONREPORTING BASIS

Each of the following Physical Damage Coverages that is indicated in ITEM TWO applies only to the types of "autos" and interests indicated below by "X".

COVERAGES	TYPES OF "AUTOS"		INTERESTS COVERED			
	New "Autos"	Used "Autos", Demonstrators And Service Vehicles	Your Interest In Covered "Autos" You Own	Your Interest Only In Financed Covered "Autos"	Your Interest And The Interest Of Any Creditor Named As A Loss Payee	All Interests In Any "Auto" Not Owned By You Or Any Creditor While In Your Possession On Consignment For Sale
Comprehensive	☐	☐	☐	☐	☐	☐
Specified Causes Of Loss	☐	☐	☐	☐	☐	☐
Collision	☐	☐	☐	☐	☐	☐

LOCATION NO.	COVERAGES	LIMIT OF INSURANCE FOR EACH LOCATION	RATES	PREMIUM
1	Comprehensive	$ MINUS $ DEDUCTIBLE FOR EACH	$	$
	Specified Causes Of Loss	COVERED AUTO FOR LOSS CAUSED BY THEFT OR MISCHIEF OR VANDALISM SUBJECT TO $ MAXIMUM DEDUCTIBLE FOR ALL SUCH LOSS IN ANY ONE EVENT; OR $ MINUS $ DEDUCTIBLE FOR ALL PERILS SUBJECT TO $ MAXIMUM DEDUCTIBLE FOR ALL SUCH LOSS IN ANY ONE EVENT.		
2	Comprehensive	$ MINUS $ DEDUCTIBLE FOR EACH	$	$
	Specified Causes Of Loss	COVERED AUTO FOR LOSS CAUSED BY THEFT OR MISCHIEF OR VANDALISM SUBJECT TO $ MAXIMUM DEDUCTIBLE FOR ALL SUCH LOSS IN ANY ONE EVENT; OR $ MINUS $ DEDUCTIBLE FOR ALL PERILS SUBJECT TO $ MAXIMUM DEDUCTIBLE FOR ALL SUCH LOSS IN ANY ONE EVENT.		
3	Comprehensive	$ MINUS $ DEDUCTIBLE FOR EACH	$	$
	Specified Causes Of Loss	COVERED AUTO FOR LOSS CAUSED BY THEFT OR MISCHIEF OR VANDALISM SUBJECT TO $ MAXIMUM DEDUCTIBLE FOR ALL SUCH LOSS IN ANY ONE EVENT; OR $ MINUS $ DEDUCTIBLE FOR ALL PERILS SUBJECT TO $ MAXIMUM DEDUCTIBLE FOR ALL SUCH LOSS IN ANY ONE EVENT.		

LOCATION NO.	COVERAGES	LIMIT OF INSURANCE FOR EACH LOCATION				
All	Collision	$ MINUS $ DEDUCTIBLE FOR EACH COVERED AUTO.				$
		BLANKET ANNUAL COLLISION RATES				
		First $50,000	$50,001 To $100,000	Over $100,000	Adjustment Factor	Premium
						$

TOTAL PREMIUM $

Continued on next page

POLICY NUMBER: _____

ITEM SEVEN (Cont'd)

Our limit of insurance for "loss" at locations other than those stated in ITEM THREE.

$ Additional locations where you store covered "autos"

$ In transit

PREMIUM BASIS – Reporting (Quarterly or Monthly) or Nonreporting (Indicate Basis Agreed Upon by "X").

☐ **REPORTING BASIS** (Quarterly or Monthly as indicated below by "X")

You must report to us on our form the location of your covered "autos" and their total value at each such location. For your main sales location identified as location no. 1, you must include the total value of all covered "autos" you have furnished or made available to yourself, your executives, your "employees" or family members and other Class II – Non-Employees, and covered "autos" that are temporarily displayed or stored at locations other than those stated in ITEM THREE above. For your main sales location you must include the total value of all service vehicles.

YOUR REPORTING BASIS IS:

☐ **QUARTERLY**

You must give us your first report by the fifteenth of the fourth month after the policy begins. Your subsequent reports must be given to us by the fifteenth of every third month. Your reports must contain the value for the last business day of every third month coming within the policy period.

☐ **MONTHLY**

You must give us your reports by the fifteenth of every month. Your reports will contain the total values you had on the last business day of the preceding month.

Premiums will be calculated pro rata of the annual premium for the exposures contained in each report. At the end of each policy year we will add the monthly premiums or the quarterly premiums to determine your final premium due for the entire policy year. The estimated total premiums shown above will be credited against the final premium due.

☐ **NONREPORTING BASIS**

Stated limit of insurance shown above applies.

Loss Payee – Any loss is payable as interest may appear to you and:

Copyright, ISO Properties, Inc., 2002.

Item Eight—Medical Payments Coverage

Medical payments coverage is for autos, garage locations and operations, or both. Item Eight indicates the type of medical payments coverage provided and what additional percentage of the liability premium applies for this coverage. For autos furnished to others or insured on a specified car basis, however, the insurer separately computes the medical payments premium under Item Nine.

Item Nine—Schedule of Covered Autos Furnished to Other Than Class I or II Persons

The insurer lists in Item Nine the autos furnished to someone other than a Class I or Class II operator or covered autos insured on a specified auto basis. As Exhibit 11-4 shows, Item Nine consists of a schedule of covered autos indicating classifications and premiums applicable to those autos for the various coverages.

EXHIBIT 11-4

Auto Dealers' Supplementary Schedule—Item Nine

POLICY NUMBER: _____

ITEM NINE

SCHEDULE OF COVERED AUTOS WHICH ARE FURNISHED TO SOMEONE OTHER THAN A CLASS I OR CLASS II OPERATOR OR WHICH ARE INSURED ON A SPECIFIED CAR BASIS

Covered Auto No.	DESCRIPTION Year, Model, Trade Name, Body Type Serial Number (S) Vehicle Identification Number (VIN)	PURCHASED Original Cost New	PURCHASED Actual Cost & NEW (N) USED (U)	TERRITORY Town & State Where The Covered Auto Will Be Principally Garaged
1		$	$	
2		$	$	
3		$	$	
4		$	$	
5		$	$	

Covered Auto No.	CLASSIFICATION Radius Of Operation	Business Use s=service r=retail c=commercial	Size GVW, GCW Or Vehicle Seating Capacity	Age Group	Primary Rating Factor Liab.	Primary Rating Factor Phy. Dam.	Secondary Rating Factor	Code	EXCEPT For Towing, All Physical Damage Loss Is Payable To You And The Loss Payee Named Below As Interests May Appear At The Time Of The Loss.
1									
2									
3									
4									
5									

POLICY NUMBER: _____

ITEM NINE

SCHEDULE OF COVERED AUTOS WHICH ARE FURNISHED TO SOMEONE OTHER THAN A CLASS I OR CLASS II OPERATOR OR WHICH ARE INSURED ON A SPECIFIED CAR BASIS (Cont'd)

Covered Auto No.	COVERAGES – PREMIUMS, LIMITS AND DEDUCTIBLES (Absence of a deductible or limit entry in any column below means that the limit or deductible entry in the corresponding ITEM TWO column applies instead.) LIABILITY Limit	LIABILITY Premium	PERSONAL INJURY PROTECTION Limit Stated In Each P.I.P. End. Minus Deductible Shown Below	PERSONAL INJURY PROTECTION Premium	ADDED P.I.P. Limit Stated In Each Added P.I.P. End. Premium	PROPERTY PROTECTION (Michigan Only) Limit Stated In P.P.I. End. Minus Deductible Shown Below	PROPERTY PROTECTION (Michigan Only) Premium
1	$	$	$	$	$	$	$
2	$	$	$	$	$	$	$
3	$	$	$	$	$	$	$
4	$	$	$	$	$	$	$
5	$	$	$	$	$	$	$
Total Premium		$		$	$		$

Covered Auto No.	COVERAGES – PREMIUMS, LIMITS AND DEDUCTIBLES (Absence of a deductible or limit entry in any column below means that the limit or deductible entry in the corresponding ITEM TWO column applies instead.) AUTO MEDICAL PAYMENTS Limit	AUTO MEDICAL PAYMENTS Premium	MEDICAL EXPENSE AND INCOME LOSS BENEFITS (Virginia Only) Limit Stated In Each Medical Expense and Income Loss Endorsement For Each Person	MEDICAL EXPENSE AND INCOME LOSS BENEFITS (Virginia Only) Premium
1	$	$	$	$
2	$	$	$	$
3	$	$	$	$
4	$	$	$	$
5	$	$	$	$
Total Premium		$		$

Continued on next page

POLICY NUMBER: _____

ITEM NINE

SCHEDULE OF COVERED AUTOS WHICH ARE FURNISHED TO SOMEONE OTHER THAN A CLASS I OR CLASS II OPERATOR OR WHICH ARE INSURED ON A SPECIFIED CAR BASIS (Cont'd)

Covered Auto No.	COVERAGES – PREMIUMS, LIMITS AND DEDUCTIBLES (Absence of a deductible or limit entry in any column below means that the limit or deductible entry in the corresponding ITEM TWO column applies instead.)							
	COMPREHENSIVE		SPECIFIED CAUSES OF LOSS		COLLISION		TOWING & LABOR	
	Limit Stated In ITEM TWO Minus Deductible Shown Below	Premium	Limit Stated In ITEM TWO Minus Deductible Shown Below	Premium	Limit Stated In ITEM TWO Minus Deductible Shown Below	Premium	Limit Per Disablement	Premium
1	$	$	$	$	$	$	$	$
2	$	$	$	$	$	$	$	$
3	$	$	$	$	$	$	$	$
4	$	$	$	$	$	$	$	$
5	$	$	$	$	$	$	$	$
Total Premium		$		$		$		$
Covered Auto No.	Person or organization to which the Covered "Auto" has been furnished (Do not include Covered "Autos" which have been furnished to Class I or Class II operators.)							
1								
2								
3								
4								
5								

ITEM TEN

LIABILITY PREMIUM FOR PICK UP AND DELIVERY OF AUTOS – NON-FRANCHISED DEALERS ONLY

NUMBER OF DRIVER TRIPS		RATE	PREMIUM
51-200 Miles			$
Over 200 Miles			$
		TOTAL	$

Garage Coverage Form (CA 00 05)

The six sections in the Garage Coverage Form are as follows:

- Section I—Covered Autos
- Section II—Liability Coverage
- Section III—Garagekeepers Coverage
- Section IV—Physical Damage Coverage
- Section V—Garage Conditions
- Section VI—Definitions

Section I—Covered Autos

Using the eleven covered auto designation symbols shown in Exhibit 11-5, the garage policy provides coverages tailored to almost any kind of auto dealer exposure.

EXHIBIT 11-5

Description of Covered Auto Designation Symbols for Garage Coverage Form

COMMERCIAL AUTO
CA 00 05 03 06

Symbol		Description Of Covered Auto Designation Symbols
21	Any "Auto"	
22	Owned "Autos" Only	Only those "autos" you own (and for Liability Coverage any "trailers" you don't own while attached to power units you own). This includes those "autos" you acquire ownership of after the policy begins.
23	Owned Private Passenger "Autos" Only	Only the private passenger "autos" you own. This includes those private passenger "autos" you acquire ownership of after the policy begins.
24	Owned "Autos" Other Than Private Passenger "Autos" Only	Only those "autos" you own that are not of the private passenger type (and for Liability Coverage any "trailers" you don't own while attached to power units you own). This includes those "autos" not of the private passenger type you acquire ownership of after the policy begins.
25	Owned "Autos" Subject To No-Fault	Only those "autos" you own that are required to have No-Fault benefits in the state where they are licensed or principally garaged. This includes those "autos" you acquire ownership of after the policy begins provided they are required to have No-Fault benefits in the state where they are licensed or principally garaged.
26	Owned "Autos" Subject To A Compulsory Uninsured Motorists Law	Only those "autos" you own that because of the law in the state where they are licensed or principally garaged are required to have and cannot reject Uninsured Motorists Coverage. This includes those "autos" you acquire ownership of after the policy begins provided they are subject to the same state uninsured motorists requirement.
27	Specifically Described "Autos"	Only those "autos" described in Item Nine of the Declarations for which a premium charge is shown (and for Liability Coverage any "trailers" you don't own while attached to a power unit described in Item Nine).
28	Hired "Autos" Only	Only those "autos" you lease, hire, rent or borrow. This does not include any "auto" you lease, hire, rent, or borrow from any of your "employees", partners, (if you are a partnership), members (if you are a limited liability company) or members of their households.
29	Non-Owned "Autos" Used In Your Garage Business	Any "auto" you do not own, lease, hire, rent or borrow used in connection with your garage business described in the Declarations. This includes "autos" owned by your "employees" or partners (if you are a partnership), members (if you are a limited liability company), or members of their households while used in your garage business.
30	"Autos" Left With You For Service, Repair, Storage Or Safekeeping	Any customer's land motor vehicle or trailer or semitrailer while left with you for service, repair, storage or safekeeping. Customers include your "employees", and members of their households, who pay for the services performed.
31	Dealers "Autos" (Physical Damage Coverages)	Any "autos" and the interests in these "autos" described in Item Seven of the Declarations.

Section 1 explains what autos the policy covers according to the symbols used in Item Two of the Garage Coverage Form Declarations. The first eight symbols of the garage form are similar to the first eight symbols of the business auto form.

Symbol 21— Any Auto can be used for only liability and auto medical payments. When the insurer shows this symbol opposite either or both of those coverages, such protection applies to all autos owned at policy inception, any newly acquired and replacement autos on a blanket and automatic basis, all nonowned autos, and all hired autos. Because the policy defines the term "auto" as "a land motor vehicle, trailer or semitrailer," the term "any auto" can include private passenger autos, trucks, truck-tractors, buses, taxis, motorcycles, and trailers of any type. This definition would also include mobile equipment. (Because the garage policy also covers general liability exposures, the insurer does not have to separate mobile equipment coverage between the CGL and auto policies.)

Symbol 22—Owned Autos Only applies to any type of land motor vehicle, trailer, or semitrailer as long as the insured owns it. When the insurer shows this symbol opposite liability or physical damage insurance, coverage also applies to any type of nonowned trailer that the insured attaches to any type of owned auto. In addition to liability insurance, Symbol 22 can be used to provide non-compulsory uninsured motorists insurance and physical damage coverage.

Symbol 23—Owned Private Passenger Autos Only can be used for liability and physical damage coverages. It provides blanket and automatic coverage on all owned private passenger autos, including those newly acquired. The symbol also covers trailers used with the autos. In addition, it can be used to provide noncompulsory uninsured motorists insurance; when a dealer wants to limit its noncompulsory uninsured motorists insurance to private passenger autos only, it uses Symbol 23.

Symbol 24—Owned Autos Other Than Private Passenger Autos Only serves the same purpose as Symbol 23, except the policy will cover any auto, as defined, that is not a private passenger auto on a blanket and automatic basis. Symbol 24 applies to liability, medical payments, physical damage, and noncompulsory uninsured motorists coverages. Dealers who may want non-compulsory uninsured motorists coverage on this class of autos can also use Symbol 24.

Symbol 25—Owned Autos Subject to No-Fault is used only for mandatory no-fault coverage. Although insurers can apply Symbol 27 to no-fault, most insurers prefer Symbol 25 to ensure that coverage is always in place and that the insured complies with the law.

Symbol 26—Owned Autos Subject to Compulsory Uninsured Motorists Law is used only in states that have compulsory uninsured motorists insurance laws giving the insured no right to reject the coverage.

Symbols 21 through 26 provide blanket and automatic coverage for vehicles that fall within the limits of each symbol. As an alternative, insurers can use Symbol 27—Specifically Described Autos to confine such coverage to specifically described autos. When the insured or insurer selects Symbol 27, the insured must specifically describe all autos for which it desires coverage. Insurers do not normally require dealers to specifically describe their owned autos on the supplementary schedule at policy inception. The exceptions are when the insurer uses Symbol 27 for physical damage, uninsured motorists, or no-fault coverages, or when the insured furnishes autos to certain persons. If the insurer enters Symbol 27 next to a coverage in the declarations, a newly acquired auto is covered for that coverage only if the following are true:

• The policy insures all autos that the named insured owns for that coverage, or the new vehicle replaces a covered auto the insured previously owned that had the coverage

• The insurer receives notice within thirty days after the named insured acquires the auto that the named insured wants the auto covered for the coverage in question

Coverage for newly acquired autos of the type described by each symbol is automatic for symbols 21, 22, 23, 24, 25, or 26.

Symbol 28—Hired Autos Only is self-explanatory. It is the same coverage as that provided by Symbol 8 in the business auto policy. Because Symbol 21, which is usually used for dealers, already includes the hired auto liability exposure, Symbol 28 is not necessary for liability coverage for most dealers. Policies covering dealers under Symbol 21 for liability can use Symbol 28 to provide physical damage coverage for hired autos.

Symbol 29—Nonowned Autos Used in Your Garage Business provides nonowned auto liability coverage and is, like hired auto coverage, included within the coverage provided by Symbol 21. Therefore, it would only be used when Symbol 21 is not shown for liability coverage. It is the same coverage as that provided by Symbol 9 in the business auto policy.

Symbol 30—Autos Left With You for Service, Repair, Storage, or Safekeeping applies solely to garagekeepers coverage. A later section in this chapter describes this coverage in more detail.

Symbol 31—Dealers Autos (Physical Damage Coverages) triggers physical damage coverage for the autos and the interests in those autos as shown in Item Seven of the declarations.

Dealers may have vehicles in their possession on consignment; for example, a dealer (the consignee) may have possession of an auto belonging to someone else, such as another dealer or an auto manufacturer (the consignor), for purposes of sale. Generally payment on consigned property is not due the consignor until sold by the consignee. Most courts consider a consignment to be a bailment, but responsibility for damage to a consigned auto may be subject to a contract between the parties that would impose greater responsibility on the consignee. The supplementary schedule under the heading "Interests Covered in Item Seven" includes a column headed: "All Interests in any Auto not owned by you or any creditor While In Your Possession on Consignment for Sale." An entry in this column would provide coverage for the consignee's and consignor's interests.

Insurers must place Symbol 31 opposite the desired physical damage coverages in the policy declarations. The insured does not have to describe specifically the consigned autos in the schedule but must show total values. If the policy is on a nonreporting basis, the insurer uses this limit in determining the premium. If the policy is on a reporting basis, the insured will include the value of those autos when it makes each report and the premium auditor will consider the values at the policy's expiration.

When a lending institution finances autos for a dealer, the autos are encumbered and no longer qualify for coverage under Symbol 31. Insurers handle coverage on encumbered autos as if the dealer owned the autos. The insurer will show Symbol 22, 23, 24, or 27 opposite the physical damage coverages in the policy declarations; however, the insured must also designate the interests of the dealers and creditor in Item Seven of the supplementary schedule.

Section II—Liability Coverage

Section II of the coverage form explains the liability coverage. It provides protection for the insured against accidents arising out of garage operations that result in bodily injury to or a property damage loss of any other person. This protection includes coverage for premises and operations liability, products and completed operations liability, and contractual liability. Because the definition of garage operations includes the operation, maintenance, and use of covered autos, this insurance combines general liability and auto liability coverage.

As long as the insurance applies, the insurer will pay what the insured is legally obligated to pay, subject to the maximum limits of liability and the exclusions. Section II begins by separately defining what the policy will pay for garage operations other than covered autos and garage operations for covered autos.

For covered autos, the policy insures the named insured and anybody else using a covered auto with the insured's permission, with just a few exceptions. These include the owner of a hired or borrowed auto, an employee when the covered auto is owned by the employee, and anyone using a covered auto in an automotive-related business other than the insured's operations. The most important limitation on status as an insured applies to customers using a covered auto. A dealer's customer is not an insured except when the customer has no other insurance (primary, excess, or contingent) or the insurance that the customer has is less than the limits required by law. When the customer has no other insurance, the customer is an insured, but only for the amount required by the compulsory or financial responsibility law. When the customer has other insurance (primary, excess, or contingent) that is less than the compulsory or financial responsibility law limits where the covered auto is principally garaged, the customer is an insured only for the difference between the customer's policy limits and the limit required by law.

Anyone liable for the conduct of an insured is also an insured but only to the extent of that liability. For garage operations other than covered autos, the policy insures the named insured and partners, members of a limited liability company, employees, directors, or shareholders, but only while acting within the scope of their duties.

The coverage will also pay supplementary expenses related to losses covered by the policy, such as expenses incurred by the insurer in defending and investigating claims, and the cost of bail bonds up to $2,000. The policy covers several other supplementary payments in the same manner as the CGL and business auto policies discussed in previous chapters.

When a covered auto is out of the state in which it is licensed, the out-of-state coverage extension increases the limit of insurance for liability coverage to meet the requirements of the state in which the insured is operating the auto. This coverage extension includes the requirements of financial responsibility laws or no-fault laws that apply to out-of-state autos. The policy increases the limits only to meet the minimum requirements. This matches the coverage in the business auto policy.

Exclusions narrow the coverage and eliminate coverage to which other insurance applies. Section II lists seventeen exclusions. Most of them are the common exclusions of general liability coverages and the Business Auto Coverage Form. From a premium auditor's viewpoint, Exclusion 7 is one of the most important. According to that exclusion, the policy provides no coverage for autos leased or rented to others except when the named insured rents an auto to a customer while that customer's auto is being serviced or repaired.

Section II also specifies the limits of liability applicable to the policy and that these limits are on a per accident basis. A $100 deductible applies for property damage to an auto resulting from work the named insured performed on that auto.

Section III—Garagekeepers Coverage

When auto dealers, repair shops, service stations, auto storage garages, or public parking facilities have care, custody, or control of customers' autos, these businesses are bailees. They may be liable for loss to nonowned autos in their possession. Even if the auto owners carry their own insurance for physical damage, the auto owners' insurers can subrogate against the garage when they pay their insureds for damages occurring while the vehicle is in the bailee's custody. Garagekeepers coverage is designed to deal with this exposure—it is needed because liability coverage excludes damage to the property of others in the insured's care, custody, or control. Although only dealers are eligible for the garage policy, garagekeepers coverage is available as an endorsement (CA 99 37) that can be attached to the business auto, motor carrier, and truckers coverage forms for other businesses with this exposure. The coverage is identical. For example, a restaurant that offers valet parking may have custody of customers' vehicles and therefore need garagekeepers coverage.

Section III of the Garage Coverage Form explains garagekeepers coverage. If garagekeepers coverage applies, the insurer must enter Symbol 30 in the declarations opposite the causes of loss the insured desires. The insured can elect comprehensive (damage from any cause other than collision or overturn— of course, like every "all-risks" form, other exclusions apply) or specified causes of loss (fire, lightning, explosion, theft, and vandalism and malicious mischief). The insured can add collision coverage, which includes overturn, or just purchase collision coverage. The insured's choices are, of course, subject to the insurer's acceptance. The supplementary schedule shows the garagekeepers coverage limit and the deductible for each location. This coverage does not penalize for underinsurance.

Under garagekeepers coverage, the insurer will pay the amount for which the insured is legally responsible when loss caused by an covered peril occurs to a covered auto or auto equipment left in the insured's care while the insured is attending, servicing, repairing, parking, or storing the covered auto or autos in its garage operations. The insurer also promises to provide defense and to pay all defense costs in any suit involving a covered loss. However, the insurer's duty to defend or settle any claim or suit ends when the payment of judgments or settlements exhausts the limit for any coverage.

For loss to a covered auto, garagekeepers coverage insures the named insured and the named insured's partners, members (if the insured is a limited liability company) employees, directors, or shareholders, but only while acting within the scope of their duties as such. In addition to paying the limit of liability, the insurer agrees to pay many other expenses and costs (or supplementary payments) similar to those covered under the Business Auto Coverage Form and the liability section of the Garage Coverage Form. The only exception is the $2,000 for the cost of bail bonds the insured must provide because of a covered accident. Garagekeepers insurance does not provide that coverage extension.

Also, there are eight exclusions to the coverage. Of these, four are similar to those in the business auto physical damage coverage and garage policy physical damage provisions. Those are loss to sound-reproducing equipment, tapes and records, radar detection equipment, citizens' band radios, telephones, and similar devices. No insurance applies to the following:

- Liability that results from any agreement by the insured to accept responsibility for loss. Such an agreement would defeat the condition of legal liability.
- Loss by theft or conversion caused in any way by the named insured, its employees, or its shareholders. It would be against public policy to pay

for theft caused by the named insured, but crime coverage (commonly referred to as a fidelity bond) can cover loss by theft or conversion caused by the named insured's employees.

- Defective parts or materials.
- Faulty work of the insured.

The last two exclusions merely reinforce the intent that defective products and faulty work are business hazards. However, coverage applies to damage of other property stemming from defective products or faulty work.

The most the insurer will pay for a loss at each location is the limit shown in the declarations for garagekeepers coverage minus any applicable deductible. This limit applies regardless of the number of covered autos, insureds, premiums paid, claims made, or suits brought.

While the garagekeepers coverage provides liability coverage, many insureds want to be sure that their customers will be paid, regardless of fault; if desired, the insurer can substitute one of two other forms of garagekeepers insurance by checking a box in the supplementary schedule. One option provides direct coverage without regard to liability on a primary basis, and the other provides the same coverage on an excess basis. The premium charge for each form of garagekeepers insurance appears in the premium table displayed on the state rate pages. Direct coverage can be purchased on a primary basis or an excess basis.

When the insured purchases garagekeepers direct coverage on a primary basis, the insurer pays losses that result from insured causes of loss without regard to the named insured's liability. No requirement exists that the vehicle owner first try to collect under its own insurance.

When the insured purchases garagekeepers direct coverage on an excess basis, the insurer pays losses without regard to the named insured's liability. Coverage applies only as excess over any other collectible insurance. The liability coverage of the garagekeepers remains unchanged; if the vehicle owner's insurer pays its insured and then asserts a subrogation claim, the garage-keeper's insurer will defend the claim and pay any judgment or settlement.

Section IV—Physical Damage Coverage

Physical damage coverage under Section IV of the Garage Coverage Form can cover owned, hired, or borrowed autos and autos held on consignment. The coverage options are the same as those available with the business auto coverage.

Insurers may use the specified auto basis for dealers who have a limited number of autos. However, insurers usually handle physical damage insurance on dealers' covered autos on a blanket basis. Insurers still adjust losses on an actual cash value or cost-to-repair basis, but the policy does not specifically describe covered autos. Instead, the dealers' supplementary schedule in

Item Seven states one amount applicable to all covered autos at each of the described locations, less the deductible that applies to each covered auto, as well as the maximum deductible that applies to all loss in any one event regardless of the number of vehicles involved. If a dealer acquires additional locations during the policy period for storage or display of autos, a separate insurance amount designated in the schedule applies to those autos. However, if an insured does not report a new location to the insurer within forty-five days, this temporary coverage ceases. The supplementary schedule for auto dealers also provides coverage while covered autos are in transit, subject to the amount specified for that exposure.

The physical damage covered-causes-of-loss options have the same titles and possible combinations as those discussed in connection with garagekeepers coverage, and two of them—comprehensive and collision—cover exactly the same perils. The specified-causes-of-loss coverage, however, lists causes of loss that are not included in the garagekeepers version. In addition to the causes of loss of fire, lightning or explosion; theft; and mischief or vandalism (which are covered by both), the physical damage version of specified causes of loss also includes windstorm, hail, or earthquake; flood; and the sinking, burning, collision, or derailment of any conveyance transporting the covered auto.

The Garage Coverage Form contains all the physical damage coverage exclusions in the Business Auto Coverage Form. In addition, no coverage applies to any of the following:

- Covered autos leased or rented to others except covered autos rented to customers while their autos are left with the named insured for service or repair.

- Loss to a covered auto with which the dealer voluntarily parted because of a trick or scheme or under false pretenses (coverage for this peril can be added by an endorsement to be discussed later).

- Loss to a covered auto the named insured acquires from a seller who did not have legal title (coverage for this peril can be added by an endorsement to be discussed later).

- The dealer's expected profit.

- Loss to any covered auto at a nonscheduled location that the insured does not report to the insurer within forty-five days after the insured begins using the location.

- Any covered auto under collision coverage while being driven or transported from the point of purchase or distribution to its destination if the distance is more than fifty road miles.

- For specified-causes-of-loss coverage, loss to any covered auto caused by collision or upset of any vehicle transporting it if the policy insures the covered auto for specified causes of loss only. Collision insurance would cover such losses.

The coverage form explains the maximum amount the insurer will pay in case of a loss. For any one covered auto, the insurer will pay whichever is less: the actual cash value of the damaged or stolen property at the time of loss, or what it would cost to repair or replace the damaged or stolen property with other property of like kind and quality. Most property forms do not define the term "actual cash value." However the Garage Coverage Form states that an adjustment for depreciation and physical condition will be made in determining actual cash value in the event of a total loss, and that the insurer will not pay for any betterment resulting from a repair or replacement. If the policy does not cover all interests, the insurer pays only an amount equal to the value of the covered interests.

Regardless of the number of covered autos involved in a loss, the most the insurer will pay for all loss at any one location is the amount stated in the dealers' supplementary schedule for that location. Likewise, the most the insurer will pay for loss to covered autos in transit is the amount shown in the schedule for loss in transit. Those limits are maximums. Whether the insurer pays those amounts depends in part on whether the dealer has complied with the other special limit of liability provisions. Which of those provisions apply depends on whether the insurer has written the coverage on a reporting basis or a nonreporting basis.

Insurers often use a reporting basis when the values of cars in stock fluctuate drastically. The dealer may prefer the nonreporting approach when dealers' values are relatively stable or when the dealer wishes to avoid the complexity of the reporting approach.

The dealers reporting is similar in concept to the reporting insurers use with property insurance. The insured submits monthly or quarterly reports of values to the insurer. The insurer then adjusts premiums based on those reported values. The insurer should check the appropriate boxes in Item Seven of the dealers' supplementary schedule.

The reporting basis approach is subject to a reporting provision under the "Limits of Insurance" section, which encourages proper value reporting by a penalizing for underinsurance. If the covered autos' value at the location in question exceeds what the insured actually reported in the last report, the insurer will determine what percentage the total reported value was of the actual value on the last report's date. The insurer then pays this percentage of the loss, subject to the limit of insurance stated in the schedule for that location. If for some reason the first report due is delinquent on the date of loss, the most the insurer will pay is 75 percent of the insurance applying to the scheduled location.

Suppose, for example, the insured reported values of $200,000 for the last month before the loss, but the actual values for the last month before loss were $400,000. The amount of the loss was $20,000. The proportion of reported values to actual values is $200,000 divided by $400,000, or

50 percent. Therefore, the insurer would pay only 50 percent of the loss, or $10,000. If the insured has not made any reports at all, the insurer will not pay more than 75 percent of the applicable limit of insurance for the location. Even if the insured overreported, the insurer would not pay more than the actual cash value.

For insurance purposes, the insured should report the inventory's actual cash value, not the value shown on the books for accounting purposes. Significant differences exist between the accounting and the insurance approaches to inventory valuation.

When insurers write coverage on a nonreporting basis, they base the premium on the total value of the covered autos stated in the declarations. A provision resembling a 100 percent coinsurance clause enforces insurance-to-value. The most the dealer can recover is the policy limit for the physical damage coverages. However, if the value of covered autos at the time of loss is higher than the policy limit, the dealer will suffer a penalty for underinsurance because the insurer will pay less than the policy limit. The insurer determines the percentage it will pay by dividing the policy limit by the total value of covered autos at the time of loss. For example, assume a dealer purchases $100,000 of comprehensive insurance on a nonreporting basis. At the time of a flood loss, the parties establish that the total value of all covered autos was $150,000. The most the insurer will pay is determined as:

$$\frac{\$100,000}{\$150,000} = 66.7\% \text{ of the loss.}$$

Section V—Garage Conditions

Section V of the Garage Coverage Form sets out the loss and general conditions applicable to the coverage; they are virtually identical to those in the business auto form. In brief, the loss conditions include appraisal procedures, the insured's duties in the event of a loss, legal action against the insurer, loss payment, and rights of recovery. The general conditions clarify the conditions of bankruptcy, concealment, misrepresentation or fraud, liberalization, bailees, other insurance, premium audit, the policy period and coverage territory, and when the insurer issues two or more coverage forms or policies.

The policy period and coverage territory condition explains that the policy covers bodily injury, property damage, and losses occurring during the policy period within the U.S., its territories or possessions, or Canada. It also explains that products liability coverage applies to losses anywhere in the world as long as the insured sold the product for use within the U.S., its territories or possessions, or Canada, and the injured party brings the original suit for damages in one of those places.

Section VI—Definitions

Section VI defines certain words and phrases relating to the garage coverage. From a premium auditor's point of view, two definitions are particularly important. Auto means "a land motor vehicle, trailer or semitrailer." Garage operations means "the ownership, maintenance or use of locations for garage business and that portion of the roads or other accesses that adjoin these locations. 'Garage operations' includes the ownership, maintenance or use of the 'autos' indicated in SECTION I of this Coverage Form, as covered 'autos.' 'Garage operations' also include all operations necessary or incidental to a garage business."

Endorsements

Insurers can add endorsements to the policy provisions to broaden or restrict the coverage. In either case, the endorsement may affect the premium adjustment. Support personnel do not attach every endorsement to the premium auditor's copy of the policy. The only reference to the endorsement may be the appearance of the form number in Item Two of the declarations. When certain endorsement numbers appear on the policy, a premium charge applies. Some endorsements have already been discussed; the sections that follow describe other endorsements that most often affect the premium adjustment.

Medical Payments

Insurers can add medical payments coverage by endorsement for auto exposures, garage locations and operations exposures, or both. Item Eight of the declarations indicates the type of medical payments coverage and the estimated premium. The additional premium for medical payments coverage is a specified percentage of the liability premium. The premium auditor can find this percentage in the manual rules and should indicate it in Item Eight. Separate endorsements provide the two types of medical payments coverage:

- Auto Medical Payments Coverage (CA 99 03)
- Garage Locations and Operations Medical Payments Coverage (CA 25 05)

Insurers must add both endorsements to the policy to cover both types.

If the policy provides auto medical payments coverage (CA 99 03), the insurer will pay medical expenses without regard to liability for the named insured while occupying an auto or while a pedestrian, when struck by any auto; if the named insured is an individual, for any family member while occupying an auto or while a pedestrian, when struck by any auto; and for anyone else while occupying a covered auto or a temporary substitute for a covered auto that is out of service because of a breakdown, repair, servicing, loss, or destruction. Under garage medical payments coverage (CA 25 05), the insurer will pay medical expenses without regard to liability to anyone whose injury arises from garage locations or operations with the following three exceptions: bodily injury arising out of the maintenance or use of an auto, bodily injury arising out of and in the course of employment, and bodily injury caused by war or insurrection.

Uninsured Motorists Coverage

Uninsured motorists coverage protects the insured, family members, and anyone occupying a covered vehicle against the inability to collect damages from the uninsured vehicle's owner or driver. Uninsured motorists insurance varies by state; the state exception pages contain the rules regarding this coverage. Many states have laws making uninsured motorists insurance mandatory if a vehicle owner purchases auto liability. In some of those states, the insured can reject coverage by signing a rejection form. For dealers, uninsured motorists insurance applies both to owned autos and to dealer, repairer, and transporter plates.

False Pretense Coverage (CA 25 03)

False pretense coverage, shown in Exhibit 11-6, broadens the physical damage coverage by eliminating the exclusion of losses resulting from someone causing the insured to voluntarily part with a covered auto by trick, scheme or under false pretenses, or by the insured's acquiring an auto from a seller who did not have legal title. Coverage does not apply to a loss in which for any reason a bank or any other drawee fails to pay.

This endorsement covers all autos the insured acquires, not just the autos covered for physical damage. If, for example, a new car dealer with physical damage coverage only on used cars had this endorsement attached, the coverage afforded by the endorsement would also apply to new cars. Although the loss is limited to $25,000 per occurrence, or a higher limit if shown in the declarations, the premium for this coverage is a specified rate per $100 of total inventory value.

Dealers Driveaway Collision Coverage (CA 25 02)

Physical damage coverage excludes coverage under collision for autos the insured picks up or delivers more than fifty road miles away. This would include all autos driven, towed, or carried on any other auto or trailer owned or hired by the named insured. Dealers frequently encounter such an exposure when they swap cars with another dealer who has in stock the exact vehicle configuration that a customer wants. Coverage for this exposure is available under the Dealers Driveaway Collision Coverage Endorsement, shown in Exhibit 11-7. A condition of this endorsement is that the insured will report, either monthly or quarterly, the number and the values of covered autos picked up or delivered more than fifty road miles away and the points of origin and destination.

EXHIBIT 11-6

False Pretense Coverage Endorsement

POLICY NUMBER:

COMMERCIAL AUTO
CA 25 03 03 06

THIS ENDORSEMENT CHANGES THE POLICY. PLEASE READ IT CAREFULLY.

FALSE PRETENSE COVERAGE

This endorsement modifies insurance provided under the following:

GARAGE COVERAGE FORM

With respect to coverage provided by this endorsement, the provisions of the Coverage Form apply unless modified by the endorsement.

This endorsement changes the policy effective on the inception date of the policy unless another date is indicated below.

Named Insured:	
Endorsement Effective Date:	
Countersignature Of Authorized Representative	
Name:	
Title:	
Signature:	
Date:	

SCHEDULE

Limit of Insurance – $25,000 unless another limit is shown below or in the Declarations.			
$ Limit of Insurance			
Named Location No. From Item Three Of The Declarations	**Total Inventory Value For Each Named Location**	**Rate**	**Premium**
	$	$	$
	$	$	$
	$	$	$
Information required to complete this Schedule, if not shown above, will be shown in the Declarations.			

Continued on next page

A. **Covered Autos** is changed by adding the following:

Any "auto" you have acquired is a covered "auto" under False Pretense Coverage.

B. **Physical Damage Coverage** is changed as follows:

1. The following is added:

We will pay for "loss" to a covered "auto" under:

False Pretense Coverage caused by:

a. Someone causing you to voluntarily part with the covered "auto" by trick, scheme or under false pretenses.

b. Your acquiring an "auto" from a seller who did not have legal title.

2. **Exclusions** is changed as follows:

a. The **False Pretense** Exclusion does not apply.

b. The following exclusion is added:

(1) The insurance under Paragraph **B.1.a.** of this endorsement does not apply unless:

(a) You had legal title to, or consignment papers for, the covered "auto" prior to "loss"; and

(b) You make every effort to recover the covered "auto" when it is located.

(2) False Pretense Coverage does not apply to a loss in which for any reason a bank or any other drawee fails to pay.

3. **Limits Of Insurance** is changed as follows:

Under False Pretense Coverage, the Limit of Insurance shown in the Schedule or Declarations is the most we will pay for all "loss" caused by any one person within any one year of the policy period.

4. The **Deductible** provision is changed by adding the following:

From our obligation under False Pretense Coverage, we will deduct the actual value of any property delivered to you in full or partial payment for title to or possession of a covered "auto".

C. The following is added to the **Duties In The Event Of Accident, Claim, Suit Or Loss** Garage Condition:

You, or someone on your behalf, must take all reasonable steps to cause a warrant to be issued, as soon as practicable, for the arrest of anyone causing a "loss" defined within the False Pretense Coverage. Failure to cause such warrant to be issued as required by this Condition shall not invalidate any claim made by you, if it is shown that reasonable efforts were made.

100 Dollar Deductible for Completed Operations Does Not Apply (CA 03 03)

By endorsement, the insured can eliminate the $100 deductible provision. This coverage requires an additional premium charge.

Broad Form Products Coverage (CA 25 01)

Broad form products coverage eliminates the exclusion under liability coverage of damage to the products or any part of the product caused by a defect existing when the insured sells or transfers the product to another person. Without this endorsement, a service station that sells a tire that blows out because of a defect has no coverage for damage to the tire. When the insurer attaches this endorsement, coverage is subject to a $250 deductible per accident.

EXHIBIT 11-7

Dealers Driveaway Collision Coverage Endorsement

COMMERCIAL AUTO
CA 25 02 12 93

THIS ENDORSEMENT CHANGES THE POLICY. PLEASE READ IT CAREFULLY.

DEALERS DRIVEAWAY COLLISION COVERAGE

This endorsement modifies insurance provided under the following:

GARAGE COVERAGE FORM

With respect to coverage provided by this endorsement, the provisions of the Coverage Form apply unless modified by the endorsement.

PHYSICAL DAMAGE COVERAGE is changed as follows:

The exclusion relating to collision "loss" to covered "autos" driven or transported more than fifty road miles from point of purchase or distribution to their destination does not apply, provided that:

1. You must include in your regular monthly or quarterly reports a statement of the points of origin, the destination and the factory price of each of these covered "autos".

2. If on the date of your last report the total value of these covered "autos", driven or transported during the period the report covers, exceeds what you reported we will pay only a percentage of what we would otherwise be obligated to pay. We will determine this percentage by dividing the total value reported by the total value you actually had on the date of your last report.

Copyright, ISO Properties, Inc., 1993.

Personal Injury Liability (CA 25 08)

Some garages want broader liability coverage than bodily injury and property damage liability. Personal injury liability coverage includes injury arising out of false arrest, detention, or imprisonment; malicious prosecution; wrongful entry into or eviction of a person from a room, dwelling, or premises the person occupies; slander or libel; and violation of the right of privacy orally or by written publication of material. The insurer must add such coverage by endorsement. The liability premium is increased by a factor shown in the CLM.

Broadened Coverage (CA 25 14)

Broadened Coverage—Garages Endorsement (CA 25 14) can be used to add personal and advertising injury, fire legal liability coverage, incidental medical malpractice, non-owned watercraft, and limited worldwide liability coverage. It also provides ninety days' automatic coverage for a newly acquired or formed garage business and adds the spouse of any partner as an insured with respect to the insured's garage business if the insured is a partnership.

PREMIUM DETERMINATION FOR AUTO DEALERS

Rules for classification and premium determination appear in the *CLM* "Division One—Automobile," Section II. The manual separates rules into those for auto dealers (Rules 48, 49, and 50) and garagekeepers insurance (Rules 54, 55, and 56).

Basis of Premium

Insurers historically based the premium for garage liability coverage on payroll; the insurer applied factors to adjust the premium for coverage modifications. This procedure assumed that losses varied in proportion to the business' size, which the insured's payroll would reflect. An ISO study, however, revealed that a substantial portion of all losses resulted from traffic accidents involving employees and employees' family members. A dealer who is generous in permitting employees and family members to use garage-owned cars represents a distinctly greater exposure than another dealer with the same payroll amount who is not as liberal about the use of garage-owned cars. Therefore, using payroll as a premium base results in considerable inequity among insureds.

Garage coverage for dealers therefore uses premium bases more directly reflecting the exposure. Liability exposure for a garage uses a premium base reflecting the number of auto operators. Insurers base physical damage premiums on the values of covered autos.

Liability Premiums

Rating unit
A measure of loss exposure used in garage liability pricing determined by multiplying the class of operators by the number of persons in the class.

For liability insurance covering garage operations and autos in conjunction with such operations, the basis of premium is the rating unit. A **rating unit** represents a person or a part of a person (that is, a factor less than one) depending on which class of operators applies. Insurers determine the number of rating units as follows: the number of operators multiplied by the applicable rating factor from Rule 49 (the Premium Determination Rule) equals the number of rating units. The liability premium is the rate shown on the state rate pages for the territory in which the garage is located multiplied by the number of rating units for each location. Two classes of operators exist: Class I—Employees, and Class II—Nonemployees.

Class I—Employees includes all the dealer's employees, including part-time employees and active proprietors, partners, or officers. Insurers count those working an average of twenty or more hours a week as full-time employees for this computation. The insurer must multiply the number of employees working an average of less than twenty hours a week (but for the entire year) by 0.5 before determining the number of rating units. Because the rating unit is an annual unit of exposure, the insurer must similarly prorate an employee who worked only part of the policy period according to the part of the year the insured employed him. For example, if an employee defined as one rating unit began working for the insured on August 1, and the policy covers the calendar year, that employee counts as 0.42 rating units (22 weeks ÷ 52 weeks × 1.00 rating unit = 0.42 rating units). The manual divides this class into the following regular operators, and all others.

Regular operators include any proprietors, partners, and officers active in the business, as well as salespersons, general managers, service managers, or any other employee whose principal duties involve operating autos or to whom the insured furnishes a garage auto. This class includes executives, proprietors, or partners even if they do not have the regular use of a dealer's auto as long as they are active in the business. Employees whose principal duties involve operating a covered auto may include tow truck drivers, parts department runners, employees who pick up and deliver customers or autos, or any other employee who uses an auto as an integral part of the job. The integral role of an auto in performing the job, not the percentage of the employee's time, determines inclusion in this class. Any other employee with the use of a company auto also belongs in this category. Mechanics who drive vehicles to and from the bay where they perform work on the cars do not belong in this class. Their principal duties are not driving the vehicle. A rating factor of 1.00 applies to each employee included in this class.

The term "all others" includes all employees other than regular operators. A rating factor of 0.40 applies to each employee in this class. The class even includes employees who do not have a driver's license.

Unless already described in Class I, any person regularly furnished with a dealer's auto belongs in Class II—Nonemployees. Class II may include inactive proprietors, partners, or officers. Class II also includes relatives of those individuals and the relatives of any person described in Class I. This class may also include a prominent local sports figure to whom a dealer loans an auto. If more than one person uses the same auto, the insurer counts only the factor for the highest rated operator in determining the number of rating units. The operator's age at the policy's inception determines the rating factor to use for Class II operators. The rating factor does not change if the Class II operator reaches twenty-five during the policy period. Insurers also use age to divide Class II into two categories.

Premium auditors should be aware that the manual also specifies a charge for furnished autos. A later section describes this charge. The charge should dovetail with the Class II nonemployees. The manual under the furnished auto rule states, "Autos furnished for regular use to other than Class I and Class II operators...." Generally, the furnished auto charge is for cars furnished to groups or organizations, not individuals.

Class II rates vary by the age of the operator. Those under age twenty-five take a higher rate than those over twenty-five. For operators younger than twenty-five, the number of such persons multiplied by 1.15 equals the applicable number of rating units.

Operators twenty-five and older are in the second category. The insurer determines the number of rating units for this category by multiplying the number of such persons by 0.50.

Premium auditors generally use the individual earnings records as their primary source to determine the number of employees. An insured normally maintains an individual earnings records for each employee, listing the payroll and the hours worked. Those records may be the only records showing the hours worked. The insured maintains those records on an annual basis. If employment terminates, the employer usually removes the record from the active file and places it elsewhere.

Some employers also (or instead of recording individual earnings) record the detail by pay period, listing all employees for the pay period. Such employers produce a new printout each pay period. The employee's duties are not shown on these printouts, which the premium auditor needs to obtain from personnel records or interviews.

At audit, the premium auditor obtains the needed records from the insured. However, the premium auditor must be sure to obtain records for all employees. The insured could neglect to provide the payroll records or information for those no longer employed, or it could lose some payroll records in handling them. Therefore, the premium auditor could be short several rating units in the calculation and not know it. Payroll records should show all employees at all times during the calendar year. If the employee terminates employment, his or her name still appears on each printout until the end of the calendar year. That facilitates the premium audit and reduces the chance of overlooking an employee. Because the premium for one rating unit can exceed $1,000, such an oversight can be costly to the insurer.

The information needed from these records includes each employee's name, the job duties or title, the employment period, the status (full time or part time as defined by the manual), and the class of employee (Ia or Ib). The premium auditor's worksheet must also list all employees. Exhibit 11-8 shows a worksheet with this information. The column totals show the number of rating units for Class I employees.

An alternative procedure that may be easier for the insured to understand is for the premium auditor to add the number of weeks worked by all employees in each category and divide the total by fifty-two (or the number of weeks in the policy period if it is not a year). This calculation yields the average number of employees in each category for the policy period. Multiplying this average number by the appropriate rating factor produces the number of rating units for each category. The premium auditor uses the number of days worked and considers 365 days to be 100 percent. The premium auditor then sums the percentages for all full-time employees and sums the percentages for all part-time employees and uses these percentages to calculate the number of rating units.

EXHIBIT 11-8

Premium Auditor's Rating Unit Worksheet

Carrier	Policy Information	Insured Name and Address	Completed By
AAA Training Insurance Company 101 W. Louisiana St., Ste. 210 McKinney, TX 75070	SMPL-HAZ1-001 Garage Liability 11/28/2004 to 11/28/2005 AuditID: 145988 Audit Method: Physical Audit Complete Type: Regular	J. Joneser Motor Co. 8040 Irving Blvd. Dallas, TX 75225	Ron Carlo Crowell & Associates, Inc. 101 Lousiana St. Ste. 207 McKinney, Texas 75069 Date Completed: 07/12/2006 FA Version: 3.0.5206 PID: 24

Description of Operations ... Audit 145988 ... Entity: J. Joneser Motor Co.

Legal Entity: **INDIVIDUAL**

J. Joneser Motor Company is a sole proprietorship which is owned by John Joneser and has been in business for 20 years. This is a used automobile dealership that specializes in 2000-2005 vehicles that are obtained from automobile auctions, local car dealerships, private owners and trade-in's. The vehicles for sale include top of the line vehicles from domestic and import automobile manufacturers, luxury automobiles and SUV's. There is an average inventory of 45 to 50 vehicles for sale and the insured sells approximately 900-1000 vehicles a year. There is a repair shop that does mechanical repairs such as tune-ups, brake and exhaust systems and minor mechanical repairs. There is no body shop operations, any exterior repairs are done by independent body shops at their place of business. Any detailing of vehicles is also sent out to outside independent shops. There are porters who wash and prepare sold vehicles for delivery to customers. The IA exposure includes John Joneser the owner/general manager. He handles all administrative and financial records, does some sales and manages all aspects of the business. Also, included in IA are 4 automobile salespersons who have been with the insured for over 10 years. The IB exposure includes the office secretary/title clerk, the shop manager, 3 mechanics and 2 porters. The IIA exposure includes Tonya Joneser, John Joneser's daughter who is furnished a vehicle for personal use. The IIB exposure includes Lucy Joneser, John Joneser's wife and Joan Joneser, John Joneser's mother who are furnished vehicles for personal use. There was no contract labor or sub contract labor used. The insured does not provide any loaner vehicles. John Joneser, the sales manager and the salespersons pick up or deliver vehicles within a 50 mile or less radius.

Dealer's Class Plan Rating Units Summary ... Audit 145988

Class	Status	Rate	Sum P/R	Prod.
I-A	FULL	1.000	6.830	6.830
I-B	FULL	0.400	4.000	1.600
I-B	PART	0.200	0.334	0.067
II-A		1.150	1.000	1.150
II-B		0.500	2.000	1.000
	Subtotal:			**10.647**
	Total Rating Units:			**10.647**

Dealer's Class Plan Detail ... Audit 145988

| Class: | I-A | Status: | | FULL | |

Name	Rate	P/R	Prod.	Gross	Start	End	Duties
Clyde Morter	1.000	1.000	1.000	209,834	12/01/2004	12/01/2005	Auto salesperson
Henry Sampson	1.000	1.000	1.000	75,000	12/01/2004	12/01/2005	
Duties:	Serviice Manager over sees the mechanics						
John Joneser	1.000	1.000	1.000	771,000	12/01/2004	12/01/2005	
Duties:	General manager - handles all administrative and financial records, does some						
	sales and manges all aspects of the business.						
Mitchell Irvin	1.000	0.830	0.830	180,400	02/01/2005	12/01/2005	Auto salesperson
Roger Stawbaugh	1.000	1.000	1.000	310,600	12/01/2004	12/01/2005	
Duties:	Sales Manager-Over sees the sales staff and approves sales						
Tim Ownman	1.000	1.000	1.000	205,000	12/01/2004	12/01/2005	Auto salesperson
Tom Achem	1.000	1.000	1.000	215,000	12/01/2004	12/01/2005	Auto salesperson
Subtotals:			6.830	1,966,834			

Continued on next page

Class:		I-B		Status:			FULL			

Name	Rate	P/R	Prod.	Gross	Start	End	Duties
John Crown	0.400	1.000	0.400	47,000	12/01/2004	12/01/2005	Mechanic
Juan Hernandez	0.400	1.000	0.400	8,000	12/01/2004	12/01/2005	
Duties:	Porter-washes automobiles						
Robert Blake	0.400	1.000	0.400	41,500	12/01/2004	12/01/2005	Mechanic
Shirley Joneser	0.400	1.000	0.400	25,000	12/01/2004	12/01/2005	
Duties:	Secretary/Title Clerk						
	Subtotals:		1.600	121,500			

Class:		I-B		Status:			PART			

Name	Rate	P/R	Prod.	Gross	Start	End	Duties
Rob Long	0.200	0.334	0.067	2,500	08/01/2005	12/01/2005	
Duties:	Porter-washes automobiles						
	Subtotals:		0.067	2,500			

Class:				II-A						

Name	Rate	P/R	Prod.	Relation	Ins	Age	Location	Start	End
Tonya Joneser	1.150	1.000	1.150	John Joneser's daughter	No	19	Dallas, Tx	12/01/2004	12/01/2005
	Subtotals:		1.150						

Class:				II-B						

Name	Rate	P/R	Prod.	Relation	Ins	Age	Location	Start	End
Joan Joneser	0.500	1.000	0.500	John Joneser's mother	No	60	Dallas, Tx	12/01/2004	12/01/2005
Lucy Joneser	0.500	1.000	0.500	John Joneser's wife	No	45	Dallas, Tx	12/01/2004	12/01/2005
	Subtotals:		1.000						

	Totals:			10.647		2,090,834

DEALER'S CLASS PLAN GENERAL INFORMATION

Number of Dealer Plates: 6	Number of Leased Autos: 0
Private passenger auto furnished for regular use but not included in Class I or II provided to: N/A	
Commercial auto furnished for regular use but not included in Class I or II provided to: N/A	
Number of trips for pick-up or delivery between 51 and 200 miles: 0	
Number of trips for pick-up or delivery beyond 200 miles: 0	
Drive-away collision mileage: 0	

General Information ... Audit 145988 ... Policy SMPL-HAZ1-001

Insured:
J. Joneser Motor Co.
8040 Irving Blvd. Dallas, TX 75225
Entity: J. Joneser Motor Co.
Phone: 214-585-4400 *Fax:* 2141-585-4401 *Mobile:* 214-585-4509
E-Mail: joneser@jjonesermotor.com
Website: **jjonesermotor.com**
Records obtained from:
J. Joneser
Dallas, TX 75225

----------------Verification Source Record----------------

Entity: J. Joneser Motor Company
Verification Source Record: Form 941
Employer's Federal ID No.: 74-2900111

1st Quarter 2005:	550,123
2nd Quarter 2005:	563,248
3rd Quarter 2005:	482,369
4th Quarter 2005:	496,358
Subtotal:	2,092,098
Add 12/01/2004 to 12/31/2004:	125,632
Less 12/01/2005 to 12/31/2005:	(126,896)
Adjusted Subtotal:	2,090,834
Grand Total:	**2,090,834**

General Information Checklist

Are there any Additional Entities?	No	Are there any Additional Locations?	No
Average Number of Employees?	See Notes	Does the Insured operate any Aircraft?	No
Is the Legal Entity correct?	Yes	Is there a 20% (+/-) difference in Estimate vs Actual?	No
Is a Signature on File?	Yes	Reference Number?	No
Was Contract Labor used?	No	Was Overtime paid?	No
Was the Cooperation from the Insured Adequate?	Yes	Was there any Board & Lodging?	No
Was there any OCIP exposure?	No	Was there any Severance Pay?	No
Quarterly Reports Available?	Yes	Were Employee Contributions to Benefit Plans paid?	No
Were Subcontractors used?	No	Were the Records Adequate?	Yes
Were there any Bonuses paid?	No	Were there any Commissions paid?	Yes
Were there any new operations?	No	Were there any Leased Employees?	No
Were there any Tips Paid?	No	Were there any Claims listed on the policy?	No
Was there any Housing Allowance?	No	Was there a difference between Quarterlies & Actual Payroll?	No
Was a General Ledger used?	Yes	Was a checkbook used or any type of disbursement record?	No
Were Individual payroll records used?	Yes		

Notes To Audit Department ... Audit 145988 ... Policy SMPL-HAZ1-001

All employees were listed by name and duties. They have been assigned to the proper classification
per their job duties.
Average numbers of employees =12
Commissions paid include additional amount of remuneration paid to automobile sales persons.
Gross Annual Sales are $19,500,000. The auditor requested monthly sales figures, however the
insured furnished a single annual sales figure.
Average Monthly Inventory is $550,000. The auditor requested monthly inventory figures, however the
insured furnished a monthly average figure.
The variance between the estimates and the actual exposure is less than 20%.

Exit Interview conducted on: 07/11/2006 at 3:02:59 PM
Interviewee: John Joneser   Title: Owner

The auditor reviewed the entire audit with John Joneser. The auditor reviewed
the operations, the duties and classification of each employee, the number of
dealer plates and non employee furnished a vehicle. John Joneser agreed with
the results of the audit

To verify the payroll amounts used in the audit, the premium auditor should total the gross payroll for the policy period from the individual earnings records used for the rating unit work sheet and compare it to the total payrolls for the same period shown on a separate source, such as the cash disbursements record, the payroll journal, or payroll tax returns. Although premiums are based on rating units, payroll provides further verification of the information gathered.

Many insureds have turned to a payroll service or their own personal computers for recordkeeping. Although convenient for the insured, this practice may create problems for the premium auditor. Some payroll services do not retain information on terminated employees or provide any employment data, such as employment or termination dates. In those cases, the premium auditor may have to refer to the insured's personnel records for this information.

Sometimes the liability premium developed in the preceding manner may not meet the minimum premium. The minimum premium for liability coverage is double the dealers' rate shown on the state rate pages for the highest rated location.

Liability—Unlimited Coverage for Customers

Item Five of the dealers' supplementary schedule states that the policy limits the liability coverage for the insured's customers in accordance with paragraph a.(2)(d) of the section, "Who Is An Insured." The insured can check the box found in Item Five to provide unlimited liability coverage for customers. If the policy provides unlimited customer liability coverage, the insurer increases the liability premiums otherwise developed by a factor of 1.25. Some states do not permit insurers to write limited customer coverage—the manual rates already allow for unlimited customer coverage, and this adjustment is not necessary.

Furnished Autos

Other information the premium auditor should seek concerns autos furnished to others, such as autos given to school districts for driver education training or to Welcome Wagon organizations. The premium auditor must make a furnished auto charge on such autos for the following reasons:

- The insurance policy of the organization that furnished the car normally excludes coverage for the owner of a nonowned or hired auto. Therefore, under that organization's policy no coverage exists for the dealer, the auto's owner.
- The other organization's insurance policy provides only excess coverage to that organization for hired or nonowned autos.
- The garage policy provides coverage not only for the dealer, but also for the other organization on a direct primary basis.

A certificate of insurance verifying coverage for the other organization does not eliminate the need for a premium charge to the dealer for a furnished auto. The insurer computes the premium according to the applicable private passenger-type truck, tractor, and trailer classification.

Liability for Pickup or Delivery of Autos Beyond a Fifty-Mile Radius—Nonfranchised Dealers Only

The policy provides liability coverage without additional charge for pickup or delivery of autos (driveaway operations) regardless of mileage. For the non-franchised dealer, an additional charge applies for pickup and delivery of autos beyond a fifty-mile radius from the limits of the city or town in which the insured conducts operations. The *CLM* uses the term "fifty-mile radius," not "fifty road miles," which may be different.

Charging nonfranchised dealers in this way is simply a rating provision. The Garage Coverage Form has no exclusions or limitations regarding liability coverage for driveaway operations. The insured, even if a nonfranchised dealer, has the coverage regardless of the premium charge.

Most nonfranchised dealers obtain used cars from car auctions, unlike franchised dealers, who obtain their used cars in trade for new autos. Both may also sell cars at such auctions. The premium auditor should determine what car auctions the dealer used. Those auctions could easily be beyond the fifty-mile radius of the city limit where the dealer's operations are located. The premium auditor must ask about those exposures. Usually, few, if any, actual records are available to determine this exposure.

The premium auditor must determine the number and mileage of trips beyond a fifty-mile radius of the city or town where the dealer is located and indicate them on the premium audit worksheet so that the insurer can charge the proper rates. Because the manual provides higher rates for trips beyond a 200-mile radius, the premium auditor must indicate on the worksheet both the number of trips between a 51- and 200-mile radius and those beyond a 200-mile radius. The rates are per driver per trip. A driver who delivers an auto and then picks up and returns a different auto would be making two driver trips.

The minimum premium for this exposure, where it exists, is the private passenger-type premium for the rating territory in which the dealer is located. If the insurer knows this exposure exists at the policy's inception, the insurer charges a deposit premium. If at the policy year end the insured has not made any pickups or deliveries of autos beyond a fifty-mile radius, then the insurer refunds the deposit premium or credits it to the insured. If an exposure exists, the minimum premium or the premium derived from multiplying the rates by the number of driver trips—whichever is greater—applies.

Medical Payments

Insurers can provide medical payments coverage by endorsement when they insure an auto dealer for liability. The premium calculation depends on the type of medical payments coverage provided, such as coverage for proprietors and executive officers, and auto and garage operations.

Insurers can provide proprietors and executive officers with medical payments coverage if the insurer includes them in the rating units used to calculate the liability premium (that is, if they are active or rated as active). The premium for such coverage for each person is double the private passenger-type medical payments premium in the rating territory in which the dealer is located. Insurers can extend spouses or resident relatives of proprietors and executive officers medical payments coverage for the same premium charge that applies to private passenger-type medical payments.

Insurers can add medical payments coverage for the auto liability exposure, the garage location and operations exposure, or both. The premium for this coverage is a specified percentage of the $25,000 liability premium. The CLM rule provides two tables showing the applicable percentage factor for each type of medical payments coverage for limits ranging from $500 to $2,000 per person. One table applies to liability premiums for unlimited liability coverage. The other table applies to liability premiums for limited coverage.

Uninsured Motorists

If the policy includes uninsured motorists coverage, the insurer computes the premium according to the procedures shown on the state exception pages. The insurer usually bases the premium on the number of dealer or transporter plates.

Physical Damage

Dealers' autos are those consigned to or owned by dealers and held for sale in the insured's business as an auto dealer. Physical damage coverage protects the insured against loss to owned autos—both autos the insured holds for sale and those that the insured separately registers. In case of loss, the insurer will directly pay the insured and any covered loss payee regardless of who is at fault.

The insurer bases the premium for this coverage on the value of the covered autos on hand. The insurer writes this coverage either on a reporting or nonreporting basis. Only coverage written on a reporting basis involves a premium auditor. The CLM rules provide for either quarterly or monthly reporting of values, but most insurers prefer monthly reporting.

Rates are annual rates and apply per $100 of inventory value. The CLM state rate pages list the rates for franchised dealers of any type. For any type of nonfranchised dealer, the insurer must multiply the manual rates by 1.10.

For physical damage coverage other than collision, rates vary according to where the insured normally stores the vehicles. Storage areas include open lots and buildings. The *CLM* divides open lots into standard open lots and nonstandard open lots. According to the *CLM* definition, **standard open lots** "are open parking storage lots enclosed on all sides by a metal cyclone or equivalent fence not less than six feet in height; or bounded on one or more sides by the wall or walls of a building, with no unprotected openings, and with the exposed sides of the lot enclosed by a metal cyclone or equivalent fence not less than six feet in height, with openings securely locked when unattended."[2] The manual defines a **nonstandard open lot** as a classification of auto storage for dealerships including "all other open lot parking locations, or unroofed space and buildings not securely enclosed and locked when unattended."[3] Buildings may include display rooms, service areas, and other completely enclosed areas that the insured locks when unattended.

A typical new car dealer often stores vehicles in all three types of locations. The dealer may have a standard open lot for some new cars; a nonstandard lot for used cars, customers' cars, and possibly some new cars; and a display room for other new cars. Because of their size, dealers usually store trucks or recreational vehicles in open lots, either standard or nonstandard. They almost always store motorcycles, however, inside a building. A typical nonfranchised dealer stores all vehicles in a nonstandard open lot.

The manual also refers to "miscellaneous types," which include ambulances, fire trucks and apparatus, funeral directors' flower cars, hearses, mobile home trailers, and special or mobile equipment. The manual divides the physical damage rates for those vehicles into buildings or open lots (for this classification, the manual makes no differentiation between standard and nonstandard).

Inventory Values

At the policy period's end, insurers may require verification of the inventory values reported. In this verification, the premium auditor may use many records.

The key information from the records is the number and values of all new and used vehicles in the dealer's inventory. The value of lease and rental units should not be included because a dealer reporting policy does not cover them, and those vehicles must be separately insured on a specified auto basis.

Also, these records should indicate other financial interests in those vehicles. When the insurer is only providing coverage for the insured's interest in financed autos, the premium auditor deducts those amounts from the inventory values listed as assets to arrive at the values insured.

Some premium auditors misunderstand the proper audit procedure in connection with cars under a floor plan. Floor plan cars refer to specific cars on which a dealer borrows money. The amount borrowed is identified with a

Standard open lot
A classification of auto storage for dealerships; parking enclosed by at least six-foot-high fencing with openings locked when unattended.

Nonstandard open lot
A classification of auto storage for dealerships including all other open lot parking locations, or unroofed space and buildings not securely enclosed and locked when unattended.

specific auto. New car dealers usually borrow from a local bank or a finance company, often a captive finance company owned by the auto manufacturer. Under this arrangement, the dealer orders cars from the factory, and the manufacturer sends the bills to the finance company for payment. The dealer is free to order new cars, and the finance company or bank pays the manufacturer as long as the dealer stays within its credit restrictions. The lender charges the dealer amounts owed against specific cars. When a dealer sells a car, the dealer must pay the amount owed on that auto, usually within ten days of the sale date. Under this arrangement, the finance organization knows not only the gross amount the dealer owes, but also the amount owed on each car.

Used cars can be under a floor plan in the same manner. The only difference is that lending a maximum 80 percent or 90 percent of the cash value on used cars is customary, rather than the 100 percent that is customary on new cars. A floor plan does not include money owed by a dealer on the car inventory unless the dealer owes specific amounts on specific units.

Occasionally, insureds suggest that insurers should not make a premium charge for cars under a floor plan. This suggestion probably stems from the fact that most companies financing dealer cars obtain physical damage insurance to cover their own interest in the financed cars.

If Item Seven of the dealers' supplementary schedule indicates that coverage exists for the named insured and its creditor's interest, the insurer would pay a loss on any auto under a floor plan. When an insurer writes a policy in this way, the premium auditor should include all covered values in the premium audit. If the premium auditor finds that the insured did not intend to cover autos under a floor plan, the premium auditor should obtain all the facts and notify the underwriter so that the underwriter can properly endorse the policy to exclude such vehicles.

Insureds often forget to report the values of service vehicles such as wreckers and pickup trucks. The premium auditor must value the service vehicles at actual cash value, not depreciated book value normally shown on the financial statement.

Insurers can provide collision coverage for dealers' autos either on a specified auto or a blanket basis. If the insurer writes the coverage on a specified auto basis, the insurer prorates the manual collision premium for the time at risk for the desired deductible and the type of auto.

When the policy insures all autos on a blanket basis for collision, the premium auditor must determine a **value per rating unit,** the total values for all autos written on a blanket basis for collision coverage for auto dealers under a Garage Coverage Form divided by the number of rating units used in determining the liability premium. **Total values** are the average values reported during the year for all autos written on a blanket basis for collision coverage for auto dealers under a Garage Coverage Form. If the policy is new, total values are 75 percent of the limit of liability shown in the policy.

Value per rating unit
The total values for all autos written on a blanket basis for collision coverage for auto dealers under a Garage Coverage Form divided by the number of rating units used in determining the liability premium.

Total values
The average values reported during the year for all autos written on a blanket basis for collision coverage for auto dealers under a Garage Coverage Form.

The premium auditor then determines an adjustment factor based on this value per rating unit. Exhibit 11-9 shows those factors.

EXHIBIT 11-9

Adjustment Factors for Dealers Blanket Collision Coverage

Value per Rating Unit	Value per Rating Unit Code	Adjustment Factor
Less than $10,000	1	1.25
$10,000—14,999	2	1.15
15,000—19,999	3	1.05
20,000—27,499	4	1.00
27,500—34,999	5	0.95
35,000—44,999	6	0.85
45,000 and Over	7	0.80

The state rate pages show the blanket collision rates. Separate rates apply to the first $50,000, the next $50,000, and for inventory values over $100,000. The rate pages show rates for $100 and $250 deductibles. The premium auditor multiplies those rates by the total reported values (or limit of liability for policies on a nonreporting basis). The premium auditor then multiplies that premium by the adjustment factor to obtain the blanket collision rate. The insurer cannot change this adjustment factor during the policy term. The premium auditor can average blanket collision rates when different rates apply to the different ranges of values.

The Garage Coverage Form's physical damage coverage limits the collision coverage for dealers by excluding losses "to any covered 'auto' while being driven or transported from the point of purchase or distribution to its destination if such points are more than fifty road miles apart." By attaching the Dealers Driveaway Collision Coverage Endorsement, the insurer can eliminate this exclusion. Note that this is for collision coverage only. The earlier discussion related to liability coverage for pickup and delivery of autos more than fifty miles away. (The liability coverage uses a fifty-mile radius from the border of the city where the dealer is located. This coverage uses fifty road miles, which is generally more restrictive.)

The premium basis for this coverage is per trip. The premium auditor determines the actual rate per trip by the following: the number of miles between origin and destination, the covered auto's cost new, and the deductible applicable to the collision coverage.

The manual table for this coverage shows the premium corresponding to the applicable combination of these three factors. Separate tables exist for blanket coverage and individual coverage (per auto per trip).

Garagekeepers Coverage

Insurers base premiums for garagekeepers coverage on the type of coverage chosen (liability, direct primary, and direct excess) and the limit of liability chosen. Rates apply per location.

Classifications

Manual rules define the auto dealers' classifications. An additional classification applies for physical damage coverage.

Dealer Classifications

The manual lists seven auto dealer classifications. Only one classification code can apply to an insured. If the dealer is a franchised dealer, the classification depends on the type of vehicle for which the insured is franchised. (Nonfranchised dealers have their own classification.) Equipment and implement dealers who do not handle vehicles and do not have any other franchise are rated according to the rules in "Division Six—General Liability." Such dealers do not belong to one of the eight dealer classes.

For each dealer type, one of two classification codes will apply. One code applies to policies that limit coverage for customers, and the other applies to policies in which coverage for customers is unlimited. To determine what coverage applies to the customer, the premium auditor should refer to Item Five of the auto dealers' supplementary schedule. If the box in Item Five is checked, unlimited customer coverage applies, and the premium auditor must increase the liability premium 25 percent unless the rates for that state already include unlimited customer coverage.

Seven dealer classifications exist, as follows:

1. Franchised Private Passenger Auto Dealer
2. Franchised Truck or Truck-Tractor Dealer
3. Franchised Motorcycle Dealer
4. Franchised Recreational Vehicle Dealer
5. Other Franchised Self-Propelled Land Motor Vehicle Dealer
6. Nonfranchised Dealer
7. Trailer Dealer

The franchised private passenger auto dealer classification applies to any auto dealer with a franchise to sell new private passenger autos. The dealer may have other franchises. However, the franchised private passenger auto dealer classification applies as long as the dealer has a franchise to sell private passenger autos.

The franchised truck or truck-tractor dealer classification applies to any dealer with a franchise to sell new trucks or truck-tractors that does not have a private passenger auto franchise. The dealer may have other franchises.

This classification also applies to a truck dealer as identified above who also sells used private passenger autos.

The franchised motorcycle dealer classification applies to franchised dealers of motorcycles, motorscooters, mopeds, and any other type of motorized, two-wheeled vehicle. If the dealer holds a private passenger or truck franchise, this classification does not apply.

The franchised recreational vehicle dealer classification covers franchised recreational motor home dealers. If the dealer holds a private passenger, snowmobile, or residence-type mobile home trailer franchise, this classification does not apply, nor does it apply to mobile home dealers. A mobile home is a large trailer designed for use as a home that its owner rarely moves.

All franchised self-propelled land motor vehicle dealers that are not franchised equipment and implement dealers and not described by any other classification are in this category. Also, auto dealers that do not have an auto franchise of any kind come within the nonfranchised dealer classification. Two additional classifications are listed in the manual: franchised and nonfranchised residence trailer dealers and franchised and nonfranchised commercial trailer dealers.

Additional Classifications for Physical Damage Coverage

Regardless of the classification of dealers, an additional classification assignment applies for physical damage coverage. These physical damage classifications differentiate the degrees of security at storage locations. Those include standard open lots, nonstandard open lots, and buildings. Any number of additional classifications can apply to one insured.

SUMMARY

Garage coverage fits the insurance needs of auto dealers, both franchised and nonfranchised, that sell any type of auto, including private passenger autos, trucks, motorcycles, trailers, and so forth. These businesses have liability exposures arising both from their premises and operations and from their operation of autos. Rather than attempting to distinguish the general liability and auto liability exposures, the garage coverage includes both. The garage form resembles the business auto form and the trucker form in its simplified language and its use of covered auto symbols in the declarations. The policy expands the declarations, however, to include a supplementary schedule for the coverages provided. The coverage form contains the policy provisions including definitions, coverage symbol explanations, the specific terms of the liability, garagekeepers section, the terms of physical damage coverage, and the contract conditions. The insurer can add, by endorsement, medical payments coverage, uninsured motorists coverage, false pretenses coverage, driveaway collision coverage, broad form products coverage, and other coverages. The insurer can also provide garagekeepers direct coverage, without regard to liability, either as primary or excess over the customer's coverage.

For auto dealers, the basis of premium for liability coverage is the rating unit, which represents the number of vehicle operators rated according to the applicable category. One class of operators includes all employees, divided into two groups (regular operators and all others) and rated according to whether they work full time or part time. The other class includes all non-employees divided into those younger than twenty-five and those twenty-five or older. The premium auditor must categorize operators into those groups to compute the total exposure in terms of rating units. The liability premium equals the number of rating units times the rate. Additional premium charges may apply for unlimited customers coverage, autos furnished to others, liability for pickup or delivery of autos by nonfranchised dealers beyond a fifty-mile radius, medical payments coverage, and uninsured motorists insurance.

Insurers base the physical damage coverage premium for auto dealers on the value of the covered vehicles. Insurers can write this coverage on either a reporting or a nonreporting basis. If the insurer writes the coverage on a reporting basis, at the policy term end a premium auditor may verify the reported values before the insurer completes the final premium adjustment. The dealer's financial statement provides the necessary information. The manual states the annual rates per $100 of value. Dealers' blanket collision premiums are subject to an adjustment factor depending on the value per rating unit. Insurers determine driveaway collision premiums from a table in the *CLM* on the basis of the factory price, the mileage driven, and the deductible.

Auto dealers' classifications depend on whether the dealer is franchised, the type of vehicles for which the dealer holds a franchise, and whether limited or unlimited customer coverage applies.

State exceptions to the general *CLM* rating procedures for the garage policy also exist. The most significant exceptions are in Massachusetts, which requires a special policy form, and Texas, where insurers still rate dealers on a payroll basis.

CHAPTER NOTES

1. There are two declarations for the Garage Coverage Form. The one described (CA DS 06) applies when the garage coverage is written as part of a commercial package policy. The Garage Coverage Form Declarations (CA 00 09) applies when the garage coverage is written as a monoline policy. The only difference between the two is the addition of several items of information to CA DS 09 from the Common Policy Declarations, making the Common Policy Declarations unnecessary.
2. *Commercial Lines Manual*, "Division One—Automobile," Section II, Rule 48.B.2.a., http://info.iso.com (ISOnet, accessed July 18, 2006).
3. *Commercial Lines Manual*, "Division One—Automobile," Section II, Rule 48.B.2.b.

Direct Your Learning

Commercial Property/Inland Marine Insurance and Premium Determination

Educational Objectives

After learning the content of this chapter and completing the corresponding course guide assignment, you should be able to:

▶ Describe the role of premium auditing in commercial property insurance.

▶ Compare the property valuation methods used in accounting and those used in insurance.

▶ Given a loss involving reporting form coverage, determine the amount of insurance provided for the loss.

▶ Describe the coverage provided by, the premium determination rules of, and the reporting requirements of the ISO Builder's Risk Coverage Form.

▶ Describe the coverage provided by and the premium determination rules of time element insurance.

▶ Describe the coverage provided by, the premium determination rules of, and the premium audit considerations in each of the following categories of inland marine insurance:

- Transportation insurance on domestic shipments
- Bailees' insurance
- Contractors' equipment insurance
- Insurance on the property of dealers

▶ Describe the coverage provided by, the premium determination rules of, and the premium audit considerations of ocean marine insurance.

▶ Define or describe each of the Key Words and Phrases for this chapter.

Develop Your Perspective

What are the main topics covered in this chapter?

Reporting form property policies with fluctuating values are subject to premium audit. Appropriate reporting benefits both the insured and the insurer. Property valuation methods appearing in policy contracts may differ from those used in accounting. A premium auditor's approach to these property and inland marine issues is addressed.

Compare property valuation methods used in accounting with those used in insurance.

▶ How does the accounting book value differ from the actual cash value?

▶ What are the significant limitations in asset accounting?

Why is it important to know these topics?

Property and inland marine premium audits occur less frequently than workers' compensation or general liability premium audits. However, monitoring these property lines ensures appropriate premium flow. Premium auditors with specialized skills to perform such premium audits increase their value to insurers through their contributions.

Consider how valuation concepts apply to property.

▶ How does the coinsurance clause affect the limit of coverage that should appear on a property policy so that the insured is not penalized in a claim payment?

▶ How does a resulting adjustment of property value affect the premium flow to the insurer?

How can you use this information?

Imagine yourself as a premium auditor advising a policyholder regarding the importance of reporting requirements under a reporting policy form. Respond to the following questions:

▶ How may claim payments be determined if reports are not timely?

▶ How may claim payments be reduced if reports are not accurate?

Commercial Property/Inland Marine Insurance and Premium Determination

Premium auditing of property insurance contracts is far less common than for workers' compensation or general liability insurance contracts, even though insurers write many of those contracts with a variable premium base. Classification is seldom as complex an issue in property insurance as it is in workers' compensation insurance. However, premium auditors' accounting knowledge, their customary role in premium determination, and their experience in communicating directly with insureds can help to protect an insurer's premium base for property lines.

This chapter focuses on premium adjustments for commercial property insurance, with particular attention to those property and inland marine contracts that are commonly written with a variable premium base. Commercial property insurance and the use of the value reporting form, the builders' risk coverage form, and time element insurance are covered. Inland marine insurance and ocean marine insurance are also examined.

ROLE OF PREMIUM AUDITORS IN COMMERCIAL PROPERTY INSURANCE

Most property loss exposures are not variable; consequently, premium auditors have not had a primary role in commercial property insurance pricing as they have in commercial general liability and workers' compensation insurance. However, some property loss exposures do fluctuate in value over the course of the policy period, and sometimes the premium auditor is the ideal resource for the insurer to use when accounting skills are required. In addition to providing accounting knowledge to underwriters and claim representatives, premium auditors assist insurers providing commercial property insurance in the following ways:

- Determining premium
- Assisting insureds
- Detecting possible deficiencies
- Valuing property
- Avoiding coinsurance penalties

Determining Premium

Most commercial property insurance policies insure property loss exposures whose values do not vary significantly during the policy period, which enables the insurer to establish a fair insurance premium at the policy's inception. However, some commercial property insurance policies provide coverage for inventory, which may fluctuate in amount—and consequently in value—during the course of the policy period.

Assisting Insureds

Premium auditors may serve as a resource to insureds who are struggling with the appropriate value to place on their property for insurance purposes. Property valuation, described later, can be confusing because property can be valued different ways depending on the purpose of the valuation. Consultation with the premium auditor may alleviate property valuation issues before they become problems. For insureds whose commercial property insurance policies require periodic reporting of property values, the premium auditor can assist by showing them how records may be set up to facilitate reporting.

Detecting Possible Deficiencies

Insureds may make mistakes in property valuation that will result in insufficient insurance coverage if a loss occurs. Premium auditors may identify these deficiencies and assist the insured by correcting property values and reporting procedures. Reporting deficiencies include the following:

- Fixed assets reported at net depreciated value instead of actual cash value or replacement cost
- Improvements and betterments on leased premises omitted
- Fixed assets omitted
- Delay in entry for stock received
- Labor and overhead expenses omitted
- Sold but not delivered items not considered
- Supplies omitted

Additionally, insureds may attempt to cut their insurance costs by deliberately underreporting property values. The attempt may take the form of shaving small amounts from the total in the hope that they will go undetected. Alternatively, an insured with sudden cash problems may gamble on not having a loss in the coming month and report drastically reduced values to cut the current month's premium. If the insured submits a corrected report, it may be because a loss has already occurred. Premium auditors should thoroughly investigate any reporting deficiency and discuss it with the underwriter.

Valuing Property

Valuation is challenging because property is often valued differently depending on the purpose of the valuation. An insured's financial records show a property's book value. **Book value (net depreciated value)** is an asset's historical cost minus accumulated depreciation. Therefore, book value is calculated on the assumption that a portion of that asset's useful life has expired. **Depreciation** is a noncash expense used to allocate the cost of long-term assets over multiple accounting periods. For example, an asset with a purchase price of $100,000 and a useful life of ten years would be depreciated at a rate of $10,000 per year. Often the insured and the insurer do not agree on the insured property's valuation because the insured is concerned with book value whereas the insurer is concerned with actual cash value.

Actual cash value (ACV) is the replacement cost of a property minus its physical depreciation. Physical depreciation refers to the actual deterioration of property over time, resulting from use as well as obsolescence. Accounting depreciation, discussed previously, affects a property's book value. Physical depreciation is generally determined by an appraisal.

Another approach to valuing property for insurance purposes is replacement cost. **Replacement cost** is the amount required to replace lost, damaged, or destroyed property with comparable property. Often replacement cost is greater due to the effects of inflation.

Underinsurance is a serious problem for insurers as well as insureds. Without some mechanism to enforce insurance to value, many insureds would purchase much lower amounts of insurance, believing that the chance of a large loss is so remote that buying higher limits is unnecessary. Because most losses are partial, the insureds would collect most of their losses in full. If the insurer set the rates assuming that all insureds carried insurance to value, it would not collect enough premium to pay losses and expenses. Of course, insurers could charge one rate for those who insure to 50 percent of value, another (lower) rate for those who insure to 60 percent of value, and yet another (even lower) rate for those who insure to 70 percent of value, and so forth. However, that type of rating system would be more complicated. Therefore, to address this problem many property insurance forms contain a coinsurance clause.

The **coinsurance clause** requires the insured to carry insurance equal to at least a specified percentage of the insured property's value. The effect of the coinsurance clause is that the insured agrees, in exchange for a reduced premium rate, to carry insurance at least equal to a specified percentage of the actual cash value of the covered property. The coinsurance percentage most commonly used is 80 percent. Coinsurance percentages of 90 and 100 percent are also available. If the specified amount of insurance is not carried, the amount of loss payable (not to exceed the applicable limit of insurance) is calculated as follows:

$$\left(\frac{\text{Limit of insurance}}{\text{Value of covered property} \times \text{Coinsurance percentage}} \times \text{Amount of covered loss} \right) - \text{Deductible}.$$

Book value, or **net depreciated value**
An asset's historic cost minus accumulated depreciation.

Depreciation
A noncash expense used to allocate the cost of long-term assets over multiple accounting periods.

Actual cash value (ACV)
The replacement cost of a property minus its physical depreciation.

Replacement cost
The amount required to replace lost, damaged, or destroyed property with comparable property.

Coinsurance clause
Clause that requires the insured to carry insurance equal to at least a specified percentage of the insured property's value.

The coinsurance formula is applied separately to each specifically insured type of property. For example, assume that Sarah operates a greeting card business in a building she owns. The building is specifically insured for $100,000 and her business personal property is insured for $200,000. The insurable value of each item is $250,000. A covered loss resulted in $40,000 in damage to the building and $40,000 in damage to her business personal property. The coinsurance formula is applied separately to each item, and Sarah is subject to a coinsurance penalty on the building loss. Even if Sarah had $250,000 insurance on her personal property, which is more than needed to comply with the coinsurance requirement, she would still incur the same coinsurance penalty on the building coverage. The coinsurance clause applies to the total of all covered property only when one limit of insurance applies to two or more separate types of property. For example, Sarah might have carried $300,000 insurance covering the building and her business personal property as one item instead of two.

The effect of the coinsurance clause is to "penalize" (by means of a lower recovery on the loss) an insured who does not insure to at least the specified percentage of value, the penalty being proportional to the amount of underinsurance.

VALUE REPORTING FORM

Value Reporting Form
A commercial property form that bases the insured's premium on the business property values that the insured reports to the insurer periodically during the policy period.

To address the issue of fluctuating property values, insurers have used a variety of reporting form coverages. One version of reporting form coverage is the Value Reporting Form. The **Value Reporting Form** (CP 13 10) is a commercial property form that bases the insured's premium on the business property values that the insured reports to the insurer periodically during the policy period. The Value Reporting Form provides a way to modify the Building and Personal Property Coverage Form (BPP) to avoid the costs of overinsuring or underinsuring business personal property.

Briefly, it works as follows: A limit of insurance is set high enough to cover the insured's maximum expected values at any time during the policy period. The insured reports values to the insurer in periodic intervals specified in the form. As long as the insured reports values accurately and on time, the insurer will pay the full amount of any loss that occurs (subject to the policy limit), even if the values on hand at the time of loss are greater than those last reported to the insurer. At the end of the policy period, the insurer calculates the average values that are exposed to loss and uses that average to determine the premium. Therefore, the final premium is based not on the policy limit but on the values reported by the insured as exposed to loss.

Major features of the Value Reporting Form include the following:

- Reporting requirement
- Limit of insurance
- Penalties
- Provisional premium
- Treatment of specific (nonreporting) insurance

Reporting Requirement

The insured must give the insurer periodic reports of dollar values covered by the policy. The period of time for which the reports of value are due is referred to as a reporting period. Five reporting period options are available. These options and the code letters used to indicate them are as follows:

DR—daily values reported monthly

WR—values as of the last day of the week reported monthly

MR—values as of the last day of the month reported monthly

QR—values as of the last day of the month reported quarterly

PR—values as of the last day of the month reported at the end of the policy year

MR, monthly reporting of monthly values on the last day of the month, is the most commonly used option.

The applicable code letters (DR, WR, and so forth) appear in the commercial property declarations page in place of a coinsurance percentage. The insured must file the required report within thirty days after the end of each reporting period. The thirty-day requirement applies to the renewal, with the same insurer, of a policy previously written on a reporting form. For coverage that was not previously written on a reporting form by the insurer, the insured has sixty days from the end of the reporting period to file the first report on all except the quarterly report basis. Different rules apply to quarterly reports; see the policy form for the exact conditions.

Limit of Insurance

Usually, a specific limit of insurance applies to property at each location. The insurer's obligation is limited by this maximum amount per location unless coverage is written on a blanket basis, in which event the blanket limit can apply at any one location.

The insured is required to report all covered property on hand as of each report date. If $250,000 worth of property is on hand and the limit of insurance is $150,000, then the insured must still report $250,000. Because the premium is based on the reported values, the insured must also pay a premium based on $250,000. However, coverage is still capped by the $150,000 limit of insurance. If such a situation occurs, the insured should increase the policy limit or should purchase specific insurance to cover the additional $100,000 of value. Insurers and producers may also set up systems to trigger a review in any case when values approach or exceed limits, but the ultimate burden of monitoring rests on the insured.

The Report of Values (CP 13 60) used to report property values to the insurer prominently displays the following notice of this potential problem: "The values you report do not change your limits of insurance. If values exceed or come close to your limits of insurance, contact your agent or broker. You may need additional insurance."[1]

Penalties

For the Value Reporting Form to work properly—and for the insurer to collect adequate premiums—the insurer must have timely information that accurately reflects the values exposed to loss. Accordingly, the form imposes penalties for failure to submit reports and for inaccurate reports.

Failure to Submit Reports

If at the time of loss the first required report of values is due, but has not been received, the insurer will pay no more than 75 percent of the amount that would otherwise have been paid. For example, assume that the insured had made no reports of value at the time that a loss occurred under the following circumstances:

Limit of insurance	=	$100,000
Reporting period	=	MR (monthly values reported monthly)
Policy inception	=	January 1
Date of loss	=	April 12
Amount of loss	=	$40,000

Because the first report was due but had not been received at the time of the loss, the insured would collect only 75 percent of the amount that the insurer would otherwise have paid. Thus, ignoring any deductible, the insurer would pay $30,000 instead of the full $40,000 loss.

If at the time a loss occurs the insured has failed to submit any required report after the first required report has been made, the insurer will pay no more than the values last reported for the location at which the loss occurred. This provision can result in a serious penalty for an organization whose values at the loss location are higher than they were at the time of the last report. However, it has no effect on an organization whose values are the same or lower at the loss location than they were at the last report date. The following loss example illustrates the provision:

Limit of insurance	=	$100,000 (single location)
Reporting period	=	MR (monthly values reported monthly)
Value last reported	=	$60,000 (first report, accurate)
Policy inception	=	January 1
Date of loss	=	June 20 (second report was overdue)
Amount of loss	=	$70,000

Because the second report was overdue at the time of the loss, the insurer would pay no more than the value last reported for that location; therefore, disregarding any deductible, the insurer would pay only $60,000, leaving the insured with a $10,000 uninsured loss. Had the loss been $60,000 or less, no penalty would have applied.

Inaccurate Reports

The Value Reporting Form replaces the coinsurance provision of the BPP with a full reporting clause, sometimes referred to as an honesty clause. (Referring to this provision as an "honesty clause" can be misleading. The provision applies even if the insured had no intent to deceive the insurer. For example, the full reporting clause applies even when the erroneous report is due to an inventory miscalculation by the insured.) The full reporting clause simply stipulates that if the last report showed less than the full value of covered property at the affected location on the report date, then the insurer will pay claims according to the following formula:

$$\text{Insurer's payment (Not to exceed limit)} = \left(\frac{\text{Value reported}}{\text{Actual value}} \times \text{Loss} \right) - \text{Deductible}.$$

To understand the consequences of underreporting values, assume that a loss occurs under the following circumstances and the insurer's claim representative investigating the loss has discovered that the actual value at the time of the last report was greater than the value reported:

Limit of insurance	=	$2,000,000 (single location)
Value last reported	=	$1,000,000
Actual value at time of report	=	$1,500,000
Amount of loss	=	$600,000
Deductible	=	$1,000

The insurer's payment would be calculated as follows:

$$\left(\frac{\$1,000,000}{\$1,500,000} \times \$600,000 \right) - \$1,000 = \$399,000.$$

In this case, the insured's inaccurate reporting resulted in an uninsured loss that was $200,000 greater than if the insured had made an accurate report. The potential severity of the penalty for inaccurate reports should deter anyone who understands it from trying to save on premiums by intentionally underreporting values. Unfortunately, many insureds do not understand the consequences of inaccurate (or late) reports until after they have suffered a loss.

As long as reports are accurate and are made on time, the penalties described do not apply; the insurer will pay the full amount of any loss (up to the limit of insurance), even if it exceeds the amount last reported. If, for example, the amount of loss in the example had been $1.8 million and the last due report, totaling $1 million, had been accurate, the insurer would have paid the full $1.8 million loss, minus the deductible.

Insured Underreported Values

A&R Supply Company, a hypothetical wholesaler that deals in seasonal products, insures its business personal property under a BPP to which a Value Reporting Form has been attached. The amount of insurance is $5 million with a $1,000 deductible. Reports of values are due monthly. The inception date of the policy is January 1.

On the following November 10 of the policy year, A&R suffered a business personal property loss of $240,000 caused by an insured cause of loss. The actual value of A&R's business personal property at the time of its last report, which was made on time, was $4 million. However, the value stated on that report was $3.2 million. At the time of the loss, A&R's business personal property had a value of $3.5 million.

Question: What amount would A&R's insurer pay for the described loss?

Answer: A&R's last report of values, although made on time, showed less than the full value of covered property on the report date. Therefore, the amount payable by the insurer is calculated using the method described in the full reporting clause: the insured will be able to collect only that proportion of the loss that the amount last reported bears to the actual value of covered property when the last report was made. The calculation is as follows:

$$\left(\frac{\$3,200,000}{\$4,000,000} \times \$240,000 \right) - \$1,000 = \$191,000.$$

Provisional Premium

Like most other types of property insurance, the Value Reporting Form carries a limit of insurance that is the most the insurer will pay for a loss. However, unlike most other property insurance limits, the limit of insurance for property subject to the Value Reporting Form is usually set for an amount that is higher than the maximum value expected at any one time during the policy term.

Because the limit usually exceeds the exposure, the initial premium, called the provisional premium, is not based on the full limit of insurance. The provisional premium is typically 75 percent of the annual premium that would be required to purchase nonreporting coverage with the same limit. Ordinarily, the provisional premium must be paid at the beginning of the policy period.

The earned premium for the entire policy period depends on the average values reported during the policy term. At the end of the policy period, an additional premium may be due or a refund may be owed to the insured. Refunds and additional premiums are calculated on a pro rata basis.

Specific Insurance

Reporting form insurance may be combined with other, nonreporting insurance covering the same property. This other insurance is then referred to as specific insurance.

Calculating the Earned Premium for the Value Reporting Form

Collegiate Supply Company (CSC), a wholesaler of school supplies, deals primarily with college bookstores. The greatest demand for its products occurs just before the start of the fall and spring terms. Therefore, CSC's inventories in the months preceding the start of each semester are substantially higher than at other times, making CSC a logical candidate for the Value Reporting Form. Because CSC did not expect its total business personal property to exceed $1 million at any time, it selected a provisional limit of $1 million. The applicable rate was $0.50 per $100 of insurance, making the provisional premium $3,750, calculated in two steps as shown below. (As Step 2 shows, the provisional premium is 75 percent of the premium that would otherwise apply.)

1. $\dfrac{\$0.50}{\$100} \times \$1,000,000 = \$5,000.$

2. $\$5,000 \times 0.75 = \$3,750.$

The reported values for the policy were as follows:

Date	Reported Value
January 31	$ 950,000
February 28	700,000
March 31	700,000
April 30	650,000
May 31	650,000
June 30	600,000
July 31	1,200,000
August 31	950,000
September 30	750,000
October 31	700,000
November 30	650,000
December 31	1,100,000
Total	$ 9,600,000
Average (Total ÷ 12)	$ 800,000
Earned premium $800,000 × ($0.50/$100)	$ 4,000
Deposit premium	− 3,750
Additional premium due insurer	$ 250

Note that the July 31 and December 31 reports exceed the limit of insurance. The full reported values are included in the earned premium calculation even though the insurer's loss payment would be limited to $1 million. Insureds and their representatives must be alert to this possibility despite the apparent advantages of a reporting form. Building a margin of safety into the original limit involves very little additional cost; the earned premium will reflect only the values reported. (The insured would sustain a loss of interest income on the additional deposit premium. For most insureds, that would be an insignificant cost.) As a further safeguard, as soon as a report approaches or exceeds the limit of insurance, the adequacy of the limit should be reviewed. In CSC's case, the $950,000 report for January 31 should have triggered a review.

The Value Reporting Form defines specific insurance as:

> . . . other insurance that:
>
> a. Covers the same Covered Property to which this endorsement applies; and
>
> b. Is not subject to the same plan, terms, conditions and provisions as this insurance, including this endorsement.[2]

Coverage on property subject to the Value Reporting Form is excess over the total of the amount due from specific insurance plus the amount of any deductible applying to the specific insurance.

If the specific insurance has no coinsurance clause, the specific coverage pays the loss up to its policy limit, and the reporting insurance pays the balance, less any applicable deductible. If the specific insurance has a coinsurance clause, the reporting form coverage is not counted when determining whether the coinsurance requirement has been met. If the specific insurance is uncollectible, possibly because of the insurer's insolvency, the reporting form insurer will deduct the amount due from the specific insurer in calculating its payments; it will not pay the uncollectible amount due from the specific insurer.

Because the Value Reporting Form is excess over specific insurance, the premium for the reporting form is based only on the excess of covered value over the amount of specific insurance at each location. Therefore, with specific insurance of $100,000 at a location and value of $250,000 in covered property, the reporting form premium rate is applied against the $150,000 difference. The insured and the insurer must be alert to any change in specific coverage. In particular, when any specific coverage expires, the change must be noted in the next report.

Advantages and Disadvantages

For some insureds, the Value Reporting Form provides an ideal way to insure values that fluctuate substantially. As long as values do not exceed the limit of insurance, coverage is adequate to cover any loss in full, with no penalty for underinsurance. Yet the insured does not pay for more insurance than is needed, because the premium directly reflects the values exposed to loss. In short, the insured can get the effect of full coverage without paying for more insurance than is necessary.

However, the Value Reporting Form must be used with extreme care. The penalties for late or inaccurate reports can be severe. Late reports are an all-too-common problem with reporting forms. The penalties present a compelling reason why a reporting form should not be used unless the insured can reasonably expect to produce timely and accurate reports. Even insureds that can generate timely and accurate reports may believe that the savings in premium do not justify the costs to generate the reports. Similarly, insurers are sometime reluctant to provide reporting form coverage because of the added expense such forms impose on them.

Insureds sometimes make inaccurate reports because they know that lower reported values will result in lower premiums. More frequently, inaccuracy reflects an inadequate system for developing the needed information. Sometimes the insured has an accounting system that cannot accurately generate reports. Other times inaccuracy results from a misunderstanding about which values should be included in the report. For example, the insured might report only inventory values even though furniture, fixtures, and equipment are also among the items covered by the policy, or the insured might report book (accounting) values rather than ACV or the replacement cost values called for by the policy.

Even with timely and accurate reporting, problems sometimes arise. As noted, when the value of the property on hand exceeds the policy limit, the insured is still required to report the value and to pay a premium for it, even though it is not fully covered. Such a situation is obviously undesirable and has been the source of litigation involving insureds, insurers, and producers.

In short, the Value Reporting Form presents a sound solution to the problem of fluctuating values—but only if the insured submits timely and accurate reports and makes sure that the policy limit equals or exceeds the maximum possible loss.

Using Sales as a Reporting Basis

Independently developed forms sometimes use annual sales as a reporting basis instead of values at risk. That solves some of the problems associated with the ISO Value Reporting Form. It is much simpler for insureds to report total sales, which are easily determinable from books and records, rather than insurable values. In addition, monthly reports are not needed because sales are cumulative for the year. Insureds also like reporting forms linked to sales because the premium expense is directly related to sales volume. However, setting the rate is more difficult when sales are used as the reporting basis. Generally, past exposures are used to calculate a rate based on sales. For example, if a firm had average values at risk during the past year of $2 million, an average property insurance rate of $0.25 per $100, and annual sales of $5 million, the rate might be calculated in two steps, as follows:

1. $\dfrac{\$0.25}{\$100} \times \$2,000,000 = \$5,000$ (Annual premium based on average values).

2. $\$5,000 \div \$5,000,000 =$ Rate of $1 per $1,000 of sales, or 0.1 percent.

Using sales as a premium base solves some of the problems of value reporting, but it introduces its own set of problems. Some of them are as follows:

- No relationship necessarily exists between values at risk and annual sales. Sales might decrease while inventories increase; a shift to just-in-time inventories might reduce insurable values even when sales are remaining the same or increasing.

- Insureds may understate the values at risk (either intentionally or unintentionally), thereby producing a lower premium with no reduction in exposure.

- Competitive pressures are harder to control. There is no base rate against which to compare the calculated reporting rate.

Basing premium on sales is an attractive option for insureds, but one that requires careful underwriting to make sure that the premium charge accurately reflects the exposure.

BUILDERS' RISK COVERAGE FORM

Insurers must handle property insurance for buildings under construction differently than completed structures because the building's value changes as construction progresses. The Builders' Risk Coverage Form (CP 00 20) provides this coverage. Although inland marine underwriters also provide a form of builders' risk insurance, the forms discussed here are those included in "Division Five—Fire" of the *CLM*.

The Builders' Risk Coverage Form covers direct damage to the building under construction, including the foundation. Also covered are fixtures, machinery, and equipment used to service the building, and the contractor's building materials and supplies used for construction if the insured intends them to become part of the structure and if they are located in the building or structure or within 100 feet of its premises. The policy covers temporary structures built or assembled at the job site (if not covered by other insurance), including scaffolding and construction forms.

Insurers write the Builders' Risk Coverage Form on a completed value basis or on a reporting form basis. The policy inception date cannot be later than the date construction starts above the level of the lowest basement floor or the date construction starts (for buildings with no basement). This requirement matches the insurance requirements common in construction loans that insurance coverage commence at the earliest project stages as a condition for the loan. The limit of insurance is the structure's value at completion (including all permanent fixtures and decorations that constitute a part of the building), but the coverage provided is the structure's actual cash value at the time of the loss.

This coverage form has no coinsurance provision. Instead of a coinsurance clause, the policy has a provision that limits the insurer's liability to no greater share of a loss than the proportion that the limit of insurance bears to the building's value on the completion date. If during the course of construction the building's estimated value at completion increases, the insured should increase the policy limits so that it will not have to share in the loss. When limits are increased, the insurer computes the premium based on the increased limit from inception.

Some question may arise as to exactly when coverage ceases. The coverage form tries to clarify this by specifically stating that coverage ceases when one of the following occurs:

- The policy is canceled or expires.
- The purchaser accepts the property.
- The named insured's interest in the property ceases.
- The named insured abandons the construction with no intention of completing it.
- Ninety days elapse after construction is complete (unless the insurer specifies otherwise).
- Sixty days elapse after any building described in the declarations is occupied in whole or in part, or put to its intended use (unless the insurer specifies otherwise).

The Builders' Risk Reporting Form Endorsement (CP 11 05) changes the Builders' Risk Coverage Form from a completed value basis to a reporting form basis. Like the reporting form, this endorsement has similar requirements for the timely and accurate reporting of values. The Builders' Risk Premium Adjustment Form Endorsement (CP 11 06) is used for value reporting. Within thirty days of policy inception, the insured must select the day of the month on which it will make reports. The insurer bases the initial premium on the covered property values existing at policy inception. When the insurer receives each report, it charges an additional premium based on the increase in values for the unexpired policy term (as measured from the date midway between the current and preceding reports to the policy's expiration date). The CLM contains a rating example to illustrate calculating premiums under a Builders' Risk Reporting Form.

Under both the completed value form and the reporting form, the insurer expects the insured to maintain accurate records of all buildings or structures insured, indicating the total completed value of each. The CLM specifically points out that the contract price does not necessarily equal the full value at completion.[3] A premium auditor's primary source for verifying submitted values would be job cost records tied back to the sales ledger.

TIME ELEMENT INSURANCE

The indirect losses suffered because of a fire or other causes of loss are often substantial and can sometimes exceed the direct damage. A manufacturer, for example, may be out of business until a key machine that must be ordered is replaced; the income lost as a consequence may be much greater than the cost to replace the machine. Furthermore, some firms fear permanent loss of business would occur if they shut down completely, or the nature of their business is such that they must remain in operation. These firms can incur extra expenses to avoid a cessation of business. Because they stay open, those firms often suffer little loss of income. Newspapers, dairies, hospitals, and banks are examples. Time element coverage provides protection for the loss of income and extra expenses resulting from direct physical damage by an insured cause of loss.

The two major aspects of time element coverages are business income coverage and extra expense coverage. **Business income coverage** is insurance coverage for the loss of net income and continuing normal operating expenses during the period of interruption resulting from direct damage to property at the insured location resulting from a covered cause of loss. **Extra expense coverage** is insurance coverage for extra expenses incurred by the named insured to avoid or minimize the suspension of operations resulting from direct damage caused by a covered cause of loss. The ISO Business Income Coverage Form (CP 00 30) covers both lost business income and extra expense. Other forms are available for just business income coverage (CP 00 32) or just extra expense coverage (CP 00 50). The two business income coverage forms also provide an additional coverage called **extended business income coverage**, which is insurance coverage for business income losses that continue after the period of restoration ends; the coverage begins when the damaged property has been restored and ends when the insured's business returns to normal, subject to a maximum of thirty days. (The ISO forms also include an option to extend the thirty-day period of coverage to as much as 730 days.)

Coverage

If a covered loss occurs, the business income forms cover the "actual loss of Business Income you sustain due to the necessary suspension of your 'operations' during the 'period of restoration.'" For a manufacturing risk, net income includes lost production. The business income form's loss determination provision states the following:

The amount of Business Income loss will be determined based on:

(1) The Net Income of the business before the direct physical loss or damage occurred;

(2) The likely Net Income of the business if no physical loss or damage had occurred, but not including any Net Income that would likely have been earned as a result of an increase in the volume of business due to favorable business conditions caused by the impact of the Covered Cause of Loss on customers or on other businesses;

(3) The operating expenses, including payroll expenses, necessary to resume "operations" with the same quality of service that existed just before the direct physical loss or damage; and

Business income coverage
Insurance coverage for the loss of net income and continuing normal operating expenses during the period of interruption resulting from direct damage to property at the insured location resulting from a covered cause of loss.

Extra expense coverage
Insurance coverage for extra expenses incurred by the named insured to avoid or minimize the suspension of operations resulting from direct damage caused by a covered cause of loss.

Extended business income coverage
Insurance coverage for business income losses that continue after the period of restoration ends; the coverage begins when the damaged property has been restored and ends when the insured's business returns to normal, subject to a maximum of thirty days.

(4) Other relevant sources of information, including:

    (a) Your financial records and accounting procedures;

    (b) Bills, invoices and other vouchers; and

    (c) Deeds, liens or contracts.

The business income coverage relies on a coinsurance condition to enforce insurance to value. Because of this coinsurance provision, insureds must frequently review their business income coverage to be certain of having an adequate amount of insurance. Premium auditors may, on a special request basis, assist in reviewing the insured's accounts to project business income loss exposure and the amount needed to comply with the coinsurance provision. The ISO business income report/worksheet (CP 15 15) can be used to determine the amount of insurance needed to comply with coinsurance and to provide a basis for estimating loss exposure. A premium auditor's skills can be useful in helping insureds complete the form.

A claim situation may also draw on a premium auditor's skills in verifying the loss. For example, the claim department may ask the premium auditor to examine the insured's books to determine the gross revenue and expenses over a given period. The premium auditor would also differentiate between expenses that would continue after the loss (salaries of key employees, for example) and those that would not (expenses directly associated with producing the product if the insured can no longer produce the product because of the loss). The premium auditor must also project revenues and expenses for the period of the loss. A premium auditor's accounting background makes this a logical extension of the premium auditor's responsibilities. In addition, it is likely to be less expensive than hiring a CPA to make the same calculations, and the insurer can maintain quality control over the process by using its own employee.

A simple example of a business income loss is as follows:

	Expected	Actual Due to Loss
Sales	$3,000,000	$2,000,000
Cost of Goods Sold	1,800,000	1,200,000
Gross Profit	$1,200,000	$800,000
Operating Expenses	900,000	600,000
Net Income	$300,000	$200,000

In this case the business income loss would be $100,000 ($300,000 expected minus $200,000 actual).

Business Income Premium Adjustment Endorsement

Premium auditors are most likely to become involved with business income coverage when the insurer writes the coverage on a premium adjustment basis. Under the Business Income Premium Adjustment Endorsement (CP 15 20), the initial premium paid is a provisional premium adjusted annually based on a report of values. The coinsurance provisions remain in effect and apply to the limit of insurance in the usual manner. As with reporting form coverage, the insurer will at no time pay more than the policy limit. The policy specifically states that the insured must request higher limits if needed to maintain adequate coverage.

The named insured must submit a report on the business income report/ worksheet showing business income values for the latest available twelve months' operating experience at the time the endorsement becomes effective. After that, the named insured must submit similar reports within 120 days following each succeeding twelve-month period for that twelve-month period. Finally, the insured must file a report within 120 days after the coverage ends or is canceled. If the named insured fails to submit the required reports, the endorsement terms no longer apply (that is, the insurer will not adjust the premium). The limit of insurance provision enforces accurate reporting because the insurer will not pay losses in a greater proportion than reported income and expenses bear to actual income and expenses.

The insurer computes the premium adjustment by multiplying the rate by the reported business income for the policy period. If this earned premium is less than the provisional premium, the insurer returns the difference to the insured. If it is greater, the insurer charges an additional premium.

Business Income Report/Worksheet

The business income report/worksheet (CP 15 15) (to be referred to as "worksheet" hereafter) is used to report values to the insurers and to assist the insured in determining the amount of insurance needed to comply with coinsurance as well providing a starting point to estimate the insureds business income exposure. Many underwriters require that insureds submit worksheets as part of the underwriting process so that they can evaluate the exposures and the adequacy of the amount of insurance requested. Insureds, producers, and underwriters often lack the accounting skills needed to correctly complete and interpret the form, and insureds' accountants and financial people generally do not understand the insurance aspects of the worksheet. Premium auditors combine the accounting and insurance knowledge that is needed to properly complete the form. The discussion looks first at completing the worksheet and then at using the values as a starting point to calculate a probable maximum loss and to select a coinsurance percentage.

Calculating the coinsurance basis is the primary use of the business income worksheet. Coinsurance as applied to business income is a source of confusion to almost all insureds as well as many insurance practitioners.

For business income purposes, coinsurance is based on net income plus all operating expenses less only those items specifically listed as excludable in the policy; payment in the event of a loss, however, is based on net income plus continuing expenses. Some expenses that are not excluded in calculating the coinsurance basis may discontinue when a business is interrupted and therefore will not be part of the loss. For example, rent paid by a tenant can be a significant expense, but it will discontinue under the terms of most leases in the event of substantial damage to the premises. Because rent may not discontinue when the building is not as seriously damaged and will, in that case, be part of the insured's loss, it is not excluded by the policy. Therefore, the coinsurance basis may be greater than the maximum that the insured can collect in the event of a loss. To compensate for this, ISO publishes rates for 50, 60, 70, 80, 90, 100, and 125 percent coinsurance. Various coinsurance percentages are also necessary because the coinsurance basis is twelve months of income and expenses, but coverage is governed by the time it will take to restore the property, which will almost certainly be different.

Exhibit 12-1 shows an example of a business income worksheet. Most of the items have their ordinary accounting meaning; therefore, the discussion focuses on areas of difference.

Notice that the first page states that worksheet must be completed on an accrual basis and that the same valuation method must be used for beginning and ending inventories. The next four pages have two sets of double columns; the left column in each set is used for manufacturing operations and the right column, for nonmanufacturing operations. The first set of double columns is completed based on the insured's most recent twelve-month financial period; the second set is the insured's estimate for the year beginning with the policy inception. Coinsurance is based on policy-year income and expenses.

The first variance from accounting procedure is the treatment of finished stock inventory for manufacturing operations. Because business income coverage for manufacturing is based on lost production, sales must be converted to production. (Lost profit on finished goods is covered by a manufacturer's selling price endorsement that is attached to the direct damage property coverage.) To convert sales values to production values, the form requires that the insured deduct completed inventory at inception (those are goods that were completed in a prior period) and add completed inventory at the end of the period (those are goods that were manufactured, but not sold, during the current period). Both inventories are to be valued at sales value. Accounting records record inventories at cost, not at sales value. Dividing the cost value by the cost-of-goods-sold percentage gives the sales value. For example, if a firm's sales for the period are $10 million and cost of goods sold is $6.5 million, its cost-of-goods sold percentage is 65 percent. For such a firm, an inventory of $520,000 on a cost basis converts to $800,000 sales value ($520,000/0.65 = $800,000). This calculation is not needed for a nonmanufacturing firm since its coverage is based on sales revenues, not production. The remaining entries on page two agree with accounting terminology.

EXHIBIT 12-1

Business Income Report/Worksheet

POLICY NUMBER: **COMMERCIAL PROPERTY**
                                                                 CP 15 15 06 95

BUSINESS INCOME REPORT/WORK SHEET

Your Name _____ MANUFACTURER, INC. _____   Date _____ 3/01/X4 _____

Location _____ 123 Any Street _____

_____ Anytown USA _____

This work sheet must be completed on an accrual basis.

The beginning and ending inventories in all calculations should be based on the same valuation method.

APPLICABLE WHEN THE AGREED VALUE COVERAGE OPTION APPLIES:

I certify that this is a true and correct report of values as required under this policy for the periods indicated and that the Agreed Value for the period of coverage is $ _____ , based on a Co-insurance percentage of _____%.

Signature _____
Official Title _____

APPLICABLE WHEN THE PREMIUM ADJUSTMENT FORM APPLIES:

I certify that this is a true and correct report of values as required under this policy for the 12 months ended _____

Signature _____

Official Title _____

Agent or Broker _____

Mailing Address _____

CP 15 15 06 95   Copyright, ISO Commercial Risk Services, Inc., 1994   **Page 1 of 5**

BUSINESS INCOME REPORT/WORK SHEET
FINANCIAL ANALYSIS
(000 omitted)

Income and Expenses	12 Month Period Ending 12/31/X3 Manufacturing	Non-Manufacturing	Estimated for 12 Month Period Beginning 4/01/X4 Manufacturing	Non-Manufacturing
A. Gross Sales.....................................	$ 10,050	$	$ 10,350	$
B. DEDUCT: Finished Stock Inventory (at sales value) at Beginning...............	- 500	XXXXXXXX	- 550	XXXXXXXX
	9,550	XXXXXXXX	9,800	XXXXXXXX
C. ADD: Finished Stock Inventory (at sales value) at End.........................	+ 533	XXXXXXXX	+ 480	XXXXXXXX
D. Gross Sales Value of Production......................................	$ 10,083	XXXXXXXX	$ 10,280	XXXXXXXX
E. DEDUCT:				
Prepaid Freight – Outgoing........	- 0	-	- 0	-
Returns & Allowances................	- 20	-	- 21	-
Discounts................................	- 30	-	- 32	-
Bad Debts................................	- 25	-	- 27	-
Collection Expenses..................	- 0	-	- 0	-
F. Net Sales......................................		$		$
Net Sales Value of Production........	$ 10,008		$ 10,200	
G. ADD: Other Earnings from your business operations (not investment income or rents from other properties):				
Commissions or Rents	+ 4	+	+ 5	+
Cash Discounts Received..............................	+ 0	+	+ 0	+
Other..	+ 6	+	+ 10	+
H. Total Revenues.............................	$ 10,018	$	$ 10,215	$

Continued on next page

	12 Month Period Ending 12/31/X3		Estimated for 12 Month Period Beginning 4/01/X4	
Income and Expenses	Manufacturing	Non-Manufacturing	Manufacturing	Non-Manufacturing
Total Revenues (Line **H.** from previous page)................................	$ 10,018	$ _____	$ 10,215	$ _____
I. DEDUCT: Cost of goods sold (see next page for instructions)......................	- 5,725	- _____	- 5,900	- _____
Cost of services purchased from outsiders (not your employees) to resell, that do not continue under contract.............	- 0	- _____	- 0	- _____
Power, heat and refrigeration expenses that do not continue under contract (if **CP 15 11** is attached).....................................	- N/A	XXXXXXXX	- N/A	XXXXXXXX
All ordinary payroll expenses or the amount of payroll expense excluded (if **CP 15 10** is attached).....................................	- N/A	- _____	- N/A	- _____
Special deductions for mining properties (see next page for instructions)................................	- N/A	- _____	- N/A	- _____
J.1. Business Income exposure for 12 months..	$ 4,293		4,315	
J.2. Combined (firms engaged in manufacturing & non-manufacturing operations)..............	$_____		$_____	

The figures in **J.1.** or **J.2.** represent 100% of your actual and estimated Business Income exposure for 12 months.

K. Additional Expenses:

1. Extra Expenses – form **CP 00 30** only (expenses incurred to avoid or minimize suspension of business & to continue operations)................. $ _____ $ _____

2. Extended Business Income and Extended Period of Indemnity – form **CP 00 30 or CP 00 32** (loss of Business Income following resumption of operations, up to 30 days or the no. of days selected under Extended Period of Indemnity option)...................... + _____   + _____

3. Combined (all amounts in **K.1.** and **K.2.**)................................... $ _____

"Estimated" column

L.   Total of **J. and K.** .... $ _____

The figure in **L.** represents 100% of your estimated Business Income exposure for 12 months, and additional expenses. Using this figure as information, determine the approximate amount of insurance needed based on your evaluation of the number of months needed (may exceed 12 months) to replace your property, resume operations and restore the business to the condition that would have existed if no property damage had occurred.

Refer to the agent or Company for information on available Coinsurance levels and indemnity options. The Limit of Insurance you select will be shown in the Declarations of the policy.

Supplementary Information

	12 Month Period Ending 12/31/X3		Estimated for 12 Month Period Beginning 4/01/X4	
	Manufacturing	Non-Manufacturing	Manufacturing	Non-Manufacturing
CALCULATION OF COST OF GOODS SOLD				
Inventory at beginning of year (Including raw material and stock in process, but not finished stock, for manufacturing risks)	$ 1,050	$ _____	$ 1,110	$ _____
Add: The following purchase costs: Cost of raw stock (including transportation charges)	+ 5,715	XXXXXXXX	+ 5,820	XXXXXXXX
Cost of factory supplies consumed	+ 25	XXXXXXXX	+ 20	XXXXXXXX
Cost of merchandise sold including transportation charges (for manufacturing risks, means cost of merchandise sold but not manufactured by you)	+ 0	+ _____	+ 0	+ _____
Cost of other supplies consumed (including transportation charges)	+ 0	+ _____	+ 0	+ _____
Cost of goods available for sale	$ 6,790	$ _____	$ 6,950	$ _____
Deduct: Inventory at end of year (Including raw material and stock in process, but not finished stock, for manufacturing risks)	- 1,065	- _____	- 1,050	- _____
Cost of Goods Sold (Enter this figure in Item I. on previous page)	$ 5,725	$ _____	$ 5,900	$ _____

On page three, the cost-of-goods-sold deduction is another area that differs from accounting procedure for manufacturers. The worksheet for cost of goods sold is on page four. Notice that for a manufacturer it is based on only raw materials and stock in process, not finished goods. Furthermore, unlike accounting calculations of cost of goods sold for manufacturers, it does not include factory overhead and factory payroll. These are not deducted; the only exceptions are those insureds that have elected endorsements to exclude or limit coverage for power, heat, and refrigeration, or ordinary payroll. Cost of goods sold for nonmanufacturing operations follows standard accounting procedures. It is common to see worksheets for manufacturing operations, particularly when the form has been completed by accounting personnel, that omit the calculations on page four and instead use the cost-of-goods-sold computation from the insured's financial statements. This substantially overstates the deductions by reducing the insured's coinsurance base and often results in an inadequate amount of insurance. Some insurers have developed their own worksheets and typically avoid the use of the term "cost of goods sold" because of this possible confusion.

The sum of each column—item J-1 or, for firms that have both manufacturing and nonmanufacturing operations, item J-2—has a misleading label: business income exposure for twelve months. It is really the coinsurance basis, not the business income exposure, because it includes expenses that may discontinue but that the policy does not permit the insured to deduct in calculating the coinsurance basis.

Once the coinsurance basis (J-1 or J-2 in the right columns) for the twelve months starting with the policy inception has been calculated, the insured can use these figures to determine its maximum probable loss for this insurance exposure and select an appropriate coinsurance percentage.

The first step is to calculate maximum probable loss. The adjustments that are necessary to convert the coinsurance basis to a maximum probable loss can be summarized as follows: period of restoration, the effect of peak seasons, changes in income and expenses during the period of restoration, noncontinuing expenses, and extra expense and extended business income.

The worksheet is based on twelve months. The insured calculates what its worst-case period of restoration would be, which may be more or less than twelve months and must be adjusted accordingly.

If the period of restoration is not exactly twelve months, peak seasons will affect the maximum possible loss. For example, some businesses do 75 percent of their business in the last three months of the year. Even if their period of restoration is only three months, their possible loss may be 75 percent of the annual income and expenses, not 25 percent.

Coinsurance is based on the twelve months starting at policy inception. The loss may occur on the last day of the policy period and continue for a year or more, depending on the length of the period of restoration. A rapidly increasing business could be highly underinsured if adjustments for future increases were not made.

Even though noncontinuing expenses cannot be deducted in calculating coinsurance, in projecting maximum probable loss, the insured may want to deduct items such as rent that may continue for a short interruption, but would be waived in the event of significant damage. The same is true for ordinary payroll if the insured has not elected the endorsement that excludes or limits ordinary payroll.

As the worksheet indicates, allowances for extra expenses and extended business income coverage must be added to determine exposure to loss.

Once the maximum probable loss (MPL) has been estimated, a simple formula can be used to select the appropriate coinsurance percentage, as follows:

Divide MPL by coinsurance basis:

- If the result is less than 0.50, use 50 percent coinsurance. Carry an amount of insurance sufficient to satisfy coinsurance.
- If the result is between 0.50 and 1.25, select the next higher coinsurance percentage. Carry an amount of insurance sufficient to satisfy coinsurance.
- If the result is over 1.25, use the 125 percent coinsurance.

The formula calls for selecting the next higher percentage because business income rates decrease as the coinsurance percentage is increased, making the cost of the higher amount of insurance little more, and in some cases less, than an amount of insurance equal to MPL written at the lower coinsurance percentage. Furthermore, MPL is based on estimates and insureds tend to underestimate their exposures; rounding up gives some protection against underestimating. In fact, it is often recommended that insureds include a specific amount as a cushion against underestimating when calculating MPL.

INLAND MARINE INSURANCE

In nineteenth-century America, traditional marine policies were adequate to cover the bulk of transportation and communications exposures. Commerce in the United States moved by water—Intercoastal Waterway, river, or canal—and the transportation system was also the only form of communication. New forms of transportation and communication, however, brought new loss exposures. When the conveyances in use diversified to include railroads, motor vehicles, and aircraft, new forms of insurance became necessary. The insurance business had to respond to the changes in the transportation industry. Marine insurers were better positioned than fire or casualty insurers to adapt their coverages to fit those new situations; the coverages became known as inland marine coverages. To distinguish the new inland marine field from traditional marine coverages, the latter are referred to in the U.S. as "ocean marine." The rest of the world still uses the title "marine insurance."

Floater
An inland marine policy that covers mobile or "floating" property.

Filed classes
The classes of inland marine business for which policy forms and/or rates must be filed with a state's insurance department before being used in that state.

Nonfiled classes
The classes of inland marine business for which neither policy forms nor rates must be filed with a state's insurance department before being used in that state.

Insurers also expanded this new line of coverage. Because they were designed to insure highly mobile property as opposed to property that remains at a fixed location, inland marine policies are often referred to as floaters. A **floater** is an inland marine policy that covers mobile or "floating" property. Inland marine policies can provide coverage for personal effects, mobile property (excluding conveyances designed for highway use), property undergoing installation, installment sales property, accounts receivable, valuable papers, equipment dealers' property, and much more. Generally, the one common feature is coverage of something of a mobile nature or related to transportation and communication.

Forms and rates for inland marine policies are either filed or nonfiled. **Filed classes** are the classes of inland marine business for which policy forms and/or rates must be filed with a state's insurance department before being used in that state. This means that a particular class's forms, rules, and rates are industry standardized and filed with the various state insurance departments by rating bureaus on an insurer's behalf or by the insurer. Individual underwriters have less flexibility in coverage or rates for filed coverages. **Nonfiled classes** are the classes of inland marine business for which neither policy forms nor rates must be filed with a state's insurance department before being used in that state. The forms, rules, and rates are not restricted by state filing regulations. Insurers write and rate policies providing nonfiled coverage in accordance with individual insurers' underwriting manuals or use forms and rates developed on an advisory basis by ISO or American Association of Insurance Services (AAIS). In many cases, insurers use tailored coverage, rules, and rates to fit the individual account's needs. Such policies may even include a manuscript coverage part instead of a printed form. This individually prepared form may specify the intended coverage, premium basis, and other conditions that match the insured's particular needs and the insurer's desire to meet them. The flexibility of nonfiled inland marine coverages is one reason for their popularity.

Whether filed or nonfiled, the policy indicates the information concerning coverage, premium basis, and rates needed for premium adjustment purposes. Endorsements can modify the terms of coverages in ways that the premium auditor must consider. Before any premium audit, therefore, the premium auditor must review the entire policy to analyze the specific coverage provided.

The ISO commercial package policy can provide inland marine coverage by including an inland marine coverage part. The Commercial Inland Marine Coverage Part consists of Commercial Inland Marine Declarations, Commercial Inland Marine Conditions, one or more commercial inland marine coverage forms, and appropriate endorsements. The coverage forms include the necessary descriptions of coverage and conditions that apply specifically to that coverage. The ISO general rules for each of the inland marine filed classes are in "Division Eight—Inland Marine" of the *CLM*. AAIS also files inland marine forms on behalf of its member insurers, as detailed in their Commercial Inland Marine Program manual. The twelve ISO classes are as follows: accounts receivable; camera and musical instrument dealers; commercial articles; equipment dealers; film; floor plan merchandise; jewelers block; mail; physicians', surgeons', and dentists' equipment; signs; theatrical property; and valuable papers and records. (Some states require that other forms be filed before insurers can use them.) With the exception of jewelers block, these forms do not develop much premium. The leading inland marine forms, in terms of premiums written, are transit coverage, builders' risk, and contractors' equipment, which are nonfiled in most states. To assist their member insurers, both ISO and AAIS publish guides to many nonfiled coverages even though they do not submit them to the states. While builders' risk is a major inland marine classification and offers several coverage advantages for insureds (availability of coverage for property in transit or storage, coverage for soft costs—advertising, financing, etc.—and broader covered perils), the inland marine forms are not very different from a premium auditing perspective from the property forms already discussed.

The Commercial Inland Marine Declarations is relatively simple because the variety of forms that insurers can attach prevents much standardized pre-printing. Sometimes, it may contain little more than the insured's name and address, the policy period, a description of the business, a premium, a list of the applicable forms, and a place for policy countersignature. Insurers use a separate declarations page for each class of coverage. The conditions and coverage form provisions deserve careful study because the specific terms vary widely.

Insurance to value is as important to inland marine underwriters as it is to property underwriters. Insurers often establish value by appraisals on scheduled items. In other cases, the underwriter may know the value of the insured property and agree with the producer and insured on an amount of insurance without an appraisal. Inland marine policies often contain coinsurance clauses or clauses that result in insurance to value by requiring the insured to report values accurately or suffer a penalty at the time of loss. An example of a clause from the ISO floor plan coverage form follows:

> If your last report before any loss is for less than the total amount required to be reported, we will pay only that proportion of the loss or damage that the amounts you reported bear to the actual total amount as of the last report.[4]

Insurers apply this reporting requirement the same as in property insurance. Although inland marine policies exist for numerous diverse situations, this section concentrates on policies written on a reporting form basis.

Transportation Insurance on Domestic Shipments

Inland marine underwriters insure domestic shipments by rail, motor truck, aircraft, or messenger. The originator (shipper), the transporter (carrier), or the recipient (consignee) can purchase policies covering such shipments. A **bill of lading** is a document that contains the contract of carriage between the shipper and the carrier and that may also serve as a receipt for property

Bill of lading
A document that contains the contact of carriage between the shipper and the carrier and that may also serve as a receipt for property being shipped.

being shipped. The bill of lading also serves as a receipt from the carrier. The carrier's liability may be limited by a released valuation provision, such as "carrier's maximum liability...not to exceed $25 per pound per package or $100,000 per incident, whichever is lower." Such a bill of lading is known as a released bill of lading. A **released bill of lading** is a bill of lading in which the carrier charges a lower freight rate (called a "released rate") in return for the shipper's allowing the carrier to limit its liability for cargo losses. The bill of lading may also function as a receipt for cash on delivery (COD) sales.

The bill of lading's provisions determine the responsibilities of the parties. The terms specify when the carrier becomes responsible for the goods and when that responsibility ends on delivery. The bill of lading is important in determining which party is responsible for a loss and which party needs insurance. Laws also specify the causes of loss for which carriers are responsible. Generally common carriers are responsible for loss or damage with only a few exceptions: damage from natural disasters (flood, hurricanes, etc.) generally called acts of God, acts of a public enemy, acts of a public authority, fault of the shipper, and damage due to the inherent nature of the goods. Contract carriers have more flexibility in negotiating the causes of loss for which they will be responsible.

The purchase order or bill usually defines when title passes and who will bear the risk of damage in transit. For example, for goods sold FOB manufacturer's plant, the title passes when the property has been loaded onto the designated carrier's truck at the manufacturer's loading dock. (FOB, an acronym for "free on board," is a term derived from ocean shipping.) If goods shipped FOB are damaged or lost in transit, the consignee must pay for the goods and make claim against the carrier for recovery even if the consignee does not receive the shipment or receives it in damaged condition; once the bill of lading is signed by the carrier, title to the goods passes and the risk of loss or damage is the responsibility of the consignee.

The appropriate insurance coverage therefore depends on the terms of the bill of lading and the insured's interest in the goods. Motor truck cargo insurance covers the carrier's liability, while transit, parcel post, and mail policies protect the goods' owner. Motor truck cargo owner's goods on owner's trucks is a first-party coverage that can be used to provide coverage for loss to the insured's own goods while on its vehicle. This exposure is also covered by most annual transit policies.

Motor Truck Cargo Liability

Motor truck cargo liability insurance covers insureds who are motor carriers for direct loss of or damage to shipments in their custody and control during the course of transit. Trucking companies differ in their operation methods, the territories serviced, the commodities hauled, and the length of hauls. Therefore, insurers designed motor truck cargo policies with the flexibility to meet the insured's individual needs. The coverage applies to lawful goods for which the carrier is liable, and most policies contain a coverage

Released bill of lading
A bill of lading in which the carrier charges a lower freight rate (called a "released rate") in return for the shipper's allowing the carrier to limit its liability for cargo losses.

extension for terminals while the goods are in the insured's custody during the course of transit (that is, the goods are not warehoused, but are temporarily stored, perhaps to be loaded onto a different truck). Insurers can write motor truck cargo policies either for a flat premium charge or on a reporting basis. When the policy is written on a reporting basis, the insurer usually bases the premium on gross receipts, which means the total amount due the insured from shippers, consignees, or other carriers for transporting property. However, gross receipts typically exclude the following items:

- Payments made to interline connecting carriers for transportation performed beyond the insured's operating rights (that is, the other carrier operating under its own permit)
- Taxes collected as a separate item and remitted directly to a government division
- Collections for cost of merchandise, including collection fees
- Warehouse storage charges (as noted, warehousing is not covered by the motor truck liability policy—a separate form is available to insure warehouse operators)
- Advertising revenues

Premium auditors can apply many of the rules introduced in Chapter 10 for truckers and motor carriers to motor truck cargo insurance. The insurer should not exclude payments to others for leased equipment or purchased transportation performed by others under the insured's rights (that is, the insured pays another carrier to deliver goods). Also, insurers should not exclude storage charges incidental to transportation. Premium auditors should exclude other operating revenues, such as snow plowing, shop work, lunchroom and vending sales, and advertising revenue. Those operations have no relationship to a carrier's responsibility for goods hauled.

The premium auditor should verify the commodities transported because the insurer uses this information in determining the rate. The policy should indicate the principal type of commodity hauled. If the premium audit discloses that the insured also transports other commodities, the premium auditor should advise the underwriting department. Another rating factor is the radius of operation. The premium auditor should also check this information.

Rates apply per $100 of gross receipts. The premium audit worksheet should always start with monthly gross receipts and then indicate appropriate deductions, individually identified. In this way, the premium auditor can verify the amounts by comparison with the carrier's reports.

Annual Transit

The **annual transit policy** is an inland marine policy purchased by frequent shippers to cover all shipments made or received during the annual policy period. It provides broad coverage for damage to the insured's property while being shipped and is particularly attractive to insureds that ship or receive a

Annual transit policy
An inland marine policy purchased by frequent shippers to cover all shipments made or received during the annual policy period.

large amount of property by various transportation modes. Typical insureds are manufacturers and wholesalers, although retailers and contractors also use this coverage. The policy can cover incoming shipments, outgoing shipments, or both. The policy indicates the transportation method covered, which can be common carrier, contract carrier, the insured's own vehicles, rail, air, or messenger. Any combination of transportation or all can be covered in one transit policy. Except for shipments in the insured's vehicles, the insurer pays claims promptly and then submits its claim as subrogee to the carrier or its insurer when the loss is due to any causes other than the excepted ones mentioned above. Naturally, when the insured uses its own vehicles rather than public truckers, the insurer cannot collect from another party. Therefore, the rates for that coverage are normally significantly higher.

Value of shipments
A premium base used for annual transit policies equal to the invoice cost plus prepaid freight charges.

The insurer usually bases premium for this annual transit coverage on the value of shipments, and the insurer requires the insured to maintain accurate records of all shipments. The policy may not cover local deliveries. The premium auditor should exclude them from the premium base. **Value of shipments** is a premium base used for annual transit policies equal to the invoice cost plus prepaid freight charges. Outgoing shipments refer to shipments leaving the insured's premises, and incoming shipments refer to shipments coming to the insured's premises. In general terms, outgoing values would be the same as total sales, providing the insured ships all merchandise, and incoming values would be the cost of raw materials or products received from others. The policy automatically covers return shipments without an additional premium charge, but the insurer does not deduct their value from the premium base. The premium auditor should record both outgoing and incoming shipments for each month. The premium is the rate per $100 multiplied by the value of shipments. Cancellation premium adjustment procedures follow the customary pro rata or short-rate rules, but policy cancellation does not apply to any property in transit on the cancellation's effective date.

Trip transit policies are similar policies written to cover a specific shipment. As trip transit policies are almost always written for a flat charge, premium auditors are seldom involved with them.

Parcel Post Policy

Shippers can insure packages sent by parcel post at the post office, but arranging the insurance on each individual shipment and collecting any claims can be time consuming. An alternative is the parcel post policy, which is nonfiled and works like the annual transit floater with a deposit premium and reporting provisions. A similar policy can be written to cover shipments via commercial parcel carriers.

Limits often vary according to the type of shipment. For example, a policy may have a limit of liability of $100 on any one package shipped by ordinary parcel post or unregistered mail and $500 on any one package shipped by registered mail or government-insured parcel post. The higher limits are allowed because the postal service typically takes greater care with those items. If necessary, the insured can usually increase the limits (valuable items such as gems, jewelry, or coins require high limits). The policy insures the safe arrival of the package and pays for loss or damage "from any external cause whatsoever" occurring while the package is actually in the postal service's custody. The premium for this coverage is the stipulated rate per $100 of shipment values in most cases.

Mail Coverage Form

The Mail Coverage Form (CM 00 60) can be used for fiduciary and nonfiduciary organizations. Mail coverage policies, if sold to fiduciaries, are a filed line with ISO rates for registered mail, first-class mail, certified mail, and U.S. Postal Service Express Mail. Policies sold to nonfiduciary organizations are nonfiled, and the insured and insurer can negotiate rates and forms. Insurers can write the policies on an annual basis or as an open policy, both with periodic reporting requirements. The filed coverage rules do not allow for insuring a single, specific shipment. Typical insureds are fiduciaries, including banks, trust companies, insurers, securities brokers, investment corporations, and others who mail valuable documents like stocks, bonds, and other securities.

The policy covers the property until it has been delivered to the addressee at the address on the shipping package, delivered at the proper address in the event of nondelivery by reason of error in address, or returned to the sender in the event of nondelivery. The policy territory for registered mail is between places anywhere in the world. For the other covered types of mail, the territory is the U.S. and its territories or possessions, and Canada.

The insured must keep accurate records of all covered property mailings, and must create such records before the loss. A record would be the covered property's description, its destination, and the type of mail used as well as the value of the property contained in each shipping package. Within thirty days after the end of each reporting period, the named insured must report the total values of all covered property sent during the reporting period.

Bailees' Insurance

A **bailment** is the transfer of personal property (such as for a repair or safe keeping) by its owner (the bailor) to another (the bailee) with the understanding that the property will be returned to the owner in the future. The **bailee** is the party temporarily possessing the personal property in a bailment. The bailee has the duty to redeliver the property to the bailor. The **bailor** is the owner of the personal property in a bailment. A simple transaction such as the bailor giving his shoes to a shoemaker (the bailee) for repair is an example of a bailment.

Unlike common carriers, which are almost totally responsible for shippers' goods in their possession, other bailees are liable under common law, in most situations, for only their own negligence. If a loss occurs because the bailee fails to exercise the standard of care expected of the reasonable and prudent

Bailment
The transfer of personal property by its owner (the bailor) to another (the bailee) with the understanding that the property will be returned to the owner in the future.

Bailee
The party temporarily possessing the personal property in a bailment.

Bailor
The owner of the personal property in a bailment.

person in the same circumstances, the bailee will be responsible for the loss or damage. The care, custody, or control exclusion in third-party liability policies, such as the CGL policy, usually exclude this liability for damage to property of others in the insured's custody. Because insurers rarely delete this exclusion, bailees need inland marine insurance for their liability for damage to customers' property.

Bailments are sometimes classified according to who benefits from the transaction. Therefore, clothing given to a dry cleaner is bailment-for-mutual-benefit (the dry cleaner will be paid and the suit will be cleaned); when a person borrows his neighbor's lawnmower, it's a benefit to the bailee; and when a person asks a neighbor to keep a dog for a few days while the person is out of town, it is a benefit to the bailor. Courts generally base the degree of care required of the bailee on who benefits most from the transaction.

A bailee can purchase a bailee liability policy, which provides coverage for any damages for which he or she is legally liable. If the bailee is negligent, the policy will respond. If the bailee is not negligent, the policy will provide the bailee with a defense but may not make any payment to the bailee for its loss. For example, if a fire caused by lightning destroys the property in the bailee's custody, a court would probably rule that the bailee was not negligent, and, while the insurer would pay the expenses to defend the bailee, it would not make any payment to the bailor. In practice, bailees usually want broader coverage than just their legal liability exposures. For example, if a laundry is destroyed by lightning-originated fire, customers would be irate if told that the laundry is sorry, but that it is not responsible for the destroyed clothing. To maintain customer goodwill, many bailees purchase insurance that will pay whether the bailee is liable for the damage or not.

Bailees' Customers Insurance

Bailees' customers insurance
A policy that covers damage by covered perils to customers' goods while in the possession of the insured, regardless of whether the insured is legally liable for the damage.

Bailees' customers insurance is a policy that covers damage by covered perils to customers' goods while in the possession of the insured, regardless of whether the insured is legally liable for the damage. It provides coverage not only for the legal liability exposure, but also for any loss that results from a covered peril. (Covered perils can be either broad named perils or "all-risks.") This dual interest insurance covers both the bailee's legal liability exposure and the property owner's interest. One of the most popular types of bailees' customers insurance is the laundry and dry cleaner policy; in fact, laundry and dry cleaners customers insurance is sometimes referred to as bailees' customers insurance. However, insurers write many bailees on this form. (Because of their different exposures and business procedures, coverage for furriers and warehouse operators is provided by different forms, discussed below.)

Bailee policies usually exclude property held in storage or for which the insured has made a storage charge. Coverage for property in storage is usually available by endorsement. The policy usually excludes damage resulting from the servicing itself (cleaning, for example); however, coverage generally applies for ensuing covered losses. The insured can also insure processing charges it is unable to collect because of the covered loss. The policy covers property at the insured's premises, the insured's agents' premises, or branch stores, and while in transit. Coverage restrictions sometimes apply to theft losses from an unattended vehicle.

Policies usually state a limit per location as well as a separate limit for the transportation exposure. Dry cleaners policies are sometimes written with no dollar limit. The policy states that it will pay no more than the property's actual cash value. This is one of the few policies for which insurers have no dollar limit.

Insurers can write the policy for small accounts on an annual basis with a fixed premium. On larger accounts, insurers write the policy on a gross receipts reporting basis with reports due monthly, quarterly, or annually. When insurers write the policy on a reporting basis, it contains a full value reporting clause. In the event of underreporting of gross receipts, this clause penalizes the insured in any loss settlement in which the insured's last report was less than the actual values at the time of the last report.

Insurers usually base premiums on gross receipts, which are the total amount charged for processing. The rate applies per $100. Because the policy excludes some items, premium auditors should exclude receipts derived from such items from the premium base if they can determine the amounts. For example, premium auditors should exclude storage charges if the policy does not provide storage coverage. The insured must also report uncollected gross receipts because they represent work that has been done, and gross receipts are intended to indicate the amount of processing the plant has done. Before the premium audit, the premium auditor should review the policy and consult with the underwriter if necessary to confirm the exact coverage and premium basis. The premium auditor should also obtain copies of the insured's reports for the past twelve months and compare them to the insured's actual records. When verifying those reports, the premium auditor should compare them to the insured's cash receipts journal or preferably to the general ledger. Credit transactions do not appear in the cash receipts journal, but premium auditors should include them in the gross receipts. If the insured operates at more than one location, the premium auditor must obtain separate figures for each location (because the rate may vary by location).

The premium audit procedure depends on the insured's recordkeeping system. The premium auditor may ask the insured to explain the records. This explanation may enable the premium auditor to understand the system and to evaluate its adequacy. The premium auditor then can suggest to the insured improvements that may result in more reliable reports and reduce the possibility of a penalty in case of a loss.

As mentioned, many insurers will extend their bailees' customers policies to provide coverage for goods owned by customers and accepted for storage by the insured. The extended coverage provided by this endorsement usually applies only if the insured has issued a receipt furnished or approved by the insurer indicating the customer's name, address, and the stored item's description and agreed value. The insurer is then liable only for the declared value amount, subject to the amount of insurance specified in the declarations. Insurers normally require insureds to submit a monthly report to the insurers indicating the total values in storage as of the last day of each month. The insurer multiplies the monthly values by the rate shown on the endorsement per $100 of values. The insured must maintain a record of all receipts. From this source, premium auditors can make a premium audit or verify monthly reports.

Furriers Customers Insurance

Furriers customers insurance covers customers' property that is made partly or wholly of furs (including imitation fur) while in the custody of furriers or others storing such property. The policy can also cover other garments, textiles, and similar articles. It is written for furriers, department stores, fur storage warehouses, and cleaners that accept such items for storage. Insurers write this coverage on a nonfiled basis. AAIS has an advisory form for use by its subscribers.

Insurers can issue the policy on a nonreporting basis or as a monthly reporting form. The reports are of the aggregate values of the amounts set forth in all the insured's outstanding receipts. Limits apply to property at designated premises or while in transit within and between the states of the continental U.S., the District of Columbia, and Canada. In addition to an aggregate limit applying to any one loss, the policy also states limits applying to storage enclosures at specified premises, locations outside the storage enclosures at specified premises, other premises not used for storage purposes, any other unnamed premises, and property in transit. Because the owners of the furs expect broad coverage, insurers write most furriers customers policies on an "all-risks" basis.

The insurer's liability is limited to not more than the amount stipulated in the furrier's receipt for each article, the property's actual cash value, or the cost to repair or replace the property with materials of similar kind and quality, whichever is less.

Insurers can endorse policies covering furriers issuing storage receipts to cover liability for excess valuation over the amount shown on the storage receipt. The insured may need the Excess Legal Liability Endorsement for customers who declare a lower value on the receipt than the stored item's value or in case the insured is held grossly negligent. The insured may also elect to insure accrued storage and service charges that are either unpaid, prepaid, or both.

The insured may also arrange to issue special fur policies by issuing certificates of insurance to annually insure customers' furs on an "all-risks" direct damage basis, whether in or out of storage. In this case, the insurer must attach a Furriers Customers Endorsement to the policy. The insurer furnishes the insured a supply of numbered certificates. The insured then submits monthly declarations of the certificates issued or voided. If the insured has issued insurance certificates to customers, the insured must keep those amounts separate from other goods received. These policies are equivalent in many respects to the owner of the fur scheduling it on his or her homeowners policy.

The insurer usually requires the insured to submit a monthly report reflecting the total value stated on all outstanding receipts as of the last day of each month. The premium reflects the total values stated in the receipts even if this amount exceeds the limit of liability shown on the endorsement. The premium equals the total values multiplied by the indicated rate per $100 of values.

A furriers customers policy contains a special cancellation provision. If the insured cancels the policy, the unearned portion of the minimum annual and deposit premium shall be returned to the insured, but such return shall not exceed one-sixth of the minimum annual and deposit premium for each of the months of June through September (or any part thereof) and one twenty-fourth for each remaining month. The summer months are when most furs are in storage. If the insurer cancels the policy, the insurer returns the unearned portion of the minimum annual and deposit premium to the insured, but the amount returned shall not exceed one-twelfth of the minimum annual and deposit premium per month.

Warehouse Operators Insurance

Insurance for warehouse operators differs from that for other bailees; coverage is almost always written on a legal liability basis. The ISO handbook for nonfiled inland marine classes points out that logistics has become an important part of warehouse and transportation insurance. **Logistics** is defined as the practice or art of moving goods from the point of manufacture to the final location of sale or distribution by the most cost-efficient means possible and available. Logistics providers have become the integrated managers of services. Because liability exposures are changing with these evolving operating services, insurers need to understand who has liability for each piece of the process.[5]

The three broad classes of property stored are furniture and household goods, frozen foods or other property requiring cold storage, and general merchandise (which is anything else). When someone leaves property with a warehouse operator, the warehouse operator issues a warehouse receipt. An amount indicated on this receipt often limits the warehouse operator's liability. If a furniture storage customer wants insurance to value, the warehouse operator can issue a certificate of insurance, which provides direct damage coverage whether or not the warehouse operator is responsible for loss or damage.

Policies to cover warehouse operators' legal liability vary considerably among insurers. Insurance generally is on an "all-risks" basis, including coverage for investigation expenses and defense and court costs in connection with claims. The insuring agreement usually states that the insurer will pay all sums for which the insured becomes legally liable for damage to or loss of property of others stored in the warehouse(s) described in the policy (subject to certain exclusions). Specialty insurers provide much of the insurance written on warehouse operators using tailor-made forms.

Logistics
The practice or art of moving goods from the point of manufacture to the final location of sale or distribution by the most cost-efficient means possible and available.

Separate rates apply to storage and to handling. Revenues for handling include fees for moving goods into and out of the warehouse, labor charges for loading and unloading vans belonging to others, and fees charged for access into and maintenance of customers' lots. When the policy covers more than one location, the insured must show gross receipts separately for each location.

If the insured's reports have been accurate, the premium auditor can easily verify them against the general ledger. If not, the premium auditor may have to refer to the cash receipts journal or other books of original entry to obtain the needed information.

Contractors' Equipment Insurance

Contractors' equipment floaters, which account for the largest premium volume of any inland marine class, can cover a wide variety of mobile equipment and machinery ranging from small air compressors, pneumatic tools, and portable electric generators to huge cranes, derricks, pile drivers, tractors, graders, and scrapers. General contractors, home builders, road builders, and other contractors often have large values in mobile equipment. Many commercial and industrial operations other than contractors have such equipment and can insure it using this form. For example, insurers often schedule forklift or squeeze lift trucks owned by manufacturers, wholesalers, or retailers on a contractors' equipment floater. Even a small apartment complex with a tractor to mow grass or a snow plow is eligible. Watercraft, aircraft, and autos are ineligible for this coverage.

Insurers schedule covered property for smaller accounts in the policy. Included are the machine's description, the model, the identification number, and a limit of insurance for that item. For larger accounts, insurers often write the contractors' equipment floater on a blanket basis. Insurers can use a combination of blanket and scheduled coverage for a contractor's smaller and larger equipment, respectively. The policy also contains an aggregate limit for any one loss or occurrence. Policies usually provide for limited automatic coverage for additional equipment and include insurance on similar property of others that the insured may lease or for which the insured may be liable. Policies can stipulate that valuation will be actual cash value or replacement cost, and some extend to provide rental reimbursement coverage as a result of damage to insured equipment. Coverage can be specified causes of loss but is more typically "all-risks." The policy usually excludes the following property:

- Autos, motor trucks, tractors, trailers, motorcycles, or similar conveyances designed for highway use
- Aircraft or watercraft
- Plans, blueprints, designs, or specifications
- Property while underground, underwater, airborne, or waterborne (except while being transported on a regular ferry line)
- Property that has become a part of any structure

- Property leased, loaned, or rented to others
- Consumable property such as fuel, grease, oil, asphalt, paving materials, building materials, and supplies
- Tires or tubes (unless the loss is caused by fire, windstorm, or theft, or is coincident with other covered loss)

A 100 percent coinsurance provision is typical for contractors' equipment floaters, although insurers may use a lower percentage in certain cases. For larger accounts, insurers can write the policy with an annual adjustment without coinsurance, subject to a full reporting clause.

Because of the hazardous conditions under which much of this equipment can be used, insurers often require a substantial deductible. For example, a grading contractor working in difficult terrain and bad weather may have a $10,000 or larger deductible per occurrence. Some policies use a percentage deductible.

The territorial limits usually include coverage while the property is in the U.S., the District of Columbia, Puerto Rico, or Canada (some policies exclude Hawaii, Alaska, or Puerto Rico) or in transit within or between those locations.

Insurers normally base the premium for contractors' equipment floaters coverage on the following:

- Insurable value of all owned and lease-purchase equipment
- Total expenditures for equipment rented or leased from others if this coverage is included

The policy contains a schedule of owned and lease-purchased equipment with corresponding values. Miscellaneous low-valued items can be aggregated and covered blanket, subject to a maximum per item and maximum per loss. If the policy provides coverage for leased or rented equipment, the insurer should indicate an estimate for this expenditure.

In determining the premium for this coverage, the premium auditor must not use the equipment's book value (net depreciated value) because a piece of equipment could be almost fully depreciated but have a much higher insurable value. Insureds often depreciate their equipment using one of the accelerated methods of depreciation because doing so legitimately reduces their income tax. Conversely, the premium auditor must be alert to a value that seems too high for a particular piece of equipment. Unless the insured's records indicate an up-to-date insurable value, premium auditors should obtain this information from a business principal. The insured must provide the value; the premium auditor must investigate any apparent discrepancy. Maintaining an inventory during the equipment's useful life, indicating the actual cash value rather than value determined using a straight-line or accelerated depreciation method, is to the insured's advantage. In the event of a claim, such a value is a more realistic measure of loss. There are many sources of information for accurate values of contractors' equipment, including trade journals that advertise equipment for sale, Internet listings of equipment for sale, and local equipment dealers.

The premium auditor values equipment disposed of before the policy anniversary date and equipment acquired during the policy period by averaging the beginning and ending inventories. Specific items of owned or lease-purchase equipment scheduled on the policy and disposed of or acquired during the premium audit term shall be disregarded in computing the average value. The premium auditor must separately compute the earned premium for such items on a pro rata basis. If such equipment is the same throughout the premium audit period, the premium auditor still does not include it in the average computation but charges for it separately at the value indicated in the declarations.

Accurately determining leased expenditures is an equally important premium auditor function. Contractors may sell seldom-used equipment and rent or lease instead as needed. The amount the premium auditor should record is the total expenditure for such rented or leased equipment. Unlike with liability premium audits, premium auditors do not add or deduct operators' wages, regardless of who provided the operators. This exposure includes any delivery or setup charge. If the premium auditor has any doubt regarding the accuracy of the indicated expenditure, reference books give territorial average daily, weekly, or monthly rental costs for different types of equipment. Although uncommon, the insured may complete a job for which the insured rented equipment before the owner can pick it up. In this situation, the lease charges normally cease, but because the equipment remains in the insured's custody, the insurer is entitled to a premium based on the rent or lease charges as if they continued until the insured returns the equipment to the owner.

On renewal business, the premium auditor needs a copy of the previous premium audit because he or she uses the total values at risk on that policy's expiration date as a base for determining the average values for the current premium audit. The premium auditor adds the total values at risk on the previous expiration date to the total values at risk on the currently audited policy expiration date and divides this sum by two to determine the average values for the current premium audit. For a new policy, premium auditors must use the declared values taken from the policy schedule, instead of previously audited values, in conjunction with the currently audited values to determine the average values. Leased equipment expenditures are total expenditures for such equipment during the premium-audited policy period.

Installation Floater

Insurers designed the installation floater for contractors who install machinery and equipment, such as plumbing, heating, and air conditioning firms, as well as manufacturers of elevators and store or restaurant fixtures. The insured can also be the property's owner or the one selling the property. The insurance covers the insured's property while in transit to the job site, while in storage away from the job site, at the site awaiting installation, during and after installation, and until the purchaser accepts the job and the title to the property passes to the purchaser. The form is generally written on an "all-risks" basis.

Policies are usually written for one-year terms but can be written to cover a particular project or on a continuous-until-canceled basis with monthly reports of insured values installed. The policy can cover building materials until they become a part of a structure, and the insurer can extend the policy to include tools and equipment the insured uses in the installation. A typical policy may exclude any loss because of error or omission in design, faulty workmanship, or equipment testing. The policies are usually subject to a deductible and to a coinsurance or full-reporting clause. A separate limit of insurance usually applies to the property in transit and the property at the job site.

The premium audit worksheet should show the location, the beginning and completion dates, and the construction type involved for each job. The premium for this coverage depends on the premium base, the most common of which are gross receipts and completed value.

When an insurer uses gross receipts, it bases the premium on the total amount due the insured from selling and installing property. The indicated rate applies per $100 of gross receipts. This premium base should exclude the sale of property sold on a customer pickup basis with no delivery or installation if the amounts are available from the records. Premium auditors should include those sales if the insured delivers but does not install the property because the policy provides coverage on covered property while in transit.

The completed value premium base usually requires a monthly report as of the last day of each month indicating the location, construction type, commencement date, and the project's anticipated value. The value is the invoice price for each job, including labor, materials, overhead, and other charges. The insured must report the same information monthly for each project under construction during the month until completion. The insurer charges monthly premiums at the indicated rate per $100 of values.

Processors Floater

A **processors floater** is a policy that covers the insured's goods while being worked on at a subcontractor's or processor's premises and while in transit to and from those premises. It covers manufacturers that send partially completed products to contractors for processing. Examples are a machine parts manufacturer that sends items to a contractor for plating, a garment manufacturer that sends fabrics out for pleating, and a furniture manufacturer that uses a contractor to apply special wood finishes. Garment contracts are sometimes written on a specialized form. The form is essentially a processor's form with a number of modifications to reflect the special coverage needs of clothing manufacturers.

The insurer schedules subcontractors' locations in the policy for specific limits of insurance, and other limits apply while the property is in transit. The insurance generally covers "all-risks" while the property is in transit and while on the contractor's premises. Some policies provide only named-perils coverage while on a contractor's premises. Coverage is usually written on a 100 percent coinsurance basis.

Processors floater
A policy that covers the insured's goods while being worked on at a subcontractor's or processor's premises and while in transit to and from those premises.

Accounts Receivable Insurance

The Accounts Receivable Coverage Form (ISO form CM 00 66 or AAIS form IM 1000) is a filed form that provides "all-risks" insurance on a reporting or nonreporting basis to cover the costs incurred as a direct result of covered loss of or damage to accounts receivable records for the following: (1) reestablishing accounts receivable records, (2) inability to collect sums due, (3) interest costs incurred because of the inability to collect accounts, and (4) extra collection expenses because of the loss. The coverage applies principally to damages resulting from occurrences on the insured's premises. The form requires that the insured store the records in specified receptacles when the business is not open or the records are not being used. Accounts receivable insurance does not cover losses arising from a debtor's bankruptcy or unwillingness to pay. Credit insurance can cover such bad-debt losses.

When an insurer writes a policy on a nonreporting basis, the premium base is the limit of insurance (which would represent the total amount of accounts receivable). When an insurer writes a policy on a reporting basis, the premium base is the average amount of accounts receivable during the past twelve months. Insurers adjust rates based on the receptacle the insured uses to store and protect the records, the insured's maintaining duplicate records in a separate fire division, and the risk's classification.

The sources of the insured values include the general ledger accounts receivable debit monthly balance, the accounts receivable ledger monthly balance, the monthly accounts receivable schedule, and subsidiary supporting records. The premium audit worksheet should show total accounts receivable outstanding for each month.

The policy may specifically exclude accounts receivable coverages for designated customers. If so, the premium auditor should indicate on the premium audit worksheet any such exclusions. The premium auditor should also carefully review the policy and endorsements to determine the premises covered.

The widespread use of computers has significantly reduced the risks posed by the destruction of accounts receivable records. Because they have regular backup copies stored off-premises, many insureds elect to retain the risk.

Dealer or "Block" Policies

Block policies
Policies that cover broad perils and a variety of property policies.

Policies that cover broad perils and a variety of property policies are often called **block policies**, derived from the French phrase *en bloc*, which means "all together." Lloyd's of London started writing a broad policy for jewelers at the beginning of the twentieth century in response to demands for fire and crime coverage in a single contract, and U.S. insurers followed suit. The policy was called the jewelers block. The Jewelers Block Policy set a precedent for other dealers policies, and special contracts were designed for furriers, camera stores, musical instrument dealers, stamp and coin dealers, and equipment dealers.

Despite their theoretical attractiveness, some of these forms are seldom used. Based on data reported to ISO and AAIS, premium volume for the filed inland marine forms for equipment dealers, camera stores, musical instrument dealers, and stamp and coin dealers totaled less than $2 million per year. It is possible that some insurers report writings for these classifications under the miscellaneous classification, but it is more likely that most insureds of this type are covered by businessowners policies that combine property and liability coverages at advantageous premiums. By contrast, jewelers block premiums have exceeded $200 million. Therefore, this section covers only jewelers block, furriers block, fine arts dealers, floor plan merchandise, and installment sales floaters.

Jewelers Block Coverage Form

When written for jewelry retailers with inventories under $250,000, jewelers block coverage is a filed, "all-risks" policy (ISO CM 00 59 or AAIS IM 1200). Nonfiled forms are used for manufacturers, wholesalers, and retailers with larger inventories. Ineligible exposures include bullion and precious metal dealers, industrial diamond dealers, fine arts and antique dealers, loose diamond dealers, pawnbrokers, and exhibition-only exposures. Jewelers Block Policies are generally written by specialty insurers or by knowledgeable underwriters working for insurers that write a large book of this business.

Coverage is generally written "all-risks," although named peril forms are available. Because of the high value-to-size ratio of jewelry, certain exclusions, in addition to customary ones, are usually added, including:

- Theft from an unattended vehicle, except to shipments in the custody of the U.S. Postal Service or other carriers
- Unexplained disappearance, shortage found after taking inventory, or shortage of property claimed to have been shipped when the package is received by the consignee in apparent good condition with the seals unbroken
- Employee dishonesty
- Theft or attempted theft of property in show windows at the insured premises resulting from the smashing or cutting of the windows
- Processing or work on the property, except for resulting fire or explosion
- Insufficient or defective packaging
- Breakage of fragile articles, except when caused by certain named perils
- Voluntary parting with any property or unauthorized instructions to transfer property to any person or to any place

The policy covers the insured's stock in trade—consisting of jewelry, precious and semiprecious stones, precious metals and alloys, and other stock used in the business, and similar property of others in the insured's care, custody, or control—and property in transit.

Deductibles can be as much as $10,000 or more. Credit is allowed for membership in the Jewelers' Security Alliance, which publishes a manual on jewelry security and effective security procedures and sends members weekly e-mail crime alerts and bulletins on dangerous jewelry criminals.

The insured must maintain the protective safeguards specified in the policy; failure to do so suspends coverage. Property is covered wherever located within or between the U.S., Puerto Rico, and Canada.

Valuation is based on the lowest of the following: the actual cash value, the cost of reasonably restoring the property, the cost of replacing the property with substantially identical property, and the lowest figure put on the property in the insured's inventory records.

The insured is required to keep accurate business records and to retain them for three years after the policy ends. The records must consist of an itemized inventory of stock in trade; records of all purchases and sales; records of the property of others in the insured's care, custody, or control; a detailed listing of traveling stock; and records of all other property away from the insured's premises. The policy also requires taking a physical inventory of all stock at least every twelve months. The application for a jewelers block policy, called a "proposal," is made a part of the policy. The application, a sample of which appears in Exhibit 12-2, requires detailed inventory information.

There have been a number of cases upholding an insurer's right to void coverage based on failure of the insured to maintain the required records or for misstatements in the proposal.[6] Checking that the values in the proposal correspond with the insured's books and records and recommending adequate recordkeeping procedures for insureds are areas in which premium auditors may assist insurers, insureds, and producers.

Furriers Block Policy

The Furriers Block Policy resembles the Jewelers Block Policy. It is an "all-risks" nonreporting policy. The policy is used to insure dealers whose property consists principally of furs, fur garments, and garments trimmed with fur, but not those firms that deal exclusively in raw or dressed skins or those that manufacture principally for the fur trade. A fur concession in a department store can be covered with minor policy modifications.

Like jewelers, furriers can buy coverage that applies away from the premises and can include furniture, fixtures, improvements, machinery, and tools. The property of others is insured for the furrier's legal liability if owned by another furrier or on a direct damage basis if in the insured's possession for repair or alteration. Property of others accepted for storage is excluded. The furriers customers form is specifically designed to cover that exposure.

The Furriers Block Policy excludes coverage while the property is being worn by the insured or any family member, relative, or friend, but unlike the Jewelers Block Policy, it does cover property while being modeled on the premises of the insured or another dealer. The "insect and vermin" exclusion is important in this policy because damage to furs from insects or rodents is a major exposure faced by insureds. Loss or damage occurring at the insured's premises is excluded if caused by flood. The flood exclusions can be removed at the underwriter's discretion.

The insured, to the extent that it controls any protective safeguards such as alarms or an automatic sprinkler system, must maintain those protective safeguards or the coverage is suspended for the unprotected period.

The policy pays for unsold merchandise at actual cash value. For sold but not delivered property, the policy pays the net selling price after all allowances and discounts. For property of others, the policy pays the amount for which the insured is legally liable (not exceeding the actual cash value), including labor performed and materials expended on the property up to the time of the loss. Like the Jewelers Block Policy, the Furriers Block requires a detailed application, often with the same questions concerning inventory.

Fine Arts Dealers

Fine arts dealers coverage is used to provide coverage for dealers in fine arts and antiques. Insurers usually write this coverage on an "all-risks" contract on a blanket basis covering property on the insured premises, while in transit, or while elsewhere within the policy's territorial limits. Separate limits usually apply to property in each of those situations. Insurers can write policies on a flat premium basis (with a 100 percent coinsurance clause) or on a reporting basis. When an insurer writes a policy on a reporting basis, the insurer can issue this form on an annual or a continuous basis, subject to the reporting of values. Verifying the insured's reports may require a detailed analysis of the insured's accounts.

Insurers base premiums on the reported values. Those values differ according to an item's status. That is, the insurer typically values unsold property at the amount shown in the insured's inventory. The insurer can also use actual cash value or fair market value. The insurer values property sold but not delivered at the selling price. The insurer values others' property at the amount at which the insured accepted the property.

Floor Plan Merchandise

Under floor plan financing, the lender loans funds to a dealer to purchase inventory; the purchased item serves as security for the loan. The loan must be repaid when the item is sold. This approach enables a dealer to display a wide selection of inventory on its selling floor (hence the name "floor plan") with a low capital outlay. To qualify for floor plan coverage, a dealer must have borrowed money from a lending institution to pay for merchandise, the merchandise must be specifically identifiable (for example, a serial number on an appliance) as encumbered, and the dealer must not be able to dispose of the property until the lending institution releases it from encumbrance. This form provides "all-risks" insurance for the dealer's single interest, the lending institution's single interest, or the interests of both. The dealer's interest

EXHIBIT 12-2

Jewelers Block Application

POLICY NUMBER: _____   **COMMERCIAL INLAND MARINE**
                                                                        CM 59 90 09 00

PROPOSAL FOR JEWELERS BLOCK COVERAGE FORM

To Be Effective With

_____
Name of Insurance Company

A separate proposal must be completed for each location and signed in duplicate. One signed copy, together with signed supplementary information, if any, will be attached to the Coverage Form.

Quotations cannot be given on incomplete proposals. If the answer to any question is none, state "NONE" or "NIL".

1. **a.**   Our firm or corporation name is _____
    b.   The names of the individual members of our firm or the officers of our corporation are
    _____
                        Floor   St. No.   City   County   State
    c.   Our premises are located at _____
    d.   The number of entrances: _____ open to the general public and _____ not open to the general public.
    e.   Usual business hours are _____
    f.   Give names and addresses of other locations of the Proposer and of other concerns engaged in the jewelry trade under the same ownership or management as the Proposer and not included in this Proposal: _____
    _____
    _____
    _____
    g.   Are the premises shared with others? If "yes", state name: _____

2. Indicate % of sales that is other than retail _____ %
3. **EMPLOYEES: a.**   How many employees do you have? _____ **b.**   What is the least number of employees, officers or owners customarily on your premises at any time during business hours or when opening or closing for business? _____

4. **LATEST THREE YEARS EXPERIENCE**

Year	Premium	Losses
_____	_____	_____
_____	_____	_____
_____	_____	_____

    —   Give statement covering all losses (insured and uninsured), whether paid in full or otherwise, during the latest 3 years involving property covered by this form, with dates, nature of loss, amount and name of company.

5. **NAME OF PRIOR CARRIER** _____

6. **BOOKKEEPING**
    a.   Do you keep a detailed and itemized inventory of your stock? _____
    b.   Do you keep a record of purchases and sales? _____
    c.   Do you maintain detailed records of the property of others in your care, custody or control? _____
    d.   How often do you take a physical stock inventory? _____

7. Are you a member of the Jewelers' Security Alliance? _____

8. **LIMITS OF INSURANCE DESIRED**
    NOTE: Limit cannot be less than 80% of average inventory values for each location.
    a. $ _____ Stock (including other people's goods)
    b.   **(1)** $ _____ In transit by Registered Mail;
             (2) $ _____ In transit by Armored Car;
             (3) $ _____ In transit by Merchants Parcel Delivery Services;
             (4) $ _____ All Other Shipments Covered by Coverage Form;
    c. $ _____ At the premises of sales agents, dealers, processors or similar custodians;
    d. $ _____ Safe Deposit Vault;
    e. $ _____ Off Premises Coverage including Travel and Messenger.

9. **OPTIONAL ADDITIONAL COVERAGES AT PROPOSER'S PREMISES**
    NOTE: Limit cannot be less than 100% of actual value for Items **(2)** and **(3)** below.
    (1) $ _____ On Money in Locked Safe against Burglary
    (2) $ _____ Furniture, Fixtures and Office Supplies
    (3) $ _____ Improvements and Betterments
    (4) $ _____ Machinery, Tools and Fittings
    (5) $ _____ Patterns, Dies, Molds and Models
    (6) $ _____ Flood
    (7) $ _____ Earthquake

10. **OPTIONAL DEDUCTIBLE**
    NOTE: This insurance is based on a $500 Mandatory Deductible applicable to all loss or damage.
    If a higher deductible is desired, _____ $ 1000 _____ $ 5000
    check one _____ $ 2500 _____ $ 10,000 _____ Other
    Do you desire a $25,000 registered mail deductible? _____

11. **INVENTORIES OF ALL PROPERTY WHEREVER LOCATED**
    If you can give your exact monthly inventories for the last 12 months attach a slip here showing these inventories with the date of each and questions **a.**, **b.** and **c.** of this section need not be answered.

    a.   The last merchandise inventory was taken on
         (give date) _____ and was exactly $ _____
    b.   The previous merchandise inventory at least 6
         months prior to **a.** was taken on (give date)
         _____ and was exactly $ _____
    c.   The maximum amount of our stock during the
         last 12 months did not exceed $ _____

CM 59 90 09 00 ☐

Continued on next page
▶▶

d. During the last 12 months the estimated
average daily amount of other people's
property in our care, custody or control for
any purpose whatsoever, whether insured or
uninsured, was $ _____

of which unset diamonds (Non-industrial) was $ _____

NOTE: This should not include property of others in the jewelry trade deposited with the Proposer
for safe keeping only.

**12.   PROPERTY ON DISPLAY IN SHOW WINDOWS AT PREMISES (INCLUDING OUTSIDE SHOWCASE
DISPLAY <u>ON</u> PREMISES) OCCUPIED BY PROPOSER**

NOTE: Property displayed in show windows and in showcases not opening into the interior of the premises is considered "protected" only when it is displayed behind swinging plate glass (or its
equivalent) secondary to window-pane or behind metal bars or grille entirely across window or
showcase, or behind shatterproof laminated glass or behind other burglary resistive glazing
material such as polycarbonate or acrylic. (Taped windows are <u>not</u> considered protected.)

a.   (1) Number of show windows _____

How many are protected against window smashing and how?

_____

How many open into the interior of the premises?   _____

How are these openings protected against theft?   _____

(2) How many showcases are out-
side? _____   How are they protected against forcible entry?

_____

(3) Number of Inside Showcases _____

Are they equipped with locks? _____

Describe locks (self-locking, key locks, snap locks, etc.) _____

_____

Are showcases kept locked during business hours except when the contents therein are
actually being removed or replaced? _____

How are showcase tops secured? _____

	PREMISES OPEN TO BUSINESS		PREMISES CLOSED TO BUSINESS	
	Protected	Unprotected	Protected	Unprotected
b. The maximum value displayed during the policy period will not exceed:				
(1) In all windows and outside show-cases	$ _____	$ _____	$ _____	$ _____
(2) In any one window	$ _____	$ _____	$ _____	$ _____
(3) In any one outside showcase	$ _____	$ _____	$ _____	$ _____
c. Limit Of Insurance to apply:				
(1) In all windows and outside show-cases	$ _____	$ _____	$ _____	$ _____
(2) In any one window	$ _____	$ _____	$ _____	$ _____
(3) In any one outside showcase	$ _____	$ _____	$ _____	$ _____

13. **SHOWCASE AND SHOW WINDOW DISPLAYS OF PROPOSER <u>NOT AT PREMISES</u> OCCUPIED BY PROPOSER**

If Proposer desires insurance on property displayed in showcases or show windows in building lobby or elsewhere than at premises occupied by Proposer, furnish full particulars of each display.

14. **TRAVEL AND MESSENGER**

The average value of property outside of the Proposer's premises during the last 12 months in the care, custody or control of the Proposer, messengers, employees, members of the firm or officers of the corporation was $ _____ per day. The maximum was $ _____ .

The maximum amount of property in the care, custody, or control of others, except as provided above, during any one period during the last 12 months was $ _____ .

15. **SHIPMENTS**

The total amount of property to be shipped at our risk during the policy period is estimated to be:

a.	Registered Mail	$ _____
b.	Armored Car	$ _____
c.	Merchants Parcel Delivery Services	$ _____
d.	All Other Shipments Covered by Coverage Form	$ _____

16. **BURGLARY PROTECTION OF PREMISES, SAFES, VAULTS OR STOCKROOM**

Protection Provided	Alarm Company	Type of Installation		Connected With		Grade Certification	
Premises	_____	High (1)	_____	U.L. Certified	_____	A _____ AA _____	
		Intermed. (2)	_____	Central Station	_____	B _____ BB _____	
		Basic (3)	_____	With Key	_____	C _____ CC _____	
				Police Connect	_____	U.L. Cert. No.	_____
				Local	_____	Expiration Date	_____
						Non-Certified	_____
						Explain	_____
Safe or Vault A	_____ _____	Complete	_____	U.L. Certified	_____	A _____ AA _____	
		Partial	_____	Central Station	_____	B _____ BB _____	
		Complete	_____	With Key	_____	C _____ CC _____	
		Partial	_____	Police Connect	_____	U.L. Cert. No.	_____
				Local	_____	Expiration Date	_____
						Non-Certified	_____
						Explain	_____
Safe or Vault B	_____ _____	Complete	_____	U.L. Certified	_____	A _____ AA _____	
		Partial	_____	Central Station	_____	B _____ BB _____	
		Complete	_____	With Key	_____	C _____ CC _____	
		Partial	_____	Police Connect	_____	U.L. Cert. No.	_____
				Local	_____	Expiration Date	_____
						Non-Certified	_____
						Explain	_____

Copyright, Insurance Services Office, Inc., 1999   **CM 59 90 09 00**   ☐

Continued on next page

Safe or _____ Complete _____ U.L. Certified _____ A _____ AA _____
Vault C _____ Partial _____ Central Station _____ B _____ BB _____
                        Complete _____ With Key _____ C _____ CC _____
                        Partial _____ Police Connect _____ U.L. Cert. No _____
                                           Local _____ Expiration Date _____
                                                           Non-Certified _____
                                                           Explain _____

Attach copy of U.L. Certificate for each premises, safe, vault or stockroom.

a. Minimum value of property kept in each safe, vault or stockroom at all times when premises are closed:
Total to agree with **18.a.** _____ % _____ % _____ %
                              Safe A   Safe B   Safe C

b. Watchperson Services—State number of your employed watchpersons maintained on duty within your
closed premises at all times _____ ; when open to business _____ .
                              (number)   (number)
Reports to _____   _____
           Central Station   On a Watchperson's Clock

c. Any other loss control security measures? If so, explain in detail: _____
_____
_____
_____

d. If premises have second or third Central Station Premises Alarm System state full particulars as
above: _____
_____
_____

17.   DESCRIPTION AND PERFORMANCE OF STOCK ENCLOSURES

(1) Give manufacturer's name   A _____
and the description of   B _____
each safe or vault: C _____

(2) Are safes on wheels?   A _____
                                B _____
                                C _____

State the Burglar-resistive Classification for each safe or vault.

Explanation of U.L. Classification Codes:

KL	- key lock, door only
TL-15/30	- tool resistive, door only for 15 or 30 minutes
TRTL-30/60	- torch and tool resistive on door and front face only for 30 or 60 minutes with concrete encasement
TRTL-15/30x6	- tool and torch resistive all six sides for 15 or 30 minutes
TXTL-60	- tool, torch and explosives resistive on all six sides for 60 minutes

	Classification	Walls*	Safe or Door	Vault
E –	60 min. Burglary Resistive as tested by Underwriters' Laboratories (U.L.) Class TRTL-60 or Class TXTL-60	-reinforced concrete at least 18" thick with four rows of #5 rebars** or three mats of expanded metal*** and **** or -U.L. Class 2 Burglary Resistive modular panel	Class 2	_____ A _____ B _____ C
D –	30 min. Burglary Resistive as tested by U.L. Class TRTL-30x6	-reinforced concrete at least 12" thick with three rows of #5 rebars** or two mats of expanded metal*** or -U.L. Class 1 Burglary Resistive modular panel	Class 1	_____ A _____ B _____ C
C –	15 min. Burglary Resistive Class TRTL-30 or Class TRTL-15x6	-reinforced concrete at least 9" thick with two rows of #5 rebars**	3 1/2" steel door with materials to resist tool and torch attack	_____ A _____ B _____ C
B –	Burglary Resistive (less than 15 min.) Class KL Class TL-15 or Class TL-30	-reinforced concrete masonry at least 8" thick or -steel lining at least 1" thick	1 1/2" thick steel with tool resistive materials to protect lock mechanism	_____ A _____ B _____ C
A –	Fire Resistive or Unlabeled or obsolete labels	-brick, concrete, stone, tile, iron or steel	iron or steel and equipped with at least one combination lock	_____ A _____ B _____ C

* Walls include roof and floor.
** 5/8" diameter deformed steel bars located in horizontal and vertical rows in each direction to form a grid not more than 4" on center.
*** Grids of expanded steel bank vault mesh placed parallel to face of walls, weighing at least 6 lbs. per sq. foot to each grid, having a diamond pattern not more than 3" x 8".
**** Other steel grids placed parallel to face of walls, weighing at least 6 lbs per sq. foot to each grid, having an open area not exceeding 4" on center.

18. State as to property insured during policy period at all times when premises are closed:
   a. The proportion by value of property ON PREMISES kept in Locked Enclosures protected as indicated under **16**:

   Total to agree with **16.a.**   _____ %   _____ %   _____ %   _____ %
                                    Safe A   Safe B   Safe C   Total

   b. The proportion by value of property ON PREMISES kept in other Locked Enclosures will be   _____ %
   (Show separate percentages where more than one such enclosure)

   c. The proportion by value of property ON PREMISES (including window display) out of Enclosures will be   _____ %
                                                         _____ %
                                                         (Total 100%)

               CM 59 90 09 00   □

Continued on next page

d. **(1)**   Indicate proportion by value of property kept in Safe Deposit
            Vault of a Bank, Trust or Safe Deposit Company   _____ %

  (2)   Name and address of Safe Deposit Vault: _____

    _____

Signing this form does not bind the Proposer to complete the Insurance, but this Proposal shall constitute a warranty should a policy be issued.

          Date   _____   Signature of Proposer   _____

                                        Title   _____

THIS SECTION MUST BE COMPLETED AND SIGNED BY THE INSURANCE COMPANY

Fire rate for stock at premises described in Question **1.c.**

Give Adjusted Rates for Highest Percentage of Coinsurance Permitted.

          Fire Contents Rate   _____   subject to   _____   %   Coinsurance

          Safe or Vault Rate   _____   subject to   _____   %   Coinsurance

          (If more than one enclosure, designate to which the safe or vault rate applies   _____   )

Expiration Date of Current Block Policy   _____

          Date   _____

                                _____

                                (Signature of Company Representative)

consists of the payments made to date by the dealer on the merchandise. The lending institution's interest consists of the outstanding balance on the merchandise. As a filed inland marine coverage, the policy cannot be used to insure autos and motor vehicles; however, similar policies are often written for auto dealers. The rules also permit coverage for manufacturers or processors.

Insurers usually collect premiums monthly. The reports and premium condition require that reports be made within thirty days after each month's end. If the insurer writes the policy to protect the dealer's single interest, the insured reports the total payments as of the last day of the month. Under a single interest form for the lending institution, the total amount of outstanding balances as of the month's last day is reported. If the insurer writes the policy to protect the dual interest of the parties, the insured reports the property's full value as of the month's last day.

Three limits usually apply to this coverage. The first limit is for property at the insured's premises. The second limit is for property at any unnamed location. The third limit applies to property in transit.

In the event of loss, the valuation of unsold property is the smallest of three amounts: the cost of restoring the property to its pre-loss condition, the cost of replacing the property, and the price the dealer paid for the property. If the insured has sold the property, the value is the selling price minus any discounts and allowances.

The policy's records and inventory condition is important for the insured to understand. This condition elaborates on the composition of the inventory the policy requires the insured to maintain and states the need for keeping records of outstanding balances, payments made or values at risk, purchases and sales, and others' property in the insured's custody. Insureds must also keep records of property sent to others. The insured must maintain those records for three years after the policy terminates. The policy requires a physical inventory of all stock in trade at least every twelve months.

Installment Sales Floater

The insured under the installment sales floater contract can be the manufacturer, the retailer who sells the product, or the financial institution that finances the purchase for the customer. Each of these parties has an interest in the outstanding balance. Even though the deferred sales contract or deferred payment plan may require the buyer to pay the balance even if a cause of loss destroys the property, most buyers are unwilling or unable to do so. This situation leads to a need for this coverage.

Insurers usually write this form on an "all-risks" basis. Like the coverage for floor plan merchandise, insurers can write this form to protect the single interest of the insured (a manufacturer, retailer, or financial institution) or the dual interests of the insured and the buyer. When the insurer writes the form to protect dual interests, some states allow the insured to issue certificates of insurance to the purchaser. Those certificates show the full sales price, the rate per $100, all insurance contract conditions, and the number of months of the installment contract.

Insurance coverage begins when the merchandise passes into the insured's shipping room for packing and delivery, or as designated in the certificate issued to the buyer. The insurance for the seller's interest terminates when the certificate expires, the buyer pays the amount owed, or the named insured repossesses the property or the buyer surrenders it to the named insured.

Whether written as a single or dual interest form, the policy is on a reporting basis (usually monthly) with a full reporting clause. If the insurer writes the policy as a single interest form, the reports must show the unpaid balances of the accounts covered by the policy. Under a dual interest form, the insured must report the full purchase price of each account covered. Premium auditors can verify those reports by the sales journal and the general ledger.

OCEAN MARINE INSURANCE

Ocean marine insurance
Insurance on vessels and their cargoes.

Ocean marine insurance is insurance on vessels and their cargoes. The three main types of ocean marine insurance are hull insurance, protection and indemnity, and cargo insurance.

Hull insurance is mainly property insurance covering loss of or damage to vessels and their equipment. Hull insurance often includes collision liability insurance as well, covering the insured's liability for damage to other vessels and their cargoes resulting from collision with the insured vessel.

Protection and indemnity (P&I) is the second main type of ocean marine insurance. Protection and indemnity covers a wide range of liability exposures and miscellaneous expenses (such as fines and penalties) that a shipowner may incur. The most notable liability exposures covered by P&I are injuries to crew members and other persons on board the insured vessel, injuries to persons on board other vessels struck by the insured vessel, damage to property (other than vessels) struck by the insured vessel, and the insured shipowner's liability for damage to cargo being carried by the insured vessel.

The third main type of marine insurance is cargo insurance, which covers a shipper's or consignee's interest in property being transported by vessels. Ocean marine cargo insurance also covers the insured goods during land transit that connects with the ocean conveyance. An ocean cargo policy can also be extended to cover inland-only shipments and international air shipments. The most common form is what is known as an open cargo policy because it covers all shipments made by the insured. For infrequent shippers, a trip transit policy can be obtained to cover a specified shipment only.

Premium auditors generally have little contact with ocean marine coverages. Only open cargo policies require premium audits, and only a few premium auditors will ever be involved even with those policies. Therefore, this chapter includes only a brief description of open cargo coverage.

The **open cargo policy** is an insurance policy that covers overseas shipments, either exports or imports or both, by vessel or aircraft. Like the annual transit policy, it is designed for frequent shippers because it automatically covers all shipments for which the insured is at risk.

The policy covers the interest of the insured (usually referred to as "assured" in ocean marine policies) or order. The term "or order" means that the insured can direct payment to the consignee, a bank, or another party that has an insurable interest in the shipment.

The property covered is typically all shipments of lawful goods and merchandise of every kind and description. A general description of the products shipped by the insured is inserted in the blank space. While all types of goods are therefore covered, the perils covered for loss or damage to goods other than those of the type specified may be more restricted.

In addition to covering the insured's interest in the property being shipped, cargo policies also cover the insured's responsibility for general average and sue and labor charge. (In maritime law, "average" refers to a partial loss to a vessel or its cargo.) **General average** is an expenditure or sacrifice of part of a vessel or cargo made in a time of damage in order to save the voyage. Flooding a cargo hold to extinguish fire that threatens the vessel is an example of general average. If the venture is saved because of the general average act, all parties—even those whose property suffered no damage—must pay a proportionate share of the cost of saving the venture. The general average clause in the open cargo policy binds the insurer to pay general average costs assessed against the insured.

The **sue and labor clause** is an obligation of the insured to take all reasonable steps necessary to preserve the property at the time of a loss. In return, the insurer agrees to pay the cost of such measures.

The open cargo policy specifies a date on and after which all shipments made will be covered. Coverage is continuous thereafter. Either party may cancel the policy on thirty days' advance notice, but any coverage continues for any shipment in progress until it reaches it destination. The policy also sets out geographic limits and types of conveyances by which covered shipments may be made.

Most open policies are written on an "all-risks" basis, subject to a few exclusions. Named perils coverage is also written, and sometimes only named perils coverage applies to merchandise other than that of the type shown as the insured's typical shipment.

Limits of insurance are set out on a per conveyance basis, with lower limits applying to shipments on deck and by aircraft or connecting conveyance. The typical valuation provision is invoice cost and any prepaid or guaranteed freight charges plus 10 percent or another agreed-upon percentage, referred to as an advance. The purpose of the advance is to indemnify the insured for any claim expenses not otherwise covered and to provide the buyer with coverage for loss of expected profit from the transaction.

Open cargo policy
An insurance policy that covers overseas shipments, either exports or imports or both, by vessel or aircraft.

General average
An expenditure or sacrifice of part of a vessel or cargo made in a time of damage in order to save the voyage.

Sue and labor clause
An obligation of the insured to take all reasonable steps necessary to preserve the property at the time of a loss.

Premium is determined in one of two ways: insureds may be required to report details of all shipments, with the appropriate rate being charged to each shipment, or the insured may be required to report the gross value of all covered shipments, with one rate being applied to the total. Premium auditing the individual reports is complex. The premium auditor will need to see all invoices and bills of lading, determine the amounts at risk, and tabulate the shipments to apply the appropriate rate to each shipment. Premium auditing gross sales reports is simpler. However, if an insured has domestic and export/import shipments or makes or receives shipments that are not at its risk, unless the definition of what is meant by gross sales is clear, it can be difficult to determine the proper amount.

SUMMARY

Insurers write many property and marine insurance forms with a variable premium base. Although premium audits occur far less often for property and marine insurance than for workers' compensation or general liability insurance, they can still be useful in monitoring and safeguarding the insurer's premium flow. Premium auditors familiar with the concepts of property insurance contracts can contribute significantly in this area because of their accounting knowledge and experience in the premium adjustment process. They can relate the valuation concepts that apply in insurance to the valuation concepts that apply in accounting.

Certain basic concepts apply to most commercial property insurance forms. Particularly significant is coinsurance, which encourages insureds to insure property to its full value. When reporting form coverage applies, the same principle appears in the full value reporting clause. An insured who does not report the insured property's full value incurs a penalty in the loss settlement. Although this penalty encourages insureds to report accurately, premium auditors can monitor and verify those reports. This role can facilitate the reporting process for the insured and increase the insurer's confidence in the reliability of the reports.

The reporting process essentially works the same way in marine insurance. When verifying the reports, however, a premium auditor must first ascertain the coverage provided by the policy to determine what values are relevant. Inland marine contracts vary considerably. Inland marine coverages can be filed or nonfiled, and substantial variation can exist in forms filed by ISO, AAIS, and individual insurers. Each of the policies written on a reporting basis involves fluctuating values suited to the reporting procedure. This chapter describes the coverage and includes examples of premium adjustments for many of those situations.

Premium auditors can also potentially help insureds, producers, and underwriters complete and interpret the business income report/worksheet, value reporting forms, and the accounting detail required by some coverage applications.

CHAPTER NOTES

1. ISO Report of Values (CP 13 60 10 00), Section E.2.e. (6). Copyright, ISO Properties, Inc., 1999.

2. ISO Value Reporting Form (CP 13 10 04 02). Copyright, ISO Properties, Inc., 2001.

3. ISO Builders Risk Reporting Form (CP 11 05 04 02). Copyright, ISO Properties, Inc., 2001.

4. ISO Floor Plan Coverage Form (CM 00 52 09 04). Copyright, ISO Properties, Inc., 2003.

5. ISO Inland Marine Handbook Warehouse Operations Legal Liability— Underwriting Information Section 1.2. Copyright, ISO Properties, Inc., 2001.

6. See: *Globe Jewelry v. Pennsylvania Ins. Co.*, 72 Misc 2d 563, 340 N.Y.S. 2nd 295 (N.Y. Sup. App. 1973); *Coin Roberto, Inc. v. Reliance Ins. Co.*, 281 A.D. 2d 319, 722 N.Y.S. 2d 497 (N.Y. App. Div. 2001); *M. Chalom & Son, Inc. v. St. Paul Fire & Marine Ins. Co.*, 285 F.2d 909 (2d Cir. 1961); and *Designcraft Jewel Industries, Inc. v. St. Paul Fire & Marine Ins. Co.*, 59 A.D.2d 857 399 N.Y.S. 2d 225 (1st Dept. 1977) aff'd 46 N.Y.2d 796 386 N.E. 2d 832 (1978).

Direct Your Learning

CHAPTER

Other Premium Auditor Roles

Educational Objectives

After learning the content of this chapter and completing the corresponding course guide assignment, you should be able to:

▶ Explain how a premium auditor may contribute to underwriting crime insurance and fidelity bonding relating to the following crimes:

- Robberies and burglaries
- Embezzlement

▶ Explain how fidelity bonds address an employer's embezzlement exposure and how underwriting and loss control considerations for fidelity bonds are implemented.

▶ Evaluate a crime or fidelity insured's internal control procedures, including general and specific controls.

▶ Describe the responsibilities of the premium auditor and audit manager in crime and fidelity loss auditing and in assisting the crime and fidelity underwriter.

▶ Define or describe each of the Key Words and Phrases for this chapter.

CHAPTER 13

Develop Your Perspective

What are the main topics covered in the chapter?

Fidelity bonds provide protection for the dishonest acts by employees, while crime insurance policies provide protection against the crimes or dishonest acts committed by nonemployees.

Identify ways a premium auditor can assist the underwriting department of the insurer in evaluating fidelity and crime coverages.

- How can understanding robbery, burglary, and embezzlement loss exposures help the premium auditor in accomplishing the audit?

- What general and specific controls of the insured does the premium auditor evaluate?

Why is it important to learn about these topics?

Losses can occur when internal controls over assets are nonexistent or inadequate in one or more areas of the insured's operations. Losses may occur from criminal activity by employees or others even when the insured takes reasonable precautions to prevent such losses.

Examine what a premium auditor must consider in crime and fidelity loss auditing.

- What is the financial audit's purpose?

- What are the responsibilities of the premium audit manager and the premium auditor?

How can you use what you will learn?

Examine the premium audit procedures in dealing with crime and fidelity loss auditing.

- What are the limitations on the premium auditor?

- Why are working papers and the narrative report important?

Other Premium Auditor Roles

In addition to the loss exposures covered in the preceding chapters, businesses also face loss exposures resulting from dishonest acts. These acts may be committed by persons employed by the business firm (for example, embezzlement) or by those with no connection to the firm (for example, robbery). Businesses can insure most of those loss exposures. One exception is that most policies covering losses committed by employees exclude losses committed by the business's owner or partner. Covering such losses would violate the general requirement that insured losses be accidental; that is, that they are neither expected nor intended from the insured's standpoint. Theft and embezzlement cause substantial losses to businesses every year. Small businesses are particularly vulnerable to such losses; in fact, crime losses are a major cause of bankruptcy. Although not mandatory, crime insurance and fidelity bonds are prudent forms of protection for businesses.

Despite the similarity of the loss exposures they cover, crime insurance and fidelity bonds traditionally have been separate underwriting fields. The essential distinction is that fidelity bonds cover employees, while crime insurance policies protect against crimes committed by nonemployees. Some crime policies, however, combine those coverages in one package. This chapter describes ways premium auditors can use their skills in aiding the underwriting and claim functions of their employers.

THE PREMIUM AUDITOR'S ROLE IN CRIME AND FIDELITY UNDERWRITING

Neither crime insurance policies nor fidelity bonds normally involve an audit for premium adjustment purposes. Therefore, those fields have traditionally been outside the scope of premium auditors' activities. Even so, premium auditors' unique training and qualifications enable them to contribute significantly to improving an insurer's book of crime and fidelity business. Premium auditors familiar with crime and fidelity coverages can verify the loss exposures and recommend improvements in the insured's internal financial controls as well as loss control measures (although this is usually reserved for the loss control department). Those recommendations help the insured reduce losses and also reduce the losses ultimately paid by the insurer.

Robberies and Burglaries

Robbery
The unlawful taking of property from the care and custody of a person by one who has caused or threatened to cause that person bodily harm or who has committed an obviously unlawful act witnessed by that person.

Burglary
The unlawful taking of property from inside a building by unlawful entry into or exit from the building. Signs of forcible entry or exit must be visible.

Small businesses in particular are exposed to robbery and burglary. **Robbery** is the unlawful taking of property from the care and custody of a person by one who has caused or threatened to cause that person bodily harm or who has committed an obviously unlawful act witnessed by that person. **Burglary** is the unlawful taking of property from inside a building by unlawful entry into or exit from the building. Signs of forcible entry or exit must be visible. Businesses may sorely need insurance protection for robbery and burglary loss exposures, but underwriters may be reluctant to provide coverage because of the adverse selection possibility. Premium auditors are well qualified to observe an insured's procedures for handling money and merchandise and to make appropriate recommendations. A premium auditor can verify that the blanket insurance amount is enough for a particular policyholder and that the additional loss exposures reported are accurate. The business's growth and inflation can necessitate adjusting previously accurate coverage amounts. Because accurate records are crucial for establishing the amount of crime or fidelity loss, a premium auditor's suggestions on maintaining records can be especially helpful to the insured. Therefore, premium auditors are positioned to provide underwriters with information about the robbery and burglary loss exposures unique to each organization so that underwriters can make appropriate risk selection and pricing decisions.

Embezzlement

Embezzlement
The unlawful taking of money or property by a person to whom it has been entrusted.

The primary manifestation of employee dishonesty is embezzlement. **Embezzlement** is the unlawful taking of money or property by a person to whom it has been entrusted. Businesses face a risk of loss due to the employee dishonesty exposure—a dishonest or fraudulent act by the employee with the intent to cause a loss to the employer and thereby obtain a financial benefit other than benefits earned in the normal course of employment. Embezzlement by employees is considered to be the single largest crime loss to business organizations. The exact amount is unknown, however, because many businesses never report employee thefts.

Some businesses retain this loss exposure. Many firms have survived by arranging for restitution directly with the employee or the employee's family. Sometimes the business even retains the employee who has embezzled, with proper appropriate controls, because his or her value is greater than a possible future loss. Also, many embezzlers intend only to borrow the money to take care of health needs, gambling debts, or drug or alcohol needs. They are often relieved the business discovers them. They discuss their problem and work hard to repay. However, countless firms go out of business or become bankrupt before they discover the employee fidelity loss.

Fidelity Bonding

Another way for employers to handle this problem is through fidelity bonding. The agreement titled "fidelity" (the historical name for employee dishonesty coverage) is the most important element of the bond; employee dishonesty accounts for the vast majority of losses, as well as the most severe losses. The fidelity agreement covers loss caused by dishonest or fraudulent acts committed by employees. Fidelity bonds are a specialized surety segment. **Suretyship** is the obligation of one entity to answer for the debt, default, or miscarriage of performance of duties by another entity. One individual or entity guarantees honest and faithful performance of duties of other individuals or entities. Despite some theoretical distinctions, suretyship in practice resembles insurance and is performed mostly by insurers. Although other fidelity situations exist, this discussion focuses on the employer-employee relationship. The insurer agrees to indemnify the employer if an employee fails to act in an agreed manner. With the widespread use of the blanket fidelity bonds, however, employees may not even know that their employer has bonded them.

Underwriting an organization requires an understanding of that organization's operations and activities. Because losses caused by employee dishonesty occur frequently, underwriters attempt to avoid bonding any questionable employees or situations. One underwriting concern with fidelity bonding is the type of business. Businesses with many cash transactions are more vulnerable than others to employee crime losses. Also vulnerable are businesses dealing in merchandise that someone can easily take or convert to cash. An estimated 15 to 20 percent of mercantile establishments have employee fidelity bonding. Another consideration in underwriting such loss exposures is the amount and value of noncurrent assets and of inventory. The organization's size is also an important factor in underwriting. Size includes the number of locations, the annual sales, and the number and types of employees. Size also affects owners' or managers' ability to closely supervise workers. A final consideration is whether the policy limits requested seem reasonable for the potential embezzlement losses.

Insurers gather much of the information to determine these factors by including questions in the insurance application. Data from many business services can verify the information on the application. Even so, no reliable way exists to estimate possible employee fidelity losses that a company may experience during a particular period.

Loss Control

However, employee dishonesty losses are responsive to loss control techniques. Two such techniques are the employer's control over assets and checks to reveal trust violations. Probably the most dependable indication of loss possibilities is the employer's attitude toward internal controls and the controls that are in force.

Suretyship
The obligation of one entity to answer for the debt, default, or miscarriage of performance of duties by another entity.

In most insurance lines, loss control activities are the loss control representatives' or safety engineers' responsibility. Loss control personnel may also make recommendations regarding fidelity loss exposures. Because of the importance of the insured's internal controls, however, premium auditors are uniquely qualified for the loss control function. Moreover, evaluating internal control is a routine step in any premium audit. By expanding their observations in this regard, premium auditors can contribute significantly to improving the profitability of the insurer's fidelity business.

Internal Control Surveys

The premium auditor is an insurance person trained in accounting and business methods as well as experienced in dealing directly with the insured or with highly placed officers employed by the insured. Underwriters want to know about the insured's accounting and business practices and internal control to determine whether they prevent theft or make detection more likely. The underwriter may request a loss control survey if fidelity claims are unacceptably high, limits requested exceed a predetermined amount, and the insured has requested the survey.

Because the time and expense involved in making a survey are considerable, an underwriter will request such a survey only when a problem occurs or the underwriter suspects a problem. The underwriter may limit the request to surveying only a particular unit or department. If a premium audit is necessary for workers' compensation or general liability coverage on the same account, an internal control survey for fidelity purposes involves little additional effort.

This survey's purpose is not to catch a particular thief and gather evidence. The survey is an independent appraisal to measure the value of management controls designed to discourage theft by employees or provide early detection of such theft. The statement that this survey will prevent employee theft could open the possibility of a lawsuit or at least put the claim department in a bad position. Preventing embezzlement may be impossible, even with effective and extensive controls.

The underwriter should help the premium auditor prepare for the survey, especially when the request did not originate with the insured. The underwriter should explain the reasons for the survey in advance, informing both the insured and the producer that the survey will first be used as an underwriting tool to judge overall controls and to determine specific areas in which losses are probable. Second, the insured can use it as an aid for improving or strengthening fidelity loss controls. Misconceptions can cause hostility towards the premium auditor and obstruct the survey. For example, insureds may perceive this action as criticizing their ability to judge their employees' character. The employees may perceive it as questioning their integrity. Such reactions are particularly undesirable because either the insured or the employees may be the same people who must also provide information for a premium audit.

To be successful, the survey must start with top management. Arrangements for the visit by the premium auditor should include appointments with the chief financial officer, the location manager, and the chief security officer (if one exists). Before the visit to the insured, the premium auditor should perform the following five tasks:

1. Review the existing files on the insured.
2. Discuss the account with the underwriter. Find out the specific reasons for the request.
3. Scan engineering reports for indications of management's attitude toward safety recommendations and physical security recommendations.
4. Review any financial and credit reports in the file for pertinent information.
5. Determine whether multiple locations exist. If so, make a preliminary decision with the underwriter as to how many and which locations to visit.

During the visit to the insured, the premium auditor should obtain an organization chart. This chart reveals the lines of authority and reporting responsibilities, departments, and other company structure information. If a chart is not available, the premium auditor should attempt to determine lines of authority.

Loss Control Techniques

Segregation of duties is a basic fidelity loss control concept. **Segregation of duties** consists of the processes that ensure that no one individual has the physical and system access to control all phases (authorization, custody, and record keeping). For example, the person who opens the mail should not also prepare the deposit slips and deposit the funds in the bank. Most embezzlers work alone, because attempted collaboration with others may disclose the theft. Embezzlement is more likely if an employee has effective control over two or more related financial areas. Separating related financial areas, such as check writing and bank statement reconciliation, purchasing and receiving, sales and collections, or shipping and billing greatly reduces the opportunity for embezzlement and the length of time for which it continues. In addition, insureds should add the responsible individuals' full names and titles to the organization chart. The same name appearing in areas of overlapping responsibilities indicates poor control. Even if names and titles are on the organization chart, the premium auditor should check both to verify they are current. Vacancies and temporary changes may have weakened controls. Also, temporary situations tend to become permanent.

Organization charts also become outdated during fast growth periods when the business expands duties and during business recessions when the business makes frequent personnel cuts.

Once the organization structure is clear, the premium auditor should examine company controls instituted by management. An easy method of examining controls is to divide them into general controls and specific controls.

Segregation of duties
Processes that ensure that no one individual has the physical and system access to control all phases (authorization, custody, and record keeping) of a business process or transaction.

General controls relate to policies and reports that apply to the business as a whole. Specific controls apply to areas that need special procedures to handle problems or loss exposures particular to that area. Premium auditors can find lists of controls and their applications in many general premium auditing texts. An increasing number of reports of internal auditors deal with detecting fraud or embezzlement for the accounting and security professions. The premium auditor's job is to confirm that the controls exist and to determine whether the business heeds and enforces them—not to perform a financial audit. An effective technique for evaluating internal controls is to ascertain the answers to a questionnaire. The questions asked and areas examined depend on the business type and the nature of the survey requested by the underwriter.

Evaluation of General Controls

Evaluation of internal controls should be made relating to the reliability of records used for a premium audit. When the objective is to reduce the potential for fidelity losses, evaluating internal control takes on a broader scope. A firm's prospects of detecting and verifying a fidelity loss depend largely on the same factors as its overall managerial efficiency. The extent of a firm's general controls can therefore be a clue to management's attitude toward safeguarding its assets.

Many small businesses may have inadequate internal controls and may lack sufficient personnel to segregate duties. They may also lack the expertise and the resources to fully develop formal internal control procedures. Direct involvement of the firm's owners in the business's affairs can make internal controls much more effective at little cost. Even elementary steps regarding regular financial audits, effective management, personnel policies, rotating duties, and physical security measures can significantly affect the potential for fidelity losses. Those general controls, therefore, deserve scrutiny in any internal control survey.

Audits

Many businesses never have an audit until they need to borrow money. These businesses therefore may need to borrow money to restore a loss or to cover lost revenue from careless business practices because they have avoided the expense of an audit. At a 6 percent profit margin, the business must generate sales of $100,000 to replace a $6,000 theft. Because regular audits are a central element of internal control, an internal control survey should ascertain the quality of the audits performed, if any. The survey questionnaire may include the following questions:

- Are regular audits performed?
- Who makes the financial audit—the CPA firm or public accountant, internal auditor(s), or both?

- If the business engages outside auditors, what are their qualifications and what is the scope of the service they provide?
- If the business has an internal audit, does a full-time staff auditor conduct it? If not, what are the auditor's other duties?

Those questions help determine both the audit's quality and the auditor's qualifications. The survey questionnaire should ask for the firms' or auditors' names. The person completing the questionnaire should describe internal auditors' education and job experience. If the business limits the total activity of all audits to preparing tax forms, without tests and controls for possible embezzlement, the audits are not a means of fidelity control.

Conglomerates, multiple enterprises, and widespread branches and divisions present special problems for internal control. Businesses have recorded immense losses because they did not consistently apply controls to all locations. New acquisitions can cause further problems. The questionnaire should therefore ask the following:

- Does an audit include all interests and locations?
- How often does the auditor inspect or visit each location?

The internal control survey should determine how often auditors conduct audits. The following are relevant questions:

- If auditors do not perform annual audits, why not?
- What was the date of the last audit?
- If not scheduled, why did the auditor perform the audit?

Existing problems can become more serious the longer the business ignores them. Even relatively small amounts stolen frequently add up to substantial sums. In one case, the chief bookkeeper had embezzled over several years an amount equal to the company's net worth at the time the business caught him. His juggling method was so elementary that even the most cursory audit would have uncovered his scheme. A request for high fidelity limits for a particular position or individual when audits are rare or nonexistent should cause the underwriter to consider adverse selection.

Even if auditors perform regular audits, the underwriter must know the depths of those audits. Sometimes an audit may only appear to exist. The internal control survey should therefore include the following questions:

- Does the auditor follow written procedures?
- Are parts of the audit unannounced?
- Are parts of the audit conducted at irregular intervals?
- Does the auditor have authority to check any records and anyone whenever the auditor considers it necessary?
- Are all direct verification replies and undelivered requests handled under the auditor's control?
- Are completed bank statements reviewed and tested?

- Does the insured have interim bank cutoff statements and make proof of cash reconciliations? How often?
- Does the auditor get a bank balance confirmation?
- Is someone in accounting who does not buy or sell noncurrent assets responsible for verifying that someone accounts for purchases, sales, trades, and other disposal of these items?

All of the preceding questions should help to reveal embezzlers' more common tricks, such as record switching, selective account deletions, and last-minute deposits.

The audit's outcome provides a clue to its effectiveness. Unless tested periodically by independent auditors, internal auditors' work can be a meaningless charade designed to create the appearance of effective internal control. An unresponsive management can undermine even an independent audit for internal control's value. The internal control survey should answer the following questions:

- Are the auditor's reports and recommendations in written form?
- Do the audit reports go directly to the owners, the partners, or a board of directors audit committee?
- Has the business implemented past recommendations for internal control improvements?

The audit report should always go directly to the owner, partners, or directors rather than a highly placed manager or officer. That procedure reduces the possibility of altering the report's substance to hide questionable findings. The internal control survey should include examining the letter to the owner if possible. If the business has not implemented its recommendations, the auditor must determine why not.

Management

When the owner, partners, or directors supervise operations on a daily basis, they are probably aware of what is happening and can take the necessary steps to protect assets. Even if the owner, partners, or directors actively participate in the daily activities, however, they should insist on the procedures discussed here, to the extent that they apply to the particular business, and should review the resulting reports.

Preparing and enforcing budgets are ways to control expenses, asset changes, and cash flow. Comparing actual results with projected results is often the first indication that something is wrong. The internal control survey should therefore determine whether management effectively uses financial information. Relevant questions in this regard are as follows:

- Does the insured compare inventory costs to sales and other standards?
- Does the insured compare income and expense accounts with prior periods and the budget?

- Does management pursue explanations for significant fluctuations that employees or others report or discover?

Management reports may satisfy the procedural requirements, but reports must lead to action if they are to have value for internal control purposes.

Management should also be certain that the same person who has control over an area is not the person who reports financial information for that area. An obvious question is, "Are duplicate deposit slips compared to the cash receipts journal by someone other than the person who has control of the journal?" This procedure helps to detect payment switching and "delayed" deposit techniques.

Management should require that invoices be verified. For example, someone can submit invoices for services or goods that are never provided. Sometimes such actions are a part of a fraudulent scheme, and in other instances they are a means to hide employees theft.

The internal control survey should also determine who approves customers for credit. Sales staff should not have authority to extend credit. Fictitious accounts often provide the means for embezzlers to manipulate funds. In a small business, an effective control is for the owner to approve all credit sales.

Personnel Policy

The internal control survey should ascertain the firm's vacation policy. Appropriate questions are the following:

- Must all employees take an annual vacation of at least five consecutive business days?
- Does someone else perform the duties of vacationing employees?
- If the company shuts down for vacations, does it keep a "skeleton" crew during the shutdown?

The bookkeeping staff and other people in key financial positions should take consecutive business-day vacations. The substitute employee often discovers irregularities. Embezzlers normally do not take vacations or sick days if they are manipulating records. Quite often insurers discover that the dependable employee who never missed a day committed the fraud.

The survey should also determine whether the company has a benefit package for all employees. Countless employee thefts have started because of job insecurity, a medical emergency, or the concern about future financial security. An employer who provides no benefits adds nothing to an employee's incentive to be honest and trustworthy.

The company's hiring practices also affect internal control. Employers should screen new employees and maintain accurate personnel files. Especially for management and accounting personnel or for employees with custody of cash or merchandise, employers should check personal and prior employment references before extending a job offer.

Rotation of Duties

Businesses should rotate key employees on an irregular, unannounced basis. These key employees include foremen, supervisors, accounting personnel, and managers. Such rotation is a good control when other business objectives make it possible.

Physical Security

A business for which employee pilferage is a problem should enclose the entire premises perimeter and protect all openings by guards or alarms. The security officer can explain the procedures for employees to remove stock or equipment from the premises. A special employee entrance with a guard could be provided. Employers may require employees to have a pass or receipt to leave with any packages. Other measures to curtail pilferage include locker room and personal accessory inspections, metal detectors, and rubbish bin inspections.

The business should store in a safe or vault all money, securities, and valuable papers that the business must keep on the premises. Reserve supplies of blank checks and other documents also belong in the safe. If the business uses facsimile signature plates, it must also protect them. Only a few secretly designated individuals should know the combination to the safe or vault. At all times, the business should guard or lock up inventories and particularly tempting items. Guards are an absolute necessity for bank messengers and any custodians of substantial funds. Unauthorized electronic access to bank card and brokerage accounts is an increasing concern. Businesses must ensure sufficient electronic safeguards are in place to protect financial assets.

Evaluation of Specific Loss Controls

The preceding discussion provides an overview of an insured's general controls—how the insured identifies, develops, and implements them. On occasion, however, bond underwriters request a survey of internal controls because of concern about a particular area. The underwriter may need the survey to acquire details about a certain area. Anyone evaluating internal controls, however, should not consider a single area apart from the total organization. Although additional details in each area should be examined, the general controls still apply. The following discussion identifies specific areas that are subject to control and describes how a business implements those controls.

Accounting

Consistent procedures and separation of duties are the most important internal controls over the accounting records. The survey should determine who maintains the general ledger. It should also examine the accounting procedures to determine whether the business uses a standard journal entry for recurring items or whether it uses special journals. All persons making journal entries should explain or document them and, if appropriate, have a responsible person approve them. The business should prohibit erasing journal entries. The supervisor of the person making the correction should initial journal entry corrections. It should also be a strict policy that the auditor should never originate accounting entries. Covering up dishonesty is easier when the accounting procedures are disorganized and when clear supporting evidence is not readily available. In most electronic accounting systems, mistakes must be corrected through offsetting entries.

Cash

A business conducting many cash transactions has obvious fidelity loss exposures. Businesses should establish internal controls for petty cash, bank reconciliations, cash receipts, cash disbursements, and expense accounts.

Insurers design questions on petty cash surveys to determine duty segregation, controls, and good recordkeeping practices. The business should not use the petty cash fund as a local banking facility. Petty cash funds are a favorite target of employees' check kiting schemes to get money or credit through fraudulent means. Invoices should all go through the cash disbursement department, which maintains better control over such payments. Such payments from the petty cash fund allow for various abuses, including kickbacks. Appropriate questions to include on the survey are as follows:

- Who keeps the petty cash records?
- Does this person have control of other funds?
- How much does the business keep in petty cash?
- Does the business impose a maximum amount for an individual transaction? How much?
- Must someone approve payments from the fund before the appropriate person makes payment?
- Does someone cancel receipts and bills after paying them?
- Does the insured cash employee personal checks from the fund?
- Can the person controlling the fund cash checks from the fund?
- How often does someone balance the fund, verify it, and count the cash?
- Do other cash funds exist?

Even though the amount in petty cash may appear to be trivial and not deserving of too much attention, someone's embezzlement of $25 per week for ten years adds up to a significant loss for a business.

Bank reconciliation procedures are an important control against manipulating funds. An assigned person should receive bank statements unopened. That person should keep the statements under strict control. The business should design procedures to uncover any irregularities and should investigate any checks outstanding for more than two months. The internal controls survey may include the following questions:

- Who prepares the reconciliations?
- Is this person independent of those keeping the cash receipts and cash disbursements records?

- How often does the business prepare bank reconciliations?
- Does anyone other than the reconciler have initial access to the statements?
- Does the insured reconcile the branches' or subsidiaries' accounts in the home office? If not, what controls exist, and what control does the home office enforce over local bank accounts?

Strict control of cash receipts requires absolute segregation of duties. An authorized person other than a cash receipts clerk should open incoming mail. This person should make a record of receipts when he or she opens the mail and should check that record against deposits. Without this procedure, the first account manipulation indication is often the number of customer complaints about incorrect account balances. This person can endorse all checks, money orders, and drafts with a restricted "deposit only" endorsement. A stamp is normally used—it should have a restricted endorsement and the account number.

The internal control survey should also determine the procedures for controlling cash receipts from shops, service and repair centers, branch offices, salespersons and collectors, vending machines, and other collection areas. The business should use prenumbered sales invoices with cash sales and should balance cash receipts daily with the invoices. When the business uses cash registers, a tally of sales by the supervisor or manager using locked-in totals and irregular audits of the locked-in total and the cash drawer often entirely prevents loss.

When feasible, daily deposit of all cash received not only safeguards the funds, but also provides better control. A daily reconciliation between the total cash received, total cash credited, and the deposits made prevents small losses from becoming big ones.

Cash disbursements include coins, bills, checks, money orders, stamps, and similar readily convertible items. This aspect is an especially crucial part of the survey because large losses are common in this area. Relevant questions include:

- Who maintains the cash disbursement records?
- Who prepares the checks?
- Are those people independent of other accounting or bookkeeping functions?
- Does the insured require that approved vouchers or invoices support all payment approvals?
- Must the vouchers or invoices be initialed to show verification or prices and terms, receipt of goods, account distribution, and final payment approval?
- Does someone who does not sign the checks give final approval?
- Must all supporting documents be attached to the voucher and be effectively canceled by either the person who controls the signature or persons who do not prepare checks or approve vouchers?
- Is the practice of drawing cash or bearer checks prohibited?

- Must the check be completed before someone signs it?
- When the insured uses a facsimile signature plate, does the insured protect and use it with the same controls as are used with an actual signature?
- Does the insured require two signatures when checks are manually signed? Must both persons review supporting documents?
- Are all checks prenumbered and accounted for by someone other than the person who signs or affixes signatures?
- Are spoiled and voided checks canceled and kept on file?
- Are signed checks mailed by someone other than those who prepared them or approved the checks' preparation—without allowing the checks to be returned to those persons or departments?

Fictitious supplier schemes become more complicated and less likely if the perpetrator does not have easy access to the means of payment.

Expense account falsification can add up to large losses. The insured can discourage such losses by applying these controls to all expense accounts regardless of who submits them or the amount. A higher-level supervisor should approve expense reports, checking them for accuracy, supporting receipts, and authorized expense type. Employees should charge all expenses on an individual expense account rather than to a company account because company accounts tend to lack personal accountability.

Accounts Receivable

A person who does not have access to cash, inventories, or invoice preparation should maintain accounts receivable records. Someone other than the person who posts accounts receivable ledgers should prepare the statements. Regular statements mailed to all debtors should ask for a reply in the event of a discrepancy. Premium auditors or other independent persons can also periodically confirm all accounts with customers. The insured should balance accounts receivable with the general ledger at least monthly. An aged trial balance of accounts receivable prepared monthly can detect the bad debts' increase, which may indicate someone's using fictitious accounts.

The credit function should be independent of the sales and receivable functions. The internal control survey should ascertain who is responsible for follow-up on past due accounts and who authorizes the write-off of bad debts.

Accounts Payable

Businesses can establish immediate control of accounts payable by sending invoices directly from the mail opener to the accounts payable department. Employees should mark duplicate invoices immediately on receipt to prevent duplicate payment. The person who approves invoices for payment should be independent of the person preparing or approving purchase orders.

The following procedures are important controls before someone approves vouchers for cash disbursements:

- Checking extensions and footings
- Verifying prices
- Matching vouchers with receiving reports
- Matching vouchers with purchase orders
- Confirming that all purchase discounts are included
- Securing approval by the designated person, especially if a noninventory item is involved

The accounts payable clerk should regularly reconcile open accounts payable with monthly statements. He or she should also regularly investigate unmatched purchase orders, receiving reports, and vendor invoices.

A detailed accounts payable subsidiary ledger balanced monthly with the general ledger is an effective control. Premium auditors can detect kickback schemes and overcharging by balancing, verifying, and investigating unmatched items. Someone from outside the purchasing department should periodically verify prices with suppliers' price lists and the supplier's home office.

Payroll

The internal controls over payroll processing are a constant concern of premium auditors. When payroll is the premium base, the premium auditor should be certain that the controls over payroll processing are good enough to ensure that payroll records are a reliable source for the audit. When evaluating internal controls as a safeguard against fidelity losses, the premium auditor should be certain that consistent procedures make it difficult to issue improper payroll checks or to mishandle properly issued checks. Important questions in this regard are as follows:

- Who authorizes adding or removing names from the payroll list?
- Who authorizes changes in salary or wages?
- Does the insured use time cards as the basis for preparing payroll?
- Does the insured post someone at shift changes to make sure that all employees punch only their own time cards?
- Does a responsible official approve time cards?
- Is rechecking payroll computations routine?
- Does the insured separate the duties of timekeeping, payroll preparation, and payroll distribution?
- Are the people responsible for distributing payroll checks periodically rotated?
- Does the insured require positive identification for check distribution?
- Does the insured vest custody of unclaimed wages to someone who does not prepare or distribute payroll?

- Does the insured require receipts when the employee claims those wages?
- Are payroll checks prenumbered and accounted for?
- How does the insured protect the supply of unused payroll checks?
- Does someone outside the payroll preparation department reconcile the payroll bank account?
- Is signing of blank checks prohibited?
- What is the payroll procedure for commission employees?
- If branch locations exist, does the home office handle payroll?
- If not, does the branch location have the same controls as the home office?

Inventories

A perpetual inventory system provides the most effective inventory control. Perpetual inventory records should reflect both quantities and values. The insured should balance perpetual inventory amounts monthly with the general ledger. Regardless of the inventory system, the internal control survey should determine whether someone other than the custodian of the physical inventory keeps inventory records.

Other appropriate questions that will provide information about inventory controls include the following:

- Does the insured compare quantities received with receiving reports and packing slips?
- Does the insured release material from inventory only on approval by authorized personnel?
- Does the insured deny unauthorized persons access to inventory areas?
- Does the insured physically count all inventory classes at least once a year?
- Do physical counts call for the following:
    - Adequate written instructions?
    - Adequate supervision?
    - Prenumbered tags that are accounted for?
    - Counting and tagging only by employees not responsible for custody of the inventory?
    - Carefully investigating overages and shortages?
- Are adequate written instructions provided for physical inventory counts?
- Are physical inventory counts supervised?
- Do physical inventory counts use prenumbered tags, and are the tags counted and applied only by employees?
- Are overages and shortages of inventory investigated?

The insured must enforce good inventory controls. The size or value of an individual item will not prevent theft. Most bonds reimburse only the actual cost of goods, not the retail value. In addition, the insured must prove an actual loss caused by an employee as opposed to bookkeeping loss or theft by others.

Fixed Assets

An insured can control fixed assets by attaching permanent identification to all items and maintaining a detailed subsidiary ledger that balances with the general ledger. The insured should periodically take a fixed asset physical inventory. The survey should determine who is responsible for maintaining fixed asset records and whether that person makes fixed asset expenditures and dispositions in accordance with established procedures.

Securities

The insured should register securities in the company's name and keep them in a safe deposit box or under comparable security. The survey should determine who has custody of the securities and whether the custodian has power of attorney. Persons who do not control the securities should inventory them at least annually.

Purchasing and Receiving

Purchasing and receiving are integrally related to accounts payable and cash disbursements. Preparing written purchase orders should be independent of approving invoices and preparing checks. Purchase orders can be prenumbered and controlled by the accounting department. The following questions relate to the control of kickbacks, or bribery, which is a white collar crime in which money or something of value is illegally given in exchange for favorable treatment:

- Does the insured use competitive bidding for all purchases?
- Are policies in effect to ensure that the insured obtains the lowest price?
- Does the insured periodically verify prices with trade and sales publications?

The insured should also establish controls for the receiving department. The person preparing receiving reports should be independent of the purchasing department and the shipping department. Those receiving reports should list all incoming goods or materials. If possible, the insured should have the receiving area physically separated from the shipping area. The insured can match receiving reports with purchase orders to detect any discrepancies between amounts ordered and amounts received. Someone should inspect goods and materials for condition and quality. That person should report defective goods so that the insured receives credit.

Sales and Shipping

Only designated individuals should prepare sales orders. The appropriate person should approve credit before shipment. It should be necessary to have a copy of the sales order attached before anyone releases a shipment. A second clerk double-checking all orders before shipment can eliminate many losses.

Someone who does not have access to cash, accounts receivable, inventories, or shipping functions should prepare prenumbered sales invoices. That person should then recheck for extensions, footings, prices, special prices, terms, and discounts.

Insureds can control sales returns and allowances by requiring that credit memos be supported by receiving documents. The insured should control freight claims for damaged merchandise on the books of account.

Scrap sales can also be a significant item in some businesses. The internal control survey should determine whether the insured verifies scrap weights, counts, or volumes before release to scrap dealers. Firms should retain supporting records and approvals in the records. The insured can verify scrap prices with independent sources. Bids can curtail kickbacks.

Drivers

The following questions are important in establishing controls if the business makes regular route sales:

- Who loads the trucks?
- Do drivers have access to the warehouse?
- Is merchandise physically checked at the start and end of each trip or run?
- Does the insured use truck seals?
- Do drivers make collections?
- Must drivers turn in and account for collections daily?
- Does the insured number and account for sales receipts and credit vouchers?
- Must customers sign sales receipts when receiving merchandise?
- Must management approve credit before someone grants it?
- Must customers sign credit vouchers for returned goods?
- Does the insured mail statements to credit customers monthly?
- Does the insured instruct customers to contact the home office directly about discrepancies?

Computer Operations

Computers present extraordinary opportunities for dishonest employees to take advantage of their position and specialized knowledge. Controls over computer operations are therefore extremely important, and the insured should have competent independent auditors periodically evaluate these controls. The insured should restrict access to the computer and make changes in the computer file possible only under carefully controlled conditions. Completely documenting all programming is also essential for internal control. The potential for abuse in this area is so large, however, that the underwriter should address any concerns by having an expert examine this operation.

Completion of Internal Control Survey

The premium auditor has not finished the internal controls survey until he or she communicates all information to the underwriter who requested it. Although the answers to the survey questions provide much information, the premium auditor should supplement the answers with his or her overall opinion of the controls, recommendations, and qualifications.

The premium auditor must remember that the evaluation compares the business's specific controls with an internal control model as represented by the questionnaire. Commenting on all deviations from the model is safest, but the premium auditor must qualify recommendations and comments in the practical context of the business. For example, lack of segregation of duties in an office in which the owner directs billing, ordering, receipts, and payments does not have the same significance as in a company in which an employee performs those functions. Likewise, the same inventory controls would not be appropriate for heavy, bulky items that one or two people could not lift as would be necessary for small, valuable diamond-tip drill bits. The premium auditor is uniquely qualified by formal training and experience to make the necessary judgments in evaluating internal controls. Internal control surveys offer a fresh opportunity for premium auditors to contribute significantly to an insurer's profitability.

CRIME AND FIDELITY LOSS AUDITING

Losses can occur when internal controls over assets are nonexistent or inadequate in one or more areas of the insured's operations. Losses may occur from criminal activity by employees or others even when the insured takes reasonable precautions to prevent such losses. When an insured with crime or fidelity coverage suffers a loss and files a claim, the insurer's claim department may seek a premium auditor's assistance in verifying the loss amount claimed by the insured in the proof of loss form.

Audit's Purpose

In requesting premium audit help, the person in the claim department wants the premium auditor to determine that the amount claimed is accurately calculated from the insured's books and records, that the amount claimed is determined in accordance with the policy provisions relating to loss valuation and adjustment, that the loss claimed does not exceed the actual loss sustained, and that the loss is not attributable in part or whole to some cause other than that for which coverage is provided.

Because of their technical training and experience in accounting and auditing, premium auditors are valuable in helping to verify the loss amount claimed under crime and fidelity coverages by auditing the insureds' books and records.

Audit Manager's Responsibilities

When claim personnel request a premium auditor's assistance, the audit manager should discuss the claim with the adjuster or claim supervisor and review the correspondence and documentation in the claim file. Through this procedure, the audit manager can determine whether a field audit would be helpful to the adjuster in the settlement of the claim. The audit manager may be able to use the insured's loss calculation and supporting documentation to verify the amount claimed without a field audit. Some claims may require only an audit manager's explanation or analysis of the insured's loss calculation from information in the claim file. In other cases, it may be apparent to the audit manager from the discussion and claim file review that a field audit will not be beneficial enough to claim personnel to justify the expenditure of the premium auditor's time.

Once an audit manager determines an audit assignment from the claim department, the audit manager is responsible for selecting the premium auditor or auditors. In selecting the premium auditor, the audit manager should take advantage of the opportunity afforded by the assignment to give training to one or more staff auditors working with a fully qualified auditor on the loss adjustment type of audit. This ensures the manager will have more than one staff member available for claim audits, thereby giving the manager some flexibility in staff use. The audit manager should avoid a situation in which he or she is the only experienced one on the staff to audit loss claims.

In assigning a loss adjustment audit under crime or fidelity coverages, the audit manager should give the premium auditor the following items:

- A copy of the proof of loss and the supporting schedules and documentation provided by the insured
- A copy of the policy or bond, or a memoranda summarizing the policy or bond provisions applicable to the loss adjustment, including limits, deductible, and basis of loss adjustment valuation
- Copies of correspondence, memoranda, reports, statements, and other items from the claim file relevant to the audit

Those items are important to the premium auditor in planning and making the audit, as well as in writing the audit report.

The premium auditor must determine from the claim file the name of the person within the insured's organization to contact for the audit. The audit manager should give the premium auditor the names of the insured's claim supervisor and of the adjuster assigned to the claim and should include with the assignment any special requests of the claim supervisor or adjuster regarding items the premium auditor should review and report. The audit manager may suggest specific areas for the premium auditor to investigate procedures to apply to those areas. If the audit manager is careful in preparing the loss adjustment audit assignment, the insurer can avoid costly follow-up work.

The audit manager should monitor the premium auditor's progress from the scheduling phase through submission of the completed audit because the law requires the insurer to respond to the insured regarding claim settlement or denial within a certain time after receiving the proof of loss from the insured, the audit manager should encourage the premium auditor to complete his or her work as soon as possible.

When the audit manager receives a completed audit from the premium auditor, he or she should review the premium auditor's working papers and the premium auditor's narrative report. This review should determine whether the audit procedures the premium auditor applied and entered in the working papers are an adequate basis for the premium auditor's narrative report and recommendation for settlement.

Premium Auditor's Responsibilities

Once assigned to an audit, the premium auditor should review all the materials and instructions included with the assignment, make arrangements with the insured to conduct the audit, and prepare the audit program to the extent feasible before examining the insured's books and records. This review should include the provisions and endorsements in the policy relating to loss adjustment, such as valuation, limits, and deductibles.

During the preparations for the audit, the premium auditor may want to discuss the audit with the claim supervisor or adjuster, who may have more recent information about the claim, the persons to contact, or additional facts about the claim that are valuable to the premium auditor. This procedure also makes the claim representatives aware that the audit process is underway.

Limitations on the Premium Auditor

Before beginning the audit, the premium auditor should understand that the claim department has authority for handling the claim for the insurer and the responsibility for settling the claim with the insured. The premium auditor provides technical assistance in verifying the monetary loss claimed by the insured but does not replace the adjuster. Consequently, the insurer does not authorize the premium auditor to make a representation or commitment to the insured or the insured's representative regarding the amount for which the insurer is willing to settle the claim. This authority and responsibility remain with the adjuster.

The premium auditor should also remember that the insured is responsible under the policy to determine the loss amount. The insurer's claim department does not ordinarily request an audit until the insured has submitted proof of loss summarizing the dollar amount of loss. To proceed with an audit before this time tends to place the premium auditor in the position of developing the claim for the insured. In practice, because of omissions by the insured or the insured's using an incorrect approach in determining the loss, the premium auditor may have to develop additional information affecting the loss amount from the insured's books and records to propose a way to settle the claim. If the premium auditor cannot trace the insured's approach in developing the claim and the premium auditor faces the prospect of determining the loss amount for the insured, the premium auditor should bring this fact to the claim department's attention before proceeding with the work. The adjuster may wish to review the situation with the insured before the premium auditor spends additional time.

Audit Procedures

The premium auditor should plan audit procedures to reconcile the amount claimed and the amount actually lost according to the insured's books and records. If the premium auditor can devise audit procedures to substantiate those amounts satisfactorily, the premium auditor will be able to verify the loss, which is the audit's primary purpose. The premium auditor should not devote time to procedures that do not work toward this purpose.

The loss type and the records maintained by the insured dictate the procedures selected. For example, claims for cash-related losses—cash receipts, cash disbursements, or petty cash—involve applying procedures using the cash-related books and records, such as cash receipts journals, cash register tapes, cash summaries, cash counts, cash disbursements journals, paid checks, petty cash vouchers, deposit slips, bank statements, bank reconciliations, general ledger cash accounts, and so on. Claims involving inventory losses require developing audit procedures relating to records such as physical inventory summaries and details, perpetual inventory records, cost records, vendors' invoices, general ledger inventory accounts, and cost of sales accounts. For instance, when an insured has evidence of an inventory loss caused by burglary or employee dishonesty, the insured may calculate a book inventory on the day the loss was discovered (or at about that time) and take a physical inventory at the same time. The amount by which the book inventory exceeds the physical inventory reveals the suspected shortage. The insured can then file a claim with the insurer for the total shortage. In this situation, many possible explanations exist for the inventory shortage other than employee dishonesty or burglary. Most crime policies exclude losses when the proof of the existence of such loss depends on an inventory computation or a profit. That is, if the only reason the insured thinks a loss occurred is a shortage of inventory, the policy will not respond.

In verifying the loss, the premium auditor must determine whether part of the shortage is because of reasons other than employee infidelity or burglary. Reviewing the insured's inventory system, including the procedures for taking and summarizing physical inventory, can help the premium auditor evaluate the extent to which the insured's inventory records are a reliable source for determining a shortage of a certain dollar amount. If the premium auditor finds numerous errors and omissions in the inventory records, the accuracy of a shortage determined from those records is doubtful.

Working Papers

The premium auditor is responsible for preparing a set of working papers as evidence of the extent of the audit. The working papers should contain such schedules and summaries as the premium auditor needs to provide a basis for the amounts he or she entered in the narrative report and accompanying schedules. If the premium auditor includes an amount in the report, it should be traceable to the working papers. The premium auditor should index and cross-reference the working papers where appropriate.

The procedures the premium auditor followed and the specific sources for the information from the insured's books and records should be clear to a person reviewing the working papers. Although an experienced premium auditor should be able to design working papers, examples of working paper formats are available in many auditing texts.

Narrative Report

A premium auditor uses a report to advise the insurer's claim function of the premium auditor's findings and recommendations. The claim department will use the report in connection with the negotiations for final claim settlement with the insured. The report can be important if the insurer and the insured cannot settle or if the insurer denies the claim and a court decides the claim settlement.

The report should include information developed from the insured's books and records. The premium auditor should not include opinions, hunches, and guesses because they are subjective and do not have a bearing on the claim settlement from a legal standpoint.

In preparing the report, the premium auditor should remember that the claim personnel requesting the audit are the audience. Generally, claim personnel are not as knowledgeable about accounting and auditing terminology as is the premium auditor, so they need a clearly written narrative with adequate explanations to make the report useful in settling the claim. The premium auditor should also avoid excessive detail because this makes it difficult for the reader to sort out the facts having a bearing on the premium auditor's findings and recommendations.

Premium auditors should include schedules in the report. The premium auditor should refer to the schedule in the narrative report, indicating the schedule's significance. Each schedule should have a title and appropriate column headings, which make the included data understandable and clear. As in the report, the premium auditor should avoid excessive detail in the schedules.

In a suggested format for crime and fidelity loss claim audits, the premium auditor arranges the narrative report according to the following sections:

- Cover page
- Index of exhibits and schedules

- Proof of loss
- Principal person responsible
- Coverage
- Persons contacted
- Method of alleged discrepancies
- Audit procedures and findings
- Audit findings summary
- Settlement proposal schedule
- Exhibits
- Schedules

The cover page is a memorandum from the premium auditor to the audit manager; it also indicates the other persons to whom the premium auditor has distributed the report. The premium auditor also enters the insured's name, the claim number, and the auditors' names on the cover page.

The exhibits and schedules index lists the exhibits and schedules in sequence by identifying number or letter and brief title or description of each exhibit and each schedule's title.

In the proof of loss section, the premium auditor refers to the insured's proof of loss, which the premium auditor should include as the first exhibit in the report. The type of loss claim—burglary, theft, or employee dishonesty—is indicated along with the date of the loss or discovery and the location. The premium auditor summarizes the loss claimed by the insured by the categories—cash, inventory, or equipment—and dollar amount. The premium auditor also indicates the persons, department, or outside firm preparing the claim for the insured. This will usually be someone from the insured's accounting or internal auditing staff or a public accounting firm.

The premium auditor shows the name of the person responsible for the theft, burglary, or dishonesty, if known, under the principal. If the premium auditor names an employee, the premium auditor should disclose the position held by the employee and the period of employment with the insured. If the premium auditor develops information concerning the principal during the audit that is contrary to the information set forth by the insured in the proof of loss, the premium auditor also enters that information under this heading.

In the report's coverage section, the premium auditor should identify by type, policy number, and policy period the policy under which the insurer provides coverage to the insured for the loss. Also indicated are the limits and deductible applicable to the coverage under which the insured claims the loss.

In the report's persons contacted section, the premium auditor enters persons contacted during the course of the audit, their position with the insured (or their title or accounting number), or their accounting firm or company affiliation. The premium auditor should not include the names of insurer personnel.

In the method of alleged discrepancies section, the premium auditor includes a brief description of how the principal allegedly committed the burglary, theft, or dishonest act. An example from one report appears in Exhibit 13-1.

EXHIBIT 13-1

Excerpt From a Sample Loss Audit Report
Method of Alleged Discrepancy

The principal, a supply clerk employed by the insured on the night shift, gained unauthorized access to the insured's high-value storeroom and allegedly stole 2,000 one-ounce containers of silver powder for his personal use or sale. The principal is alleged to have had a key for the storeroom made from the set of keys assigned to the warehouse supervisor.

In the audit procedures and findings section, the details of the audit procedures and the premium auditor's findings are included for each item or categories of items shown in the insured's proof of loss. The premium auditor can describe general audit procedures under this topic, followed by the reporting for the specific items or categories.

The premium auditor can also include a description of the insured's accounting system and controls over the specific items or categories in this section, along with comments on the premium procedures applied by the auditor in reviewing the system and controls, and the premium auditor's findings or recommendations. The premium auditor describes the adjustments to the amount claimed for each item or category in this section. The premium auditor indicates the amounts in the report or in a schedule to which the premium auditor refers.

The summary of audit findings section includes the premium auditor's recommendations. If the premium auditor recommends claim settlement, he or she should refer to the settlement proposal schedule included with the audit report. If the premium auditor cannot recommend settlement or recommends denying any payment on the claim by the insurer, he or she should explain the basis for this recommendation.

The settlement proposal schedule section begins with the claim amount on the insured's proof of loss. The premium auditor then describes adjustments to the loss claim developed by the premium auditor and added or deducted from the amount claimed to arrive at an adjusted claim total before the deductible. The premium auditor enters the deductible next on the schedule to arrive at the loss amount as adjusted. This is the amount for which the premium auditor is recommending that the insurer's claim department settle the claim.

The premium auditor selects exhibits and schedules for inclusion with the report. The exhibits section generally includes the insured's proof of loss together with other documentation from the insured's records. The premium auditor prepares schedules included with the report. The premium auditor can modify the report format according to the reporting requirements on a particular audit.

SUMMARY

Crime and fidelity coverages have traditionally been specialized areas of insurance operations with little involvement from premium auditors. The trend toward package policies and account underwriting makes those past divisions less meaningful. Fidelity coverage, whether the insurer provides it as part of a combination crime policy or as a separate fidelity bond, requires judicious underwriting if the insurer is to have a profitable book of business in this line. The insured's internal controls are the most significant underwriting consideration because effective internal controls make embezzlement more difficult to execute and easier to detect. Although evaluating internal controls is conceptually equivalent to other loss control activities, premium auditors, among insurer personnel, are uniquely qualified for the task. Premium auditors' evaluation of internal controls, either as a supplement to a premium audit required by another coverage or as a response to a fidelity underwriter's specific request, capitalizes on their skills and adds to the overall success of the insurer they represent.

A premium auditor's skills can also contribute to an insurer's claim operations. When a loss occurs, a premium auditor can assist in verifying the loss amount by examining the insured's records. The premium auditor's resulting recommendations can greatly assist in settling the claim according to the actual loss amount indicated in the insured's books and records and according to the policy provisions relating to loss adjustment and valuation.

Index

Page numbers in boldface refer to definitions of Key Words and Phrases.